Myth of Iron

T0385459

Also by Dan Wylie

Savage Delight: White Myths of Shaka (2000)
Dead Leaves: Two Years in the Rhodesian War (2002)

Myth of Iron

Shaka in history

Dan Wylie

James Currey
OXFORD

Ohio University Press
ATHENS

University of KwaZulu-Natal Press
PIETERMARITZBURG

University of KwaZulu-Natal Press
Private Bag X01, Scottsville, 3209, South Africa
Email: books@ukzn.ac.za
Website: www.ukznpress.co.za

Ohio University Press
The Ridges, 19 Circle Drive, Athens, Ohio 45701, United States of America
Website: www.ohioswallow.com

James Currey Ltd
73 Botley Road, Oxford OX2 0BS, United Kingdom
Website: www.jamescurrey.co.uk

© 2006 Dan Wylie
First published in 2006

All rights reserved. No part of this publication may be reproduced or transmitted in any form
or by any means, electronic or mechanical, including photocopying, recording, or any information
storage and retrieval system, without prior permission in writing from the publishers.

ISBN: 978-1-86914-047-2 (UKZN Press Hardcover)
ISBN: 978-1-86914-153-0 (UKZN Press Softcover)
ISBN 10: 0-8214-1848-3 (Ohio University Press Softcover)
ISBN 13: 978-0-8214-1848-2 (Ohio University Press Softcover)
ISBN: 978-0-85255-441-8 (James Currey Softcover)

British Library Cataloguing in Publication Data
   Wylie, Dan
   Myth of iron : Shaka in history
   1. Shaka, Zulu Chief, 1787?-1828 2. Zulu (African people) -
   Kings and rulers - Biography 3. KwaZulu-Natal (South
   Africa) - History
   I. Title
   968.4'039'092

Editor: Andrea Nattrass
Cover concept: Dan Wylie
Cover designer: Sebastien Quevauvilliers, Flying Ant Designs
Cartographer: Sue Abraham
Typesetter: Patricia Comrie
Indexer: Cynthia Harvey-Williams

Contents

List of boxes

List of maps

A note on language and terminology

Public perceptions of the Zulu continue to be dominated by the stereotypical imagery of massed warriors – extravagant feathers waving, short stabbing-spears rusted with blood – pouring down grassy hillsides. Similarly, Shaka's part-murderous, part-brilliant responsibility for creating this allegedly monomaniac 'military machine' continues to be dominated by the language of warfare, an awkward mixture of inflexible discipline and frenzied rapacity. The strict language of rank, regimentation, and weaponry lies unsettlingly alongside metaphors of animality, volcanoes, storms, and other uncontrollable natural forces. Together, these forms of expression articulate in almost all the readily available literature a world apart, a specifically Zulu cult and culture of romanticised yet rigorous brutality.

Such language is in every respect misleading, even dangerous. Almost every aspect of these expressions, ranging from the translations of terms such as *ibutho* and *ikhanda*, to the use of the overarching term 'Mfecane', needs redefinition, if not excision. If one thing has become clear to me in the writing of this book, it is that what happened to and around the Zulu people in Shaka's time cannot be politically, geographically or socially divided off from what was happening in near or far neighbourhoods, or in the world at large. Shaka's reign was not a self-enclosed, *sui generis* process; there was no Zulu-centred, spontaneous, isolated explosion of inexplicable violence that can be adequately contained within a single politico-geographic rubric like 'the Mfecane'. Even geography has to be redefined.

Hence, I have tried to find a way of overcoming the historiographical quirk of dividing south-eastern Africa according to colonial boundaries, by which 'Mozambique', 'the Cape', and 'Zululand' were treated as largely independent entities even when discussing pre-1840 times. Those earlier movements and processes were rather governed by ecological rhythms, environmental necessities, economic opportunities and political interchanges, all of which spanned these regions seamlessly. I have therefore eschewed appellations such as 'Natal' and 'Zululand', which are fraught with colonial connotations, and the more inclusive but anachronistic 'KwaZulu-Natal', in favour of a clumsier but physical term for the broader region within which Shaka forged his career: '*the Thukela-Phongolo catchment*'. Strictly speaking, it ought to be the 'Mzimkhulu-Thukela-Phongolo catchment', but the shorter term serves to delineate a region that is geographically unified by its major river systems and, with the exception of some fringe activities to the far south, pretty much covers the Zulu sphere of interest, from around Delagoa Bay, west across the headwaters of the Black and White Mfolozi, Mzinyathi, and Thukela rivers to the Drakensberg foothills, and south to the vicinity of Port Natal (Durban).

Zulu terms have too often been simplistically translated into English equivalents that distort their meaning. Most prominent are those terms that have come to imply a far-too-rigid division in the Zulu social mind between military and non-military modes and functions. One such term is *ibutho* (plural *amabutho*), usually misleadingly translated as 'regiment': the *amabutho* were much more complex labour- and age-based units of social organisation the function of which was only partly and sporadically 'military'. Congruently, an *ikhanda* was not simply a 'barracks', but a full-blown settlement around which agricultural, colonising and ritualistic practices revolved, as well as defensively or aggressively military activities. In this regard, 'kraal' has fallen into disfavour, being too vague (anything from whole settlements to small cattle enclosures), too Afrikaans, or too 'animal'. Hence, I mostly use the Zulu term for homestead settlements, *imizi* (singular *umuzi*), retaining 'kraal' only in quotations. A third important term is *isigodlo* (plural *izigodlo*), which was not a 'harem' or 'seraglio', as earlier writers thought of it, but both an architectural as well as a socio-political feature of larger settlements involving an awesome complexity of marital, gender, ethnic, ritual, and political dimensions.

In these and other cases, then, I try to explain the meanings of the terms early on and thereafter use the Zulu terms only, which hopefully carry with them their full weight of meaning.

There have been changes in Zulu orthography over the decades and, by and large, I have attempted to use the more modern orthography. 'Shaka' has come to predominate over 'Chaka' or 'Tshaka', 'Dingane' over 'Dingana', and so on. Similarly, colonial-era spellings have been superceded: 'Tugela' is now spelt 'Thukela', 'Umtata' is now 'Mthatha', and so on. Two particularly common orthographic conventions have changed, involving *dh/d* and *th/t*. Thus, for example, the older *'isigodhlo'* has become *'isigodlo'* and, conversely, *'takata'* is now spelt *'thakatha'*. I have retained old-style spellings only where they appear within quotations, as they frequently do, especially in quotations from *The James Stuart Archive*.

In only one aspect have I resisted advice to use modern orthography throughout, and that is in the spelling of James Stuart's informants' names. For economy's sake, I have referenced *Archive* sources by informant's name only, indicating this with small capitals (for example, MGIDLANA); this also prevents confusing informants with other people whose names are sometimes the same. The five published volumes in the *Archive* contain the informants in alphabetical order as follows: Volume 1: ANTEL–LYLE; Volume 2: MABELE–MAZIYANA; Volume 3: MBOKODO–MPATSHANA; Volume 4: MQAIKANA–NDUKWANA; and Volume 5: NDUNA–SIVIVI. To avoid difficulties in finding the informant in the relevant volume, then, I retain Stuart's old-style spelling.

Acknowledgements

In the course of a project that has taken some twenty years to mature, numerous debts accrue. Some of them may have been forgotten; for these I apologise. Others have been acknowledged in my first book on Shaka, *Savage Delight*, and I will not repeat them here.

From the bottom of my historiographical heart, I must thank two exceptional teachers, whose work and presence permeate this book. The first is Julian Cobbing, whose energised, innovative, and uncompromising teaching got me going on this subject way back in 1982. I have frequently disagreed with him and have been frequently shaken to the roots by his unflinching criticism, but he has enthusiastically stood by this project, reading and annotating it many times at different stages, without which it would be a much lesser work. In this book, his kind gift to me of the three volumes of Leverton's *Records of Natal* at last bears fruit.

The second teacher is John Wright, who has done more work in early Zulu studies than any other scholar. He is the primary giant on whose shoulders I stand. John has not only done the groundwork for me: he has discussed endlessly, hosted me, walked me off my feet in the 'Berg, and read the whole manuscript, his meticulous comments saving me from committing a thousand orthographic horrors. Any that remain are, of course, my fault. As I am not proficient in isiZulu, I have relied entirely on his massive work translating the James Stuart material; he also kindly allowed me to read some of those translations before they went to print. So formidable yet generous a scholar is difficult to disagree with, though I do so from time to time, with trepidation if not apologies.

Other scholars whom I have met only tangentially or not at all, yet on whose work this book has been partially built – David Hedges, Alan Smith and Carolyn Hamilton in particular – will find themselves, I hope, adequately acknowledged in the notes.

For reading parts of the manuscript and commenting fruitfully, I must thank Paul Maylam and Wayne Hugo in particular; for many lunch-time discussions and supportive noises, Cathy Gorham; for some very juicy and useful items of information, Jürg Richner; for helpful contact and correspondence on archaeological issues, Len van Schalkwyk and Martin Hall; and for pretty much everything else over the last three years, Ann Smailes (who wisely calmed my frenzied search for the truth about Macingwane and the Chunu by reminding me that 'Massive Guano and the Huge Poohs' were all deceased anyway; it was okay). Also to Ian for – I forget what, exactly.

The English Department at Rhodes University, Grahamstown, has provided an unimpeachably cushy ambience in which to work; and the university itself has granted sundry bits of research funding to make it possible. Thanks also to Sue Abraham of the Rhodes University Graphics Unit for her uncomplaining and attentive work on the maps. The staff of the following archives have been endlessly friendly and helpful, some over many years: the Cory Library, Grahamstown (especially Mr Zwel Vena); the Cape Archives, Cape Town; the Natal Archives, Pietermaritzburg; the Killie Campbell Library, Durban; the British Library, London; the National Maritime Museum Library, Greenwich; and the SOAS missionary archives, London. None of this work would be possible without all the half-concealed archivists at these institutions.

Last but not least (in a gesture that is becoming almost habitual), I must thank my editor, Andrea Nattrass, for her meticulous, intelligent and sensitive editing, which has prevented me from perpetrating at least my worst stylistic solecisms, and has been irreplaceably instrumental in helping me to produce a more readable work.

In memoriam my father, Jack Wylie.

. . . I spoke with survivors and witnesses and searched through newspaper archives and official documents, and I realized that the truth did not lie anywhere.

Gabriel García Márquez, *Living to Tell the Tale*.

Preface

We know very little for certain about Shaka. This statement might come as a surprise, since over the decades we have heard a great deal about this most famous – or infamous – of Zulu leaders. Nevertheless, we do not know when he was born. We do not know what he looked like. And we do not know precisely when or why he was assassinated. In Shaka's case, even these most basic facts of any person's biography remain locked in obscurity. So it's exceptionally difficult to say anything definite about how he conducted his wars, what he thought about at night, or what his sexual life was like. It's equally difficult to make out and summarise his character, his political philosophy, or his personal ambitions.

Many people will be familiar with a cluster of dramatic stories about Shaka, derived from school or university textbooks, museum displays, the film *Shaka Zulu*, television programmes, or word of mouth. Shaka – the stories usually go – was illegitimate, bullied as a child, and exiled as a youth. He nevertheless, starting with a previously insignificant clan, founded the Zulu nation, welding all the people of 'Zululand' into a unified whole. This took about ten years. He was an innovative military genius who won every battle he fought. He was a brutal dictator who killed off thousands (if not a million) people, including many of his own, whom he slaughtered for cowardice, or arbitrarily tossed off cliffs. He was sexually dysfunctional. He was mainly responsible for sending other predatory groups of people scattering all over the subcontinent, as far afield as Tanzania, an explosion of violence which eventually became known as the *mfecane*. He was assassinated by his half-brothers because he went crazy.

Most of these stories have come to sound so familiar that they generally pass unquestioned. In fact, virtually everything about this portrait is wrong.

1

Can I say this, having already asserted that we know almost nothing for sure? I believe I can, for the simple reason that there is no solid evidence for any of it. Such evidence as we have, though it's frequently thin, is none the less rich enough and full enough to point in very different directions. Let's take two brief examples. It is almost always asserted that Shaka invented the 'chest-and-horns' military formation. This has become practically *the* symbol of Shaka's military expertise; many of you might recall its dramatic and picturesque representation in Bill Faure's deeply misleading television series *Shaka Zulu*. Yet there is not a single account in anything that could be regarded as 'evidence' (that is, in eyewitness accounts by travellers, in the accounts of people who spoke to those eyewitnesses, or among the numerous Zulu oral testimonies gathered in the course of the next 80 years) which says anything of the sort. Similarly, it is almost always asserted, right through to the *Encyclopaedia Britannica*, that Shaka's greatest victory was won at 'Qokli Hill', where Zwide of the Ndwandwe, Shaka's main rival for regional power, was finally defeated in 1819. Yet there is not a shred of credible evidence anywhere that this battle occurred. In fact, it turns out to have been invented by E.A. Ritter in 1955, in his novel *Shaka Zulu*. We have to start looking elsewhere for more truthful depictions of Shaka's military systems.

Astoundingly, Ritter's *Shaka Zulu* is practically the only book that even pretends to be a biography of Shaka, despite Shaka being probably the most famous black southern African leader besides Nelson Mandela. But Ritter's book is unquestionably a *novel*. Shaka seems somehow to have remained immune to searching scholarship, at least until the last fifteen years or so. Almost all the new research remains relatively inaccessible in academic theses and specialist journal articles. Meanwhile the public image juggernauts on – truly a 'myth of iron': a myth of iron aggression, of a Zulu 'mailed fist', and a myth apparently as durable as iron itself. It seems that the conventional tale is so intriguing, so dramatic, so archetypal, and sometimes so politically useful, that few have ventured to subject it to proper scrutiny.

On the one hand, Shaka is *the* primary icon of Zulu nationhood, and to suggest that he may not have been as great and heroic as the legend says, is to lay yourself open to the charge of demeaning the Zulu nation itself. On the other hand, for those who have grown up with the image of a pathological mass-murderer, to suggest that he wasn't, is to lay yourself open to the charge of opportunistic political correctness. Conversely, any suggestion that the white eyewitnesses of Shaka's reign, who are usually presented as beacons of civilisation, were actually violent and lying ruffians whose accounts cannot be trusted, can also be seen as an attack on entrenched white values generally. Similarly, to assert that Zulu oral testimonies – oral testimony being the historiographical flavour of the month – are equally difficult, contradictory and suspect, can be interpreted as being downright racist.

In this book I intend to run all of these gauntlets in the interest of laying out, as far as possible, all the available evidence on Shaka's reign, and deciding, item by item, what we can make of it. What emerges is not so much a biography, as an 'anti-biography'. This is not to say that I disapprove of biography as such. But this book is an anti-biography in several senses. In the first place, it re-examines what *pretends* to be the biography of Shaka – the popular narrative briefly outlined above, the essence of which I have captured in the epigraphs to each chapter. I find this pseudo-biography to be profoundly flawed in both conception and detail, and so I present an alternative narrative.

Secondly, however, as my opening remarks hint, this book also suggests that it's scarcely possible to write a biography of Shaka at all. When reading biography we usually expect a reasonably full and connected account of the progress of a person's life; a chronologically clear sequence of events; some sense of the effects of ancestry and parentage; some sense of how the childhood affected adulthood; some sense of the day-to-day cultural life. We presume an adequate supply of credible eyewitness anecdotes and observations, leading to a more or less clear impression of what the person thought about him- or herself, a plausible psychological insight into what drove the personality, and some basis for finally summing up the character. We expect to be able to say something about the importance of the subject to his or her times. In almost every aspect, the evidence on Shaka often leaves us in the dark, or at least in considerable doubt. So part of the purpose of this book is to show why a biography in the fullest sense of the word just isn't possible.

Thirdly, I try to embed the story of Shaka's life, or what we can discern of it, more extensively in the regional context than might be the case with a more narrowly focused 'biography'. This is because that context has generally been either ignored or distorted, so that our understanding of Shaka – what it was logical and possible for him to achieve, what was new or reactive in his policy, what was important or trivial in his behaviour – has also been distorted. Three aspects of Shaka's context are important and have been examined with varying degrees of success by recent scholars: the influence on the 'Zululand' region of global communication and trading networks (including the slave trade); the environmental or ecological matrix within which the Zulu inevitably lived; and the role of the first white adventurers to settle and trade from isiBubulungu or Port Natal (now Durban). I try to draw these dimensions together into a more integrated understanding. So if I spend time examining the careers of Shaka's near and distant neighbours, it's because we can't understand the scale and nature of Shaka's own operations without them. And if I focus on the final four years when whites were present and writing down things, it's because part of my project is to query the nature of their documentation itself. Questioning the historical status of surrounding events and how they were later presented is a vital part of questioning the status of Shaka himself.

These two dimensions of this book – Shaka's geo-political contexts and the development of a legend-riddled 'history' – are also a product of the nature of the sources available. Paradoxically, there is quite a lot of material to work with, most of it in the form of Zulu oral testimonies, which I mine more comprehensively than most writers have to date. These testimonies are as flawed, shallow, distorted, patchy, and contradictory as the few written white eyewitness accounts. They tend to recall violent but minority movements and heroic actions, not the static peacefulness of the majority. Their many charming but scattered personal anecdotes are often riven with improbable mythology, subsequent politicisation, and misremembrance. Yet they are detailed, pithy, suggestive and fascinating in themselves. This book, then, is as much about the process of the search itself as it is a new narrative of Shaka's life. 'History' is not just the presentation of a 'factual' narrative of the past. It is also the *process* of sifting the evidence, asking questions about who wrote or spoke it, in what circumstances and why. It is not just about arriving at a conclusive answer to the perennial question, 'What *really* happened?' History is also about investigating the question, 'How does this particular *image* of what happened get put together?' History, in the end, is a creative literary medium. It tries to say something verifiable about the past, but the past is ultimately a construction of language; it's something imagined.

If you question differently the language in which the evidence is couched, you are likely to come up with a different kind of narrative. In Shaka's case, the language in which he has been conventionally portrayed is a particularly fascinating and politically fraught case – a case of a narrative being constructed actually *in defiance of* the evidence.

While I tend to regard written history as a sub-species of literature, this doesn't mean that I want to do away with 'facts' altogether. In this book, I try to interrogate every facet of the evidence in order to find out just how solid it is. There are some cases in which we can be pretty certain that this or that 'really happened'. In others, the *probability* is strong, though not finally provable. In many more instances, we will have to settle for mere *possibility*, for hypotheses supported by logical inferences from surrounding circumstances or, even more shakily, analogies from other similar scenarios. And in quite a few cases – as in the three I mentioned at the start of this Preface: Shaka's birthdate, his looks, and the details of his assassination – we will simply have to say, 'We don't know,' and leave it at that. Most importantly, we need to resist the temptation to make things up in order to fill the gaps, which is what has all too often happened in the popular Shaka story.

THE BUTTOCKS PROBLEM: A BRIEF DISCUSSION OF SOURCES

There are two basic problems with the sources available. Firstly, they are rather meagre in many areas, particularly on the early and middle years of Shaka's life. Secondly, many of the sources were written or recorded many years after the events they describe, with memory loss, political concerns, racial bias and other factors all potentially serving to distort or fragment the views of informants. In documentary terms, exploring Shaka's life is a bit like exploring Attila the Hun's or Jesus of Nazareth's. Hefty attention is paid to the end of his life, while earlier years and other areas attract no evidence at all. Contradictory accounts are written up and re-edited years afterwards. In the absence of hard facts, legends and invented anecdotes flourish. Ideological concerns frequently become stronger than factual ones.

There are two essential sets of source material. The first, most important group comprises the oral histories recorded by a Natal administrator, James Stuart, roughly between 1890 and 1922. This – *The James Stuart Archive* – is my primary source. Shaka was assassinated in 1828, so these accounts were written down between 50 and 80 years after Shaka's death. Innumerable distortions have inevitably crept in over this time period. The information is rich, but very fragmentary and contradictory. What are we to make, for instance, of the fact that one informant says that Shaka had broad buttocks, 'showing he was a king' – but another, apparently no less reliable, claims they were narrow and honed, the buns of a compulsively athletic dancer? How are we to judge the reliability of the first informant, who is young but intelligent and the son of one of Shaka's own warriors whose accounts he claims to be faithfully reproducing, as against the second who, though he was a tiny child at the time, asserts that he actually *saw* those regal buttocks with his own eyes? The short answer is that we probably can't trust either person. The question of the shape of Shaka's rear – let alone deeper and more complex issues – is never likely to be settled.

The personal affiliations of the many different informants play a crucial role in how they speak of Shaka. As a result, from time to time in this book, I foreground the lives of the informants themselves, to remind us that these testimonies once issued from the mouths of real people, with their own inhibitions and opinions, strengths and limitations, agendas, pleasures and fears. Often we don't know enough about these informants to judge fully their possible biases. A few of them had been born before Shaka died, but were obviously then still too young to remember him. A number could remember their fathers or grandfathers serving under Shaka, and relayed their tales. Even this closeness to eyewitnesses, of course, doesn't eliminate problems: not even eyewitnesses are reliable, and in some respects they are the *least* reliable. Moreover, James Stuart's own collecting techniques, though astoundingly tireless and attentive, were hardly what a modern anthropologist would judge professional, and often we can see his own opinions or agendas dictating the way the questioning goes. In certain contexts, Stuart could come across as just as appallingly racist as any of his less-informed contemporaries. Nevertheless, this massive archive of oral testimony is the most important existing source of information on Shaka's reign. Still under-utilised, it provides a very necessary counterweight to the second set of sources: white eyewitness accounts. Indeed, a profoundly different narrative emerges from *The James Stuart Archive* – the history as Zulu people and some of their neighbours recalled and reconstructed it.

White adventurers encountered Shaka only in the last four years of his reign. In documentary terms, three of these eyewitnesses are most important. Henry Francis Fynn was the most literate amongst them, and over the years he wrote a number of overlapping accounts of his time with Shaka, some of them for patently self-serving purposes. These various papers were mined, edited and at times substantially rewritten, mostly by the same James Stuart already mentioned. The result – *The Diary of Henry Francis Fynn* – was published in 1950, and rapidly became a primary source for historians. Of course, it was not a diary at all; nor were many of the original papers meant to be unvarnished accounts of Fynn's time amongst the Zulu. The nearest we have to a diary is a notebook written up sometime in the 1830s, not all of which has survived. Its style shows that Fynn was nowhere near as articulate or perceptive as Stuart's version in the *Diary* implied. Wherever possible, then, I have turned to Fynn's original papers for information, rather than the largely fraudulent published version. At least we have a reasonable idea where those papers were coming from; we can relate them directly to Fynn's subsequent, colourfully troubled career as a colonial magistrate and his periodic attempts to extract land from suspicious authorities, usually on the basis of an entirely mendacious claim that Shaka had ceded land to him.

We do not have the luxury of resorting to original papers in the case of a second eyewitness, Nathaniel Isaacs. Less literate than Fynn, Isaacs was young (seventeen when he was shipwrecked at Port Natal in 1824) and ignorant, but cunning. In 1836 he was able to get published an evidently ghost-written account of his time in 'Zululand', *Travels and Adventures in Eastern Africa*. Even on a superficial examination, this two-volume work is full of gaps, contradictions, and implausibilities. If it is indeed based on an original (now lost) diary, as it purports to be, it contains so many obvious lies that it has to be regarded with considerable suspicion.

The white settlers had plenty to lie about and cover up: they acquired harems of local wives and spawned numerous children whom they subsequently abandoned; they ran guns and possibly slaves, fighting in a mercenary capacity for Shaka and eventually against him; they conducted their own violent raids on their neighbours, and generally behaved in a thoroughly disreputable manner. Not surprisingly, none of this emerges in their own accounts. Indeed, a great deal of what they were doing they eventually found it necessary to project onto Shaka, so creating the basis for the monstrous portrayal of the Zulu leader which is now so familiar. In the absence of anything else, it was Nathaniel Isaacs's image of Shaka as a terrifying, pathological brute that dominated the literature for a century and more.

This distortion is more obvious when laid alongside the third white eyewitness account, that of the even younger Charles Rawden Maclean, who rather mysteriously entered semi-legendary history as 'John Ross'. Young though he was (maybe ten in 1824), Maclean spent more time actually in Shaka's court than the rest of the whites put together, and he supplies a much more measured and intimate portrayal of the man. Unfortunately, his account is also thinned by long retrospect – it was only written up in the 1850s – and by remaining unfinished. Still, he is a crucial corrective to the vitriol of his money-grubbing compatriots.

These two groups of primary evidence are complemented and moderated by a scattering of further references. Some documentation was channelled through the officialdom of the Cape Colony. This includes some letters from Francis Farewell, James Saunders King and John Cane, three other prominent adventurers in Shaka's territory. All of them unfortunately met their deaths not long after Shaka himself, and so left no accounts more substantial than these few notes. We also find a smattering of oral evidence taken down by the occasional traveller or missionary, both from indigenous people and from the white eyewitnesses and their closer friends. Amongst the most important of these is a list of Natal 'tribes', gleaned in the 1850s by the famous administrator Theophilus Shepstone, in the course of establishing various land claims. As far as we can tell, some fourteen informants supplied these all-too-brief and uncorroborated histories. In the form in which they were eventually published in John Bird's *Annals of Natal* in 1888, they are still a useful corollary to *The James Stuart Archive* for that rather limited area.

They are also interesting in that they appear to be a major source for an unavoidable presence in the field of Zulu history – the work of A.T. Bryant. An Oxford-educated priest, amateur anthropologist and Zulu linguist, Bryant's voluminous works – especially the 1829 *Olden Times in Zululand and Natal* – have until recently been regarded as all but the last word. Overly florid in style, racist in undertone, and densely interwoven, on a first reading *Olden*

Times appears both highly detailed and based on a wealth of oral tradition. In fact, on close analysis, Bryant's sources on Shaka are limited almost entirely to Shepstone's historically rather meagre material, and to some of James Stuart's records as encapsulated in a series of Zulu school readers which Stuart generated from the accounts now transcribed in the *Archive*. The rest of Bryant seems to be conjecture, or spun out of hints in the white sources, or sheer invention. If – on the occasions he differs markedly from the other sources – he is drawing on independent oral informants, these are generally neither named nor verifiable. To a large and surprising extent, therefore, Bryant is either plain wrong or can be ignored.

That's all we have. I have deliberately refrained from interviewing living 'old men' in KwaZulu-Natal, though I have been frequently enjoined to 'ask the King, he will know the true story'. I doubt very much that there is anything to be gained from this. Even by James Stuart's time, 'feedback loops' – in which white and black inventions alike were leaking back into allegedly 'pure oral Zulu' accounts – are evident. This danger has multiplied with the spread of literacy. A current informant – even so crucial a repository of the national memory as the King – will either repeat a story we already know from earlier sources, or will present a new story which is *not* present in earlier sources, and which is by that very fact completely unverifiable. Consequently, I have elected to use only the earliest available testimonies, those with the most direct links to people alive in Shaka's own lifetime. This book presents the picture suggested by those testimonies alone.

It is a rather different picture from the one we are used to.

1

Stones from a distant grave

The question of Zulu origins

The Zulus and the neighbouring clans were the purest Nguni, as the
Scandinavians are the purest 'Teutonic' race today.
E.A. Ritter, Shaka Zulu (1955, 7).

A man leans against the rough but solid drystone wall of his cattle pen.
Evening light, reddening over the massive snow-rimmed escarpment
to the west, tints his skin a dark bronze. He has slightly prominent cheekbones
and hair with a knotty peppercorn effect. He is tall, pot-bellied, a man of
local substance. Short-horned cattle chew the cud in the pen behind him;
some fat-tailed sheep are kept in check by his dark-skinned sons nearby. He
carries a pair of honed iron spears, bought for a goat from people living on
the edge of forests several ridges away. At his feet, in a russet-and-black clay
pot, several handfuls of sorghum are mixed with wild tubers, some herbs,
and a few locusts. The pot's flared rim is etched with chevrons in the latest
fashion. The man lifts a hand to brush away the flies. His wrist is adorned
with several bracelets: one of twisted genet fur, one of beaten copper, others
of glass beads. The beads were manufactured somewhere way to the north,
though he bartered for them locally from some visiting traders. They were
narrow-faced, shanky; he could barely understand them.

The man heads an extended family – a number of wives, a scattering of
children, an even bigger number of cousins. He has labour and time enough
to build stone walls. He is a ridge-dweller who migrates with his cattle over
short distances. Winter is about to force them down through dense forests

11

and into the spreading river-courses; the cattle need sweeter grasses. Most years he'll burn a hillside somewhere nearby to bring up the green shoots. Cattle are the heart and soul of his culture.

He has heard of the sea, several days' travel to the south-east, but has never seen it. They eat fish there: horrible. To the north-west, beyond the dramatic escarpment, he knows that others live, different again in language and custom. Even more foreign to him are the little brown people subsisting on the escarpment itself, living in caves, supplying herbs and ironwork. They are strange even though they are the people of his own grandmother; he himself uses some of their words, sharp with clicks. It's said that people further north laugh at him and his clicking kind.

And the little people raid his cattle. He has to keep an eye out.

In the reckoning of the European peoples who made some of the beads he wears, it's AD 1300, but he knows nothing of them. He'll be a couple of centuries dead before the first Portuguese sailors touch on the eastern seaboard. He also knows nothing of the Indians the Portuguese will be looking for, though the ancient ancestors of the grey-humped cattle he owns originated in India. Nor does he know that the sorghum he grows on the fertile valley floor in summer comes from beyond the Niger River and the forests of the Cameroon. His fat-tailed sheep are originally from the Middle East. Some local artefacts of iron and, further north, gold, may well find their way back there. The greatest gold-makers, with their cities of stone (to which his own humble pens and house complex are distantly related), live far to the north. He has heard no more than the faintest rumours of the empire centred there – Zimbabwe – at this point just reaching its influential peak.

The man's horizons are limited, but influences from the north drift down, subtle as dust. He is already being integrated into the world economy.

Where does he *think* he came from? One strand of his ancestry – his grandfather's line, dark and rangy – he may think of as having migrated from the north somewhere. Those origins are so far back that they are beyond the reach of even the oldest of the stories regularly recounted around the evening fire. The biggest movement he's actually aware of has been from the ridge just to the east. That is still his father's ridge; it may become his own eldest son's ridge once the old man dies. Or the son will form a settlement of his own, just far away enough to give his own cattle the grazing they need.

Which is hardly further away than hailing distance. There's plenty of space; groups of people, though related, can live almost entirely distinct from each other.[1]

HISTORY AND PURITY

Who were all these people, whose individual lives – as the reconstruction above implies – we can only imagine? The story as it is usually told (or written) is that the people who came to be known as 'Bantu-speakers' originated on the borderlands of Cameroon and Nigeria. They 'occupied' east Africa around 3 000 years ago, and crossed the Zambezi river into the south some centuries after that. Some writers have pictured this 'Bantu migration' as the greatest movement of peoples in history: violent, catastrophic.[2] But given that it was only some 5 000 kilometres in 500 years, it was certainly more complex, and much slower, than that.

There is no direct evidence that there was ever an actual 'migration' at all. Genes can flow through populations with scarcely a body leaving home. If actual individuals moved, it was more likely in small groups, one river valley at a time, in fits and starts, sometimes by intermarriage, sometimes by raid, sometimes by short-term conquest and colonisation.[3] New people brought new technologies, others were discovered and invented. Trade probably pushed these technologies ahead of them, so that by the time 'they' arrived in southern Africa, they encountered indigenous peoples already carrying water in so-called 'Matola' or 'Chifumbaze' clay pots, planting sorghums, forging iron, herding cattle and sheep.[4]

This brings us to our imaginary man's second ancestral strand: that of his grandmother. She is short, big-bottomed, a pale creamy bronze; she speaks the clicking language. She thinks of herself as one of the originals – an autochthon, her people have been here for as long as there have been human beings.[5] The two strands are in the process of cross-fertilising each other. It is sometimes the autochthons who have become the ironsmiths for the newcomers. The 'natives' have imposed something of their language, even their spiritual beliefs, on the immigrants.[6]

In short, it was not, as the usual story would portray it, a straightforward case of invasive, superior, sophisticated mixed farmers ('Bantu') obliterating simple-minded nomadic hunter-gatherers ('Bushmen'). Relations were variable: sometimes hostile and destructive, more often cordial. Genes mixed as marriages, minor migrations, and no doubt sometimes rape occurred.[7] The 'San' who survived this ponderously slow mutation were those who already lived in areas that were inaccessible to cattle and therefore unattractive to the farmers. Most likely many adapted, even as they tried to preserve their own traditions: the hunting techniques, the herbal lore, the art of their ancestors. In the richer agricultural areas, the original people were probably eliminated more by assimilation than by conflict. Some conflict there surely was: the term 'Twa' or 'Ntwa' survived into literate times as an insulting term for the little people; and more northerly peoples called their southern neighbours, with their click-inflected speech, 'Abathwa' too.[8]

This brings us to the question of how the imaginary man in our story would have thought of himself. What labels or names might he have attached to his identity? What groups did he see himself as representing and belonging to? The short answer, of course, is that we have no way of knowing. The lack of written records has condemned him to absolute silence. We cannot know quite what language he would have spoken, though the distinct dialects we find much later must have been forming throughout this era.[9] He would certainly not have thought of himself as 'Bantu' – a term coined only in 1862 by the German ethnologist W.H.I. Bleek – any more than his grandmother would have labelled herself 'San', 'Bushman', Khoikhoin', or 'Khoisan', all names bandied about by European academics obsessed with classification.[10] Nor would he have thought of himself as 'Nguni', a term popularised still later, in 1929, by another amateur European missionary anthropologist, A.T. Bryant.[11] And certainly not 'Zulu', 'Ndwandwe', 'Thembu', 'Mbo', or any of the other 'tribal' names that would eventually characterise the people of this south-eastern corner of Africa – what I'm calling the Thukela-Phongolo catchment (see Map 1 on page 15).

As these names actually came into local use, it was often with very different connotations. *When* they came into use, we will never really know. The same must be said of 'Zulu' itself. There is no clear evidence of when anybody first came to think of themselves as 'Zulu'. Even when people do eventually record themselves as 'Zulu', it remains slippery, changeable, one of several possible

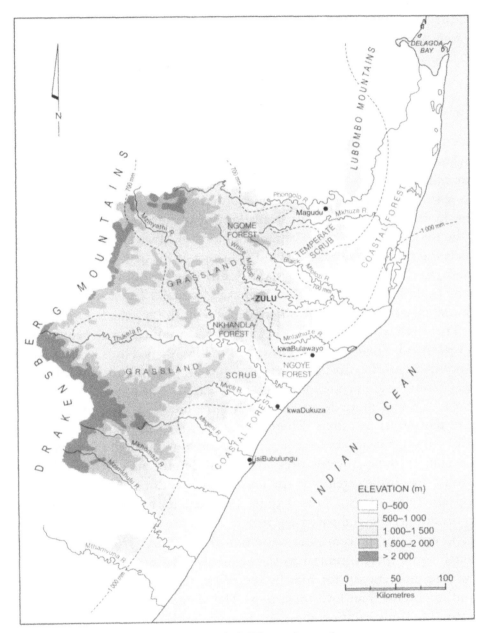

Map 1: The Thukela-Phongolo catchment

simultaneous identities. Contrary to the epigraph at the start of this chapter, there is no such thing as 'pure Nguni' or 'pure Zulu'.

In matters of identity and ancestry there is no such thing as purity.

NGUNI, NTUNGWA, LALA

Let's take a leap some 500 years forward in time. It's now around 1750. Imagine another man, standing on the very same ridge. He is tall, quite dark-skinned, able-bodied if paunchy, and (if we could place him alongside the first, earlier man) clearly a genetic descendant. Let's imagine further that the ridge is one that has become known as the Gcongco, leading down to the middle reaches of the White Mfolozi river. (By a strange coincidence, this is the place where Shaka would fight one of his major battles, and also where, in 1985, a film-maker named Bill Faure would build, and then dramatically burn down, a replica of Shaka's 'capital'.) The man looks around him. What's the same, what different, from all those years before?

There is – we can surmise – less forest and wildlife, more people, cattle and grassland. There are many clusters of beehive-shaped huts in view, almost all on the ridges, heavily palisaded with poles and thorn-bush. Little building is happening in stone nowadays. This society is in some respects more mobile than it was, and more defensive. Life is more crowded, safer in some ways, more dangerous in others. There's a new form of heavy grain available – maize – though it's tricky to grow, and the sorghums are still the staple grain. The man is, today anyway, dressed in considerable finery: he is about to attend a first-fruits ceremony, the *umkhosi*, which can only occur when the local chieftain says so. This is quite new; chieftains are becoming more important, getting comparatively richer. There are more trade goods going in and out from the coast; beads are now the primary form of bride-wealth, though cattle remain central to the economy. The man is about to gain a new wife, one chosen for him by the *inkosi*, the chieftain: politics can be more important than love these days. The woman is also a reward for his loyalty. Men are banding together, because raids – mostly for cattle – are becoming more frequent; some say there are pale-skinned marauders from the coast who also take people away in great shells and eat them on the high seas. He himself has been out quite often now hunting elephants; the teeth are hacked out and sent on the heads of war-captives to feed the pale coastal strangers. His particular arrangement of genet skins, monkey tails and crimson lourie feathers distinguishes his group (they are of his age and were circumcised together). In his hair he wears two gall bladders: signs that he has killed in battle, something even his own father had never done. One of his three spears is specifically designed to stab people. Society is indeed changing, he can feel it happening; it's slow, but it's as palpable and alarming as the onset of drought.

How might *this* imagined man have identified himself? Who and what are the groups he might have associated with? It's possible he thought of himself in some way as 'Zulu', or 'Mthethwa', or 'Langeni'. Almost all Western historians of precolonial peoples have thought in terms of such 'tribes'. These are sometimes refined into 'clans' or 'septs'. Interpretation has been dominated by these ethnic criteria, by genealogies of blood-relations. But these are not the only identities that people have. The man – now making his way to join not only his own circumcision-band, but others he scarcely knows or even cares for, but who, like him, pay periodic tribute in cattle or iron or exotic feathers to the same chieftain – has several other names for himself, too.

(This shouldn't be surprising. I, for instance, might describe myself as 'European' [by ancestry], either 'Rhodesian' or 'Zimbabwean' [by birth], 'South African' [by current domicile], or 'African' [by political conviction], depending on circumstance. Most of us do this.)

By way of example, three other names, or labels of identity, seem to have been important to the people of the Thukela-Phongolo catchment: *Nguni*, *Ntungwa*, and *Lala*. These cut across, enrich, and complicate the 'ethnic' labels.

An immediate problem is that there's considerable muddle amongst indigenous informants, most of them recorded in the late nineteenth century or early twentieth century. They are seldom in agreement even about what these names refer to. Some informants think of the names as primordial 'tribes'. For others they're simply insults. There are those who connect them with geographical areas or use them to highlight linguistic differences. On occasion, one name will act as shorthand for something else, in the way that

'Protestant' and 'Catholic' connote deeper ethnic and historical divisions in Northern Ireland. Some, like Magema Fuze, writing just after 1900 in the first extended history published by a Zulu author, use the terms in all these senses at once. According to Fuze, the 'Ntungwa' were a western stream of immigrants, the 'Nguni' an eastern one; they settled in different places and spoke differently. The Ntungwa - it seems - felt no shame in going about naked.[12] But no other indigenous informant supports Fuze on this point.

First, let's consider the name *Nguni*. Most, but not all informants are agreed that the Zulu are 'abeNguni', along with the Xhosa. This is one man's list of Nguni peoples: Qwabe, Makhanya, Chunu, Zulu, Biyela, Langa, Ntombela, Magwaza.[13] Other informants think of the Xhosa as the 'true Nguni'.[14] Some say that there was an original Nguni tribe who preceded the formation of the Zulu and Qwabe people, also known as *umzantsi*.[15] Another speculates that the Nguni came from the east coast somewhere.[16] Still others feel that 'Nguni' implies a local, not an immigrant, identity.[17] In this last view, the Zulu themselves did not come from anywhere, but came into existence *in situ*, right where they were still to be found in the 1910s.[18]

The *Ntungwa* - our second label - are thought of by some as coming from the north, as having, metaphorically, rolled down 'by means of a grain-basket' - that is, carrying their provisions with them. They were immigrants, invaders. One informant says that the word comes from *intungwa* grass, used for thatching huts.[19] The Bhele, for instance, thought of themselves as Ntungwa. They 'rolled down in a grain-basket'. A piece of fat appeared in the basket. The person with the piece of fat ran away to the Zulu country, and was followed by the rest.[20] Several peoples use this allegory to explain their origins.[21]

But many an informant will throw an assegai into the historical works by claiming, for instance, that the Xhosa are the great Nguni precisely *because* they came from the north.[22] Or that it was the Zulu themselves who rolled down from eLenge, Job's Kop, in their grain-basket.[23] Or that 'the amaChunu are Ntungwa like the Zulus; also the Qwabe, but as they lived *down*-country near the Mthethwa they *tefula*'d' - that is, they spoke differently.[24] Or that the Zulu were all of them at once: 'abeSutu, abaNguni, amaNtungwa, abakwaZulu'.[25]

What are we to make of this confusion? MAZIYANA,[26] one of James Stuart's most thoughtful informants, makes some telling observations:

> Qwabes and Zulus speak of themselves as abeNguni, *though they are really amaNtungwa*. One cannot say which arrived first, amaNtungwa or abeNguni, but as the Qwabe, who were Ntungwas, *came to speak of themselves* as Ngunis, so it seems to me there was a small settlement of Ngunis here first, and these Ngunis *modified their Ntungwa dialect.*[27]

There are three important statements here, which I've highlighted in italics. Firstly, the comment that the Zulu are '*really amaNtungwa*'. They were, in this view, not local but intruders 'from the north'. But they didn't want to be thought of as such. They wanted to belong, to be rooted, to feel naturalised here. They preferred to think of other peoples, like the Mphungose and the Zondi, as Ntungwa, as foreign.[28] Indeed, they felt deeply offended if they themselves were called 'Ntungwa'. Shaka was gravely insulted in this way on a couple of occasions. Phakathwayo, an obstreperous leader of the Qwabe, taunted Shaka, 'Little Ntungwa who came down by means of a grain basket'. Mande of the Cele likewise snorted, 'Never will I come under the protection of an Mntungwa [Shaka] who wears the shell of the *intongwane* fruit as a penis-cover'.[29]

This is a clue. People raise verbal smokescreens. They call themselves by labels that will advantage them; they deny those that demean them. They invent etymological connections and histories, if only to ridicule the size of an opponent's manly organ. There is no *necessary* correlation between what people say and the historical 'truth'. We cannot tell from these statements alone whether the Zulu really did 'come from the north', or developed as self-conscious 'Zulu' in one place. But what we *can* say is that the Zulu – or at least some Zulu – were extraordinarily sensitive about the question of their origins. Why? The whole issue is pervaded by an air of discomfort, as if they feel they shouldn't really be there at all. Shaka seems to have felt particularly uncomfortable.

There's another clue in MAZIYANA's second italicised statement. People change their views of themselves over time; they '*c[o]me to speak of themselves*' as this or that. So it was said, 'We [Zulu] were called abeSuthu because we lived upcountry (*enhla*). We left the abeSuthu, who were of different kinds, and by living so long apart from them we have become another people.'[30] Equally, the criteria by which a particular grouping was distinguished might change. So it seems with the label 'Ntungwa':

> To foster the growth of a sense of corporate identity among them, people in this category were encouraged by their Zulu rulers to regard themselves as all being of common descent, viz. *amantungwa* (or 'upcountry') descent. In time, many of them did, in fact, come to think of themselves as sharing a common origin and culture. *Ntungwa*-ness thus came to constitute an ethnic identity which, like all ethnic identities, developed in specific political circumstances.[31]

One important kind of change is in the way people spoke: 'the Ngunis *modified their Ntungwa dialect*' is MAZIYANA's third point. There's nothing strange in this. People have always distinguished themselves by accent and intonation and differences of dialect. They have always modified their accents in order to belong, or to align themselves with those who wield power and patronage.[32]

The third label of identity involves a stronger distinction that was made between those who called themselves 'Ntungwa' and those known as the 'amaLala'. This was partly a matter of accent: Shaka called the Cele 'Lala' because he said they spoke with their tongues lying flat in their mouths.[33] Like the Mthethwa, to whom the Cele were related or at least attached themselves, they said '*inkonane*' for '*inkonyane*' (a calf).[34] They *tekeza*'d or *tefula*'d, spoke in a manner associated with the region south of the Thukela river. But it could also cut the other way: the Zulu, too, were reported by some to *qotshamisa* – to hold their tongues low in their mouths.[35] Shaka himself is said to have spoken like this, saying, for example, *kona loku* rather than *kona yoku*.[36] By others, this would be derided as an actual speech defect; it becomes difficult to say whether Shaka really did have a physical deformity, or whether these informants are just being nasty about his accent. All of this adds up to the vital realisation that the same term can have utterly opposite connotations, depending on who is using it when.

Almost certainly the term 'amaLala' had been in use before Shaka's time.[37] In other southern African societies a similar word was applied to outsiders, serfs, the impoverished. Generally speaking, it may have meant something like 'menial'.[38] Only in Shaka's era did the term also come to have geographical, even ethnic, connotations. It was refined to apply to those who lived along the Natal coast; they were despised by the Zulu as lowlanders, idiots, and foreigners, all at once. So Shaka scoffed that the Cele, being amaLala, didn't have the cunning to make something out of nothing, couldn't distinguish between good and bad, and had filthy habits. They 'farted on the mimosa tree and dried it up'. When they went to sleep they lay (*lala*) with their fingers up their bums – and at dawn sucked the finger and spat at the sun.[39] The amaLala were known for scarifying their faces or, like the Bomvu, cutting off a joint of the little finger. Ntungwas wouldn't dream of doing that. The terms also came to have class or status connotations. As Mqaikana says, 'We Zondi are amaLala, having been called so by the Zulu who defeated us, so insulting us'.[40] Eventually these lowland folk would start calling *themselves* 'amaLala'.

The terms, in short, were never intrinsic; they were acquired and changeable. They were vigorously contested at the time, and continued to be contested later. As we will see, some inherited meanings were certainly altered by Shaka's intervention and power. They had probably changed before, and would be changed again after him, as Zulu history unfolded. Nor were the three 'categories' that we have looked at here the only ones.[41] People picked up labels as they moved in place, status, and time. They used them to ingratiate and to insult. They stole them, massaged them, lied about them. Nevertheless, these strategies are themselves essential to our history. They *are* history. Identities are always tangled and multiple. In reading historical testimonies, we are always witness to the dynamics of identities in the very process of being forged.

TIME AND THE ANCESTORS

Was Shaka born into a people who already called themselves, thought of themselves, as distinctively 'Zulu'? Did he invent the name, or just give an old name a new lustre? If it was already being used, how old was it?

It turns out that such 'tribal' or 'clan' identities, the labels that most of us are familiar with, are just as troublesome as *Nguni* or *Ntungwa* or *Lala*. For one thing, the terms are now riddled with Western anthropological prejudice. The peoples of present-day KwaZulu-Natal do, of course, define themselves in part by those terms that we have come to know as 'tribal'. So we can't ignore or avoid them, but we have to remember that they are less stable than is generally believed.[42]

Not surprisingly, there are conflicting ideas amongst informants about just where the Zulu 'came from'. They range from 'very far away and out of antiquity', to 'right here in KwaZulu and relatively recently'. The most distant alleged connection seems to be with the 'Suthu', who occupied the chilly plateaux beyond the Drakensberg. This was not because they were related; they were just close to each other.[43] Even that is not very far away: perhaps a couple of hundred kilometres. Although this connection is sometimes associated with a move from 'the north', this makes little geographical sense. The Drakensberg mountains are almost due *west* of the Mhlathuze and Mfolozi valleys, which is where we meet the Zulu next. Often, though, the term informants use is simply *enhla*, or as we've seen, *ntungwa*, meaning 'upcountry'.

So maybe, just maybe, some of the ancestors of the Zulu people moved east or south-east from the mountains.

When might this have been? Oral traditions take no account of the question; archaeology is almost useless in this regard. We have practically no outside documentation – not until the 1820s. The Portuguese records are largely confined to the coast, and are at most suggestive and sketchy.[44]

Perhaps the best we can do is to work back through recorded Zulu genealogies, the list of ancestral leaders, the *amakhosi*. In some versions, this goes back seven or eight generations. One informant refers to a decidedly mythical-sounding original forebear: 'Bhekaphezulu was the first. He had a son Mntungwa, whilst Mntungwa's son was Nnja. Now it so happened that the Lembe people fought with Nnja and gave him the opprobrious name Lufenulwenja', an insult associated with a dog's bottom.[45]

The insulted Nnja begat Malandela who begat Zulu and Qwabe, two brothers – the first ancestors of whom we begin to hear any detail. Zulu, as we'll see, is the man who is thought of by some as having made the move into what would become the Zulu heartland – and who gave his name to the 'tribe'.

A.T. Bryant, in his monumental *Olden Times in Zululand and Natal* (1929), embarked on a quest to establish the chronology of this notional Zulu line. He rightly noted that there were a number of variations on the family genealogies as recorded over the years from a variety of sources. He eliminated some of the more speculative entrants, and boiled the rest down to what he thought was the closest he could get to the 'true' genealogy. This was misguided, as such testimonies can't be 'boiled down'. The contradictions are precisely the point: they reflect the politics and desires of the different informants. At any rate, Bryant then decided, after comparing various other African and European genealogies, to assign eighteen years per reign. He worked his way back, and decided that Malandela must have died around 1691. In this view, Zulu's move *might* have happened at around that time.[46]

Bryant knew that he was being wildly speculative. Even so, he took no account of possible variations in lifespans, accidents, usurpations, periods of regency, wars and peace. He could not be sure whether these alleged members of the line were in fact direct ancestors at all. This method of establishing a chronology has now been thoroughly discredited,[47] and an undisputed genealogy simply doesn't exist (see Box 1 on page 33).

In any event, it is only with reference to the Mhlathuze river, which loops and curls through deep valleys between present-day Babanango and Richard's Bay, that some detail begins to emerge in the recorded traditions. Somewhere around the headwaters of the Mhlathuze, most informants maintain, the Zulu began. Their beginning is captured in a story, which is almost certainly no more than that – a story.

A TALE OF TWO BROTHERS

There were – so the narrative goes – the two brothers already mentioned, Qwabe and Zulu. They might both have been members of an existing people known as Chunu or Chunwini, or not.[48] Their people were known as hawkers of tobacco, or of medicines, roots and herbs.[49] They lived close together, and also near to others whose names we'll meet again and again: Buthelezi, Mabaso, and Khumalo. In one account, some Zulu are said to trace themselves to a Langa ancestor, Sibiya.[50] These various folk lived on neighbouring ridges, even on the same ridge. They collaborated in times of threat. Perhaps they spoke a common dialect, thought of as *Hofe*, a name associated with an Ntungwa oath, 'Ho, *ofe!*'[51]

Qwabe and Zulu were sons of Malandela and Nozidiya.[52] Qwabe was the eldest. In a crucial event in the ancestral memory, they separated at the Mhlathuze river. Most versions say there was a quarrel – apparently because their mother Nozidiya palmed off a goat on Qwabe, while secretly giving Zulu a white heifer, and a productive one at that. When Qwabe spotted Zulu's herd of white cattle on the hills, he headed off in a huff down to the 'great reed-bed' of the Mhlathuze proper.[53] Zulu either stayed behind, or moved away himself towards the White Mfolozi, where we'll rejoin him shortly.

This is also, more or less, the story related by Bryant in *Olden Times*, which was henceforth uncritically accepted by historians as 'fact'.

The tale of the white heifer could be a cipher for a succession dispute.[54] But other informants assert that there was no dispute at all. MBOVU, himself a Qwabe, argues that Qwabe simply wanted to get to warmer, lower ground. Zulu remained behind, at a gorge or donga called Thathiyana (old spelling Tatiyana), because he actually preferred herding goats.[55] MMEMI, also a Qwabe, tells another story, involving not Zulu, but another brother, Ngema (or, confusingly, Mcineka). This dispute centred on a hunt, the outcome of which was supposed to decide seniority between Ngema (or Mcineka) and Qwabe. Qwabe's people killed a duiker, ceremoniously smeared its anus with blood, and won.[56] This succession dispute brought about the split.

The whole story resonates with the structure of numerous cultures' origins myths.[57] The differences between versions make nonsense of any attempt to find a 'core' of truth. The alleged wanderings make little geographical sense. The name Malandela never appears in Qwabe genealogies, which usually portray quite independent origins. The contradictions between the genealogies expressed by later Qwabe ruling lineages, as opposed to those 'remembered' by so-called subordinate lineages, expose the way later manipulations happened. After Qwabe power was largely absorbed by Shaka's Zulu, the ruling lineage invented ancestries that would legitimise the new distribution of power; but it was never quite strong enough to repress the historical memories of subordinate lineages like the Makhanya.[58]

In short, the story of Zulu and Qwabe was invented, probably in early Shakan times. It is a metaphor: retrospective, colourful, and effective. It does not state the facts of Zulu and Qwabe roots – but it does express rootedness. It was intended first and foremost to explain the present. We will come across lots of tales of this kind.

One way or another, the 'Qwabe' established themselves on the lower Mhlathuze river. (We can't be sure when they began to think of themselves as such, either.) But what happened to Zulu – or to 'the Zulu'? The contradictions between accounts further highlight Zulu's mythical nature. By some, he is said to have hiked across the hills to the White Mfolozi river, settling at Mzinhlanga, near where the great Zulu *umuzi*, settlement, Nobamba would later be built. This was possibly Shaka's birthplace.[59] Another tradition, however, states that 'the Zulu' actually didn't hike in from anywhere: they came into being around Nhlazatshe, a little further north, and moved south to Nobamba from there.[60] Either way, the Mhlathuze isn't very far: about 30 kilometres; one good day's walk.

The consensus has to be, I think, that 'Zulu' self-consciousness emerged right there, probably during the mid-1700s. This is the case whether a chieftain named Zulu did exist, giving his name to the emergent group (this is not unusual), or whether he was invented later to 'explain' the group's name. Historically speaking, we're sure of nothing, but the story has undeniable power. It has become an integral part of Zulu identity.

As for the composition of the group itself, there is absolutely no reason to believe that it comprised a core of ethnically pure 'Zulu' whose 'blood' somehow flowed unadulterated into the future to make 'the Zulu nation' what it was. Members of the dominant group – a core which could be later termed 'royal' – would of course be trying to spread their genes. They would command power precisely in accordance with their ability to procure more wives, have more children, acquire more wealth in cattle, and exercise greater influence through family ties. These original 'Zulu' were certainly accompanied by other groups – the Mabaso, the Buthelezi – with whom they were intermarrying, as the principles of exogamy demanded. This practice of marrying outside the clan ensures, inevitably and mathematically, a steady watering-down of any one family strain. So to hold onto a notion of 'Zulu-ness' as a biological given or constant is absurd.

ANCESTRY AND RESPECT

When we move on to the next rung of the genealogy, we begin to get some concrete support in the form of gravesites. At least one informant thinks Malandela himself was buried at Nobamba, though his gravesite has never been located.[61] Zulu is said by some to have been buried near the site of Dingane's great *umuzi* Mgungundlovu (now a museum).[62] The graves of Malandela's other sons are barely better attested. Whether there are any actual bones in the various gravesites, no one has ever checked, but it hardly matters now. The sites express Zulu belonging; they accept that this is where the people truly began and consecrated the ground with their deaths. The chieftains would have been buried within the thorn-wood walls of their respective central enclosures, and the bush allowed to grow back over their bones. The graves' closeness to one another suggests there was very little movement of their people over four or five generations. The area would become known retrospectively as *Emakhosini*, 'the burial place of kings' (though the petty family heads who preceded Shaka hardly deserved that title). This is where the great ceremonies of respect for the ancestors would forever be performed, and you can visit the graves today – south of the Mpembeni stream which flows into the White Mfolozi, on the farms Bergvliet, Heelgoed and Pandasgraf. However, as H.C. Lugg warns, 'their correct allocation is open to considerable doubt'.[63]

Of the actual men said to be buried there, we know next to nothing. There is also more confusion. JANTSHI asserts that Zulu had three sons, Mageba, Phunga, and Ndaba, who stood in the dynasty in the same way as Shaka, Dingane, and Mpande stood.[64] This is possible, but sounds suspiciously like a justification for the later trio. Other informants point out that most *izibongo* praises say, 'Phunga kaMageba', the 'ka' indicating that Phunga was Mageba's son.[65] Cetshwayo, the *inkosi* who lost his battle with the British invaders in 1879, had a somewhat different version:

Umalandela . . . was succeeded by his son, Undhlana, who was succeeded by his son Zulu, who was succeeded by his son, Untombela; who was succeeded by his son, Ukosinkulu, who was also called Mamba; who was succeeded by his son, Umageba; who was succeeded by his son, Uphunga; who was succeeded by his son, Undaba; who was succeeded by his son, Ufaina, who was the father of Senzagacone.[66]

No other informant agrees with this in its entirety, though, which goes to show that even royalty has no monopoly on accuracy.

Most informants place Ndaba as following Mageba and Phunga. Ndaba's grave seemed to be the biggest, the most revered in the collective memory. The grass was burned around it every May.[67] It was Ndaba's praises that were recalled as being sung at the great first-fruits ceremony, the *umkhosi*, as late as Mpande's time (the 1840s). It's worth lingering on this festival a while because, although the descriptions below refer to after Shaka's time, they almost certainly were fully practised well before him. These ceremonies express the continuities in Zulu history and culture: beneath the political turbulence, the raids and counter-raids, and the incursions of foreigners, they form the symbolic artery that most firmly and beautifully runs from the present back into the most distant and most rooted past. They *are* the Zulu sense of belonging; if we are to find the heart of the 'Zulu character' anywhere, it would have to be here. MTSHAYANKOMO describes the *umkhosi* ceremony:

The *umkosi* in the Zulu country began in the month of the *inyatelo*, the month of uZibandhlela [October–November]; that was the little *umkosi*. It would be the younger warriors who assembled; the more senior ones would remain at home. It would be the Mbonambi regiment that would assemble, even if incompletely, even if only two companies (*amaviyo*) were present, or even only one. The Kandempemvu and the Ngobamakosi regiments were assembled to gather firewood in the bush country of the White Mfolozi. The wood would be for burning the bull. This bull would be fetched from foreign parts, stolen from the grazing grounds. It would be a fighting bull, pitch black in colour, a big, old one, that would rip out people's innards. We had to have its tendons slashed because it overcame all the warriors, until we Ngobamakosi were set on to help them. We blocked it off in front.

The bull was eaten by the young boys, those who had not yet reached puberty, the carriers of mats and blankets. Older youths,

those who had reached puberty, did not eat it. These younger boys
were called into the inmost enclosure, the *isigodhlo*, where the king
was *nqwamba*'d - a strip of the skin draped around his shoulders -
and the bull burnt. The king was given protective medicines. He did
not partake of any of the food until the next day. The boys were not
allowed to leave; they were shut up in the king's washing enclosure
until the next day, without being allowed to defecate or urinate. At
dawn the bull would still be burning. The fire was fed continually and
the bull was burnt, the flames crackling. Strips of meat as long as
one's arm were continually cut off. It would burn for two days. The
king would stand on a rush mat and be treated by *izinyanga*, medicine-
men. On the third day the burning would be over.

Then followed the ceremony of asking for rain at the place of the
kings - Senzangakhona, Ndaba, Phunga, and Mageba - there where
they were buried. A small herd of royal oxen, black in colour, without
markings, and which were not to be touched, was driven along by the
regiments, all those from the Emahlabatini country. The men who
drove them dressed in the finery which they wore at the time of the
umkosi. Only their ox-tail decorations were left in the huts. These
were not worn as they would get wet. There was no thunder; only a
drizzle fell. When they left the sky was clear; there were no clouds, for
it was very dry. They passed Bulawayo, Ndabakawombe, crossed the
White Mfolozi, passed Siklebeni, and crossed the Mkumbane. There
they broke into a chant. They halted. All the regiments came up and
stood together in one place, with the cattle grazing in front of them.
They broke into the great chant (*irubo*):

> *O ye, iye he yiya! Ha! O hu yiyi!*
> *Ha! O ho hu. Oye iye! Iya! Ha o,*
> *Hi i ya! Ihi.*

Then the great *imbongi* Magolwana, standing in front, cried:

> *Now hear! Somnandi ka Ndaba!*
> *You have never even kissed the mouths.*

Now hear! Sihlopeside tree of the Gumede people!
The buffalo which goes leaning over the river crossings,
The hunter of the place of Mamfakane's people,
He does not forget his shield,
Even though the old men have forgotten theirs,
The one of variegated colours waters him with tears,
The ubenyane grass of Ndaba breaks his ribs.
The persecuted one of Ndaba!
The obstinate one who refuses to listen to whispers.

. . . Then it began to rain.[68]

We assume that there are some historical events shadowing these cryptic, vivid enchantments, but they have been lost to memory. We can learn nothing definite about Ndaba from this. But the names and imagery would resonate in the excited minds of the people, re-affirming their place in the world through honoured and honourable ceremony. They would re-connect their often turbulent present with the timeless presence of their revered leaders, whose graves they would now proceed to tend in strict order:

The kings were buried at one place, at Nobamba and esiGezeni and at Siklebeni. At all these graves the people would form a circle at a distance; no one would go close. A clump of trees grew on each grave; no one would go into the trees. We formed a single circle surrounding all the graves . . . On the westward side would be the Nobamba, Ngwegwe, Dukuza and Siklebe regiments . . . The Tulwana were close to the grave of Mnkabayi, near esiGezeni. The Nobamba would be standing near the grave of the king who had been buried on that side . . . When this was done the regiments began to do the *ukuketa* dance, section by section. We sang:

> Come (asking for rain),
> Come then; come here; come, then; come here.[69]

The *amabutho* would then disperse to their *imizi*, their homesteads, wet with the falling rain, chanting. They would sacrifice cattle, and ululate again the

praises of each of the ancestors whose graves they had honoured. At other
times, the graves would be honoured with gifts from the sites of *amakhosi*
who – like Shaka and Dingane – had been buried elsewhere. Senior headmen
of Senzangakhona's stock – the *izinduna* – would dig up a tree from the
faraway grave, and replant it ceremoniously amongst those on the ancestral
graves at emaKhosini. Or a stone would be brought and placed there. This
was called the *isithombe*. In this way, the spirit was brought back to the ancestral
resting-place, where it could be *thetha*'d, praised. Cattle could be properly
sacrificed.[70] History itself is thus consecrated.

GRANDFATHER JAMA

Ndaba, the earliest *inkosi* whose praises have survived in any bulk, had at
least four sons, including Xoko, Mbuzo, Nkwelo and Jama – Shaka's
grandfather.[71] Jama is the man usually – but not always – credited with
building the *umuzi* at Nobamba, a central node of Zulu occupation.[72] Jama is
also the first Zulu *inkosi* recorded as having other peoples *khonza*, swear
allegiance and fealty, to him: namely, the Buthelezi and the Bhele.[73] These
are hints, perhaps, that the Zulu were beginning to show some muscle; that
circumstances were changing sufficiently to prod people into joining forces
in a rather more organised fashion than before; and that power was being
wielded and distributed in a new way. Jama certainly had a good number of
children, perhaps a sign of some influence. Mnkabayi, Mawa, Mthembase
and Mmama were amongst his daughters. We will meet these women again.
His sons included Sojisa and Senzangakhona – Shaka's father – as well as
Khekhe, Magunza, Nomaphikela, Nobongoza and (controversially) Nkwelo.[74]
    Jama died while Senzangakhona was still quite small.[75] His daughter, the
formidable Mnkabayi, reigned for some time as regent. Shortly after his
death – one account goes – a younger widow was *ngenwa*'d, that is, given over
as a new wife, to another son, supposedly named Vubukulwayo. This widow
was Mntaniya. She and Vubukulwayo then plotted to have their own son
become the next *inkosi* rather than Senzangakhona, who had presumably
been named the heir. They sent a girl along to Mnkabayi and Senzangakhona
with some poisoned beer. They were suspicious, though, and didn't drink it.
Instead, they sent the girl off on a pretext, then concocted a complimentary

pot filled with Mnkabayi's own beer, laced with some of the poisoned stuff. This changed the colour of the beer a little, so the girl was told to take this mixture to Mntaniya with the message, 'Even the cream-coloured drink is sweet'. Mntaniya and Vubukulwayo both drank, and died.[76]

This is melodramatic stuff. Did people really try to poison their own closest kin? There are plenty of these sorts of stories, and after all Shaka himself was killed by his half-brothers. But most likely the stories hold the same relationship to reality as the swarms of violently entertaining Hollywood schlock movies hold to the reality of American society. They reflect particular fears and psychoses; they are not credible representations of what really goes on. Stories work to defuse anxiety, to distance it, to make it manageable. It only takes a few actual incidents to make this a necessity.

In any case, there's no other record of a son of Jama called Vubukulwayo. The only Vubukulwayo we hear of wasn't a Zulu at all, but a Qwabe, a son of Khondlo who much later ran into trouble with Shaka and defected to Zwide of the Ndwandwe. We will meet him again.

As for Mntaniya, the other alleged victim, at least one account names her as the mother of Senzangakhona who protected the baby Shaka from his own father.[77] She didn't die of poisoning at all. More than likely the tale reflects a folk memory that there was some kind of succession dispute, that Senzangakhona had to overcome various obstacles to his taking over. This might have been particularly the case if there was a period of regency until he came of age.

We have arrived at the time of Shaka's birth. We are little the wiser about the chronology. We know almost nothing for certain about his ancestors, or about their identity as 'Zulu' or otherwise. The old ideas about mass migrations from the north owe more to European prejudices about barbarian hordes than to actual evidence. I speculate that a network of families calling themselves 'Zulu' had been in existence for at least four generations before Shaka. Almost certainly they came into being as self-conscious 'Zulu' more or less where the Zulu heartland remains to this day. Like all such groupings, the network was fluid in its composition, constantly added to through political and marriage alliances, and constantly diminished as family members came of age and split away in the usual fashion. Such earlier splits and alliances are expressed metaphorically in tales about disputes and migrations. The identity of 'the Zulu people' is thus as much a matter of stories as of facts, and a great deal of what we've explored in this chapter likely has been invented in retrospect.

We have focused so far only on one tiny segment of the picture, on one small corner of the Thukela-Phongolo catchment, almost on a single spur overlooking the southern bank of the White Mfolozi river. But Shaka's genealogy was not unfolding in a vacuum. We need now to take a much broader view and to consider the regional situation into which Shaka was born.

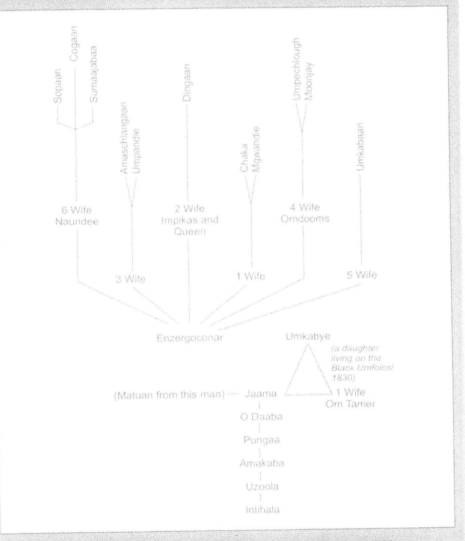

Box 1

Zulu genealogies

Shaka's family genealogy according to Andrew Smith in 1832
(in Kirby, 1955, 88).

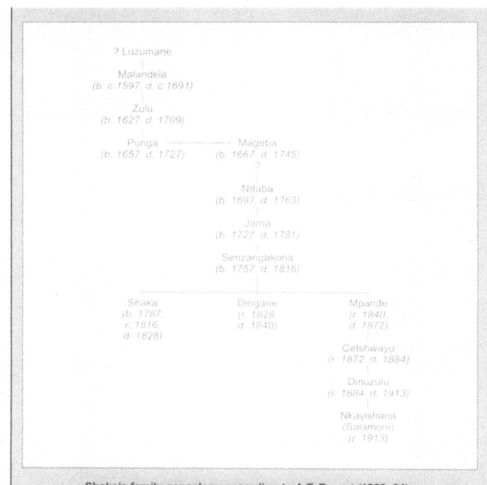

Shaka's family genealogy according to A.T. Bryant (1929, 34).

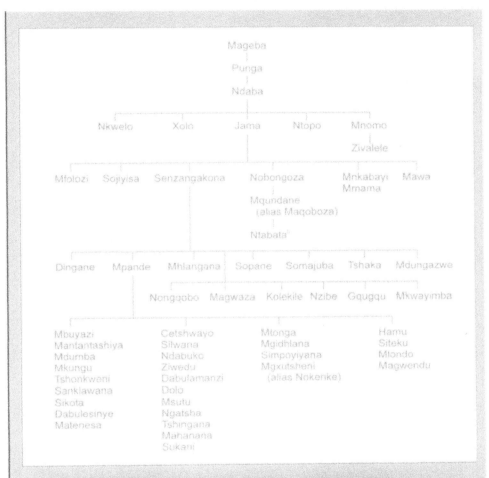

Shaka's family genealogy according to MGIDHLANA (110).

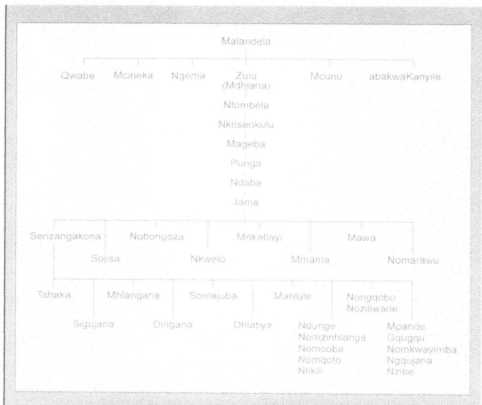

Shaka's family genealogy according to MMEMI (265).

2

Under pressure

Regional contexts, c.1780

> In the 1820s the mounting population pressure in the black half of
> South Africa caused an outburst of political violence, the *mfecane* or
> 'time of troubles'. At the eye of the storm was the dreaded Shaka
> [whose] leadership transformed the Zulu . . . into the master race of
> the south-east.
>
> Colin McEvedy, *The Penguin Atlas of African History* (1985, 94).

Within a few short decades of Shaka's death, the idea that he had been
single-handedly responsible for an abrupt and massive eruption of
'total war' had taken a very firm hold on the public imagination. Shaka was
the monster; all warfare before him was gentlemanly and negotiable. This
was not just an invention of white men; many Zulu people came to believe it,
too. In 1900 LUGUBU told James Stuart:

> In the fights that took place in former days, the men would hurl
> assegais at one another. They did not approach closely. If one side was
> defeated and a man was left exhausted, he would say, 'Mo! I am
> defenceless!' He would be taken captive, but never killed. When the
> fighting was over his family would come and ransom him with a beast.
> That was the custom in former times. Chiefs had not yet begun putting
> people to death, even if they had done wrong. Women were not killed
> in war, nor was a man who was running away, for he was like a woman.
> Only a man who was engaged in fighting was stabbed. The practice of

37

stabbing a man who was running away, or one who was left wounded, was begun by Shaka. Small boys, children, used not to be killed. The practice of killing even women was begun by Shaka. Chiefs are responsible for acts of madness.[1]

This image of Shaka is a myth. People everywhere love to dream of a paradisal era before some apocalypse or other fell upon them. There was surely at least *some* unbridled violence in south-eastern Africa before Shaka's time. In 1688, for example, one group, named by castaways as the 'Makanaena', reputedly did 'great injury' to their more peaceable neighbours, stole their cattle, and did 'not spare women and children, inhumanly murdering them'.[2] Nor – as we will see – did negotiation come to a sudden halt when Shaka came to power. And, no doubt, even in a period of apparent upheaval, most people carried on living much as they always had – just as, at about the time of Shaka's birth, there were many folk living in France, blissfully ignorant that there was a 'revolution' happening at all.

Still, LUGUBU's testimony raises crucial questions. *Was* there an upsurge of violence associated with Shaka? If so, how do we explain it? What were its roots? How extensive was it? Was it really all Shaka's fault? What was the environment Shaka must have had to work within? What constrained him, provoked him, opened up opportunities for him? Was he a magnificent genius who could conquer all obstacles, or really a mere twig on the tide of greater historical forces? Or was he just a competent muddler doing the best he could in a whirlpool of influences?

Let's begin exploring these questions by outlining the regional situation around the time of his birth.

A SKETCH OF 1780

When, in or around 1780, Shaka's mother-to-be, Nandi, set about wooing Senzangakhona, we can imagine she took particular care over her array of beadwork. She had already passed on to him through giggling intermediaries a 'love-letter' or two - *isibhebhe* - colourful little pendants woven in beads. Now, as she made her way along a hillside path towards a region of little-frequented bush, where a wooing shelter had already been constructed, she wore several adornments. Around her waist was a skirt of freshly cut fibrous grass, set off by a girdle of beads, *isigege*, predominantly red in colour, signifying fertility. She had slipped this in herself, though her neckpiece, *imibhizo*, was of staggered white and yellow, colours chosen for her by her father, Mbhengi. Some of the family head's control of 'his' women – both his actual and his tribute-donated 'daughters' – was exercised through control of the beads brought in. He dictated who wore what. The colours carried complex genealogical and ethnic signals, as well as personal ones. Naturally, Nandi was determined also to be fashionable, and had smuggled in some brilliant blue glass beads that sparkled against her bronzed skin, and clinked against her brass armbands. The imported items lay quite comfortably alongside local ones – a brief rear covering of cowhide, some small gourds at her side, a couple of black-and-white porcupine-quills tucked perkily in her extravagantly worked hairstyle.

Senzangakhona, picking his way towards the rendezvous along the cattle-paths that wound between white-thorned acacia bushes, had also adorned himself. As the son of a substantial chieftain, the *inkosi* Jama, he could afford a little more: particularly striking was a panel of beads slung down his chest from a broad neckband, beautifully done in zigzag patterns of red, white and black. At his side, poking out from the somango-monkey-tail skirt, was slung a small gourd snuff container, *ishungu*, also richly covered in beads. This was a gift from *his* father, paid for in locally mined iron and agricultural produce. The raw iron would make its way to people living to the east, among the forests where there was plenty of firewood for their kilns. There they would hammer out assegais, not only a vital accoutrement for a young man, but increasingly necessary in disturbed times. Moreover, the smiths were supplying the needs of the local elephant hunters, who were hefting increased tonnages of ivory eastwards across the hills and down the river-lines to Delagoa Bay.

At almost the same moment as Nandi and Senzangakhona neared their meeting-point – we can speculate a bit further – the Dutch ship *Jagtrust* was offloading a fresh consignment of Bombay beads and rough English cloth at Delagoa Bay. The captain of the *Jagtrust* had pointedly ignored claims from the director of the Austrian-owned 'factory' on the north bank of the Espirito Santo river, that the Ostend East Africa Company had monopolised the trade. What were the Austrians going to do, shoot him? Despite their treaties with local chiefs, they couldn't even protect the ivory caravans coming from the interior; the carriers were regularly robbed by the intermediate peoples, precisely because the Austrians hadn't the wherewithal to pay them transit fees. The Dutch, by contrast, could pay for good quality ivory from well inland; prices had doubled in the previous ten years. So into the small Tsonga canoes went a few more bales of beads, many of which would soon be making their way back into the Zulu country.[3]

There is a danger, in what I have imagined here, of reading back too directly from mid-nineteenth-century knowledge. In fact, there is very little detailed information on what people wore prior to the 1840s, when beadwork developed and changed rapidly as beads became even more available. However, around the 1780s, Xhosa country had become so saturated with beads that they lost much of their value; in 1800, the Tswana leader Molihaban already displayed a keen eye for bead quality and type. There is no doubt that beads had become a crucial part of self-expression and a culturally loaded medium of exchange throughout the Thukela-Phongolo catchment by this time. Beads were just one aspect of a culture that linked its most intimate and secretive rituals – the very whisperings of lovers – with commerce and communication on a global scale.[4]

Consequently, explaining Shaka's context is a tall order. The scope is wide and the sources are meagre. Oral traditions barely begin to kick in with historical credibility around this time, and they are thin. Otherwise, we have only the accounts of various coastal sailors to go by. Onwards from Vasco da Gama, making landfall at Ilha da Mozambique in 1498, these sailors are mostly Portuguese. For three centuries they battled their way in their frail caravelles and *nãos*, en route to India, up and down the treacherous coast lying between the Mzimvubu and Maphuta rivers. For hundreds of leagues there were no easy ports, no navigable rivers. So they seldom made landfall here, and then usually only because their vessel had been smashed to planks on the rocks. A few parties survived these wrecks, making their way on foot northwards to the tenuous settlement at Delagoa Bay, or even further to Mozambique Island. Some were helped by locals; others died from starvation, disease, or the spear. Some refused to walk any more, and stayed to add their genes to the region's pot-pourri. But such travellers were few and far between, and they understood little of what they encountered. (Trying to explain conditions in the whole Thukela-Phongolo catchment through these survivors' tales would be like trying to explain South Africa's 1994 transition to democracy through two accounts written long after the event by parties of semi-literate, hungry and frightened Russian carpenters who just happened to walk along the Garden Route, one in 1990 and the other in 2000!) Nevertheless, these marginal sources are all we have.

We also need to remember that it's fatal to generalise. The Thukela-Phongolo catchment contains many different micro-environments. People in one part might react in one way to drought or slave-raids, and their counterparts in the very next valley in a completely different way. The movements of these peoples are also astoundingly complex and fluid, and for the period up to 1780, we really don't have the detail we need.

However, as KwaZulu-Natal poet Douglas Livingstone said, 'best buckle to'. Here – before we dig deeper into such evidence as we have – is a very brief overview of the situation in about 1780, the time of Shaka's birth.

Three rings of influence

Let's start at the centre: the Zulu heartland, and its immediate environs. By 1780, the Zulu people would have found themselves surrounded by several larger, more powerful groups (see Maps 2 and 3 on pages 42 and 114 respectively). Mostly they got along, often through exchanges of produce, goods, and women – wives-as-politics. Sometimes, though, these groups were aggressive raiders, demanding tribute from their neighbours, using force to get it when threats failed. To the south of the Zulu, near the coast, were the Qwabe. A little further north, on the upper Mhlathuze river, the Mkhize. To the east, the Mthethwa, who were probably trading regularly with middlemen and, ultimately, the Portuguese and other Europeans at Delagoa Bay. The Mthethwa's main rivals in this regard lay further north, centred on the middle Phongolo river: the Ndwandwe, a particularly militarised grouping. In between these agglomerations, sometimes joining them, sometimes moving away, sometimes fighting, were a welter of tiny groups of varying size and importance. The Zulu were one of these. This we can think of as the inner ring of influences.

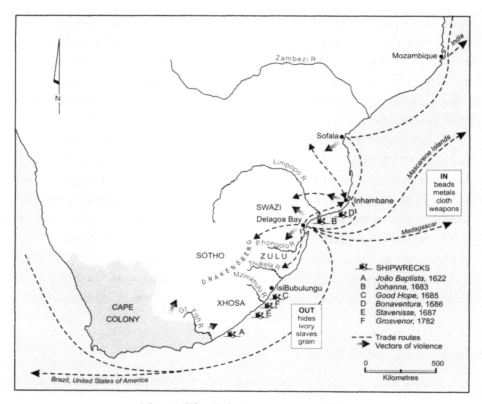

Map 2: The Zulu in context, c.1780

A second ring of more distant but not irrelevant peoples would have been known to the Zulu. Further south, beyond the Qwabe, the Cele and the Thuli, the Mpondo would become important actors in Shaka's story. The Mpondo lived around the Mzimvubu river and were related to the various peoples known collectively as the Xhosa, who occupied the space between the Mpondo and the borders of the Cape Colony. North-west, beyond the Drakensberg, the Sotho were also forming the beginnings of a kind of state, in response to violence building up along the Orange (now Gariep) river valley and amongst the northern Tswana-speaking peoples (Tau and Rolong). North-east of the Zulu and on the fringes of the Ndwandwe polity, the Ngwane, the Hlubi, and the Dlamini (later to be known as the Swazi) all appeared to be reacting in various ways – fight, surrender, or flight – to increasing aggressions from their neighbours. Finally, closest to Delagoa Bay, the Thembe-Tsonga and Mabhudu polities also influenced the Zulu heartland, mostly through their role in international trade.

This introduces the third ring, perhaps better pictured as a vast pincer movement. In some ways, the Thukela-Phongolo catchment *was* a backwater. Its forbidding coastline, which was short on harbours, together with the tricky winds and currents of the Mozambique Channel, meant that relatively few Europeans had landed there, let alone wanted to occupy it. 'The beach is generally very foul,' lamented one early traveller, 'and full of steep rocks'.[5] But through the eighteenth and early nineteenth centuries, its inhabitants would become increasingly boxed in and penetrated by outside invaders. Europeans had of course occupied the Cape to the west; the century since 1652 had seen them steadily encroaching eastwards. By 1780, the first major conflicts between white settlers and the Xhosa in the region of the Great Fish river were already boiling up. Outriders from this colony seldom penetrated directly to the Thukela river; more worrying were the northern offshoots – primarily Griqua and Kora or Koranna – who, equipped with firearms and horses, would soon be sowing unprecedented mayhem along the Orange and Caledon river valleys.

Of greater impact on the early Zulu, however, was the eastern jaw of the European pincer, hinged on the Portuguese settlement at Delagoa Bay. Portuguese influence was weaker here than further north where Inhambane, Mozambique Island and Kilwa were more important ports. And southern

Mozambique also lay just beyond the outermost fringe of the great Arabic-Indian trade-system of the east coast. Nevertheless, through Delagoa Bay, international trade in ivory, metals, cloth, grain, hides and slaves had been flowing since at least 1600. This increasingly affected societies well inland. Although the Europeans themselves had little capacity to commit aggressions at any great distance from the port, more subtle effects reached everywhere.

Just how this 'pincer' worked, from one decade to the next, even from year to year, was often sharply affected by events at an even greater distance. The activities and policies of Cape Colony officials, or of Portuguese traders at Delagoa Bay, were frequently altered by dynastic wars in Europe, Arab and Indian price wars in Oman, the development of sugar and cocoa markets in the Mascarene islands or Brazil, anti-slaving legislation passed in Britain, and so on. Consequently, what might appear on the surface to be a purely local affair in the middle of Zulu country – a very private encounter between a Zulu youth and a Langeni girl, for instance – often contained international dimensions.

STATES OF UNREST

Two important points must be made about my sketch. Firstly, it implies that there was a considerable amount of violence going on before Shaka was even born. There is no longer any real question about this. From about 1750 onwards, an upsurge of conflict was happening more or less simultaneously on the western Xhosa frontier with the whites; amongst the Tswana-speakers on the highveld;[6] and amongst the peoples living near and inland of Delagoa Bay.[7] What is still questioned is the extent of the violence, its sources, and its effects on local societies. A short answer is that it was different for different groups. Overall, however, it's safe to say that, on the one hand, most earlier European writers ignored evidence for violence before the 1810s and 1820s, preferring to blame it all on Shaka. On the other hand, when they did bring violence up, they tended to exaggerate the scale of it. The important point is that a certain increase in violence preceded Shaka's period of rule by a good half-century. Blaming Shaka alone is ludicrously facile.

The second important implication of the sketch is that quite a number of groups were gathering together into more or less centralised, more or less

militarised, 'mini-states' or, to use the term that I prefer, polities.[8] Though he
might have been more successful than most, Shaka was neither the inventor
of nor the only practitioner of this kind of process. So was there anything
new in the structure of the Zulu polity? Was it different from its neighbours
in kind, or only in degree? What exactly were its precedents in the region?

None of these questions is easy to answer. For a long time, the historical
assumption was that all African societies in the subcontinent were small-scale
and family-based: a minor chief or headman ruled a limited set of
genealogically related folk, who carried on a pastoral lifestyle that remained
static for centuries. The impression of one late seventeenth-century Dutch
traveller was carried over into anthropology and history and simplistically
generalised: 'They live together in small villages, and the oldest man governs
the rest, for all that live together are of kin, and therefore they submit to his
government'.[9]

Such assumptions are reflected in the very structure of many historical
texts about this region, which are conventionally divided into an introduction
frozen in an 'ethnographic present', followed by an explosion into narrative
'history', with Shaka often the starting point.[10] In this way, statehood, violence,
and history are presented as coterminous; a pattern I have made strong efforts
to break with in this book.[11]

The dynamics were not so straightforward. Though small kinship-based
units would remain one fundamental component of these societies, there
were other, wider allegiances, too, which waxed and waned over the years.
As early as 1589, the survivors of the *São Thomé* wreck got the impression
that 'All this land of Fumos [probably northern KwaZulu-Natal] belongs to
the king called Viragune', whereas further south 'there are no kings, but all
is in the possession of chiefs called Ancores [*amakhosi*], who are heads and
rulers of three, four and five villages'.[12] Another shipwreck survivor's account
of 1688 noted five larger groups, recognisably some of those that would survive
into the nineteenth century: the Thembu, Mpondomise, Mpondo,
Mathimba, and Griqua.[13] At least one of these groups could muster a force
of a thousand armed men. The Griqua were particularly ferocious. (Similarly,
in the 1690s, not much further south, a traveller subsequently known as the
'French boy', Guillaume de Chalezac, reported a Xhosa battle in which 'all

were massacred, men, women and children', with four or five thousand men involved.[14])

The remains of stone buildings (mentioned in Chapter 1) indicate some quite substantial centres of settlement. By the mid-eighteenth century these had been abandoned – perhaps because of increasing violence, perhaps because of ecological stress. We have no precise chronology, no firm evidence.[15]

Nevertheless, it's now clear that by the mid-eighteenth century a number of centralising polities were being formed. The most important of these groups were the Tsonga-Thembe, the Mabhudu, the Dlamini-Swazi, the Ndwandwe, the Qwabe, and the Mthethwa. These efforts at consolidation were partly novel, involving new kinds of hierarchy, and new ways of distributing resources. But they also strongly clung to the established patterns of kinship and patronage. The consolidation was still a fairly gradual process: the ejection of the Dlamini from the Delagoa Bay area, for instance, didn't fully firm up until the reign of Zikode, who probably began ruling the 'Swazi' around 1795.[16] The average person would scarcely have seen it all happen within his or her whole lifetime.

Relations between peoples weren't all hostile, either. All these groups were intricately intermarried; what they had in common probably played a much bigger role in their relations than open warfare. For example, Zwide's Ndwandwe might have attacked the Swazi, but the Swazi 'queen mother' at that very point was Zwide's own sister.[17] Obviously blood relationships didn't prevent conflict, but they must have complicated things hugely. Such connections could be, and were, regularly used as bargaining chips to sue for peace. This was partly because these groups weren't all that cohesive in the first place. Even the Mthethwa, the Ndwandwe and the Zulu could fragment along pre-existing kinship lines at the drop of an assegai. Hence, attacks were seldom between one huge power block and another, like 'Britain' fighting 'Germany' in 1940. They were more often raids on one or another *section* of the 'Swazi' or 'Mthethwa', frequently in conjunction with some dispute or other which could provide an excuse for pinching a few cattle or some youths for the slave-trade. None of these raids ever 'destroyed a nation'.

The groupings also varied considerably. Around Delagoa Bay, the Tsonga-Thembe people (European transcriptions of the name being as problematic as any) had apparently regarded themselves as a kind of unit since at least the

1550s. Even at that time their reach, in trade if not in political dominance, extended as far as the Mhlathuze river. This was a reach as great as, if not greater than that of Shaka's Zulu at their height. However, the Tsonga-Thembe weren't particularly militarised, despite – or perhaps because of – squabbling endlessly. Many of the squabbles were clearly over trade with the Bay. This was the case as early as 1726, when a Thembe raid on the neighbouring people of Machavane lightened them of both cattle and other marketable goods. These conflicts extended well to the west and to the south, but weren't of a scale to disturb trade much.[18]

More strongly militarised – and perhaps the first to form recognisably military units, around 1750 – were the Mabhudu (Maputo). We know little about them. They established themselves in the southern marches of Thembe country, taking their name from Mabhudu, a son of the Thembe leader Mangobe. Mangobe, paramount leader in the Delagoa Bay area from around 1750, spread Thembe influence as far west as the Lubombo hills and some twelve days' journey – maybe 200 kilometres – south of the Bay. He moved his own establishment southwards to the Usuthu-Phongolo confluence.[19] Mangobe divided his area of influence amongst his sons, one of whom was Mabhudu who himself moved still further south, across the Usuthu, ousting the Matshabane people, but apparently without violence. Following Mangobe's example, Mabhudu may have been most responsible for continuing to elbow out the Dlamini, and for introducing beads as a primary form of *lobolo*, bride-wealth payment.[20] This influence was closely tied to his ability to control the trade with Delagoa Bay, behind the backs of the minor chiefs – his own nephews. Mabhudu was remembered as proud, intelligent, warlike, the 'one who lit the fire' and 'founded the nation'.[21] Part of his power was based on the forging of some or other early version of the *ibutho* military unit. Mabhudu ruled until 1795 or so, by which time he had come to dominate even the Khumalo inland, and the Ntuli around Kosi Bay. His influence stretched at least as far as the Mthethwa, who may have been trying to forge some kind of trade alliance to outflank the growing power of the Ndwandwe in between them.[22] Although they remained a formidable group even in the 1830s,[23] Mabhudu – or 'the Mabhudu' – were gradually overshadowed by the Ndwandwe to their west.

Mabhudu's southward thrust – perhaps partly distancing himself from the intense in-fighting and slaving around Delagoa Bay, and perhaps partly seeking new opportunities – is just the first of a distinct movement of several groups away from the Bay. This trend would eventually affect the Zulu, too. The movement was associated with the gradual formation of age-units with specifically military functions, mostly built up from age-based circumcision schools. The Dlamini-Swazi began moving westwards, shouldered out by the Thembe and Mabhudu.[24] At least some of the Hlubi moved westwards out of the Lubombos around the 1750s. Under Bhungane, who took over as chieftain around 1760, the Hlubi established control over some 5 000 square kilometres, centred on present-day Newcastle. Bhungane probably began forming some militarised units; his successor Mthimkulu definitely did. The Hlubi almost certainly traded directly or indirectly with Delagoa Bay, and were visited by whites in the late eighteenth century.[25] People later mistakenly called the 'Mantatisi', or 'Mantatees', also originated near Delagoa Bay and were forced west sometime before the 1790s – these might have been either Ngwane or Ndwandwe offshoots of the Dlamini.[26]

However, this movement away from the Bay should not be exaggerated: it was neither wholesale nor catastrophic. The Qwabe were also consolidating, and pushed the Cele and Thuli southwards, but more likely in response to sporadic slaving and other factors around Port Natal than to that around distant Delagoa Bay (see more below).

We don't know a great deal more about the early Ndwandwe. They also seem to have originated near Delagoa Bay, but had drifted or had been forced south-westwards via the Phongolo river valley to settle around Nongoma, the easily defensible hilly country north of the Black Mfolozi river.[27] Quite when this was, if true, is unknown. Who ruled, with what effect, before Zwide, apart from his father Langa, no one seems to remember. Under Langa of the Nxumalo line, they were still most likely a semi-united conglomerate of peoples, including and at times even dominated by the Jere and Gaza. Zwide may have taken over the leadership around the time of Shaka's birth – 1780 – but even that is a guess.

As we'll see, it was Zwide who was more likely than Shaka to have been responsible for regional disruptions in the early nineteenth century. The fact that the Ndwandwe became the most aggressive of all these groups, including the Zulu, with a number of major settlements and distinctively named *amabutho* or regiments, implies a higher than usual degree of social stratification. Again, these *amabutho* were forged well before Shaka took over the Zulu leadership. Other than these meagre details, we know nothing at all about the structures of Ndwandwe society.

We do know a little more about the last of the emergent groups, the Mthethwa – the Ndwandwe's main rivals for regional power, and Shaka's immediate mentors.

THE MTHETHWA WANDERER

The Mthethwa were probably beginning to move towards consolidation as early as, or almost as early as, the Mabhudu. They had also come traditionally from 'the north', taking their name from 'a man who found fault' (*thetha*'d) and was huffily told that if he felt like that he could go off and build his own place.[28] Under Khayi, the Nyambose ruling lineage of the Mthethwa settled between the Mfolozi and Mhlathuze rivers, and *khonza*'d, swore allegiance to, the resident Mbokazi. This was probably around 1750. Jobe, Khayi's son, married an Mbokazi woman, Mabamba ka Nzimase. It was an excellent elephant-hunting region, and the Mthethwa were said to have tapped straight into the Delagoa Bay ivory trade.[29] Probably under a mixture of aggressive pressure from the north, and a desire to increase their muscle in the market-places, they began to form alliances with other local groups. The Mkhwanazi under Cungela were the first to *khonza* the Mthethwa. The Cambini, just to the south, were brought in or conquered. The Dletsheni, under pressure from the Ndwandwe to the north (presumably under Zwide's predecessor), *khonza*'d. So did the Gengeni. All four groups then claimed common ancestry with the Nyambose ruling lineage. This would be the pattern in the future: a lineage would establish itself as dominant, and subordinate lineages would then creatively rework their own genealogies as a way of cementing a new, more helpful identity.

When Jobe took over from his father, perhaps in around 1770, regional trade was stepping up – at least 75 000 pounds of ivory were being exported from Delagoa Bay each year in the 1770s.[30] Slaves were also being taken out, possibly in increasing numbers. Not coincidentally, the first Mthethwa *amabutho* – partially militarised groups of young men – date to this period. Jobe was embarking on a sterner campaign of corralling tributary groups.

The Sokhulu, who had first *khonza*'d Jobe's father, now worked as a kind of client mercenary for Jobe; their job seems to have been to control certain low-lying areas where sugar cane (*umoba*) could be grown. The reward included a daughter of Jobe's in marriage to a prominent warrior. The Dube and Ncube people were also incorporated, and were given land near St Lucia Bay – that is, right next door to the Mabhudu.[31] So long as relations with the Mabhudu remained friendly, the Mthethwa had a clear corridor to Delagoa Bay.

It isn't clear from the traditions just how solidly these groups were glued onto the Mthethwa main body. There are hints that they might have been refugees in the first place, and that they didn't have to raise their own *amabutho*.[32] We'll never know exactly. But we can see here the first traces of the system of building up supportive subordinate client-chiefdoms which Dingiswayo, and Shaka after him, would refine and strengthen.

At this point we come to the man who would be so instrumental in Shaka's own rise to power: Godongwana, later to be renamed Dingiswayo. Godongwana-Dingiswayo would get to attract quite a few legends himself. It would become commonplace to characterise Dingiswayo as the great persuader, Shaka as the brutal bone-crusher. The truth is certainly more complicated.

Godongwana was one of Jobe's several sons, born of an Mbokazi woman. Jobe named another son, Mawewe, as heir. There was a scuffle; a third brother, Tana, was killed; Godongwana fled. These bare bones apart, we never find out much about these succession disputes. Godongwana first took refuge amongst the Qwabe, a little to the south. The Qwabe were also in the process of consolidating, though they never seem to have stiffened their internal structures as much as the Ndwandwe or the Zulu. But by the time Shaka came to power they had formed a few *amabutho* of their own and, as we will see, could dish up a fair bit of trouble.

For some unspecified reason – the story goes – Godongwana couldn't stay with the Qwabe. He wandered north-east to the Langeni – Shaka's mother's people – where an Mthethwa *impi* attacked, presumably trying to get rid of him.[33] They failed.

When Jobe died, in about 1780,[34] Godongwana seized the opportunity to return to the Mbokazi, his mother's people, and launch a challenge for the

Mthethwa leadership. He won the battle; Mawewe fled, also to the Qwabe. (This was a tribute to the comforting strength of the Qwabe, as well as to the strong genealogical links between the peoples of the region; the conflicts of interest here were intense and fearsomely complex.) Godongwana renamed himself Dingiswayo – 'The Wanderer' – and set about toughening the embryonic militarised structures he had inherited.

He was doubtless blissfully unaware of the birth, at almost the same time and under somewhat shadowy circumstances, of a son to Senzangakhona, the heir to the not-very-significant Zulu chiefly line.

QUESTIONS AND APPROACHES

These then were the main contenders for power in the region: the Mabhudu, the Dlamini-Swazi, the Ndwandwe, the Mthethwa, and the Qwabe. In a swathe, running roughly from east to west, all these groups were socially centralising and militarising, forming 'military units' of some kind.

Let's linger for a moment on an essential question: just how 'military' were these various outfits? They seem to have been gradually evolving out of the common circumcision schools. Circumcision, in fits and starts, was being discarded or actively abolished. Shaka's father Senzangakhona, for instance, was probably circumcised; but Shaka almost certainly was not. If Dingiswayo can be regarded as representative, this was being done because the young men needed to be fighting fit, not isolated in the bush nursing their doctored members. People were evidently being called upon to fight in increasingly organised ways. But the very word 'military' is misleading. A.T. Bryant pointed out a long time ago that even under Shaka the so-called 'regiments' were 'essentially multifunctional organized labour gangs rather than regiments of professional soldiers'.[35] Hereafter, then, I will use the term *amabutho*, meaning something like 'multifunctional gatherings', rather than 'regiments'. The *amabutho* were as much a way of controlling labour division, marriage patterns, and territorial occupation as they were a way of conducting war. Though the formation of *amabutho* must imply an increase in violence, fighting remained seasonal and sporadic, never a full-time occupation. The *amabutho* were not a standing army. They were formed in response not only to violence, but also to a more complex wave of change.[36] This upheaval was affecting almost every aspect of society, especially relations between elders and juniors, and between men and women.

This returns us to the central questions: *why* were these various groups, amongst others, firstly, moving away from the Delagoa Bay hinterland; and, secondly, beginning to militarise in the second half of the eighteenth century? *How* exactly did the Zulu 'state' emerge from the mix of influences? Neither question has yet been adequately answered, despite some provocative hypotheses.

In the sections that follow, I'll be treading a line somewhere between the three main approaches encountered in the literature. There is the 'strongman' theory, which suggests that everything happens mostly because charismatic leaders drive history. Dingiswayo, Zwide and Shaka, some have argued, were such leaders. This overlaps to some extent with the 'Africanist' theory, which tries to compensate for old colonial prejudice by valorising Africans' ability to, for instance, build centralised 'states' entirely independent of outside (read European) influence. The Africanists run into conflict with a third school – let's call it 'neo-colonial' – which suggests that Africans were mainly passive victims of outside (read European) forces that were simply irresistibly superior; Africans just reacted uncreatively to what was thrust upon them.

In their extreme forms, each of these theories is absurd. It is more obvious to us now that while invasive global forces sometimes had overwhelming localised impact on unprepared societies, both charismatic leaders and ordinary people could, and did, respond actively and creatively, in highly individualistic ways that made cultural sense to them.

So the question is: why *this* particular response at *this* particular point in history? Precisely because there isn't a great deal of information about the pre-Shakan era to work with, historians have come up with a number of ideas. Because these hypotheses remain controversial, and because a clear understanding of the wider context is vital to understanding Shaka's career, we will treat them in some detail. There are four main ideas that we will explore in turn: population pressure, climatic or ecological crisis, trade, and slaving.

TOO MANY PEOPLE?

The epigraph to this chapter captures the idea that 'mounting population pressure . . . caused an outburst of political violence', with Shaka at 'the eye of the storm'. This was essentially the picture, marginally refined, presented by J.D. Omer-Cooper in his influential book, *The Zulu Aftermath* (1966). There is almost nothing to recommend this scenario, which rides on the back of the presumption that the whole 'Bantu migration' could 'only be explained [by] continuous population growth',[37] and more covertly on prejudices about Africans' allegedly rampant fertility.[38]

As we have seen, the mass-migration theory has now been all but discarded. Population growth there may well have been: archaeologists have argued fairly persuasively for a gradual increase up to this date in the highveld region.[39] Nevertheless, there is no solid evidence that it had reached any kind of critical threshold in the late eighteenth century. We have no idea what the population was in the first place.[40] We don't know what the carrying capacity of the country was. Seventeenth-century travellers observed that the country was 'incredibly populous' (but compared to what?). They said that there were 'an infinite number' of settlements (but how many is 'infinite'?). They gave no indication that there was any ecological stress; on the contrary, people seemed abundantly supplied.[41] A century later, while it makes superficial sense that there would have been a certain increase in numbers, there simply isn't any direct evidence for it. Some have speculated that the arrival of maize as a new crop stimulated a population explosion, but its introduction elsewhere in the world never had this effect,[42] and it also doesn't seem to have been a significant food item in the region until the mid-nineteenth century.[43]

Furthermore, an increase in people does not *inevitably* lead to an escalation in conflict. More importantly, the overpopulation thesis fails to explain the precise mechanism by which the particular structures we find amongst the Mthethwa or Zulu came about. As Jared Diamond notes, 'correlations [between state size, population density and social stratification] do not tell us precisely how population variables function in a chain of cause and effect whose outcome is a complex society'. Rather, he suggests, reorganised food production, population growth and political centralisation reinforce one another.[44] But as we'll see later, I can find no sign that political stratification within the Zulu polity was accompanied by a greater density of population anywhere, except perhaps in the immediate vicinity of the 'capital'.

So we can more or less dismiss the overpopulation hypothesis. At best, we might surmise that certain areas became overcrowded, resulting in some local movements, possibly accompanied by friction. Possibly.

'EAT WHAT YOU CAN AND KEEP QUIET'

In 1815, the volcano Tambora in Indonesia erupted, killing 80 000 people and covering the planet in a swathe of volcanic dust. It was the biggest eruption on record since 1500, and had widespread climatic effects. In the course of an argument for an environmental cause for the rise of the Zulu state, Charles Ballard named Tambora as the primary suspect in causing major droughts in the early 1800s. This was a first cause for the consolidation of 'states', in Ballard's view. We can now see that the timing of this is quite wrong, and there is another problem, too. The droughts, says Ballard, caused 'a serious *breakdown* of social, political, and economic institutions'. So how did this mutate into polities of considerable social *cohesion*, 'capable of providing a more efficient organization of the agricultural economy'?[45] (Anyway, as we will see, there was no real breakdown of social institutions – rather there was a creative extension of the existing ones.)

In 1929, the unavoidable A.T. Bryant argued, with suspicious precision, that in 1802 a massive drought struck the Thukela-Phongolo region. It was called the 'Madlathule' drought, meaning roughly, 'Eat what you can and keep quiet'. Although Bryant did not link this famine directly with state-building, others did. In fact, Bryant more or less rejected it as a cause: Mthethwa *inkosi* Dingiswayo's capacity to build a polity was rather based, Bryant thought, on his meeting a vagrant European, Dr Cowan (see Box 2 on page 74). At the same time, Bryant admitted that the famine 'may have been five years earlier'.[46] Nevertheless, because he pictured Shaka suffering through the famine as a child, the drought hypothesis got almost irreversibly attached to Shaka's desire to build up power, and another brick in the myth was laid.

Environmental or ecological explanations in history are fashionable these days. In some ways, they are unavoidable: after all, the environment is always there, it must have *some* effect. How much more so when a society is completely dependent on agricultural and pastoral produce, on rainfall, grazing, the immediate fertility of soil, and so on. In times of ecological crisis, subsistence margins are narrow. As we've seen, however, polity-consolidation had been slowly happening for decades. It makes no sense at all that a single famine, whatever its timing, would have had so dramatic or general an effect. Previously recorded great droughts (in the 1640s, in 1705, and in 1734), had not visibly had this impact.[47] Even a series of droughts or famines is unlikely to have done so. On the contrary, wherever we have evidence, the effect of drought on precolonial societies has been to bring about not consolidation, but scattering. Survival depended on fanning out over the country to supplement decimated herds and grain supplies with more thinly spread wild animals, roots, berries, and so on. These were well-developed survival tactics.[48] Sometimes the starving might move into the shelter of a people who were unaffected by the crisis; but this begs the question of why those people were already consolidated. In short, even if droughts temporarily enhanced certain groupings and stimulated raids on neighbours' resources, as they well might have, there *must* have been other factors involved.

There's also a difference between *drought* and *famine*. Even an extremely serious drought very seldom brings about all-out famine, in which many people actually starve. Famines – as has been shown repeatedly, even in the most recent examples in Africa, from Ethiopia to Zimbabwe – are almost always generated by humans. They almost always result from the disruptions of war or of political failures. Shaka himself would be blamed for inducing famine through his wars.

A further difficulty with the drought hypothesis is that we have no real idea when, where, or with what local effects, drought or famine struck in the region. Unbearable weight has been placed on *one* study of the ring-patterns of *one* tree in *one* corner of the region (the Karkloof, near Durban). In this study, Martin Hall argued that what the tree-rings showed was that 1774 was an exceptionally dry year, 1787-9 were abnormally wet, and the final decade of the eighteenth century was drier than normal.[49] This is fascinating and suggestive, but far too limited to support conclusions about political effects over half a century and throughout the region. It doesn't help to explain what was happening *before* 1774. There is some additional evidence for a dry period in the 1790s, and possibly the early 1800s – at least in southern Mozambique,[50] but we might as easily speculate about the state-building propensities of floods, which are arguably just as disruptive to agricultural production. It all begs the question of *how* and *why* people would have reacted to ecological stresses by consolidating politically.

The most sophisticated attempt to answer this question has been made by the eminent historian Jeff Guy. His theory is that the late eighteenth century saw progressive deterioration of soil fertility throughout the region, an inevitable consequence of overgrazing.[51] In my view, Guy is too dependent on that same unproven assumption of an overpopulation problem (whether of people or cattle). He probably concentrates too fixedly on cattle-herding as opposed to grain-cropping, though he does rightly note that most labour-power was expended on crop production.[52] In addition, he leans very heavily on J.P.H. Acocks's seminal but somewhat broad opinion that the Thukela-Phongolo region was experiencing a vegetation change from forest and scrub to grassland. There was undeniably long-term human impact (cutting and burning), but this arguably increased rather than decreased available grazing and cropland (indeed, that was its purpose). In fact, Guy has to rest his case on the phrase 'It seems possible'; and his proposal that the increased conflict in the region was actually over natural resources seems to rely on only a single informant's testimony.[53] The thesis is not implausible – but does it explain everything? I would say not.

What Guy has very valuably done is to focus attention on the overall ecological conditions within which the Zulu polity necessarily grew, as well as on the pragmatic activities of ordinary people at the level of the homestead. It's worth dwelling on these aspects here, because they will crop up (literally) time and again in the rest of this book.

The homesteads

Where people went and settled, who they raided for what, what they planted when, whether they moved or fought – all these things were deeply affected by the topography, rainfall patterns, and vegetation.

The Thukela-Phongolo catchment consisted, at the risk of oversimplification, of a hotter, wetter coastal plain, prone to human and

cattle diseases, more heavily forested with only some sourveld grazing; and a
generally drier inland plateau deeply cut by major winding rivers, whose valley
floors provided sweetveld grazing and good soils for grains, and high ridges
of mixed or sourveld grasses and some soil for grains (see Map 1 on page 15).
By Shaka's time, according to Guy:

> The forest and scrub forest which dominated Zululand had been
> reduced drastically leaving forest relics on high wet ridges, and scrub
> in areas protected from fire, along watercourses and on the coast. In
> those places where it had been removed, it had been replaced by sour
> grass. The savanna vegetation types had spread from the depths of
> the valleys, and the wooded elements had been reduced by regular
> burning which favoured the grass understorey.[54]

The first requirement of any settlement – especially one dependent on cattle
– was for access to both summer and winter grazing. This meant the freedom
to move from sweetveld to sourveld areas, according to the season, as well as
to remain within easy reach of both water sources and fertile, well-drained
places to grow grains and vegetables. Gaining such access would be a factor in
both territorial control and in peoples' movements. They could not survive
otherwise. The distribution of cattle would inevitably mesh closely with the
distribution of political influence. Still, this had been the case for decades, if
not centuries; it doesn't go far enough in explaining the *particular* structures
developing around 1780. These controls operated first and foremost at the
level of the household.

Most people lived in small homesteads (*imizi*; singular *umuzi*), under a
head (*umnumzana*), who divided his resource-control amongst his sons and
wives. The men principally hunted; the women principally grew crops. They
strove for self-sufficiency, supplemented by some trading. Most importantly,
they traded cattle (or, it has been suggested for this period, beads) for new
wives for the sons, who would move off to create their own *imizi* and lineages.
There was always a certain centrifugal impetus, working against any pressure
to centralise. If a chief began, by whatever means, to accumulate more wives
(one feature of centralisation), there were consequently more sons wanting
to move off to found independent households. There was also potential for

greater conflict, over inheritance on the one hand, and over raiding for cattle to pay for the wives, on the other. Cattle were certainly the main marker of wealth and status, and therefore of political power. The symbolisms of production and reproduction – of cattle-wealth and the lineage – were thus tightly interwoven. But it would take a big push for such headmen and chiefs to give up their independent power-bases.

In the 1680s, if the Dutch observers from the wrecked *Stavenisse* are accurate, some controls wider than the *umuzi* also existed, but they were fairly loose.[55] The role of older, prestigious leaders was more to arbitrate than to command tyrannically. A century later it is quite clear that the mechanisms of control – over cattle, women, and cultivation alike – were a great deal tougher, and in certain ways quite new. Leaders began to intervene increasingly at the household level, wielding more influence over the distribution of women, cattle, crops and trade goods. They needed, in the last resort, coercive means to do it: either persuasive ideas, or sharpened assegais, or both. This was not necessarily a more efficient use of resources,[56] but it changed the relationships of power and control. The question is, why did headmen agree to join up into such larger units for the long term? What did they have to gain? The drought hypothesis fails to explain this. There was, quite bluntly, 'no general ecological crisis'.[57]

Ecological factors in polity-building are inevitable, and therefore seductive. But, I suggest, they are factors, not causes. The physical and natural environment helped to structure peoples' social strategies, but did not cause radical changes in them. We need to look for new causes, not well-known influences for which survival strategies were already highly developed. What was new in the Thukela-Phongolo catchment in around 1780?

THE BEAD-CARRIERS

Dingane, Shaka's successor, had the thick wooden poles of his main hut encrusted with hundreds of thousands of European-made glass beads. Perhaps Shaka did, too. Ostentation is power. Even by Shaka's time, beads were the main medium of exchange – *lobolo* – when a man acquired a wife.

Beads were not the only trade item. Though copper and iron were mined locally, they were traded, too (and extracted from wrecks where possible).

The metals were one way of distinguishing status: iron and copper ornaments were worn by some as a sign of bravery.[58] In small ways such as these, international trade helped in the stratification of society. Since the pioneering work of David Hedges and Alan Smith, the 'trade hypothesis' has become an essential ingredient.[59] It is a much more plausible theory than the over-population or ecological hypotheses. But was there enough trade to provoke the build-up of 'states'? Was competition intense enough to provoke major wars? Who was doing the trading, in what volumes?

The evidence, as before, is scanty. Most trade was certainly local, based on 'use-value': cattle bartered for iron assegais, grain for hide shields, and so on. We have no way of measuring the levels of such exchanges, nor any way of knowing whether much changed in the eighteenth century. In the absence of any local invention that suddenly increased production, however, it was most likely international trade which would induce societal changes. So how much trade with the outer world was there?

For many years, along most of the coast, trade with outsiders was opportunistic rather than organised, the by-product of occasional visits and shipwreck. As early as 1589, though, the native peoples of the St Lucia area were apparently familiar with ivory trading.[60] Further sporadic observations come from the survivors of the *Santo Alberto* (1593), and of the *Johanna*, wrecked at Delagoa Bay in 1683. The former noted a persistent ivory trade at Delagoa Bay, serving an annual Portuguese vessel.[61] The *Johanna*'s people made it all the way back to Cape Town with (it was reported) unstinting hospitality from the local people along the way.[62] In an epic trek in the opposite direction, the castaways of the *São João Baptista*, wrecked near present-day East London in 1622, found a man, apparently an ex-slave from Angoche in the Mozambique Channel, as far south as the Great Kei river – one indication of how far links had penetrated. Closer to Delagoa Bay, they found a distinct correlation between the spread of trade goods (including varieties of Indian cloth), the Portuguese language, and organised violence.[63]

The *Good Hope* was an English ship wrecked at Port Natal (present-day Durban) in 1685. Some of the survivors built a boat in which the captain continued up the coast to trade in copper and slaves. Those who remained were able to exchange neck-rings and beads for about three tons of ivory and enough food to live off. They were shortly joined by some survivors of the

Bonaventura, which had been washed ashore at Cape Corrientes, near Delagoa Bay. Some were murdered by locals; others died of starvation. In 1687, survivors of these parties and of the Dutch ship *Stavenisse*, wrecked at the mouth of the Mzimkhulu river, made it back to Cape Town. They had found the local people mostly hospitable; food supplies, elephants and other game were plentiful. Metal-working in iron was so well developed that few locals were interested in trading for it. Internal and external trade were clearly flourishing. Together with the goods rescued by the English survivors of the *Good Hope*, the foreigners had enough copper and beads to keep them in food 'for fifty years'. They found they could exchange an arm-ring, worth one rix-dollar, for a fat ox.[64] Only two years later, the *Noord* was sent to look for the *Stavenisse* survivors, and to purchase 'Natal' for beads or cutlery to the value of 29 000 guilders. Back then Europeans thought they could do that: buy a whole region for a boxful of spoons. The purchase was made, but from whom is not recorded.[65]

It was the first of many imperialist incursions into this difficult coast.

Ten years after that, in 1699, a wrecked Dutch captain, one Joanis Gerbrantzer, 'bought' the whole place again, this time for a mere 20 000 florins. Only three of his men survived with him to stagger into Cape Town. When he returned to take up his purchase in 1705, the former 'Natal' ruler was dead. His son shrugged and said it had nothing to do with him; sorry, no deal.[66] Just how important this local 'king' was, or how extensive his domain might actually have been, we have no idea.

There is also some evidence for more regular use of the natural harbour at Port Natal, despite its tricky sand bar. English mariner William Dampier recorded in 1700 that his 'ingenious friend', one Captain Rogers, had been amongst 'some of our English ships' that had visited it a number of times. For what purpose, Dampier doesn't say, and his impressions of local society are crude and rather unenlightening (and unenlightened).[67]

The Delagoa Bay hinterland

The major trading activity in the region emanated from Delagoa Bay. This had been mostly in Portuguese hands since the mid-1500s, but only in the 1700s did it begin to gain in importance. A Dutch report of 1721 found the

stories of vigorous trade at Delagoa Bay in ivory, amber, wax and gold-dust
exaggerated; it took the writer all day to bargain for a pathetic little five-
pound tusk – and that had been hoarded for years. The Dutchman thought
the locals were being difficult, but more likely they were being discerning:
they wanted a particular kind of yellow bead that he simply didn't have.[68]

More successful traders were reporting quantities of weightier 'teeth'
trickling in, from '40 or 50 leagues' away – perhaps 200 kilometres – that is
to say, as far away as 'Zulu' country.[69] In 1723 the crew of the *Northhampton*,
anchored in Delagoa Bay, were able to purchase 11 000 pounds of ivory and
gold-dust from traders of the far interior, probably from as far north as
Manica.[70] Two years later, Hlanganu people from well north-west of the Bay
brought in more ivory.[71] In 1756, men from Delagoa Bay were encountered
at St Lucia, trading in ambergris and ivory.[72] Tsonga traders from the Bay
area were found as far south as the Mfolozi river, and ivory from that general
area was said to be making up a substantial proportion of the Bay's trade.[73]
The Tsonga traders even made it as far as Xhosa country.[74] Even more
spectacularly, at least a few traders from the east and west coasts met in the
middle of the continent, 1 500 kilometres from anywhere, or made it right
across, like some Portuguese traders from Angola around 1800.[75]

The Portuguese hold on the coast, some legalistic claims notwithstanding,
was light, consisting of little more than a smattering of trading posts. These
were fatally dependent on support from – and vulnerable to attack by – the
local populations. Delagoa Bay was no exception. In fact, for Europeans, it
was a fever-ridden hellhole. The Austrian agent there in 1779 complained
that he had never been in such a miserable situation, surrounded by
'crazymen', seriously short of food, ill-armed, and prey to the extortionate
demands of local chieftains. The following year he had to bundle his tiny
garrison into boats and watch helplessly while a local force of 400 men
ransacked his fragile establishment.[76]

Nevertheless, the Bay was an obvious base, almost the only place on all
that coast with a decent harbour and navigable rivers. But even those didn't
go far. This made trade more difficult than along the Zambezi river, for
instance, so the *prazo* system that developed there didn't penetrate the
Thukela-Phongolo catchment. Attempts to establish factories on the Bay's
islands repeatedly faltered. It was occupied by the Dutch between 1721 and

1730, but by 1750 no single power commanded it. Throughout this period trade was relatively slack, despite the desire of the locals to promote it.[77]

Then, around mid-century, trade throughout the region accelerated. The Mascarene islands, in particular, became a major market after the 1740s, acting as a way-station for a massive Indian trade. The English began to do 'big business' in the area.[78] An Englishman named Edward Chandler ran twelve boats, manned by Goan Indians, up and down the Maphuta river between 1756 and 1768. The French also became more active, taking advantage of successive anti-monopoly measures in France. A distinct briskness of competition galvanised the Delagoa Bay communities. Europeans of different nationalities worked through local or *mestizo* (mixed-race) middlemen who played off traders against one another, hoarded goods to push up prices, and occasionally got their way through violence. The Tsonga became famous throughout the region as the source of metal, though how early is hard to say. They became especially known for *umdaka* – rough lengths of copper or brass – which would be hammered into *ingxota* (neck-rings) and bangles by smiths in the forests of the interior. We know that people wore these as early as the seventeenth century.[79] The coppersmiths were rewarded with cattle.[80] Well into the nineteenth century Tsongas would bring ivory to the Zulu in return for cattle, and the ivory would go on to the whites of Natal – to some degree patterns that, we must surmise, had been established a century before. (At least in Dingane's reign, and perhaps earlier, a Portuguese trader known as Dinisa resided in Tsongaland: he dealt in locally grown tobacco; ivory was bartered for *utshodo* [black cloth], *izimbedu* [heavy brass bangles] and *amasinda* [lighter arm bangles], which were taken inland to be exchanged for wildcat skins, sheep, goats, sleeping mats, and shields.[81] These, too, are probably very like the transactions of the previous century.)

By 1777, when the Austrian Asiatic Company of Trieste, run by an Englishman named William Bolts, took over the Bay, ivory was rapidly becoming the main trade item: prices quickly doubled those at Mozambique Island, and the Inhambane trade in ivory declined by comparison. In 1777, the ship *Success* loaded 69 000 pounds of ivory; in 1779, two ships took aboard another 40 000 pounds; the same weight was loaded on another Austrian ship in 1780. These were just some of the shipments, almost accidentally recorded. An estimated 100 000 pounds of ivory were being exported every year, which meant some 4 000 elephant deaths a year, a substantial toll on the local ecology. Bolts worked to maintain links already established with 'Nguni' suppliers deep in the interior.[82]

American whalers were also frequenting the Bay more often; both Arabic and Indian traders were visiting, and some were even staying. William White, visiting in the *Lion* in 1798, noted that several 'Parsee' (Indian) vessels had traded in the recent past, and that a 'Mahomedan priest' and a few other Muslims were actually living there. He recommended that 'Ships coming here to furnish themselves with a good stock of fresh provisions, should bring coarse blue linen cloth, old clothes, brass rings, pieces of copper wire, glass beads of different colours, the larger the better, tobacco and pipes, knives, hats, wigs, shoes and stockings'.[83]

The growth in trade coincided exactly with the growing amalgamation of native groups, most notably near Delagoa Bay. The early 1760s saw the rise of Thembe dominance of the region, until by the 1790s, according to William White, they had secured some control maybe a hundred miles inland.[84] Exactly what this control consisted of is difficult to say, but that it was in some way related to trade is undeniable. It is also undeniable that trade items had acquired profound symbolic value amongst local societies. There was little or no money in the region in the eighteenth century, though some travellers refer to trade in 'specie', coins. However, it's unlikely that these were used as money, as a disembodied medium of exchange. The local economy had always been, and continued to be, based on use-value, although there were deeper levels. Obviously, the accumulation of goods could also signal political clout. Women wore massive brass neck-rings as 'a mark of rank'.[85] Cattle, brass necklaces, and beads, were all valued by a leader not just because they were aesthetically gorgeous, but because they also usefully displayed his power over *other* useful resources. Such aesthetics, in addition to all the localised trading in plant, animal and metal products that was going on constantly, would take on added importance as larger polities developed.

We have established that there was an increase in trade in the region, but it's much more difficult to judge how far this trade, however extensive it was, actually *caused* amalgamation and aggression. Groups certainly clashed over trade routes and access. This was especially the case near Delagoa Bay. In 1726, for instance, the Thembe attacked Machavane, the minor chief living closest to the Bay itself, in order to secure their trade routes.[86] The Thembe were themselves under attack from the west and south by various groups, probably for the same reasons. This pattern was often repeated. Many attacks came from minor bands of freebooters, regularly characterised as 'cannibals' (see Box 4 on page 223).[87] They probably operated on principles similar to those of the pirates working out of Madagascar at the same time: mobile, small-scale, and extremely violent.

The growing scale of ivory trading has prompted some historians to speculate that more elephant hunting meant bigger bands of people, embryonic *amabutho*. Competition meant the development of military honour; this spiralled into larger 'state' formations. This is not a convincing argument. It is true that the ivory trade was expanding, but there is no evidence that it was big enough or organised enough to have this effect; or that there were so few elephants as to provoke such severe competition (indeed, the opposite seems to be true). It's far more likely that for elephant hunting 'a flexible, semi-nomadic association was required, not a territorially determined fief'.[88] Professional elephant hunters later discovered working for Shaka, mostly Bushmen, operated in precisely this way. Although tusks were periodically purloined by disgruntled middlemen or marauders, there is not a single recorded actual case of anyone clashing over access to elephants. While some hunting methods *may* have carried over into military tactics, this would be a spin-off of the process, not an explanation for it.[89]

The important point is this: generally speaking, fruitful trade depends on peace, not war. A report from Delagoa Bay in 1729 lamented that 'continual wars near us, originate generally from one tribe supposing another to derive greater advantage from our trade than themselves; and that these wars are great impediments to the trade itself . . .'[90] This is also clear in the case of Makua-Portuguese hostilities in northern Mozambique in this same period.[91] In other words, trade tended to serve as an in-built brake on conflict, even conflict over trade itself. The various groups within the Thembe usually preferred to collaborate with one another to provide better frameworks for the peaceful passage of goods. Warfare is the mother of organised theft, not of exchange-based trade. Warfare would have stimulated only certain kinds of trade – in weapons, or in items of military finery. Cattle-raiding seems to have become a primary activity of the militarised polities; this was because

militarisation had, almost incidentally, made it easier. It doesn't mean that
cattle-raiding *caused* militarisation. It has been suggested that capturing cattle
to feed American whalers at the Bay was the cause, but there is no evidence
that this was extensive enough to provoke such far-reaching social changes.[92]
The fact that ordinary, peaceful trade seems to have persisted throughout
the Shakan period is one indicator that regional violence was less than totally
consuming.

Finally, at least up until 1780, and even beyond, we simply have no idea
of how much trade was happening. There are few figures, and the situation
is complicated by the existence of both sea and land routes between Delagoa
Bay and ports further north – especially Sofala and Inhambane – so that
impressions of trade at the Bay itself may be misleadingly under-represented.[93]

International trade was unquestionably deeply implicated in the growth
of bigger polities in the southern African region. The effects of trade were of
long standing. In Zimbabwe between the fourteenth and sixteenth centuries,
for instance, the growth of Mwenemutapa and its successor states had been
founded largely on trade – and they collapsed mostly because of the loss of
trade. But that state had a massive supply of gold as its motor: even the ivory
of the Thukela-Phongolo catchment couldn't match the attraction of that.
Nevertheless, trade did help to mark off greater differences between groups,
and between classes of people within groups. This was also later a feature of
Zulu organisation. More importantly, it generated a certain level of
dependency, to the extent that relationships of power within a polity depended
on imported goods such as beads, or on the control of exportation of, for
example, ivory. However, trade alone doesn't seem to me to be sufficient
cause for the Thukela-Phongolo polities to develop in the way that they did.
Australian historian Norman Etherington is right in his assertion that 'there
is no automatic linkage between trade and the growth of kingdoms'.[94]

There is one more candidate for the primary cause of centralisation – a
controversial but ultimately more convincing one: the slave trade.

TRADING MEN

In 1731, the Dutch ship the *Snuffelaar* dropped anchor in Delagoa Bay. The
first Dutch attempt at settlement there had been abandoned the previous

year. The crew of the *Snuffelaar* tried to buy some slaves. There were none.
The problem, according to the local Tsonga, was that there had been no
wars; hence there were no captives to sell.[95]

This is the fundamental dynamic, a macabre dance of unholy twins: war
and slavery. And if there were no wars to generate slaves, then the wars
themselves must be generated. William Bolts shrewdly noted in 1777 that
inland succession disputes could be exploited to produce slaves.[96] Bolts himself
didn't have much success, but others would.

Was slaving from Delagoa Bay a crucial – if not *the* crucial – factor in
stimulating polity-building in the Thukela-Phongolo catchment? Like a
lightning bolt, this possibility was delivered to a complacent South African
historical establishment by Julian Cobbing, beginning with an article published
in 1988. The subsequent furore proved to be one of the most energetic and
fruitful debates ever seen in South African historiography; and the case still
isn't closed (see Box 11 on page 437).[97] There was slaving from Delagoa Bay
throughout the eighteenth century; that much is beyond dispute. But was it
sufficiently extensive, damaging, and dangerous, to stimulate widespread
militarisation? Was the timing right?

If the evidence for the extent of trade in the region is slight, it is even
more so for slaving. As we've seen, the Bay wasn't exactly a great place to
keep meticulous records. Much trade, and even more slaving, was done by
private individuals, at first trying to keep things secret from competitors,
later (in the early nineteenth century) trying to evade the law. There was no
central recording office. Slaves were shipped out all over the world. Piracy
was rampant. Such records as we have (from Mauritius and Brazil, for example)
sometimes recorded slaves as being 'Mozambican', but this could mean
anywhere from Delagoa Bay to north of the Zambezi river. As with the other
theories, the argument has to proceed by a mixture of trying to fit the local
scene into the general situation; evaluating what specific evidence we have;
looking for analogies from similar scenarios elsewhere; and daring a bit of
creative speculation.

What of the general slaving situation, then? The great trans-Atlantic slave
trade from the west coast of Africa was booming in the eighteenth century,
feeding mostly the Caribbean plantations. Down the east coast, slavers –
Arabs and their proxies – had been raiding for 200 years, and by the

eighteenth century had driven south at least as far as Sofala. The Portuguese
pursued a complicated relationship with this end of the trade, sometimes in
collaboration with Arabs, sometimes at war, as they supplied slaves to their
enterprises in the Far East as well as South America. As intersecting imperial
ventures burgeoned worldwide in the seventeenth and eighteenth centuries,
Omani Arabs, Portuguese, Goanese Indians, and later French, Dutch,
American and English traders fought each other, employed each other, bribed
each other, sailed fraudulently under one another's flags, and died in large
numbers from disease and attack. Pirates, especially from Madagascar, raided
anyone who came within range. The prospect of enormous profits kept
everyone going.

We need to keep two warnings in mind. One: trade in slaves accompanied
trade in goods in complex and variable ways. Sometimes they could piggy-
back on one another: men out, beads in, for instance; or slaves were captured
to carry ivory. But the two forms of trade could also work against each other.
Slave-wars were frequently depicted as disrupting normal trade. The dynamics
are very different. When people trade their excess produce for goods they
desire, they do it willingly, by definition. But no person willingly becomes a
slave. Slavery meant disruption, aggression and violence: this was inevitable.
If we're looking for an enemy against which the peoples of the interior needed
to defend themselves, this is the most obvious candidate – but not necessarily
in every single case.

A second warning to remember: it is a mistake to think simplistically of
aggressive European slaving nations stealing people from passive non-slaving
victim nations. The term 'slave' covers a continuum, from varieties of domestic
vassalage within African societies, through African middlemen supplying other
African groups with slaves for their own use, to those same middlemen
supplying slaves to European traders for export to foreign plantations.
Throughout Africa, very few Europeans ventured inland to capture slaves
themselves. They waited at the coast for local warlords to supply people; they
were often at the mercy of the business acumen of the African traders. The
hapless chattel-folk, for their part, could be the unwanted of the society itself,
captives of deliberate slaving raids, captives in wars fought for other reasons,
or famine victims desperate for alternatives and incapable of offering
resistance, even selling their own freedom. It is more useful, then, to think

of 'The Slave Trade' not as a one-way plunder system imposed from without, but as 'an appendage to the internal African market'.[98]

Slaving at Delagoa Bay

Slaving activity along the east coast of Africa mounted through the eighteenth century as a result of several factors: 'a revival of older patterns of trade in the wake of Portuguese decline, increasing demand for ivory and other African produce in India and Europe, a demand for slaves by Europeans and Asians, the availability of Indian capital to finance trade, and the initiative of Africans in bringing goods from the interior to coastal ports'.[99] Accurate figures are extremely difficult – indeed impossible – to come by. Most estimates are based on exports from Mozambique Island and Quelimane. According to Patrick Manning, exports from Mozambique climbed steeply from 1760 onwards, until about 1790, then crashed until about 1805, when they sky-rocketed again.[100] In the 1760s, a steady but slight flow of slaves was going out to Brazil, Cuba and the Caribbean. The VOC company commanding the Cape Colony also maintained a stream of slaving expeditions to feed the Cape Colony, including in 1755, 1756 and 1759. Only about six of these, however, were recorded as having slaved on the Mozambique coast, carrying out at least 1 600 slaves before 1786.[101] The main stimulus, however, was the opening up of plantation society on the Mascarene islands, Mauritius and Bourbon (Réunion). The Mascarenes imported less than 500 slaves a year before 1725; by the 1770s this had swelled to 5 000 a year. The French alone loaded some 40 000 slaves from the East African coast during the 1780s, mostly from Mozambique.[102]

Did Delagoa Bay participate in the upsurge of the slave trade between 1760 and 1790, or was it for some reason exempt? Although many ships apparently avoided southern Mozambique because of its offshore currents, there can be no doubt that at least some slaves were coming through from Delagoa Bay.[103] Some 'Mozambicans' were shipped via Madagascar to join the many slaves being exported from that island. One known case of slaves from the Bay being channelled through Madagascar dates from 1823, but there is no reason to preclude this from happening habitually earlier on.[104] The Tsonga-Thembe, long established in southern Mozambique, were the region's first proxy slavers. They had slaved from as far back as 1560.[105] In 1593, about 200 slaves aboard the *Santo Alberto* when it was wrecked were described as 'Kafirs', when Tsonga were said to be raiding a hundred leagues from the Bay.[106] The English slaver *Mercury*, under one Captain White, slaved from Delagoa Bay in 1719, and off Port Natal, too. The Dutch, setting up station there in the 1720s, found locals who spoke passable English, implying more regular visitations than we have direct evidence for.[107] Tsonga chiefs offloaded slaves onto a Dutch ship in 1724; the chieftains had gone off to procure slaves 'of their own free will'. They were demanding guns in exchange – a sure sign of escalating violence. In 1727, Muslim intermediaries to the Tsonga shipped 31 slaves onto the Dutch ship *Victoria*, en route from the Bay to Inhambane. The following year, some Tsonga themselves were enslaved by a Portuguese punitive expedition from Inhambane; this was probably tied up with conflict at the Bay and the fact that Tsonga were beginning to replace Muslims as proxy slavers and getting bolshy in their negotiations. This temporarily made the Tsonga understandably cautious about further dealings.[108] Some slaves may well have been fed out through Madagascar, where the trade was diabolically active: between 1675 and 1725 some 12 000 slaves were exported from the strife-torn island to the Americas alone.[109]

Port Natal, closer to Qwabe and Zulu country, also attracted some attention, despite its tricky entrance. Robert Drury, the Madagascan castaway, joined the slaver *Mercury* in 1719 and recorded buying '74 Boys and Girls' at Natal; these slaves ended up in Virginia.[110] Doubtless there were other visits, by Drury's mentor Captain Rogers amongst them. But the area seems largely to have been saved all but the occasional visit of a Cape ship for timber, and the wreck of the *Grosvenor* in 1782. The crew of the *Happy Deliverance* (built from the wreckage of the *Doddington* at Algoa Bay), reported from the St Lucia area in 1756 that the locals 'had never heard of any commerce along this coast'.[111]

On the one hand, then, the general upsurge of trade and slaving along the whole Mozambique coast between 1750 and 1790, combined with evidence of more ships visiting Delagoa Bay than before, implies that we can include the Bay in that upsurge. We can propose that slaving into the interior was indeed a crucial factor in the growth of centralised polities there. On the other hand, it has to be admitted that *direct* evidence of slaving from the Bay up to 1780 remains limited.

The slavery spiral

There are some further points to be made in favour of the slaving theory.
I've already suggested that other theories don't quite cut the ice. I keep coming
back to the imaginary headman, finding himself in a position to *khonza* –
become tributary to – a neighbouring leader, and choosing to do so instead
of fighting or simply moving away. What did such a headman (and his
dependants) have to gain? In many ways, he lost, often losing control over
the distribution of his cattle and grain, over his women, even over his judicial
and ceremonial functions. He had to pay tribute; he had to relinquish
manpower to serve the overlord's own wars; he lost full command of even
local trading links. Since – as was usually the case in such a submission – he
was going to stay right where he was, it wasn't a particularly good way of
overcoming any ecological scarcities. He might get handouts from the overlord
– but then he could have gone to get the same supplies himself, or simply
moved off.

The only answer, I think, is that the overlord could provide a defence
against some outside threat that was too big for the headman to handle
alone. Whatever was lost in control was more than offset by the gains:
protection against even more damaging plunder by others. One obvious,
and evidently pervasive, type of plunder was cattle-raiding. Since cattle were
the primary form of wealth, it was inevitable that unscrupulous people would
covet their neighbours' goods, and attempt periodically to make off with
them. An accumulation of cattle-wealth would aid in differentiating the
wealthy from the inferior and poor, and could ramify into other advantages:
pride in belonging to a more powerful group or family, to which one could,
albeit fictitiously, even attach one's own genealogy; and backhander-wealth
in the form of patronage if one behaved well. However, as we've already
noted, cattle-raiding was age-old. Something else was stimulating even greater
wealth accumulation, greater internal differentiation between classes, and
greater aggression. Trade for external goods was one strong possibility, but it
is not entirely convincing. To generalise dangerously: people gather
defensively, and commit counter-aggressions, because they are under threat
from other aggressions. New forms of political organisation arise in response
to new kinds of threat, need and (it is often forgotten) opportunity. The
most obvious candidate in the Thukela-Phongolo catchment was a new level

of aggressive slaving. This did not have to be massive in order to trigger an escalation in a spiral effect. (An analogous effect can be seen in contemporary Johannesburg. There, crime has escalated – markedly, but neither abruptly nor catastrophically, and for deep historical reasons. Some residents have banded defensively together to build high-walled housing villages, guarded by quasi-military security firms. This has become almost fashionable, has formed a different sense of community – sometimes distinguished by distinctive architectures – and reinforced certain rich-poor divisions. It has also stimulated changes and improvements in the techniques of theft. In other parts of the city, residents have taken the more counter-aggressive route of forming vigilante bands, sometimes only marginally different from the armed gangsters they combat. A mini-arms-race is in progress.[112])

The spiral worked to reinforce itself. Vital defence involved some militarisation; this raised the possibility, in other quarters, of accumulating power through coercion. This in turn was signalled by the accumulation of both local and international trade goods, including cattle, beads, metals and even women. The social crisis involved in losing manpower to slavers – or even the mere threat of such losses – meant that small groups were willing to sacrifice their independence and their access to wealth in return for participating in armed protection. This would have the effect of intensifying the relationship between militarisation, social stratification and centralisation, and wars involving trade of all kinds. Some groups, through geographical chance or charismatic leadership, proved more successful in managing this emergent spiral than others. They could take advantage of droughts, succession disputes, and trade opportunities to consolidate still further.

This picture can be supported by many analogies from elsewhere in Africa (accepting that analogies are the weakest form of historical argument). The growth of organised, centralised and aggressive polities has throughout Africa been associated with the radical superior-inferior relations of slaving. Some forms of organisation were designed to participate in the overseas slave trade, to extend such local systems of vassalage and plunder into the overseas market. The Ndwandwe were probably a polity of this kind; the later offshoots, the Gaza and Jere, unquestionably so (see Chapters 6 and 8). Other forms of organisation, though superficially similar in some respects, were primarily defensive, committing aggressions more opportunistically than habitually. A well-documented case of this kind is that of the extraordinary Queen Nzinga Mbande in seventeenth-century Angola. Like Shaka, she was characterised as 'Unconquerable'. Resisting Portuguese attempts to undermine her, she moved a portion of her people inland, consolidated by attracting minor potentates to join her, played foreign powers off one another, sold a few war captives when she could, and fought aggressively to stave off the destructiveness of European commercial encroachment.[113] Shaka's Zulu polity, I will be suggesting throughout this book, was a 'state' of a very similar kind. Queen Nzinga was not the only such case. In fact, the phenomenon is so widespread that, as the doyen of African history Basil Davidson asserts, 'the slave trade became inseparable from the workings of chiefly rule. Wherever the trade found strong chiefs and kings, it prospered almost from the first; wherever it failed to find them, *it caused them to come into being*'.[114]

A NUGGET OF COAL

You may well object that the scale of slaving in the eighteenth century was simply not great enough to have had so dramatic an effect. Indeed, much of what I've covered in this chapter remains arguable. Partly this is because up to 1780, the process was still developing and murky. There was clearly an upsurge in violence, at least some of it attributable to slaving. The upsurge was nevertheless relatively gradual. It mostly radiated from the Delagoa Bay region. The westward and southward movement of peoples away from Delagoa Bay was likewise slow, taking several decades of accumulating pressure. This was still not an outright catastrophe or sudden holocaust. But it was greater than what had come before, and it was setting the stage for further intensification of all these processes. Slaving provided one essential stimulus for quasi-militarisation of circumcision schools or other age-based organisation, part defensive, part aggressive. Trade and competition for goods intensified the process, feeding into other foundational factors such as, perhaps, local population pressures, drought and flood distress, and succession disputes. The result was a ponderous but profound social upheaval touching every level of many societies in the region. The pincer movement represented by encroaching global influences would tighten over the next 50 years, taking its ultimate form of expression in outright white invasion and colonisation.

The Zulu polity, amongst others, would emerge from this process as loose vegetable matter is transformed into a nugget of coal – under pressure.

Perhaps the most important point to take from this chapter is this: there can be no one all-explaining cause for the emergence of 'states' in this region, only complex sequences with specific local triggers and a diffusion of more general influences.[115] All of these factors would go on playing their part in the period that followed Shaka's birth.

Box 2

Dr Cowan disappears

Never, perhaps, in all of South African historiography has such a nonentity been credited with such dramatic effects.

In September 1808 one Dr Cowan left Cape Town, accompanied by a Lieutenant Donovan, and a motley band of followers: '20 of the Cape regiment, a boor, and a person from Klaar Water', according to one source;[1] one Jacob Kreiger, two English soldiers, and fifteen Hottentots, in four wagons, according to another.[2] Cowan's goal was to cross the subcontinent from west to east and emerge at the Portuguese settlement at Mozambique.

He never made it. What happened to him and to his party has never been ascertained. He was of little importance to the community he left, and he certainly achieved nothing. He appears in no dictionary of South African biography or history. Yet his story – or non-story – niggled the fears and consciences of the Cape colonists for decades. In 1815 Campbell, travelling to Lattakoo, worried that the local people would see his party as an expedition sent to avenge Cowan's death.[3] In 1820, the Cape official Andries Stockenström suggested using a search for Cowan as a cover for sending a commando into Griqua and Koranna territory, since Cowan and Donovan had 'lately been said to exist amongst some of the remoter hordes'.[4] The traveller William Burchell noted in 1821 that there was still no certainty.[5]

The mystery of Cowan's disappearance inevitably spawned overheated rumours. However, it was only many years later, when the Shaka phenomenon had emerged and passed, that the notion arose that Cowan had had a crucial influence on Shaka's rise to regional power. Henry Francis Fynn was perhaps the first to speculate that Dingiswayo, while visiting the Hlubi chief Bhungane, encountered a white man who had performed some successful surgery on Bhungane's injured or arthritic knee. This was 'probably' Dr Cowan, wrote Fynn, and since there was no other way of explaining Dingiswayo's surging and militarised power (he couldn't *possibly* have thought it up himself), 'there is a probability that during the time he [Dingiswayo] was with Dr Cowan he acquired much information from him, and that on this were founded his plans for the future'. That this was no more than the thinnest of speculations is shown in Fynn's vagueness about the date: 'in the year 17—'.[6] In *The Diary of Henry Francis Fynn*, James Stuart mendaciously changed this to '1806', which was also wrong.[7] Bryant surmised on no evidence whatsoever that Fynn had meant '1750'.[8] This was, in fact, at least thirty years too early for Diniswayo's rise (as I have argued in the main text).

Despite this obvious error, the Dr Cowan legend stuck. Most responsible for perpetuating the story was A.T. Bryant. He scorned Theophilus Shepstone, who had 'almost succeeded in establishing a myth' that the fugitive Godongwana/ Dingiswayo had wandered as far as the Cape Colony and observed British troops at drill. Bryant was obliged to recognise that Cowan had, from all the available evidence, gone nowhere near Mthethwa-Zulu country. Cowan had – as Stockenström knew – travelled to the Karoo, then due north over the 'Boggeveld', crossing the Orange river somewhere west of the present-day Gariep Dam, to Lattakoo, near present-day Kimberley.[9] Bryant cited Campbell's record of rumours that Cowan had been murdered by the 'Wankatzens' people (Ngwaketsi), east of Lattakoo, and that their chief 'Makkabba' had been seen in red-and-white clothing, presumably Cowan's, and winning local squabbles with Cowan's guns. As it happened, this was probably wrong,[10] but Bryant could do no more than now openly speculate that it was 'some survivor' of Cowan's expedition who gave Bhungane and Godongwana their instructions in military techniques. He had therefore to surmise that Shaka had assumed power in 1816, and Dingiswayo eight years before,[11] which is far too late.

If Bryant allowed some doubt about all of this, not so E.A. Ritter in his novel *Shaka Zulu*. While clearly using Bryant as his source, Ritter stated quite firmly that Dingiswayo 'had no doubt talked of politics with Dr Cowan', and insinuated that this was directly responsible for Dingiswayo's abrupt institution of a regimental system – which he passed on to Shaka.[12]

Now Dr Cowan appears in every Zulu history. This encapsulates the process of the whole Shaka myth-industry: a mistake, tainted with prejudice, spawns a speculation, which is then disseminated far and wide as fact.

While we can dismiss the Cowan legend for the nonsense it is, his tragic tale is still of interest in other ways. It shows how difficult it was for ignorant white men to make their way through the southern African interior (the fate of the *Grosvenor* castaways a few years before was similarly salutary). The reality of events could also be swallowed up by distance and distortion. It never became clear just what had happened to the Cowan party. It was said that Cowan had reached the Limpopo.[13] It was said that he had 'passed Malela at Molopo, then west to the Bawenkets, then to the Baquana, afterwards to the Bamangwato, and then came to a large river and in attempting to cross the river they were all drowned'.[14] It was said that they had died of fever.[15]

Yet news did travel, right across the subcontinent. The captain of the English ship *Beaver*, interviewing the Portuguese governor at Mozambique on 19 August 1812, was assured that Cowan and Donovan had been murdered somewhere between Sofala and Inhambane, '40 leagues from the coast'. Trade links with those parts (around the present Mozambique-Zimbabwe border) were well established, he said.[16] This is likely to be the closest we will ever get to the truth.

Of this much we can be certain: Dr Cowan had nothing at all to do with early Zulu history, and can henceforth disappear from our accounts.

3

Behind the matting screen

Birth, c.1781

Ironically Shaka Zulu, certainly the greatest ever warrior king of the awesome
Zulu nation, was born under a shadow, being the illegitimate son of a strikingly
beautiful mother, Nandi . . .

Ted Partridge, Shaka Zulu (1990, 11).

Far from knowing that Nandi was 'strikingly beautiful', we don't have the
faintest idea what she looked like. Our few white witnesses who actually
met her, leave no physical impression at all. One much later informant would
claim that she was medium in height, strongly built, dark-skinned,[1] and
another that she was tall and rather light in colour.[2] So we can take those
impressions for what they're worth.

Gloriously romantic tales, containing astonishing detail, would be told of
how Nandi and the young Zulu man, Senzangakhona, met, made love, and
fell out. Popular stories, of course, are just that – popular. Popularity can be
misleading. The fact that a story appears frequently doesn't mean that it's
true, only that people love it. People love the Rags-to-riches story, or the
Murky-origins story, or the Well-what-can-you-expect-when-they-started-like-
that story. Detail isn't always a guarantee of truth, either; it may only be
proof of embellishment.

QUESTIONS OF LEGITIMACY

Shaka's alleged illegitimacy has become a kind of pointer to the rest of his
rule. It has been seized on as the psychological fount of his tyranny, or,

conversely, as the measure of his heroic triumph over adversity. Such interpretations really tell us more about the writers' desires than about Shaka.

It is by no means certain that he was illegitimate at all. What did 'illegitimate' mean in Zulu society anyway? Did Nandi and Senzangakhona marry, or didn't they? Did a bride-price, *lobolo*, change hands, or not? Did Shaka subsequently grow up in his father's place, or in exile? Was he ever acknowledged as eldest son and as heir? It's significant that the sources are so divided over these questions. Clearly, the question of the legitimacy of his birth has long been a central factor in judging the legitimacy of his entire rule.

But what, first of all, of the two people who produced him?

Details of Nandi's ancestry are sketchy. She was probably the daughter of the Langeni *inkosi*, Mbhengi. Mbhengi's parents were Mhlongo and Mfunda; Mfunda was the daughter of Phakathwayo of the Qwabe.[3] So Nandi embodied the strong, ongoing Qwabe connection with the Zulu.[4] Her grandmother, Phakathwayo's wife, may have been a Mthethwa - another important link.[5] And, apart from Fynn's assertion that Nandi was of a 'violent, passionate disposition', for which he gives no real evidence, we are told nothing of her character whatsoever.[6]

We do have a little more information about Senzangakhona. He is said to have got his name when his father, Jama, exclaimed to his wife as the boy was born, 'You have done well, Nkosikazi, you have done well [*wenze ngakona*] by producing a son for me'.[7] He was, most accounts agree, a rather colourless character. He did not have many idiosyncrasies, *imikhuba*.[8] This doesn't quite match the pounding lines of his praises, his *izibongo*:

Tree with fragile trunk;
He whose body was beautiful even in the great famine;
Whose face had no fault,
Whose eyes had no flaw,
Whose mouth was perfect,
Whose hands were without defect;
A chest which had no blemish,
Whose feet were faultless . . .[9]

And so on. We would be deluded to believe all that. Not that *izibongo* are necessarily all sweet-talk. On the contrary, they can be sharply critical. One of the jobs of a praise-singer, the *imbongi*, is to voice with impunity the worries of the populace. So Senzangakhona is also depicted as being a bit of a dresser, a ladies' man, a somewhat frivolous hunter. He had an unpredictable streak:

> I was almost eaten up by the mamba
> Which lay in the thickets and creepers . . .
> Gurgling water of the Mpembeni stream,
> I don't even know where it's going to,
> Some runs downhill and some runs uphill . . .
> Expresser of sympathy, here is a magical stone
> Not falling on the neck it will fall on the shoulder,
> It will play a trick and fall on the flank . . .[10]

Still, he was seen as doing his best to secure the interests of his people, though not in the aggressive manner of Ndaba – or of Shaka. Nathaniel Isaacs claimed that Senzangakhona 'kept the neighbouring tribes around him in great terror and subjection',[11] but this is not supported by anyone else. The *izibongo* picture more of a negotiator:

> He who went in darkness to the Mazolo people and returned by
>   moonlight,
> And the men turned to vicious critics,
> He who went with criticism and returned with praises.
> He whose head-dress was wet with the journey.
> He who spoke and his words were resisted but presently accepted,
> It was as if the darkness was coming with the rain.[12]

As so often with these praises, the original incident has been lost, but the tenor is deliberately chosen. Only one or two lines of Senzangakhona's *izibongo* indicate aggression: 'He captured a woman, the wife of Sukuzwayo,/And destroyed Sukuzwayo and his sons'. Most informants think he was not a particularly formidable personage, and did not have a huge following – though it must have been greater than that of his predecessors.[13]

According to BALENI, Senzangakhona even had a hard time succeeding to the position of *inkosi*. He probably had to take over from Mnkabayi's regency after Jama's death, which had happened while he, Senzangakhona, was a youngster. Fighting broke out. Senzangakhona fled to the Phathe stream, below Mthonjaneni mountain to the south-west. The opposition, led by his brother Mkhasana kaJama, had ousted Senzangakhona from the Nobamba *umuzi* so unexpectedly that one of his daughters got left behind, squalling in the forecourt. BALENI claimed one of his ancestors, Khuba, happened to be there and rescued the infant.[14] With this brave and generous act, Khuba initiated, or cemented, a lasting friendship between the Zulu and Khuba's Mphungose people. Khuba's son, Ndlovu, then helped Senzangakhona to kill Mkhasana; they cut him down on the slopes of Sihlungo hill, near Babanango.

In this violent manner Senzangakhona became *inkosi* of the Zulu.

Somewhere in the middle of the fracas – certainly before he actually took over – Senzangakhona met Nandi.

How did Shaka's birth happen? The sources are divided – and the controversy is itself fascinating. It gives us a quite detailed glimpse into the making of historical myths, myths arising as much from the biographies of the informants as from anything that might have actually *happened*.

Crudely put, there are two opposing versions of Shaka's birth. There is the romantic version, exemplified by the testimony of NDHLOVU kaThimuni; and there's the pragmatic version, as held by MADIKANE kaMlomowetole. Looking at the stories through the lenses, as it were, of these two informants' own lives, helps us to understand how and why the stories arose in the first place, as well as how and why they were used. Let's begin with the romantic version.

BOY MEETS GIRL

James Stuart met with NDHLOVU kaThimuni several times between 1902 and 1919. Stuart described his informant as 'medium-height, light-coloured, talkative, agreeable, intelligent', very 'frank and open', with a consuming interest in the past and in current affairs. In 1902 NDHLOVU was about 45, and had heard his stories of Shaka from his father Thimuni. Thimuni had been called up late in Shaka's reign as a member of the Ndabenkulu section of the old but expanding iziMpohlo *ibutho*. This was probably in around 1826.[15] The men of this section were not permitted by Shaka to marry, but were later *juba*'d (given permission to marry) by Dingane. So Thimuni came of age during Dingane's reign, and he initially benefited from Dingane's liberality. It is probable, then, that stories of Shaka which stuck in Thimuni's mind, to be related to his curious son, were stories developed in Dingane's time, and quite possibly concocted by Dingane to discredit his predecessor. Thimuni's relationship with Dingane himself could not have been simple, since he fled from Dingane under threat of death; quite why, unfortunately, NDHLOVU doesn't say. Thimuni – and thus NDHLOVU – continued to live in Natal under white protection and patronage, until NDHLOVU himself (after a spell of work in the Kimberley mines) became a chief in the Maphumulo division south of the Thukela river. Unlike his father, NDHLOVU approved of Theophilus Shepstone's disastrous divide-and-rule policy for Zululand.[16] A certain anti-mainstream streak also emerged in NDHLOVU's apparent support for Mbuyazi, who was Mpande's choice of heir but not supported by the majority of Zulu massing behind Cetshwayo. After Mbuyazi was killed at the internecine battle of Ndondakusuka in 1856, NDHLOVU seemed to throw his support behind Mkhungo, another son of Mpande's whose bid for the Zulu throne was patronised by Shepstone. NDHLOVU's sympathies were perhaps also influenced by a sense of being from the 'left-hand' (*ikohlo*) side of the ruling house, which is to say, the secondary side. This had to have been keenly sharpened by the knowledge that his own grandfather Mudli, a prominent adviser to Senzangakhona, had been murdered by Shaka. As we'll see, NDHLOVU's (and Thimuni's) testimony is deeply coloured by a desire to place Mudli at the centre of the action at every stage.[17]

Though he is by no means wholly one-sided, NDHLOVU can be seen in a number of ways to nurse a certain grievance against the house of Shaka, and so to have become a vector for anti-Shaka stories. In this regard, his differences of opinion with other informants, including, interestingly, his own elder brother MRUYI kaThimuni, are revealing.

So here, slightly edited, is NDHLOVU's romantic version of the story of Shaka's appearance in the world:

A man of the Langeni went out one day from eNguga, accompanied by a youth, his baggage carried by a smaller boy. Out in the veld they found Senzangakhona and other boys, herding cattle. They slaughtered young steers, ones with horns broader than the width of a hand. Senzangakhona gave them meat; they ate; they went on with their errands. On their return, Senzangakhona fed them again. When they got home to Langeni country, they related the story to the girls, including Nandi. 'Who was this man who gave you meat?' Nandi asked. 'It was Senzangakhona,' they said. 'How I wish to see him!' Nandi exclaimed. The man replied, 'I could show him to you.'

Nandi gathered the girls of her place, many of them. She went with the man, and the boy, to the place where the boys were. They watched the herdboys from amongst the bushes to one side. The boys could not see them. They were playing with branches, hitting each other. The man pointed out Senzangakhona, 'There he is!'

Every day the girls would go there with the man. One day the cattle wandered close to where they were hidden. The boys, heading the cattle off, found the place where the girls had been sitting. They saw bones, and beer, and smelt *umutwa* perfume. 'Hau!' they said. 'People have been sitting here, watching us. They must be girls. The places where they have been sitting have turned white with use.'

Senzangakhona and the boys returned home to sleep. Next day, they found the girls had already arrived. Four boys went forward, and made the discovery. The man, the youth, and the boy then left and went home. The boys who had been sent to investigate returned to Senzangakhona. 'Go and call them,' said Senzangakhona. They did so, and the girls came to them.

The boys asked of them, 'Where are you going?' The girls replied, 'We have come to see the son of the chief, Senzangakhona.' The boys asked, 'Can you point him out?' The girls replied, pointing, 'There he is!' The boys asked where the girls were from; and having found out they were from eNguga in Langeni, asked, 'So who is this daughter of Mbengi who has come to see Senzangakhona?' They pointed out Nandi, who said, 'I have come to see him because I like him.' They asked, 'On what account?' She said, 'I want to *soma* with him; I want him to be my lover, my *isiklebe*.'

Nandi then went forward, took Senzangakhona by the arm, and went into his makeshift herdboy's hut. She went in with several of her attendants, her *izigqila*, those whom she liked and who cooked food for her at home. Rush mats were spread for them; they sat and drank beer, talked and ate meat. At sunset they went home. Nandi said, 'Let the four boys who were staying in this hut remain here, and sleep in it.' They would guard it; the girls gave them cloaks to sleep in, and food. Then they went home.

Nandi told her attendants to go and dig up *incombo*, some earth from an antheap, and put it into water. The man previously referred to had been building a hut at his place; he had made a wicker door, cut timber for rafters; everything was ready. Next day the man said Nandi should look for youths to carry the hut to that place amongst the bushes. Girls would carry mats, woven over many days, to put on the roof of the hut. So people came and carried off the framework of the hut; holes were dug and it was put in place; the framework was thatched. That finished, the floor was laid. Then the makeshift hut which Senzangakhona was using was repaired. It became the hut in which his meat and other food was cooked, and his beer vessels stored. He stayed in his own hut.

Senzangakhona now *hlobonga*'d, had non-penetrative sex, with his girl. Her stomach began to swell.[18]

So far, so ordinary. This story relates the commonplaces of step-by-step, partially supervised courtship, the kind of thing that would have been happening every day in Zulu society. There is nothing individuated or unique about this process, which is highly ritualised, open, and common to all. Senzangakhona and Nandi are ordinary teenagers, making an ordinary kind of error – Shaka-as-mistake.

However, absolutely none of NDHLOVU's story can be verified or corroborated. Where could such details have come from? The anonymous man? But he is, in the terms of the story, not privy to all these conversations. One of the girls? Nandi or Senzangakhona themselves? The same limitations apply. Possibly NDHLOVU's grandfather, Mudli, himself put different accounts together. But then, if Thimuni was still a babe-on-the-back when Mudli died,

he must have heard it from yet another party. Or, of course, he could have
invented a lot of it himself. *Someone* must have made things up. Whichever
way we look at it, this is a composite, partly imaginary depiction. It is an oral
account of a presumption, fleshed out with all the drama of the performance,
with that relish we all display for the intricacies of a love story. But it's little
more than speculation.

Accepting that, there isn't much point in quibbling over details, balancing
NDHLOVU's version against the equally dodgy details from other accounts, or
even noting all of the inconsistencies. Most telling of all, NDHLOVU's was the
minority opinion in Zulu circles, even a century later. James Stuart himself
recognised this in 1919, when he asked NDHLOVU why the story was, even at
that time, 'so little known throughout the country'. NDHLOVU replied that
Shaka's illegitimacy was hidden by the *abanumzana*, the important women.
This is possible, but why would they have done that? Stuart penned into his
notebook a number of other searching questions. Why did the Langeni people
report the pregnancy to Mudli, and not to Jama, or to the regent if Jama was
dead? Wasn't Mudli actually too young at the time to have taken part at all?
They were questions to which, apparently, he got no reply.[19]

Not even NDHLOVU's own brother Mruyi agreed with him. And after
lunch on 9 November 1902, when NDHLOVU and his followers left James
Stuart sitting at his magistrate's desk, another informant, NDUKWANA
kaMbengwana, took the opportunity to disagree strongly. It was news to him,
NDUKWANA said, 'that Nandi bore the child outside marriage (*esihlahleni*) and
did not marry Senzangakhona'. Stuart further noted that Fynn, Isaacs,
Shepstone, and the informant MKANDO all disagreed with NDHLOVU. He still
defended NDHLOVU's curiosity and Thimuni's apparent closeness to events,
but conceded that though NDHLOVU's story 'was told straight off without
hesitation . . . probably a little fiction was brought in here and there'.[20]

The real sticking-point, as Stuart also picked up, was in these next few
sentences of NDHLOVU's marvellously fluent narration:

> She [Nandi] was pregnant with Shaka. Her people saw this and said,
> 'Hau! What is the matter with the child of the chief?' They said, 'Hau!
> She has an *itshati* – that troublesome intestinal beetle.' 'How can she
> be pregnant when the girl has not yet menstruated? Has she indeed

not got an *itshati?*' They saw that her breasts swelled and her nipples grew darker. It became clear that she was pregnant.[21]

This, the story then went, was how Shaka got his name. He was named after an intestinal beetle. The potential ironies in this were of course irresistible. A.T. Bryant popularised the *itshati/itshaka* story beyond recall in 1929. Stuart rightly couldn't figure how *itshati* got translated into *Shaka*. Wasn't the beetle usually known as *ikamba?* He was aware that Henry Francis Fynn had written it as 'Cheka' (though Stuart couldn't resist 'indigenising' this to *itshaka* in his editing of the *Diary*[22]). Fynn had anyway translated this as 'a looseness of the bowels'; Isaacs had similarly written of 'chekery, or dysentery'.[23] Informants are likewise bemused by the issue.[24] According to MAPUTWANA, Shaka *hlonipha*'d the term – that is, made it disrespectful to use – and replaced it with another, *iqagana* or *iqangala*.[25] This was a neat way of avoiding the problem. It doesn't necessarily mean that the naming happened, only that Shaka disliked the closeness of the sound. This innocuous kind of *hlonipha* was often done.

NDHLOVU also couldn't clearly answer another of Stuart's questions. Who would then have actually named the child, if it was all so covered up, and the baby smuggled off, as his story went on to describe? For there was another tradition, that the child had a completely different name. One informant thought he was initially called Mandlesilo, after a former chief of the Langeni.[26] Others say – and this is the version that I am most inclined to believe – that Senzangakhona never called his son Shaka at all: he named him Sikiti. Shaka 'used to call himself "*uSikiti, uSikit' omnyama!*"', and indeed seemed at one stage to have resented being called Shaka at all: 'Let there appear the man who will call me Shaka!' he once challenged. 'Do I shake (*tshakaza*) the gourd of his people?'[27] The name Shaka was bestowed much later, in recognition of his fighting deeds. Dingiswayo first knew Shaka as Mandlesilo. 'Shaka' derived from a praise-name endowed by Dingiswayo, 'He who beats but is not beaten' (*uSitshaka ka sitshayeki*).[28]

Despite its problems, it's the romantic story that has taken the strongest hold in the literature: Shaka was a child of passion, born illegitimately when both Nandi and Senzangakhona were still quite young, and unmarried. Just how young, it is impossible to say. JANTSHI avers that Senzangakhona and his companions (Zivalele and Sithayi among them) were all but men, more than mere teenagers.[29] But they could have been anything between twelve and twenty. Senzangakhona could have been even older. In any event, informants are at odds about Sikiti-Shaka's illegitimacy.

To repeat: the notion that Shaka was formally illegitimate was for a long time the *minority* opinion. There was no hint of it in the early missionary accounts of the 1850s and 60s, for instance.[30] Even Nathaniel Isaacs, who took every opportunity to throw aspersions on the man, did not quite say that Shaka was illegitimate. By 1875, however, on the cusp of the Anglo-Zulu war, Theophilus Shepstone was proclaiming it authoritatively.[31] Where Shepstone got the idea from is unclear. It was almost certainly spread about by Dingane's propaganda machinery after his assassination of his brother. It suited enemies like Shepstone to believe it. Most Zulu people, by contrast, continued to object to the story as a deliberate slur.[32]

A half-concealed birth

Despite its various holes, was there something valid in Ndhlovu's version? How otherwise could it have risen plausibly at all? Let's follow his dramatic story through:

> [On discovering Nandi's pregnancy] the Langeni people came to Kwa Nodunga, the place of Senzangakhona's people. They met Mudhli. Mudhli asked, 'What is the matter? What brings you here?' They replied, 'We thought we had an *itshati*. In fact she, Nandi, is pregnant. She says a man from here is responsible. She says that she *hlobonga*'d with Senzangakhona.'
>
> Mudhli summoned Senzangakhona. He came. Mudhli said, 'Do you know these people?' He replied, 'No, I do not know them.' Mudhli said, 'They come from the Langeni. Do you know anyone amongst the Langeni?' He replied, 'No. I know girls from there. I know Nandi, from where we were herding. I know her from staying with her and *soma*ing with her.' Mudhli said, 'Yes, these people have come to report on her. She is sick. She has an *itshati*. Go now.'
>
> After Senzangakhona had gone, Mudhli said to the Langeni men, 'O! Men! This matter you have come to us about. It will make it so

much easier for us if you take care of this child of ours. I would be glad if it were a boy, for among our people it is not spoken of when the chief has a child. Do not mention the matter to anyone else. Hide the child for me. Do not let the mother suckle it; let it suckle from the grandmother. The mother should not squeeze the milk from her breasts, so they dry up; it should not be seen that she has suckled a child. When the child is born, come and tell me, but tell no one else.'

In due course the child was born; it was called Shaka. They came to inform Mudhli . . . . Some time passed without anyone knowing of the matter. Then Mudhli revealed it to Senzangakhona's mother. He did so when Senzangakhona was taking a wife. She asked, 'How big is he?' He replied, 'I don't know, I asked them to keep the matter secret.' She then said, 'I would like you to go and see it for me.'

Mudhli found the child with its mother's mother. He was a sturdy child, already well-grown. The mother of Senzangakhona then plucked some *umuzi* grass and twisted it into a string. She said, 'I would like you to go back and put this string around the child's waist. Measure the size of the child, put the string around its chest and tie a knot in the string to indicate his size.' He went off and did this . . .

Time passed. Then the mother of Senzangakhona said to Mudhli, 'You said that you would make a plan for me to see the child. Have you done it? I see that your heart is no longer in it.' Mudhli replied, 'No, *mame*. Put it out that you are ill, that you have a pain in your bones. People will go and fetch an *inyanga* who heals illnesses. He will make medicines. This will be so that I can fetch the child to you without old people coming to visit you, for the preparation of medicines for you will have begun.'

It was noised about that the *inkosikazi* was ill. A healer was fetched. She told girls to weave a large rush mat for her to screen the pots of medicines. She told boys to bring her white torches of dry *ugugane* wood, so that when she took medicines at night she would have light to do so. Mudhli then fetched the child and placed it behind the screen. The grandmother could now see him for herself all the time. Only she and Mudhli saw him.

Then one day the chief came to hear that his mother was hiding
something in her hut. Mudhli hurried off to take the child away,
thinking, 'Habo! They have let the secret out! They are destroying
my plan!' He took the child out by a side-entrance during the night.
They kept quiet, and heard the order given, 'When it is dark, go and
surround the kraal and kill the thing, together with that little old
crone who is my mother.' Mnkabayi and the chief's other sisters came
to hear about this, that it had been revealed to the chief that there
was an *impaka* which their mother played with every night, and that
she was to be killed. The girls came to their mother's hut together
with those who were coming to put her to death, and prevented them
from entering. The Zulu force assembled, surrounding the hut. They
built fires. At dawn the girls were still sitting before the door. When
it was light the girls called out, 'Come out, mother!' She did so. The
men went inside and pulled away the matting screen. They brought it
out and handed it to the girls. The girls said, 'Bring out our mother's
impaka; bring it here so we can see it.' The men said, 'There is nothing
there.' . . . Senzangakhona said, 'Hau! So people have been concocting
lies about my mother! Go and kill them all. Destroy everything, even
the dogs of the place.' Senzangakhona was referring to the eBaqulusini
umuzi, at Kwa Mfemfe. It was these people who were put to death,
for it was they who had said that there was an *impaka* in the home,
meaning Shaka.[33]

This is all very dramatic: the future king escapes an early death by the skin of
his teeth. An exactly parallel story – complete to the detail of the matting
screen – would be told about Shaka himself, about to kill Nandi for harbouring
a secret child. This is another conventional story, then, suspiciously
stereotyped. It strongly resembles the great archetypal hero monomyth, which
seems to have an extraordinary degree of similarity across diverse cultures.
(It sounds, for instance, very like the birth of King Arthur.) On a more
mundane level, the story might be an attempt to restore the reputation of
the murdered Mudli. It is, any way you look at it, a literary artefact.
      Nevertheless, a number of informants roughly follow the essentials of
this version: that Nandi's pregnancy was hidden, that Senzangakhona wanted

to get rid of the child, and that the infant Shaka was eventually raised among the Langeni.[34]

The usual reason for Senzangakhona's alleged viciousness is hinted at by NDHLOVU, above, when Mudli claims, 'among our people it is not spoken of when the chief has a child'. NDHLOVU's father Thimuni had told him, 'A Zulu chief does not father children, i.e. he is not supposed to father children; he takes precautions.' This was to follow the example of the leopard and the lion, whose mothers take a male cub away, for fear that its father will kill it. NDHLOVU cites the example of another chief, Mtonga, who 'has not appointed a chief son for this very reason, that it will cause a disturbance in his tribe'.[35] JANTSHI similarly states that 'royalty were not allowed by custom to be suckled by their mothers'.[36]

This is a curious set of claims. Generally speaking, a healthy brood of children is all to the good – a sign of wealth, health and status. *Not* appointing a chief son would surely cause as much disturbance as appointing one. It's true that sons can cause trouble: Shaka is said to have caused the death of his own father; Shaka and Dingane are both said to have avoided sons for fear of being usurped by them. However, rather than reflecting some kind of personal pathology, this may have been a product of the times they were living through. (In Shaka's case at least, it is far from clear that he was in fact childless.) At any rate, these generalisations of NDHLOVU and others simply don't wash. Ndaba, Jama, Mpande, Cetshwayo and Zwelithini were all perfectly happy to have children and to acknowledge them. Senzangakhona isn't said to have had such problems with any of his other children – only Shaka. Moreover, Senzangakhona *wasn't* the chief at the time anyway.

Something more specific, half-concealed, is happening in Shaka's case.

NDHLOVU's version of these later events is also not universally accepted. A number of informants assert that, on the contrary, Shaka was born *in Zulu country*.[37] Some say that he was born at Nobamba;[38] others say esiKlebheni, one of Senzangakhona's other major *imizi*.[39] One or two do insist that Nandi and Senzangakhona never got married at all.[40] Most, however, say that they *were* married, and that *lobolo* was paid once Senzangakhona admitted his error of passion.[41] BALENI goes so far as to say that this was quite customary, hardly an occasion for branding Shaka with a terrible stigma: the future king Dinuzulu was just one other case in point.[42]

On balance, it seems most likely that Nandi was an *ingodosi* – a girl who is betrothed, but has returned home after a run-away visit to her sweetheart and is waiting for *lobolo* to be paid. Any delay in the *lobolo* negotiations could put the embryonic child in a very awkward, transitional position.[43] In any event, Nandi almost certainly married Senzangakhona, just when we cannot be sure. NDHLOVU says that Shaka was already a small boy by the time his parents married.[44] The traditions are equally unclear on where Nandi stood in relation to Senzangakhona's several other wives. At any rate, far from being bundled immediately into exile, she probably bore other children to Senzangakhona.[45]

Still, the initial ambiguity of the situation later became fruitful ground for bizarre rumours. In one particularly unlikely scenario, Nandi has already been admitted to Senzangakhona's *isigodlo*, his circle of wives or prospective wives and their attendants. Nandi, out of favour for some reason, secretly sneaks in instead of another woman one night, and Senzangakhona – noticing nothing unusual – gets her pregnant that way.[46]

What is interesting is that Senzangakhona had an *isigodlo* in the first place. It is the first of two important signs of the times. The second important sign involves the issue of circumcision, that act of ritual mutilation, at once so private and so publicly important. This is where we can bring in the pragmatic version of Sikiti-Shaka's problematic birth.

CIRCUMCISION RITES

MADIKANE kaMlomowetole is a more pragmatically minded informant than NDHLOVU. When MADIKANE was interviewed by Stuart in 1905, he was a sprightly 75. He was born just a few years after Shaka's death in 1828; it was the time when Dingane *juba*'d those *amabutho* whose marriage Shaka had delayed. He was born on the Nsuze, near Nkandla, and crossed over into Natal just ahead of Mpande in 1839. He became a *kolwa*, a convert to Christianity, and subsequently a 'teacher of the Bible', an educated man.[47]

MADIKANE's father Mlomowetole was of the Maqadini people, related to the Cele. They had voluntarily *khonza*'d Shaka at the height of the troubles; Shaka was their protector. Mlomowetole had become a warrior in the iNtontela *ibutho*, had fought against Zwide and Sikhunyane, and had taken a wound high on the forehead in Shaka's second Mpondo campaign. He himself wasn't well known in Zulu country, since he belonged to a client-chiefdom, but he recalled going up to Dukuza to *khonza*, and seeing Shaka himself *giyaing*, dancing the warrior's boast. Mlomowetole, MADIKANE told Stuart, had died as recently as 1888.[48]

Mlomowetole's position was therefore close, but not too close, to the Zulu centre. There is no great reputation to be saved, no secret to conceal, no axe to grind. It's as good a basis for 'objectivity' as we're likely to get. His father was MADIKANE's main source of information, but not his only one. He also got information from others, and noted his father's sources, too: notably one Makobosi kaNdlovu, and Hlathi of the eMgazini, who had been a member of one of Senzangakhona's *amabutho*.[49] Probably at Stuart's behest, MADIKANE went to quiz a man named Magudwini, then over 100 years old. Magudwini had been a member of the Intenjane section of Shaka's Ndabenkulu *ibutho* (coincidentally the same unit to which Thimuni, NDLOVU's father, belonged), and an *umphakathi*, a member of the central council.[50] In his delivery, MADIKANE is blunt, forthright, to the point, even telegraphic. This may, of course, be partly due to James Stuart's mode of note-taking at the time, but the air of considered, unemotive realism is palpable.

MADIKANE related the story of Shaka's birth twice, once on 8 July 1903, and then again on 17 August 1903. This is the second version:

> Shaka was not illegitimate. Nandi had come to Senzangakhona to marry by becoming one of his *isigodhlo*, and it was while she was living there that she had intercourse with Senzangakhona and, becoming pregnant, bore Shaka. Now Mnkabayi, Senzangakhona's sister [and then regent], heard of this and reported the fact to Senzangakhona. Senzangakhona exclaimed, 'It seems ridiculous that I am who am still so young and have not been circumcised should be said to have a child.' Mnkabayi at once replied, 'Oh, seeing the child was a boy I have already put it to death by giving it poison.' This satisfied Senzangakhona. Mnkabayi at once communicated with Nandi, directing her to go home with the child. This she did, and returned at a later time with Shaka to show Mnkabayi. Some person or other reported the arrival to Senzangakhona, who at once took steps in the

matter. Nandi, however, thanks to Mnkabayi, succeeded in escaping, got back to the Langeni, and then went to marry among the Qwabe.

Mnkabayi afterwards caused the man who had made the report to Senzangakhona to be put to death.[51]

MADIKANE's summary includes one element missing from most other versions: the issue of circumcision. The problem in this view was not so much that Shaka was conceived 'out of wedlock', by accidental passion, but that Senzangakhona hadn't yet been circumcised. He couldn't believe – or at least found it deeply embarrassing – that he could father a child before being circumcised, before he had been proven a man. Or so he said. This is the meaning of the term often translated as 'illegitimate': *o wa se sihlahleni*. It was a violation of a whole network of norms and restraints. Moreover, a premature male offspring could cause horrendous succession issues later – as indeed it did.[52] What Mnkabayi, already here entering into her historic role as 'kingmaker' amongst the Zulu, was thinking of in preserving the child, is anyone's guess. At any rate, to save the situation, hasty arrangements had to be made. Senzangakhona was hurriedly circumcised.[53]

According to MADIKANE, there was no formal ceremony between Nandi and Senzangakhona, but the Langeni came to demand restitution anyway. *Lobolo* was paid, and Nandi was brought into Senzangakhona's *isigodlo*. MADIKANE's story is not without problems. At another point, he says that Nandi was *already* in the *isigodlo*. (This might have been Jama's *isigodlo*, left over from his early death.)

Its contradictions aside, MADIKANE's version ties in persuasively with other informants,[54] and with elements of the earliest accounts by Isaacs and Fynn. For once, Isaacs had little need to lie. He scoffs at the notion that the Zulu *believed* conception before circumcision was impossible, calling it 'preposterous'.[55] Isaacs almost certainly misreads the situation: Senzangakhona couldn't have been the first errant boy in tribal memory to have perpetrated an unintended pregnancy. But the correlation with the circumcision ceremony is unavoidable. Fynn pretty much agrees. He also claims that the ceremony could be long delayed for a chief, up to the age of 30 or 40. This seems a little exaggerated. But Fynn – like MADIKANE – states that when Senzangakhona impregnated Nandi, he already had a number of betrothed women in his own *isigodlo*, and was *soma*ing away, trying not to impregnate anyone.[56] And as Fynn put it elsewhere:

> It was then the custom of kings not to connect with their wives as married women but merely to satisfy their inclinations on the outward part of the female which custom is supposed to exist till the King is circumcised which they are generally backward in performing and never till 30 or 40 years old, apparently under the idea that they may be considered younger than they really are. However, Nande [sic] had been but a short time betrothed to Senzangakona before she was in the family way . . .[57]

The whole thing places Nandi's pregnancy, and Shaka's birth, in a curious half-light. The birth is caught in that transitional stage in a young father's life when marriage alliances, arranged and otherwise, are in the air. But he is not yet formalised in his manhood. He has no formal right to have a baby. Marriage is hastened on; the baby is born, despite its accidental origin, barely within the bounds of propriety. It's easy, if this sequence of events is right, to see how both kinds of story could then arise. Yes, Shaka was illegitimate; no, he was not. The reality was a little fuzzier than either version. Conceived, but not born, out of wedlock. The eldest son, but not of the chief wife-to-be. This uncertainty would have a dramatic impact on Shaka's eventual claim to the Zulu leadership.

And *when* did the birth occur? At this – the first fundamental of anyone's biography – I can only hazard a roughly calculated guess: it was in 1781 (see Box 3 on page 101).

The stories of the birth also encapsulate two new, wider developments: the decline of circumcision; and the growth of the institution of the *isigodlo*. Why were these happening?

We saw in Chapter 2 that society in the Thukela-Phongolo catchment generally was undergoing some long-term upheavals. The ceremonials themselves were changing. Circumcision was falling into disuse. It's near impossible to say now just what the timescale of this was, but it is important. The age-based circumcision schools, the *intanga* groups, were probably in many cases the basis of the 'regimental' system, the core of the *amabutho*.

Phakathwayo of the Qwabe, Macingwane of the Chunu, and Magaye of the Cele probably all based their emergent *amabutho* on age-sets. Others may have organised their units more on a territorial basis, and it seems possible that sometimes the two methods could have coincided.[58] At any rate, the transition from one mode to the other was doubtless erratic, patchy, and constantly argued about.

In former days, the circumcision ceremony went something like this. At some point after puberty, the boys would be taken off into the bush. Their foreskins would be cut using assegais sharpened on stones, sharp enough, but only just. The boys would be housed in temporary shelters in the bush and instructed in more than merely losing their foreskins. They called themselves *abakwetha*, the 'sequestered ones', and would stay out until the penis had healed. They would return to the settlements only at night, to see where the women had urinated, and urinate there themselves. Some died. No mourning was allowed. A man who had been circumcised wouldn't wash in public for fear of being laughed at. He would wear a penis-cover, at first made of ox-hide; in later days, of banana-leaf.[59]

Not everyone seems agreed on why circumcision was done in the first place. Many connected its origins with the Basotho people. Obviously it was a rite that welcomed boys into full manhood. In psychological terms, the detachment from the mother and the domestic scene was an important step towards manly independence. It also served to bind a man to his peers of the same age-group; they were isolated together, suffered pain and healing together. There were other beliefs attached: some felt that circumcision prolonged a man's life, or made him strong.[60]

Almost all informants are agreed that the practice finally died out in Shaka's time.[61] MINI's father Ndlovu, a contemporary of Senzangakhona's, was circumcised, but not his children.[62] Nogandaya, the father of one of Shaka's greatest warriors, was circumcised, but not his famous son.[63] Among the Thembu, the practice was discontinued during the rule of Ngoza, Shaka's contemporary.[64] Magaye, another chieftain who was closely associated with Shaka, wasn't circumcised.[65] The picture isn't uniform. Another of Shaka's warriors, Ndlela, brother of Bhibhi, *was* circumcised.[66] Langalibalele of the Hlubi, who was born around 1818, was also circumcised, and this couldn't have happened earlier than 1834.[67] People from further south, where circumcision lingered, would join the Zulu polity and still offer their skinned members for ridicule. Nor did the symbolic meanings of circumcision disappear overnight. Shaka himself is said to have been insulted about the paltry size of his penis-cover: a slight on his manliness. He didn't have to be actually wearing one to feel the sting; we don't know whether he was circumcised or not. Most likely not. His brother Dingane apparently wasn't – and felt so insulted when one Makata referred to him as a 'good-for-nothing that has not been circumcised', that he killed him.[68] Eileen Krige is almost certainly correct to say that Shaka simply pushed into oblivion a practice already on its way out.[69]

But why was this the case?

The rite of circumcision, importantly, embodied a certain kind of relationship between elders and youngsters. The abolition of circumcision entailed the imposition of other forms of control. As we will see in more detail later, these controls increasingly involved the *inkosi*'s distribution of labour-power (production) and the timing and form of marriage ceremonies (reproduction).[70] It also meant that manhood would be valorised in other ways, primarily by conduct in warfare. Young men had normally been circumcised between the ages of sixteen and eighteen, and they were generally *butha*'d, called up for military service, around eighteen. The implication is that either more men were being required to fight, or that there were now fewer men around. Either way, they were being *butha*'d younger, and in bigger units. If this is right, the decline of circumcision is testimony to increasing turbulence. Fynn understood that Dingiswayo had already let circumcision fall away, or actively prevented it, because it was interfering with his men's involvement in conflicts of greater urgency.[71] Not much later, Mswazi of the Swazi did something very similar, for similar reasons.[72] MMEMI puts this in a nutshell:

The Qwabe and the Mtetwa practiced circumcision, as did the Amampondo. The reason why it was discontinued was because those who were circumcised were obliged to remain away in the field far from home until *all* had recovered. Some of their constitutions were bad, some good. Poor constitutions took a long time to heal. The fact of a large number of young men being away from home, and for a considerable period, was thought to render the tribe, or they themselves, liable to attack.[73]

Shaka would most thoroughly refine this general transition from scattered, small-group circumcision ceremonies to larger, centrally controlled agricultural, military, and marital ceremonies. Several informants state that Shaka stopped circumcision because he wanted to perpetuate his men's youth. He claimed that it *reduced* virility and power; he wasn't going to have his warriors castrated like cattle.[74] Although this doesn't make sense in any literal way, the symbolic power of the rite is all-important. Its place in the general structure of the society is at stake. In short, the dynamics of violence increasingly governing local conditions made circumcision simply impractical, even dangerous.

Senzangakhona was amongst the last of the Zulu to have suffered the dreaded cut.

CONTROLLING WOMEN

The decay of circumcision seems to have been happening at the same time as the growth of the other means of controlling production and reproduction: the *isigodlo*. This institution also grew out of long-established customs. At the homestead level, it had probably long been customary for the chief, the *indlunkulu*, to dispense his own daughters and other girls or women, given in tribute or taken captive in wars, in strategic marriages of his choice. This was the system of *ethula*, and the other side of the coin was the payment of *lobolo*. Girls were generally *ethula*'d very early, aged six or so, and grew up as members of the new homestead, even taking on the family *izibongo* and name. The *indlunkulu* had the first say in the labour that women performed. He controlled their tools, the very hoes that they dug with. He dictated what they wore. They were, in addition, excluded from working with cattle, the main form of wealth, and prevented from participating in the most important rituals. They were further subjected to a whole raft of observances and taboos, especially ones associated with menstruation.[75]

A word of warning: we have even less information about pre-Shakan women than we do about pre-Shakan men.[76] Not all women were chattels to be tossed from hand to hand. Even before Shaka's time, some women were powerful political figures. We've already seen Mntaniya's apparently implacable hand at work in relation to Shaka's own birth. The difference between élite women and chattel women would become accentuated in Shaka's time. At least it's reasonably clear that pre-Shakan chiefs like Senzangakhona, and even his father Jama, had an *isigodlo*. The other major figures of the time, Dingiswayo and Zwide, apparently did, too. And it's reasonably clear that the *izigodlo* extended the system as it operated at homestead level to a broader 'state'-controlled level.

The *isigodlo* was, for a number of reasons, tightly guarded. One reason was protection of the body of the *inkosi* and of his most important womenfolk against both actual invasion and magical malpractice. A second reason was to prevent misbehaviour amongst the women themselves, many of whom never wanted to be there in the first place, and most of whom were being prevented from freely expressing their physical desires.

But there may have been another necessity for guarding the women so rigidly, one that has been neglected. Historians have tended to follow a quasi-Marxist line that the domination of women in this way was based on 'surplus labour'. The idea is that in order for the systems of *ethula* and *lobolo* to work, there had to be more women than the immediate household needed (so they could be 'given away'); and the women had to generate more produce than was immediately needed (so that they could be paid for). Up to a point, I can accept this line of thinking. The centralised control of Senzangakhona, Shaka and others meant that the overlord purloined some of this surplus from the household head. Yet this was only ever partial, as far as we are able to tell. Was there then an even greater surplus of labour, a surplus of women? If so, why? One possible reason – and it fits rather neatly with the idea that men were being called up for military service at a younger age – is that there was a shortage of men. Given what we argued in Chapter 2, this shortage – at least in its initial stages – might well have been the result of slaving. The *izigodlo* were one product of a relatively new imbalance between the numbers of men and women. Moreover, in threatening times, women had to be physically more securely guarded.[77]

This wouldn't have been the only, or – amongst communities at a further remove from slavers' effects – even the main benefit of the *izigodlo*. There were spin-offs that could acquire a momentum of their own. The *isigodlo* was a further sign and tool of élite power and accumulation of wealth. The *isigodlo* and its inmates were sacrosanct, barred by fences and an intricate panoply of rituals and observances, the conduct of which were in the hands of the men. It became a mark of especial favour or power to be granted an *isigodlo* of one's own, as old Ngomane was, or Shaka's half-brother Ngwadi.[78] The *isigodlo* was, as Carolyn Hamilton puts it, 'the local nerve centre of royal administration', its concentration of important people and huts giving it 'the sense of being an inner cabal of limited access – the hub of the nation – where future events were determined'.[79] In the Zulu case, many of its prohibitions, though often extensions of well-established ones, seem to have been put in place by Shaka, and held to particularly strictly; although his successors retained the *izigodlo*, many of the restrictions outlined earlier would be relaxed.[80]

It was an arrangement that developed out of the long-established *lobolo* system, which involved the obligation by a junior house to transfer the eldest daughter to the senior house in return for cattle or other payment. This was called *ukwethula*. The richer a man, the more such women dependants he could attract. They would be brought up in his household as *umndlunkulu*, his to dispose of in marriage as he pleased. Since the richest men were those patronised by the *inkosi*, and they were generally of the closest clans, they got a lot of young women to dispense. The *inkosi* got the *lobolo*. A woman considered less attractive could be sold off for between 30 and 50 cattle; while a well-favoured woman could go to a prominent *induna* for anything up to 200 cattle.[81] It was a way of expanding the wealth and resources of the ruling élite without the *inkosi* himself having to marry.[82] In addition, it was a way of influencing the group or clan into which an *umdlunkulu* girl would marry. So, for example, Shaka's half-sister Nomcoba was married off to Mayandeya kaMbiya of the Mthethwa, cementing particularly closely that historic link.[83]

In these and other ways women were thus a fundamental source of wealth for the patriarchal élite: a means of manipulating power and of redistributing both local trade in cattle and international trade for metals.

I've run ahead of the story a little here in order to show where this trend was heading. The institution of the *isigodlo* was nevertheless already sturdily developed in Senzangakhona's time. In short, both the decline of circumcision and the rise of the institution of the *isigodlo* were accompanied by complex new sets of prohibitions and norms reflecting new power relations between chiefs and commoners, between men and women, between free and enslaved. Little wonder, then, that there was a certain amount of consternation when Nandi fell accidentally pregnant. The incident violated all the controls that were then developing as a response to increasingly troubled times. The 'Nandi/Shaka problem' continued to pursue Senzangakhona even as, having finally taken over from Mntaniya, he responded to the troubled times by attempting to consolidate his patrimony. He would continue to do so for the next 25 or 30 years.

Meanwhile, where was Shaka, alias Sikiti?

Year	King	Mini	Mntaniya	Holden	Nomcoba
1791					
1790					
1789					
1788					
1787					
1786					
1785					
1784					
1783					
1782					
1781					Median
1780					
1779					
1778					
1777					
1776					
1775					
1774					
1773					
1772					
1771					
1770					
1769					
1768					
1767					

Calculating Shaka's birthdate

Box 3

Calculating Shaka's birthdate

Estimates of Shaka's date of birth have up to now depended on a single view: that of the white adventurer **James Saunders King**. How good was King at estimating black men's ages? We don't know. At any rate, King in 1824 estimated Shaka's age as 38, so placing his birth in 1786 – though for no obvious reason this has been changed to 1787 in most accounts. It is, at least, one legitimate estimate, though I'd like to build in a margin of error of, I think, 5 years towards the older side. After all, Shaka was already going grey at the time.

Some other rough calculations can also be made. They are all fuzzy; all have to have even larger margins of error built in. These margins are indicated as shading in the diagram on page 100. Nevertheless, the results are suggestive. These estimates are calculated as follows.

James Stuart's informant **Stephen MINI** was three or four when Shaka died, so was born in c.1824. His father had died in 1839, already 'an elderly man'. He was a man 'of Senzangakhona's time'. If we take 'elderly' to mean 75 (likely margin of error 5 years either way), he would have been born around 1864. If we take 'of Senzangakhona's time' to mean an exact contemporary, and we assume that Senzangakhona was about 20 when Shaka was born (margin of error 3 years), this would place Shaka's birth in 1784 (overall margin of error 5 years either way).

Mntaniya, Senzangakhona's formidable mother and predecessor as regent, died in 1825 aged (Fynn and Isaacs estimated) 95. If this is right, she would have been born in 1720 (margin, 5 to 10 years downwards, that is, towards 1730). Since she would have had to be well-established to take over as regent (say, aged 50, margin of 5 years either way), and she must have taken over when Senzangakhona was quite young, say 10 (margin of 5 years either way), she would have been about 30 years older than Senzangakhona. This would date Senzangakhona's birth to 1760, and Shaka's (following the assumption made in the previous calculation) to 1780 (overall margin of 10 years either way).

William Holden, a missionary, claimed that he received much of his information from one 'Abantwana' (Bantwana), a brother of Nandi and therefore an uncle of Shaka's (though elsewhere he confusingly says 'nephew'). NGIDI affirms that Bantwana was of an age with Senzangakhona and Mgabhi, of the age of the Mbelebele *ibutho*. If, however, Bantwana was 12 to 14 when Shaka was born, as Holden says, he must have been a bit younger than Senzangakhona. When Holden met him, he was 'aged'. Let's say, again, 75 (margin of error at least 5 years). Unhappily, Holden doesn't say exactly when he met Bantwana during his 26-year stay in Zulu country (1840–66). If we assume (on no evidence at all) that they met early on, 1840 or shortly thereafter, Bantwana would have been born around 1765, and Shaka around 13 years later, in 1778. Since Holden might have met Bantwana later on, and Bantwana might have been anything up to 95 years of age (the two possibilities might even cancel one another out), the margin of error here is quite great: at least 10 years).

Nomcoba, a slightly younger sister to Shaka (say 5 years younger), died in 1856, aged about 80. This would place her birth in 1775, and Shaka's therefore in 1770 (margin of error 5 years, in the direction of a later date).

If we take these estimates for what they are – extremely rough – and simply work on the median, we emerge with 1781. The cumulative suggestion, then, is that Shaka's date of birth needs to be pushed back from King's estimate by at least 5 years. As we'll see, this makes some sense in terms of the probable pace of developments during Shaka's life.

However, the long and the short of it is this: we do not know when Shaka was born.

4

Escaping the father

Growing up, c.1781–1800

For all his normal life the scars of his childhood were still upon him.
Donald Morris, *The Washing of the Spears* (1966, 46).

In 1928 (exactly a century after Shaka's death) Sigmund Freud, by then a
notoriously influential psychoanalyst, published a short piece entitled
'Dostoevsky and Parricide'. In this essay, Freud held up the profound fictions
of the Russian writer as a mirror to his own ideas about sons' relationships
with their fathers:

> The relation of a boy to his father is, as we say, an 'ambivalent' one.
> In addition to the hate which seeks to get rid of the father as a rival,
> a measure of tenderness for him is also habitually present. The two
> attitudes of mind combine to produce identification with the father;
> the boy wants to be in the father's place because he admires him and
> wants to be like him, and also because he wants to put him out of the
> way.[1]

Only the following year, A.T. Bryant published, in *Olden Times in Zululand
and Natal*, his account of Shaka's relationship with Senzangakhona. He drew
for comparison on a different story:

> History sometimes repeats itself in the records of the world. Carcinus
> of Rhegium, like Senzangakhona, begat a son who, the Delphian
> oracle informed him, would prove a source of great evil both to Sicily

103

and to Carthage. Determined to rid his house and country of so evil
a portent, he had the child thrown out into the wilds to die. But its
mother, unknown to her husband, rescued the babe, and, giving it
the name Agathocles, had it nursed in the home of Heracleides. When
the boy was seven years old, the father, Carcinus, came to a sacrificial
festival on the invitation of Heracleides. There he saw a boy at play
with his fellows and admired his superior strength and ability . . .[2]

For Carcinus, read Senzangakhona trying to kill the infant son; for
Heracleides, read Dingiswayo. As the story goes, Dingiswayo, many years after
Shaka is smuggled away, invites Senzangakhona to a festival. Senzangakhona
remarks on the agility of a particular dancer. Of course, it turns out to be his
son Shaka. Bryant relates the consequence in terms strongly redolent of
Freud. Dingiswayo primes Shaka for a gesture of usurpation:

Then, when his father was seated in his hut, he was to enter and
stand in such a way that his shadow would fall upon his father. That
an inferior should remain standing while the royal Presence was seated
was, of course, a piece of dumbfounding audacity. But it was more
than that, as Dingiswayo knew – it was magic; for, working
subconsciously between the two parties, the standing personality would
gradually impress and impose itself so profoundly upon that sitting,
as to gain a sure and complete ascendancy over it.[3]

Senzangakhona subsequently – or, rather, consequently – dies. So the
conventional story of Shaka's youth travels this path: from the father
unsuccessfully attempting infanticide, to the 'infant' successfully performing
parricide.

SEDUCTIVE ANECDOTES

Freud used a fiction to illustrate a theory about something that he thought
affected everybody. Bryant used a fiction to 'verify' an historical singularity,
a much more dubious tactic. What in fact the parallel shows is not that history
repeats itself, but that stories repeat each other. Stories 'cast their shadow'
over facts. People often bend facts to suit a narrative that everybody can

relate to. The story of the boy-in-exile who comes back to take the crown is as common in African tales as it is in the European hero-myth. We have already seen it in the story of Godongwana-Dingiswayo himself; we will find it again in Makhedama, chief of the Langeni. In other words, it is a metaphor, used to explain a certain attitude towards the subject. It shows that he is regarded as an outsider of some kind, or it captures one aspect of a succession dispute. But this does *not* mean that Shaka actually went 'into exile'.

Nevertheless, the early-exile story seems to have been put about very shortly after Shaka's own time, if not actually during it. Shaka might even have put it about himself. Shaka's 'pet white boy', Charles Rawden Maclean, recalled in January 1854 that 'Shaka raised himself, from being a persecuted wanderer in the bush, where he and his mother had to fly from his father's vengeance (when he was but an infant), to rule the Zulu nation'.[4] *Why* the initial eviction happened has subsequently been interpreted in purely psychological terms (though so crudely that Freud must be turning in his grave). The psychological explanation largely ignores another Zulu perspective, one that is far more political in its implications:

> [Shaka's] mother hid him as [Senzangakhona] would have killed him, for by our custom if a man's first child is a boy, and he allows the boy to grow up, this boy will fight and oust his father, therefore he must be put to death whilst still young.[5]

As we've already seen, the existence of such a *custom* seems doubtful. Our informant Yenza (speaking here within a decade of both Bryant and Freud) nevertheless captures a central problem: successions to chieftainships were often bitterly, even fatally, contested.

This is not to say that the exile story is totally without foundation. But I will suggest that Maclean, who is in some respects our most reliable white eyewitness, is in this case wrong. His version captures the two popular anecdotes by which many writers, over the course of a century and a half, have been seduced.

The first anecdote is that Senzangakhona evicted Shaka and Nandi when Shaka was either unborn or very small, launching him on a poverty-stricken journey of bitter exile. This is said to explain why Shaka was so ambitious.

The second anecdote is that Shaka was bullied as a boy, especially by his cousin Makhedama. This is said to explain why Shaka was so nasty.

Both of these anecdotes are fiction, and we need to explore how and why they might have arisen.

WHAT DOES 'EXILE' MEAN?

As I argued in Chapter 3, Shaka was born, if not conceived, *legitimately*, in *Zulu* country. Nandi *was* formally married to Senzangakhona.

Was Shaka then chased away at all?

The most common version of the exile tale claims that Nandi and Shaka went back to the Langeni, Nandi's people, and lodged with Nandi's mother, Mfunda.[6] One or two people think that he went to live amongst the Qwabe, Mfunda's people, a bit further south.[7] NDHLOVU - who as we've seen has a tendency to romanticise and embellish - thought that a brother of Nandi's, Mbikwana, had a role in this, smuggling Shaka yet again out of sight of his vengeful father.[8] Others claimed that he went even further, to Macingwane of the Chunu, or even the Cube, but this seems even less likely.[9]

Some alleged that it was Nandi who found herself 'disliked' by Senzangakhona, and so ran off on her own accord; she felt that she was a woman of rank, but wasn't being treated accordingly.[10] Yet elsewhere her nature was said to have matched her name, *unandi* meaning 'sweet': she was 'known for her good nature in the Zulu country; she was well-liked'.[11] This contradicts Fynn and Isaacs who had a vested interest in portraying Nandi as a violent harridan: it 'explained' Shaka. Subsequent stories about Nandi beating Senzangakhona about the head, and indeed of Shaka misbehaving violently as a boy, so provoking his own exile, find little support amongst the traditions. (He was said only by one informant to have attracted ire for killing some Langeni cattle without permission.[12])

One story goes that Nandi went off and married, or settled in with, a man named Gendeyana who, according to some, lived among the Mbedweni section of the Qwabe.[13] By Gendeyana, Nandi is said to have had two more children, a daughter Nomcoba, and another son, Ngwadi. Ngwadi would become known as 'The stick of the one who cuts down trees (*intonga yomagwuli*)',[14] and he would stand by Shaka throughout, accordingly being assassinated by Dingane shortly after Shaka himself.[15] Nomcoba (also sometimes called Nomzinhlanga) lived to a ripe old age, dying in around 1856. A prominent and good-natured citizen, she had her own *imizi*. Apparently she had Shaka's prominent nose, and was light in colour.[16]

Other informants categorically deny that Nandi ever remarried or ran off, dismissing this story as pure slander. Nomcoba and Ngwadi were Senzanga-khona's children.[17] Bryant claims that Nomcoba was Senzangakhona's child, but Ngwadi was Gendeyana's.[18] Another informant thought that Nomcoba was Senzangakhona's daughter, but by another wife.[19] Since Gendeyana disappears from the record, it seems impossible to say now, one way or the other. However, since Nomcoba seems to have been married off by Senzangakhona, the weight must lie with *his* paternity.

In the popular story, only a single incident is used to 'prove' that Shaka spent his childhood amongst the Langeni. He is said to have had a fight or fights with a cousin, Makhedama kaMgabhi:

> Shaka complained of the way in which he was treated by Makedama; he complained, whilst still a boy, of Makedama's objecting to Shaka drinking water higher up a stream than where he was drinking; and of picking out the best of Shaka's stones, which represented cattle in the games they played. 'Kraals' of cowdung were built and stones were selected and put inside. Shaka's stones were better than Makedama's and he objected to Makedama's jealously seizing and putting them in *his* 'kraal'.[20]

Makhedama would be accused of other cruel acts, too, such as pouring hot curds over Shaka's hands.[21] There were many other torturous variations, but there is evidence to indicate that the bullying was made up after the event. It was not a part of Shaka's childhood exile.

The informants are also hopelessly at odds about what this alleged exile consisted of. MBULO, for instance, related that his father Mlahla, who was the same age as Shaka, actually *lived* with Shaka in Langeni country, where Shaka 'was made to thresh *unyaluti* millet, and they gave him a louse-ridden blanket, even though he belonged by birth'.[22] These kinds of details are vivid and plausible; they appear superficially to 'make sense' of Shaka's later alleged cruelties. Thus they, too, like the 'illegitimacy', became an irresistible ingredient in the tale.

What could 'exile' have possibly meant, anyway? Senzangakhona's and Mbhengi's respective *imizi* were barely more than a day's journey apart.[23] After all, the distance hadn't hindered Nandi from meeting her future husband. Family networks were so intricate, and gossip surely so pervasive, that it defies the imagination that a child could have been concealed so deftly, for so long, so close by. I am not completely discounting the story that Shaka spent time amongst the Langeni. However, there is plenty of information to allow us to put together an alternative narrative to the simplistic 'exile' story; a narrative that is at once much richer, more nuanced, and more sensible.

This alternative narrative has to be set within the broader circumstances of Senzangakhona's whole period of rule.

As we saw in Chapter 3, Senzangakhona had a rough time on his way to the Zulu chieftainship. He was chased out of his own Nobamba *umuzi* for a time, having to abandon a baby daughter as he fled. If true, this is an interesting detail. If Shaka was Senzangakhona's first child, this daughter must have come later, indicating that Shaka himself must have been growing up in that very turbulent time of regency and succession dispute before Senzangakhona formally took over the Zulu chieftaincy. This was not a good time for a baby son to be around. Could Shaka have been temporarily removed for his own safety?

Serious tensions – mostly involving Shaka – would arise during Senzangakhona's reign over the succession problem. This was rooted in the particular sequence and ranking of his many wives. Where and how he got his wives was in many ways a product of the alliances and conflicts he was involved in with surrounding peoples. Those conflicts in turn were partly a product of that even wider 'third ring' of influences, reaching as far as the coastlines. Consequently, we need to outline wider events, as far as we can make them out. We'll look first at the regional situation between about 1785 – roughly the beginning of Senzangakhona's reign – and 1800; then at Senzangakhona's own activities around the Zulu heartland; and, finally, come back to what was happening within the very walls of his *umuzi* with his wives and children.

THE THUKELA-PHONGOLO REGION

We left the regional situation in 1780 in a state of increasing turmoil as slaving and trade activities intensified. Several polities were already in the process of consolidating: the Qwabe, south-east of the Zulu; the Mthethwa, due east; the Hlubi, due north; the Ndwandwe, north-east; the Ngwane-Dlamini further north; and the Mabhudu, nearest to Delagoa Bay. Amongst many of these groups, there was a discernible shift southwards or westwards away from the Bay, and a noticeable tendency to relocate to defensible hilltop areas. All of these processes were further developed in the twenty-year period from 1780 to 1800.

Trading and slaving continued to escalate throughout Mozambique at least until 1795. At Delagoa Bay, whaling ships were visiting in increasing numbers, maybe fifteen a year from 1787 onwards.[24] Trade at the Bay became something of a free-for-all as Portuguese control slipped.[25] At the same time, there seems to have been a downturn in the local ivory trade, even as prices continued to rise.[26] Food, some have suggested, became the main trade item going out to the boats. Since the immediate Bay area was infested with tsetse-fly, it wasn't particularly good for cattle, and they were being brought in from further afield. According to one argument, this created a pressure to raid more aggressively for cattle inland. There is, however, no solid evidence that the numbers of cattle required would have had a dramatic effect any great distance from the Bay.[27] Instead, the movement of several important groups to defensive hilltop locations indicates that they were defending themselves against something more vigorous than mere cattle-theft. People were attacking *each other*.

Importantly for the future, the Ndwandwe established themselves, under Langa and then his son Zwide, in the Magudu hills, between the Mkhuze and Phongolo rivers. From there they in turn helped to push the Ngwane-Dlamini groups into defence in the Lubombo hills north of the Phongolo river. Similarly, the Jere and Gaza were forced to defend themselves on hilltops in the southern Lubombo, including Tshaneni, the gravesite of the Gaza ancestors, and along the edge of the St Lucia lowlands.[28] For some time, it seems, the Ndwandwe survived in an uneasy equilibrium with the Jere and Gaza. When Zwide's father died in around 1780, Zwide himself may still have been a minor. Hence the Ndwandwe as a distinct entity only gained real dominance in the early nineteenth century.[29]

To the west of Ndwandwe country, the Hlubi were establishing a sturdy presence. They, too, appear to have migrated westwards, after their *inkosi* Dlomo had been murdered on his hilltop position in the Ngome. Dlomo's enemy is unspecified in these traditions, though I suspect the emergent Ndwandwe. The Hlubi – or at least some of them – moved to the Phongolo-Thukela watershed (around present-day Utrecht). There, Bhungane built up a substantial polity,[30] and became a key figure in the area: a respected hunter, warrior, and trader. Hlubi trade links with the Bay seem to have been retained even after the move westwards.[31]

One of Bhungane's close associates was the power-broker living a couple of days' journey to his south-east: Dingiswayo of the Mthethwa. It's doubtful, as some traditions have it, that Dingiswayo was sheltered by Bhungane during his 'exile'. The two did, however, spend time together in the 1790s, and learned much from one another. Bhungane was also already forging early versions of the *amabutho*. One somewhat dubious tradition holds that Shaka later accompanied Dingiswayo when he visited Bhungane at his *umuzi* kwaMagaloza, on the Mzinyathi river, near present-day Newcastle.

> Dingiswayo came to ask about chieftainship. 'When you overcame the nations, how did you do it?' Bungane received him kindly, and instructed him . . . He treated him with medicines in various ways, and when he had finished he gave him further instructions when a buck appeared. Bungane said, 'Go to that *inyamazane*.' Dingiswayo went and went and went, until he began to fear it and wonder what kind of buck it was. When he appeared to hesitate Bungane ordered that he be told to approach it. The buck remained standing; he eventually went up, took hold of it, and milked it. He milked it thoroughly! Bungane then doctored him with this milk, let him go, and Dingiswayo returned with Shaka.[32]

MABONSA goes on to say, it wasn't a buck; in fact, it was a *lioness*. Dingiswayo plucked some of its hair! He heard this from Sisiyana, who was actually there!

At any rate, MABONSA adds darkly, 'The Hlubi now blame themselves for teaching Dingiswayo.'

The precise timing of these interactions remains open to some speculation. Fynn wrote that Dingiswayo came to power in 1780. In publishing *The Diary of Henry Francis Fynn*, James Stuart arbitrarily changed this to 1795.[33] David Hedges favours the earlier date, but notes that it could have been as late as 1802.[34] Such are the uncertainties. Part of the problem is a dearth of Mthethwa traditions. James Stuart's main Mthethwa informants, NDUKWANA and MAGIDI, are disappointingly ignorant about early Mthethwa history. Both of their fathers had joined Shaka, and so retained none of the traditions of the chiefly line, which Shaka had dispersed. Another Mthethwa informant, NHLEKELE, did have connections with the ruling family, but only with the junior lineage associated with Sokwetshata – who in turn appears to have been one of Bryant's informants. Sokwetshata's father Mlandela was a nephew of Senzangakhona himself, and Sokwetshata married one of Senzangakhona's daughters. This is obviously no guarantee of accuracy; and the testimony has to be read through the fact that the Mthethwa chiefs who remained in the 1880s joined the anti-Usuthu (ruling Zulu family) faction during the civil war, 'possibly in an attempt to restore something of the lost greatness of the chiefdom'.[35]

Everything considered, an earlier date for Dingiswayo's troubled accession is more likely. He needed time to build up alliances and forces.[36] He was not, of course, inventing his polity out of thin air. As we saw earlier, Dingiswayo had inherited the polity built up by the Nyambose lineage of his predecessors. Their territory centred on the ridge between the Black and the White Mfolozis, and came to dominate that part of the wide coastal plain. The confluence of the Mfolozi rivers was a prime elephant hunting region, as evidenced by the extensive game pits in this natural funnel-trap.[37]

This has fuelled the theory that Dingiswayo's power was built on, and designed to defend, trade links with Delagoa Bay. Certainly the name 'Nyambose' was well known at the Bay, so much so that the name would be attached to entirely unrelated groups for decades to come. But detailed evidence is hard to pin down. Almost all the historians have laid great weight on a single paragraph from *The Diary of Henry Francis Fynn*. This relates that, having overthrown his brother Mawewe:

Dingiswayo now collected several Delagonians who were in the habit of bringing small quantities of beads and barter among his and neighbouring tribes. Such bartering he now claimed as a personal privilege. He rewarded them well for their beads and sent chiefs with presents of oxen and ivory to the Portuguese and to a native chief in their neighbourhood called Makhasane, requesting the former to let him have a company of soldiers to assist him in attacking his neighbour Phakathwayo. He promised Makhasane that, having become the sole merchant, he would trade only with him.[38]

Proponents of both the trade and the slaving hypotheses have cited this paragraph as a clear indication that firearm-wielding mercenaries were at large in the Thukela-Phongolo catchment, and were quite likely extracting slaves.[39] However, this passage does not appear in Fynn's original account of Dingiswayo, nor, as far as I can see, amongst his original papers. It seems to have been slipped in by James Stuart himself, and what *his* evidence is, no one knows. It *may* have been based on information from an informant named Matshwili, a grandson of Dingiswayo, but unfortunately, Matshwili's original testimony has been lost.[40] Temptingly dramatic though it is, this account has to be regarded with some suspicion. There is no indication in any other traditions about the Mthethwa-Qwabe clashes that firearms were used, or indeed that Dingiswayo won any decisive victory at all over his robust southerly neighbour.

Still, there are various suggestions that trade with the Bay was a serious factor in Dingiswayo's politics. Assertions that he came anywhere near a 'monopoly' of the trade are misguided. What does seem to be the case is that during the 1790s, disruptive civil war amongst the Thembe in the vicinity of the Bay allowed inland groups (including the Ngwane-Dlamini, the Ndwandwe conglomeration, and the Mthethwa) to gain better purchase on the trade routes. Shortly after 1800, the Thembe were overrun by an unnamed group from the interior. Such conflicts were also certainly generating slaves, as noted by William White of the *Lion*, anchored in the Bay in 1798. Slaves were also being taken off by the numerous whaling ships from time to time.[41] Ivory was certainly exiting through the Bay in some quantity during the 1780s and 90s, brought in from well to the south.[42] This continued until the price fell radically after 1795. Around the turn of the century, the trade situation in the Thukela-Phongolo catchment entered a strange lull.

Meanwhile, whether or not on the strength of trade, Dingiswayo was certainly able to exert his dominance over other neighbouring peoples. He moved his father Jobe's main *umuzi* site southwards, from the lowlands to the upper ridges of the Ntseleni and Mfolozi watershed, retaining the name oYengweni.[43] Dingiswayo is said to have killed the Thembu chieftain, Jama, and exerted some form of dominance over the Mbokazi (his own mother's lineage), the Nxumalo in the lowlands, and the Ngadini and Xulu to the west.[44] Initially, he was possibly aided in this by a detachment of Hlubi allies, the Bizini; and by two *amabutho* supplied by Mbangami of the Dube people. Finally, dominance was extended over the Khumalo on the White Mfolozi, the Buthelezi – and Senzangakhona's Zulu (see Map 3 on page 114).

Though Dingiswayo forged his own *amabutho* in a more thoroughgoing manner than his predecessors, this did not apparently lead to anything like full integration. He still depended on marriage links to hold the northern border in stable allegiance. He gave, for instance, his daughter Nomatuli to the Nxumalo chief, Malusi. In the lowlands, the Mbonambi had to *khonza* with spear-heads and maize (still something of a luxury item, it appears). To the south, the Ngadi, Qadi, the Chunu and, perhaps from time to time, the Qwabe, were pressured into paying tribute, but the Mthethwa yoke lay relatively lightly on their shoulders. The Mthethwa polity remained an association of tributary chiefs, rather than a newly integrative system. Most of the chiefs retained their own *izigodlo*, for instance.

By the turn of the century, then, Dingiswayo was ready to embark on another phase of expansion. He was holding his own against the emerging Ndwandwe polity in the north, though this was not too great a threat as yet. In the south he was extracting tribute from several groups. As Carolyn Hamilton sums it up, 'It was Dingiswayo's policy to remove recalcitrant chiefs and to replace them with minors or known Mthethwa loyalists from amidst their ranks'.[45] This, in effect, is Shaka's method prefigured.

And just at this point – around the turn of the century – Shaka himself turned up on Dingiswayo's doorstep. But I'm running a little ahead of our narrative. What were the Zulu doing in these twenty-odd years?

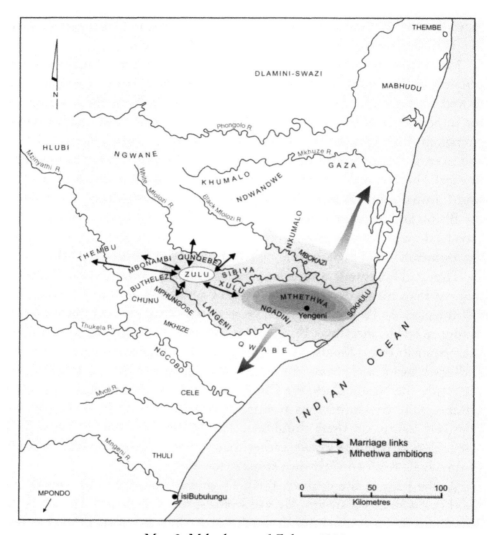

Map 3: Mthethwa and Zulu, _c_.1800

SENZANGAKHONA RULES

Amongst the peoples who were tributary to the Mthethwa, either under Jobe or Dingiswayo, were Senzangakhona's Zulu. We know practically nothing more of relations between the two peoples. Senzangakhona himself, however, was trying to build up his own power-base by marrying into, allying with, or bullying into submission his various small neighbours. Some of his alliances were based on older ties. The informant JANTSHI related how he had been shown the remains of former settlements around Nhlazatshe, where 'the Zulu, Mabaso, Kumalo and Butelezi people used to build . . . their respective kraals close to one another, more or less in a line, and that way occupy a single long ridge'. This, JANTSHI explained, 'was employed to enable the members of the tribe to be quickly called together in case of sudden attack'.[46] Similar defensive arrangements dominated further developments.

Another group that established early ties with the Zulu was the Mphungose. The Mphungose also claimed to have originated at Nhlazatshe. You will recall that an Mphungose man, Khuba, was the hero who so kindly rescued Senzangakhona's daughter and helped him to murder his brother (see page 80). Khuba then formally *khonza*'d the still poorly supported Senzangakhona. Together they set about trying to subdue the nearby Chunu people, with indecisive results. Macingwane of the Chunu was said to have fought with Senzangakhona quite regularly, though it never amounted to more than burning down each other's huts.[47]

It may not have been the string of outright assaults it appears; this is retrospective Zulu military pride speaking. BALENI kaSilwana, anxious to promote the memory of Ndlovu kaKhuba, his grandfather, says at one point that this fight against the Chunu took place under *Shaka's* rule. He relates in some detail how the Chunu, having already defeated Shaka's men, were repulsed after Ndlovu, who liked to fight alone, killed three of them. (Such were the tiny 'forces' often involved in these conflicts.) At another point, however, BALENI claims that Ndlovu and Senzangakhona died around the same time, in which case Ndlovu obviously *couldn't* have fought for Shaka. BALENI may be confusing his grandfather Ndlovu with his father, Silwana kaNdlovu, who did indeed fight under Shaka. This evidence as a whole needs to be taken with some caution. BALENI, speaking in 1900, thought the Zulu generally an 'angry, vindictive' people, and was obviously keen to promote the reputation of his Mphungose ancestors.[48] It bears repeating that virtually every 'fact' about Shaka's life carries a similarly fraught burden of complexity and qualification.

The Mphungose-Zulu warriors then took on, and defeated, Xabatshe of the Xulu, who lived east of the Zulu, around the Mfule river. (Since the Xulu are also said to have been tributary to the Mthethwa, it is possible that this 'campaign' was conducted under Dingiswayo's orders or aegis.) Khuba's son Ndlovu seems to have been the military leader in these forays. He was rewarded with tracts of land around Thaleni, and jurisdiction over the Xulu inhabitants. Ndlovu might have headed one of Senzangakhona's first named *amabutho*, the Nobamba, which was called, as many such units were, after the homestead or village from which its members were mostly drawn. The Mphungose were, or became, so close as to be all but indistinguishable from the Zulu in these early days.[49] Khuba had an *umuzi* very close to Nobamba. His son Silwana separated off, along with a brother, while a sister, Ncitha, married a Zulu man. One of Silwana's wives – BALENI's mother – was actually living in Senzangakhona's Nobamba homestead. Silwana himself was a member of Senzangakhona's esiKlebhi *ibutho*. A son of Silwana's, Gawozi, also became an *isikhulu*, a man of high standing, under Shaka; he survived to become a great favourite of Cetshwayo.[50] Other clannish families that split off from the early Zulu (like the Gazini, the Mandlakazi, the Mataka, the Fazini, and the Biyela) would continue to provide the core from which Shaka's power élite would be drawn. Senzangakhona, likewise, needed these alliances to bolster his position as *inkosi*.

Thus from the earliest stages the organisation of the *amabutho* meshed closely with the concentration of political control within certain families; marriages were political. At the same time, the usual family movements could be used to extend territorial domination: the fissiparous or splitting-off dynamics, with sons finding, being allocated, or more forcefully occupying new homestead sites, could be used as a tool for stronger centralisation, too.

Senzangakhona went on to call up a number of *amabutho*: the isiPhezi, the iWombe, the esiKlebhi, the iNtontela, the Mbelebele, and the uMnkangala. These were probably a mix of age-group and locality in organisation. The iWombe, for example, was named after an *umuzi*, and most of its men appear to have been uncircumcised.[51] It was said to have been enrolled in imitation of Dingiswayo.[52] Several of Senzangakhona's sons were inducted into the iWombe, including Ntunja, Dingane and Mpande, despite quite wide differences in age.[53] The iWombe also contained older men, like Nduvane, the younger brother of Senzangakhona's wife Bhibhi, and Mqundane, Senzangakhona's uncle. Later, it was swelled by not only 'core' Zulu, but others, including Langeni men.[54]

In short, the *ibutho* was a hotchpotch, not yet governed by any secure principle of selection, certainly put together in haste, in increments, and out of pressing necessity.

Senzangakhona built more *imizi* than any of his predecessors, though the important ones remained those that he had inherited: esiKlebheni, iNtontela, and Nobamba, which one informant called 'the Jerusalem of the Zulus'.[55] There is no indication that he began the practice of barracking *amabutho* in more specialised settlements, *amakhanda*, as Shaka would do. But evidently he was, like many of his neighbours, dealing with – and dealing out – more conflict than had been the case in the past.

In the process, Senzangakhona built up a substantial family. The origins of his wives also give us some idea of the influence he could command or attract in terms of marriage alliances. One wife was Zitshungu kaMudli. Mudli was himself a grandson of Jama, a cousin therefore of Senzangakhona's. The marriage of Senzangakhona and Zitshungu comes perilously close to inbreeding.[56]

Another wife was Langazana, a Sibiya woman. The Sibiya would be known as either a section of the Zulu people, or of the Chunu, depending on which period we are looking at. They would be amongst the first to be more thoroughly incorporated by Shaka, since they lived so close by, immediately west of the Zulu.[57] It was another exceptionally close genealogical liaison, since Senzangakhona's own mother, Mntaniya, was a Sibiya woman. Langazana became the chief wife at esiKlebheni, which Senzangakhona had taken over from his father.

Mnkabi of the emaBeleni people was said by some to have been the first and greatest wife. She was partially saved from the succession disputes because she had no sons, only a daughter, Nozilwane. However, it was probably her establishment into which Nandi was placed, *ngenisa*'d, which might have had repercussions on the succession issue.[58]

There was Mpikase of the emaQungebe who were situated just north of
the Zulu, in the Mfolozi valley. She was the mother of Dingane, Shaka's
future assassin.[59] Songiya kaNgotsha was of the Hlabisa people, who were
settled among the emaBhedlane hills across the Mfolozi river.[60] Songiya was
much less well known than either her son, the future *inkosi* Mpande, or her
brother, Mbopha, who would participate in Shaka's assassination. Magulana
kaNtshongolo of the emaNgadini (a Qwabe offshoot) may have been an
important link to the large Qwabe polity. Sondaba, mother of a boy named
Bakuza, was, according to Bryant, a Buthelezi,[61] and there were others whose
origins are unknown: Nomarawu, Ngoto kaMhuyi, Ngaca kaMncinci.[62]

Senzangakhona's chief wife, and the most beautiful, was Bhibhi. If Bryant
is correct, she was a Bhele, from relatively far away, westwards across the
Mzinyathi river.[63] The Bhele thought of themselves as having 'come down'
in a grain-basket, were descended from 'cannibals', and *khonza*'d the Zulu
when Jama or Ndaba was ruling. (In another version, Bhibhi's own father,
Sompisi or Nkobe, was the first to *khonza* Senzangakhona.) Bhibhi was slightly
younger than her brother Ndlela, who would become one of the most
prominent of warriors under Shaka. She would bear Senzangakhona an
important son, Sigujana.[64] A proverb arose around her: 'You must be the
possessor of some beautiful virtue, like Bhibhi, whose star was in the ascendant
whatever king happened to come into power.'[65] Senzangakhona is said to
have objected to his wonderful wife's ancestral name: 'How is it that my wife,
who is so beautiful, and whom I love, should be called a Bele? Why should
she be addressed as "Mbele"? It's difficult for the tongue to say "Mbele" to my
wife. Does it mean that she is the *ibele*, the front covering, of an *imbila*, a
dassie?'[66]

He asked the old Bhele folk what their *isithakazelo*, their praise-shout,
was. 'Mbele! Ntuli!' they replied. So Senzangakhona declared the people's
new name to be Ntuli. No one was going to call his beloved wife a rock-rabbit
again.[67]

Senzangakhona's sons and daughters – and they were numerous – likewise
were used to bolster political alliances with the neighbours. So, for instance,
his daughters Nomanqe, Ntikili, Nomcoba and Mathenjwase all married
into the Mthethwa, whose alliance would prove so crucial in Shaka's career;
Manthongela married into the Buthelezi, Sikhakha into the Mbatha,
Mthembazi into the Mgazini.[68]

If we map out these varied alliances, conquests, and marriage-links, it appears that Senzangakhona, during the period of Shaka's youth, established a patchwork of dominance and connection over an area roughly to the White Mfolozi valley to the east and north; to the headwaters of the Mfule to the south-east; somewhat across the upper Mhlathuze to the headwaters of the Nsuze to the south-west; and tentatively to the Mzinyathi valley to the west (see Map 3 on page 114). It is an area maybe 100 kilometres long and 40 kilometres wide. Under Senzangakhona, Zulu influence grew amoeba-like, partly independently and partly parasitically, within the bigger body-politic of the Mthethwa sphere of influence.

This would ultimately be Shaka's patrimony: the Zulu heartland.

AN ORDINARY BOYHOOD

Even though Shaka grew up in a time of turbulence, the chances are good that he generally enjoyed an ordinary Zulu boyhood. It would have been filled with the games and duties of conventional kinds, and punctuated by conventional rituals of growth and maturity. As it happens, we have several accounts, *not* embedded in long fanciful tales, of precisely such rituals.

After his birth, Shaka would surely have been doctored in the approved ways against disease and witchcraft. Although we are reading later conventions back into Shaka's time, he and his mother most likely would have been secluded for a week or so. Then, his mother purified with *intelezi* water and herbs, the hut swept out and plastered with fresh dung, he would have emerged into the sunlight with much ululation. Shaka would have met his father for the first time, and been passed between the man's legs in benediction.[69] He would have been named: 'Sikiti!'

Shaka would then quite naturally have been carried off to his mother's people, the Langeni, to be weaned at the age of two or three.[70] He would normally have gone to visit the Langeni at later stages, too. This may be the core of the idea that he 'went into exile' there. He would, in the normal working-out of family relations, have done at least part of his usual boyhood herding-training under his grandmother's fond eye. Another famous South African leader – Pixley Seme – described the importance of this activity:

For in the Zulu country looking after cattle was the great school for boys. Boys had their own *izinduna*, the *izingqwele* who gave them orders, like soldiers, and who were obeyed by all the other boys. They also knew, and were the guardians of, all the customs (*umteto*) followed by boys. All disputes (*amacala*) among the boys were resolved there; they were dealt with while the boys were out looking after the cattle . . . . For boys did not fight at their homes . . . At their homes they showed great respect for the customs of the older people. A boy did not answer back; he did not argue with an adult, for at his home there was no one to side with him. He could put his trust only in his own swiftness of foot. This caused boys to form their own little group (*ibandhlana*) as they grew up . . .[71]

Undoubtedly, these groups could form the nucleus of secessionist or other political challenges to the rulers.

As Shaka emerged from puberty, he would have embarked on a series of important rituals. These events are crucial to a Zulu boy's sense of growth and acceptance, and so they are usually remembered with some precision. The first event would likely have been his first nocturnal emission, his inaugural wet dream. As it happens, we do have a story about this event in Shaka's life:

One day Shaka awoke with his thighs covered in dried slime. He asked the Zulu *izinduna* about it. 'You have come of age, Mntwana,' they replied. 'Go back into the hut and wait there.' They said this although as a matter of fact Shaka was a man. They flattered him. He went indoors. Girls then sang a song all over the country; they gathered at the *isigodlo* where Shaka was, and sang, '*Ya i ya i*, see, the Mntwana has come of age.' They were being acceptably lewd – they *bina*'d – in saying this. 'The Mntwana is in seclusion.' This process of being taken through the ceremonies of puberty took several more months.[72]

This was, MAYINGA added, a well-known event in Shaka's life. Most importantly, it happened at esiKlebheni, the *Zulu* homestead to which Nandi had originally been assigned. One informant even asserts that Senzangakhona had actually built the *umuzi* for Shaka and his half-brother Sojisa;[73] this is almost certainly wrong, but the implication is that esiKlebheni was Shaka's normal home.

MAYINGA's story is odd in one respect: the assertion that Shaka was already a *man* when the emission occurred. In biological terms, that first wet dream would have happened around the age of twelve, or perhaps slightly older.[74] Possibly MAYINGA's tale is another slur on Shaka's manhood. Usually, the boy, having been thoroughly educated by his peers, would know exactly what had happened. He would sneak out before dawn and disappear with his father's, and sometimes the neighbour's, cattle. His group, or *intanga*, knowing instantly what had happened, would search for him – the harder the search, the better – and 'drive' him back, like a beast himself: he was not properly human until the whole ritual process was complete. He would be cleansed with *intelezi* medicines, wash in a sacred pool, and be closed off in a hut, attended only by his *intanga*. He would be reborn in this womb-like space, become a full member of the group. He would eat special food; he would be called *umakoti*, a bride, because like a bride he was about to be added properly to the family. Finally, seclusion would end with sacrifice of a beast, a feast, and a great dance.[75]

Under normal circumstances, the growing boy would, after he had *thomba*'d, have suffered through having his ears pierced, the *qhumbuza*.[76] This was an important sign of increasing responsibility. Shaka *did* have his ears pierced.[77] (He probably wasn't circumcised; as we've seen, this ritual was already falling away.[78]) After the *qhumbuza*, he would be in a position to get permission to marry, be *juba*'d or *jutshwa*'d. After that, he could sport the *umutsha* loincloth.[79]

There seems no reason to doubt that Shaka went through all of this in the usual way. He would have continued to spend most of his time in or around esiKlebheni. Only as he grew older does he appear to have begun to run into trouble with his father, that he became known to some as an *itshinga*, a troublemaker.[80] Possibly he then spent more time away, as this odd story implies:

When Shaka had become an *insizwa* amongst the Langeni, Senzangakhona came to hear of him, and wanted to send for him. Mudhli secretly sent his *inceku* [personal attendant] to Shaka with

this message: 'Mudhli says you are about to be summoned to the
country of the Zulu. Do not, when you arrive there, sit down. Remain
standing. You will see me there. I shall wink at you if there is any
danger, whereupon you must make off immediately'. The invitation
was duly made, and Shaka arrived in the Zulu country with twenty
izinsizwa of his own age, armed with large war-shields. They found
the Zulu seated in a large semi-circle. This was probably at Mfemfe
kraal, which Senzangakhona had attacked before when attempting
to kill Shaka. Shaka took up a position, not too close, but some distance
off, standing a little in front of his companions. He looked about
him, and made out the *inceku* in the crowd. The *inceku* was winking,
so they immediately took to their heels.[81]

The interesting implications of this improbable (and uncorroborated) story
are that Shaka could at this point command a following of his own; that
there was warlike tension between the Langeni and the Zulu; and that *now*
there was tension between Shaka and his father. This is borne out by other
evidence, too. NDUKWANA asserted that Shaka was still at esiKlebheni when
he ran into trouble with his father.[82] Nathaniel Isaacs had a similar
understanding:

> As Chaka *advanced towards manhood* [he] attracted the notice and
> ultimately the jealousy of his father, who resolved that he should die
> . . . Chaka's precocity, shrewdness and cunning soon enabled him to
> learn the intention of his father; and he fled . . . to a neighbouring
> tribe, called the Umtatwas.[83]

For once, I am inclined to believe Isaacs.

'ITSHINGA', TROUBLEMAKER

Sikiti-Shaka almost certainly spent the bulk of his early and teenage years *in
Zulu country*. Towards the end of his youth, things became more complicated.
We have only a scattering of hints as to what was going on, and any picture
that we deduce must be tentative. However, of this much we can be sure: the

situation involved more than a mere personality clash between father and son.

It seems that relations between the Zulu and the Langeni were close, but not without problems. Mgabhi and his Langeni people were independently minded, and Senzangakhona may have been competing for their allegiance with other groups, including the Mthethwa, his overlords. Another such group was the Thuli, just to the north-east. This is one account of that little war, conducted during Shaka's youth:

> Vezi [of the Luthuli section of the Thuli] fought against Mgabi kaMhlongo of the Langeni. The latter was defeated and *khonza'*d Vezi. The Langeni people proposed an *umjadu* dance with Vezi. Vezi agreed. The dance was held. The Langeni danced first. War shields were taken by the Langeni and hidden at night where the *umjadu* was to be. Vezi then went the next day to dance with his *impi*, having no war shields. Mgabi then fell upon those at the dancing place, killed Vezi, and seized the people and land. The people then *khonza'*d Mgabi.[84]

This story of the dance as a pretext for slaughter is so common that we need to be thoroughly suspicious of its credibility. However, it may be a further sign that the conflict with groups to the north was intensifying.

The strain showed in an internal Langeni succession dispute. When Shaka was young the Langeni *inkosi* was Mgabhi. When Mgabhi died – I speculate that this was in around 1795 – Nxazonke, Shaka's uncle on his mother's side, took over as regent until some or other son of Mgabhi's came of age. Nxazonke appointed, presumably after a suitable interval, Mfundeko, but a majority favoured another son, Makhedama. Makhedama at this point seems to have been away at *his* mother's folk, the Xulu – another leader-in-waiting in exile – or he had been sent away for his own safety.[85]

This is the same Makhedama who is said to have bullied Shaka as a boy. You will recall the 'stones-in-the-kraal' game (on page 107). Here's a fascinating sidelight on that story – and a potential clue. NGIDI, one of the most knowledgeable and detailed of Stuart's informants, and himself a Langeni, stated that the 'stones' spat occurred *after* Makhedama returned from the

Xulu, as virtually a grown man. At this point, he was important enough to
have had an *inceku*, an attendant named Nsindwane. Nsindwane 'took up
the stones belonging to Shaka and threw them into Makedama's imaginary
cattle kraal'.[86] It's highly improbable that these grown men would have been
playing with make-believe cattle in miniature kraals of cowdung: it is a
metaphor for a deeper disagreement.

Shaka, with his close ties with the Langeni, had somehow become
embroiled in the succession dispute, and come down on the wrong side. So
close were his ties, indeed, that according to NGIDI Shaka had been, alongside
Makhedama, actually inducted into a Langeni *ibutho*. (We have to treat this
with caution, though, since NGIDI says at one point it was the isiBubulungu
ibutho, at another the Amananana.)

This is nevertheless interesting, because there seems little doubt that Shaka
was finally *juba*'d by his own father, and then called up into the Zulu *ibutho*,
the iWombe, along with his brothers.[87] Only after this did he go to
Dingiswayo.[88] Shaka would always remain fond of the iWombe regiment; it
was his own. He would put it in the vanguard of a number of subsequent
campaigns, including against the ferocious Zwide.[89] Shaka and Ndengezi would
have met here, along with others who would eventually support Shaka in his
bid for the Zulu leadership. Without his having spent this time in the *ibutho*,
forging connections and friendships, that bid would have had a much slimmer
chance of success.

Could Shaka have been inducted, *butwa*'d, twice at the same time – once
amongst the Langeni, again amongst the Zulu – or only at different times?
Much depends on the timing – which we don't know. At the very least, the
situation seems to indicate divided loyalties. The Langeni succession dispute
intersected with a succession dispute brewing within Zulu circles at exactly
the same time. Both disputes affected the power tussles between the Zulu
and Langeni and Shaka was caught in the middle. This is murky water, but I
suspect something like the following happened.

Shaka found himself the subject of disputes within the Zulu family about
who was to succeed Senzangakhona. Shaka was the eldest boy, but Nandi was
not the favourite wife: Bhibhi was. Mnkabi was the first wife, but had no
sons. However, Nandi was of Mnkabi's establishment and so *her* son, some
argued, had precedence.[90] The dispute exploded when Sigujana, Bhibhi's

son but one of the younger boys, was announced as the chosen one. This was not supported by a substantial number of the influential women, including Mnkabayi, Mawa, and Mmama.[91] The situation was exacerbated by Senzangakhona's announcement that the men of the iWombe were not to be permitted to marry.[92] (This is an interesting pre-empting of Shaka's orders to the same effect later; it was probably intended to keep men in fighting mode for longer than usual.) A not unexpected consequence was that many of the men went off looking for satisfaction anyway. Their *hlobongaing* with unauthorised women gave Senzangakhona the pretext for sending his sons away, except Sigujana. Dingane, Mhlangana, Ngqojana, Sopana, Mfihlo, Mbudhlele, Somajuba and Mdungwaze, all ran off to the Qwabe. Shaka went back to the Langeni.[93]

Here, Shaka found himself at loggerheads with his cousin, Makhedama, the new Langeni *inkosi*. Perhaps Shaka resented now being put down by his erstwhile playmate; maybe Makhedama asserted himself with unnecessary arrogance. The images of bullying all have this aspect of subordination about them: Makhedama made Shaka drink the *amalaza*, the first and inferior milk; Makhedama made Shaka drink downstream of him.[94] Almost certainly, the bullying stories are a metaphor for this later disagreement, projected back into their childhood.

Makhedama, praised as 'the horse (*injomane*) of Mgabhi', was, by all accounts, both ferocious and self-centred. He became a vigorous, even vicious leader. He is recorded, for instance, getting involved in a dispute between Mvunyelwa kaMandiza of the Embo (or Mkhize), and his brother Zihlandlo (a man we will see much more of later). Mvunyelwa took refuge with the Langeni, but Makhedama collaborated secretly with Zihlandlo, and killed the fugitive. He used, it is said, a short-hafted stabbing-spear – the one that Shaka is mistakenly credited with 'inventing'. Makhedama apparently brought the idea back with him from the Xulu, saying grimly, 'People are afraid. Are people like buck that they should be stabbed at a distance? They must come to close quarters and be stabbed with one assegai.' Even more alarmingly, Makhedama is said (and let's beware of exaggeration) to have impaled people with barbed assegais (*izinhlendhla*), laying them on their backs and driving assegais in through the neck, the breastbone, and through hands and feet.[95]

It's possible, if NGIDI is right, that Shaka witnessed one campaign in which the stabbing-spear was used, a joint venture between Nxazonke and Makhedama. The campaign was against the Vilakazi. After stabbing many to death in the hapless homestead they attacked, they returned with an *isikhulu* of the Vilakazi, Ngiyashumayela. Ngiyashumayela was then incorporated as an *induna* in one of Makhedama's regiments.

Was this another increasingly widespread idea – assimilating good fighting men from amongst the defeated – that Shaka picked up and refined? Very likely. NGIDI also insisted that Shaka learned the technique associated with the short stabbing-spear from Makhedama.[96]

Perhaps as a result of this very ferocity, Nxazonke, the erstwhile regent, fell out with Makhedama.[97] Shaka sided with Nxazonke. This may have been because Makhedama had made some sort of play for dominance over the Zulu. The missionary William Holden drops an intriguing hint (his source possibly being 'Abantwana'), that Makhedama actually tried to take over the Zulu leadership, though only on Senzangakhona's death.[98] As this is genealogically impossible, perhaps political dominance was meant. NGIDI even asserts that Makhedama had tried to kidnap Nandi herself, as he supposedly did 'with other women married elsewhere'. It was *he* who married Nandi off to Gendeyana.[99] These stories are unlikely, but herein might lie the seeds of Shaka's disaffection – and defection. Moreover, another tradition speaks of two men coming from the Zulu at just about this point in the proceedings to *khonza* the young pretender, Shaka:

> Two men left the Zulus and went to *konza* Shaka among the Langeni, Silwane kaNdhlovu and Nomleti. Makedama made war with an *impi*. He attacked with Shaka and the other two men, and succeeded in winning. Shaka also killed people. Makedama then *lungisa*'d [rewarded] the warriors who had stabbed. He left Shaka alone; he did not *lungisa* him. Shaka questioned him, saying, 'Is not the *impi* I stabbed yours?' Makedama replied, 'You do not belong to us.' Shaka became angry and left his uncle [and] ran off to the Mtetwa.[100]

If we put these scraps together, it seems quite possible that as the question of who would succeed Senzangakhona began to brew, Makhedama and Shaka found themselves on opposite sides of more than one issue.

The upshot, in any event, was that Makhedama evicted or lost Nxazonke, who left, along with the unfortunate Mfundeko kaMgabhi, and a handful of others: Mbikwana, Mendameli and Ngceba. Shaka joined them, and they all headed east to *khonza* Dingiswayo and the Mthethwa. There is no sign that Shaka took the initiative in the departure, though for obvious reasons he is best remembered. The group fled first to a man named Daleni. There they were attacked by a party of Makhedama's men. Once they had beaten them off, Daleni suggested that they go to Dingiswayo.[101]

That Shaka *did* go to Dingiswayo as a young man is one of the few undisputed 'facts' of his life.

So much for the legends. Shaka, if he did go into 'exile', went as a young man, not as a baby. He was largely the victim of wider political forces, none of which were of his own making. There is no sign here of him being an *itshinga* or troublemaker at all. His personality had little or nothing to do with it. The influence of childhood events on character and the future is, of course, one of the staples of any person's biography. In Shaka's case, all evidence of such influence evaporates on close inspection. We possess no psychologically useful information about his childhood whatsoever. As for the terrible revenge he is supposed to have exacted later on the Langeni, and on Makhedama in particular; that, too, as we'll see, is nonsense.

There was no trauma; no need for vengeance.

5

Waiting in the wings

Accession to power, c.1800–12

The chivalrous knight was not yet dead in this African Arcady.
A.T. Bryant, *Olden Times in Zululand and Natal* (1929, 100).

It's evening. A breathless *inceku* bows deferentially to his *induna*, Ngomane kaMqomboli, then blurts out the news. A group of men has arrived, having travelled hard. They are from Langeni, some from Zulu. They have come to *khonza* Dingiswayo. It is thought that one of them is the son of a chief.

Ngomane procrastinates politely. After due ceremony, the men are brought before him. They sip beer, look respectfully away from each other, and comment on the weather. Then to business. One man nods; he introduces himself as Sikiti, the son of Senzangakhona kaJama. Ngomane's jaw drops. He waves his *inceku* close and whispers against his cheek: 'Tell Dingiswayo.'

A SURROGATE FATHER

Such, perhaps, was the scene. At least most informants are agreed that when Sikiti-Shaka arrived in Mthethwa territory, it was at the *umuzi* of Ngomane. Who he came with is disputed. I stated in Chapter 4 that he arrived with Nxazonke, Mfundeko, Mbikwana, Mendameli and Ngceba. There are, however, other versions: that he came with Silwane kaNdlovu and Nomlethi;[1] that he was alone;[2] that he was accompanied by his mother Nandi, his sister Nomcoba, and Ngqengelele of the Buthelezi.[3] However, there is no further evidence that Nandi ever stayed with the Mthethwa, and the presence of the last two women seems unlikely. Claims that so-and-so accompanied Shaka here or there are often ways of saying that so-and-so was important to Shaka later. This is certainly the case with Ngomane and Ngqengelele, and I'll return to this issue in Chapter 6. The truth is that we don't know for sure.

Nor can we be certain how old Shaka was when he arrived: he could have been anything between sixteen and twenty-five.[4] I tend towards the older estimate, because by that age Shaka would have become a serious pretender to power within Zulu circles, he could have spent some time in the iWombe *ibutho*, and he would have been old enough to start gathering a few loyalists to himself. I'll hedge my bets, and settle speculatively on an age of twenty-two. This means that – if my estimate of his birthdate in 1781 is about right – he arrived in Mthethwa country in around 1803.

Shaka probably lodged more or less permanently with Ngomane, who was appointed to be his 'father'. One informant does say that he was made an *inceku* to Dingiswayo himself at the main Mthethwa *umuzi*, oYengeni; he milked the special cows that Dingiswayo drank from.[5] This is uncorroborated. Another informant claims that Shaka was lodged alongside Dingiswayo's chief son (who remains unnamed). They ate from the same wooden bowls together; each was given a *wasakasi* beast, black with white beneath the belly.[6] This is also not corroborated. Both of these stories may be simply trying to let royalty rub against royalty: it enhances the general shine.

The politics of such a submission are complex. What could it have meant, that a pretender-son of a subordinate chieftain (Senzangakhona) *khonzas* the very overlord his father also pays tribute to? It *had* to generate tension. It meant, at the very least, that Dingiswayo had a lever to play power-blocks off against each other, both within the Zulu polity and perhaps elsewhere. It suited him, evidently, to induct Shaka into one of his own *amabutho*, and initiate him into the ways of a warrior. Within this *amabutho*, if we can believe even half the tales of derring-do and valour, Shaka began, over the next ten years or so, to build himself something of a reputation.

A BREATHING SPACE

The years between 1800 and 1810, or even 1815, present a peculiar problem for the historian of the Thukela-Phongolo catchment. Suddenly, there seems to be a gap in our knowledge, a dearth of traditions, a drying-up of documentary sources from the coast. There seems to be little trade going on; there is almost no evidence of slaving. Everybody claims that Zwide's Ndwandwe were rapidly expanding and causing greater friction, but there is almost no evidence to support this. David Hedges's thesis makes an unexplained leap from the 1790s, in his Chapter VI, to the 1810s at the beginning of Chapter VII.[7] Similarly, Alan Smith's thesis can provide almost nothing about the southern Mozambique situation before 1815 or so. Julian Cobbing's attempt to locate the 'motor of change' in the slave-trade was criticised in part because he couldn't show that any slaving was happening in this, the crucial period. Even John Wright, despite his exemplary attention to detail, can say no more than that the Ndwandwe were, 'in the early years of the 19th century . . . attempting to expand their power' against the Dlamini and against the Jere-Gaza polities.[8] This is altogether too vague to be satisfactory.

There are two ways of interpreting this 'silence'. The first is to surmise that there is an accidental hiatus in the documentation. (Explaining this hiatus then becomes a whole historiographical problem in itself.) In this view, trade and slaving and warfare and polity-consolidation were going on as before, but we just happen to have no record of it all. The assumption is that we must trace a more or less steady progression from the 1790s through to the 1820s. If this is the case, there is nothing more to be done, and we must move on and pick up the trail where we can.[9]

The second way is perhaps more interesting. This is to surmise that the lack of evidence is related to an actual lack of activity – or, perhaps, to a certain redirection of activity, the nature of which has yet to be fully explored.

The clue comes, I think, from the few snippets we can pick up about what was going on around Delagoa Bay. There, the Portuguese had, from 1799 onwards, managed on the one hand to prevent almost anyone else from trading in the Bay (there is only a single English ship recorded as calling, in 1801; the East India Company, caught up in the European Continental wars, didn't send another until 1815). No doubt some unrecorded ships called, but British naval reports of 1809 indicate no great traffic from Delagoa Bay.[10] On the other hand, the Portuguese had inadvertently managed to cramp their own trading, too, by imposing absurdly high tariffs on ivory and other goods. This is not to say that trade stopped altogether: after 1800 the Tsonga were more actively sending people to trade into the far interior, including to the Sabi and Musina, and into Ngwane and Qwabe country.[11] A route apparently ran all the way from the Bay to Lattakoo in Tswana territory.[12] By 1810 the Tsonga were aggressive and cohesive enough to launch a major raid on Inhambane. But generally the evidence points towards a downturn in trade between 1800 and 1815. Even more so than for the preceding decades, statistical precision is impossible to find.

The situation is similar with the slave-trade. Slaving continued apace in the northern Mozambique ports, where French ships plundered the Portuguese, Brazilian slavers were beginning to call more frequently, and perhaps 12 000 slaves were being exported annually up to 1812.[13] Indeed, there was a marked upturn after 1805, with French slavers supplying the Mascarenes, Madagascar slaving internally as well as acting as a transit-station, and American and Spanish slavers supplying the Cuban market.[14] On the face of it, it would seem odd if a commensurate proportion of slaves were not being taken off at Delagoa Bay. An 1809 report by one Captain J. Tomkinson of the British naval sloop *Caledon* gives just a hint that the Bay continued to be involved. According to Tomkinson, 'the coasting trade from Delagoa Bay (Cape Correntes) to Cape Delgada, the value of which in negroes, elephants' teeth, gold-dust, and specie, is estimated at five hundred thousand dollars'.[15] His comment is frustratingly ambiguous and vague. In the final analysis, it has to be admitted that there is simply no direct evidence for much slaving around the Bay in this period.

By contrast, there was still some activity inland of the Bay. The Portuguese garrison continued to be extremely shaky, but they were, by dint of their firearms, able to intervene successfully in various phases of the local civil wars that had been rumbling since the 1790s. By about 1800, then, while trading had shrivelled, Moamba of the local chieftains, and Makhasane a little further south, were enabled to consolidate their respective polities more thoroughly than before. These interventions by firearm-wielding Europeans and their black proxies were precursors to those of the 1810s and 20s, when wars would be more deliberately fomented in order to generate slaves for an exploding market. They also presumably had some ripple effects inland, especially amongst the Ndwandwe and related groups along the Lubombo hills. For the moment, however, it was relatively quiet.

Further inland of these new coastal powers (or, more accurately, new arrangements of old powers), there also appears to have been a breathing space. There is no sign, importantly, that Zwide's Ndwandwe launched any major attacks on anyone before 1810. Perhaps it was a period of internal consolidation for his polity. The Dlamini-Swazi (or Ngwane, depending on how you read the genealogies) under Ndvungunye were establishing themselves among the hills north of the Phongolo river, but cannot be said to have suffered or launched any major forays.[16]

Let's assume, as I argued earlier, that these polities had by 1800 begun their processes of consolidation, stimulated in certain crucial ways by trade in goods and slaves. Assume further that in this decade these sources of wealth and prestige partially dried up. What then were these leaders to do in order to maintain their positions? They needed to find other, locally available means of asserting their dominance and continuing to signal their status. Most likely, then, they turned more strongly to reforming the traditional means of acquiring wealth – primarily their control of women and cattle. The embryonic *amabutho*, initially forged under pressures of defence, could be utilised now for more vigorous but localised cattle raids. They could also be used to back up more coercive interventions in neighbours' domestic politics. The control of men and marriage rituals could also be reworked slightly to forge more distant or lucrative marriage alliances, and to control more centrally the production and distribution of agricultural produce. As far as we can see, this was the primary purpose of the *amabutho* under Dingiswayo, Shaka and their fellow-chieftains; so it's hardly a great stretch to propose that the rudiments were being put in place during this period.

My line of reasoning is frankly speculative, but it makes more sense to me than proposing, for example, a high level of slaving for which we have no evidence at all.[17] It is supported by an impression that there were no major conflicts going on. Zwide's Ndwandwe were probably contending with[18] the Gaza and Jere to the east, the Nxumalo to the south-east, the Dlamini-Swazi to the north of the Phongolo, and the Ngwane to the north-west. But this is still more of an assumption than a certainty. We assume that the Ndwandwe were gradually building up the capacity to launch the major attacks of the following decade (see Chapter 6), but we possess no details.

We do have some information on activities further south, however. There – along the southern bank of the Mfolozi river – Dingiswayo's Mthethwa were very active indeed.

SEIZE THE GOURDS

The oft-repeated assertion that Dingiswayo's main aim in life was to build up, monopolise and protect his 'trade route' to Delagoa Bay is based on a single passage from Henry Francis Fynn:

> In the first year of his chieftainship, [Dingiswayo] opened a trade with De la Goa Bay, by sending 100 oxen and a quantity of elephants' tusks to exchange for beads and blankets. Prior to this a small supply of these articles had been brought to that country from De la Goa Bay by the natives. The trade thus opened by Dingizwayo was afterwards carried on, on an extensive scale, though the Portuguese never in person entered his country. . . . A kross (karosse) manufactory was also established, a hundred men having been generally employed in that work.[19]

One or two other passing references apart, this paragraph is the sum total of our evidence for Dingiswayo's trading connections. It is assumed, rather than evidenced, that Dingiswayo and Makhasane forged a friendly agreement over trade.[20] However, it seems much more likely that, like his neighbours, Dingiswayo was turning his attentions inward. Rather than battle for trade against stronger groups between himself and the Bay, he now worked on consolidating his dominance over his immediate neighbours.

Rather than fighting with them, he cemented a marriage connection with the Nxumalo branch of the Ndwandwe, offering his sister Nomathuli kaJobe to the Nxumalo chieftain Malosi kaMatshuku.[21] He forged something of an alliance of mutual respect with Bungane's Hlubi, held together largely by opposition to the common antagonist, the Ndwandwe. Other local lineages were probably incorporated into the structures of the *amabutho*.[22] Having thus stabilised his northern frontier, Dingiswayo turned his attention to the east and south. He secured tighter tributary relations from the Mbonambi and the Dube along the coast. Near the mouth of the Mfolozi, Nqoboka kaLanga of the Sokhulu was boosted into the chieftainship; in return he had to extend Mthethwa domination over the lower Mfolozi river area.[23] Further south, near the Thukela and Qwabe country, he forced chief Madlokovu of the Ngadi to *khonza*, and similarly, the Qadi. Another southern chief, one Mjezi, was obliged to give up his *isigodlo* – a sure sign of losing political independence. Dingiswayo was also said by some to have obliged Macingwane of the Chunu to surrender both *isigodlo* and cattle, but it seems unlikely that this was a lasting arrangement.[24]

To the west, Dingiswayo pursued a similar policy of assassinating or ousting incumbent chiefs and replacing them with his own appointees. This was the case with Jama of the Thembu; Jama's heir Ndina, a minor, was forced to *khonza*. Xabatshe kaDanda of the Xulu was also killed, and a new dynasty under Mapholoba installed.[25] Since the Xulu were also periodically in a tribute relationship to Senzangakhona's Zulu, as were the Buthelezi, over whom Dingiswayo also tried to assert himself, the potential for trouble and tension was enormous.

Though Dingiswayo was later pictured by some as the local 'chivalrous knight',[26] his interventions weren't so kindly remembered by those he subordinated. One informant says that the Mthethwa became notorious for seizing people's goats and eating them as they marched; they would 'go into people's huts and seize the gourds and pour the contents into their mouths, to such an extent did they believe themselves masters of the land they passed through'.[27] At the same time, the common phrases of awe shouldn't be taken too literally: 'People said the country had been destroyed by the man of Mthethwa, Dingiswayo, for he killed all the nations. He finished them off and brought Shaka to power.'[28] All this means is that power changed hands in the upper hierarchies of the various groups. And we should definitely not believe Fynn's list of Dingiswayo's 'conquests': 'the Kwabis, Amalanga, Amakwadini, Amazulu, Amatyaleni, Telayizi, Kuyivane, Amatembu, Amaswazi, and the Amakose. The only chief he had not subdued was Zuedi, chief of the Endwandwe.'[29]

The Mthethwa polity was certainly becoming more cohesive than most of its neighbours. Dingiswayo was following others in the region in forging *amabutho* units, though not apparently of girls (something Shaka would do from time to time).[30] He did have the power to marry girls off by command,[31] another invention mistakenly attributed to Shaka. But apart from absorbing a number of fairly minor groups, Dingiswayo could do little more than hold his own against the larger ones. There were always tensions threatening to break his polity up again – as indeed it readily did on Dingiswayo's death. Other neighbours remained untouched. There is actually no evidence that he tried to incorporate peoples along his alleged trade route past St Lucia. And he never, for instance, attacked the nearby Langeni, 'for reasons best known to himself'.[32]

Dingiswayo also never fully managed to subdue his southern neighbours, the Qwabe. Apparently these two peoples had related amicably enough, frequently intermarrying. The Qwabe asserted dynastic links with the Nyambose-Mthethwa. During the seventeenth and eighteenth centuries, they had established themselves firmly between the Mhlathuze and Thukela rivers, based on the Ngoye heights. Control of coastal trade in ivory, metals, beads and possibly slaves very likely spurred some of their accumulation of power. A couple of dozen local lineages were incorporated, especially during the eighteenth-century reigns of Kuzwayo and Simamane.[33]

Then, sometime in the early 1800s, a dispute blew up between the two sons of Khondlo, the Qwabe *inkosi*. Khondlo named Nomo as heir, and he was supported by the Mthethwa. However, the Qwabe majority objected to Khondlo, on the grounds that the Mthethwa were 'amaLala'.[34] They supported Phakathwayo instead. The conflict between the brothers was allegorised as one over a famous ox.[35] Nomo went off to the Mthethwa, accompanied by Goduka kaMboli. (It's possible that Nomo had already *khonza*'d Dingiswayo.) Phakathwayo came up after him with his own extensive delegation, presumably with the intention that Dingiswayo should mediate. Other sons of Khondlo were amongst them. Dingiswayo quizzed them carefully, then slaughtered a steer, prepared medicines and burnt them in a potsherd, and finally squeezed the steer's intestinal juices over them. Dingiswayo then said, 'Come and show me the son of Khondlo that you have come to instal as chief.' They came up, dipped their fingers in the medicines and sucked on them. Somehow at this point an unseemly scuffle broke out between two of the brothers, Godide and Nakile. The latter got the worst of it and was grated into the dust. The potsherd got broken.

Dingiswayo harrumphed, 'I see how it stands now.' He got new medicines. This time, Phakathwayo came forward and symbolically scoffed the lot.

The Qwabe contingents then returned to oDwini, Khondlo's kraal on the Mhlathuze. Further symbolic disputes arose over another (or perhaps the same) missing ox. The account that I'm following here is very muddled, but the upshot seems to have been that Nomo was harried back into the arms of the Mthethwa. Dingiswayo protected Nomo against an assassination attempt by the Qwabe *ibutho*, the iziNkondo. In the middle of it all, Khondlo died, 'for a chief does not live when there is a dispute'. Phakathwayo was immediately installed as the Qwabe *inkosi*.[36]

If the chronology is right, Dingiswayo then attacked Phakathwayo in an attempt to reinstall his protégé, Nomo. The young Shaka may have been involved in these campaigns, of which there may have been several.[37] Some sort of connection was possibly forged between Shaka and Nomo, who is said by some to have accompanied Shaka to Nobamba on Shaka's accession. Some body-servants of Phakathwayo were also thought to have defected with a man named Sopana, who gave them to Shaka, who in turn passed them on to Nomo. When Shaka later defeated Phakathwayo, Shaka gave the captured cattle to Nomo.[38]

Neither the Mthethwa nor the Qwabe seem to have had the wherewithal to permanently cow the other; both are recorded as having chased each other into the eNtumeni forests.[39] One version, from an unknown source printed in 1864, says that Dingiswayo once captured Phakathwayo's entire household – women, children, the lot. He performed a war dance in front of them, and then – chivalrous knight that he was – let them go home. Shaka thought that this was just feeble-minded.[40] The two polities would remain in hostile equilibrium until Shaka, as we will see in due course, was able to assert his overarching supremacy. Nevertheless, Dingiswayo laid down much of the basis for Shaka's own strategies and power.

THUNDER IN THE OPEN

What part did Shaka play in these events? Later romanticists would go as far as claiming that Dingiswayo wouldn't have won a battle without Shaka, but this is certainly nonsense.

Shaka was presumably inducted into one of Dingiswayo's *amabutho*, probably the isiFazana.[41] He may even have become an *induna* as he began to distinguish himself in battle.[42] He was said to have killed a madman who had fended off practically whole armies; not a particularly credible tale.[43] There were other deeds, too, of a sillier and more boyish kind. One incident seems to indicate a certain big-headed truculence. Shaka had been banned from milking Dingiswayo's cows because he had recently killed in battle. When he returned to his duties he felt that he was on top of the world. Some girls came along, carrying food for Dingiswayo. Shaka blocked the gate and refused to let them through. The girls told the *izinceku*; the wary *izinceku* told some *izinduna*; the equally wary *izinduna* told Dingiswayo. Dingiswayo ordered, 'Go! Tell Shaka to let my food through.' Shaka did – but not without retaliating. He got some boys to bring a whole heap of stones, and he proceeded to pelt the offending warriors with them.[44] In another anecdote, Shaka blocked a gate by gripping the sides with both hands and wouldn't let anyone through; in another, he flung a man through the air, shield and all, and so on and so forth.[45]

There are also tales of a less savoury kind. Shaka had the habit, it is said, of ambushing girls, who belonged to commoners, on the bush paths. He would have intercourse with them – the informants hesitate to say 'rape' – and impregnate them. Dingiswayo would just shrug and say, 'What can one do with this wrong-doer from the Zulu (*itshinga la kwa Zulu*)?'[46]

It's impossible to know how much weight to give such stories, which may well be coloured by vengeful hindsight.

More than one source claims that Shaka had a wife or wives amongst the Mthethwa. He wore a headring, like other married men.[47] NGIDI was quite definite on this:

Shaka had wives at Dingiswayo's: one of these had a son, Zibizendhlela, who, when Shaka broke up (*cita*'d) his kraal, fled to Faku in Pondoland. Zibizendhlela *konza*'d there and refused to return at a subsequent period. Monase, the mother of Mbuyazi, was Shaka's wife. . . . Monase, when given by Shaka to Mpande, was said to be pregnant by Shaka, only her state was not showing. Mbuyazi is believed to be really Shaka's son.[48]

This is somewhat controversial. Others claim that Shaka had neither wives nor offspring; anyone who fell pregnant was forced to abort with *izimbiza* or *imxukuzo* drugs.[49] No one seems quite certain whether Zibizendhlela was actually Shaka's or Mpande's son; likewise with Mbuyazi.

At any rate, if Shaka did take wives amongst the Mthethwa, they were subsequently disowned, or 'given away' in an acceptable traditional style.

More positive anecdotes tell of Shaka's reckless courage in Dingiswayo's campaigns, and hint at the beginnings of his involvement in regional politics. He certainly learned much of the arts of fighting under Dingiswayo, not to mention the cunning arts of statesmanship. He acquired some praises: 'Heavens that thunder in the open, where there is neither thorn nor mimosa tree; willow tree which overhangs the deep pool'.[50] Dingiswayo himself sang of him, 'He whose fame spreads even while he is sitting.'

Very likely it was Dingiswayo who gave Shaka – up to then called Sikiti, or Mandlesilo – his more famous name, praising: 'Shaka who is not beaten, the axe that surpasses other axes, the impetuous one who disregards warnings.'[51] Shaka is said in several anecdotes to have exceeded his brief, even as a noted warrior, an *iqawe*. He is said to have been sent out by Dingiswayo to attack Malusi of the Nxumalo people; he launched himself alone into battle, stabbing ferociously about. Dingiswayo reproved him, telling him that the son of a chief shouldn't be courting danger like that.[52] The same might have happened with the Mbatha: Shaka not only defeated them, but pursued them to their death, and plundered all their cattle.[53] Once again, though, it is wise to be wary of retrospective exaggeration.

If we are to believe one anecdote, Shaka didn't always get the better of his opponents. A fight was said to have occurred between the Mthethwa and Zihlandlo of the Mkhize (a man who we will see more of later). Shaka came face to face with one of Zihlandlo's warriors, Bacwali. They kept stabbing each other with their assegais, until Shaka eventually wavered and fell into a donga. Bacwali appeared above him, hooting triumphantly, 'Qope! Jeje!' (his sister's name, apparently). Shaka did not rejoin the fight, but clambered out the other side of the gully, and Bacwali went back to the fray. At a later date, Shaka tried to hunt Bacwali down, but Zihlandlo shielded him, and he carried on living in Zulu country.[54]

Shaka probably remained with the Mthethwa for nearly a decade. It is highly likely that during this time he again drew the attention of his now ageing father, Senzangakhona.

AN OEDIPAL MOMENT

I speculate that sometime between 1805 and 1810, Shaka encountered Senzangakhona face to face. It appears as a classic Oedipal moment, when the son is given the opportunity to kill – or at least overthrow – the father. The alleged meeting has been retold with relish, with a dozen variations. Like other suspiciously detailed anecdotes of the kind, it's hard to know how much is a genuinely remembered historical happening, and how much is an elaborate metaphor for an ugly seizure of power. Nevertheless, for what it's worth, here is the story.

Senzangakhona decided to go down to Dingiswayo's to look for some wives. This may have been no more than a pretext to see the long-lost Shaka, about whose fame he had heard. There are disagreements in the traditions about who came with him. One account has Zwide of the Ndwandwe also turning up to look for some wives. This is not an impossibility, since, for all their hostility, Dingiswayo had given away at least one of his daughters to Zwide. It was a good way of staving off conflict. If Zwide and Senzangakhona did indeed sit alongside one another, watching Shaka go through his paces, it was a supremely ironic moment.[55]

A few accounts have Senzangakhona arrive along with a chieftain named Nkomo kaTshandu of the Mbatha people. Like the Zulu, the Langeni, the Buthelezi, and various other small groups, the Mbatha had khonza'd Dingiswayo. However, Nkomo still had pretensions to independence. Dingiswayo had sent messengers who inquired whether there were any chiefs greater than Dingiswayo. Nkomo brusquely killed them. Dingiswayo would, or could, do nothing – until the moment when Nkomo arrived with Senzangakhona. When Nkomo left, Dingiswayo instructed an *impi* to intercept Nkomo on the path. 'Do not kill him,' Dingiswayo ordered, 'Just stand around him in a circle and beat on your shields.' It was a horribly intimidating tactic, which worked: Nkomo sank to his knees on the spot, and Dingiswayo came and stepped over him in the classic gesture of supremacy. Overcome with fear, Nkomo died. The gift of cattle which Dingiswayo had deceptively given him were driven back.[56]

This is remarkably similar to what, as we'll see shortly, happens to Senzangakhona – which is probably why it is told in this way and place – not necessarily because it happened at the same time. Indeed, as the Mbatha had probably also *khonza*'d Senzangakhona, or even Jama,[57] asserting power over one was tantamount to asserting power over the other.[58]

In a third version, JANTSHI claims that his own father Nongila was in the delegation, along with Mudli, and Menziwa, and Senzangakhona's brothers Zivalele and Sithayi. Other brothers of Shaka's were there, too, including the ill-starred Sigujana.[59]

At any rate, the story goes, Senzangakhona arrives with his retinue, is well received and housed for the night. The following day a grand dance is staged. The Zulu dance first, then the Mthethwa. Dingiswayo has instructed Shaka first to conceal himself, then to come forward and dance. Shaka *giya*'s in front of his father, waving his war shield, the rents from enemies' assegais stuffed with the skins of genets and meerkats. Dingiswayo asks Senzangakhona if he recognises the dancer – another echo of the great hero-myths. Some say that the Zulu *inkosi* saw the resemblance immediately, others that he denied it, that Dingiswayo had to tell him. Senzangakhona was overcome with fear. He retired trembling and sick to his hut.

Yet another version is perhaps closer still to the realpolitik of the situation; it points more clearly at the power relations involved:

Senzangakhona was sent for by Dingiswayo. He went to Dingiswayo in company with my [MRUYI's] grandfather Mudhli and *amakosikazi* [great wives]. A hut was set apart for him. In one hut, whilst seated there with Dingiswayo, a large number of young men of Dingiswayo's tribe entered the hut by pre-arrangement. Shaka also came in, unknown at that time to Senzangakhona. He stood as if there were no place for him; he did this on instructions from the Mtetwa chief, ie. according to a preconcerted plan. Shaka had on horns about his neck and the *iziqu* amulets of a man who had killed in battle; he was, moreover, one of Dingiswayo's heroes. He stood for a moment and looked about for a place to sit down, and before finding one, stood immediately before Senzangakhona so that his shadow fell on his father, and as soon as he had done this he sat down. A silence fell upon all in the hut. Dingiswayo asked Senzangakhona, 'Do you see your calf here?' Senzangakhona was silent, and looked about among the young men. He then pointed at Shaka. Dingiswayo laughed, and proceeded to sing Shaka's praises. Senzangakhona's wives then one and all moved forward and kissed Shaka's arm. Shaka then asked Senzangakhona for an assegai. A number of assegais were produced and he was presented with one of them. Again was the young hero praised by the Mtetwa people, after which ordinary conversation took place for some time.[60]

Dingiswayo is clearly the manipulator here. Of interest, too, is the supportive gesture of the Zulu women. The stage is set for Senzangakhona's demise.

In most versions, that night Shaka, doctored by Dingiswayo himself with appropriate medicines, climbs on top of Senzangakhona's hut and washes himself with the medicines. They drip through onto his father's bed; Senzangakhona awakes, sends someone out to look; they see only a shape flitting away. But they know all too well it was Shaka. Senzangakhona fearfully packs to go home; Dingiswayo sees him off with a present of cattle and some insincere platitudes. On the way back to Zulu country, Senzangakhona falls ill, and dies shortly afterwards, clearing the way for Shaka's accession.

The modern mind might baulk at this magically induced demise, but it cannot be dismissed out of hand. Zulu society was then, and in many places remains, steeped in unquestioning beliefs in the power of witchcraft and sympathetic medicines. Whatever the historical status of the story, it gives us insight into vital, pervasive and real motivations, fears, and methods of asserting supremacy or dislike or desire. Debilitating fear could easily be the result of such an encounter. Zulu people were sensitive to the mix of pharmacological and psychological effects of such actions. So some versions say that Senzangakhona fell ill out of pure panic, others that it was the physical effect of the dastardly medicines. This is not an isolated incident. There are later events from which magic and the belief in magic (or 'witchcraft') cannot be excluded from the historical account.

Such magic also features in another tale about this meeting. According to JANTSHI, Shaka's half-brothers were there in force as well. At one point in the proceedings, Shaka paused in his *giya* dancing in front of Senzangakhona and shouted, 'Father! Give me an assegai and I will fight great battles for you!' A pile of assegais was brought. Senzangakhona said, 'Take one yourself.' Shaka replied, 'No, rather let it come from your hand.' Senzangakhona ran his thumb along the blade of this one and that one, chose one and handed it to Shaka. Shaka resumed his dance, then walked over to where his brothers Dingane, Sigujana, Mhlangana, Ncgojana, Mpande and Maqubana were seated. He went up to Sigujana, said, 'Greetings, my brother,' and tapped him on the head with the assegai.

Days later, Sigujana went out with a Zulu impi to fight with Donda of the Khumalo. He was struck in the head by an assegai, on the very spot where Shaka had tapped him, and he died.[61]

Since other information about Sigujana's death disagrees with this (most believe that Shaka himself killed Sigujana, or had him killed later), this whole incident with the assegai is probably a fabrication. However, it captures precisely the state of the power-play between these members of the family: between Senzangakhona and Shaka, jockeying for the privilege of choosing the assegai, which is to say the responsibility for the succession, and between Shaka and Sigujana, the heir-designate.

Another account – that quoted earlier by MRUYI kaTimuni, another grandson of Mudli of the romantic birth version (on pages 81 to 83) – claims that Mudli was again at the centre of the action. Mudli, watching the dance, saw exactly which way the wind was blowing, and actually advised Senzangakhona to *feign* illness in order to get out of there sooner. Perhaps Dingiswayo tried to get Mudli to side with him in engineering Shaka's accession; he is said to have sidled over to Mudli during the dancing and offered, 'Here is Shaka, I am bringing him to you.' Mudli replied, 'How can you expect me to protect and look after Shaka, when I am already protecting his father?' So Dingiswayo later told Shaka, 'This Mudli refuses to have anything to do with you, he does not care for you. Do not spare him. He is the leading *induna* of the Zulu. Put him to death, or you will never reign.'[62] Which, in due course, Shaka did. MRUYI's desire to valorise his grandfather aside, this is likely much closer to the grimy politics of the situation.

As so often happens, the shift in a power relationship would come to be figured in a highly coloured, symbolic story, in this case also MRUYI's. On the day of the dance,

> large numbers of Mthethwa came together. A circle was formed. Dingiswayo went out and played and danced. Mudli joined him, whilst Senzangakhona remained indoors, ill. Whilst the dancing was going on, a feather fell from Dingiswayo's head onto the ground. *Izinceku* stepped forward immediately to pick it up, as it stood upright on the ground and remained so. Dingiswayo, however, checked them and said the feather was to be left alone. The dancing proceeded. When the playing was over, the feather was picked up.[63]

As with other accounts of this weirdly upstanding feather – at least three involving Shaka himself – what initially appears to be an omen of no good, is turned by the leader into a symbol of future success. So it is here, but it is a myth created in hindsight.

At any rate, Senzangakhona died – on the way home, amongst the Makhoba people,[64] or very shortly after he got back,[65] or after some considerable time,[66] or even after Shaka had already arrived himself with a whole column of Mthethwa in support.[67] Indeed, Senzangakhona may have died quite peacefully at home, 'in his bed', as the missionary David Leslie heard in 1865.[68] If this is true it virtually cancels out the entire 'meeting' story.

Hovering over all this is the question of whether, in the end, Senzangakhona *wanted* Shaka to take over, or whether he felt obliged to give in to Dingiswayo's obvious pressure, allied with less obvious pressures within the Zulu polity. One account has Senzangakhona say, as he feels death creeping over him:

> 'People of Zulu, I am dying. You must abandon the idea of appointing as chief my son [Sigujana]. For when I die there will come up the madman who was borne by a woman of Mbengi's people [Nandi]. He, Shaka, is not human. If you argue that he is not a chief he will kill my people, and destroy them. You must make him chief. For he will not be made chief by me; he will make himself chief . . .'[69]

After this outburst of mixed signals, Senzangakhona dies. In another version, Senzangakhona says: 'Let this matter that we were talking about (viz. appointing Sigujana as heir) not be discussed; let it be avoided, because Shaka is at Mthethwa *where we are ruled*.'[70] We don't need to believe that Senzangakhona said any such thing, but the tradition captures the atmosphere of threat, the sense that the Zulu, whatever they thought, didn't have much choice in the matter. In effect, it was Dingiswayo who would decide.

Whichever way it was, the result was the same: Senzangakhona's death meant that Shaka's path to power was open.

TAKING OVER AS LEADER

When Senzangakhona died, Shaka came up to Zulu country with full and essential Mthethwa support, a whole column of them.[71] He had been living at Ngomane's *umuzi* much of this time, poised on the very edge of Zulu territory; the takeover had probably been contemplated for years. Mthethwa *amabutho* drove ahead of them herds of cattle, the mobile wealth that Shaka would need to establish his patronage.[72] Mthethwa warriors accompanied him, including his mentor and 'father', Ngomane. Shaka came 'with high-ranking men of the Mthethwa who took him to Mahlabathini'.[73] So long had he been amongst them that, it was said, he spoke the Mthethwa dialect.[74] Others reported to have come up with him were Ndwetsha, Mkhono and Luphuzi (all Thembu men), Makula kaVavane of the Qwabe, Mbikwana, Mfundeko kaMgabhi, and Nxazonke of the Langeni.[75]

Shaka's core 'Zulu' support-group was thus already a hotchpotch. Probably these people formed the nucleus of the *umuzi* Shaka quickly established, kwaNogqogqa, which was soon renamed Mkhandlu. This was both a physical homestead and a distinct band of people, a following he had established in Mthethwa country with Dingiswayo's blessing and support.[76] The strategy was typical of the manner of control that Dingiswayo had already employed elsewhere, and which Shaka would refine in the course of his own reign.

On arrival, Shaka went into the main cattle enclosure (presumably of Nobamba kraal) and formed his contingent into a semi-circle. The Zulu people came out, joined the circle, and together they chanted *amahubo* songs – a particularly revered form. Carrying his war shield, Shaka advanced into the

circle, demanding, 'Where are the cattle for my father's funeral?' The cattle
were brought, and Shaka slaughtered them, 'slaughtered them as if he were
destroying the herd', as MKEBENI put it. In this way Shaka asserted his right.
The Mthethwa column, suitably provisioned, then returned to Dingiswayo
to report.[77]

On Dingiswayo's instructions, Shaka assassinated all of those who might
be opposed to him, even (if we credit NDHLOVU at all) the man who had saved
him as a child, Mudli. According to NDHLOVU, Mudli had actually sent to
Dingiswayo asking him when he intended to install Shaka, begging him not
to do it while Senzangakhona was still living. Despite this muted approval,
Dingiswayo wanted Mudli dead. Once he had called the bulk of Mudli's
followers over to his side, Shaka moved swiftly to eliminate four prominent
men who might offer opposition: Mudli himself, Zivalele, Sojisa, and
Nobongoza – the last three all sons of Jama, brothers of Senzangakhona.
Elsewhere, NDHLOVU somewhat contradictorily states that these murders
happened while Senzangakhona was still alive. In his version, Shaka went to
kwaNodungu, Mudli's kraal, killed him, and then Sigujana (here called
Nomkhwayimba), and also Nomaphikela kaJama of the chiefly house. The
deaths were reported to Senzangakhona: 'They have been put to death by
the one who beats but is not beaten.' Even as the report was being made,
Shaka arrived, his Mthethwa *impis* chanting, 'These cattle are a great bone
of contention.' And Senzangakhona fainted dead away.[78]

The most brutal – and from Shaka's point of view, essential – act, was
the murder of his half-brother Sigujana, the heir-designate, a young man
apparently of his own age. There is very little evidence as to what exactly
happened, none at all to say that Shaka himself did the terrible deed. Fynn
claimed that Shaka's other half-brother on his mother's side, Ngwadi, was
the appointed assassin.[79]

Despite the dubious legitimacy of such a coup, the Zulu, willingly or
otherwise, seemed to have accepted Shaka as new leader without further
demur.[80] There are indications that Shaka had strong support already: he
may even have been called, in a sense, by a clique consisting of Menziwa
kaKoko of the Biyela (a sub-section of the Zulu), Mnkabayi, Mawa, and Mmama
(all Shaka's aunts; remember them kissing his arm at Dingiswayo's). They
objected to Sigujana being named heir, since Sigujana's mother Mpikase was

not a woman of rank, whereas Nandi, Shaka's mother, was.[81] There may even have been a short interregnum by Mnkabayi. In the end, as NDUKWANA put it, 'Senzangakhona had no one to stand armed by his grave as his successor. Sigujana did not stand thus, for when Shaka got up, people accepted him without a fight. No one was ousted by Shaka.'[82]

In all probability this is the true meaning of the Shaka-Senzangakhona meeting story, and of Shaka tapping Sigujana on the head with the fatal assegai: Senzangakhona had already engineered, or perhaps bowed to the inevitability of, Shaka's succession.

As for Shaka's other brothers, they seem to have chosen discretion over valour. Dingane, at least, fled to the Qwabe, and was only permitted to return much later.[83] He, Mpande, Mhlangana, and the others almost disappear from the record until the very final act, in 1828. As a result, Shaka would become well regarded as a man who 'killed none of his relations'.[84] Even BALENI, who was usually only too keen to regale James Stuart with sensationalist stories of Shaka's cruelties, admitted, 'We used to say that Shaka was the king for he did not kill his father's sons.' Dingane, by contrast, 'was a bad king for he killed his own relations'.[85] This was not entirely true, but compared to Dingane's accession some twenty years later, the bloodshed was light indeed.

Perhaps, for the most part, the Zulu saw that Shaka was their best hope at a time when the country seemed quite suddenly to be under greater threat of external violence than ever before. If the period from 1800 up to 1810 or 1812, when Shaka took over, had been something of a breathing space in the Thukela-Phongolo catchment, a period for polities to consolidate internally, the next decade would prove to be dramatically different.

6

Laying the foundations

Early reign, c.1812–17

> The Zulu nation, as built up by Shaka, was merely an agglomeration
> of mutually hostile elements held together by nothing more stable
> than brute force.
>
> A.T. Bryant, *Olden Times in Zululand and Natal* (1929, 390).

I think that Shaka took over the patrimony of Zulu in about the year of
Napoleon's disastrous advance on Moscow: 1812. This is to push his
accession back further than most historians have allowed, but they have based
their dating almost entirely on an estimate by the white adventurers Francis
Farewell and Henry Francis Fynn. These two counted the number of annual
umkosi first-fruits ceremonies over which Shaka was said to have officiated:
eight before 1824, indicating that Shaka came to power in 1816.[1] This has to
be taken from whence it comes, of course: from two very recent arrivals,
limited in their understanding of the local language and customs, and working
with traditions not famed for accurate numeracy. The one other Zulu
informant with an opinion on the matter asserted that Shaka ruled for eleven
years, coming to power therefore in 1817.[2] This is very clearly too late.

I'm proposing an earlier date for a number of reasons. Firstly, it seems
relatively clear that Shaka was able to field a very substantial force to defeat
the Ndwandwe by 1819. He would have needed more than a mere three
years to build such a force. The number of *amabutho* he could command by
then well exceeded three; and although it's no longer accepted that one-
ibutho-per-year is an accurate guide to the chronology, it's unlikely that all
these units could have been organised in under five years.

149

Secondly, Shaka had had to retreat from the Ndwandwe *twice*, and deal with the aftermath of Dingiswayo's death in a separate Ndwandwe campaign. While again it's not a hard and fast rule, it is unlikely that the Ndwandwe were capable (any more than Shaka was later) of launching more than one major long-distance raid in a fighting season. And they had been launching other raids on the northern peoples, too. This argues for an Ndwandwe expansion covering five, perhaps six, years, before the final confrontation with the Zulu.

Thirdly, Shaka evidently had had time to get involved in a range of local political wrangles, wars, and interventions, requiring several years to unfold, before the initial Ndwandwe assaults.

And finally, a single decisive date for the accession may be simplistic; as we've seen, the relationship between Senzangakhona's death, Shaka's arrival, and a possible period of regency, is impossible to determine precisely. All in all, however, this slightly longer, less explosive perspective pushes his accession back to about 1812.

This is to disagree, though only in nuance, with John Wright, who states that the 'installation of Shaka inaugurated a new period of rapid political change and of sharply intensified conflict in the mid-White Mfolozi region',[3] and with Carolyn Hamilton, who writes of Shaka injecting 'a new military imperative into the western reaches of Dingiswayo's domain'.[4] Their language reveals a persistence of the 'explosive Shaka' stereotype. I'm picturing a rather slower transition, with the violent changes being initiated further north, not by a still-quite-weak Shaka.

This is fuzzy stuff. We can easily give or take a couple of years. It's another crucial date in Shaka's 'biography' of which we will never be sure.

THREE CHARACTERS

One morning, early on in his reign, Shaka noticed a stalwart, somewhat older man busying himself around Mntaniya's *umuzi*, cooking for his mother, Nandi. Shaka gave the man an order. He was apparently ignored. Shaka saw then that the man was an *isancute*: he hadn't had his ears pierced – *boboza*'d – as Zulu men usually did. Shaka joked that evidently the fellow couldn't hear too well with his ears looking like that. 'Seize that *isancute* and pierce his ears,' he ordered.[5]

The man was Ngqengelele kaMvuyana, a Buthelezi who had found himself working as a menial, 'a hewer of wood and drawer of water, a nurse', at Mntaniya's place. He had arrived with no following and so was an *inkulelane*, a 'stranger who has been adopted, having no home of his own'. He was, nevertheless, thought of as being 'one of the original inhabitants', and thus even Shaka had respect for him.[6] Getting his ears pierced was a sign of belonging perhaps, a symbol of being brought into the central Zulu circle. Ngqengelele rose quickly in Shaka's estimation. He became, it is said (though the privilege is claimed for any number of people), the only one who could openly challenge Shaka: 'Here, boy,' he is supposed to have rebuked Shaka much later, 'why are you finishing off the people of the chief?' He became one of the most prominent individuals in Shaka's reign, with a string of *imizi* of his own.[7] He was 'a dominant figure who commanded the attention of the whole nation',[8] and a commoner made good who, unlike most of Shaka's great men, survived Dingane's purges and enjoyed the 'privilege' of dying naturally.[9]

A similar rise from the bottom ranks is attributed to a second character.

It is maybe two or three years later. The situation is critical. The northern barbarians have been burning homesteads in the very heart of the motherland. The beaten warriors have been forced to retreat. The *inkosi* must resort to some cunning strategies to enthuse the flagging troops. Shaka gathers them together in the council place of his remaining *umuzi*. He sticks a new and unstained assegai in the dusty ground, points to the north and shouts out: 'There is Zwide, still following me. Let there come forward one Zulu warrior. He who takes this assegai will earn these praises of mine: *The one who was astonished at insults even as he insulted Dlungwana at Embelebeleni!'*

But the warriors are afraid. They think that they might be seen as pretending to be equal to the *inkosi* himself. Shaka returns to his seat, invites them to *giya* instead, to dance the war dances and demonstrate how savagely they will stab.

Hovering at Shaka's elbow is a young *inceku*, a very dark man of medium height. He is a Qwabe, of the Ncwane section. He steps forward to seize Shaka's assegai. His name is Khomfiya kaNogandaya.

Khomfiya had run into trouble amongst his own people, who lived around the lower reaches of the Mhlathuze river, some 40 kilometres south of the

Zulu. When climbing over the brow of a hill, Khomfiya and a few cohorts had inadvertently sighted some Qwabe princesses cavorting, stripping the bark from *ubendle* plants to make girdles. He and three of his companions were spotted. The Qwabe *inkosi* was known to have a ferocious temper. Rather than be accused of anything, the young men fled – to Shaka. In this, Khomfiya was following the example of his father Nogandaya who, dissatisfied with Qwabe rule, had headed off north. Nogandaya was said to have been buried under a cabbage-tree, somewhere in the country of the Ndwandwe.[10]

When Khomfiya arrived to *khonza* Shaka, he shuddered with fear as he approached because he and his companions were mere commoners. Khomfiya was chosen to present the fugitives' salutations. Khomfiya's own son MKOTANA related:

> They then went to Shaka, and when they got to him they saluted him. Then my father saluted him [and] praised him in the ordinary way. Shaka was seated on top of a heap of earth which had been dug out of a hole in the ground, elevated some two feet, on a large reed mat . . . Komfiya saluted him, 'You are the heavens!' An *inceku* was sent to them to find out who they were, for they stood far off. . . . The *inceku* shouted his questions at them, but Komfiya replied to the *inkosi* direct in a loud voice. 'Tell them to approach,' said Shaka. They approached a little and then stood for fear. Shaka said, 'Tell them to come closer.' They did so. Shaka said then, 'You, boy, whose son are you?' 'I am the son of Nogandaya, *inkosi*.' Shaka said, 'Where are you going?' They said, 'We have come to *khonza*. We have got into trouble.' Shaka then said, '*Halala!* Celebrate, Zulu people, for I am chosen as a husband!' Everyone present then saluted, '*Bayete!*' thereby signalling their congratulation. The four were then given to Tshoba of the Lembe people among the Ntuli. Shaka told Tshoba to take care of these people, for they had come with no cattle.[11]

This account provides a nice insight into the protocol. Another son of Khomfiya's adds that Shaka, perceiving Khomfiya's terror, said gently, tapping him on the head with his nails, 'Don't show fear here among us. If you do not fight fiercely your meat will be soaked in water, like an infant's. You will be a close friend, for you are of our people; we originated together with you. We are amaNtungwa together with you.'[12]

If this is anything like what Shaka actually said – and how can we know? – it is a moment of conscious invention. The Qwabe and Zulu were scarcely related at all (see the discussion in Chapter 1). Shaka was creating a new family.

Finally, a third character represents Shaka's ready-made 'family', the one with whom he arrived in Zulu country. We have already met Ngomane kaMqombolo of the Mthethwa. He was Shaka's surrogate 'father' in Mthethwa country, and remained with Shaka throughout his reign. He became part of the innermost circle of advisers.[13] Ngomane was possibly already quite old at the time of Shaka's accession, and would not accompany the *inkosi* on his final campaigns.[14] He would die 'during Dingane's reign', most likely during the fighting with the Boers.[15] Otherwise, we know little about his role.

However, James Stuart did record an argument about Ngqengelele and Ngomane between two of his informants, JANTSHI and NDUKWANA. It's quite an instructive exchange.

A dispute arises between Ndukwana and Jantshi in regard to the status of Ngqengelele and Ngomane. Ndukwana contends that Ngqengelele, a man of the locality (not a Buthelezi, as Magidi said, above), was Shaka's 'father'. Shaka and his brothers grew up in his charge. He had no homestead of his own; he was a menial among the people of the *nkosikazi* Mtaniya, but as I do not know exactly where Shaka grew up, I am rather puzzled.

Jantshi replies that Shaka arrived already a man in the Zulu country with Ngomane [when he returned to take over power].

Ndukwana says Mdhlaka was the great *induna* of the country, and certainly Ngomane was not as big as he was. Assuming Ngomane, as Jantshi avers, had an *isigodhlo*, there is nothing remarkable in that. He was made a present of it. I know of Ngomane's having 'come up' with Shaka from the Mthethwa, but it is new to me to hear he was the most powerful man of the nation.

Jantshi replies: I have stated merely what I heard from my father, and although I admit Ngqengelele was one of the heads of the people, still I deny he had anything like the influence of Ngomane, to whom Shaka showed the signal favour of giving him (or allowing him to keep) an *isigodhlo*.[16]

There are some interesting points to be made about this extract. One is the way in which the 'facts' about Shaka's arrival at Ngomane's get mixed up in, and influenced by, disputes about the *later* status of Ngomane in the Zulu state. The earlier event has to be read through the filters of the later ones. A second point is how even these informants – and JANTSHI, being the son of Shaka's spy Nongila, is about as close to the horse's mouth as we're likely to get – become muddled and self-contradictory, admit to doubt, and learn new things from each other. In effect, they can only repeat what they've been told – which may or may not be true.

A third point is perhaps the most important: the muddle may arise because there never was a clearly defined hierarchy in the first place. Promising men were incorporated and elevated at different times, for different reasons, and often under immediate pressure of events. Ngomane gained prominence by virtue of his long and fatherly association with Shaka, his age, and his connection as an *induna* of the overlord, Dingiswayo. Ngqengelele gained prominence partly because of his family connections with the oldest inhabitants of the country and the Zulu's strongest allies, the Buthelezi; and partly, perhaps, because of his independent and astute personality. Khomfiya, having been drafted into an *ibutho* in order to help meet an urgent crisis of invasion, gained prominence through his warlike valour, not as a councillor. Each would be rewarded in his own way: with permission to own an *isigodlo* of women, to build an *umuzi*, to govern a territory, or to lead an *ibutho*.

The careers of these three men (and we will see more of Khomfiya in particular) give us some insight into the ways in which Shaka began to build the foundations of his new polity. In these initial years, he was sharply restricted. In the first place, he was still tributary to the Mthethwa. His early campaigns were almost certainly dictated primarily by Dingiswayo's ambitions, not his own. These forays weren't particularly extensive. As David Leslie noted in 1868, Shaka probably 'reigned peaceably enough for two years'.[17] He must have spent the bulk of his time not fighting, but attempting to consolidate internally: forging alliances, organising *amabutho* and food supplies, building new *imizi*, gathering a core of supportive and able men, as well as redistributing power and resources.

In the second place, Shaka was restricted by the increasing incursions of Zwide's Ndwandwe. New upheavals in the northern half of the Thukela-Phongolo catchment were sending alarming ripples across the region.

FIRST MOVES

In the first six or so years of his reign, during which Shaka operated under Dingiswayo's protection and domination, the Mthethwa-Zulu strategy seems to have been two-fold. Firstly, they tried to tighten their control over the little polities that still buffered them against the Ndwandwe. Secondly, they tried to persuade or coerce the polities to their south to join them in a wider and more powerful alliance. In all cases, negotiated intervention was the first option, coerced taxation the second. Their goal was to tap as many resources as possible. Occasionally this might involve a judicious assassination. Essentially they needed cattle for wealth and patronage, and land for cattle. They needed men to fight and trade, women to plant and build, and both to breed. The 'Zulu' did not develop, overnight, some kind of pathological murderousness. The goal was never to obliterate entire peoples.

It's impossible now to establish the exact sequence and chronology of Shaka's various operations (see Map 4 on page 156). Here we will look at them in the most geographically sensible sequence: the smaller and closer groups first, the larger and more problematic ones next. Although traditional accounts tend to speak of single decisive and dramatically devastating 'wars', in reality there were probably several overlapping campaigns against some of these groups. There were certainly subtler, extended negotiations going on that have been lost to view, masked by the more exciting memories of bloody confrontations and heroic 'battles'.

According to NGIDI, Shaka, under Dingiswayo's direction, first turned his attention to those peoples living between the White and Black Mfolozi rivers: the buffer zone between the Mthethwa-Zulu area and the Ndwandwe. These included – going roughly from east to west – the Mpanza, the Sibiya, the Zungu, the Mabaso, the Makhoba, and the Buthelezi. There were others,

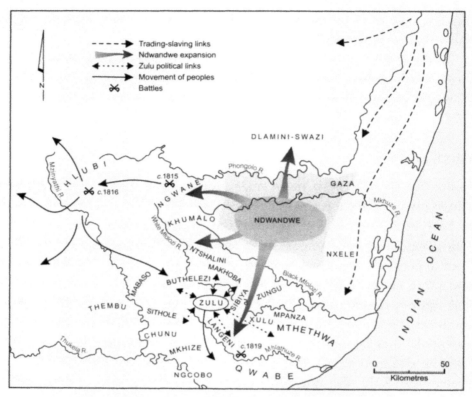

Map 4: Ndwandwe and Shaka's early politics, *c.*1810–20

too, whose precise locations we don't know: the Phisi, the Mthimkhulu, the Qungebe, the Mbuyeni, the Xulu, and the Sikhakhane.[18] One informant says, contradictorily, 'There was intermarriage with them. Shaka attacked and killed off these tribes; he crept up on them in the night.'[19] The first sentence cancels out, or at least complicates, the second. Since there are no records of actual fights with these little clanlets, we can assume that they *khonza*'d readily enough. This was certainly true of the Sibiya.[20]

Amongst this first 'wave' of groups to be brought under the Zulu wing, the Buthelezi – later to be so important in Zulu politics – is almost the only one on which we have any detail. The Buthelezi had long *khonza*'d the Zulu, in Senzangakhona's and maybe even Jama's time.[21] It seems that they gave their allegiance to Shaka without resistance. The chief, Phungashe, feared that Shaka might attack. Melodramatically, it is said that a Zulu *impi* was already heaving into sight across the Nhlazatshe ridges, whereupon Phungashe hastily sent white oxen with the message, 'We do not want war.' Shaka responded, 'Hear! My Zulu brothers. He fears the lion of Zululand. He says that he will not fight the Zulu nation. He is a man, this Phungashe. He will survive to a great age; the army will never go against him again.'[22] That much was true, and the Buthelezi became thoroughly integrated into the growing Zulu structures.

Almost due north of the Buthelezi and across the White Mfolozi, the Ntshalini would give a little more trouble. Indeed, Shaka never secured full allegiance from them. They had probably already *khonza*'d Zwide when Shaka came to power. Both Dingiswayo and Shaka made attempts to win or bully them onto their side, possibly more than once.[23] According to MADIKANE, they were the first to be attacked by Shaka himself. But they presented sturdy resistance.[24] At some point Shaka killed Khondlo, the Ntshalini chieftain. (Since this assassination has also been attributed to Dingiswayo, it almost certainly occurred during this period – Shaka executing his overlord's orders.) Khondlo's chief son Hlangabeza fled who knows where, but later reappeared, still aligned with the Ndwandwe under Sikhunyane, Zwide's son.[25] Under Hlangabeza, the Ntshalini are later still recorded as having attacked Shaka and been repulsed, and finally as deserting entirely towards the north (see page 491).[26]

In the Buthelezi and the Ntshalini, we have two poles of reaction to Shaka's gradually increasing power: relatively unproblematic allegiance and integration, and highly problematic independence resulting in flight.

We have a few details of one other operation in the 'buffer zone'.[27] The Zungu people lived a little east of the Zulu, above the confluence of the White and Black Mfolozi rivers. They, along with the closely aligned Makhoba, became a particular bone of contention. They lived athwart a particularly lush area of diverse vegetation, ideal for cattle and agriculture.[28] A Zungu succession dispute resulted in one faction calling on Zwide, the increasingly powerful chieftain to their north, to assist. The other faction called for the 'armed intervention' of Shaka.[29] There were already marriage connections between them and the Zulu.[30] Shaka's attack on the Zungu was transformed into a revenge story.

According to this tale, a wife or wives of the Zungu chieftain Mtshitshizelwa refused to give Shaka a drink of water on a hot day. 'Go and lap it up from the stream yourself,' they laughed. Shaka 'later' sent men to go and kill these women. It was also said that on this visit he hlobonga'd with some Zungu girls; he 'caught hold of one and penetrated her, causing her to be pregnant'. Dingiswayo was informed, but shrugged it off, saying, 'What can I do to this Zulu wrongdoer, this itshinga?'[31] Mtshitshizelwa himself fled and khonza'd elsewhere.

In other words – the story implies – Mtshitshizelwa was politically ousted, and the Zungu clan was obliged to submit to Mthethwa-Zulu domination. Shaka supported the installation of Sidinanda, cementing the alliance with the gift of a Zulu bride. This was also perhaps one of the earliest campaigns in which Khomfiya kaNogandaya participated.[32] As a very similar rape story is attached to other peoples and scenarios, it is certainly a metaphor for political conflict, rather than a simple representation of Shaka's personality.

Following the Buthelezi, the Zungu joined the Zulu polity.[33] They were substantial enough to form, in time, a cohesive Zungu ibutho, known colourfully as the amaNkenetshane, the Wild Dogs. This outfit survived as a unit for decades, right into Cetshwayo's reign.[34] Alongside their offshoot Mphungose, they would take pride in their martial contribution: 'It was the capacity of the Mpungose people to get very angry in wartime that caused so deep an alliance to spring up between them,' said an Mphungose informant. 'By "angry in war" I mean so staunch, brave and absolutely true to the Zulus.'[35]

Zwide was infuriated at losing the Zungu. He launched an attack on the Zulu-Zungu forces, such as they were, and beat them. This was the first of Shaka's losses and retreats before the Ndwandwe onslaught.

Here we need to backtrack a little to trace out the beginnings of that onslaught amidst broiling disturbances to the north.

'EPIDEMICS OF CRIME'

In *Olden Times in Zululand and Natal*, Bryant comments:

> We occasionally hear tell of 'epidemics of crime', in which a whole group of individuals, even of nations, becomes swayed by some common mentally-overwhelming impulse. Such a wave of political animosity, panic, fear, or general unrest seems to have invaded the South African native mind in the earlier decades of the past [nineteenth] century – or even, indeed, the whole negro race-mind; for we find evidence of similar political upheavals at the same period also in other parts of the Dark Continent. The distemper had entered upon its earlier stages even prior to the days of Shaka and Dingiswayo; but it reached its crisis in them.[36]

This kind of racialist claptrap will no longer serve for historical explanation, but an upheaval there was; and in that last sentence, Bryant is certainly right. The 'distemper' preceded Shaka. But what had sparked the new upsurge?

Many writers, Bryant included, discern its beginning in an attack of peculiar ferocity. As we've seen, the Ndwandwe, less a cohesive polity than a bundle of interrelated but competing lineages, had been wrestling for regional influence with several neighbours. Under Zwide in the 1810s, the ruling lineages had achieved greater centralised power. Zwide had spawned an extensive ruling family with a number of well-remembered sons, including his successor, Sikhunyane, whom we will meet again.[37] Zwide formed a number of feared *amabutho*: the amaPhela, the abaHlakabezi, the isiKwitshi, and the amaNkaiya. At least some of these *amabutho* were well established before Shaka's rise to power. The polity got big enough to split off again into semi-autonomous sections, including the Nxumalo, the Manqele, and the Phiseni.[38]

In conjunction with the development of this ruling hierarchy, the nature of the Ndwandwe raids achieved a level of unprecedented violence. Sobhuza of the Dlamini-Swazi was attacked north of the Phongolo river over several years, but in about 1815 he was struck with much greater force. His people were ejected, in stages of increasing destitution, onto the ridges of the highveld. The Ndwandwe invasions 'very nearly obliterated' Sobhuza's polity. This was despite the fact that Zwide had married off his daughter Nompetu – or perhaps it was Lazide or Mphandzeze – to Sobhuza himself.[39] The Dlamini, already long under pressure from the east, were amongst the first peoples of this region to be substantially and abruptly displaced in the nineteenth century. Roaming bands of Ndwandwe marauders were distracted only by other conflicts to the south.[40]

Zwide also launched attacks on the two main branches of the Khumalo, led by Donda and Mashobane respectively. These people lived between the upper Mkhuze and White Mfolozi rivers; only the Ntshalini buffered them from the Zulu. Zwide assassinated Donda and routed his weaker forces. Mlotha of the Ntshalini was likewise killed.[41]

Then, around 1815, came what may be the key attack. Matiwane of the Ngwane, having concluded various judicious alliances with the Hlubi and the Mthethwa, was ensconced in the area between the Bivane and upper Mfolozi rivers, immediately north of the Khumalo.

> But while Matiwane was priding himself inwardly on this easy triumph, behold! suddenly from the east a second invader, as mighty as Dingiswayo, but without his mercy, Zwide, the Ndwandwe king, swept up irresistibly upon the amaNgwane and drove them in headlong panic before him.[42]

I am usually suspicious of this kind of overwrought language, but for once the consequences indicate that it's almost justified. The subsequent career of Matiwane's Ngwane is one of the great migration epics of the subcontinent, ranking almost with Mzilikazi's, and more tragic. Though the language of praises is likewise conventionally exaggerated, Matiwane's extensive *izibongo* proved no idle boasts:

The Supporter, like unto Gasa, who props up the uBombo.
The father of girls through the begetting of daughters.
Matiwane, our royal bird with the red knees
Red-eyed, and red on the lips
From drinking the blood of fighting men.[43]

Though conflict with Zwide is only hinted at in these praises, his attack was savage enough to force Matiwane's people to move off en masse. Though virtually nothing else is known about these new Ndwandwe invasions, their evident ferocity demands explanation. What had changed?

The only obvious answer lies to the north-east, in a resurgence of trade from Delagoa Bay, particularly the trade in slaves. I suggested in Chapter 5 that in the period 1800 to 1811 there was a decline in the Bay trade, necessitating an inward turn amongst the inland peoples, a move primarily to more violent and organised cattle raids. After 1811, there was an upsurge in slaving throughout south-east Africa. Although in 1807 Britain had banned its own nationals from slaving, an illegal trade flourished. Anglo-Portuguese treaties of 1810 and 1815 confined Portuguese slaving to south of the equator, forcing a greater concentration of attention to Mozambican and Angolan sources for captives. Smuggling to Mauritius and Réunion continued apace throughout the 1810s and 20s.[44] Halting attempts were being made to eliminate Madagascar as a slave source, and the slavers were looking elsewhere. Mozambican slaves were still being filtered through Madagascar, however, and even more indirectly through the Seychelles.

The Madagascar dynamic undoubtedly reflects that developing in the Thukela-Phongolo catchment:

In the year 1816 Governor Farquhar [of Mauritius] opened a communication with Radama, a chief in Madagascar, with a view to establish relations that should lead to the suppression of the slave trade in that island. The father of this chief of a tribe called the Ovahs had carried on successful wars in the country, and had realized much treasure from the sale of his prisoners. Radama, who was young, had also engaged in these wars, which were fomented by the slave-traders, to whom many of the captives were sold, and the expeditions to the islands of Mozambique seem to have had the same object.[45]

At least some of those Mozambique expeditions are likely to have called at Delagoa Bay, as they certainly did a few years later.[46]

Most importantly, the Brazilian market for slaves mushroomed. In 1811, the Portuguese opened up the subordinate Mozambique ports to the Brazil trade. For these slave ships, Delagoa Bay was 1 200 kilometres closer than Mozambique and an obvious entry-point. By the end of the 1810s, 10 000 slaves a year were being exported from Mozambique, and 20 000 a year a decade later.[47]

How much Delagoa Bay participated in the upsurge remains controversial. Documented details from the Bay area are lacking. Almost all we know comes from reports of the early 1820s, which are patchy and biased towards underplaying the slave trade. Reading back into the early 1810s is tricky. Certainly *some* slaving was happening again. Much of our information comes from hints dropped by one Captain W.F.W. Owen, the British navy commander of a survey team that dropped anchor in Delagoa Bay for the first time in September 1822.

Although Owen claimed in official despatches that there were 'very few' slaves leaving Delagoa Bay at the time, he was less sure in private. In truth, he had little information to go on. He seemed undecided as to whether the local Africans, 'Like all other African Nations' – a conventionally gross generalisation – made 'slaves of their enemies' and sold them to the Portuguese, or whether they had 'a decided aversion' to slaving. Nevertheless, the Bay had been 'very much frequented' by whalers, by British, French and Dutch ships, and at least one vessel from Bombay with Hindi speakers aboard, over the previous decade.[48] This doesn't necessarily amount to much in itself, but it at least negates the Portuguese claim that they had a lid on the trade. Though the Portuguese were able to chase off the British East India Company ship *Perseverance* in 1815, there is sufficient evidence that a stream of other ships visited – 'a constant source of vexation', the officials of Mozambique reported in that same year.[49] There were almost certainly more ships than anyone recorded. Owen wrote privately that there had not been an 'annual' Portuguese slaver in the harbour for three years, implying that this vessel *had* been a regular visitor prior to 1820; it would touch at all the ports between Mozambique and 'Lorenzo Marks' (Delagoa Bay) around February or March, and with 'ivory, horn & slaves' depart again in May. Female slaves were also

regularly being bought into prostitution in exchange for clothing. Though
other, equally unquantifiable, items of trade should not be ignored, slavery
was the primary purpose of the Portuguese presence from 1811 onwards.
While the Portuguese had sustained only what Owen called a 'precarious
tyranny' over the years, there had also been 'much communication with the
Ships of all Nations who come here to fish the black Whale', and generally
ongoing 'traffick with the natives for Ivory, Rhinoceros horns, tiger skins,
Cattle, Slaves and Hoes in return for coarse blue Dungarees, beads, brass
wire and bangles'.[50]

The increase in trade was almost certainly responsible for further
consolidation of the Thembe polity nearest the Bay. The Thembe were robust
enough in 1810 to launch a serious raid on Inhambane, far to the north.
Such conflict was in part retaliation for the Portuguese garrisons' own policy,
increasingly applied, of fomenting wars inland in order to generate slaves. In
1813, for instance, Portuguese firearms decided a Moambo-Mfumo conflict,
although they weren't strong enough to prevent the slaughter of a party
trying to set up a new whaling factory in 1817. In that same year, the governor
complained that the Bay garrison 'often did more to create disorder than to
resolve it'.[51] Captain Owen later concurred: the Portuguese were guilty of
'Murder and Rapine' in the interior.[52]

Zwide was almost certainly amongst those chieftains angling for a greater
portion of the expanding Bay trade. There is little question that commerce
of all descriptions was traversing the Thukela-Phongolo catchment: a report
of 1811 noted that Bay traders had travelled south all the way to the borders
of Xhosa country. Some Tsonga from the Bay area were becoming
professional traders, and were travelling well inland themselves.[53] They
supplied cloth and beads for women's dancing-girdles; in time they would
add carafes of liquor in wickerwork covers and, doubtless, weapons. The
Tsonga also supplied secretary-bird feathers and monkey tails from the lowland
forests, increasingly staples of military finery: a stronger ethic of martial pride
was developing. Carriers were hired from minor chiefs – *amakengana*,
inferiors – sometimes 50 or 100 at a time.[54] We need to be cautious about
the timescale here, but there is some evidence that a 'caravan' system was
coming into use in the early years of the century.[55]

The coincidence of an upsurge in trade of all kinds, most importantly slaving, and the increase of more violent attacks by more organised *amabutho* in the immediate hinterland, is, at the very least, deeply suggestive. We do not have the 'smoking gun' – an unambiguous report that the Ndwandwe sold off slaves to the Bay at this point in time. Nevertheless, I think it's safe to say that slaving was the most important factor in stimulating the kinds of attacks being made by the Ndwandwe conglomerate on their neighbours. They were after more than just cattle for personal enrichment. The dynamics involved so closely resemble those of the early 1820s and later, when clearly documented slavers worked the Bay area, that this conclusion is all but unavoidable.

THE SHATTERING OF THE BOTTLE

Matiwane's praises lament: 'If he were not found by the Ndwandwe, He would be found by the Nxumalo.'[56] Yet Matiwane was no helpless victim of Zwide's attacks. He had built up a sturdy, partly militarised polity himself. Despite the vigour of the latest assault, the Ngwane weren't wiped out. Matiwane was able to lead a large Ngwane group away with remarkable cohesion. They maintained an indomitable military punch. This kind of capacity hadn't been developed overnight: it must have been in existence for a while. Though taking severe casualties, they fended Zwide off and shifted westwards. Nor were the Ngwane about to *khonza* feebly to anyone. They descended disastrously on the Hlubi, who were numerously but loosely settled along the Mzinyathi river.

Wright argues that the attack happened no earlier than 1815;[57] James Stuart thought that it happened around 1820.[58] For reasons that will become clear, I'd say that it was probably 1816.

It may not have been the first raid from the Ngwane that the Hlubi had suffered. Fynn claimed that the Ngwane marauded in the area north of the Mfolozis' headwaters for a period of ten years.[59] Possibly both Bhungane, Dingiswayo's old friend, and his son-successor Mthimkhulu, were attacked at different times, as they are sometimes conflated.[60] Though the Ngwane intermarried with the Hlubi, they weren't on particularly good terms with them.[61] This is captured in a story in which Mthimkhulu succumbs (like Dingiswayo) to splashing his semen unwisely about: some Ngwane girls seduced him, then took the sperm off to a renegade Hlubi doctor named Zulu kaMafu to bewitch. The result was that – like Dingiswayo later – Mthimkhulu waved away his attendants and retreated to a garden at a place called Ejiyaneni – where there just happened to be some concealed companies of Ngwane warriors . . .[62]

No doubt there were more far-reaching political conflicts at work, too. There's a suggestive hint that slavers may have reached the Hlubi themselves before this: a meeting between Mthimkhulu and three white men, *izinkawu* (a word also used to describe monkeys – and albinos). They were dressed 'like Scotch troops', the informant thought; the sun scorched them; they must have come from the Cape. But they would more likely have come from Delagoa Bay.[63]

In any event, this particular Ngwane attack on the Hlubi was catastrophic. It was, the informant MABONSA said, 'like the breaking of a bottle into a thousand fragments'.[64] It was an *izwekufa*, a state of ruin, literally 'a country of death'. Sections of the loosely integrated Hlubi scattered in various directions. Some went north to rejoin older family connections; some, under Mpangazitha kaBhungane, went across the Drakensberg and into the Caledon valley; some drifted as far as Matatiele in the present-day Eastern Cape. Some, under Maranqa, stayed where they were, and *khonza*'d Matiwane as the new force for stability in the area. (Given this information, let's not exaggerate even this *izwekufa*. Even the Ndwandwe's comparatively fierce attacks probably only shunted survivors off a matter of tens of kilometres before they settled on some or other available land to rebuild, replant crops, and raid on their own account.) Most importantly for our story, some Hlubi, including the dead chieftain Mthimkhulu's sons Mndebele, Mananga and Ntambana, headed south to *khonza* Shaka. They would form the nucleus of the iziYendane *ibutho*, a ruthless group who would act for a time as Shaka's shock-troops. (Since the iziYendane participated in Shaka's confrontation with the Ndwandwe in 1819, the Hlubi break-up can at least be securely dated to 1818 or before.)

This highlights an aspect of Shaka's rule that is badly underplayed in the literature: the emerging Zulu polity as a haven. Even in these early years, Shaka was coming to be seen less as a threat than as a stabilising influence; a leader who quelled minor squabbles in order to present a safer front to the bigger threat. Zwide, it is said, chased a lot of people into Shaka's arms, including some of his own Ndwandwe.[65] We do know of one Ndwandwe who ran south to *khonza* Shaka around this time: Mpangazitha kaMncumbata (who is not to be confused with Mpangazitha kaBhungane of the Hlubi). He was possibly accompanied by others, including his brother Kokela.[66] Mpangazitha later became an important Zulu *induna*, commanding the Fasimba regiment.[67]

This growing stability was captured in a saying, 'Bellow, beast, you who will never leave this place.' This saying, according to MKANDO, 'did not exist until Shaka's reign. People felt secure; no other state would dare to attack.'[68]

But Shaka was not entirely secure yet.

MOVING SOUTH

Dingiswayo's and Shaka's efforts on their northern borders along the two Mfolozi rivers seem to have been primarily a holding operation. They involved groups who were, like the Buthelezi, mostly already relatively friendly. However, the two needed further resources, and so they turned their attention more acquisitively to the south. Here, a string of rather more difficult prospects faced them. From west to east, in a chain between the Mhlathuze and Thukela rivers, lived the southern branch of the Khumalo, the Sithole, the Thembu, the Chunu, the Mkhize (or eMbo), the Ngcobo and, at the coastal end of the chain, the formidable Qwabe. Just a little closer to home base were the Langeni.

Shaka's relationship with his mother's people is the site of another hoary misapprehension of the mythology. Because Shaka was bullied as a boy amongst the Langeni, the myth goes, he bitterly lined the whole tribe up and slaughtered them. This gave rise to the legend of 'Tatiyana Gorge', which Shaka was supposed to have tried to fill up with Langeni corpses. Henry Rider Haggard gave the tale even more romantic currency in his novel *Nada the Lily*. However, since there *was* no bullying, there was no need for vengeance. The story is nonsense.

Whether Shaka moved to incorporate the Langeni first amongst these southern polities we don't know, though it makes geographical sense. It would have been logical for him to cement an alliance with his mother's people first. Despite occasional differences, the Langeni had collaborated with the Zulu for a long time before: they were so close that they used to bring fire for each other (*okhelana umlilo*). Probably, as Fynn related, the Langeni 'freely submitted in the expectation of receiving favourable treatment', their daughter Nandi having 'taken charge of Shaka's household'.[69] A Shakan onslaught was more rumour than fact, as implied by the experience of Mpitikazi, a Langeni man. Mpitikazi's son Baleka relates the story:

> [Shaka] hunted my father Mpitikazi because he had told the Langeni people of his mother's house to flee, for Shaka was coming to kill them. Shaka heard that Mpitikazi had said this, causing the Langeni to run away. He sent out an *impi* to kill him. Mpitikazi fled; but there was no place to run away to. A person would simply wander about in the land until he was eaten by wild animals. . . . Father climbed into a tree. The *impi* searched and searched for him, but did not see him. They gave up. He ate filth from the river; he no longer knew food. He slept in the forests.
>
> He then went to the place of Mbopa kaSitayi, and did not appear at the Great One's place. Then he was sent by Sitayi to the king himself. And he went, because he had been found, and was afraid to refuse. He saw that there was no help for it, for Sitayi would kill him. So he went off, travelling alone, knowing that he was going to die.
>
> He arrived and went into the cattle-kraal to the *izinduna*, to Ngqengelele. He walked forward reluctantly and limply to the upper end of the cattle-kraal; the *izinduna* were sitting inside.
>
> Shaka came out of his hut. He said, 'I think I know this person, my Zulu. Look at this red-skinned fellow; I would say it is Mpitikazi.' Then his mother Nandi came out. Reciting Shaka's praises, she said to him, 'Surely you will not kill Mpitikazi? What is Mpitikazi that you should kill him, he who is just a dog?' Shaka said, 'Go fellow, you with the little red ears. Your "mother" has saved you. Go, genet of the wilderness that outwitted the dogs.'[70]

The story is virtually a parable of the non-destruction of the Langeni, indeed of the relationship as a whole: initial apprehension, unnecessary flight, reconciliation, and incorporation.

This is not to say that the relationship remained totally trouble-free. At some point early in Shaka's reign, he and his Langeni cousin Makhedama, now *inkosi*, fell out. Possibly it was a result of Shaka trying to exert a new regime of dominance. The spark was said to be an insulting song that some Langeni unwisely uttered at one of those fateful *umjadu* dances:

Give us the he-goat, the he-goat of the daytime!
The people say, 'He-goat, lie down.'
So it lay down, it lay down, *e-ya-he!*
What is this? I see the friends roving about.
They said, 'Ha! Let the concubine rove about at the place of Mcube.'
We said, 'Because we were roving about with the Abawane,
It was said they had run away.'
As for us, we are rejected at the place of the Langeni
While other men are carrying off cattle.
So it was we who were gored in the hand,
We shall be given a he-goat . . .'[71]

Whatever this meant at the time – and it seems to contain dark hints of rejection, of competition for cattle – Shaka is said to have taken offence. He attacked. Makhedama beat him off. Shaka attacked again and was once more repulsed. For his third attempt (NGIDI, our Langeni informant at this point, is fond of things happening in threes), Shaka enlisted the help of the Qwabe and of Sinqila of the Nyuswa. Makhedama prudently withdrew to the shelter of the Nkhandla forest, or perhaps sent most of his people there while he dug himself in behind some stone enclosures down on the Mhlathuze river. Shaka's men went into the Nkhandla, drubbed the resistance there, and made off with some incidental cattle. A further attack on the Mhlathuze stronghold was repulsed. Having run out of steam and of options, Shaka went home. If this account is at all accurate, it shows how short the Zulu's military stamina was at this time.[72]

Makhedama was sufficiently rattled, however, to send a message to Shaka: 'If you kill the people who follow me, I shall pass on beyond you.' By which he meant that he would, with at least some of his followers, go and *khonza* the next best bet: Zwide.

This temporary and partial dispersal – and the eventual return – may be what's figured in the following delightful story. Having scattered (a few of) the Langeni, Shaka

> felt sorry for what he had done, and sent all the orphans to be carried off to the Mthethwa district, where he himself had grown up. The country was pleasant, he said, and they could get nice curds for their children. They were accordingly accommodated there. But one day a lion began to roar near their cattle, which all ran into the temporary kraal. This was in broad daylight. The men came and started to sing various ceremonial songs in honour of the lion, for according to belief the lion was their chief. The lion went to the back of the kraal and began roaring. The cattle then went out and moved off, and the women, having packed up all their belongings, moved after them, laden and leading their children. They were followed by the men, and last came the lion. On and on they went until sunset, paying no attention to the lion, fearing nothing. The lion, after all, was their chief. At sunset the lion moved ahead of the cattle, turned them back, and they grouped together. The lion pounced on a beast and killed it, but did not eat it; it left it to be eaten by the people.
>
> This went on day by day until the party reached their old lands by the Mhlatuze. Their arrival, and the peculiar circumstances, were reported to Shaka, who selected many cattle to be slaughtered in honour of the lion, the chief. The lion then, for the first time, killed a cow to eat itself. Shaka said, 'Woh! They have been fetched by their chief. I thought I was sending them to a good place, but he does not want them to leave their old lands.' He then allowed them to live on their old lands, where they remain to this day.[73]

If nothing else, this legend shows Shaka to have been quite flexible. He also continued to use Langeni manpower throughout his reign. At least one Langeni warrior, Mpukane kaMbandakazana of the Magwaza section, is recorded as a member of Dingane's Mkhulutshane *ibutho*.[74] Nxazonke and Mbikwana kaMbhengi, both Nandi's brothers and variously credited with roles in Shaka's childhood, also survived throughout as prominent individuals under Shaka.[75] Both were present, for instance, at Nandi's burial at kwaBulawayo,[76] and Mbikwana may have gone with Sotobe on Shaka's delegation to the Cape Colony in mid-1828.[77] One Langeni girl, a great-granddaughter of Mbhengi, is recorded as being in Shaka's *isigodlo*.[78] Ndikindi, Mpande's younger sister, married Mbikwana's son Vokoba, testament to how integrated these peoples became.[79] They were neither wiped out in a holocaust, nor assimilated to vanishing-point.[80] In fact, the Langeni still cohered to the extent that, as we'll detail in due course, Makhedama felt justified in trying to reassert his independence. It would cost him his life.

The Langeni were sometimes loosely associated with another southern conglomerate of little groups, including the Qadi, the Nyuswa, the Ngongoma and others, who collectively thought of themselves as Ngcobo. This was probably the second group to be dealt with. Shaka seems to have needed both Nyuswa and Qwabe assistance to get the upper hand over the Langeni; and – if we can trust anything in the traditions' garbled sequences – he seems also to have attacked those Ngcobo groups at much later stages as well. They were recalcitrant, needing constant coercing into submission.[81]

There is, in sum, no single discernible sequence to these groups' deeply entangled histories.[82]

The Mthethwa experienced long-standing trouble with the Ngcobo, particularly with the Nyuswa segment. Either before or after Shaka's accession – and quite possibly during both periods – Dingiswayo despatched Shaka to try to extract allegiance from the Nyuswa.[83] Of particular importance seems to have been Mthethwa intervention, possibly at the request of the Nyuswa themselves, in a succession dispute between Sihayo and Mgabhi, two sons of the chief Mapholoba. Such requests for mediation were common – even though the consequences were sometimes fatal for one or another of the parties. In this case, the antagonists were said to have been quarrelling over some castor-oil seeds; this subsequently became the subject of a Zulu war song. (Doubtless it was a little more serious than that.) Shaka is said to have taken Sihayo's side, dispersing Mgabhi's adherents and depriving them of their cattle. Sihayo, however, declined to take or to hand over his share of the booty, so Shaka had him killed.[84] The Nyuswa were thereafter firmly kept in check by having a Zulu-Mthethwa *umuzi* or military post established amongst them, the iNtontela. This effectively became an *ibutho* and, as one

informant puts it, all the Nyuswa 'became iNtontela'.[85] This was probably
one of the earliest examples of the main strategy that Shaka would use to
command his fragmentary subject peoples.[86]

The Qadi, another Ngcobo branch, voluntarily *khonza*'d Shaka when
under Dube kaSilwana.[87] Other groups, such as the Sithole, were evidently
friendly, but Shaka was in no position to move towards incorporating them
all yet. This was even more the case with the bigger groups, such as the
Thembu, the Chunu, the Mkhize and the Qwabe. While both Dingiswayo
and Shaka almost certainly had relationships with these people in these early
days, their full nature isn't known. They were all distracted by the growing
pressures from the north. Even the sizeable Chunu polity, feeling the ripples
of the Ngwane assault on the Hlubi, moved cautiously southwards a short
distance, across the Thukela and on to the headwaters of the Mvoti (near
present-day Greytown). Macingwane's Chunu had a history of squabbling
indecisively with Senzangakhona,[88] and with their other neighbours, the
Mphungose,[89] the Ndlovu and the Bayeni.[90] Macingwane, like Shaka,
spawned legends of both ferocity and stability, if his praises are anything to
go by:

> Croucher like a beast sneaking into a maize-field . . .
> Antheap that is pale amongst the brown burnt ones;
> Large headland of rocks at Nkandla,
> That could shelter elephants in bad weather.[91]

Macingwane was notorious for murdering his own sons, fearing their rivalry.[92]
One son, Mfusi, grew alarmed and *khonza*'d Shaka. Macingwane sent Shaka
an ox, hoping that he would send the boy back. Shaka refused – and kept
the ox.[93]

The Chunu's strongest connections may well have been further to the
north. MAYINGA offers the interesting clue that the Chunu were apparently
in the habit of calling on a diviner from the Gaza people, up the coast near
St Lucia, a man named Mnisi. For reasons not made clear, Mnisi was killed
off on his way home by a Chunu *impi*. His women and children were captured.
Other Gaza scattered to the Zulu, some to Sotshangane.[94] MAYINGA thought
that this scattering of the Gaza happened before Shaka's reign, though the
main movement certainly happened much later, after Shaka's defeat of Zwide.

He may be conflating events. But his account also echoes an allusion in Macingwane's praises, to the effect that Macingwane 'captured the cattle of the traders'.[95] And one of Macingwane's *amabutho* was named the abaThwa. 'Vatwahs' was the generic name given by whites at Delagoa Bay to inland marauders. It's thin, but suggestive of at least a possibility that a trade route from the north ran through this territory, and that this was a factor in the violence and militarisation here, too – a violence entirely independent of that generated by Shaka.

Still, there might have been an early Zulu-Chunu spat that helped to precipitate the move to the Mvoti river; it would have been before Zwide first attacked Shaka, and before Shaka moved south against the Qwabe.[96] One informant thought that the scrap happened at Thaleni, just west of the upper Mhlathuze river, on the eastern fringes of the original Chunu territory. Only three Chunu were killed.[97] Such a minor fracas would hardly have by itself impelled them into a wholesale move. In fact, Shaka may have attacked only one section of the Chunu, the Ndawonde, who had unaccountably captured the chief of Shaka's southern neighbours the Cube – and the Cube 'worked Shaka's *itusi*', his brass, for him.[98] Several Ndawonde would be involved in the big 'Mvuzane fight' against Zwide in 1819, indicating that at least some must have *khonza*'d Shaka by then.

The main regional pressure now, in about 1817, was emanating not from the Mthethwa-Zulu alliance, but from the Ndwandwe. The northern hammer was descending again.

'THE WHOLE COUNTRY WAS UPSIDE-DOWN'

The sequence of actual attacks from the Ndwandwe, and how they dovetailed with Shaka's campaigns to the south, will probably always remain elusive. NDLOVU's comment captures something of the upheavals of the time:

> Shortly after Shaka's accession, Zwide attacked Dingiswayo; then disturbances broke out in every direction. Men were sent one way, only to be sent another after returning from a bloody and successful mission. Presently the whole country was upside-down, and it continued until subdued by Shaka's energetic action.[99]

Informants seldom agree, and often telescope what must have been separate battles, sometimes producing geographically impossible contortions. Only the clashes with the Zulu emerge from the traditions in any detail. At first the Zulu fared badly. They are said to have been defeated *twice* by the Ndwandwe's amaPhela and amaGugu regiments at Kwa Gqokli hill, on the White Mfolozi.[100]

(Stuart and Bryant write the name as 'kwaGqori'. E.A. Ritter would pick up on the name as a venue for his imaginary battle in *Shaka Zulu*, in which he depicts the Ndwandwe as decisively defeated. Although you will find this battle re-inscribed in detail in every school and university textbook, encyclopaedia and museum display in South Africa, it did not happen. It is a non-battle.[101])

The Ndwandwe burned many of the Zulu *imizi*, including Mbelebeleni and Shaka's very own *ilawu*, his personal enclosure, at iNtontela. Shaka was obliged to retreat all the way across the Thukela. It is possibly this withdrawal that was remembered by some as a kind of 'scorched earth' retreat: the Zulu burned their own fields, drove off their cattle, and hid their grain in pits covered with hides and earth, to deprive the Ndwandwe, who were known to travel light on supplies.[102] What happened to the women and children is not explained.[103]

It may have been on this retreat that the Mdadasa *ibutho*, commanded by one Lukhilimba, made some kind of tactical error and clashed with Zwide's forces, getting mauled. Shaka was deliberately avoiding battle. When he heard of the damaging mistake, he angrily banished Lukhilimba to the wilderness. Lukhilimba went to the lower Mzimkhulu with a whole section of the Mdadasa – only to be welcomed back much later.[104]

Shaka had to swim across the Thukela at eDhlokweni with his troops and a lot of cattle. He came to Magaye and the Cele, warning them not to try helping themselves to his livestock. It may be at this point that he asserted himself, of necessity, over the Maphumulo, killing their chief Mthimkhulu kaDibandhlela (not to be confused with Mthimkhulu kaBhungane of the Hlubi), and leaving his own appointee, Nodokwana, in charge of them.[105]

For all his truculence, Shaka was weak. He was trapped between the hammer of the Ndwandwe and the anvil of the big polities along the Thukela, and was seriously displaced from his central lands and resources. His own adherents back in the central Zulu area were loosening their ties: it was probably at around this point that Makhedama of the Langeni left and went to *khonza* Zwide.[106] Very likely, too, Shaka wanted security in the Nkhandla forests, close to Qwabe territory.[107] It was probably now that he first called upon the Qwabe for help.

PHAKATHWAYO AND THE QWABE

The Qwabe were not to be trifled with. They had pushed several substantial polities, including the Cele and the Thuli, further down the coast, had centralised to a relatively high degree, and had a number of *amabutho* at their disposal. A number of these units had been lumped into a huge body named the iziNkonde – so huge, related KAMBI with some exaggeration, 'that if it began to enter the *umuzi* in the morning it would take until sunset to pass through'.[108] There were also the Izengqana, the Izilinda, the uBede, and others.[109] Phakathwayo boasted a number of *imizi* whose names we know: eMtandeni, eNtoyeyeni, eyiDedeni, eNdlekezeni, eMaganukeni, and oDwini.[110] Phakathwayo's importance is further reflected in the richness and length of his *izibongo*: he was the 'calf that is like a white-spined ox, the muscles of which are as hard as a dried hide; it overcomes even those who are offensive'.[111]

However, there were internal rifts in the Qwabe polity, too, which presented an opening for Shaka. As we have already seen, the problems dated back to the days of Phakathwayo's father and predecessor, Khondlo, and even before. The early Qwabe seem to have emerged as an awkward welding of various lineages, some local, some 'foreigners', some drawing perilously close to inbreeding. Incorporating them and falsifying the genealogical links was a way that the ruling lineage found to keep power just a little more concentrated in their own hands.[112] The result was a polity rather more centralised than most at the time, but which hadn't entirely overcome divisions dating far back in genealogical history. The Makhanya section of the Qwabe, for example, had set themselves up on the south side of the Thukela, naming themselves after Makhanya himself. They were, or became, a junior lineage; they had to ask Phakathwayo for permission to hold their *umkhosi* first-fruits ceremony. But they retained pretensions to greater independence, with distinct origins: 'The Makhanya jumped over royalty', they claimed.[113] Before Shaka's accession Makhanya quarrelled with Phakathwayo, who crossed the Thukela to attack, saying he would 'cause the gourd of his place to be filled'.[114] But the Makhanya successfully rebuffed him.

Not long after that, Phakathwayo scuffled with his brother Nomo; Phakathwayo was obliged to take refuge in the bush for so long that he ended up eating raw hides. Khondlo, their father, was still alive but apparently ineffectual. He had nominated Nomo as heir, but Nomo's mother was a Mthethwa – a sister of Dingiswayo's – and some Qwabe objected to this connection. Nomo went to Dingiswayo for mediation. It failed. For some reason, Khondlo also expected the Makhanya to help sort it out. They didn't. Khondlo fumed: 'What do you mean by looking on?' The Makhanya chieftain Mnengwa armed himself, came to Khondlo's assistance, and chased Nomo off. The Mthethwa-backed counter-offensive from Nomo failed. This was when Nomo joined Shaka permanently in Mthethwa country.[115] As we'll see shortly, Phakathwayo's other brothers grumbled in the shadows.

Other Qwabe would cross over to Shaka, too, most importantly Sophane kaMncinci and Nqetho kaMncinci,[116] who came to *khonza* Shaka just before the big confrontation with Phakathwayo happened. And, of course, the famous Khomfiya.

For the moment, in 1817 or so, it was Shaka who was looking for help. He asked Phakathwayo for grain, obviously not having had the time or opportunity to plant any.[117] Another account figures the contact as a bead exchange. Phakathwayo starts an argument by asking Shaka for beads, the fine *ingwele* beads from the Nhlengwa (a derogatory name for the Tsongas; this may be some indication that trade matters were involved). Shaka gives the messengers some beads, with due praises; Phakathwayo responds in kind. Phakathwayo then asks for a shield and for 'some of the fat cattle of Mahlabathini'. Shaka gives him some; Phakathwayo sings the customary praises. But then, not only do the Qwabe insult the paucity of Zulu numbers; they accuse the Zulu of rubbing nasty *intelezi* medicines into cuts at the base of the cows' tails! Shaka responds, interestingly, by planting a settlement in Qwabe territory, an *ikhanda* – more of a military barracks than a homestead. This may have been the rebuilt Mbelebeleni, presumably meant as an interim base, named after the original that Zwide had ransacked. The Qwabe resented this impertinence, and burned it down. The Zulu rebuilt it. The Qwabe burned it down. Shaka himself came, and ushered in the final act.[118]

The more common version of this build-up is rather different – and also less credible. It involves one of those dreaded *umjadu* dances, which you are beginning to recognise, I'm sure, as a metaphorical way of saying that old friends have fallen out for some reason. This is how one version goes. Shaka proposes a dance. Phakathwayo sneers:

> How do you hope to surpass me, son of Senzangakhona? I will not dance with a man whose forces are no greater in number than the few beads needed for a necklace, with that little Ntungwa fellow from upcountry, whose penis stands erect.[119]

Or, even more colourfully:

> The little Nguni who wears as a penis-cover the fruit-shell used for snuffboxes! Where did he get an *impi* from? Is the *impi* from up-country like the rain? It is nothing but a little string of beads that doesn't even reach the ears. The Nguni who, when mixing food, holds it in his left hand and his spoon in the right, and has to hit the dog with his head![120]

Nevertheless, Phakathwayo agrees to the dance. Shaka goes to Mthandeni, Phakathwayo's *umuzi*, with his warriors. No assegais are allowed, so they hide them in a nearby river, arriving dressed only in their dancing-costumes of ox-tails and headbands worn so thick that their bodies are completely, respectfully hidden. Shaka's men dance first, and dance well. Then the more numerous Qwabe dance. Phakathwayo shrills, 'We have stabbed them!' meaning that the Qwabe have danced better. Already stung, Shaka is further insulted when Phakathwayo says, 'I killed a beast for you yesterday, son of Senzangakhona, and won't do so today, so you might as well go home.' Shaka pretends to leave, but retrieves the weaponry from the river, waits until dark, and goes straight to Phakathwayo's hut and kills him.[121]

In another version, Shaka makes use of a roving medicine man named Mqayana, an Nzuza who has already been chased out by the Qwabe. Shaka asks if his medicines might kill Phakathwayo. Mqayana thinks that they might. Shaka proposes the dance, and is duly insulted. Mqayana mixes Qwabe excrement with hyena dung, dirt from the dance-floor and various *intelezi* medicines, secretly putting them in grass baskets sunk in the Qwabe drinking pools and releasing infected cockroaches around the Qwabe huts. Shaka despatches an *impi*, taking the Qwabe by surprise. Phakathwayo is found seated at his ekuDabukeni home with only a small section of his Abatungwa *ibutho*. The latter try to fight but, bewitched by Mqayana's medicines, they begin to mess themselves as soon as the Zulu heave into sight; their strength fails; they sink to the ground. Phakathwayo is captured; Shaka leaps over him; he shortly dies of pure fear and humiliation.[122]

Or, there is indeed a fight of greater or lesser intensity with Qwabe soldiers, with Phakathwayo escaping to hide in a grove of palm trees, only to be discovered, huddled and alone. Then he is leaped over, and dies, as above.[123] If there *was* a struggle (there's one tradition of the Qwabe being defeated at a fight on kwaHlokohloko hill, near Eshowe[124]), casualties were probably minimal. In one variant, Shaka does not actually want Phakathwayo to die, even sacrifices cattle for him, but to no avail.[125]

In this welter of versions, only one or two things are certain. Firstly, there was *no* massive slaughter of Qwabe, with Shaka trying to fill up a whole donga with corpses, as an aberrant version avers.[126] Nevertheless, this story became one of the staples of Shaka's alleged brutality, and was also sometimes attached to the Langeni, as we've seen. The second certain thing is that, although the majority of Qwabe seem to have *khonza*'d without further ado, directed by the *induna* Sikwayo,[127] Shaka was faced with a fearsomely complex task in trying to incorporate the Qwabe into his own rather shaky polity.

Indeed, there's something of a paradox here: how could the well-organised but nevertheless fugitive Zulu have so rapidly asserted themselves over the much more sizeable Qwabe? Partly (as the various stories attest) by Shaka's apparently boundless cunning – but also through a hidden factor, one that has been buried by Zulu-centred traditions. The hidden force is surely the weight of the Mthethwa, who must have been as keen to keep Shaka in support as they were to exert long-cherished dominance over their southern neighbours.

Happily – and despite this obvious gap in the records – the process of the Qwabe's assimilation is one of the best-documented we have.

A struggle ensued, involving Phakathwayo's own potential heirs. He had no sons, so the contest was between his several grumbling brothers. Godolozi, an older brother of Phakathwayo's, had at first been sidelined by his father Khondlo when he favoured Nomo, but in compensation had been given some status under Phakathwayo himself. Although Godolozi came into greater prominence after Nomo was bundled off (to play no further part in the saga; he apparently died in Mthethwa country), Phakathwayo still held on to power. When Phakathwayo died, however, Godolozi, Godide and Vukubulwayo, all brothers of Phakathwayo's, took themselves off to Zwide to *khonza*. Just to muddy the waters further, Nqetho, another son of Khondlo, and Sopane kaMncinci, Nqetho's uncle, had probably already gone over to Shaka.[128] Their flight was figured as the result of an impenetrably tangled disagreement over what wives they could or couldn't have.[129] Nqetho, as a member of the senior house, now argued that *he* should take over the Qwabe.

Nevertheless, when it came to the crunch, Shaka preferred to follow protocol. Godolozi was the rightful heir.[130] As he was senior, he had also *ngena*'d – formally taken over – Phakathwayo's wives.[131] But Godolozi and the others had gone to Zwide, although they weren't there long. Zwide asked them, 'Since there is more than one principal here, who is the chief?' Some of the Qwabe men who had come with them, indicated the youngest, Vukubulwayo. Zwide couldn't see it: since Godolozi was the eldest, it surely ought to be him. Despite this mark of favour, Godolozi decided not to stay there. Maybe he got nervous about the Ndwandwe's general suspicion of these Qwabe intruders: they were, the Ndwandwe sneered, unnaturally fond of warming themselves over a fire. Leaving some Qwabe sticking it out with Zwide, Godolozi returned to take his chances with Shaka. So did Godide and others.

'So you have come back, have you?' said Shaka to Godolozi. 'Why did you pass by me? Because you regard me as having murdered your house, and shed blood!' Godolozi admitted that this was true. Well, said Shaka, there were no heirs to Phakathwayo's domain, no sons, so Godolozi and the others should return to the Qwabe lands, take wives, and procreate – which they did.[132] Shaka gave Godolozi a large tuft of made-up feathers (*idlokolo*) as a mark of friendly respect.[133] (Nevertheless, it seems that Godolozi, Godide and Vukubulwayo were all assassinated by Shaka eventually; Godolozi because he himself was erratically killing off others amongst the Qwabe.[134])

Thus it was Nqetho who became Shaka's client-chief over the Qwabe territories.

'FAR-SEEING METHODS'?

The Mthethwa-Zulu incorporation of the Qwabe shows Shaka to be a tough and canny politician, but no more. Everything he did was tightly constrained by circumstances, ranging from his subordination to Dingiswayo to the exigencies of climate. He succeeded as far as he did because his strategies made cultural and political sense to his supporters, not because he was a visionary of near-mystical powers, as the legends (like the following) would have it:

> Had [any ordinary man] lived to be a hundred he and his kind would never have understood Shaka's far-seeing methods which had already begun to carve a nation from the raw bush.[135]

Even by Shaka's time there was probably not a great deal of 'raw bush' left. Centuries of settlement, grazing of livestock, burning, agricultural planting and path-making had modified the landscape of much of the region beyond recovery. Vast tracts of forest or thornveld had already been reduced to grassland. Of course, there was still a lot more bush than there is today, and many more elephants around to supply apparently insatiable white traders with ivory. In places the population was so thinly spread that white travellers, used to British or Dutch congestion, thought that the country was entirely empty. Yet such bush as persisted was already criss-crossed and patched with human influences, scarred and thinned by axe-blade, hoof, and tooth. The people lived with and through nature. Variations in season and rainfall had instant effects. Everything – absolutely everything – depended on a group's ability to feed, and feed off, cattle, wildlife, and crops. Vegetation, weather and terrain were paramount in every person's life. Ideologies, military systems, marriage ceremonies: all of these were shackled to the most important thing: the demands of the stomach. The margins were small; starvation was always close.

In any case, it is a peculiarly Western idea that a 'state' could or should be carved out of 'raw bush'. It's a mistake to think of the new polities in the Thukela-Phongolo catchment as somehow halfway to 'civilised' conurbations. Even the bigger settlements were still quite small and relatively mobile. It's also an error to think of a rigid distinction between 'wild' and 'tamed'. The bush was as much a resource as a threat. It provided wood for iron-smelting furnaces, monkey tails for soldiers' regalia, tusks for trade, and roots for essential medicines. Forests harboured leopards, but were also refuges in times of flight. Mountains hindered trade, but were great for defence. Whatever a 'state' was going to consist of or be organised by, it was always going to be commanded by three resources: fertile land to grow crops, grazing for cattle, and men and women to tend and defend them. In only a few cases – unless he were actually raiding *for* people, to enslave them – would a chieftain want to destroy productive centres of a society. This was even more the case when the fundamental stance was one of defence against an outside aggressor.

Shaka, in short, didn't have much room to manoeuvre. He had to have access to resources – cattle and agricultural lands – and he had to have people to fight and to farm for him. His alliances and his attacks were designed to ensure both. His allegedly 'far-seeing methods' were mostly, by necessity, extensions of practices already in existence. Though in the first few years he was partly on the run, he also had time to begin the foundations of a stronger polity. The Qwabe case highlights some of these foundations.

The primary method at this stage was to continue the practice of calling up *amabutho*, groups of men who could both fight and work. Shaka inherited some *amabutho* from his father: the isiKlebhe, the Nobamba, the Mbelebele, and the isiPhezi. When he came to power, these were already ageing, and probably had to be augmented by youngsters. The members of the isiPhezi, perhaps amongst others, were obliged to cut off the headrings that signified their status as men eligible to be married. This was almost certainly not a nasty prank on Shaka's part, as it is often portrayed, but a necessary move to prevent for a time the interference of marriages and the splitting-off of new families. Every fighting man was desperately needed.

At the same time, Shaka started collecting new *amabutho*, increasingly on an age-group basis, but sometimes with an ethnic core. His first experiment was the Fasimba. The name signified the distant haziness of hills. They would be distinguished by their all-white shields, and by incisions cut in the calves of their legs.[136] Wright and Webb are of the opinion that the Fasimba were *butwa*'d in 1818, but this seems to me to be somewhat late.[137]

The Jibingqwange followed the Fasimba in age, so were probably *butwa*'d the following year, just as Ndwandwe raids were intensifying. They were given speckled grey shields and were also, having just attained headring status, ordered to cut them off again; they were to *kleza*, to 'drink from the udder like boys again', said Shaka. This was a way of saying that they would have to be ready for a long fight before they could attain mature independence.[138] The manipulation of eligibility had always been a mode of chiefly control, but Shaka toughened and broadened the process. It worked something like this:

> A man asks for a girl. . . . She is a mature woman (*iqikiza*), but has not put on the topknot. The man would pick out a beast. This is known as 'gathering' (*ukuka*), choosing. The beast is taken to the king. The man will begin by taking the beast for the putting on of the topknot, and then he begins to *lobola*, after the king's consent has been granted.
>
> Men act with cunning when they 'gather' a girl. They say, 'She is my wife's sister (*umlam' wami*)'; they say this to the king when going to ask for her . . . . Girls are *ibuto* of the king, for they are not yet *jutshwa*'d [released to marry]. No man without headrings (*izinsizwa*) would ever be married, even if old. Only mature men (*amadoda*), those with headrings, could take a girl. Only in exceptional cases, to raise up seed in a big kraal, the king might give a man without a headring permission to put on the headring and marry. No *lobola* could begin before the king's sanction had been granted.[139]

The process was perhaps not as stifling as it sounds. Some were allowed by Shaka to take *izingodosi* – 'betrothed girls' – but not formally to marry. And many men took wives illegally; it was called *guqaing*.[140] Nevertheless, at least in those areas centrally under his control, Shaka was able to call men up to fight and, just as importantly, he was able to manipulate their marital arrangements and geographical location, in a more rigorous manner than before. He could 'plant' them in semi-colonised areas, in homesteads of their own – *amakhanda* – to keep an eye on the client-chieftains. Far from displacing people from their familiar lands, then, Shaka's strategy was to get them to stay. Over the established networks of chiefly and family-head authority he laid a parallel network under appointed *izinduna*. Building an *ikhanda* in Qwabe territory was probably the first in a series of such moves.

Shaka was seldom in a position to impose his will simply by force. It was much more a question of balancing and playing localised powers off one another.

Other units were also *butwa*'d – in what order is unclear. Shaka *butwa*'d the Dhlangubo, for instance, and 'threw it into' the older iNtontela *ibutho*. Though an early unit (regarded by some as Shaka's earliest), it included at least one Chunu warrior, of the Ndawonde section, Zembe kaNgobe.[141] (It is frequently difficult to tell from the sources whether a name refers to a larger *ibutho*, or just to a section of one. Sometimes names were changed: the Mbonambi became the Zibolela, for example.[142]) Certain *amabutho* were brought in from elsewhere, and had an ethnic slant. The iziYendane members brought their name from their Hlubi homeland in about 1816. The Mgumanqa was formed the following year largely of Qwabe: their service was part of the tribute that they had to pay their new overlord. It was not mere servitude: as a sense of militaristic pride was enhanced, names and finery were becoming more important. The iziYendane's all-red shields would become widely feared; the Mgumanqa, their red shields spotted with white, enjoyed the resonance of their name and *ithakazelo* praises – 'that which stands threateningly in the patch of burnt grass, the Nomandela which is at Mateko'.[143] As in most such organisations, it is difficult to know where coercion ends and loyalty begins.

By 1818 or 1819, when Shaka confronted Zwide's Ndwandwe in the first really pitched battle, he had at least four more units: the Dhlangezwa, slightly junior to the Mgumanqa; the Zibolela; the Ngqobolondo; and the Mnkangala. These dozen or so *amabutho* would remain the core of his military strength throughout his reign. The elevation and distribution of *izinduna* would, as we'll see, become increasingly concentrated on an élite, tightly interrelated Zulu core, with a ring of semi-independent client-chiefs, such as Nqetho, around the centre.

In 1818, however, Shaka was displaced to the south of the gravesites of his forebears. Though many Zulu people doubtless remained pretty much where they were, or returned as quickly as they could after the marauding Ndwandwe bands had swept through, it would be a while before Shaka could re-colonise that heartland south of the White Mfolozi river.

'The bulls of the herd have met'

Turning points, c.1817–20

He finally succeeded in establishing a sort of *Zoolacratical* form of
government, (if I may so term it, for I do not know of anything
resembling it in either ancient or modern history), a form that defies
description or detail; that can neither be comprehended nor digested,
and such a one as gives protection to no living creature . . .
Nathaniel Isaacs, *Travels and Adventures in Eastern Africa* (1936, I 269).

We last saw Khomfiya kaNogandaya in Chapter 6 (see page 151), stepping
forward at Shaka's invitation to seize an assegai quivering, at once
dangerous and inviting, in the earth of the dancing-ground. It was the raiding-
season in 1817 or 1818. Shaka had tried to reoccupy his old home-site of
Mbelebeleni, and had rebuilt the others that Zwide had burned down.[1] But
now the Ndwandwe were advancing again in frightening numbers into
Mthethwa and Zulu territory.

As his warriors stabbed the air and chanted their boasts on that day,
Shaka whispered in Khomfiya's ear: 'Why are you silent, Khomfiya? If you
are silent, it may be that the army will have to retreat, and have to be sprinkled
with medicines for war all over again.'[2] With this encouragement, Khomfiya,
the obscure *inceku*, the personal menial, stepped forward, his hands still
smeared with cowdung. He may already have been involved in Shaka's lesser
campaigns. In fact, as a young *insizwa* he is said to have fought against
Macingwane of the Chunu, possibly on that first brush mentioned in Chapter
6, and against both the Mbatheni and the Zungu, smaller groups who had

khonza'd Shaka quite early.[3] Indeed, an *inceku* needed to have proved himself to be allowed so close to the *inkosi*. Now Khomfiya thrust his own old assegai into the ground and seized the new one. He cried out:

> These praises are mine! I 'choose' – I *qoma* – the warrior Mvundlana kaMenziwa; I shall stab before he does. I choose the warrior Sigwebana kaMudli; I shall stab before he does. I choose the warrior Magaju; I shall stab before he does. *Inkosi*, if any of these three warriors stab before I do you may put me to death. They will return with wounds in the back: mine will be in my chest.[4]

'Well,' rejoined Shaka, 'We will hear about that when the army returns.'

'KISI!'

Shaka gathered his warriors around to give them their instructions.

> He said, 'Let the army approach.' The sun was going down. He said, 'Now do you hear, men? Today we shall fight the fight of "Kisi".' (The fight was to take place by moonlight.) 'Call out, saying, "Kisi" once. Do not say it twice. If a man does not reply "Kisi", stab him; he will not be one of ours. You will hear one another this way.'[5]

Then, according to NDUNA, occurred one of the several legendary occasions on which Shaka's distinctive long, blue crane feather fell from his headband and stood quivering in the sand. He called, 'Cry out, "Ji! I have overcome Zwide!"' Klwana kaNgqengelele moved to take up the feather, but Shaka struck him away with the haft of his assegai, saying, 'Leave it, *mnawami*, my brother.' And then, astoundingly, a white python appeared at the feet of the men; it made for the feather and coiled itself around it. Shaka cried, 'Cry out, "Ji!"', and they did, and hammered enthusiastically on their shields.

Shaka gave command of his forces to Klwana kaNgqengelele. Khomfiya was apparently dissatisfied: he pointed out that Shaka had arranged the army in entirely the wrong order, with the younger men at the back, and the older men in front. He wanted to get out there and initiate the fight, make an *inhlakava*, spark them off. Consequently, Khomfiya took two *amabutho*, the uDlangezwa and the imiHehe, and sent them forward to provoke the fight, then to draw the enemy on by retreating. At this point – it was now nightfall – Khomfiya piled in; one moment he was there at the end of his line of troops, the next they heard him yell in the darkness: 'I have eaten, I, the heavens which thunder in the open!' In the mêlée, the Zulu warriors recognised each other by their 'Kisi' password.[6] It wasn't a foolproof strategy: Khomfiya still managed to stab one of his own men, one Mbazana, an *inceku* who failed to give the sign in the moonlight.[7]

The 'kisi' fight would become legendary, but we actually know very little about it. We don't know where it happened, or exactly when, how many men were involved, or what the casualties were. We don't know what the outcome was, apart from the insinuation that it was a Zulu victory. Perhaps it was.[8]

As for Shaka's 'military genius', forget everything that you've been told in the stories, have read in the textbooks, or have seen in the films. The 'kisi' fight is the solitary – the *only* – instance in all of the traditional and eyewitness literature of an original tactical idea coming from Shaka. And it is not a particularly earth-shattering one.

Anyway, this fight was where Khomfiya earned his first praises, which would in time be magnified into *izibongo* of considerable substance:

> Exploder like a flame of fire,
> Fly of great courage,
> He who exclaimed at the insulting language [Zwide's]
> That was directed against Shaka at Mbelebeleni . . .
> Antbear that digs a burrow in which it does not lie,
> Trampler across the burnt grass of the enemy,
> Giant that raided the Pondos,
> He who refused to be limited because he imposed no limit on himself.
> Huge chest on which tears were shed,
> Arm that defended the vitals
> From the warriors of Mzilikazi,
> Huge frame that was like Kranskop,
> Fire that raged like a furnace.[9]

These words would resound around the cattle-pens of the kwaBulawayo *umuzi*. Khomfiya would be renamed Zulu – Zulu kaNogandaya – one of the great figures of Shaka's reign. He is an excellent example of a protégé of Shaka's who sometimes seemed as much of a nuisance as a help. As we'll see, he excelled himself further against the Ndwandwe, and was involved in other campaigns, including against obstreperous members of his own Qwabe people. He was a man of the Mgumanqa *ibutho*. Shaka established him at some point at Ntshaseni, on the hill of Ndondakusuka, near the mouth of the Thukela, in the heart of Qwabe country.[10] He later became head *induna* at the Black Hlomendini *umuzi* under Nongalaza kaNondela, also in Qwabe country. Of medium height, barrel-chested, dark, eyebrows heavily jutting, he was awe-inspiring. If he called you, you immediately wondered what you'd done wrong. When he was angry, sitting out in the open catching flies and flinging them down one by one, people gazing at him even from a distance would find themselves filled with misgivings. He eventually acquired some 80 wives – or perhaps it was a mere 45.[11] Zulu was 'The rock of the one who killed the hyena; the one who stands menacingly in the place where the grass is newly burnt'. He ate alone; there was no one of sufficient rank or courage to eat with him.[12] He virtually made sure of this: if there was another *induna* making superior noises, Zulu kaNogandaya would scatter the man's forces and seize his cattle. Shaka couldn't, or wouldn't, do anything about this, saying, 'The son of Nogandaya has surpassed all other men. His name is known there where Sikhotha is, "Sikhotha, the long grass into which there is no entry".'[13]

Zulu was not always, perhaps, as secure or as heroic as his *izibongo* make out. If his grandson MANDHLAKAZI is to be believed, he would fearfully head off into the bush if there was a threat, and later come back dressed in his finery, having raided some other poor unfortunate and plundered his cattle. There's a story about how, despite his 'hardness of heart', he had the tables turned on him by one Sithunga, a brother-in-law, who marched into Zulu's Ntshaseni *umuzi*, ordered everybody about, including Zulu's own wives, and helped himself to a whole lot of food. Zulu couldn't do a thing.[14]

It's possible that this particular anecdote reflects something of the tensions within the Qwabe polity, which Zulu both stimulated and held in an uneasy balance. Zulu kaNogandaya became Shaka's semi-independent man in Qwabe country, an acolyte placed there to counterbalance Nqetho's authority.

Divide and rule – it was Shaka's number one method of exercising influence.

INCORPORATING THE QWABE

Nqetho himself rapidly became something of a favourite of Shaka's, and lived for a time at Shaka's own *umuzi*. One story relates how at first, when Shaka wanted to see him, he would simply yell for him. Nqetho would not, as Zulu protocol suggested he ought, call back; he would just silently come along when it suited him. Shaka remonstrated: 'Nqetho, what makes you fail to reply, when I call you, and I know you can hear me? Are you a dog?' Nqetho replied: 'I am deeply aggrieved, that seeing I am the son of Khondlo and you the son of Senzangakhona, that you should treat me like a dog in your own *umuzi*; I belong to the same tribe as yourself.' Shaka consulted his elders, Ngomane and Mdlaka. They said that Nqetho was in the right. From then on, Shaka wouldn't just shout for Nqetho, but would send a messenger to murmur in his ear, as befitted an important man.[15]

In another story meant to illustrate the same relationship, Shaka, having slaughtered some cattle, was said to have sent the head of a beast to Nqetho. Nqetho took this up and dumped it unceremoniously in front of Shaka's hut, refusing to eat meat that the ticks ate. Wasn't he the son of a king? Shaka admitted as much, and at once ordered the more appropriate rib-meat to be sent to him.[16]

Dealing with Nqetho was just one facet of the complicated task of getting the Qwabe to stay in one place and remain loyal. As a way of defusing opposition, Shaka incorporated other Qwabe more closely into his inner circle. One such man was Mbokazi kaMombo, a descendant of the Qwabe chief Khuzwayo. Mbokazi had apparently had the courage to question Phakathwayo's original insult about the Zulu – and he got his reward. On his way to attack Phakathwayo, Shaka stopped to visit at Mbokazi's tidy homestead; and after Phakathwayo's demise, Shaka called for Mbokazi, 'Tell him to come here with all his property, all his wives, come to be with me. Nothing of his is to go amiss.'[17]

An extension of the practice of incorporating such individuals was more subtle and long term. Shaka – and others – employed a technique that had long been in use, but now was put to grander purposes. The genealogies of the groups, particularly of the Qwabe, were progressively reworked in order to give the impression that they were really of the same family. The Zulu and Qwabe now claimed that they could trace themselves back to a common ancestor – Malandela – a figure so far back in 'history' that he had no praises and no gravesite. He was, in short, a myth. However, as a result of this notional ancestor, the upland Zulu and the lowland Qwabe could both start calling themselves 'ntungwa', or 'Suthu'. They could begin to forge a common identity. Despite being attacked by Shaka at one point, for instance, the somewhat maverick Makhanya branch of the Qwabe would later boast that they 'ruled with Shaka'.[18]

This process of assimilation didn't happen overnight, or smoothly, or completely. Shaka never would entirely overcome Qwabe resistance to being swallowed up, or entirely quash genealogies that didn't agree with the 'official' one. Hence, in the traditions, you find insuperable contradictions in the genealogies that people recall. These are signs of ideological positions clashing with each other and never really getting resolved.[19] Nevertheless, as the frequency of the 'official' idea in the traditions implies, it wasn't an ineffective strategy, either.

Meanwhile, Shaka had to make sure that errant sections were suppressed. To this end he made a foray across the Thukela against that independent-minded section, the Makhanya. Some of these people then raided the Cele, further south, and gobbled up their gourds. When the Cele complained, Shaka said, 'Let those wrong-doers perish!' They needed no more than the warning, and the country quietened down. When bandits appeared, Shaka was able to do the same.[20] He could be aggressive, but he was also a peacemaker. The last thing that Shaka wanted was people scattering off across the country, depriving him of manpower. He had lost some Qwabe to the Ndwandwe and some to the Mthethwa;[21] a few others had gone to polities further south. He needed whoever was left.

It is vital to emphasise this: Shaka's strategy was never to obliterate people. Even later in his rule, he probably never had the capacity. Rather, through a slew of opportunistic techniques, he tried to persuade 'conquered' people to join him against an enemy that threatened them all. Most homesteads were left exactly where they were; their headmen were required to pay tribute, or to help feed new establishments that Shaka built amongst them. (This strategy is a little like the current relationship between 'traditional leaders' and the Westminster-pattern parliamentary structures in South Africa; the former, though highly modified and somewhat disempowered, haven't disappeared, despite the imposition of an overseeing, parallel political system. And naturally there are sundry niggling conflicts between them.)

Whatever coercion was necessary obviously needed military muscle. As he formed new *amabutho*, Shaka built them settlements or barracks, *amakhanda*, within Qwabe territory. He was doing the same elsewhere, establishing, for example, the eNdlamate *ikhanda* in Langeni territory.[22] It's not clear what the exact sequence was, but at some point not long after the quelling of the Qwabe, Shaka built the *umuzi* Gibixhegu, nestled up against the Ngoye forests and overlooking the Mhlathuze valley. It was an excellent defensive position – particularly against attacks from the north. It was also a good 60 kilometres south-east of the Zulu heartland – a measure of how seriously Shaka had been displaced. Gibixhegu, and other nearby *imizi*, would provide the rallying-points for military units into which Qwabe men could be summoned. The Qwabe informant Mmemi's father Nguluzane, for example, was called up into the Mgumanqa *ibutho*.[23] Others were incorporated into the iziYendane, the Hlubi-based outfit that would shortly be driving Shaka's power south of the Thukela river. It also wasn't necessarily a case of one *ibutho* per *ikhanda*: the Mbelebele *ibutho* would eventually have four *amakhanda* it could call its own, either for different sections, or because Shaka's forces were so thinly spread that they needed to be moved around periodically.

The establishment of *amakhanda* was accompanied by a network of ritual observances, some military in nature, and some domestic. These rituals also became part of the evolving identity of the Zulu polity. The *ikhanda* was not just an all-male barracks: it was a domestic establishment in its own right, with a complement of women, cattle and fields. The warriors wouldn't spend all their time there, but it was their military home when needed, a rallying-place for soldierly camaraderie. Costumes and shields to distinguish *amabutho* were more precisely established. 'War medicine' was becoming a more refined speciality for specific *izinyanga*, traditional doctors. By Dingane's time, all the usual panoply and ceremony of military discipline and pride was evidently well developed: there were dances, songs, names, praises, and the display of *iziqu* – amulets of willow-pod – signifying that a man had killed in battle.

While it is with caution that I read back in time descriptions of *amabutho* ceremonial from later reigns, something very similar was developing under Shaka. There was a complex and intricate process of initiation and cadetship. This process was as much integrated with the agricultural activities of the community and with its sexual mores as it was with the military structures; there was no obvious division between them. One informant, BALENI kaSilwana, remembers how loyalties were built up through service to the *inkosi*'s own cattle before being *butwa*'d or called up to the *ibutho* proper:

> We used to drink milk from the udders of the *inkosi*'s cows. We used to sleep in huts *nga kwesikulu*, that is, on the right side going in, and near the gate of the cattle enclosure. . . . We drank from the cows at midday and at sunset, for there were two milkings. What happened was this. The cattle would all be driven into the great cattle enclosure. Those for the *inkosi*'s or *isigodhlo*'s use were driven to their accustomed spot, a little way up the enclosure, whilst the main lot stood below. After a time, the *inkosi*'s milk pail would emerge from the *isigodhlo*, carried by the *inceku*, who would whistle out loudly. This whistle would be heard and responded to by several in different parts, who would shout, 'Zi jubekile!' [they have been set apart]. Upon this, whilst the *inkosi*'s or royal cattle were being milked, we cadets would make for the main herd and proceed to drink from the cows . . . . The oxen were kept separate; they were herded separately in the field by men. These men used to be given the foreleg of the animal on a beast's being killed . . . .
>
> The cadets used to collect firewood and thornbush for the *isigodhlo*. The thorns are very painful. The thornbush would surmount the *isigodhlo* fence. Cadets also hoed the fields, carried the *amabele* sorghum when it was being reaped, and threshed it . . . .
>
> They used to perform war dances at the meeting-place in the cattle enclosure. They would do this alone. They have no assegais, only sticks and small- and large-knobbed kieries. They also practised stabbing at plant bulbs while herding at the river. They used to eat lung. The fat

on top of a beast's heart is *ubedu*. This was eaten only by the leading herdboys, cut up into small pieces.

Cadets *kleza*'d [drank milk from the udder] for two or three years, when they were *butwa*'d. They would have their local home-enclosure built. They would be given a name. When first *butwa*'d they would go to the *inkosi's umuzi* to attend the men's assembly. This would last only one day. The *inkosi* would present them with cattle which they would take off to their military headquarters [*ikhanda*] and there slaughter. It would be after that they would come together and build their homestead. The giving of these cattle is to make them mature; they are given meat.

Practices such as these took place in Shaka's day, also in Dingane's.[24]

This kind of ceremonial intricacy and order would be carried on into the calling-up of *amabutho* in times of emergency, into the doctoring of the troops before fighting, to their behaviour on the march, and to post-war cleansing.[25] Many of these ceremonials drew on well-established rites, but they were clearly being expanded and reinforced by Shaka to make a formidable impression on prospective enemies. Appearance was at least as important as actual ability to inflict damage.

Nevertheless, capable of inflicting damage Shaka's forces were in about 1818, when Zwide's Ndwandwe made yet another massive foray southwards. To combat the threat, Shaka was also trying to glean more support from other groups south of the Thukela.

'MY YOUNGER BROTHER'

In December 1826, Nathaniel Isaacs was wandering around Shaka's Dukuza *umuzi*, when he noticed the odd sight of a 'venerable-looking man washing his feet'. Isaacs was seventeen, very far from home, and in possession of only the sketchiest knowledge of Zulu. He misunderstood much of what he heard and saw. Nevertheless, perhaps correctly thinking that washing one's feet was a rather disrespectful thing to be doing in the *inkosi's* own courtyard, the curious Isaacs got the man to talk to him.[26] He turned out to be Zihlandlo, the chieftain of a sizeable group of people, the eMbo or Mkhize, who lived a day's journey away, among the Nkhandla hills overlooking the northern bank of the Thukela. Isaacs painted a rather sorry picture of Zihlandlo, a once-proud leader who had been 'subdued' and was now living as a 'dependant'. Oddly, he said that this was because 'no tribute having been agreed on, he had not become tributary' to the Zulu. At the same time,

> He, as well as others similarly circumstanced, are compelled to accompany Chaka to war, and to furnish people to carry the baggage of his army, which consists only of mats to repose on. They are not permitted to fight as auxiliaries, because it is a Zoola custom that a subdued enemy is an 'eggualor' [*igwala*], or coward, and that he is at the command, and, which is far worse, at the mercy of his conqueror.
>
> Their [such chiefs'] principal study is to please the savage into whose grasp they may fall, so as to appease his wrath, and obtain the unenviable rank of a tributary chief.[27]

So was Zihlandlo 'tributary' or wasn't he? Isaacs obviously didn't have a clue. Everything is linked to his need to demonise Shaka. Nothing in the traditional record supports Isaacs's perceptions of the relationship between these two chieftains. Still, there's probably one grain of truth there: the ambiguities in the relationship between Zihlandlo and Shaka made nonsense of Isaacs's obsession with tyranny, precisely because the relationship *was* ambiguous.

The Mkhize were another group who nursed memories of having at some point been forced southwards by troubles in the Swaziland area.[28] When Shaka took charge of the Zulu, the Mkhize were already powerful and under the firm control of Zihlandlo kaGcwabe – and would remain so throughout Shaka's reign. Shaka may have tried to meddle in Mkhize affairs while Zihlandlo's father Gcwabe was still alive, if the praise he acquired has any basis in events: 'He [Shaka] ate two sweet-reeds, one being Zihlandlo, the other Gcwabe, but spat out only one leaf.' Which was to say, JANTSHI explained, he didn't kill them, but only caught them.[29]

Though Zihlandlo elected to *khonza* Shaka, it was not without internal resistance; he may even have had to kill his own brother Matshukembele to enforce the decision. (Several lines of Zihlandlo's *izibongo* refer to him wiping out Matshukembele's family.[30]) Matshukembele, appointed by Zihlandlo to go and *khonza* the Zulu leader, contrived to keep the tribute cattle for himself, with the result that Zihlandlo, with the help of another brother Sambela, killed him. Shaka was rather fond of Matshuku, as he nicknamed him; but, as Nandi reminded him, he was even more fond of Zihlandlo.[31] He had, in fact, dubbed Zihlandlo his 'younger brother, *mnawe wami*', and promised him, 'I will never raid or seize your stock, not to my dying day.'[32]

This was a vow that he kept, despite his jealousy of Zihlandlo's own power. This envy is remembered in a famous story. In it, Shaka and Zihlandlo go down to the sea. Shaka says, 'Let us throw sticks into the waves, and the one whose stick is returned will be a greater chief than the other.' They throw their sticks; Zihlandlo's returns. Though they search for a month, Shaka's stick is never found. Shaka broods, 'I must kill Zihlandlo' – but reconsiders, 'No, he is my brother; I'll let him be, since it was I who challenged him. But if it had been the other way round . . .'[33]

If anyone was causing mayhem in those days along the Thukela, it was the Mkhize. Zihlandlo's *izibongo* make several references to his having power over at least a section of the Dlamini, living to the west, to his independence of other local chieftains (he was the 'Utter ignorer who ignored Dube of the Ngcobos'), and to his marrying into the Bomvu.[34] The disturbances were, however, mostly the fault of Zihlandlo's brother Sambela.

Sambela was a particularly wild and uncontrollable character, a compulsive fighter. He might have been an albino, and a small man. He'd been tempestuous since boyhood: after his first nocturnal emission he went out with a gang and killed twenty goats and ate them. When he came back from herding he would smash up the pottery. He was ungovernable (*uhlanya*).[35] As an adult, he attacked everyone, and even wanted to kill Shaka, but Zihlandlo restrained him.[36]

Shaka evidently thought that this lust for battle could be useful, and suggested that he should make Sambela one of his commanders; Zihlandlo demurred. Shaka worried, 'Zihlandlo, *mnawe*, look at those eyes, piercing, as if he wanted to kill you.' Zihlandlo replied, 'No, he will never kill me.'[37] He was right about that. Since Sambela at least initially didn't have his own *amabutho*, and only commanded Zihlandlo's, he didn't have entirely free rein. And Zihlandlo possessed a number of *amabutho*, attesting to his strength. He had inherited four of them – the Umtshungu, the uTshwele, the uTiyatiya, and the Imbisi – from his father Gcwabe, and thus they certainly pre-date

Shaka. Zihlandlo also formed some *amabutho* of his own: the uDliki, the isiHlabane, the iziMpohlo, and the iNguqa.[38] The last-named is one that Shaka borrowed or took over.[39] For his part, Sambela, aggressive as he was, also began to set up his own *amakhanda*, military garrisons.[40] (This is a choice bit of information. The chronology is, once again, a problem, but it suggests that there were two somewhat different military systems in operation at the same time. It may even indicate that a recognisable 'barracks' or *amakhanda* system preceded Shaka's efforts. Alternatively, something like it was at work outside Shaka's control. But it's probably impossible now to establish this exactly, or to say just who might have been learning from whom.)

At any rate, the irrepressible Sambela exercised himself quite independently of Shaka, sometimes even killing important men amongst the Mkhize. Some of the principal men advised that he be done away with, but one counsellor, Bhambatha, advised Zihlandlo to give Sambela his own *umuzi*, Emngeneleni. Zihlandlo also gave Sambela an *isikhulu* elder or two, Mbungu and Zihlangwana, probably in the hope of restraining him. All the cattle that Zihlandlo gave him as a resource base, Sambela slaughtered, cutting the hides up for war shields and giving surrounding peoples the meat. They were grateful and Sambela built up a substantial following in this way. He gathered up an *impi* and attacked and killed Nomanaka kaNgcongo, then Mandaba of the Vezi, then Mpongo of the Ndlovu, then Majiya of the Phephetha across the Thukela. He killed Mziki kaThoze, both Mkhubane and Phakhathwayo of the Manyane, Nosongolwayo and Nombombo of the Hlele, and Zisingwana of the Mguli.[41]

Zihlandlo made Sambela a chief in his own right, with the privilege of holding his own *umkhosi* first-fruits ceremony: a singular favour. Shaka grew jealous of him, too. He asked about Sambela's praises: 'the one whose fame resounds even while he sits at Mngenela; it resounds among his enemies; it resounds at his home.' Shaka said huffily: 'It is I who am "the one whose fame resounds even while he sits; the son of Menzi; the axe which surpasses other axes; the bird which devours others".' So he appropriated Sambela's praise, but nothing more was said. Sambela continued to be praised thus anyway – a fair indication of his continuing independence.[42]

Indeed, Shaka never touched the Mkhize principality; they were mutually supportive. As MBOKODO put it, 'Shaka got Zihlandlo to co-operate with him when building up his power.'[43] When Shaka attacked the Zondi people, south of the Thukela, he failed to liberate their cattle from their stone enclosures. He asked Zihlandlo to attempt the same, and he succeeded. This feat found its way into Zihlandlo's *izibongo*:

> He who climbed the trackless Bhacu mountain,
> Going to get the cattle that were at Dlaba's kraal,
> These people had got into a dispute with Shaka;
> He captured the cattle.[44]

Shaka exclaimed, 'You are indeed my younger brother! If I had succeeded myself, I would have suffered from *isimanga* – I'd have had to forswear certain foods, or pay a fine.' By this he meant, I suppose, that he would have missed gaining a splendid ally.[45] Shaka then directed Zihlandlo to fight Mtsholoza of the Nxamalala people, another of the splinter groups living south of the Thukela (a phase of action that we will cover in detail in Chapter 8). As we'll also relate in the proper places, Zihlandlo's forces eventually accompanied Shaka's on the campaigns against Sikhunyane's Ndwandwe, and against the Mpondo to the south. Tall, not too dark, shiny-skinned, Zihlandlo commanded Shaka's willing respect. Even when Shaka impulsively picked off a cow of Zihlandlo's that he thought would make a particularly fine shield, he courteously replaced the beast.[46] Indeed, Zihlandlo seems to have been a very different man from the sorry character that Nathaniel Isaacs described.

OTHER SOUTHERN FRIENDS

We will probably never know exactly what the sequence was, but roughly during this period, Shaka was also making the first attempts to forge alliances with some other southerners: the Thembu, the Sithole, the Chunu, and the swathe of disunited smaller groups between the Chunu and the Cele. In this initial phase, however, he made little headway, and would only be able to renew his efforts two or three years after the defeat of Zwide.[47]

North-west of the Mkhize, in the Qudeni district and astride the Mzinyathi river, were the Thembu. The Thembu had been expanding under the leadership of Ngoza kaMkubukeli for some years and Shaka was wary, or jealous, of Ngoza's growing power. Ngoza was once, around 1817, unwise enough to send messengers to stick a reed in front of Shaka, a gesture of defiance. He was possibly supported in this act of provocation by Macingwane of the Chunu.[48] Shaka was enraged, but the messengers did not back down. Shaka 'commended them for sticking to their chief'. His quarrel was not with them, he told them, but with their master. He gave them three oxen, and sent them home with the threat of an attack at the next new moon.[49] In short, having failed to get Ngoza to *khonza* voluntarily, Shaka tried to force his hand by attacking him. According to the Thembu informant, LUNGUZA:

> Shaka attacked Ngoza twice. The first time was at night at Malakata. Ngoza then fled across into what is now the Umsinga Division, to the vicinity of Pomeroy at a hill called eMmbe. A battle took place here and the Zulu army was defeated, Ngoza following his usual mode of fighting, i.e. having women in the immediate rear of the troops. This battle took place in the day-time. There was great slaughter of the Zulus. Shaka then said, 'As Ngoza has defeated the Bekenya, let the Dhlangezwa go out.' But when the Dhlangezwa regiment arrived, Ngoza was no longer at eMmbe, having come down to Mpumulwana (south side of the Thukela and lower down), and having attacked the Kuze . . .[50]

So much for the oft-alleged invincibility of the Zulu army. Another version is more complex in its politics. Ngoza had been tributary to the Buthelezi, and grew anxious when they were brought under Zulu control. Ngoza killed off Nomagaga kaMkubukeli of the Khuze people, 'to clear a course for his retreat' from the dangerous Shaka.[51]

> The ejected [Khuze] tribe complained of Goza's [Ngoza's] attack to Chaka; the latter sent a force to dislodge him. Goza resisted and defeated Chaka's force. Chaka himself had accompanied his army, and was directing or observing its operations from a position he had taken up on the Qudeni Mountain; he was accompanied by only a few attendants. While there he encountered one of Goza's headmen, Jobe, also accompanied by a few men. Chaka entered into

conversation with Jobe as to the probable issue of the battle; and the two remained together most of the day, Jobe not knowing who his companion was. After the Zulu forces were defeated, a messenger arrived in breathless haste, and after accosting Chaka with the royal salute, abruptly reported the loss of the day. Chaka, annoyed at the intelligence and the imprudence of the messenger in discovering [sic] his identity to the strangers by whom he was surrounded, and thereby placing his life in great danger, ordered his immediate execution, and he was accordingly put to death on the spot. Jobe and his party, confounded and alarmed, neglected to take advantage of the opportunity, and Chaka safely escaped. It is said that from this accidental meeting sprang the attachment between Chaka and Jobe, which lasted until the death of the former, but the tribes in Natal were long in the habit of reviling Jobe for his neglect of the opportunity to rid the world of its – in their idea – greatest disturber, when Chaka was in his power. Goza, although he had thus defeated Chaka's first attempt, felt too weak to stand any further attack, and immediately commenced moving south . . .[52]

Ngoza moved initially just south of the confluence of the Thukela and Mzinyathi rivers. Shaka then left the Thembu alone as he was preoccupied with the Ndwandwe.

For their part, the Sithole under Jobe became staunch Zulu allies. We have little indication of Sithole-Zulu relations before Dingiswayo's death, apart from Sithole acquiescence in Mthethwa over-rule. By the time the Thembu moved off again south-west under Ngoza – probably in around 1822 – the Sithole under Jobe were already well in Shaka's favour. In the interim, Shaka appointed Jobe suzerain over a fertile and healthy region between the Thukela and Mzinyathi. Jobe, a squat man with a broad beard that went quite white in his later years, was given considerable autonomy. He was allowed even to kill off people on his own account, in return for tactfully denying himself the title of *inkosi* – that belonged to Shaka. Jobe brought stability to his region. He cemented marriage alliances, himself marrying one of Shaka's sisters. He handed a son to one of Shaka's *isigodlo* women. His area became known for the quality of its hides: the royal cattle entrusted to him became

the main source of Zulu shields, as well as blue monkey skins and lourie
feathers from the Nkhandla forests, which fell under his jurisdiction. At
least one powerful reason for establishing such loyal client-chiefs, then, was
Shaka's need to control the best resources.[53] (This process took years, and
runs over the limits of this chapter, but it was certainly in the early stages of
being set up in 1816 to 1819.)

The Chunu connection to the Zulu was probably the closest. Rather like
the Qwabe, the Chunu eventually felt tied enough to the Zulu to generate,
possibly quite falsely, an origins myth that linked the two groups. 'Zulu crossed
over; Chunu remained behind; Qwabe went off down the Mhlathuze,' as
one informant altogether too neatly puts it. Zulu and Chunu were sons of
one man; they were all Ntungwas; they were all *abarwebi*, hawkers of
medicines. This genealogy was probably manufactured by those Chunu who
survived the upheavals and remained tributary to the Zulu. Up to a point,
they were actually on good terms. They pierced their ears, wore the headrings,
and 'resembled the Zulu in every way'. It seems that Dingiswayo himself
never attacked them.[54]

Macingwane of the Chunu built up a substantial polity near the Mvoti
river – perhaps even with initial Zulu acquiescence (see Chapter 6, page 171).
He had a string of *imizi*: Engonyameni, eLangeni, eNkanini, eNkomba,
eNkawulweni, eMdakeni, eMbangwini, and eBathweni. There were at least
a dozen distinct sections or clanlets of people under his wing. He boasted at
least five *amabutho*: iNgagu (the oldest), abaThwa, iziKwenkwezi, uMungu,
and amaTshanga. He was strong enough to fend off at least one attack by
Zihlandlo, and another by the unruly Sambela.[55] There seemed every reason
for Shaka to hope to make accord with the Chunu, but this did not happen.
As we will see later, Macingwane was unwilling to be a client-chief to anyone.

These larger groups aside, there was a patchwork of little peoples between
them. It's difficult to say whether, to what extent, or how many of the smaller
groups who lived along the banks of the Thukela were incorporated at this
stage. Probably they were assimilated quite slowly, by degrees. It does seem
clear that almost all – including the Ngcolosi, the Zondi, the Bomvu, and
the Nganga – tendered their allegiance with little or no violent persuasion.[56]
One story survives of Shaka's relations with the Bomvu:

Shaka's *impi* surrounded the Bomvus at oPisweni [a mountain south-
east of the Thukela-Mzinyathi confluence]. We [Zulu] knew the
Bomvus as amaLala. They had their cattle on top of the hill in a kraal
having but one entrance. There are precipices or very steep ascents
on all sides. Shaka, finding the enemy in this stronghold, examined it
and found that by putting ladders against wild fig trees his men could
go up. So during the night this was done, and the men succeeded in
getting up and emerged at the upper end of the kraal, ie. on the far
side of the one gate where the enemy were posted. The women then
shouted out that Shaka and his men had entered their stronghold.
All the men ran and tumbled over the cliffs, and all the cattle came
out and were captured. There was no actual fighting.[57]

A few other groups had a more difficult time of it. Some, like the Nxamalala
and the Dunge, were possibly mauled by Zihlandlo, either on his own initiative
or at Shaka's behest.[58] The Khabela also suffered this fate, but Zihlandlo's
sway over them would be successfully challenged by the Zulu themselves.[59]
The Ndlovu may have been brought under influence of the Mkhize, too,
since at least one Ndlovu man is recorded as an *inceku* to Sambela, Zihlandlo's
brother.[60]

Shaka looked down on these smaller peoples as inferior, grubby: they
were amaLala; they *tefula*'d (mouthed their words oddly); they couldn't
distinguish good from bad. They were, collectively, the 'iNyakeni'. The
Ngcolosi, the Khabela, the Mphungose, the Nxamalala, the Hlongwa, and
those further south were also all unsavoury iNyakeni.[61] Some of them had to
be weaned away from allegiance to the Cele.[62]

As for the Cele themselves, relations with the Zulu seem to have been
tenuous but friendly. Their relationship was solidified only after the defeat
of Zwide, however, so I will leave their complete story for Chapter 9. Indeed,
generally, apart from some tentative forays across the Thukela, it seems most
probable that Shaka's big, more determined drive to the south was to come
a good while later.[63]

Meanwhile, a disaster was unfolding on the northern frontier.

DINGISWAYO DIES

While Shaka was grappling with Phakathwayo's Qwabe and the other southerners, Zwide's marauders had continued to clash with the Mthethwa. This probably explains the apparent lack of direct Mthethwa involvement in Shaka's forays to the south. As a result of the fact that both Mthethwa and Ndwandwe traditions have largely vanished, we know no details of these clashes. Apparently, for all his ferocity, Zwide couldn't quite get the upper hand over Dingiswayo. So, the story goes, Zwide resorted to subterfuge and dark medicine. He pretended to be all cowed and friendly, and sent a daughter to Dingiswayo, offering her as a wife. He instructed her to collect some of Dingiswayo's semen in an *umfece*, a small snuff-case made from a cocoon, and bring it back. This she duly did.

(Another account claims that Dingiswayo's own men, internal rebels, collected Dingiswayo's *izidwedwe* – personal effects, bodily bits – and betrayed him to Zwide.[64])

Zwide stirred the semen into nameless medicines until they frothed. Dingiswayo suddenly, quite unaccountably, called up the army. His *izinduna* objected, 'Hau! Without even telling the people why!' Dingiswayo donned all his finery, and picked up his long blue crane feather, a symbol of leadership. Suddenly a number of locusts settled on the feather. The feather fell: a terrible omen. The *izinduna* cried, '*Inkosi*! The army has been injured. Let it be prepared with medicines again.' Dingiswayo replied that he would do it himself in Zwide's country when they got there. And off he went.[65]

What happened next is uncertain. Some say that Dingiswayo simply marched straight into Zwide's *umuzi*, leaving his *impi* floundering behind.[66] Others recount that there was something of a fight, possibly involving Dingiswayo's last regiment, the iNyakeni,[67] during which Dingiswayo was captured. He had somehow (as a result of being bewitched) wandered off on his own, or with his girls from the *isigodlo*,[68] or he was just sitting apart from the main army, watching the battle from a small hill, when a small Ndwandwe force crept up behind him and captured him.[69]

There is absolutely no evidence in the traditions that Shaka 'secretly communicated' with the enemy and so betrayed Dingiswayo, as Fynn alleged.[70]

However it happened, Dingiswayo was taken to Zwide's main establishment, Nsingweni. The informant MAKUZA has a colourful and doubtless largely imaginary rendering of what happened:

The sun was just coming up. The Ndwandwe soldiers took the one chief up to the other. The order was given, 'Take all Dingiswayo's people to that hut.' They went in. Then Zwide asked, 'Who is as great as you, Dingiswayo?' Dingiswayo replied, 'No, I am no longer as great as you, for I have left my people and my soldiers.' Zwide said, 'So then, could I now fight with you, Dingiswayo?' And Dingiswayo answered, 'No, I could no longer say that I could fight with you.'

Zwide then left Dingiswayo and went some distance away. He danced a war dance, and then came back and jumped over Dingiswayo. Then he called his *izinceku* to take him to the cattle enclosure where he, Zwide, used to wash, and where he had stirred the medicines. He then summoned all his *izinduna* and said, 'My *izinduna*, do not kill the chief by hitting him with sticks, for he is already dead. You will bury him at sunrise tomorrow.... I have killed him with the medicines which I ate.' They replied, 'We have heard, *inkosi*. Tell us where we are to bury him.' 'Bury him at the Mahlabaneni hill. While some are digging, let others cut posts. When you have prepared them, fix them in the ground, build a fence right round the grave, so that no evil person will be able to come and cut open this chief for the purpose of killing the chief who lives.'[71]

There would be more gruesome, contradictory, and legendary versions of the assassination. Some informants think that Zwide was inclined to spare Dingiswayo's life, and that it was his infamously vicious mother Ntombaze who insisted on killing him.[72] Others say exactly the opposite: that Ntombaze and the *induna* Nombona opposed the killing, but Zwide insisted on cutting his head off.[73] Yet another, more dramatic, version recounts that Zwide had Dingiswayo staked spread-eagled on the ground, face up, and drove a herd of cattle over him.[74]

In a touching epilogue, a number of Dingiswayo's wives are said to have gone all the way to Zwide's *umuzi*, climbed on the roofs of his huts, and wailed their grief. Zwide kindly let them exhaust themselves and leave unharmed.[75]

Historical explanations that have been offered thus far, either for the Ndwandwe invasions or for Dingiswayo's defeat, have been brief, vague and unsatisfactory.[76] They are dependent on the rather dubious sketches by Fynn and Bryant. It is unlikely that we will ever be able to fill this gap. If Zwide was after the resources of the Mthethwa lowland plains, there is no record of him ever being able to use them. He does not appear to have taken over the trade route that Dingiswayo avowedly cherished. There is no evidence of him even plundering Mthethwa cattle, though he probably did, nor of him taking prisoners off and selling them to the slave ships, though, as before, this seems the most obvious explanation for the savagery of the attacks.

Whatever the case, the death of Dingiswayo left a huge leadership vacuum south of the Mfolozi rivers. Shaka seemed to be the only one available to replace him as a regional power broker.

The Mthethwa polity's fragility showed itself immediately: it fell apart. Its various tributary segments each tried to reassert their independence. Some elected to *khonza* Zwide; others stayed where they were and acknowledged Mondisa, Dingiswayo's brother, as the Mthethwa leader; some *khonza*'d Shaka.

Shaka had to move quickly if he was to assume the Mthethwa mantle. His first task was to deal with Mondisa, who was, for a moment, alarmingly bolstered by the sudden arrival of a fresh body of adherents.

These new arrivals came courtesy of our Langeni friend Makhedama, whom we left a while ago (in Chapter 6) having *khonza*'d Zwide. This had not proved a good move. Zwide had started to court some of the Langeni girls. The girls insulted him: 'What does this old, dried-up thing (*ugogo*) want with us? We want his sons, Sikhunyane and Nomahlanjana.' Zwide threatened to kill Makhedama who consulted the Langeni elders. They pointed out that they had scarcely finished building their new *imizi*, and hadn't even reaped the red ears of their *amabele* sorghum crop yet. They would rather not move again. The younger *izinsizwa*, by contrast, preferred to head for the hills and fight there than court an undignified death by staying. Makhedama gathered up his womenfolk and children and went back south to *khonza* the Mthethwa again.[77]

Shaka grew uneasy. He couldn't afford an able leader like Makhedama supporting the upstart Mondisa, right on his doorstep. Apparently he – surprise, surprise – invited Mondisa to an *umjadu* dance where Mondisa was ambushed by hidden spearmen and killed. The immediate excuse was said to have been that Mondisa sang a risqué song that Shaka interpreted as alluding to him.[78] Makhedama, it seems, then came back within the Zulu fold, though only to make a nuisance of himself later. Mondisa was replaced with a nominee of Shaka's, a close ally named Mlandela (or Myandeya). Mlandela was a son of Mbiya kaTshangane, who was a 'cousin of Dingiswayo'.[79] He was thus high up in the Mthethwa hierarchy, listed amongst the *izikhulu*, but not so high as to be a threat. Shaka introduced him into his own family by marrying off both his half-sisters, Nomcoba and Nomzinhlanga, to him.[80] Administratively, however, he kept him on a tight leash. Mlandela was not permitted, as some other client-chiefs were, to perform his own *umkosi* ceremonies or to *butwa* people. He wouldn't dare; he would be said to be challenging the *inkosi* himself.[81]

Sections of the Mthethwa who were loyal to Mondisa, and objected to the installation of Mlandela, elected to follow Dingiswayo's young heir, Somveli, who at a later stage decided to leave.[82] Somveli's departure signalled the fact that Shaka's hold over at least some Mthethwa sections was still tenuous.

Shaka's second task was to secure, or re-secure, the allegiance of peoples who were threatened with assimilation or destruction by the Ndwandwe. He likely concentrated on the buffer zone along the two Mfolozi rivers. At the western end of that zone, the Khumalo lived, split into several independent sections. Dingiswayo is said to have attacked the section under Donda in his home area between the esiKwebezi and the Black Mfolozi rivers.[83] So did Shaka, probably under Mthethwa auspices. It was Zwide who killed Donda off, though. Likewise, Zwide killed Mashobana, chief of a second Khumalo section living on Ntumbane mountain near the upper Mkhuze, and extracted tribute from his son Mzilikazi.[84] Bheje kaMagawozi headed another Khumalo section (in the present-day Nongoma-Vryheid area), steering a difficult course between the bigger polities. He would continue to cause Shaka considerable trouble. It seems that Shaka was unable to assert his dominance fully over these people until after his defeat of Zwide.[85]

Next in line, just to the east of the Khumalo, lay the Makhoba and the Zungu, who were closely related.[86] Shaka had probably already formed an alliance with Manzini of the Zungu against Zwide, and acquired the Wild Dogs *ibutho* previously mentioned (see page 158).[87] Zwide may have tried to oust Manzini and promote another pretender, Mjiza, to the leadership.[88]

At around the same time, Shaka may also have been sent by Dingiswayo to subdue the Makhoba.[89] Shaka now likely attempted to reaffirm those links.

The Sibiya, sandwiched between the Zungu and Makhoba on the middle reaches of the Mfolozi, had probably already submitted to Shaka; now, their largesse with cattle and other riches helped Shaka to build up resistance to the Ndwandwe incursions. '*Nampo-ke aba kwaSibiya, nga nkomo abanye bebiya ngamahlahla*', it was said of Sibiya wealth: 'The Sibiya fence their cattle byres with cattle, where others use branches'. The nearby Mbatha, too, probably acceded to Zulu rule and would help to stiffen the Zulu defence.[90]

With the acquisition of manpower and resources from these various portions of the collapsing Mthethwa confederation, Shaka was finally in a position to weather a major confrontation with the Ndwandwe.

'THE BULLS OF THE HERD HAVE MET'

Zwide was not letting up after Dingiswayo's ignominious capture and death. In subsequent seasons, perhaps in 1819 and 1820, he continued to conquer other groups. (The dating is problematic in two ways. John Wright notes that there is no obvious explanation for why the Ndwandwe waited a year or more after Dingiswayo's death to attack the Zulu.[91] Probably they could only manage one major expedition a season. Julian Cobbing notes that after Bryant's speculative dating of the 'final' Zulu-Ndwandwe clash to 1819, the focus has been solely on this one allegedly decisive battle.[92] But the battle itself is the communal memory's compression of many, longer-term clashes.) The Vundla people were said to have been captured by Zwide at this time,[93] possibly Matshobana's Khumalo as well. Zwide continued to raid into the traditionally Zulu lands. Shaka may have made one unsuccessful attack into the Ndwandwe heartland, on the main *umuzi* Ndweneni itself.[94] The Ndwandwe for their part raided south again and burned – not for the first time – the almost sacred centres of esiKlebheni and Mbelebeleni, driving the Zulu ahead of them.[95] The Zulu forces had to make another strategic withdrawal ahead of the Ndwandwe advance before they were able to position themselves to fight successfully. Maybe bread was cooked and taken along, grain was burned or hidden (again?). The cattle were driven off, to serve as a mobile larder.[96]

The traditional accounts would dress this retreat up as a cunning decoy tactic. There was mention of 'decoying with bushes'.[97] Did this mean brushing over their tracks? Or did MMEMI mean that they made it look like there were more tracks than there really were? The most likely meaning is the second. Perhaps the Zulu *wanted* the Ndwandwe to follow, to fall into an ambush.

Of course, Shaka's upcoming victory would later be characterised as a triumph of medicines. When he is beaten off again, he turns the tables – does a Zwide on Zwide himself. Shaka calls some doctors who volunteer to go and live with Zwide for four months, pretending to *khonza*. They will bewitch his army, which will be magically drawn along the ridges, and as soon as they see the Zulu *impis* they will start frothing at the mouth and thrashing about. This is, however, JANTSHI's aberrant account of an attack on kwaBulawayo itself.[98]

All the other accounts that we have are quite different from JANTSHI's, more bloody and ordinary – and also, for once, largely in agreement with each other. This fight was the big one. It was well remembered.

Whether or not some lure was dangled and the Ndwandwe followed, the battle developed something like this (see Map 5 on page 208). The Zulu were forced to abandon the Nobamba and esiKlebheni *imizi*. They crossed the White Mfolozi, went up Mthonjaneni mountain, then crossed the Mhlathuze, high up, north of the Nkhandla forests. The Ndwandwe, possibly following the light, fast, bush-dragging Zulu decoy, came past Mpandleni, over Nkhandla, down along the Gcongco ridge (which faces towards the Thukela), then round eastwards towards Nomveve. In the vicinity of the Mvuzane stream, where it flows into the Mhlathuze (near present-day Bull's Run, north-west of Eshowe and due south of Melmoth), Shaka had hidden his main force, and waited.

BALENI and MANDHLAKAZI are agreed on this route.[99] MMEMI and MANGATI have the decoy swinging even further south, off the Nkhandla heights and almost down to the Thukela at Ndondondwana before turning east again, perhaps even doing another gyration or two before joining the final battle in the vicinity of the Nomveve.[100] MMEMI has the main Zulu force swinging eastwards, closer to Eshowe and eNtumeni, circling rather oddly – perhaps trying to shake the pursuit off, after light contact on the Mpofu ridge – before dropping down to the confluence of the Mvuzane with the Mhlathuze. The details of the approach paths aside, everyone is agreed that this is where the decisive fight with Zwide happened.

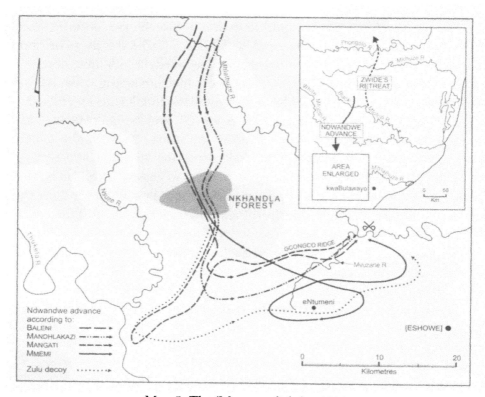

Map 5: The 'Mvuzane fight', *c.*1820

At around this point, in some accounts, Shaka was busy exhorting his warriors in preparation for the assault, when the following happened:

Shaka retired . . . to the top of a hill and there halted. This was very early. When the sun was about one hour above the horizon, Zwide's *impi* appeared, and advanced towards the heart of the Zulu country. Shaka's men, seeing this, said: 'The enemy are in our homes! Let us loose at them!' Shaka sent his force in to the attack. As he was marshalling it, his crane-feather plume came loose from his headband. It fell to the ground, where it stuck in and stood swaying about. His attendants ran to pick it up. The army cried out, 'We are full of fear! The king's plume has fallen just as he is sending us out to fight.' Shaka said, 'Leave it! There is another that will fall.' The attendants left it. He said, 'Look, Zulu! When you come up to the enemy, if they go up onto the hill and get you down below so that they can attack you from above, leave them.' After sending off his force, he told his attendants to fetch the plume. They did so, and he put it back in his headband . . .[101]

Maybe there is some less esoteric core event behind *this* version of the 'falling feather' story, something like that related by BALEKA:'[Shaka] took his crane feather and stuck it in the ground, where it stood swaying . . .'[102] This rather more prosaic act of defiance has, perhaps, been recharged in the memories of the people as a colourful, retrospective way of saying that Shaka was, as it were, divinely or magically graced. He was powerful enough to turn the omens in his favour. The story's importance is not so much in its factuality (or lack of it), but in what it reveals of the way in which Zulu people have recalled their past and given it significance.[103]

Feather or no feather, the Zulu won. The 'Mvuzane fight' (as I will call it from here on) may not have been a single confrontation. In BALENI's rendering, the armies first made contact through their outrider spies in the afternoon. Shaka unleashed his warriors. But it was only at dawn on the next day that the real clash happened. At that point, Shaka sent in the isiKlebhe *ibutho* first, while he sat on a nearby hill and watched, urging the men to get in close with their stabbing spears. Amongst the heroes said to have started the action were the brothers Mvundlana and Magidi kaMenziwa, Myakayake kaNdosi, Ndosi kaNondumo, and Manqondo kaMazwana.[104] According to DINYA, it was the 'multinational' iziYendane *ibutho* that went in first, led by Mdlaka. It was followed by the iNtontela, the Dlangezwa, the Mgumanqa, and others. The fight took place on the south bank, and lasted until nightfall.[105] MMEMI related that the fight took place actually in the swirling waters of the river. The Mbelebele, the Dukuza, the isiKlebhe, the isiPhezi and the iWombe *amabutho* went forward, while Shaka remained behind with the 'black' or younger units, the Dlangweza, the Dlangubo and the Mnkangala. He urged on his soldiers, and vilified the invaders: 'I shall hear, then, men of the elephant. It has come to the home; it has trodden in the excrement of the children.'[106]

Zwide, for his part, had the isiKwitshi *ibutho* (those that came from his mother Ntombaze's place), and the amaPhela,[107] and had thrown many of his own sons into the battle: Mphepha, Dayingubo, Nomahlanjana, Notokasa, and Nombengula – many of whom, if not all, were killed.[108] The Ndwandwe were forced once across the river; they returned, and then Shaka unleashed the 'black' reserves. This was too much for the Ndwandwe: they fled, to be pursued all the way to Zwide's main base, Ndweneni.[109]

That is all we know about this most decisive of all Shaka's confrontations with his primary rival. We don't know when it happened. The conventional date given is 1818 or 1819: my inclination is the latter, and maybe even 1820. This correlates better with the aftermath, which we'll come to in Chapter 8, but we can't be sure. We also don't know how many warriors were involved, what the casualties were, or even, those few heroes aside, who was there.

Units and heroes

If we look a little more closely at the *amabutho* involved in the 'Mvuzane fight', it might give us some more clues, however slim, about whom Shaka could commit to such a fight. Who did he trust? Who could he call on from amongst his half-integrated allies to the south? How far, in fact, had integration progressed?

We can put together a provisional list of *amabutho*. It was once thought that a chronology could be established, one *ibutho* per year, more or less. It turns out, however, that there was no rigid schedule: units could be formed, more than one at a time if opportunity or necessity presented itself, be split and dissolved, and reconstituted. This happened frequently as Shaka expanded the Zulu polity. And, as MAGIDIGIDI noted:

> There was a practice of *butaing* [calling up *amabutho*] under which, though men were *buta*'d all together, some would be cut off and established in some kraal, taking with them a separate name, although they were recruited at the same time as the main body. So later on confusion arises as to whether they were an independent regiment or merely a section of one, e.g. the Dlangubo.[110]

Nevertheless, let's take a look at what we know of the *amabutho* named by the various informants.

Shaka had inherited some of the *amabutho* from his father. The oldest was probably the isiKlebhe, consisting essentially of men from the esiKlebheni kraal. Distinguished by its grey shields,[111] the isiKlebhe dated back to grandfather Jama's time.[112] There was the iWombe, which we've met before; probably the unit that Shaka himself joined (not to mention his brother Dingane, who may thus be imagined participating in the 'Mvuzane fight', though there's no record of his presence). The Mbelebele, an offshoot of the isiKlebhe, had been used by Shaka against Phakathwayo, so was presumably better seasoned.[113] The hero Mvundlana kaMenziwa, a Biyela, was a member of this unit.[114] The Mnkangala was possibly one of Senzangakhona's creations, later led by Maphitha kaSojiyisa of the Mandlakazi, a family closely associated with the Zulu chiefly house. It would be housed at kwaBulawayo when that *umuzi* was built.[115]

The iNtontela was the last of Senzangakhona's *amabutho*.[116] The great *induna* Ndlela kaSompisi was a member of this unit. He was tall, brown, thin-legged, big-chested, the brother of Senzangakhona's beautiful wife Bhibhi and thus Shaka's uncle. Ndlela's own homestead, significantly, had been set up on Macala mountain, another defensive position cum control-point almost on the Thukela river (near present-day Jameson's Drift), only just beyond the reach of the Ndwandwe.[117] This was also right in the middle of Zihlandlo's Mkhize country. The iNtontela also included (though not necessarily at the

'Mvuzane fight') a Cele man named Mlomowethole, who had voluntarily *khonza*'d Shaka while the Cele were still under Dube.[118]

Then there was the isiPhezi, the first *ibutho* called up by Shaka himself;[119] they were the 'old men', the scrapings of whatever was available when Shaka came to power. Some of them were old enough to have been circumcised, and included (though it's hard to say when he came in) the *induna* Nongadi kaDlaba of the Dladla people.[120] The unit was named for the phrase, 'I will make them stop, *phezisa*,' an allusion to Shaka binding the peoples together. It was also robustly called the 'wall of Madilika',[121] and was known for wearing the *umnaka* – brass neck-rings made from Portuguese brass.[122]

The hard core of the army at the 'Mvuzane fight' thus was 'old' Zulu, those closely aligned to the ruling house. They were supported, however, by a fair number of men from the new allied chiefdoms: mostly, as far as we can tell, Cele, Hlubi, and Chunu.

Next in seniority may have been the Mgumanqa, praised as 'that which stands threateningly in the patch of burnt grass'.[123] They carried red shields spotted with white,[124] and were said to dress their hair up like cockscombs.[125] This *ibutho* included Gwalala kaManyala of the Ndawonde, a Chunu section, indicating that some Ndawonde had been incorporated. The Mgumanqa would be used to chase after Macingwane of the Chunu, but whether this occurred before or after the 'Mvuzane fight' it is hard to say.[126]

Another seasoned unit was the iziYendane with its red shields. This was Hlubi-based, but with a hotchpotch of others thrown in, and led by a Zulu *induna*, Mdlaka. As we'll see in Chapter 8, the iziYendane would later cause havoc further south.

There was the Dlangubo, led by another Ndawonde, Zembe kaNgobe. It was probably the scion of a regiment originally named the uPhoko, then changed to Gibabanye, which was in turn split in two, the one section being the Dlangubo.[127]

The black-and-white shields of the Dlangezwa, 'the stand of last season's grass',[128] were led by or included yet another Ndawonde, Zaviyana kaNdhlongo.[129] The Dlangezwa had already fought Zwide's men in the 'kisi' fight.[130]

And of the Dukuza, we know nothing more than its name.

There is great rivalry amongst informants over who were the prominent heroes in the 'Mvuzane fight'. Those remembered were all, not surprisingly, from the Zulu leading families: the collateral branches of the Biyela or Mdlalose. For DINYA, Mvundlana kaMenziwa of the Biyela and Nkayitshana kaKhuzwayo were the great names.[131] For MADIKANE, the main man was Ndengezi kaKhuzwayo of the Mdlalose. Shaka had said, 'The warrior who drives away Zwide's army will be given so many cattle that when a stick is placed across their backs it will find no room to fall as they move off.' Ndengezi attacked Zwide's army (you would think he had driven it off single-handed), stabbing and shouting, 'U ya Babaza!' (meaning Shaka). Ndengezi later complained that he hadn't got all the cattle he'd been promised, and Shaka promptly banished him.[132]

Of course, there was always the ever-ready Khomfiya kaNogandaya, an exceptional Qwabe in this company of tight-knit Zulu. This fight was where he earned the name 'Zulu'.[133]

For his part, MANGATI singled out Hlati kaNcidi and Ndlela kaSompisi for special mention:

The Ndwandwe were routed by the iNtontela regiment and driven towards the Mhlatuze. But the two men were lying badly wounded where the fight had taken place. The Ndwandwe were utterly defeated. Ndwandwe and Zulu corpses were lying across one another where the armies had met.

Those who could do so returned to Shaka, those with wounds and without. They said, 'Hlati fought fiercely, until at last he fell. Ndhlela too fought fiercely, until at last he fell.' The inkosi asked, 'Are they dead?' The men replied, 'They are still groaning; not yet dead.' Shaka sent out his izimbongi with oxen to call on the ancestors with praises so that the two men should recover, 'For if they die then I too am as if dead.' Praises were given. The two men regained consciousness during the night, revived by the cold. Lifted by the arms, they vomited blood. They were taken to a nearby homestead, treated with medicines; horns were used as emetics, to draw blood. They eventually recovered, and received large gifts of cattle. Shaka asked Ndhlela, 'What is your elder brother's kraal named, then?' He answered, 'eManweleni.' Shaka said, 'No. Let that name be dropped. I now name the homestead eManxebeni, after the wounds, the amanxebe, which the Ndwandwe gave you.'[134]

This is a fascinating glimpse into how Shaka cared for his men – or at least some of them – and developed a martial spirit with its system of rewards and loyalties.

It's not much to go on, but what is striking is that – the Chunu participants excepted – there are virtually no people mentioned from outside the closest leading Zulu branches: no Mthethwa, no Qwabe apart from Zulu kaNogandaya, no one from the smaller Thukela valley clans. It looks as though Shaka was still – perhaps by design – fundamentally dependent on the relatively small nucleus that had always constituted the central Zulu polity. This may be deceptive. It would be understandable if later Zulu historians didn't want to give any credit to outsiders for their great victory. Indeed, we have to recognise that Zulu traditional historians have played up both the scale of this battle and its effects in order to burnish their history to a satisfying sheen. Shaka himself is said to have crowed:

> The bulls of the herd have met. Let the boys who are herding them go out and separate them. Let there go out Noluju [the Ndwandwe *induna*] and Ngqengelele [Shaka's *induna*]. Ha! The one with the red tail [his own *impi*] has gored it! The fancies invented by the Ndwandwe on their way here are finished. They have finished today.[135]

In fact, although Zwide was defeated, the Ndwandwe threat was far from completely overcome.

TACTICS

JANTSHI kaNongila arrived at James Stuart's apartments at 2 Norfolk Villas, Durban, in the early afternoon of 9 February 1903. He had been extricated with some effort from his home near Stanger (kwaDukuza) by NDUKWANA, another of Stuart's informants. NDUKWANA came with him, as well as JANTSHI's own son, and a *kolwa* – a convert to Christianity – named Mbovu. Over the next three days, Stuart questioned JANTSHI and NDUKWANA together on Zulu history. JANTSHI had been born in around 1848 at Nyezane in Zululand, and was originally of the Mabaso people. The Mabaso liked to think of themselves as having originated alongside the Zulu at Nhlazatshe, though they were not a collateral clan of the Zulu. This is why JANTSHI's father Nongila was in for a surprise.

> [W]hen Shaka required spies he said he wanted them from his old tribal people living at Mtonjaneni. Nongila did not come forward to offer his services. Shaka repeated his wish and still Nongila, who had lived many years in the [Zulu] tribe, would not come. Shaka then asked him why he refrained from coming forward, when Nongila replied, 'Because I saw so many others of the Zulu tribe about.' 'Oh! But you too belong to the tribe. You must become one of my spies.'[136]

Nongila *did* subsequently become a spy for Shaka, which is why JANTSHI was particularly interesting to Stuart. Unfortunately, though, the 55-year-old man wasn't an entirely satisfactory informant. As JANTSHI himself admitted: 'I have not given all my father told me. Much is omitted owing to forgetfulness.'[137] He was also frequently wayward in his sense of chronology and may have been distracted, during those three February days, by the illness of one of his sons who was suffering, Stuart thought, from 'consumption'. Nevertheless, through his father, JANTSHI could supply some particularly intriguing information.

Nongila became one of Shaka's more illustrious spies. JANTSHI related:

> Shaka gave my father directions not to sleep in people's *imizi* but in the bush. He depended for food on what he stole from place to place. He did not carry food with him, or mats. He carried a shield, two stabbing-spears, and a stick. That was all. I have one of the assegais he used to carry. The two assegais were given [to] him by Shaka. My father never took clothing with him or even a skin blanket . . . . He never went on a spying expedition without consulting the *inkosi* beforehand and being doctored by him . . . . The spy would carry medicine with him too, which would be tucked away on the inside of his shield . . . . He would never be told the name of the *inkosi*'s medicine. Whenever he approached an *umuzi* he would eat some of this medicine and then enter. This would cause those at the *umuzi* not to question him as to where he came from and so on . . .[138]

Nongila once made it all the way to the Cape, reporting back to Shaka on the presence of white men. He took part in the 'kisi' fight with the Ndwandwe, getting injured in the middle knuckle of his left little finger; he was never able to straighten it out after that. He joined the ill-fated 'Balule' campaign in 1828, nearly dying from malaria. After Shaka's assassination, he narrowly escaped being murdered by Dingane in one of his staged purges, crossed into Natal with Mpande, and was on hand to spy for Mpande before the clash between the Zulu brothers at Magongqo. He served Mpande, and tried to stop Mawa, Mpande's sister, from taking royal cattle across the Thukela river on her celebrated defection in 1843. In the ensuing confusion he feared for his life, and finally crossed a second time to Natal where he encountered, amongst others, the controversial Bishop John Colenso. He eventually succumbed to dysentery in the Durban area; and JANTSHI himself took his father's body to be buried near Mount Edgecome.[139]

Other spies, such as Bovu kaNomabuqabuqa and Nomgqula kaNsizwazana, were famous, too. They carried great trust, and so were generally drawn from the 'old' Zulu of the original heartland.[140] As Shaka's extensive use of these reconnaissance men implies, encounters were generally carefully planned rather than unleashed in a welter of uncontrollable frenzy, as the stereotype would have us believe. They were also part of a style of warfare that to some degree replaced an older one:

> In old times, forces would fight in a strange way. For they would go out to fight at a river, with women and children also going to the attack. On one side of the river the womenfolk would stand behind the men; on the other side would be the other *impi*, also with its womenfolk behind. They would not approach closely, but would hurl assegais at each other. They would cry, 'Ho! *Yaka-yaka!*' The men and women would shout this. If an assegai stuck into a person, then those people were regarded as defeated. There would be a cry, 'See it snarl! See the dog show its gums!' And so they ran away; they were now defeated.[141]

How far, and in what ways, did Shaka really move beyond this pattern? His alleged martial genius is a centrepiece of his present-day image, but, in fact, there is almost nothing to be said about it. No doubt the Zulu warriors used tactics of *some* sort. Sometimes these were decidedly sneaky, as we've seen, but otherwise we have few details. The principal feature of their encounters seems to be that opposing warriors stabbed each other – not a particularly new or interesting tactic.

Although Shaka is widely credited with inventing the stabbing-spear, this is clearly not the case. However, we can *perhaps* credit him with refining its use. Evidently by Shaka's time, or by Dingane's, different kinds of assegai had acquired specific names. There were even two kinds of stabbing-spear: the *isijula* for going in to the attack with, the *iklwa* for use after the enemy began to flee. This 'tactic', if it can be called that, was called 'stabbing the *ibece* melon', because the warriors stabbed people's backs like melons as they ran.[142]

The stabbing-spear, then, was associated with a totally new, more destructive kind of warfare, usually credited solely to Shaka and summarised by one informant as follows: 'Shaka, when giving instructions to his *impi*, would direct them to make away with everything, even a dog or a hearthstone . . . "Let no one remain alive," he used to say – every soul was to be killed, even a child being nursed on the back.'[143] As we have seen so far, there is no concrete evidence whatsoever that such orders were regularly, if ever, carried out.

Shaka is said to have early scoffed at Mthethwa troops throwing their spears away: 'Wo! If these men were mine I would cut a single assegai for each of them. I do not want them to bear wounds behind. A good man should have wounds on his chest.' He wanted the men to abandon the overhead manner of holding the spear (*ukukabukomo*), in favour of the lower grip, blade thrusting upwards (*imfukule*).[144] However, it seems likely that throwing tactics would also have been used from time to time (as apparently they were in the Sikhunyane fight; see below on page 380). And the tactic of showering the enemy with thrown *izinti* assegais, rather like an artillery barrage before the hand-to-hand stuff is engaged, was said to have been the norm under Dingane.[145]

The stabbing-spear tactic is conventionally correlated with another aspect of Shaka's customary mode of attack: its swiftness. 'When attacking, Shaka told the men to carry their shields under their arms and only to bring them out once they were among the enemy.' They were to run into the attack, stooped down, at a great rate.[146] (The story that Shaka made his troops abandon their sandals and toughen their feet by dancing on devil-thorns in order to increase their mobility was invented by E.A. Ritter and there is no contemporary evidence for it.) That said, it is wrong to think of Shaka's warriors as usually rushing into massed battle in ranks of the kind that were later developed to combat the white invaders.

As for the 'horns-and-chest' formation, so unforgettably demonstrated in Bill Faure's television series *Shaka Zulu*, there is virtually no evidence that Shaka ever used this device. Allegedly developed from hunting tactics, it might have been used *once*, again in the 1826 Sikhunyane fight, and that was with muddled results. Plausible though it is, it is essentially another piece of the legend.

Most often, as Francis Farewell wrote, attacks were made swiftly and at night. This swiftness suited both the deployment of smaller forces and the kind of political impact that Shaka sought. He was not seeking widespread destruction, only widespread respect. 'Shaka did not put to death the [chieftains] he defeated if, when he proceeded against them, they ran away and did not show fight. He made them *izinduna*.'[147] In just one example, Kutshwayo of the Dube 'like many others, was attacked merely to make him pay tribute, to reduce him to become a subject and then instate him as an *induna*.'[148] Similarly, NGIDI commented: 'Shaka's policy at first was to attack one tribe at a time and take care not to embroil others. He would take special pains to warn adjoining tribes that he was not attacking them in any way, and so his enemies would be reduced to clearly defined limits.'[149]

At every level, the use of military terror was highly selective: 'No one was allowed to use an assegai when fighting against their tribesmen, in faction fighting or fighting between individuals.' This was strictly enforced in Shaka's day.[150] Nathaniel Isaacs confirms this: 'It is not the Zoolas' system of warfare to meet their enemy openly, if they can avoid it: they like to conquer by stratagem, and not by fighting; and to gain by a ruse what might be difficult for them to achieve by the spear.'[151] Occasionally, of course, open battle *couldn't* be avoided.

One final point is interesting to note about Shaka and tactics. He never personally fought in the battles, and seldom directed the details of tactics on the ground. As Farewell noted, Shaka 'never goes with the army himself but remains generally five or six days in the rear . . . so that he never incurs any personal risk'.[152] This was only sensible, and it makes nonsense of the common impression that 'Shaka himself took shield and arms and with his own hand killed people.'[153] Except for certain times during the period of Shaka's apprenticeship under Dingiswayo, there is no evidence for this whatsoever.

In fact, Shaka's real talent lay in organisation of rather more subtle kinds. This would become more fully apparent and be implemented to a greater degree after Zwide was gone.

GHOSTS OF ZWIDE

Zwide was sitting at home at his mother Ntombaze's eziKwitshini *umuzi*, waiting for news of the Ndwandwe expedition against the Zulu. The dust of an approaching column was announced, and the women ran out, ululating, anticipating good news. It was not, however, for the column was Zulu – the Mbelebele *ibutho* that had pursued, scattered and overtaken the retreating Ndwandwe army. Zwide barely had time to flee out of a door at the back of the *isigodlo*.[154] In his mother Ntombaze's hut, the Zulu warriors found pure horror. It had always been said that if anyone entered that house, tears would come to his eyes. It was festooned with gleaming rings of brass, castor-oil bushes – and human heads, hung on pegs at the back, ready for medicinal use.[155] The hut was burned to the ground, but what became of the horrendous woman herself, no one seems to know. According to (only) one account, the place was razed and the children impaled on posts.[156] Then, the Zulu pursuers

> sought Zwide's trail, and found it. They followed it across the Black Mfolozi. On the other side of the Black Mfolozi they turned back. Zulu [kaNogandaya] said, 'Let us return. We shall tell the *inkosi* that he has escaped.' They 'ate up' the cattle of the Ndwandwe; they collected them from all over Zwide's country . . . When they engaged with Zwide's army, they had left it at the Mhlatuze, at the Nkhandla. They said, 'Lay down your shield,' to each man. Those who refused to throw down their shields were stabbed. Those who obeyed were

collected into Shaka's army . . . . Shaka praised the army. He
proceeded to build the iNtontela [*umuzi*] in Zwide's country.[157]

The conventional picture drawn by historians, from Fynn and Bryant onwards,
is that Shaka in this way instantaneously effected domination over the entire
region, all the way up to the Phongolo river. People scattered in terror in
every direction. This, as we will see in Chapter 8, is rubbish. Zwide did shift
his centre of power north of the Phongolo, but not just because he had been
dusted up once by Shaka. His presence lingered on powerfully in the southern
marches. In 1824 Henry Francis Fynn was still under the impression that the
Ndwandwe were 'Zwide's people' (as they were: Zwide only died in 1825 or
so). In fact, Zwide's memory would linger on for decades. In 1868, the
missionary David Leslie recorded a charmingly macabre legend about Zwide.
As Leslie's informant put it:

> Many years ago a tribe called 'Endwandive' [*sic*] lived hereabouts, a
> numerous and powerful tribe . . . . All the chiefs in the country, even
> the Zulu, paid homage to the Endwandive 'Zweeti', who was loved by
> his people, and respected everywhere his name penetrated – and
> where did it not? At last came the bad time, when the country went
> wrong – when all the tribes fought against themselves until the rivers
> ran red, and even the corn took a redder tinge. The end of that was,
> that the Endwandive were scattered, their chief killed, and Chaka
> with his Zulus became king over all.
>
> While Zweeti lived he did everything like a king. When he wanted
> to kill any of his wives or girls he always had them taken to the same
> place, the pool below the falls on the Umkool. When any of his captives
> or the common people were to be the sacrificial victim, the wood
> over the hill there, was where they had to submit to the will of their
> chief; and his own relations were conducted into the wood before us
> on such occasions; and he himself was 'flung in' there after his death,
> and there he keeps his state now.[158]

In Leslie's rendition, this is historical memory cum Zulu lore already
transmuting subtly into European folktale. It is historically inaccurate with
regard to Zwide's death, and it exaggerates Shaka's subsequent dominion (as

Zulu storytellers were understandably liable to do). But it's worth noting in passing the ambivalent portrait of Zwide and, more importantly, the perception that Shaka brought the mayhem to an *end*. The informant goes on to relate how his brother had died, been 'flung away', and had apparently come back in a perfectly acceptable way, as an *idlose* spirit. But something was wrong:

'My brother went about the kraal, but he seemed continually to mourn for the good things he had left; would speak to no one, and wandered about as if he did not belong to us. At last it began to be whispered that he must be an Esemkofu - one raised from the dead by witches, his tongue cut out, sent back able only to moan, "Maieh! Maieh!" . . . It was agreed that I should take him to that wood - the Emagoodo - which was known to be haunted, and, if he fraternised with the others, it would set the matter at rest, and we should get rid of him from the kraal. To avoid giving cause for suspicion, I told my brother to get axes to cut wood; without saying anything he did so, and away we went - I with fear and trembling; he seeming to care for nothing. I had heard the wood was full of Zweeti's people, and that the "*Bayete*" ("King of Kings" - the greeting to majesty), was often heard mysteriously soughing through the trees . . .'

'We entered the wood . . . I cut a wattle. Immediately the sound [as of a moaning wind] increased in density - came nearer us, round us, over us, under us, and, I may say, in us; and amidst it I seemed to hear half-broken ejaculations of the human voice. I looked towards my brother; he seemed to be wakening up, more life was visible in his face. Cheered by this I cut another wattle. No sooner had my axe struck the wood than immediately were heard on all sides exclamations of surprise and anger; the sound increased in loudness, and a heavy pressure seemed to be upon me. I could scarcely breathe, and felt as if something was fingering my axe and assegais. I looked towards my brother; he evidently was now alive to his situation; terror was in his countenance, and he looked beseechingly towards me. Convinced now that he was no Esemkofu, I shouted aloud for joy . . .'

'My brother was, of course, rehabilitated in his tribe . . .'[159]

The account is testament to the lingering presence of Zwide's Ndwandwe. As for the *bayethe* salutation, to be made so famous by Shaka and his successors, it does indeed seem originally to have been Zwide's. It was a sign of Shaka's growing power that he assumed it for himself, along with various other of Zwide's *izibongo*. At least one Zulu ceremonial song came from Zwide, who in turn had got it from Sobhuza.[160]

Much of Shaka's 'warfare' was, in fact, conducted not on the 'battlefield', but on this linguistic level, the level of posturing and propaganda. The informants' 'memories' of dashing warriors and bloody confrontations are part of the propaganda, neither wholly lies nor wholly the truth. John Wright's summary is just:

> Far from being the cohesive, centralised polity under the rule of a powerful despot which is depicted in the stereotype, the Zulu polity was in reality a loose alliance of chiefdoms hurriedly brought together under the leadership of Shaka, partly by force, partly by persuasion, and partly by a common fear of the Ndwandwe.[161]

After Zwide's defeat on the Mvuzane river, Shaka's strategies for 'state-building' didn't change. Rather, their efficacy was confirmed and he continued in the same vein as before.

Box 4

Cannibal tales

Over the years 1821–3, which were precisely the years in which Shaka's iziYendane *impi* was conducting its murderous *izwekufa* south of the Thukela river, the Spanish painter Francisco Goya was painting his terrifying masterpiece, *Saturn eating his children*. The mad-eyed monstrous god rips off the head of its buxom victim; his maw gapes. In 1888, D.C.F. Moodie's compendium of South African historical tales, *Battles and Adventures*, featured an equally dramatic etching depicting Shaka: body poised in exaggerated diagonals, fanged mouth slavering, apparently about to take a bite out of a fallen foe. This is just one of many not-so-subtle imputations of cannibalism, if not to Shaka himself, at least as a product of his savageries.

The terror and condemnation of cannibalism haunts all cultures. In her wonderful book, *No Go the Bogeyman*, cultural historian Marina Warner writes that much of the world's 'lurid cannibalistic material acts as metaphorical disguise for issues of authority, procreation, and intergenerational rivalry: it relates ways of confronting the foundations of the sense of identity and the self and of the self's historical and social place'.[1]

As interesting to us as the question, '*Were* there cannibals in Shaka's time?' is the issue, 'Why did stories of cannibals arise – and persist?' In the popular literature, Shaka is repeatedly blamed for reducing conquered peoples to such a state of dislocation and hunger that they ate poisonous roots, dry grass, and each other. It went along with the images of rampaging *impis* destroying everything in their path. The Zulu *themselves* were apparently too aristocratic, too martial, to indulge in anthropophagy, but – so the literature has it – large numbers of others were forced to.

Writers as early as Henry Francis Fynn noted that folktales of cannibals had long been regaled to wide-eyed Zulu children – as they are in almost any culture you can name. In the late eighteenth and early nineteenth centuries, however, such a repository of cultural images – used for education, control and amusement – would take on specific historical inflections. Cannibals were said to arise when other social controls broke down: when people were reduced to incoherence by slaving, warfare, famine, or all three. The missionary-anthropologist Henry Callaway, while recording Zulu cannibal tales as folklore, also made the connection between cannibals and slavers. It was readily believed, on south-eastern shores as well as elsewhere in Africa, that white slavers ate their victims. Magema Fuze caught the flavour in his image of 'this enormous monster that used to move about collecting black children, filling its capacious stomach and then making off with them'.[2]

It was a short step from there to characterising local habitual raiders – anyone who challenged the established order – as cannibalistic. This was probably the source of Nathaniel Isaacs's impression that Zihlandlo of the Mkhize was a 'cannibal'. He was, rather, an accomplished raider who (as the Zulu phrase metaphorically put it) 'ate up' both men and cattle. Related confusions probably arose from the ritual use of human body parts for *muti* (medicines) – a practice that continues to the present – or (it was thought) of human fat for the working of iron.[3] Fynn liked to titillate his younger listeners such as William Bazely with cannibal tales; Bazely claimed to have gone off himself and found the very bones of cannibals' victims. Fynn himself wrote of cannibalism as a consequence of Shaka's wars only once.[4] He claims – as it appears in the *Diary* – that on his first journey *southwards* to the Mthatha river in 1824, he saw 'six thousand' unhappy refugees grubbing about for roots, and devouring each other. However, nothing like this appears in his original 'Notebook', and the allegation is made in the service of justifying Fynn's gathering up a substantial private following of his own. Moreover, as related in the main text, by 1824 Shaka's forces hadn't penetrated anywhere near this area. It's nonsense.

Almost all other references similarly dissolve on close inspection. In the whole of *The James Stuart Archive*, only 22 references to cannibalism are indexed. Two refer to the distant past. One informant thought that cannibals had originally existed far to the 'west' (possibly referring to the Sotho).[5] Another characterised all 'Ntungwas' as 'cannibals': in other words, they were the original foreign raiders.[6] This association informed MAZIYANA's observation that the Thembu were early on harassed by 'bandits or cannibals'.[7] Four further references are to incidents in post-Shakan times, including the alleged capture of the Hlubi chief Langalibalele by cannibals; an unlikely story from J.W. Shepstone; and the alleged survival of some cannibals from Dingane's time into the late nineteenth century.[8] Macingwane of the Ngwane was thought to have been eaten by cannibals, but nobody actually knew.[9] And one informant recalled a story that a certain chief had had to 'contend with' cannibals after an attack from Ngoza's Thembu.[10]

Of the twenty-two references, only *three* state that cannibals emerged during or as a result of Shaka's wars. They are rather vague. One informant thought that some cannibals had shown up on the Mngeni, 30 kilometres from Port

Natal; another named the Mhlathuze; and a third, Camperdown.[11] Two noted that the cannibalism had arisen as a direct result of famine (whether or not caused by warfare); one thought that this had once arisen earlier, too, amongst Mthimkulu's Hlubi.[12]

Only in a single instance does some agreement seem to emerge on a case marked with any precision. A cluster of people, variously named but all closely related, were said to have been 'formerly' cannibals. They were called Dunge, or Mbambo, or Ntuli, and occasionally Bhele (each being an offshoot of the following one). All traced themselves to a cannibalistic ancestor named Mahlapahlapa, whose fate was uncertain but certainly pre-dated Shaka.[13] Whether Mahlapahlapa actually ate people, or was just an anarchic raider, remains unclear. Fynn wrote that he had been reduced to cannibalism by Matiwane, who had taken all his cattle.[14] However, by Shaka's, perhaps even Senzangakhona's time, this had come to an end.

In short, there is next to no credible evidence that cannibalism was induced by Shaka's raids. Indeed, one informant thought that the effect was the opposite: Shaka 'scattered the cannibals', who went off north.[15] It remains only a *possibility* that *some* people were reduced temporarily to cannibalism by the *izwekufa* in Natal, leaving the scars of distaste on the cultural memory. As MQAIKANA vaguely but resonantly put it:

> When Shaka destroyed the country, people took to sleeping in the veld and wandering about, attacked by hyenas etc. Then other people started hunting human beings and eating them. In later years they stopped the practice. But those who resorted to it formerly are known and are pointed out, though they greatly resent being told they used to be cannibals.[16]

8

Holding the centre

Consolidation, c.1820-3

Tshaka . . . like a desolating scourge, over-ran Natal with his armies,
making his name a terror to all who heard it, until no nation dared to
stand before his wrath, but all fled, like frightened birds or deer.
William Holden, *History of the Colony of Natal* (1855, 41).

You can still find the site of Shaka's best-known *ikhanda*, his most famous
'capital' – kwaBulawayo. Some twenty kilometres north-east of Eshowe,
the road twists up the escarpment of the Mhlathuze valley; you turn off left
along a gravel road. Not far from another spot marked as 'Cowards' Bush',
the Maqwakazi ridge crests. This is the site of kwaBulawayo, and you can see
why Shaka chose it. The slope drops steeply away on the north side – from
which the most dangerous threats would have come. You can see the
Mhlathuze far below; the sheltering heights of the Ngoye forests are within
easy reach to the south-east. As Nathaniel Isaacs noted, it was 'partly compassed
by a deep ravine', the whole 'surrounded by high and irregular land, covered
with lofty and thriving timber'.[1] On the dolerite cap of the hill, its
northernmost point, remains have been found that suggest this might have
been the so-called Cele village, outside the main palisade.[2] This would have
been Shaka's private quarters, fittingly the most elevated.

CAPITAL SITES

Fynn and Isaacs said that kwaBulawayo was between two and three miles in
circumference, and that it contained as many as 1 400 huts.[3] The archaeology

227

suggests that it was nowhere near this size. It was probably no more than 350 metres across at its widest, the distance between the *isigodlo* at the top and the lowest gate. Dingane's much bigger establishment at Mgungundhlovu, some 600 metres in length, contained about 1 100 huts. KwaBulawayo, by analogy, held perhaps only half that number.[4]

To be fair to Isaacs and Fynn, it's possible that they were including the 'informal settlement' that probably gathered patchily in the lee of the leader's enclosures. More likely, their exaggeration is simply another of the inflated tales they spun about the rest of Shaka's rule: his violence, the number of people he slaughtered, and the extent of the territory he conquered. (If we were to believe Fynn, Shaka's conquests extended from Delagoa Bay to the Cape Colony frontier, and from the Limpopo to the sea.)

The two white adventurers further delighted in believing that the names Shaka assigned to his settlements were derived from some heinous act of arbitrary murder. The building of kwaBulawayo had been preceded by that of Gibixhegu. 'Gibi Caigu', Fynn wrote, meant: 'turn out the old ones' because, after defeating Zwide, Shaka 'collected all the aged men in the country whom he had killed, and sung a song composed for the purpose the words of which were:- "Produce the cowards ect [sic]" each regiment producing them they were carried off and killed, the home name of the kraal from that time changed to Umbulwaio, i.e. they are all killed'.[5] Hence 'Cowards' Bush': a highly improbable legend becomes concretised in a geographical spot that can be visited and stared at while the imagination runs wild.

Gibixhegu may in fact have been the name of a former *umuzi* back in the Makhosini area, the valley of the 'kings' along the Mkhumbane river, with no connection to killing old men at all.[6] In another derivation, Shaka is said to have scoffed, 'I won't think of fighting an old man, *ixegu*, who used to fight with my father'.[7] NGIDI, alternatively, traces the name to a memory of Shaka washing over his father's hut: he *giba*'d him, got him out of the hut and so, symbolically, out of the chieftainship.[8] Most likely the settlement was, as NGIDI says elsewhere, an offshoot which *phuma*'d, split away, from Shaka's Mkhandlu *umuzi*, the one he originally set up with Mthethwa help,[9] or of the Mbelebeleni settlement that Zwide had burnt down.[10] At first Gibixhegu was built in the Ndlangubo district, close to and overlooking the protective Ngoye hills and forest, on the eastern side of the Matheku stream's shallow valley.[11] (See Map 6 on page 229.)

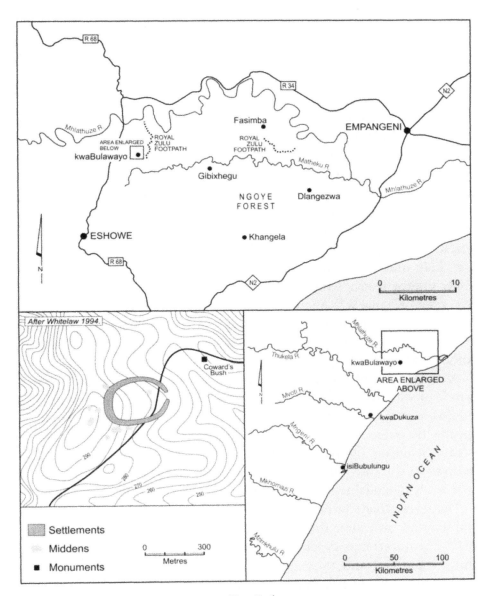

Map 6: KwaBulawayo

The timing is not entirely certain. Since it was well inside Qwabe territory, Gibixhegu must have been built after the incorporation of the Qwabe. One set of informants thinks that it was built after Zwide's defeat; another that it was before. It makes most sense to me that Shaka established Gibixhegu in its ridge-top defensive position, still more than 60 kilometres from his old home, while in the throes of his first attempt to resist Zwide's raids, and possibly after his first temporary victory in the 'kisi' fight.[12]

Several *amabutho* were also stationed in the district. Some of these can be quite exactly located. The Dlangezwa *ibutho*, formed at precisely this time, was situated nearby, on Entondweni hill, 'opposite and above Ngoye'.[13] The loyal iWombe was kept at kwaBulawayo itself; close to the *inkosi*. The Fasimba built between the Mhlathuze and what is still marked on survey maps as the Zulu Royal Footpath.[14] The Mbelebele, the iNtontela and the isiPhezi – also 'core' Zulu units – were likewise housed nearby. So was the Mqumanga, the mostly Qwabe *ibutho*, who built a new establishment on the lower Mlálazi river, called Khangela.[15] As time went on, a large number of *imizi* would be established by Shaka in the Eshowe area. Among the ones we know about are: eSiyembeni, Gibibanye, kwaFojisa, uPhoko, eNzondeni, and eKuqobhekheni.[16]

All this speaks of – at least initially – a defensive bunching as the primary reason for this shift so far south-west of Makhosini. One informant claims that Zwide attacked Shaka actually at kwaBulawayo; this seems aberrant, but captures the sense of the Ndwandwe danger.[17] The continuing Ndwandwe threat – whether before or after the 'Mvuzane fight' – may have also precipitated the next move, to the eastern side of the valley, the final and more easily defendable site. The new *umuzi* was named kwaBulawayo.

There are other sources that assert that Shaka moved from Gibixhegu to kwaBulawayo only after the assassination attempt in 1824 (see below, page 311).[18] The uncertainty developed possibly because the same people made up both settlements, and thus many continued to think of the new one as 'Gibixhegu'. NGIDI noted, 'When the Bulawayo kraal was built at Maqwakazi it was composed of Gibixegu people, so Gibixegu ceased to exist'.[19] Nathaniel Isaacs, visiting in 1825, the year after the assassination attempt, evidently knew it as 'Gibixhegu',[20] while Charles Rawden Maclean, who visited at precisely the same time, remembered it as 'Bulawayo'.[21] An alternative may be that both *imizi* remained in existence, though Shaka and his 'court' shifted.

The site of kwaBulawayo – both in its defensive geography and in the confusions over its name – can stand as a symbol for Shaka's reign. An initial stage was stimulated by the need for defence, and the need for allied manpower. A slow-maturing second stage involved greater exploitation of local resources of all kinds: good grazing, for example, and wood for iron-working.[22] It was, in all respects, an attractive region. In time, the Zulu presence became a pretty thorough act of colonisation, and the place could, in a final phase, serve as a base for more aggressive forays.

LAND RITES

In the regions that Shaka came to control most firmly, the use of the local resources was the single most important aspect of centralised power. The everyday stuff of Zulu domination involved dictating land use, cattle distribution, grain growing, and assegai manufacture, as well as the flow of trade items such as beads and brass. These regions were fairly limited in extent: the Makhosini and eventually (between the Mfolozis) Mahlabathini areas; the Eshowe-Mhlathuze valley area; and, for a brief period after 1826, the kwaDukuza (later Stanger) area. As we will detail shortly, Shaka did establish some *amakhanda*, a scattering of cattle-posts, and resident *izinduna* in a wider arc both north and south, between the Phongolo and the Mzimkhulu rivers. Very occasionally he raided even further. However, he never controlled those tracts in the same tight way. The regions over the Black Mfolozi to the north and the Thukela to the south were the realms of the client-chiefs, more or less friendly allies, tendering tribute in manpower or goods as the situation demanded.

Within the scope of Shaka's forces, land was the basis for all political business. *Amakhanda* and smaller *imizi* were planted on occupied territories, and the *izinduna* were given powers of distribution and reward. The position of *induna*, while preceding Shaka, seems to have arisen as part of the development of the *ibutho*, and there seems no reason to doubt that Shaka refined the *induna*'s role to an unprecedented degree. The *izinduna* sat on a kind of council, the *isiqoqo*. Here it was decided who would be 'allowed to have authority, and who would preserve power for themselves'.[23] This implies that it was not entirely up to Shaka. In theory, men of low rank but

outstanding ability could be elevated – remember Zulu kaNogandaya – but
in practice awards went mainly to men of the established ruling families. As
one informant wryly noted, the *izinduna* 'masked many [genuine] heroes
through mere self-seeking. A hero who had killed maybe 3 or 4 would be
silenced by its being said by the *izinduna* that some other man, some special
favourite (like a prince) had killed a couple of the very men named . . .'[24]
Once assigned to an *ikhanda* or barracks settlement, an *induna* wielded
considerable power. He was responsible for dispensing the *inkosi*'s bounty,
getting the crops in, arming his men, gathering tribute, distributing captive
women, and punishing wrongdoers, with death if necessary. An *induna* who
was permitted to punish by death was regarded as bearing a very high degree
of the *inkosi*'s trust; such men may not have amounted to more than a dozen
or so, even under Shaka.[25] The *izinduna* were the necessary agents of the
extension of Shaka's political reach, but they often verged on independence,
and sometimes on uncontrolled abuse:

> It was the *izinduna* who were responsible for the indiscriminate killing
> off that went on. Sometimes a man rewarded with cattle by the king
> would be killed just as he reached his home, and his cattle seized.
> These cattle . . . would be taken off to the *izinduna*'s kraals, and they
> would report that nothing in the shape of cattle was at the kraal.[26]

In short, the *izinduna* were an élite. They showed off their status with displays
of brass bangles, beads, and particular birds' feathers. Local and international
trade were important both to these displays and to their ability to dispense
rewards in brass collars and armlets, which the *inkosi* supplied for the
purpose.[27] In this way, they distinguished themselves from the petty chieftains
and headmen who remained where they were on the land, paying tribute to
the new authorities when obliged to. The mechanism worked something
like this:

> The land of Zululand belongs to Shaka, he who unified all of it. Shaka
> would take a fancy to a man and then, having conquered some chief's
> land, would say this man might go and build at any spot Shaka might
> indicate. Men used to be given land by Shaka, and a man might be

given permission to occupy land even though other people might be
living on it at the time. The old resident would not be called upon to
quit. If, later on, a quarrel were to arise, it might end in the two going
to Shaka, who would generally cause the old resident to move to some
other locality . . . The land at all times, all of it, belonged to the king,
i.e. since Shaka's federating or unifying the small, previously existing
amakosi. Any man who speaks of land as belonging to him means it is
his because given him by the king. Those who were conquered were
not required to ask permission to remain. There was no necessity;
they merely continued to occupy as before.[28]

Hence, there was no real reason for Shaka to assign boundaries:

The boundaries of the country were determined by the *izizwe* (tribes)
defeated, i.e. the lands occupied by them. Shaka defined no boundaries,
for the territories he conquered and whose occupants tendered their
allegiance to him were already sufficiently defined and known.[29]

On both the small scale and the large, 'boundaries' would remain very fluid,
marked if at all by rivers and hills. The new Zulu authority also did not
necessarily prevail:

Disputes over land were usually settled by the *izinduna*, and were not
taken to the king. Only a great quarrel, i.e. between *izikulu*, would be
brought to the king's notice [. . . the king might say, 'Go, So-and-so,
and set up your homestead in such-and-such a place'. . .] Matters were
settled by priority of occupation. A man coming to live next to an old
established kraal might be told to leave and not to provoke the old
settler.[30]

Moreover (contrary to the proponents of the overpopulation thesis), there
was still plenty of land to go round: 'even before Shaka came to the throne
there was a lot of vacant land . . . Cattle might graze and go three or four
miles without coming to a kraal'.[31] Minor problems of overcrowding were
easily resolved:

Separation was caused by growth of numbers (*qalwa nge zifu*). The *umnumzana* [head man] divided up the land for his own kraal, i.e. gave garden lands to his wives; that has nothing to do with other kraals. In time other kraals encroach. Objecting to this, he might decide to leave the neighbourhood and go elsewhere. He would pick out another vacant space and build there, *because there was no law restricting occupation of land.*[32]

In other words, the *inkosi*'s authority had limits; it was designed only to fulfil certain tributary and military purposes. The homesteads would have lost men for short periods to military service. They would have lost a number of women, mostly young daughters, to the centralised *izigodlo*. There would be periodic demands for grain, cattle duty, or attendance at increasingly centralised rituals such as the annual first-fruits ceremony.

Otherwise, local daily life on the land continued in much its usual way.

Indeed, it was one of the advantages of being 'beneath Shaka's armpit' that this could continue to be the case.

POURING THEM TOGETHER

Elsewhere in the Thukela-Phongolo catchment, things were not so stable. Even Shaka, despite his defeat of Zwide, was far from fully secure in 1820. To the north, more upheavals were in the making.

The myth states that the crushing of Zwide sparked a panicked scattering of various peoples all over the subcontinent: the Gaza into Mozambique; the Jere (becoming the Ngoni) all the way to Malawi; and the Khumalo (becoming the Ndebele) all the way to Zimbabwe. All this was supposedly Shaka's doing. He was, in this instant-pudding view, now the undisputed tyrant of a seamlessly unified 'kingdom' stretching to Delagoa Bay.

The reality is that Zwide was not 'crushed', although he did shift the centre of his polity northwards, to the amaNzambomvu, a tributary of the Nkomathi.[33] The defeat at the Mvuzane may have been one crucial factor in this move, but equally strong may have been the attraction of the Delagoa trade. If Fynn is correct, after Dingiswayo's death Zwide tried to corner that part of the trade previously commanded by the Mthethwa.[34] The name 'Zeite', sometimes arbitrarily attached to different inland groups, was certainly well known at Delagoa Bay by 1823.[35] Zwide retained enough punch and cohesion to keep Sobhuza of the Dlamini-Swazi in check, then to move even further north and practically smash the Pedi polity on the Steelpoort river.[36] Trade opportunities, involving well-developed Pedi links with both Delagoa Bay and Inhambane, may well have played a part in Zwide's decisions here.[37]

It may also have proved easier for him to shift gradually northwards than to compete with either Shaka or his own Ndwandwe family offshoots: the Msane, Jere and Gaza groups. All three – led by Nxaba, Zwangendaba and Soshangane respectively – had probably maintained some measure of independence from Zwide. Now, prompted by Shaka's growing power, Zwide's shift northwards, and an attractive explosion in the slave trade, they gradually moved closer to the Bay.

Shaka had little to do with these subsequent movements. He was preoccupied in absorbing southern Ndwandwe and Mthethwa segments into his polity. This process was mostly peaceable. Some segments stayed stubbornly in place, and carried on doing pretty much what they had always been doing. At a future point they would be on hand to support Zwide's son, Sikhunyane. Sikhunyane had said to the retreating Zwide, 'Shaka has overcome you, for you are an old man. He will not overcome my age-grade (*intanga*).'[38] Sikhunyane would return and build at the Mhlongamvula river, in the lee of the Ezindololwane hills. From there, after his father's death in about 1825, he would come into further conflict with the Zulu – but more on that in its proper place.

Some Ndwandwe *khonza*'d Shaka directly. A particularly prominent example was Somaphunga, a son of Zwide himself. Somaphunga became a well-respected *isikhulu*, a kind of councillor, under Shaka, Dingane, and on into Mpande's reign.[39]

Other Ndwandwe sections were merged with their neighbours. In one complicated negotiation of the new reality, a previously semi-independent section of the Mthethwa under Mkhosi kaMgudlana shifted from wherever he was and *khonza*'d Shaka. Possibly his father Mgudlana was himself still alive, and also *khonza*'d. Shaka accompanied them to a new spot on the upper Black Mfolozi, on the border of Ndwandwe territory, and helped them to build a new *ikhanda*, Mphangisweni. It was built close to a mountain, Ngome.

The name was chosen because, Shaka announced, 'They have come hurrying, *phangisa*, to pay tribute; we have poured them together in one place with the Ndwandwe'.[40] Mkhosi's brother Nquhele was made *induna* of the new colony – an example of the checks and balances of power that Shaka was refining. It included men of the Mbelebele, was supplemented by Mthethwa people, and was also under direct 'royal' supervision. Its primary purpose was probably to watch over the Khumalo sections, especially after the departure of Mzilikazi (see page 252). Mphangisweni would become the main conduit for the ongoing recruitment of Ndwandwe elements into Zulu structures.[41]

Another strategy that Shaka was developing in order to balance potentially troublesome authority-figures against one another, was to appoint one of the grand old ladies – the *amakhosikazi* – to oversee the affairs of particular *amakhanda*. They were extremely powerful figures who controlled the women of the *izigodlo* and enforced their taboos, oversaw marriage alliances, directed the distribution of provisions, and generally 'exerted a direct royal monopoly over access to the products of women's agricultural labour'.[42] Their own marriages were both politically prestigious and materially lucrative. Crucially, they represented the Zulu ancestral spirits to whom the major ceremonials were addressed.

There was Mawa, a half-sister of Senzangakhona's, at Ntonteleni,[43] who later became most infamous for defecting with a band of followers to Natal in 1843. Nomahawu became the chief woman at kwaDukuza,[44] and continued to hold influence under Dingane.[45] Langazana was of the emaBeleni people, and commanded a number of *imizi* apart from her central one, esiKlebheni: eZembeni, eNkonjeni, eNdlwayini, eNtoleleni, eTsheni.[46] Allen Gardiner met Langazana during Dingane's reign, when she was middle-aged, 'of a very dignified size', and with 'a mild and intelligent countenance'.[47] She presided over esiKlebheni until she died in 1884.[48] And, of course, there was Shaka's own mother, Nandi, who presided at Nyakumbi and Ndulinde, attached to kwaBulawayo,[49] and became the patron of the iziYendane *ibutho*.[50]

Perhaps the most important of these women was Mnkabayi kaJama, Shaka's paternal aunt.

We have already seen Mnkabayi play a pivotal role in bringing Shaka to power. Tall, light-skinned, and indomitable, she was 'the great she-elephant', an *isitubesikazi*, distinguished by her great soft bulk.[51] She presided over the major rites performed in February or March, when the army went out on campaign. The warriors would be treated by the doctors, then make their way via Makhosini and the ancestors' graves, to Mnkabayi's establishment. At first this was Nobamba; she also at times ruled over esiKlebheni, and probably kwaMfemfe, too.[52] She died during Dingane's reign, and her grave became a place to which refugees could fly for safety, as sacrosanct as a chapel.[53]

Perhaps around this period (1820 or 1821) Mnkabayi took over Emahlabaneni, established in former Ndwandwe territory between the Black Mfolozi and the Phongolo. There, NGIDI noted in 1904, the Zulu army was *thetha*'d – ritually blessed for war – 'to this day'.[54] Her presence was a powerful signal of Shaka's intention to colonise this border region. No one was better suited for the job than Mnkabayi. As the first line of her recorded praises indicates, she was seen as being as formidable as a man:

> *USoqili!* Father of guile!
> Cunning one of the Hoshoza people,
> Who devours a person tempting him with a story;
> She killed Bhedu amongst the medicine men,
> And destroyed Mkhongoyiyiyana amongst the Ngadinis,
> And killed Bheje amongst the diviners.
> Morass of Menzi [Zulu 'royalty'],
> That caught people and finished them off . . .
> Maid that matured and her mouth dried up,
> And then they criticized her amongst the old women.
> She who allays for people their anxiety,
> They catch it and she looks at it with her eyes.
> The opener of all the main gates so that people may enter . . .
> Sipper for others of the venom of the cobra . . .[55]

Mnkabayi would go on to command another important outlying northern *ikhanda*, Qulusini. This was built in the north-west, near Hlobane mountain, recently the scene of Hlubi and Ngwane violence. Qulusini was placed under the oversight of an Mdlalose collateral clan member, Mdlaka.[56] His own Mdlalose followers – colonists – would be joined by Mthethwa and Ndwandwe elements. Some of the Vundla people, once led by Nxaba, returned with

Somaphunga kaZwide to *khonza* Shaka, and they were sent out to Qulusini. They were always treated with some disdain, though, as 'mere Tongas'.[57] Qulusini's inhabitants collectively became known as the 'Baqulusi', neither an *ibutho* nor a clan, but a new kind of multinational entity. In this sense, and at least in these outposts, 'the importance of the *amakhanda* had eclipsed the importance of the clan insofar as the relations of its members to the state were concerned', because their composition directly 'represented the power of the Zulu royal house, not a pre-Shakan chiefdom'.[58]

Of other *amakhanda* on the borders of Ndwandwe country, we know little. There was at least one, uMyehe at Masipula kaMamba's, on the Black Mfolozi – but exactly when it was built is uncertain.[59]

These outposts were thinly spread. The intensity of Shaka's control over these regions is not likely to have been high. Nevertheless, these northern *amakhanda* proved surprisingly long-lived. The fact that they weren't overrun by anybody seems to indicate that such turmoil as there was along the Phongolo wasn't a particularly strong threat to them as such. (Only Sikhunyane's resurgence would cause a ripple, in 1826.) It's likely that the Zulu outriders were finding ways of *participating* in whatever was going on, and probably acting as a stabilising influence. In any case, they weren't such a huge distance from the heartland: the furthest, Qulusini, was only about 70 kilometres from Mahlabathini, the area just north of the White Mfolozi, in which Shaka was really concentrating his colonial enterprises.

In Mahlabathini, over the years following Zwide's defeat, Shaka established a relatively dense cluster of *imizi*. Under Mmama, Mnkabayi's twin sister, oSebeni was built at the western end of the district, at Nhlazatshe mountain.[60] A little to the east of that were built kwaKandisa, oNyange, kwaGuqu, Mdadasa, and Nomdayana. (These are just the ones that we can roughly locate; see Box 5 on page 263 and Map 8 on page 264.) These settlements were certainly in aid of integrating previous Mthethwa sections and adherents.

Then there was Maphitha kaSojiyisa, who presents a particularly interesting case. He was a stubby, dark man, almost shiny-black.[61] He belonged to a group called the Mandlakazi, a line very close to the Zulu chiefly family, but not as close as some of the so-called collateral clans. This was because Sojiyisa's beginnings – rather like Shaka's own – were ambiguous. He was the son of a foundling, Ngwabi, who was integrated into the Zulu chiefly family, adopting the Zulu *izibongo* (unlike the collateral clans, which retained their own praises and identity). Ngwabi died while Sojiyisa was still in the womb. His widow was 'given to', and Sojiyisa raised by, a son of Jama, Mhlaba. Hence, some would subsequently claim that Sojiyisa was a 'royal prince' of Jama's line, and others that he wasn't. Sojiyisa's descendants, like Maphitha, were raised as members of the Zulu chiefly family, but could never be either fully integrated or become real contenders to inherit the chiefdom.[62] Maphitha was, however, close: exactly Shaka's age, and a member of his iWombe *ibutho*.[63]

In short, a man like Maphitha was ideally placed to be given the semi-independent status of a client-chief.

In about 1820, Shaka appointed Maphitha to govern the southern portion of what had been Ndwandwe territory, centred on the Mona river. There, Maphitha built an *umuzi*, after which the whole area, and then the people he governed as well, became known as Mandlakazi.[64] Here, Maphitha was permitted to govern with increasing autonomy. He could execute people, assign lands, and conduct major ceremonies. Oddly, he was said not to have had an *isigodlo*,[65] though he must have controlled the local distribution of many women. He also did not formally become an *isikhulu*, one of the central 'elders' of the Zulu inner circle; that status was generally accorded on hereditary lines.[66] Nevertheless, Maphitha became hugely important as a military leader and policy-maker, remaining such right into Cetshwayo's reign. He would be remembered in his praises as both a courageous warrior and a ruthlessly cunning diplomat:

> Stabber that cannot be denied
> He who rolls back the mountain so that the sun appears
> Fierce piercer of the stomach . . .
> Jackal that escaped the trap
> When others had been caught the previous day.[67]

He established something of a family spread in the northern marches, assigning swathes of land to his brothers:

> The king used to say, 'How are matters in Mapita's country?' Mapita had charge of all the northern part of the country, and he used to

locate heads on land. Mapita ruled for the king . . . Tokotoko and Domba were Mapita's brothers, sons of Sojisa too, and had land of their own but under Mapita.[68]

As far as the record shows, with the solitary exception of the raid against Sikhunyane in 1826, Shaka never visited these north-eastern regions. He either didn't feel that he needed to, or didn't want to, as he himself moved still further south. As for Maphitha, he subsequently resisted all the Zulu *inkosis*' attempts to move him or to move other people onto his land, land 'held by him as a gift from Shaka in trust for his people'.[69]

While this process of colonising and stabilising the region between and just north of the Mfolozi rivers was going on, more violent events were unfolding further north, in a great arc running from Delagoa Bay to the Drakensberg.

THE VATWAHS ARE COMING!

On 5 July 1821, the governor of Delagoa Bay, Caetano da Costa Matoso, reported that the inland Thembe had been attacked by a huge force – some 8 000 men. They were, it was said, after 'beads and bangles [for] necklaces and bracelets'. Just who these people were is not entirely clear. They were led, apparently, by one 'Chief Inhamboza, dominating some territories south of Santa Luzia [St Lucia Bay]'.[70]

'Nyambose' was a common synonym or *ithakazelo* for the Mthethwa; the name probably derived from an early collateral group.[71] Indeed, it was intimately connected with the very origins of the Mthethwa amongst the Tsonga themselves; so it's hardly surprising that there continued to be trade links, built on and amplifying ancestral ones.[72] It was the Mthethwa who commanded precisely the area described by Matoso; and, as we've seen, they had a well-established trade link along this coast. But were the Mthethwa still able to raid so far, and in such force, two or three years after Dingiswayo's death?

One possibility is that it *was* in fact the Mthethwa, the offshoot led by, or at least accompanied by, Dingiswayo's son and heir, Somveli. Somveli was still quite young at the time of Dingiswayo's death, and seems to have hung around for at least a couple of years. At some point, however (probably early to mid-1821), he left. According to NGIDI, he and Shaka were one day jesting with each other in the cattle enclosure at kwaBulawayo.

> Shaka said to Somveli, 'Do you think your Yengo kraal [Dingiswayo's capital] ever equalled this one in size?' Somveli said, 'Of course it was. How could it be otherwise, since you were my father's protégé, having been given to Ngomane with orders that he was to look after you? You have forgotten your old condition.' They had more words, and Somveli returned home, only to arm and leave for the north on the ground that he and Shaka had quarrelled, for Shaka seemed to think the Mthethwa tribe was dead. Shaka had not driven him away, but Somveli saw that Shaka *ka ntelelani na munt' a lunge, a kule.* That is, no person that Shaka had once joked with ever prospered.[73]

Some of Mondisa's followers were also killed; others went off with Somveli, leaving a group from the *ikholo* or left-hand house of Dingiswayo's family to *khonza* Shaka without further ado. This would become Mlandela's bailiwick.[74] Consequently, it's possible that the incursion noted by the governor was indeed 'Nyambose': Somveli and followers attempting to forestall or subvert the incursion into the Thembe region of the dangerous 'Ndwandwe' groups.[75]

Another possibility is that Governor Matoso was – as coastal observers so often were – confused or misinformed about who was involved, and the attack was actually made by one of the 'Ndwandwe' groups: Soshangane's, Zwangendaba's, or Zwide's own. In September 1822, the British Captain W.F.W. Owen anchored in Delagoa Bay, ostensibly on a surveying mission, and shortly recorded that 'it appears not long since Mapoota was overrun by Vatwahs', led by a king named 'Zeite', a cousin of 'Soongundava' (Zwangendaba).[76] This seems more likely. At much the same time, though, Owen recorded the presence of 'Cinchingany' (Soshangane), also in charge of a large party of 'Zoolas'.[77] In the end, we can't be sure, but the confusion itself is significant. It indicates that if the Mthethwa/Nyambose were not the culprits this time, they had been before. Their methods were not dissimilar. Soshangane's group would apparently be called 'manhambozes' even in the

1830s.[78] Captain Owen commented: 'To the southward of Mapoota there exists a tribe of warlike Kaffers, called Zoolos, but by the Portuguese Vatwahs, being the same as the ancient term Batwa, or Butwah: the people of Delagoa call them Hollontontes, doubtless a corruption from Hottentots . . .'[79] All but interchangeable, the names were more a description of general appearance, of methods of warfare, or of simple foreignness. 'Vatwa' would become common. The name probably derives from a general disdainful term, 'baThwa', applied with a sniff of fear to practically anyone from afar. It was in use at the coast for peoples of the interior at least as early as 1730.[80] In addition, the chief's name was often attached to the whole people he led; so literally for decades all the various Ndwandwe offshoots would from time to time be termed 'Zwides'. In 1838, for instance, a reporter from Delagoa Bay called Soshangane's people both: 'Vatuas or Massuitas'. In 1844 Nxaba was also said to be 'one of the Vatua kings'. There are plenty more examples.[81]

This much is certain: the 'Vatwahs' were *not* Shaka's Zulu.[82] Shaka naturally had every interest in keeping the area peaceful, and the links with Makhasane and the Maphuta open. William Threlfall, temporarily a missionary at Delagoa Bay, noted that Shakan envoys to the Bay were quite peaceable.[83] In early 1823, for example, Shaka sent a present of 30 elephant tusks to the governor, who (possibly in return) made an ineffectual attack on Zwangendaba.[84] Owen, who visited Makhasane personally and noted his peaceful liaison with Shaka,[85] recorded the arrival in 1823 of a caravan of 1 000 porters, bearing 300 or 400 tusks and driving a large number of cattle; it is almost certain that these came from Zulu country.[86] If Fynn can be believed, Shaka and the Zulu regarded the Tsonga as 'being the only people who possessed beads and brass'.[87] He came to some kind of tribute-arrangement with Makhasane. (He did not, as Smith asserts, have the authority to have 'granted virtual independence' to the Maphuta.[88]) The trade route ran through Maphitha's north-eastern territory, and Maphitha is recorded as having disputes with Mbopha (Shaka's future assassin) over ivory, which unquestionably was being traded at the Bay in 'considerable' quantities.[89] There is even a story (from Fynn) about 'Chaqua' (Shaka) being offered a wife named 'She Shaqua' from the Bay area for 55 bullocks. 'He refused to give that price and sent a small band of Orentonts to take her by force which however *they did not accomplish*'.[90] To the extent that trade continued (and

that extent is unknown), Shaka would have supported those elements of the
Ndwandwe offshoots who were *not* destructive raiders, but who settled
amongst the Tsonga and even, according to Owen, added considerably to
the group's industriousness.[91]

In sum, Shaka's links with the Bay were persistent, but fundamentally
peaceful. Only some retrospectively written accounts would *later* suggest, quite
wrongly, that Shaka's sway extended all the way to the Bay. This, I suspect,
includes an account allegedly quoted from an unnamed officer aboard one
of Owen's ships, the *Barracouta*. It appears to have been written in late 1822.
On the surface, this might be taken to be the outside world's very first exposure
to the name, Shaka:

> At this time the work of depopulation was carried on with savage
> rapidity by the merciless and destructive conquests of a tyrannical
> monster named Chaka, whose bloody proceedings promised soon to
> leave the whole of the beautiful country, from the river St John to
> Inhamban, totally desolate.[92]

This is supposed to have been diarised in 1822, but, like other parts of Owen's
Narrative of a Voyage, it was almost certainly worked up by an 1833 editor or
ghost-writer with access to other sources. By then the mythology of Shaka
was already well developed. The exaggeration sounds far too much like
Nathaniel Isaacs to be above suspicion. In addition, the officer could not
have had much evidence of the beauty of the country all the way down to the
St Johns river, 200 kilometres *south* of kwaBulawayo. Shaka hadn't got
anywhere near there – and never would. The same applies to Inhambane.

Such forays as Shaka does appear to have made in the direction of Delagoa
Bay were failures. He had already failed to prevent Somveli and a sizeable
portion of the old Mthethwa hierarchy from making off. Probably close on
Somveli's heels, Nxaba and the Msane left. Nxaba probably *khonza*'d after
Zwide's defeat, coming all the way down to Gibixhegu with ten girls from his
father's *umuzi*. It's said that he found Shaka dancing in his usual expert style.
Shaka spontaneously composed a song about a stocky companion of Nxaba's
named Lubedu: 'Etshe, Lubedu of the place of Masondo! Now at last we see
you!' Lubedu laughed. Shaka fumed, 'So the small fat toad is laughing at me!

Take him away.' And Lubedu was taken off and killed, even though he was only laughing because he approved of what the *inkosi* had done. Nxaba was alarmed, but controlled his anxiety. In return for his girls, he was presented with 100 cattle. Subsequently, one of the girls fell sick, and Shaka had her sent home. This was all very well, but it kept happening with the other girls, until there weren't any left. None of them came back to Shaka. Fearing retribution, Nxaba decided to head off north, joining up temporarily with Soshangane.[93]

In one account, Nxaba is indeed attacked by Shaka while he is in Tsonga territory. Either he was getting in the way of the trade, or breeding white cattle when he shouldn't have been,[94] or taking cattle that Shaka was demanding in tribute. Makhasane, the Tsonga chief, is said to have had designs on those cattle himself, but the upshot was that the Zulu *impi*, possibly led by the tireless Zulu kaNogandaya, got them instead.[95] Zulu is said to have 'defeated' Nxaba by dint of killing an *imbongi* praise-singer 'and one other'.[96] This hardly describes a major military confrontation. And if MKEHLANGANA is referring to St Lucia when he says that this encounter took place near 'a large sheet of standing water', it shows that Shaka's men were still a very long way from Delagoa Bay.

In fact, there's little solid evidence of an outright fight. Nxaba and Soshangane left voluntarily; they might as easily have *khonza*'d, as other Ndwandwe groups did. Their movement was not the product of vicious predation and pursuit from Shaka, but the result of a failure of Zulu diplomacy. They also did not speed over the horizon as fast as their legs could carry them.[97] Even if a later date of 1820 for the 'Mvuzane fight' is correct, Nxaba and Soshangane took well over a year to travel less than 100 kilometres northwards. Nxaba seems to have taken a particularly circuitous route, via the Drakensberg and the Limpopo, before descending on the Bay region, and then to have lingered around his cousin Soshangane and Delagoa Bay until 1827, before moving north into the Sofala area.[98]

These movements worked more like a slow viscous oil than a shower of sparks.

Similar misapprehensions, amplified by deliberate rewritings of the record, bedevil accounts of the third Ndwandwe chieftain: Zwangendaba. Hence, in his 1833 *Narrative*, Captain Owen-and-ghost-writer said:

> King Chaka expelled his uncle, Loon Kundava, and upwards of 5 000
> of his adherents [who] threatened to destroy the Portuguese factory;
> whilst, strange to say, the commandant and soldiers of the said factory
> actually carried on traffic with them, through native traders, for their
> spoil of both cattle and slaves . . .[99]

How does this 'Loon Kundava' become Shaka's *uncle*? A comparison with
Owen's original report of May 1823 reveals all. 'Loon-Kundava' is a
mistranscription of the original, 'Soongundava' (Zwangendaba).
Astonishingly, 'Chaka' has replaced 'The present King Zeite of the Vatwahs'
(Zwide). It is *Zwide*'s 'uncle Soongundava [who] took the Government until
his nephew should come of age, but being then unwilling to resign a War
ensued and Zeite turned his uncle and all his adherents out of the country to
find another for themselves; for two years these latter have been more
destructive than a swarm of locusts'.[100]

By such untruthful editorial changes are the legends entrenched. Shaka
had nothing whatsoever to do with the depredations around the Bay.

If it was not Shaka chasing the Msane, Gaza, and Jere *into* the Delagoa
Bay area and northwards, why did they go there? And why did they stay
there?

Zwangendaba's initial incursion in mid-1821 makes the answer quite clear:
slaves. The coastal peoples found themselves quite unprepared for the ferocity
of the Jere attacks, which burned settlements and destroyed crops. People
both south and north of the Bay scattered to hiding-places. The Jere even
threatened the Portuguese 'factory', claiming to be looking for cattle, beads
and copper. In a complicated deal, the Portuguese essentially bought their
way out of trouble. Slaves formed part of the exchange, according to Captain
Owen, arriving shortly afterwards. The Portuguese were able to convince
Zwangendaba to withdraw, while securing some control over the adjacent
peoples.[101]

This episode was the culmination of a long process in which slaves had
become the prime commodity exiting the Bay. All three 'Ndwandwe' groups
worked over the Bay area for a while, before moving to fresh fields to the
north. Zwangendaba established himself in the lower Limpopo valley,
supplying slaves to both Delagoa Bay and Inhambane. Soshangane did much

the same a little further north. Nxaba attacked Inhambane in 1824, taking off cattle and slaves for both foreign sale and domestic absorption.[102] These raids combined with other internecine wars, and with drought, to progressively devastate the region inland of the Bay.

Owen, visiting the Bay in late 1822 and again in 1823, was angling from the beginning to oust the Portuguese, and forged two 'treaties' with local potentates in an effort to outflank the Portuguese domination of the Bay.[103] In doing so, he seemed to be caught between two impulses: on the one hand, to underplay slaving and violence in the area, so making his (illegal and, as far as the British government was concerned, undesirable) treaties seem less of a trap; and, on the other hand, presenting himself as heroic in his efforts to stamp out the abhorrent trade in human beings. In official despatches, he tended to minimise the slaving; in other communications, he was less guarded. His comments are nevertheless crucial indicators of what had been happening in the early 1820s. They are worth lingering on, too, for the perspective that they open up on Shaka's (alleged) participation in regional violence.

Owen reached Delagoa Bay for his second visit on 22 July 1823, where he offloaded the intrepid but ignorant young missionary, William Threlfall. According to Owen:

> The warlike, but restless Zoolos, under Loon Kundava [Zwangendaba], had settled on the right bank of the King George River . . . With a view to please Chaka, of whom the commandant was in some dread, he detached nearly all his officers and forty soldiers of his garrison to hunt them out of Cherinda . . . [H]aving lost two or three men in a skirmish, the remainder returned to pursue the more peaceable occupation of traffic . . .[104]

The traffic, however, unquestionably included slaves: the commandant himself was caught red-handed with slaves destined for Brazil, awaiting the 'annual ships from Mozambique'.[105] (If this allusion to 'Chaka' is correct – and I have some doubts – it is one of the very few indications we have that Shaka was already 'hiring' gun-bearers, most likely in conjunction with a slave-raid.) Threlfall noted that three weeks before their arrival, fever had swept the ships parked in the Bay, and *150* bodies had been thrown overboard. These could only have been slaves.[106] In a private letter of 15 April 1823, Owen pictured serious devastation and corruption:

> [There is continuous] traffick with the natives for Ivory, Rhinoceros horns, tiger Skins, Cattle, Slaves and Hoes in return for coarse blue Dungarees, beads, brass wire and bangles . . . Their ivory, horn & slaves [the Portuguese] send to Mozambique when they can, & the usual mode is by an annual vessel which leaves Mozambique in Feb[ruary] or March, touches at Quelimane, Sofala & Inhambane with their commissions, & lastly at Lorenzo Marks.

Although there had been no official Portuguese vessel for three years, there had been

> much communication with the Ships of all Nations who come here to fish the black Whale[. To] these they supply Cattle & vegetables for money; the Portuguese soldiers also collect a number of female slaves, whom they send on board such ships as enter the river, quite naked, the seamen indulge a natural propensity & in return clothe the women.

Meanwhile the local peoples were 'overrun and devastated by the outcast Vatwahs or Olontontes', while the Portuguese were 'on good terms with the invaders from whom they bought the spoil they had taken'. The Portuguese, Owen ends, 'have principally the capture of slaves as their object [occasioning] many wars'.[107]

Henry Francis Fynn was also in Delagoa Bay, making his own first contact with the Thukela-Phongolo catchment, at exactly the same time. He wrote:

> The various tribes in the vicinity of Delagoa, like all other native tribes of Africa, are constantly engaged in petty warfare, and, wherever there is a Portuguese settlement, these contests are encouraged, and, not infrequently, one or other of the rival parties is aided by Portuguese soldiers. The prisoners taken by each tribe are purchased by the

Portuguese to become slaves. Mayetha, chief of the Tembe country at the time of my visit, had recently been defeated and many of his subjects sold into slavery.[108]

This comment has no doubt been rewritten by Stuart, but the observation – racial slurs notwithstanding – is accurate enough. It was confirmed by John Philip, the humanitarian, who wrote, 'the policy pursued by the Portuguese at this bay is to keep the natives in a state of constant hostility amongst themselves, and if the conquerors refuse to sell their plunder at the price fixed upon by the purchasers they are instantly crushed by the arms of the factory or by some other tribes employed in the interior'.[109] This was Owen's impression throughout the region. When he headed north in September 1823, he noted the massive upsurge in slaving for the Brazilian and Mascarene markets. Quilimane had become 'the greatest mart for slaves on the east coast', with between eleven and fourteen Brazilian vessels arriving annually; a 300-ton brig could accommodate 'upwards of seven hundred males and females'.[110] Further south, Inhambane was less favourable for slaving, but there was sufficient incentive to keep people warring with each other who otherwise 'would in all likelihood remain in peace and amity with each other'.[111] Owen thought that Delagoa Bay was least vulnerable to slaving, noting that the Portuguese bought slaves from the 'Vatuahs', but not in great numbers.[112] This is certainly an understatement. Owen himself noted that

Like all other African nations all the countries around the Bay make Slaves of their enemies, but of the enemies only. The proximity of this point and the Bazaruto Isles to the Cape and to the French Islands offered to the Cupidity of some Europeans too strong a temptation to resist. English, French, and Dutch vessels have been known to visit these places to entice the people on board and then steal many of them, so that even now the Inhabitants have no confidence in Europeans, but watch the slightest symptoms of movement to make their escape, until they have acquired some knowledge of the parties.[113]

Owen's subsequent statement, that 'very few Slaves [are] exported from this place', thus doesn't ring true. Moreover, not all slaves caught in the Bay region necessarily left through Delagoa Bay. Owen also noted that 'couriers pass[ed] unmolested overland between Sofala, Inhambane and Delagoa', and that 'Vatwah' raiding and slaving was endemic.[114] Commodore Nourse, arriving from Cape Town on another visit to the Bay, learned that on the appearance of Owen's surveying ships, the Portuguese guiltily released 180 slaves from the fort. Some of these slaves, Nourse understood, would be carried to Mozambique and thence to the Brazils.[115] In October, Owen found seven ships at Mozambique, with 1 200 slaves aboard. The total being exported, he estimated, could not be 'less than 15 000 annually'. At least some of those would have come from the Thukela-Phongolo catchment. Quilimane, Owen learned, had been visited by sixteen ships that year – that he knew about – shipping 10 000 slaves. He continued:

> From Inhambane however, the trade in slaves is very limited compared with that of Mozambique and Quellimane. Nevertheless, wars are excited solely to make slaves to pay for merchandize. The same also occurs at English River [Delagoa Bay] to a still smaller extent, yet *sufficiently so to keep the neighbouring tribes in a ferment and a continual state of warfare.*[116]

Overall, the south-east coast from Mozambique to Delagoa Bay, *officially* exported some 13 000 slaves annually in the years 1820, 1821, and 1822, with a sudden dip in 1823.[117] At the Bay and Inhambane, the glut of slaves had by 1824 reduced the price of a slave to just 'a few shillings'.[118]

The numbers of slaves being taken off will likely never be ascertained. The question is probably less important than what the impact was on inland societies. This could vary hugely. Some patches of the Bay area evidently survived, and continued to grow foodstuffs (a lot of it increasingly geared to the demands of the visiting foreign sailors). Makhasane's sturdy and long-lived polity south of the Bay was a case in point. In the 1830s he still ruled over 10 000 subjects. As Etherington has rightly said, 'the long reign of Makhasane poses a continuous challenge to the legend of invincible Zulu expansionism and rapacity'.[119] In contrast, some areas and peoples were devastated. Extensive tracts suffered a tragic congruence of slaving and drought:

The desolation of famine filled the baracoons with the starving and the destitute . . . Agriculture and trade contracted, artisan communities were dispersed, and the only form of commercial life was slaving . . . . The ability of communities to defend themselves collapsed and only the warlords and the militarised society of their followers were able to survive in a world of increasing violence and endemic banditry.[120]

In 1823 Owen described the chiefdom of Matolla as once 'populous and rich, now in waste, poverty and famine'.[121] Starving Thembe hid in the woods; chief Mayethe lamented the reduction of his people 'to a famine' by the 'Orentontes' invasion.[122] Though slaving dipped in the years 1823–7, John Cane, walking from Port Natal to Delagoa Bay in 1827, recorded that swathes of country inland of the Bay were 'nearly depopulated in consequence of the slave trade being in active operation'.[123] The effects were exacerbated by the spread of tsetse-fly and smallpox.

This was the situation in the immediate hinterland of the Bay. Further inland the impact is less easy to measure. The slave raids certainly spilled over the Lubombo hills, driving up the Phongolo river into the headwaters of the Mfolozis and the Thukela. There, the Delagoa Bay slaving system began to overlap with that of raiders from the west, mostly Griqua on horseback. The effects spread onto the highveld, where it caught up with – amongst many others – Mzilikazi and his nascent 'Ndebele' polity. Having moved beyond Shaka's reach in 1821 (see below), he became subject to (and contributed to) a further swathe of violence which affected the Ngwane under Matiwane, the Dlamini under Sobhuza, the Hlubi under Mpangazitha, the Tlokwa under MaNthatisi, and the Sotho under Moshweshwe. There was a massive arc of *izwekufa* raids, drawn across the northern edge of the Thukela-Phongolo catchment as far west as the Caledon river valley. This is what was stimulating the growth of defensive but militarised conglomerates such as the Zulu and the Sotho (see Map 7 on page 251).

Much of this broiling activity lies beyond the scope of this book – mostly because Shaka had very little hand in it.

It is possible that Shaka and the Zulu did nevertheless participate in the far-reaching slave-trade. Fynn (albeit through Stuart's dubious rewriting) alleged as much: 'The ivory procured from the Zulus and Ndwandwes together

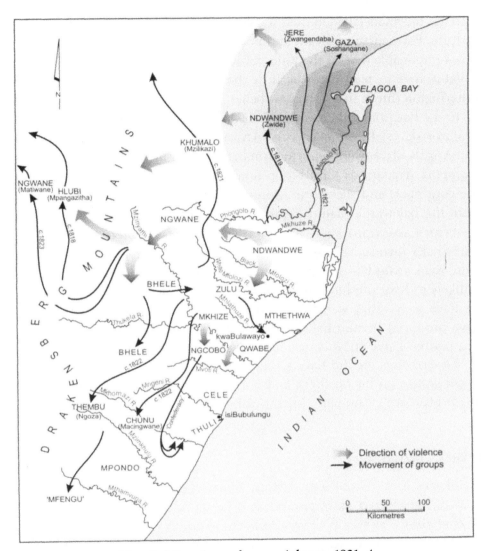

Map 7: Migrations, slavery, violence, 1821–4

with the prisoners taken in their wars (which they sold as slaves) they bartered with the Portuguese for beads and brass.'[124] This is slightly ambiguous, but it is not impossible that, as the Zulu polity absorbed Ndwandwe elements, they collaborated to feed captives into the slave market. Although Norman Etherington thinks that it 'beggars belief' that slaves could have been brought up to the Bay from Zulu country,[125] the logistics are perfectly feasible: if ivory, why not slaves? In other parts of Africa, including northern Mozambique and Angola, slaves were being force-marched over huge distances to the coastal entrepôts. Traders, as John Philip noted in 1823, were practically spanning the continent, and slavers, according to the traveller Arbousset, penetrated from the Bay to the Maluti mountains of Lesotho.[126]

Fynn's assertions apart, however, we have no concrete evidence at all that Shaka involved himself in slaving at this point. Distance is less of an issue than attitude – and opportunity. The main reason why the Zulu are unlikely to have produced many, if any, slaves in the early 1820s is that – as we have seen – they weren't involved in the kinds of conflicts that would have produced them. Shaka's attitude was still fundamentally defensive in this period. Later on, this may have changed.

Nevertheless, he did have a role to play in the movements of the other, closer groups on his northern and north-western borders between 1820 and 1823: Mzilikazi's Khumalo, Mpangazitha's Hlubi, and Matiwane's Ngwane.

LOSING MZILIKAZI

Mzilikazi's role in southern African history lasted many more years than Shaka's; he covered more ground, and he founded a nation – the Ndebele of Zimbabwe – almost as illustrious as the Zulu. Consequently, some people have found it hard to accept that he played only a minor part in Shaka's life. The paucity of Zulu traditional memories of Mzilikazi shows it; only Ndebele nationalists and allied white popular writers have elevated the relationship between him and Shaka to epic (and fictional) status.

The Khumalo people lived, in several semi-independent portions, sandwiched between the Zulu and Ndwandwe polities among the headwaters of the White Mfolozi. They claimed very similar origins: they were also *ntungwa*, having 'rolled down in a grain basket'. They may once have been attacked by the Zulu, but before Shaka's time, when they were ruled by Donda.[127] Possibly as a result of such pressure, Mzilikazi's father, Mashobane, may have shifted some 50 kilometres north from there to the vicinity of Ntumbeni mountain, overlooking the south bank of the Mkhuze river. This may have entailed a closer tributary relationship with Zwide; apparently both Mashobane and Mzilikazi married into the 'house of Zwide'. Some traditions suggest that Mashobane was more independent than that, until he was finally killed off by Zwide.[128]

What happened after that comes down to us in roughly two versions. These interpretations are neatly captured by the missionary Thomas Morgan Thomas. In the first interpretation, Mashobane dies, Mzilikazi succeeds him in a fraught situation when neighbouring chiefs were 'always ready to take advantage of any such opportunities to gain a few cattle and slaves'. Shaka does just that, defeats and captures Mzilikazi, and instantly makes him 'commander-in-chief of his army'. Mzilikazi illegally retains some captured cattle; Shaka invites the young reprobate to a dance in order to kill him quietly, but Mzilikazi escapes and flees.[129]

The notion that Mzilikazi actually became an *induna* of Shaka's – though it fed back into at least one Zulu tradition[130] – is not supported by the more credible sources. Some Khumalo certainly seem to have ended up living in Zulu territory: one informant claimed that his Khumalo father Jinjana was taken from his *umuzi*, Kabingwe, built 'beyond the Bulawayo *umuzi*', sent to Ntonteleni and killed.[131] However, the notion that Mzilikazi himself lived at Kabingwe is unlikely. The consensus seems to be that he 'was told to come cook meat at Bulawayo', but refused, and eventually 'made off in the night'.[132] This refusal was captured in his *izibongo*: 'White-spotted one who was seen by his face in a crowd,/Who refused to eat the leg at Bulawayo'.[133]

This is closer to the second interpretation given by Thomas, which he considered more plausible, as do I. In this version, obtained from an 'old man', Zwide kills Mashobane, and keeps Mzilikazi 'in bondage' – whatever that might mean. Mzilikazi is only able to escape when Zwide gets embroiled in his final conflict with Shaka. The Khumalo never fight with Shaka, but simply leave, 'plundering the whole country before them'.[134] Similarly, JANTSHI asserted that Shaka had no quarrel with Mzilikazi at all: 'he was merely an ambitious man who wanted to become wealthy in cattle'.[135] This seems something of a simplification, but this version of events is supported by a more detailed account, that of a Khumalo woman named Zitshibili:

> Mzilikazi and Zwide were on good terms with one another. After Dingiswayo died, Shaka succeeded him, and attacked and defeated Zwide. As Mzilikazi was tributary to Zwide, Shaka directed he should become his Bulawayo *induna*. Mzilikazi demurred on the ground that he was an independent chief in his own right, even though Zwide had been defeated. In order to prove his ability to be an independent chief and to be recognised as such by Shaka, Shaka called on him to attack another chief, Maconi by name, of the tribe Ntshingila, living further north. Mzilikazi did so, and succeeded in putting the man to death. This he did by decapitating him. This tribe then became tributary to Mzilikazi. In addition, Mzilikazi seized a large number of cattle from the Ntshingila people, which he appropriated for his own use. Shaka, seeing this, demanded the cattle and, as Mzilikazi refused to give them up, a quarrel arose which was the cause why Mzilikazi fled . . .[136]

All things considered, Zitshibili's account is probably the most credible we are likely to get. The traveller Andrew Smith heard something similar in 1834: Mzilikazi declined subordination to Shaka, 'knowing that [Shaka] would kill him and take his people.' Smith also heard that Shaka sent out a second *impi* after Mzilikazi, as far as 'the river to which he fled, which was in the country where he formerly resided. This commando killed many of [Mzilikazi's] wives and friends. After that he fled to the Liqua [Vaal river]'.[137] It is likely that there were other, confusing pressures: Andrew Smith also heard from a Khumalo councillor in 1835 that Mzilikazi was driven out by 'Ziete Kalanga' (Zwide kaLanga) and remained under Shaka's aegis a very short time.[138] Zwide was far from being a spent force, and may have raided Mzilikazi even as he moved off north out of Shaka's reach.

Almost certainly, after the 'Mvuzane fight' Mzilikazi initially remained at Ntumbane mountain, but found himself obliged to pay some form of tribute to the Zulu: he would have acted as a kind of military outpost, and proxy cattle raider. Shaka employed other chieftains in the same way. I can find no other reference to 'Maconi and the Ntshingila'; other accounts have Mzilikazi raiding someone equally obscure, one 'Somnisi'.[139] This – if it's true – seems to have been the one and only operation ever conducted by Mzilikazi under Shaka's auspices.

It is not clear, either, that the Khumalo and the Zulu subsequently fought, as some Ndebele traditions assert. These accounts tend to inflate Mzilikazi's ability to beat off Zulu attacks on his stronghold on Ntumbane mountain; indeed, in one version he succumbs only to treachery.[140] At any rate, Mzilikazi seems to have been able to leave with almost no cattle and only a small body of people – some 300, Fynn thought, though what Fynn's estimate is based on is not clear.[141] From the start, his followers were a mixture. A Cele *inyanga*, Mkwebi kaDibandlela, went with him; Mkwebi had *khonza*'d Zwide with Mande of the Cele, but refused to go back with him to Shaka.[142] At least some Ndwandwe also went with Mzilikazi, including (perhaps) one Khokhela kaMncumbata, who had been with Zwide's iPhelagugu *ibutho*, and would fight for Mzilikazi against Dingane,[143] as well as the abakwaZikalala, a group formerly tributary to Zwide.[144] He had to sustain himself immediately by raiding, possibly inflicting his presence at first against a small group under Nyoka, tributary to Shaka,[145] before easing north onto the highveld and out of our narrative.

Etherington decides to 'suspend judgement' about what happened to Mzilikazi between 1821 and 1825, since the sources seem insuperably confused.[146] Only in 1825 does Mzilikazi's position on the upper Vaal become certain. My hypothesis is that he moved rather slowly between the two regions, getting attacked in 1822–3 by both the Ndwandwe and the Pedi en route, as some traditions say, and maintaining contact with trade and slaving routes to Delagoa Bay. This much is certain: a *possible* initial brush aside, Shaka had nothing further to do with Mzilikazi, whose movements northwards thereafter were mainly impelled by Boer and Griqua raiders.[147]

When exactly Mzilikazi left remains fuzzy. Rasmussen relies rather heavily on quasi-legendary references to an 1820 solar eclipse, but there's enough circumstantial evidence to credit MADIKANE's impression that Mzilikazi was the first of the breakaway groups to leave, a shade before Nxaba,[148] which is to say in late 1820 or early 1821.[149] If Mzilikazi had hoped to remain somehow independent on the fringes of Shaka's polity, he failed. Even his *izibongo* referred painfully to his history of serial evictions:

The expelled one of Zimangele,
Who was kicked out by long feet
And by short ones;
The expelled one of Zimangele,
Mzilikazi son of Mashobana;
The wounded one whom they stabbed with wounds,
Whom they tripped up with short feet
And with big toes.[150]

If Shaka had hoped to retain Mzilikazi as an able tributary leader, an ally against the raiding pressures of the 'Ndwandwe' offshoots and their slaving accomplices, he too had failed.

A HORDE OF ROVING DEMONS

There is another northern myth that remains to be overthrown. We left Matiwane of the Ngwane in about 1817, having displaced large segments of the Hlubi, trying with some success to re-establish himself on the upper Mzinyathi river, about 50 kilometres west of the Zulu. Some of the Hlubi, including three of the old chief Mthimkhulu's sons, moved south eventually to *khonza* Shaka and form the nucleus of his iziYendane *ibutho*.[151] Another large section under Mpangazitha moved westwards, first to the headwaters of the Thukela. A short stay there was soon ended, perhaps by a combination of drought and further pressures from the Ngwane. It was followed by a move across the Drakensberg into the territory of mNthantisi of the Tlokwa and her son Sekhonyela. The Tlokwa were attacked by Mpangazitha in 1822, sending a ripple of further raiding north across the highveld. Both Mpangazitha and MaNthatisi moved west into the Caledon valley looking for further pastures.[152]

The Ngwane, probably feeling continuing pressure more from the raiding systems to the north-east than from Shaka and the Zulu, had elected to move a little further west.[153] Perhaps in 1820 or 1821, Matiwane resettled his people in the upper Thukela region, having carved his way along 'the line of least resistance' through the lightweight Bhele and Zizi chiefdoms. The Ngwane were certainly concerned to avoid conflict both with the Zulu and with the vortex of violence developing to the north-west, stimulated particularly by Griqua, Kora and other motley mounted commandos who, by the early 1820s, were ranging widely across the highveld. Perhaps more than any other group, the Ngwane found themselves trapped between converging raiding systems.

Matiwane's progress, rather like Shaka's, would be characterised as a scorching trail of mindless destruction in which 'infants and females, aged and sick alike' were 'mercilessly burnt or butchered' by 'a roving horde of human demons'.[154] Though that language is unnecessarily inflated, there was certainly some fairly severe dislocation. The Bhele and Zizi scattered. Of the Zizi, the only record that we have is of those who fled Matiwane to take up residence amongst the Xhosa peoples, some ending up as 'Fingos' in the Cape Colony.[155] This is probably only half their story; the rest is lost to us. Some Bhele stayed in their home area around eLenge (Job's Kop, a little north of present-day Weenen and the Sundays River); some moved south into the Mzimkhulu-Mzimvubu region of the present-day Transkei; and some moved east to take refuge with Shaka.

The last was probably a natural enough move, given that, as you will recall, the Bhele had khonza'd the Zulu for a couple of generations. Senzangakhona's favourite wife Bhibhi kaSompisi was of the Bhele people. Her brothers Ndlela and Nduvana were both butha'd into the Zulu forces. Ndlela became one of the most prominent men of the Zulu hierarchy, perhaps the greatest of all Shaka's izinduna. A tallish man, dark-brown (nsundu), with shanky legs and a barrel chest, he was distinguished by wearing the long grey tail-feathers of the red-faced mousebird, in addition to sporting the blue crane feather of the topmost élite. He was even-tempered, often disagreeing when people were sentenced to death.[156] One measure of the trust placed in him was that two former wives of Mondisa, Dingiswayo's heir-designate, were given to him by Shaka after Mondisa's assassination.[157] He was given jurisdiction over an important area between the Mpaphala flats and the Mfongosi river, and would continue to have a distinguished career under Dingane.[158] By chasing more Bhele people into Shaka's arms, Matiwane ironically helped the further consolidation of the Zulu haven-state.

While Matiwane was ensconced in the upper Thukela area, he built up widespread influence, centred on his *umuzi* esiNyondweni (east of present-day Bergville). In this position he was doubtless felt to be a rival power by the Zulu, which may have provoked a Zulu raid or two. However, the vigour of such raids is far from certain. Drawing on a number of late nineteenth-century sources, John Wright draws a picture of a massive 'onslaught' in which the Ngwane polity was 'broken up' and 'driven' onto the highveld.[159]

It seems to me more likely that the Zulu attack was lighter than this. Firstly, having moved north, Matiwane retained considerable (though not invincible) power in the Caledon valley – enough to wrest some form of submission from Moshweshwe of the Sotho.[160] Secondly, if (as Wright himself notes) the Zulu had little capacity to raid in force 100 kilometres or more to the north, there's no reason to suppose that they could do so to the west. The one James Stuart informant to give us any information on this, MABONSA, indicates that the Zulu raid was little more than opportunistic interference in the ongoing fights between Matiwane and Mpangazitha. An ad hoc cattle-raid is a more likely motive than trying to secure Zulu ambitions further south, as Wright suggests. The Zulu attack may also have been partly a product of Hlubi resentment. MABONSA's own uncle, a Hlubi named Mangena, had gone south to *khonza* Shaka after Mthimkhulu's death, and joined the mainly Hlubi iziYendane *ibutho*. He claimed to have taken part in the Zulu attack. MABONSA's chronology is confused, but interestingly he does say that only certain sections of the Ngwane were 'chased'; other sections continued to live there.[161]

It was presumably this tussle between big chiefs that Magaye, chief of the Cele, would shortly celebrate in a song of his own composition. He addressed Shaka:

> With what nations are you going to make war?
> The elephant took what belonged to it,
> The people refused it.
> It had been challenged by Matiwane,
> How great is Matiwane who challenges the elephant?
> How big is your assegai, Matiwane?
> For we took that of the Ndwandwe,
> Broke it in pieces, and drove it into the ground.[162]

It would not be the last time that Hlubi elements in Shaka's army, doubtless harbouring bitter feelings of revenge, would try to 'chase' Matiwane (see below, page 406).[163]

To summarise up to this point: across a great arc from Delagoa Bay westwards across the headwaters of the Phongolo, the Mfolozis, and the Thukela, the period 1818–23 was subject to a wave of violence. The wave travelled mostly from east to west. Slavers from the coast, in conjunction with the various 'Ndwandwe' components (Zwide, Nxaba, Zwangendaba, and Soshangane), devastated the region immediately inland of the Bay. They further attacked the Zulu, Ngwane, Dlamini-Swazi, Pedi and Hlubi peoples. The Hlubi, followed by the Ngwane, carried the momentum over the Drakensberg and into the Caledon and Orange river valleys, where they would overlap with the upper Vaal predations of Mzilikazi and MaNthatisi, the nascent state-building of Moshweshwe's Sotho, and the eastward-driving Griqua-Kora slave- and cattle-raiders from the northern Cape Colony. The scene was set for a backwash, then, into the Thukela-Phongolo catchment. The subcontinental European pincer movement, one jaw hinged on southern Mozambique, the other on the northern and eastern frontier of the advancing Cape Colony, was closing in.

In the middle, Shaka was working to consolidate control over a core polity centred on the area between the confluence of the White and Black Mfolozis and the lower Mhlathuze valley. Militarising quickly, and combining this with increasingly élitist control of wealth distribution in produce, trade goods and people, he had built up enough capacity to beat off Ndwandwe incursions, though not yet enough to make any more than the most tentative of long-distance raids. Shaka contributed almost nothing to the violence in the north and north-west of the catchment area in the early 1820s.

At exactly the same time, he was giving a great deal of attention to developing his links in the south. So were another set of characters.

'PERFIDY MEETING ITS REWARD'

We have already seen Captain W.F.W. Owen of the Royal Navy anchored in Delagoa Bay on 27 September 1822. In the ships *Leven*, *Barracouta* and *Cockburn*, he would visit the Bay several times over the next three years. He was followed by Commodore Nourse, commander at Simon's Bay in Cape Town, who sailed the *Andromache* into Delagoa Bay and met Owen on 26 December 1822.[164] Nourse's brother, Henry, was a prominent businessman in Cape Town who helped to sponsor some of the more central white players in our story. Such was the small, suffocatingly closed circle of the Cape Colony.[165]

When Owen next sailed into the Bay, on 1 March 1823, he met two trading vessels, the *Sincapore* from Calcutta, and the *Orange Grove*, one of Henry Nourse's ships. What they were trading in wasn't specified. The stopover also decimated Owen's crew who succumbed to malarial fevers. Owen left hastily on 11 March, having 'add[ed] twelve naked negroes to my physical strength' (voluntarily or otherwise is not stated).[166] He sailed for Port Elizabeth, more than 1 000 kilometres down the coast, and at that time the eastern-most coastal outpost of the colony. There, Owen met up with two other vessels, the *Jane* and the *Salisbury*, commanded by one James Saunders King.

King was a wheedling small-time merchant on the make. He was an ex-midshipman of the Royal Navy who had found some work ferrying troops between Simon's Bay and Port Elizabeth. It was dull stuff and, after an abortive attempt to get permission to trade in seals and fish on the Chaos islands off Algoa Bay, he was looking further north.[167] King was operating in collusion with another ex-Navy man, a bluff go-getter named Francis Farewell. Farewell had distinguished himself in the Napoleonic wars, and had batted desultorily around African and Indian ports for a few years. According to their companion-to-be in Zulu country, Henry Francis Fynn, King and Farewell had been linked for some years: Farewell, being 'of a speculative disposition', had bought and later sold a 400-ton ship called the *Princess Charlotte*, then chartered the *Salisbury* from King, in which they speculated together between Rio, St Helena, the West Indies and Mauritius, until a 'close intimacy sprang up between them'.[168]

On 28 May 1823 Farewell had hired the ship *Julia* from one James Gosling, telling his insurers vaguely that she was 'bound on a voyage to Port Natal, the river St Lucie on this side of Delagoa Bay, to Delagoa Bay and possibly to Inhambane and back to Table Bay with liberty to touch, trade, stay and barter at all intermediate ports and places on the coast of Africa. The value of her return cargo is quite uncertain . . .'[169] James Saunders King was to follow in the *Salisbury*, which Farewell had hired for 160 pounds a month, with the proviso that it was not to go past Delagoa Bay. 'Saint Loucie' was again named as a destination.[170] There would be much subsequent wrangling over who was really in charge of this expedition.

On 23 June 1823 the *Salisbury* left Cape Town, carrying some supplies for Captain Owen, and anchored at Port Elizabeth five days later.[171] Owen was helpful. He transferred to King's care two native interpreters, both ex-convicts from the prison of Robben Island who had accompanied Owen throughout his voyage. They were dubbed 'Jackot' and 'Fire'.

Jackot particularly interested his companions. He was a tall, powerful and self-assured Xhosa man from the Cape Colony frontier who had been jailed for sheep-stealing, and may already have been acquainted with James Saunders King (see Box 6 on page 305).[172] Owen bartered with King: he would let King have his very rough sketches of the Natal coast, if King would pass back a detailed chart of Port Natal harbour once he'd made one. (King later reneged on this, taking his chart directly to a connection in the Admiralty in London, and claiming that he had discovered the harbour all by himself. Moreover, he was only prepared to give up the chart 'on condition of being made a lieutenant'. The Admiralty told him to get lost, and Owen and his ghost-writer remarked with smug nastiness that King's subsequent shipwreck on Port Natal's sandbar was a case of 'perfidy meeting its reward'.[173])

Owen's and King-Farewell's parties left Port Elizabeth at about the same time in July 1823 and headed north.

Back at Delagoa Bay, Owen crossed paths with that other important figure in the Shakan landscape: Henry Francis Fynn. Fynn, by his own account, had landed in Cape Town in 1818, and had wandered around the Eastern Cape frontier region and back to Cape Town, before latching onto another of Henry Nourse's mercantile ventures. It was the opinion of the respected Eastern Cape official C.L. Stretch that Fynn was actually on the run from the law, having robbed the store in the frontier hamlet of Bathurst.[174] In about June 1823 Fynn had left Simon's Bay as supercargo on the *Jane*, followed by another brig, the *Mary*. Twelve days later they anchored in Delagoa Bay. Although, according to Fynn, Owen arrived in the *Leven* at much the same time as the *Mary*, Owen never mentions the *Mary*. Fynn is either misremembering, or concealing his true movements.[175] He also claims that Owen was just then beginning his survey, which as we have seen was actually late 1822; I suspect that Fynn had actually been in Delagoa Bay longer than he cared to admit.[176] The issue is important inasmuch as it generates further suspicion that all of these adventurers were involved in slaving from early on. Fynn seems to have left the Bay in about December 1823.

In the meanwhile, King and Farewell were suffering setbacks on the shores of St Lucia. Farewell, in the *Julia*, had anchored off Port Natal on 7 July, sailed north to St Lucia and had been forced to stand off for a couple of weeks due to bad weather, returning to St Lucia on 16 September. Here (though King in his initial report for some reason did not make this obvious) he met up with King and the *Salisbury*. King attempted to land a boat loaded with beads and bangles for trading, but it overturned and everything was lost. He tried again with another boat, and lost three men drowned in the surf.[177] King related the incident in the following way:

> Lieutenant Farewell and Mr Alex Thompson accompanied me in the *Salisbury*, on a voyage to the East Coast of Africa. Having arrived in the neighbourhood, where we intended to commence trading, we attempted at several ports, but it appeared impossible to land. The boats were then sent on shore at St Lucia, on the coast of Fumos. Mr Farewell's upset, but, although considerably bruised, he providentially escaped being drowned. Several days after, Mr Thompson met with a similar accident, his boat being overwhelmed when nearly a mile from the beach; they all gained the shore by swimming, except three poor fellows, who perished in the attempt. We now determined on abandoning the spot . . .[178]

King neglected to mention what would later become almost legendary: the fact that they abandoned a number of men on shore, including the interpreter Jackot. Farewell later lied that *four* men, including Jackot, had drowned.[179] Later still, he and King lied that they thought Jackot had been murdered by locals.[180] The actual scene must have been more complicated: a landing or an attempted landing, men tumbling and sliding back under the surf, flounderings on the beach, shouts, Jackot apparently exchanging blows with the sailor named Thompson. At any event, when they came to leave, Jackot had vanished – but it would not be the last they saw of him.

Box 5

Shaka's *imizi*

Northern outposts

Mandlakazi	On Mona river, Ndwandwe territory (*E*, on Map 8).
eMhlabaneni	Between Black Mfolozi and Phongolo rivers (*C*).
eMkanthlwini	Top of Ngome, Khumalo country (*B*).
eMpangisweni	North of Black Mfolozi (*D*).
uMyehe	On Black Mfolozi river.
Qulusini	Near Hlobane mountain, Hlubi/Khumalo country (*A*).

Mahlabathini (between the Mfolozi rivers)

kwaGugu	
kwaKandisa	
Nomdayana	
oNyange	
Mdadasa	
oSebeni	Near Nhlazatshe (*F*).

Heartland (Makhosini, around Mgungundlovu)

esiKlebheni	South side of White Mfolozi, near Mgungundlovu; inherited (*G*).
Nobamba	Near Mgungundlovu; inherited.
Mbelebeleni	Near Mgungundlovu; inherited; moved to Ntumeni, near Mhlathuze river (*H*).
KwaMfemfe	Near Mgungundlovu; inherited.

KwaBulawayo and environs (Eshowe district)

KwaBulawayo	Formerly Gibixhegu, south of Mhlathuze river.
Dhlangezwa	Near Ngoye, Entondweni hill.
kwaFojisa	At Mlali.
ewaKhangela	Near Mhlathuze river, downstream of Eshowe (possibly not established by Shaka).
eKuqobekeni	On Mhlathuze river, near kwaKhangela, below Mandawe.
eNdulinde	Attached to kwaBulawayo.
eNzondeni	Near kwaKhangela, 6,4 kilometres from Mhlathuze river.

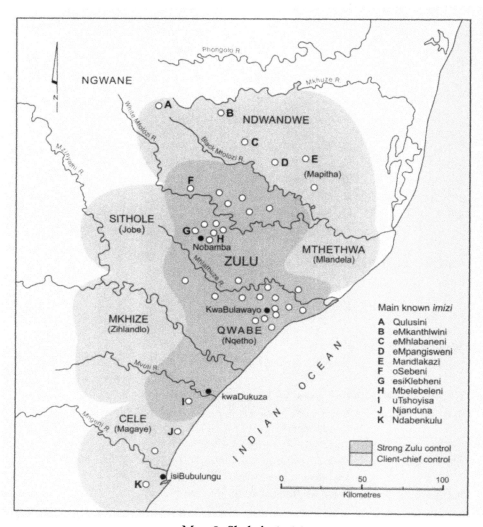

Map 8: Shaka's *imizi*

esiYembeni	Near Ntumeni and Zakaliya.
Gibabanye	Near kwaBulawayo at first, temporarily moved south of Mzimkhulu river to Fynn's area.
Mgumanqa	On lower Mlalazi river, near Eshowe.
Ntonteya	Near Tigulu river, near Gingindhlovu and Ombane hills.
isiPhezi	
uPoko	

KwaDukuza and the south (Stanger district)

kwaDukuza	Stanger (KwaDukuza).
kwaTshiyabantu	Near Emdhlazi, in Cele country.
Njanduna	On Mdloti river, in Cele country (*J*).
Nyakumbi	Just behind kwaDukuza.
Ndabenkulu	kwaMpofu flats, near Bellair, Thuli country (*K*).
uTshoyisa	South of Mvoti river, near kwaNyatikazi hill (*I*).

Not precisely locatable
uMotha
eZinyosini
Mkandhlu
eKanqetani
oBanhlaka
eTsheni
eKwenganeni
Vunganeni
iNtshamate
uBekenya
uQekete
esiYendane
oZwelini
uTekelweni
oBimbini

9

Southward bound

On the move, c.1821–4

Finding themselves face to face with so monstrously conducted and so wholly unjustifiable a series of campaigns, as unconscionable as Germany's submarine policy was for us in the late war, it might well be anticipated, had breathing-time or opportunity been afforded, that numbers of more or less connected though theoretically independent tribes would, in the hour of a common supreme danger, have formed powerful confederacies to withstand and possibly turn the tables on [Shaka's] rapidly and, therefore, seemingly insecurely constructed army. Such confederacies were, indeed, arranged, especially in Natal, though nowhere can it be said that they met with success, certainly no success in stemming the onflow of lava from the human volcano ever rumbling and thundering at Bulawayo, plotting new mischief.

James Stuart, 'Tshaka, the Great Zulu Despot' (1924, 101).

Nowadays, the Durban Bluff is smothered in the suburbia of the city, and looks over the grey-rimmed, ship-cluttered harbour, bristling with cranes and waterfront hotels. The southern point above the harbour entrance is topped by a signal tower; the Bluff's inner side is ribbed with the concrete wharves and rail lines of the coaling station; and its western side still reveals the remains of a whaling factory. Not far behind the nose of the Bluff, is a suburb named Fynnlands, legacy of our main white eyewitness to Shaka, Henry Francis Fynn, and the huge, multi-hued family that he and his brothers fathered. On the other side, known as The Point, what was a near-wasteland of lower-class houses, abandoned warehouses, and a destitutes' refuge has been transformed. A massive, multimillion-rand entertainment park has been constructed for the use of the leisured wealthy. With the richest of unintended ironies, it is named the uShaka Marine World.

CROSSING THE POINT

Back in 1824, the Bluff must have been all rock and low bushes, haunted by wild pigs, dotted with a few small homesteads. Passing whites in the eighteenth and nineteenth centuries knew the Bluff and its attendant, almost entirely enclosed, oval-shaped harbour of water as Port Natal, infamous for being so attractive and so dangerously guarded by a treacherous sandbar across its narrow mouth. The local people knew it as Emateku or iTeku (The One-Testicled Thing), or isiBubulungu.[1]

Perhaps, at an exceptionally low tide, it was across this sandbar that Shaka was actually able to lead his *impis*: a mundane explanation for the following delightful story of biblical resonance:

> Shaka, on the occasion of his first Pondo *impi* [in early 1824], crossed at the Point, Durban. He struck the water and it divided into two, and he and his regiments crossed over. He crossed to the Bluff and thence along the ridges to Mpunyungwana hill, below the Sipingo and between the Mlazi and Zimbodoko streams, where he slept.[2]

On their way back from Mpondo country in 1824, having completed their raid, some of those warriors might have spotted a solitary white man on the edge of a beach a few kilometres north of the port, staring inquisitively as they travelled past. This, had they been able to ask him, would have turned out to be Henry Francis Fynn. As it was, they could only exchange some gestures of mutual misunderstanding, though Fynn thought that one warrior was asking for beads to adorn his neck. What they made of his button nose and mutton-chop sideburns can only be imagined. Fynn later claimed that there were 20 000 warriors of fearsome discipline and swathed in finery – a characteristic exaggeration.

A few days before, Fynn had been able to manoeuvre a small boat from the sloop *Julia* across the dreaded sandbar, without mishap. It was mid-May

1824. He was there with 'stores and three mechanics, Ogle, an Englishman, a Prussian, and a Frenchman, also Michael, a Hottentot servant, and Frederick, a Kaffir interpreter from the Cape frontier'.[3] After spending the first night fighting with a storm and a pack of hyenas, Fynn set out to find Shaka. He ended up at the tiny settlement of a man whom he calls Siyingila (Sinqila kaMphiphi of the Cele), where he was advised to await Shaka's pleasure. This duly arrived in the form of 60-year-old Mbikwana, that trusty Langeni uncle who had accompanied Shaka on his very first defection to the Mthethwa, over twenty years before. Fynn wrote:

> On approaching me, with four large oxen being driven before him, Mbikwana made a long speech in honour of Shaka, his nephew; he related his greatness and his valiant deeds as a warrior, and added that he, Mbikwana, acting on behalf of Shaka, who had not yet heard of my arrival in his country, presented me with four oxen that I might not starve in the country of so great a king.[4]

The 'active and intelligent' Mbikwana took Fynn to his own, more substantial homestead. That this appeared to be not too distant is an indication of how far south, by 1824, Shaka had managed to plant his colonising *imizi*.

Let's now turn our attention to the story of Shaka's southern enterprises in the period 1821–4.

Remember that in about 1821, the chastened Zwide has left for the hills of southern Swaziland. His quasi-Ndwandwe allies under Nxaba, Zwangendaba and Sotshangane are also about to go, headed for the lucrative source of trade, Tsonga country and Delagoa Bay, where the demand for slaves is experiencing a marked upswing. Mzilikazi is on his way north, too. Matiwane and the Ngwane, ousted by the Ndwandwe and/or their slaver allies, have shattered the Hlubi 'bottle', and are thinking of moving further west to the headwaters of the Thukela, nestled in under the ramparts of the Drakensberg. Shaka is spending much of his time finding diplomatic ways of absorbing Mthethwa and Ndwandwe sections. He is starting to colonise the area between the Mfolozi rivers (Mahlabathini), and the Mhlathuze valley around his 'capital' kwaBulawayo, on the walls of which the mud-and-dung *daga* plastering is scarcely dry.

At the same time, the southern borders of Zulu territory are demanding Shaka's attention. He is southward-bound in more than one sense. In crucial ways, he is bound – beholden – to the power of the southern chieftains. Without the support first of Dingiswayo, then of Jobe's Sithole, Zihlandlo's Mkhize, and Nqetho's Qwabe, Shaka would not have been able to hold off the Ndwandwe assaults and begin to consolidate a centre of control. After the crucial turning-point of the 'Mvuzane fight', Shaka could work with these established client-chiefs to extend his influence further south.

Shaka was also south-bound in that he was shifting southwards himself. He would remain at kwaBulawayo for only a few years before making a further southward move, to kwaDukuza (later Stanger, now kwaDukuza again). This continuous drift southwards will need some explanation. While he didn't give up his grip on the Mfolozis region, or even the northern outpost *amakhanda* in Ndwandwe territory, he was starting to pay increasing attention to the region south of the Thukela. This would be the focus of his first major long-distance raids, starting with that against the Mpondo in 1824.

The story of Shaka's 'parting of the waters' is a neat symbol of his growing interest in moving southwards.

AN AUTOCRATIC PARTNERSHIP

Later history – after the white colonisation of Natal – made the Thukela river the great southern boundary of the Zulu kingdom. This wasn't always the case, although in the early 1820s, it does appear to mark a difference in Shaka's policies towards subordinate peoples. North of the Thukela, he was able to apply a policy of steady incorporation, reorganisation of families, arrangements of marriages, and so on. Even this probably held only in the area immediately south of the Mfolozis (the old Zulu heartland and Mahlabathini) and the lower Mhlathuze region around kwaBulawayo. South of the Thukela, Shaka was obliged to adopt other strategies. He pursued one strategy in relation to the bigger polities, another in relation to the slew of little ones that created a complex patchwork in the area between the Thukela, the upper Bushmans, and the Mngeni rivers.

To the east, closest to the Zulu, the landscape was dominated by the Thembu; to the south-east by the Chunu. These two groups were keeping to the middle Thukela and Mvoti valleys respectively for now. They were wary of what was happening to the north, reluctant to get embroiled in anything too damaging.

South of them, astride the Thukela, the Mkhize under Zihlandlo, aided by his rather over-zealous brother Sambela, were extending their influence southwards. The relationship that Shaka struck up with Zihlandlo, as we've already seen in Chapter 7, was perhaps the ideal. Shaka may have wanted to enter into the same kind of arrangement with Ngoza of the Thembu and Macingwane of the Chunu, but, if so, he failed.

As we've also seen, the Mkhize had already been responsible for much of the violence south of the Thukela. MBOKODO's description does compress the campaigns of several years, but it gives the general idea:

> [Zihlandlo] attacked Macingwane in the Cunu country, but he failed to kill him. He killed, however, Sondonzima keLuboko, brother of Macingwane. On returning from there, Zihlandhlo attacked Matomela kaNdhlovu in the Bomvu country. He killed his chief, Zipundulu. He killed also Sotshenge keNdhlovu, a man of high birth. Zihlandhlo then made Nzombane kaMatomela chief. On returning from this, he attacked Tshitshi near the country of the Pepeteni. He killed him, and returned. He attacked Nomagaga of the Nadi people, and ate up their cattle. Dibinyika was Nomagaga's heir, of the Zondi tribe. He next attacked Dhlaba of the Zondi, and ate up his cattle. He attacked Voyisana living higher up, and ate up his cattle. He attacked Nguza of the Dhlamini people . . . He killed him. He attacked Bodeyana of the Dhlamini people . . . He attacked Nzombane kaMatomela. He captured him, but did not kill him. He however seized his stock . . . Zihlandhlo attacked Sibenya of the Wutshe people living in the vicinity of [present-day] Cedara, and killed him. He killed Mbonjeni. He attacked Nomagwayi of the eMazolweni people, and killed him. Zihlandhlo also killed the *isikulu* Mnqundu kaMzaula of the Ndhlovu people. He killed Ngebe kaMzila of the Ngcongo. He killed Madonjeni of the left-hand house, among the Embo people. He caught Nsele kaGcwabe of the Embo people, but did not kill him, for [his brother] Sambela objected. He ate up his cattle. He killed Ntiti kaGcwabe and took his cattle.[5]

Not even Shaka has ever been accorded such a detailed and relentless series of killings.

The Mkhize depredations were partly at Shaka's behest and partly on their own initiative, as demonstrated by one episode, already mentioned on page 194:

Zihlandhlo once sent [his brother] Matshukumbele to Shaka to *khonza* there. When Matshukumbele returned after staying some days, Shaka gave him a present of five heifers. Matshukumbele did not bring any of the cattle to Zihlandhlo. Zihlandhlo shortly afterwards paid Shaka a visit. Shaka said, 'Hau! My *mnawe*, do you not give praise for what I gave you?' He referred to giving it to Matshukumbele. Zihlandhlo said, 'Nkosi, I had forgotten.' Shaka said, 'My brother, did he duly pass the present on to you? It would appear not.' Zihlandhlo said nothing more and there the matter dropped. Had Zihlandhlo said that Matshukembele had concealed the matter from him, he would have been put to death forthwith. Zihlandhlo then went home. He slept the night. Next day Matshukumbele arrived with the *impi* of his place. He entered the cattle enclosure. Zihlandhlo was seated with but a few people. Matshukumbele arrived carrying assegais. Matshukumbele said, 'Let us discuss the thing which it is said you are going to do.' Zihlandhlo replied, 'No, no, my brother. Sleep, and tomorrow I shall give you blue-monkey-skins.' Matshukumbele then went in to sleep.

Zihlandhlo then sent a man to Sambela at Mngengeleni. The message was, 'Come quickly, or you will find that Matshukumbele has already killed me. He is here at my place. Come armed.' Sambela too then assembled the *impi* of his place. As dawn was breaking he arrived. He entered the homestead at its upper end, and came to Zihlandhlo in the cattle enclosure. Zihlandhlo rose to go outside. He then asked Sambela to come with him outside the homestead. Sambela then loosed his *impi* on both sides of the kraal, directing it to kill Matshukumbele. Zihlandhlo then said Sambela was to tell his men to kill not only Matshukumbele but all those with him, as well as others who were at the kraal, for they had looked on instead of proceeding to stab Matshukumbele on his threatening Zihlandhlo. Sambela refused, saying, 'We'll kill only Matshukumbele and his son Sibabili, and a few others.' . . . Upon this he was put to death.[6]

This account is likely embellished with detail, but an illuminating portrayal of the dynamics of patronage and power nonetheless.

In the middle Thukela region, Shaka had to rely heavily on Zihlandlo's willingness to subordinate people without himself becoming a rival. Shaka tried to balance things out a bit by appropriating some of Zihlandlo's younger *amabutho* – the Nguqa and Mpiyakhe – for his own purposes; he would use them to colonise other areas.[7] (Rather like South African security companies today using Zulu guards in Xhosa-speaking parts of the country, this might have been to prevent anti-authority collusions developing.) Shaka had to trust his 'younger brother' to send back appropriate tribute, although he would send Zulu *izinduna* to oversee operations when he could. This effort is caught in a story about Shaka setting Zihlandlo up to attack the Nxamalala. It's a vivid anecdote worth citing at length for its insight into the mix of politics and military tactics that probably characterised many of these minor clashes: the posturing, the heroics, the language, and the rivalries.

When Shaka set Zihlandhlo and Mtsholoza [of the Nxamalala] on to fight each other, he brought *izinduna* to watch. These *izinduna* accompanied the *impi*. Among them were Nsizi and Sikunyana. Sikunyana was sent to Mtsholoza; Nsizi came to Zihlandhlo. Zihlandhlo was of course with Sambela, his kinsman. Mtsholoza had with him Gayeni, his kinsman. Zihlandhlo's *impi* was prepared for battle. When this was being done the lesser chiefs and the *izinduna* – the great *induna* was Nomagaga kaViliza – addressed the *impi*, saying, 'We shall get rid of that thing over there; it is nothing,' referring to Mtsholoza's *impi*. They said, 'We shall also get rid of that other thing,' referring to the Mngenela of Sambela. Zihlandhlo then directed that the Mngenela troops were not to intermingle with the Simahleni lot, but stand apart outside the cattle kraal. They accordingly remained outside. Zihlandhlo then took out the Isimahla and crossed the Tugela with it (for Mtsholoza was on the south side of the Tugela). Zihlandhlo then

summoned the Mngenela. He prepared them for battle. He then
ordered Sambela not to allow his men to perform a war-dance. An
isikulu, of Sambela's people, then came and took a pole of the cattle-
kraal gate and carried it to Zihlandhlo. He placed it on the ground in
front of him. He said, 'You can kill me if I am not the first to capture
a man with my hands.' Zihlandhlo then said, 'Let it go out,' adding, 'I
do not know what you will have to complain of, since you are my
carrying-skin, the carrying-skin in which I am carried on the back.'

The *impi* then went off and slept at Enkilingini (a kraal of
Zihlandhlo's, up the Tugela and on its banks). The Mngenela section
remained behind. The Isimahla crossed the Tugela by a lower drift
the same day. As the latter crossed, Mtsholoza's *impi* saw them. A
large body hid at one spot and the other portion hid about two or
three miles away on the other side. Zihlandhlo's men had been seen
by Mtsholoza's, but had not located their enemy. On their going
forward, Mtsholoza's men sprang up on all sides to attack, and stabbed
them, taking them at a disadvantage, for some still had their shields
rolled up. They stabbed the Isimahla and scattered it. They killed
Nomagaga, the chief *induna*, and carried off his shield.

After the Isimahla had been defeated and dispersed, word was sent
to that effect to Zihlandhlo. He then said, 'Then let the Mngenela
section be summoned and told to come to me.' Gayeni, Mtsholoza's
induna, then said to Mtsholoza, 'Let me go out; I shall overcome
him; he is my equal. For you have overcome your equal.' Zihlandhlo
then said to his messengers, sent to call the Mngenela lot, to give a
message to the *induna* Kombe. Kombe refused to come as the Isimahla
had been defeated. Zihlandhlo's order was sent to the Mngenela when
they had already gone forth to attack in accordance with the plan.
Kombe refused to desist from the plan, saying, 'Leave me; I too shall
die.' Zihlandhlo sent to Sambela, who was with the Mngenela: 'I
directed Kombe to return with the forces.' Sambela replied, 'Let them
die.' Kombe then took the *impi* across the river during the night. He
took it to the summit of the hill. Shortly after breakfast time the two
bodies came in sight of one another. Gayeni was leading, followed by
Mtsholoza. The armies met. Kombe sent out his, throwing out the

two horns to move around, deploying to right and left, whilst the central body, consisting of two groups (*amabandhla*), was to halt. Kombe then sent to Zihlandhlo to say he was to leave his kraal and take up his position on a hill, Isimungwana, and look towards Esokeni, one of Mtsholoza's own kraals, and see if it would not be burning by midday.

The two forces now clashed together. Mtsholoza's *impi*, with Gayeni, was driven off. Gayeni's section came on Sambela's lot first, and, being driven back, fell on Mtsholoza's section and the two, meeting, turned and fled. A hero, Godhloza, a big man, seeing what was happening, directed that the central section was to move to the attack. When Kombe saw this, he struck at them, killing a man, and ordered them to remain where they were as directed. Presently the enemy turned and fled. Kombe, seeing this, was delighted, as the enemy had fled without the central body being engaged. This central body at the same moment sounded on their shields, beating on them with sticks, sounding acclamation. Gayeni's *induna*, Gwabumbuya, was killed. Tokozwayo, the man who had brought the gate pole to Zihlandhlo, caught a man, Kanyekanye of the Nxamalala, and handed him over to be held as a prisoner in order to be delivered by Tokozwayo to the chief.

After repulsing the *impi*, they [chased them for] some twelve or fifteen miles. They surrounded Mtsholoza's homestead, Esokeni. Mtsholoza in the meantime had escaped. The kraal was burnt. They surrounded the homestead at Nguqa, finding he had deserted from there too. They burnt it. They attacked Ehlanzeni, another kraal, burning it and finding he had deserted. They attacked Embungeni, finding him fled. They then burnt it. They then seized all the cattle they could find, and turned back.

The chief, on the Isimungwane, saw all that was going on. 'Look, now his homestead is burning!' His whole *impi* returned, to find Nzizi, Shaka's *induna*, had put on his war-dress. He had threatened to set on the *impi* on seeing that the greater section of Zihlandhlo's *impi*, the Isimahla, had been defeated, but Zihlandhlo said, 'Wait a bit, the carrying-skin has not yet arrived,' that is, the Mngenela. Nzizi then

set them free, refraining from setting on his *impi* and killing off
Zihlandhlo's people . . . . The other *induna* of Shaka's with Mtsholoza,
seeing all the cattle had been swept off by Zihlandhlo, returned to
Shaka.

That is all.[8]

This is an astonishing recital: skilfully organised, evenly paced, lucid, and
more detailed than any fight of Shaka's on record, even the vaunted 'Mvuzane
fight'. The positioning of Shaka's *izinduna*, half in diplomatic aloofness, half
threatening, is particularly interesting. The battle is half-arranged, neither
spontaneous nor one-sidedly predatory. Casualties are few, indeed deliberately
minimised. Prisoners are taken with the intention that they be enslaved.

The way in which Zihlandlo was gathering up power for himself was
something so far unseen in this region – a model, really, which Shaka was
both helping to build and choosing to follow. As John Wright summarises it:

> The Mkhize expansion represented a new departure, for it entailed
> incorporation not simply into an enlarged nexus of chiefdoms, such
> as constituted the Qwabe, Thuli and Cele polities, but into an
> emerging if still loosely structured state system dominated by an
> increasingly closed Zulu elite. Tribute extracted from homesteads at
> the bottom of the political hierarchy more and more went to support
> not a reasonably accessible and at least partly accountable leadership
> but a socially and geographically remote aristocracy which to a greater
> extent maintained its dominance by force.[9]

It was, in short, an autocratic partnership, in which Shaka also allocated
izinduna to oversee Zihlandlo's activities on a more permanent basis. Isaacs's
portrayal of 1826 is certainly skewed (Zihlandlo was a lot less craven than he
makes out), but it captures the intensity of Shaka's oversight:

> [Zihlandlo] seemed anxious to know if Chaka was acquainted with
> my being in this quarter to obtain ivory; which led me to suspect that
> he had ivory, but was afraid to part with it on account of that monarch,
> it being an article he always took to himself for the purpose of making

presents to the European party. In this I was not wrong, as messengers had arrived from the Zoola king to ascertain the quantity of ivory that Sischlanslo had collected, which was, he said, eleven teeth, and which he had been inclined to present to me, but, being afraid of exciting the wrath of Chaka, he begged me to accept of four bullocks . . .[10]

One of Shaka's overseeing *izinduna* was probably Manjanja kaNhlambela, who was in charge of a Zulu *impi* that subdued the Dunge and the Madliwa, as well as Mathomela of the Ngcobo.[11] Manjanja subsequently (under Shaka or Dingane is not entirely clear) was settled in Khabela country to supervise matters.[12] Until that time, however, he was primarily a raider. Bryant calls him Shaka's 'prize-raider', who inaugurated a 'system of wholesale raiding on the southern side of the Thukela'.[13]

For once, Bryant's overblown language may be appropriate. It's just possible that Manjanja was operating with that Hlubi-based, by now battle-hardened *ibutho*, the iziYendane.

'DRIVEN OUT BY A PORCUPINE'

'It does not go in by itself; it goes in by force.'[14] The metaphor is violently sexual; the subject is Shaka's iziYendane *ibutho*. This unit, mostly Hlubi from the north, was distinctive with its all-red shields and the lank hair of its members. The unit's very name referred to the swaying motion of the men's shoulder-length plaits, from *ukuyenda*, 'as a man who is sleepy sways to and fro'.[15]

As we have seen, some rather savage violence characterises several of the conflicts covered thus far. However, almost none of it has been perpetrated directly by Shaka. In the first ten or so years of his rule, we've encountered scarcely a single act of gratuitous brutality. Battles, yes; rapier-like assassinations, a few; but (a couple of wispy rumours aside) very few of those horrible flick-of-the-wrist, gruesome and inventive murders that we've been led to expect of Shaka. There have also been no wholesale, genocidal massacres. This was about to change, as the iziYendane began to encounter the patchwork of tiny clanlets that jockeyed for position and safety amongst the larger polities along the southern bank of the Thukela. The iziYendane was the vehicle of Shaka's second strategy for the south: not attempted 'colonial' incorporation, but assertion of dominion through more straightforward raiding.

Even here, Shaka did not abandon more diplomatic methods, including intervening in succession disputes, but cattle-raiding seems to have been the primary form of extracting irregular tribute. Periodic raids were, presumably, the most effective way of deriving resources from often mutually antagonistic groups who were too small and thinly scattered to make fully-formed political relations worth the effort. Raids were nevertheless also a way of asserting dominance without obliterating the sources of wealth. A balance needed to be struck, and Shaka wasn't always successful in controlling this. The iziYendane in particular was to take up its duties with rather more vigour than he had anticipated or desired.

It's difficult now to work out who attacked whom, and when. Zulu cattle-raids, Mkhize proxy tribute-raising expeditions, and internal disputes become inextricably entangled. The Khabela, for instance, just across the Thukela, were subdued by Zihlandlo, though they stayed in place, hiding out in the forests until the danger had passed.[16] Suffering a similar fate were the Nxamalala, the Phephetha, the Zondi, and the Mphumuza – all living in that neighbourhood. The Nyuswa, who lived a little further down the Thukela, were placed by Shaka under Zihlandlo's jurisdiction, after the *inkosi* had successfully intervened in a succession dispute.[17] In addition, the iNtontela *ibutho* was stationed there, on the north bank of the river. The Mkhize themselves, doubtless with Zulu acquiescence, now began the same process, planting an Mkhize *umuzi*, kwaNyakenye, in Khabela territory south of the Thukela.[18]

The Khabela were also attacked by the Bomvu, who were moving across the river, perhaps under Zulu pressure.[19] The Khabela seem to have raided the Bomvu in turn, as well as the Sithole, despite being married into them. Hence there were ridiculous complications. For instance, the Bomvu chief Somhashi found himself exasperatedly having to return plundered cattle to his own relatives: 'Why are our efforts in seizing cattle in warfare all in favour of our fathers-in-law?'[20] The following story may be read more sensibly as Shaka organising squabbling peoples into a more stable arrangement, than as the expression of pathological resentment, which is what it appeared to be to SINGCOFELA, a disgruntled Bomvu informant:

It was Shaka who chased our [Bomvu] tribe out of Zululand. [Our chief] Zombane was killed by Shaka. Shaka killed Zombane because he was so handsome that it seemed as if he should become the chief of the Zulu country. Shaka said that when he looked into the water (our former looking-glass) he found himself ugly and not so handsome as Zombane who had a nice long neck, whereas Shaka's nose was so large that it filled much of his face – was as big as a toad. Shaka said that looking on Zombane it seemed as if he, Shaka, should salute (*kulekela*) him. Shaka sent for Zombane, his object being to kill him, which was done at the eMateku. . . . The result of the chief being killed was that our tribe crossed into Natal. Somhashi [the heir] then went to Jobe [of the Sithole] as, the chief having been killed, the people were depressed and slack and disorganized.[21]

Politically, it was a fairly typical assassination, intended to get the remainder to khonza either Shaka himself, or a client-chief such as Jobe.

Still, considerable turbulence ensued in its wake. Around the same time, the Hlongwa clashed with those Nyuswa who came south.[22] Groups split up. The Phephetha khonza'd with a little persuasion, putting up some stiff resistance on Phisweni mountain; then some of them stayed, while some shifted off to the south.[23] The Zondi were likewise attacked, held out for a while, but a portion then moved south in conjunction with others.[24] It's also hard to judge the timing; it seems that in some cases there was more than one attack. Probably Zulu domination was quite lightly felt by many. Tribute was extracted only periodically when an *impi* could be sent. There was no single, destructive campaign that either slaughtered whole 'tribes', or sent them all fleeing. Hence, for example, Shaka is said to have renewed raids on the Nganga and Maphumulo in the later 1820s, long after they had been initially subordinated. It was almost habitual. Shaka used to pretend that he was going for snuff, when he was really going to raid for cattle: 'Tomorrow I shall not come. I am going to ask for snuff from the Nganga. Don't expect to see me, assembly of my kraal Dukuza! Don't you see that it's painful to be like an antbear, which digs a hole and then doesn't live in it, being driven out by a porcupine?' There was always the threat of having his authority usurped or challenged, it seems, by some prickly 'porcupine' or other.[25]

The middle southern areas, sandwiched between the Mkhize and the Cele, across to the Mvoti river, were inhabited by a second band of smaller groups: the Xesibe, the Ndelu, the Dunge, the Maphumulo, and the Bhaca. These peoples bore the brunt of the iziYendane attacks. The iziYendane was based at kwaBulawayo now, under the special sponsorship of Nandi herself. The men didn't have a secure *ikhanda* to call their own, but around 1821–2 they seem to have ensconced themselves somewhere between the Thukela and the Mvoti. They had helped to fend off Zwide; now they were joined by a smattering of Mthethwa, Nyuswa, and Ngcolosi men from north of the Thukela. They began to raid further south, gathering Maphumulo and Nganga recruits into their ranks. They had adopted a Zulu war chant, and were said to have transformed themselves 'into Zulus' – though this may be an injustice to the Zulu.[26] They were so feared that, as the Thuli informant MAZIYANA, who grew up in the shadow of their marauding, dramatically put it, people hearing them coming would dive into swamps to hide.[27]

They were probably originally sent out by Shaka to gain cattle and at least temporary affirmations of tribute, but in the three or four years up to 1824, the iziYendane got seriously out of hand.[28] Almost certainly it was the skeletal results of their marauding that the first whites at Port Natal noticed (see Box 8 on page 345 and Map 10 on page 346). In their published accounts, the whites blamed Shaka directly and entirely. They would claim that virtually the whole area south of the Thukela had been 'depopulated'. In fact, wholesale slaughter was the last thing that Shaka intended. He would find himself in the unpleasant position of having to use force to rein in his own people.[29]

It was not the only time that Shaka's *amabutho* disobeyed orders. Sometimes, the annoying porcupine was within.

FLIGHT TO THE SOUTH

In mid-May 1916, when MQAIKANA kaYenge was 85 or 86, James Stuart had him brought in by train from his home at Laduma, a few kilometres west of Pietermaritzburg. The old man was stooped, darkly bronzed, with a 'rather Romanish nose' and long grey hairs under his chin. He was intelligent and knowledgeable, less about Zulu affairs than about those small Natal peoples south of the Thukela: the Zondi, the Nxamalala, and the Mpumuza. Stuart calculated that he could exhaust MQAIKANA of valuable testimony in about seven to ten long but not inconvenient days. (Factoring in rail fares, the gifts of a rug and a shirt, and the price of a photograph, Stuart figured that the elder's testimony cost him a bit over two pounds.) If anyone could throw light on the complex politics of Shaka's southern ventures, MQAIKANA could.

Nevertheless, even he had his limits. 'I used to listen to old people speaking,' he said, 'telling us what they chose, but we did not especially interrogate them, much less commit to paper . . . . I am very sorry indeed I never learned to write. Had I learnt, I would have put down all my father told me, and read it nowadays. I allowed this to escape me.'[30]

It is only through a haze of half-remembered facts, patchy and tentative, that we can approach the tangled events of the period.

Without question, increasing pressure from Shaka (approved and otherwise) and from the Mkhize, amplified by worries about the south-western drift of the powerful Ngwane, caused numbers of people to edge away southwards. This wasn't always the tragic and precipitate flight that it has been portrayed as, but the movement was significant.

The other two sizeable polities from the upper reaches of the Thukela, the Thembu and the Chunu, elected to move away. Their piecemeal flight, like Mzilikazi's, represented a failure of Shaka's essential policy to intervene in the structures of local groups in order to access more resources. The last thing he needed was for these people to move out of range. Their movements are complex, but can be simplified to two phases. We've already seen the shifts of the first phase, which occurred around 1815–17 (see above, page 171). In that phase, the Thembu had moved only a short distance, south of the Thukela. At much the same time, the Chunu had moved to the upper Mvoti.

Now, in the second phase, around 1822, the leaders of both peoples moved a much greater distance (see Map 7 on page 251 and Map 9 on page 282). Ngoza's Thembu took a northern track, ending up amongst the headwaters of the Mzimkhulu. Macingwane's Chunu took a more southerly route, ending up on the middle reaches of the Mkhomazi river. It was a quite substantial movement of people, accompanied by more upheaval than even this turbulent region was used to.

Let's first follow the Chunu. Zihlandlo, not Shaka, was possibly at fault here. Zihlandlo attacked the Phephetha around 1821 or 1822, and ran into

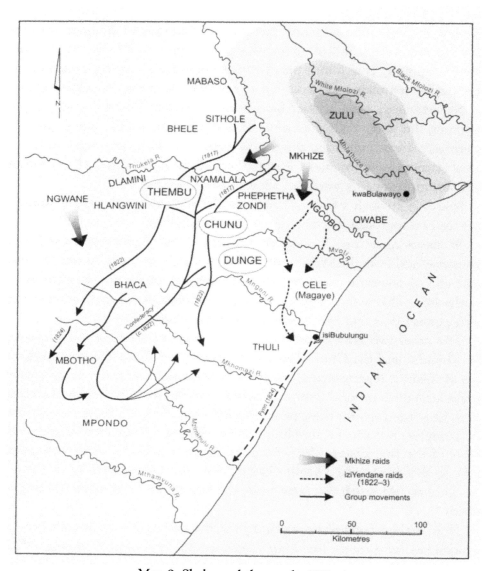

Map 9: Shaka and the south, 1821–4

Chunu raiders from the upper Mvoti (around present-day Greytown).[31] Macingwane had established a sizeable polity that was well settled and well armed. It doesn't make sense that a minor clash with Zihlandlo would have made him uproot all over again. Like Ngoza, Macingwane perhaps also decided to avoid future complications (and there may have been other *attractions* that we don't hear about). At any event, in about 1822, Macingwane pre-emptively took his people considerably further off, to the Mkhomazi river and the present-day Pietermaritzburg area. That he was *not* directly hounded by the Zulu is indicated in Shaka's own *izibongo*:

> The little-pester [Shaka] had long been wanting to get at them,
> He wanted to get at Macingwane, at the Ngonyameni kraal.
> But there, at Macingwane's, it is 'show your teeth, and he clears'.[32]

Macingwane's passage was accompanied by considerable violence.[33] He ran into stiff resistance from a female *induna* named Macibise, and had to turn a little further north. He also encountered one Madikane of the Bhaca people, with whom he had had some relations before,[34] and more or less dragged Madikane along, too. Macingwane finally built his *umuzi* iGqunu in open country near the Ifafa (or Lufafa) river, 150 kilometres from Zulu country.[35] There he stayed, for a while, but Shaka was not finished with him.

Most historians have followed A.T. Bryant in assuming that Shaka followed up immediately, chasing Macingwane all the way to Nsikeni mountain and shattering the Chunu polity for good in 1822.[36] Evidence is very thin, but it seems to me more likely that Macingwane met his end closer to the time at which Madikane of the Bhaca and Ngoza did, in late 1824 or early 1825. It doesn't seem likely that Shaka had the capacity for such a destructive attack, over such a distance, as early as 1822. I'm frankly not fully convinced either way, but I'll put my money on an 1825 raid, and make the case in Chapter 10.

Ngoza and the Thembu were still just south of the Thukela. When the Chunu moved, and under increasing threat from both the Mkhize and the iziYendane, he must have felt even more insecure. There was also possibly a Zulu raid on the nearby Mngeni. So around 1822 Ngoza moved south and west again, sucking along with him various adherents amongst his Dlamini,

Mabaso, Mbatha, Sithole and Nxamalala neighbours.[37] As always, relationships between these peoples were extraordinarily complex. Here's one little insight.

A Nxamalala man, Sondaba, is said to have gone to Ngoza, hearing that he was going to move south and wanting to join him. Sondaba's brother, Lugaju, was already related to Ngoza through his mother. When Ngoza arrived with his *impi*, he put up in Nxamalala country. Meanwhile, Sondaba was at loggerheads with Xesibe of the Zondi, or was trying to head off some of the Zondi cattle for the journey south. However, when it came to the crunch, Sondaba's people mostly declined to move. Only a few went with him, and the Nxamalala were left in place under another brother, Mtsholozi. Subsequently, when Ngoza eventually met his end in Mpondo country, Sondaba and Lugaju came back, only to run into a complicated – and for them fatal – tussle for the leadership.[38]

Ngoza's flight path was a little north of the Chunu's, possibly moving with them for a while. His passage was also marred with violence. 'In his course,' LUGUBU testified, 'he killed many chiefs indeed.' According to LUGUBU, Ngoza got lost and described an inadvertent circle via the Mpofana stream and the Ngome, before getting his bearings, and heading off towards present-day Howick and then down across the Mkhomazi.[39] There, he ran into the Bhaca between the Mngeni and Mkhomazi rivers.

The Bhaca – sometimes called the amaWushe – living under Madikane on the Mngeni river, were another fairly substantial people. They would relate themselves very closely to the Zulu, looking back on – or inventing – an ancient history of peaceable separation.[40] They had assimilated so thoroughly into the local scene that they were known as amaZotsha – people who had changed their original dialect.[41] (Or the term referred to their habit of scarifying their faces and wearing their headrings high and forward.[42]) They were probably already in conflict with their neighbours before Shaka's ventures started to have ripple effects. The Bhaca then moved, in several stages and alongside the Chunu, as far as present-day Mount Frere, under a combination of distant Zulu, and rather closer Thembu threats.[43]

These were the two major southern movements of these years, 'defections' that grieved Shaka. He was not attempting to chase these groups off, and later would welcome refugees from both Chunu and Thembu washing back into the Zulu haven. The main point of detailing this history is that at no point in this 'flight' can we see Zulu *impis* raising the dust in pursuit. There was Zulu pressure, to be sure, but it was hardly the volcanic 'lava' flow of irresistible predation, as James Stuart put it in the article quoted in the epigraph to this chapter.

A VERY BRIEF CONFEDERACY

In the meanwhile, fragments of the smaller groups of people were also attempting to get away to the south. They probably *were* feeling the steely edge of Mkhize and iziYendane raids. A temporary confederacy of those minor groups was getting itself together to try to punch through the ring of resistance presented by the Chunu, Thembu and Bhaca polities, and get to more comfortable ground. There wasn't much space to manoeuvre, what with the Cele and Thuli polities commanding the Mkhomazi region, and – as they would discover to their cost – an Mpondo polity to the south that was less than welcoming.

It is difficult to tell just how cohesive this 'confederacy' was (the term was applied to the grouping by Theophilus Shepstone in the 1860s, and picked up by Stuart, but it has a shaky relationship to the reality). The story is that several of the petty chieftains – Baleni and Nombewu of the Hlangwini, Mdingi kaLanga of the Bhele, and Xesibe of the Zondi – got their cattle together and fought their way through to the Mpondos. Some of the Dunge, under pressure from Zihlandlo and, I suspect, the iziYendane, might have joined them, leaving others to resort to foraging and banditry in an increasingly uncultivable landscape.[44] (Assertions of extended cannibalism need to be treated with extreme caution; see Box 4 on page 223.) Collectively they, too, became an *imfacane*, a marauding caravan, obliged to live by force off the land.[45] Even so, their combined power wasn't likely to have been very great; they were defeated by the Bhaca in one clash, and once they were through the Bhaca-Chunu-Thembu ring they splintered. The Mpondo were having none of this ragged invasion, and sent them packing. Xesibe was killed near Howick; his followers began to move in dribs and drabs back towards their ancestral homes. Mdingi also came back, only to be killed by the Cele.[46]

For all their disarray, the 'confederacy' helped to push the bigger polities even further away. Some Bhaca joined the Chunu in another move across the Mzimkhulu river. It seems that they had a close relationship for a time. Madikane was said to have depended on the Chunu for medicinal and magical drugs: from them he got the idea of doctoring a heifer in certain ways in order to overcome other chiefs. Together they thumped the Mbotho people on the Mzimkhulu. Madikane had a relationship with the female *induna* Macibise, and possibly worked temporarily with her to fend off the Zondi, Dunge, and whoever else was encroaching on his tenuous space. After a couple of years of marauding, Madikane would be hemmed in by an ad hoc league of Xhosa and Mpondo and killed off. If MAHAYA is right that this happened at dawn on the day of a solar eclipse, it might just have been – according to the almanacs – on 20 December 1824.[47]

Meanwhile, in around late 1822, the Chunu had separated from the Bhaca somewhere north of present-day Kokstad. They stopped in a forest near Nsikeni mountain and the Ngwagwane river, some 50 kilometres south of where the Thembu had halted around the headwaters of the Mzimkhulu. Further to the north, Matiwane and the Ngwane were still dug in beneath the Drakensberg.

All three would later suffer another Zulu attack, but up until 1824 or so, it's striking how little of the violence south of the Thukela had anything directly to do with Shaka. He was partly a victim of, and only partly a cause of, a whole ripple of activity which had begun fundamentally with Zwide and the northern slaving groups and spread southwards, bumping up against and exacerbating localised tensions and conflicts. The mayhem that did happen in his actually rather cautious and patchy intrusion across the Thukela, occurred without his direct approval or intention. Though much stronger than he had been four years previously, Shaka was still essentially looking for security and for resources across the Thukela river.

To this end, he was beginning to negotiate a relationship with, importantly, Magaye of the Cele.

ANOTHER 'YOUNGER BROTHER'

Shaka had doubtless been in contact with the Cele for some years. When he first had to retreat across the Thukela ahead of Zwide's invasion, it was hinted that he'd visited Magaye of the Cele. It makes sense that once the Mthethwa and their historical trade route through to the Tsonga were under Zulu suzerainty, Shaka would try to extend his coastal reach to include the well-disposed Cele.

> 'Among the peoples here a fire will burn at two doors – among our
> people (at the place of Nandi), and among your people (the place of
> Siwetu). Both will be ours, so that when the fire of our people's place
> goes out, it will be lit at Siwetu's; and when the fire goes out at your
> people's place, it will be lit at Nandi's.'[48]

This is Shaka, addressing Magaye. Well disposed the Cele remained, and they were powerful, too, numbering both Qwabe and Thuli peoples among their adherents.[49]

The Cele adamantly traced their history back through the Mthethwa to Tsonga origins.[50] It was said that Magaye's grandfather Mkhokholeli had migrated from the region between the Mfolozis to build his main base near Stanger – where Shaka would build his last 'capital' kwaDukuza. Some of Mkhokholeli's people had left him to rejoin the Tsongas, only to migrate back to him much later.[51] Mkhokholeli married a Thuli woman, Masivuba, mother of Dibandlela. Dibandlela, succeeding Mkhokholeli, had a number of sons, notable amongst them Magaye and Mande. Mande was apparently the older son, but because Magaye was the son of an upper-rank Qwabe woman, Siwethu, he was designated as the heir.[52] He was said to have been smuggled away (much like Shaka) to live out his youth amongst his mother's people; Dibandlela evidently anticipated trouble.

The trouble began when Mande heard about this youthful heir and got cross. He tried to persuade the elderly Dibandlela to come with him to rule at his Emfeni kraal. He – really or metaphorically – pulled so emphatically on his father's arm that the old man fell over. Dibandlela swore then by his sister Nonqina that he would pit Mande against a 'young, poking bull' – meaning, presumably, Magaye. Dibandlela called all the Cele together and informed them that there was no *inkosi* because Magaye was still too young. (Quite what role Dibandlela had in mind for himself, still the nominal *inkosi*, isn't clear.) Mande retorted, 'Is there any people as large as ours that has no chief?' Then the fighting began. Such at least is one version.[53]

The recorded accounts fall into contradiction here. MELAPI – a son of Magaye himself – says that Mande defeated and usurped his father somehow;

Dibandlela went off and built another *umuzi* at eNyenyezeni. Mande ruled for a while, until Magaye, now grown, came back from his exile, strolling provocatively past the gates of Mande's homestead, trailing a meagre three cows and two goats. Then the conflict started up again.[54] In another version, Dibandlela persuades a third son, Mziboneli, to help him give Mande a fatherly chastising. After several inconclusive skirmishes, Mande and his men are defeated; Magaye comes back and builds an *umuzi* at the Mhlali river, named eMdlazi.[55] DINYA has a slightly different version again.[56] In any event, the tussles went on for some years, Magaye probably getting the upper hand. The ageing Dibandlela seemed entirely unable to impose order.

Then Shaka came into the picture.

The timing remains unclear. It was certainly well after the incorporation of the Qwabe. MAZIYANA's assertion that Shaka attacked Mande before his defeat of Zwide seems wrong, since it would appear that iziYendane forays were part of the mix in Shaka's intervention;[57] MAZIYANA also compresses a whole lot of attacks on people south of the Thukela into one alarming sweep, which was surely not the case. Likewise, DINYA's statement that it happened after Shaka crossed over to kwaDukuza is certainly wrong; Shaka would not have built his central *umuzi* there unless the Cele were already firmly under his suzerainty.[58] Magaye was in the Cele chieftaincy when the first whites arrived at Port Natal in mid-1824; and since he quickly and unquestioningly referred them to Shaka, I would guess that Shaka had successfully intervened in the Cele dispute well before that, probably 1823, but quite possibly even earlier.

Magaye's position as chief was ambiguous. Whether or not by invitation, Shaka attempted to mediate, calling on Zihlandlo, Nqetho of the Qwabe, Nzwakele of the Dube, Duze of the Makhanya, and Nodokwana of the Maphumulo. Old Dibandlela, who had already advised against trying to resist Shaka, was now too decrepit to attend.[59] (If nothing else, this list of chieftains shows, firstly, that Shaka *hadn't* wiped out everyone in the region, and, secondly, that he didn't feel free to do things unilaterally.)

The consultation may or may not have been window dressing as Shaka not-so-secretly favoured Magaye. Either – as DINYA relates it – he heard both Magaye and Mande out, then made his decision; or – in MAGEZA's version – he tested their possible reactions by sending gifts of beads.[60] Magaye, conscious

that he would be unlikely to stave off a man who had overcome the great
Phakathwayo, gave the messenger a beast to eat; Mande insulted the size of
Shaka's member. Shaka set off – or sent men – across the Thukela to restore
the honour of his offended organ. It seems unlikely that Shaka personally
accompanied this expedition; he very seldom did.

Mande was attacked and driven to Nzala of the Ndlovu, on the Mvoti
river, where they were both defeated. Mande was not killed immediately.[61]
He may even have gone off to *khonza* the Ndwandwe but, like Makhedama
before him, couldn't remain there. He came back, saying, 'I shall not take
refuge with aliens while a child of my father is still ruling the Cele.' Magaye
built him an *umuzi*, eMfeni, at the Mhlali.[62] However, Mande lasted only a
few months. The iziYendane came and killed him, and burned the homestead
to the ground. MELAPI says that Shaka ordered it; Shaka was said to be almost
afraid of Mande: 'When he looks at me, though I am Shaka, my eyes drop to
the ground and give way before him'.[63] It is, however, probable that even
this quite useful assassination was unintended. In fact, it seems to have been
the last straw as far as Shaka's tolerance of the iziYendane's indiscipline was
concerned.

Magaye was left holding the Cele reins of power – or such power as Shaka
allowed him. This was considerable. Magaye came to hold the same position
of affection as Zihlandlo did: he was Shaka's *umnawe*, his 'younger brother',
and was invited to major festivities. Perhaps Shaka could afford to do this for
someone who had little military force, with no *amabutho* to speak of, but a
large resource in manpower. Shaka gave Magaye an *ibutho* to fight with, and
sent him at some point to harass the Mbili people further south. Magaye was
able to build up a huge family – some 20 to 30 wives and at least 28 known
sons[64] – and to erect several *imizi*. He had his own *isigodlo*, and could put
men to death independently.[65] In fact, the balance between these two groups,
Zulu and Cele, was a fine one:

> Shaka entertained great affection for Magaye, and spoke even of taking
> him onto his lap. He was, however, afraid of doing this on account of
> the ill-feeling that would be given rise to. It seems that Shaka and
> Magaye used to hold dances together. At these, on occasion, Magaye's
> men sang a chorus about 'The one who is choked with meat' and
> 'The circle of men will turn around.' Shaka could not understand

what was implied by these phrases. He was apprehensive lest Magaye meant that the time would come when Shaka's own men (circle) would leave him and join Magaye, presumably in the same way as Mande's men had come round to him. Shaka did not like this, especially as, with . . . recent additions . . . the [Cele] tribe had become a very large one, and he questioned Magaye, who thereby became frightened.[66]

Nevertheless, Shaka's hand over the Cele remained both affectionate and light. Even though he eventually moved south and built his capital kwaDukuza in the middle of Cele territory, he is recorded as having visited Magaye only once. MELAPI, Magaye's son, was there: a very little boy who peered through the fence and noted – or said he did – Shaka's dark brown skin and tight buttocks, the adornments of crimson lourie feathers. Shaka came from kwaDukuza with the still unmarried Dibinhlangu and Gibabanye *amabutho*. They carried no war shields, but wore their dancing-dress of cow-tail bunches, bead girdles, decorations of the *umkhokha* plant, and *usundu* palm at elbow and knee. They danced; Magaye first, to *tshaya* – that is, to prepare the dancing-ground for Shaka. Then Shaka danced, and sang this song:

> The kraal of Nzala kaMangqatshi
> Will no more be mentioned,
> Ask among the Nsomi people.

And then,

> Kukuluku, the cock crowed,
> Who placed it there?
> Vutani and Gubutuka praised him,
> The husband enters,
> You must carry *imincwazi* berries,
> I am not a goat to be made terrified in the kraals,
> I am not a gate-keeper such as is collected by kraal-owners;
> I am a great warrior there in the Zulu country,
> I am foremost in the place of headrings [there where affairs are
>   discussed].[67]

Magaye himself was a tall, good-looking man, *insundu* – dark brown. Shaka said to him:

> 'If I were to kill you, I would be laughed at by the whole country, for they would say I killed you because of your being handsome. I would be doing myself harm if I killed you. Even though it is said I am in the habit of killing people, I will never kill you. If I did, the various states and the Zulus would laugh at me, saying I had killed you because I am *isinkotshela* – ugly, with a protruding forehead.'[68]

We might well doubt that such words were ever uttered, or that MELAPI's memories of infancy could be quite so sharp three-quarters of a century later. Nevertheless, they do express the same thing: Magaye's favoured status. It was a kind of compliment, too, that Shaka, having taken his breakfast on that same visit atop a nearby hill, then wandered through Magaye's *isigodlo*, and commented on Magaye's young men: 'Are these young men yours? They are very handsome; they have such long legs! They must become my men.' Magaye agreed – not that he had much choice. Shaka built these men a homestead on the Mdloti river in their own country, not taking them off to Zululand as he did with other units from the southern region, like Zihlandlo's. He did, however, take their name – Njanduna – and Magaye had to rename his own *ibutho* Hodi (old spelling Rodi), or uQogi.[69]

This was perhaps the most important alliance of Shaka's reign. It was untroubled and loyal and provided him with a retreat from further troubles in the north. It was a base closer to the resources of the south: Magaye would soon help Shaka in other longer-range expeditions. The first of these was against their immediate southern neighbours, the Thuli.

IN FAVOUR WITH SHAKA

The Thuli had occupied the area around Port Natal at least since the later eighteenth century. They had been pushed south by the Qwabe, and visited a certain amount of violence on the people that *they* displaced. The Thuli leader, Dole, is said to have impaled children on posts and (pre-empting Shaka) used the stabbing-spear. In 1823 and 1824, they were relatively disunited, riven with succession squabbles – a perfect target for Shaka. The Thuli were probably first raided by the iziYendane. One victim whom we know about was Maguda, the sister of Mnini, a later Thuli leader. Maguda was hunted into the bush around the Bluff, lived a fugitive life in rough shelters, and was eventually eaten by hyenas. Mnini himself was a minor at the time, and his section was under a regent. A more important result of the iziYendane *izwekufa* – with some encouragement from Magaye, perhaps – was that this same section of the Thuli went north and *khonza*'d Shaka. They were led by the regent himself, a man named Mathubane kaJombela.[70]

Shaka then helped Mathubane into a position of dominance over the Thuli by sending a double column, one led by Magaye, the other by our old friend Makhedama of the Langeni. (Makhedama had, of course, since returned from his temporary submission to Zwide.) They attacked another Thuli claimant, Ntaba kaMyebu. Makhedama swept through the upper regions of Thuli country, near present-day Pietermaritzburg, and seized Ntaba's cattle. Magaye advanced along the coast and captured cattle along the Ilovu river and the kwaMkhobu forests. They were shadowed by a trusted Zulu *induna*, Mthobela kaMthimude, head of the ekuWeleni *umuzi*. Mthobela apparently appropriated the cattle seized by Magaye, presumably intending to pass them on to Shaka, but was compelled to return them by Makhedama. Shaka, incensed, sent an *impi* to kill Makhedama, which they did at eHlungwini, a hill opposite Maphumulo. He had always been a troublesome character, and doubtless Shaka was glad for an excuse to have him removed. It was not a deed that went unquestioned: this was one of the two occasions when Nandi spoke up against the more violent acts of her son, asking: 'Why are you finishing off the house of Langeni, your own relatives?'[71]

Other claimants to ascendancy over the Thuli were quietly sidelined. They weren't killed off, and not all of them were defeated or incorporated: one Mkhaliphi kaNombuya of the Nyamvwini section was never subdued, and he continued to evade even Dingane's search parties.[72] Overall, however, Shaka was able to take advantage of the ambiguities of power, notably between Mathubane and Dlemula. MAZIYANA explained:

> Dhlemula was a mature man but not of Matubane's age. Before the 'Izwekufa', when the tribes were disturbed by the iziYendane and others with them, Dhlemula was the acknowledged tribal guardian.

Matubane, after the depredations of Shaka's troops, *konza*'d Shaka. Shaka took a fancy to him and gave his orders to him; he spoke to him direct and not to Dhlemula. As Matubane was in favour with Shaka, so he superseded Dhlemula and became the *de facto* guardian of the tribe and responsible to Shaka for its good behaviour.[73]

Dlemula would die in the 1828 'Bhalule' campaign (see page 484), and Mathubane take over entirely. Young Mnini, for whom Mathubane had acted as regent, was thought of as having 'grown up among the Cele', since Magaye's Cele were now the Thuli's immediate overlords. He nevertheless continued throughout the atrocities of the *izwekufa* to live on the Bluff.[74] We can imagine him watching, first, the Zulu *impis* coming back from their campaign against the Mpondo and, shortly afterwards, the alarming sight of pale-skinned men washing up out of the sea.

At just about this time, Shaka discovered the full extent of the iziYendane *izwekufa*. His grip on the south was so patchy, his attention so divided between north and south, that he hadn't heard half of it. It was Magaye who told him that the iziYendane had been conducting its own campaigns, killing many people, and keeping the cattle that should have gone to Shaka. Magaye is also said to have asked Shaka about the circumstances of the murder of his brother Mande; Shaka knew nothing about it. He was enraged. He called in those who had made the attack, and had them killed off on the grounds that they were mere bandits.[75] A small section of the *ibutho* under the *induna* Makhatha presumably remained loyal to Shaka, since Makhatha was later killed in Dingane's purges.[76] The rest of the *ibutho* was dispersed: some were killed, some fled north, and a remnant joined Nqetho of the Qwabe when he eventually moved south.[77] Dingane was meanwhile making accord with other iziYendane, a suspicious circumstance to which we will return.

The iziYendane's former head *induna*, Nonzama, was punished with the death sentence, and Shaka gave Nonzama's cattle to Mathubane, his latest favourite.

THE MELON EATERS

By mid-1824, Shaka seems to have started feeling more secure. The northern marches were relatively quiescent. He had brought a substantial swathe of the coastal region under some kind of alliance in which he was the dominant partner. From north to south, the Mthethwa, the Qwabe, the Cele and the Thuli all acknowledged his suzerainty in some form. Inland, the Sithole and the Mkhize were in fruitful partnership. The Chunu, the Thembe and the Bhaca had moved far enough away to offer neither resources nor threat.

Shaka was finally in a position to be more aggressively adventurous.

It may be, as MAZIYANA states, that Shaka was seeking to 'fetch' Madikane of the Bhaca from where he had lodged himself in the northern Transkei. If this was the case, he failed.[78] Another informant thought that Shaka's aim was to chastise Faku's Mpondo for killing Ngoza of the Thembu, although why this should have upset Shaka isn't clear; nor is the timing quite right.[79] Most likely, Shaka was simply after more cattle, and perhaps hoping to gain some sort of tributary arrangement from Faku. The prominent *induna* Mdlaka was put in command. He was accompanied by elements of the Fasimba *ibutho*, under Mpangazita kaMncumbatha; of the Nobamba, under Nomapela of the Ndwandwe people; and of the Mbelebele, under Klwana kaNgqengelele.

On this occasion, Shaka underestimated both his enemy and the demands of the distance.

> The army crossed the Thukela into Natal well above Greytown (say opposite Msinga) and travelled right under the Drakensberg – they skirted along the Drakensberg range. The force travelled southwards, sweeping round, slightly entered Mpondo territory, and made its way along the coast back to Zululand, crossing the Mzimkulu in the neighbourhood of Port Shepstone. . . . The force then entered Pondoland, coming to Manci's territory (a Pondo *induna*). They merely affected [sic] an entrance and made a slight seizure of cattle. The Pondos came to the attack. The Pondos *sika*'d – stabbed – three regiments. Seeing this, Mdhlaka reinforced the three regiments being defeated by [that is, with] youths, and got the better of the Pondos. After this the Zulus came back homewards.[80]

The units sent by Shaka were probably small – *amabandla* rather than the larger *amabutho*. It wasn't intended as a massive assault and wasn't entirely successful. On the long way there, or on the journey back (the sources are divided) the Zulu warriors ran out of food. They didn't even have enough cattle to feed themselves and had to resort to a scrabble for *amabece* melons that they found lying about in abandoned hamlets.

From then on, this expedition was known as the *amabece* campaign.

In the folk memory, the outcome was blamed on Faku's ability to summon supernatural forces: he set hyenas on them, which ate both cattle and men and followed them back almost to the Thukela.[81]

The Zulu did return with a few cattle, which they gave to Shaka who was waiting back at the Mthwalume river. These he passed on to Mathubane to look after for him. En route, they also discovered Lukhilimba who, you will recall, had been banished by Shaka for making a mess of the retreat before the Ndwandwe, several years before. He had now established himself north of the Mzimkhulu, with an *isigodlo* imitated from Shaka.[82] Shaka directed Mathubane to fetch Lukhilimba to come and see him, which he did. Lukhilimba's initial apprehensions about this summons proved unfounded. Both of them received cattle from the *inkosi*. Lukhilimba gratefully gave some of his share to Mathubane, saying 'I would not have received what I have but for you'.[83]

(The ironic postscript to this episode is that Lukhilimba somehow became subordinate to Fynn, who established himself in precisely that Mzimkhulu area from 1825 onwards. In the tangle of betrayals and machinations that characterised the whites' dealings with Dingane in 1832, Lukhilimba was judged a traitor, and Fynn simply shot him.[84])

All things considered, it must, in fact, have been a rather battered, hungry, and not very imposing force that encountered Henry Francis Fynn on the beach north of Port Natal on that day in the middle of May 1824.

WILD BEASTS FROM THE SEA

Fynn doesn't even mention Mathubane, although Nathaniel Isaacs does. According to Isaacs, Mathubane was a 'tall, athletic man, about six feet three inches high; active and muscular and capable of considerable exertion'. He was the only man of his mostly fish-eating people to possess cattle. Isaacs quite misjudged the relationship between the local chieftain and Shaka:

The tribe of which Mataban was chief, had been subdued by Chaka, but having rallied the remains of it, with them he had sought a settlement between the forests, where they took refuge from the incursions of the Zoolas. The innumerable persecutions to which they had been subjected by their more powerful and sanguinary neighbours had tended to render them timid and apprehensive. On the approach of strangers they would flee with their valuables into the innermost recesses of the forest . . .[85]

The first whites misjudged a great deal of what they initially encountered on that strange shoreline. Of course, so too did the locals. You would also run if you had never seen a white-skinned apparition in flapping clothes, emerging mysteriously out of the belly of a winged shell from the sea, later attached to the back of a snorting black monster that resembled a distorted zebra.

(Ironically, on the only other occasion on which Isaacs mentions Mathubane's people, they *were* running away from him, because they knew that he wanted to coerce them into unpaid work – temporary slavery, if you like.[86])

Fynn and company were not the very first whites to have landed at this spot. Both the shipwreck narratives and the oral traditions testify that a remarkable number of whites had made their presence felt. Even this far north, people remembered, for instance, survivors of the St Johns river wreck of the *Grosvenor* in 1782. These included a woman who was married off (for a snuff-spoon) by her rescuers to one Mbukwe; she gave birth to Mntengwane, a fair-haired grandfather to MAHAYA kaNongqabana, one of James Stuart's informants.[87] MAZIYANA recalled seeing a man in the early 1830s, Mphazima kaBoko, who was descended from a white who had landed in Dole's day (that is, probably in the early 1800s). He also spoke of 'Mas-dirik', a white who arrived in Shaka's reign, and might have come 'from the Portuguese at or near Delagoa Bay'.[88] MCOTOYI knew of another of Boko's mixed offspring.[89] Magaye recalled a white man from the Cape turning up in Dingiswayo's day; the people chanted, 'Ngqabangaqwba, go away!', but finally decided to kill him.[90] Shaka himself mentioned to Fynn perhaps the same white man being killed by the Cele only three years previously.[91] Slavers had landed at both Port Natal and St Lucia in the past; no doubt Portuguese and mestizo traders had passed through, too, and Isaacs would shortly meet a Portuguese man at

Shaka's *umuzi*. In a bizarre twist to this, Fynn once suggested that Shaka himself was of 'white extraction'.[92]

MAZIYANA, who was Thuli-connected, insisted that it was Mathubane who first introduced these new whites to Shaka, and was duly rewarded with cattle. It made sense, of course, seeing as he lived right there at isiBubulungu.[93] MAQUZA's account is different from that of both MAZIYANA and of Fynn, quoted earlier:

> Europeans came first to Mpipi, who lived just across the Tongati. . . .
> He took the Europeans to his chief, Magaye, who lived on the Mhlali
> in his kraal Emdhlazi. Magaye then said they must go on the king,
> Shaka. He sent them on by Hasazi, Mpipi's son . . . Shaka asked
> where they had come from. 'From the sea,' they replied, 'in an
> *umkumbu*' [a ship], though this word was not known then. In those
> days natives thought the sea was a lake.[94]

Fynn also never mentions Magaye, but again, Isaacs does: 'a fine, stout, well-proportioned man, of a commanding appearance, familiar, but not liberal'.[95] They obviously did stay at Magaye's regularly, as another informant, DINYA, insisted. DINYA's account, though doubtless as riddled with fictions as the whites' own, provides something of a corrective, a Cele-Zulu perspective.

> The first white man arrived with Nhlamba the interpreter at the
> kraal of Sinqila kaMpipi, chief of the Amangati tribe (an offshoot of
> the Cele). Sinqila went out to look for his beast which had calved in
> the veld. He found all his women and children running away from
> the wild beast, a white man who was mounted on a horse. . . . They
> said his hair was like cattle tails, and the horse some strange bogey . . .
> Sinqila sent at once to report the incident to his chief Magaye. Magaye
> was then living at Mhlali in his Mdhlazi kraal. Sinqila gave a full
> account of the white man, saying how he was dressed, that he had an
> *imbenge* [literally, a shallow grass basket], that something (a bottle in
> which he carried milk asked for at the kraals visited) was very peculiar,
> inasmuch as it shone, and the gun he carried. All these features were
> surprising, and all this Sinqila, having brought a gift of food for the
> small children, reported . . .

Magaye sent for the principal members of his tribe. He called his *induna* Nhlasiyana kaNomunga, the *induna* Cunge kaNodinga, Mvivinyeki of the Emanhlokweni tribe, and Mpangu of the Gumbi, a section of the Qwabe tribe which *konza*'d to the Cele. Others came, too. . . . Magaye proposed the man should be brought to him to see. Sinqila said he must not run away on seeing the monster. Magaye, after Sinqila went off to conduct the stranger to him, called up his regiments and set them on both sides of him as he sat in the open space in front of the cattle kraal. His children and relatives stood behind.

Presently the stranger arrived, mounted on a horse, with hat on head, gun in hand, hair like cattle tails. All present were moved with wonder and awe, so much so that the regiments shuffled back as far as the fence, whilst Magaye himself moved backwards with such vigour as to sprain [*sic*] one of the girls behind him. When the white man halted and got off and stood, the onlookers were reassured, the more so when he did as asked by Magaye through his interpreter, namely to remove his hat, to turn round and so forth in order that full opportunity should be given of surveying him well at a distance.

Magaye now ordered that an ox should be presented as food to the stranger. A dark-brown one was got and given him, and he was told to go and pass the night at Mziboneli's kraal, this man being a brother of Magaye and a son of Dibandhlela. Mziboneli was much concerned at having to receive this monster into his own household, kwaMabola, but did in accordance with orders. Here the dark-brown ox was slaughtered. It was not stabbed, it was shot, and as the shot was fired all lay down on the ground. The white man proposed this, and after warning all to be on the lookout for a report like a thunderclap, fired at and killed the beast without touching it. He then cut its throat to let it bleed freely. He asked what part should be presented to the chief. They told him the meat covering the ribs, as well as the ear . . . . Magaye was much impressed with this stranger, and in view of what had occurred decided at once to report in person to Shaka . . . .

He directed Nhlasiyana to take a detachment of 30 to 40 men with him and conduct the white man to Bulawayo kraal; he would go on ahead himself and be present when the party arrived. When the party got to Bulawayo they found Magaye there, seated with Shaka. They had been directed by Magaye to enter the kraal by both gates and then to advance up to the meeting place of the council towards the *isigodhlo*. They were to halt with their charge as soon as they got a short distance off it, and then one and all to raise their right arms into the air and together exclaim, dwelling a long while on each syllable, as if singing, 'Magaye says that the cockroaches are crossing the council place!' This expression was to be sung out three times – an expression meaning that good luck has befallen one.

. . . No sooner did Shaka hear them exclaim thus than he ran out of his hut, dragging his skin cloak with him, to see what it meant.[96]

This account conveys the richness of careful ritual and protocol to which Fynn himself was, at least then, largely blind. What DINYA omits, of course, is that Fynn was accompanied by several companions.

Fynn had been followed to Port Natal by Francis Farewell in the *Antelope*. On 1 May Farewell and thirteen other men had been given permission to sail from the Cape. His passengers included his own father-in-law, Jan Peterssen.[97] On the same day, he wrote to Cape Governor Henry Somerset, outlining his intentions to trade, and received the government's blessing on condition that he entered into no 'territorial acquisitions'.[98] Like Captain Owen in Thembe, Farewell would shortly ignore this inconvenient constraint.

(He also omitted a fact often missed in the histories: he and James Saunders King had already, the previous year, sailed in and out of Port Natal. At St Lucia, King had taken on board from Farewell several cases of unspecified goods as well as 40 elephant tusks and 168 smaller teeth, presumably hippo. Trading and hunting was already under way. Between 4 October and 1 November 1823 they had been able to run the sandbar and shelter for the first time within the confines of Port Natal. This was possibly the more historic moment.)

According to Fynn, Farewell had conceived an outlandishly exaggerated idea of Shaka's wealth and influence, and had seriously overcapitalised. (Perhaps this is where the psychological heart of the later mythology lies. Once they had conceived of this gargantuan king in the first place, everything that the whites then saw was interpreted in that light; and they could not let go of it.) Fynn nevertheless had eagerly offered his services to the speculation. Equally troubling, the party was riven by differences between Dutch and English. As Fynn slyly put it, 'Only the hope of speedily gained treasure would have induced persons of their character to enter into such a speculation which they were so unfitted for in all its points'.[99]

James Saunders King, meanwhile, had left for London to promote his case for trade in south-east Africa. In July 1824 he was writing to Earl Bathurst, punting the 'salubrious' virtues of Port Natal and his unique map of it, his own 'upwards of ten years' service in the Navy as midshipman, and the terrible privations of his previous trip. The number drowned at St Lucia was now elevated to six, and twelve men had been abandoned on shore, he said, for 'five weeks'.[100] He made no mention of the missing 'Jackot'.

The ill-assorted Farewell, Peterssen and company arrived at Port Natal a few days after Fynn. The new invasive tribe now numbered 35. A select group, including Farewell, Petersssen and Fynn, set off via Magaye to see Shaka.

It took the whites, slowed up particularly by the 63-year-old Peterssen, about two weeks to cover the 100 miles to kwaBulawayo. Given 'the badness of the roads which were only footpaths, the bogs and the inconvenience of crossing rivers,' wrote Fynn, it felt more like 300 miles.[101] They were conveyed, according to Fynn, on a circuitous route via the homesteads of 'Siyingila' and Mbikwana, and some of Shaka's *amakhanda* – all of which seem to indicate that the country was more densely populated than they later alleged. In fact, Fynn noted that there were 'kraals' not far north of the Port, which he had previously observed from aboard ship,[102] and King remarked that in the vicinity of the bay itself Indian corn was being grown 'in great abundance'.[103] Indeed, they seemed to meet people at every turn. While the iziYendane *izwekufa* had ravaged some areas, 'depopulation' was hardly the universal horror that the whites subsequently portrayed (see Box 8 on page 345).

As the men approached kwaBulawayo, 'regiments' and herds of cattle and groups of women seemed to be converging from every quarter. The whites assumed presumptuously that it was purely for their benefit. Fynn later exaggerated everything wildly: kwaBulawayo was '2 miles in circumference'; on their arrival they were surrounded by '12 000 men in war attire'.[104] Farewell's estimates were more sober:

The king received us surrounded by a large number of his chiefs and about eight or nine thousand armed men, observing a state and ceremony on our introduction that we little expected, and his subjects appeared to treat him with such submission and respect as to rank him far above any chiefs I believe known in South Africa, whilst the nation he governs in manners, customs and mode of ornamenting themselves are so different from any hitherto known as to at once astonish and please us. . . . I fancy he [Shaka] assembled all his disposable force on the occasion of our visit and probably fifty thousand souls, fourteen of which might be fighting men on a push, forms *the whole population of the large territory he is possessed of.*[105]

Fynn was also deeply impressed by this 'most exciting scene, surprising to us, who could not have imagined that a nation termed "savages" could be so disciplined and kept in order'.[106] Mbikwana *bonga*'d (praised) Shaka; an elephant tusk was presented to Farewell; then Shaka 'sprang out from amidst the Chiefs which had surrounded him and striking the Shields of the Chiefs which stood on each side the whole body ran to the lower part of the Krall leaving us alone . . .'[107]

Oddly, Fynn seemed quite unable to describe Shaka. He gives us only a clumsily written though detailed account of what he wore, as if he couldn't see past the finery to the man himself:

[O]n his forehead he wore a Turban of Otter Skin with a feather of the Crane in the front full two feet long earrings made from the Sugar Cane dried carved round the edge with white ends of an inch in diameter for which the loose part of the Ear is cut to admit it across from each shoulder small bunches 3 inches in length of Monkey and Gennett Skins twisted appearing like the tails of the animals these hang half down the Body round the ring on the head . . . were a dosen bunches of the red feathers of the Lorie tastefully tied to thorns which were stuck in the hair round his arms were white Ox tails cut down the middle so as to allow the hairs to hang round the Arm to the number of 4 on each round the waist a petticoat resembling the Highland plade made of Monkey and Gennett skins . . . small tassels round the Top of the same and the petticoat reaching the Knee under

which were white Ox Tails to fit round the legs so as to hang to the
Ancles a white Shield with one black spot and 1 assgai . . .[108]

It may be no more than a mischievous fiction, but DINYA pictures Shaka
beautifully turning the tables. The 'anthropological gaze' – almost universally
the pose and preserve of the European voyeur of the foreign and exotic – is
reversed.

> Shaka said, 'Hear, my people! Magaye says the white men have arrived
> in his country.' He presently noticed the white object among them.
> He gave the bystanders various orders as regards making the white
> man do this and that. He took it into his head to cause the white man
> to undress and put on his, Shaka's, loin-cover, which was fetched from
> his hut. Having a sense of decency, Shaka ordered 30 or 40 men to
> stand round about the white man so as to hide him while he undressed.
> This was done, and Fynn presently appeared in the garb of a Zulu, his
> flesh as white as milk . . . The loin-cover was of blue monkey skin
> with genet skin in front . . . .[109]

Fynn himself did not care to record this undignified exposure.

The white party were in for a number of surprises, but one of the greatest
on this, their very first day in Shaka's presence, was the discovery, in that
crowd of strangers, of a familiar face: 'Jackot'.

Their erstwhile servant and interpreter, the Xhosa ex-convict who had
vanished amongst the long reeds of St Lucia the previous year, had somehow
inveigled his way right into Shaka's court. He, who had before been known
as Jacob Msimbithi, had now acquired the nickname 'Hlambamanzi' – 'Swim-
the-Seas' – in honour of his strange mode of arrival. He now appeared to
have a village and even wives of his own and, more importantly, Shaka's ear.
Captain W.F.W. Owen later related second-hand Farewell's understanding
of how 'Hlambamanzi' had managed this extraordinary feat (see also Box 6
on page 305):

> When Mr Farewell, previously to settling at Natal, visited in a
> mercantile voyage that port, as well as Delagoa and others along the
> coast, he prevailed upon Fire and Jackot to accompany him; the former

was shot accidentally some time afterwards, and Jackot deserted at St Lucia, and was supposed to have been murdered by the natives. But when Mr Farewell formed his settlement at Port Natal, he found that Jackot was with Chaka, with whom he was a great favourite, serving as an interpreter, with the rank of 'chief', and the surname of 'the voyager', and in possession of a large establishment and many wives. The manner in which he contrived to insinuate himself into the good graces of this tyrant was thus related: 'The Kaffers have an idea that when a king dies, an evil genius in the shape of a cat performs the office of executioner. Jackot availed himself of this to obtain the favour of Chaka, who he well knew could not bear to contemplate the idea of death: accordingly he repaired one evening to the king's residence, and there, with his spear commenced a most furious combat with vacancy. Chaka and all present were astonished, and Jackot, after he had continued his exertions until he was exhausted from fatigue, stopped, and exultingly informed the King, "that he had killed the cat which was about to take away his life".'[110]

Whatever the truth of that, Msimbithi (which is what I will call him from now on, since it's as close as we can get to his original name) had doubtless told Shaka much about the white people's background and manners. Shaka couldn't have been taken totally by surprise by their arrival. As far as the whites were concerned, Msimbithi had already said too much. He had not been complimentary, nursing an understandable antipathy that the whites tried to hide. Fynn scratched out of his 'Notebook' a passage that is still legible:

> in calling the interpreter [Msimbithi] who was in a hut close by and could not help but hear me made no answer after several times calling on my repeating to call him he asked me insolently what I wanted with him he proceding on with me I reproached him for his insolence when he told me we were not in the Colony now.[111]

This anecdote about sums it up. Over the next four years, Msimbithi would play a strange and ambiguous role in Shaka's dealings with these motley white men.

Box 6

The astonishing career of 'Swim-the-Seas'

Jakot, Jackot, Jacob, Soembitchi, Msimbithi, Hlambamanzi. What he was born as is guesswork: in this book I call him Jacob Msimbithi. The man's career is as protean as his name. That career, touched on at various points in the main text, is worth focusing on here for several reasons. He is a man who crossed several boundaries, accommodated himself within – and fell foul of – several cultures, as fate and his own energies carried him back and forth across the subcontinent. He isn't perhaps pivotal to our history, but he is one of those colourful minor characters in whom all the cross-currents of the times converge and clash. He is one of the many whose obscure lives form the substrate of recorded history, someone whose path makes nonsense of any attempt to isolate one area of southern African history from any other. (He was far from the only such person we know about in this time and region: the survivors of the *Grosvenor* wreck in 1782, for instance, discovered a man named 'Trout' [perhaps Traut], a runaway Javanese slave living amongst the Mpondo, as well as survivors of a previous shipwreck, including a white woman known as Gquma, now fully assimilated into local culture.[1])

What we know of Msimbithi is largely filtered through the embittered accounts of Fynn and company, who unanimously perceived Msimbithi as plotting against them – as well they might. At any rate, according to Fynn, Msimbithi, 'a man of considerable notoriety and influence', was born amongst the Xhosa people under the chief Ndlambe. Early in life Msimbithi was captured by Dutch labour- and cattle-raiders on the Cape Colony border, who named him 'Soembitchi', and from whom he learned some Dutch. He escaped, thereafter pursuing a shifting career as an interpreter and guide to Xhosa cattle-raiders. Arrested, nearly executed, dragged behind a horse, and *sjambokked*, he barely escaped alive. He was briefly recaptured and used as an interpreter by one Major Frazer, before absconding homewards again. Finally, after trying to sell an elephant tusk at the mission station at Theopolis, he recompensed himself with some cattle; he was pursued, arrested, and dragged in chains first to Graham's Town, and then, alongside the Xhosa chieftain Nxele (then sometimes called Lynx, sometimes Makanna) to imprisonment on the infamous Robben Island.[2] Nathaniel Isaacs claims that it was his friend James Saunders King who carried them there in the brig *Salisbury*; that King loosened Msimbithi's chains, even allowed him a little 'grog'.[3] The aim of this information was, however, to valorise King and hence highlight Msimbithi's later ingratitude, so I remain suspicious.

In any event, Msimbithi was somehow picked up, along with six other prisoners, in 1822 by Captain W.F.W. Owen to help interpret whilst on his eastern coast survey. Msimbithi was, Owen said, 'very handsome, strong and tall and possessed of a commanding figure'; having been 'a chief in his own country', he was scornful of the inhabitants of Delagoa Bay, and distinguished himself in a winning display of spearsmanship. He learned a little English, but it could hardly have been extensive; James Stuart wrote that he was 'said to have entirely failed as interpreter'.[4] When he was passed on to Farewell in the middle of Owen's voyage, however, he was clearly sufficiently disgusted with his treatment to escape once more, this time into the aegis of Shaka, as detailed in the main text. He certainly made himself useful; had an *umuzi* at eMlazi, in Cele country, became an interpreter to Magaye as well as Shaka; had a number of sons, including Pili and Mnkunzi; and became admired enough for the great warrior Zulu kaNogandaya to name one of his own sons Hlamba after the Xhosa refugee.[5]

Msimbithi walked a difficult, devious, and dangerous path between the desires and unthinking attitude of ownership of the Port Natal whites on the one hand and, on the other, his new position of some distinction among Shaka's Zulu.

Not surprisingly, he met a sticky end. Msimbithi had accompanied King's embassy to Algoa Bay in 1828 in which (Fynn alleged), he had 'played the usual role of deceiver', though there is really no evidence to bear this out.[6] He was accused of being equally devious when sent by Dingane to accompany John Cane on two further journeys to the Cape, and of inducing Dingane to raze Cane's *umuzi* in April 1831. Fynn endeavoured to persuade Dingane of Msimbithi's 'atrocious character'. What ensued was a turbulent morass of plot and counter-plot; of Zulu raids involving the whites, a detachment of soldiers from Delagoa Bay, and Msimbithi himself; the whites' assassination of Lukhimbila; and a panic-stricken exodus of the whites from Port Natal. In the midst of it (Fynn and Isaacs claimed), Cane was given 'permission' by Dingane to kill Msimbithi. I suspect, however, that – releasing years of pent-up frustration at a man who had spent his life evading their categories and strictures – they did it on their own initiative. '[Henry] Ogle undertook to do [the assassination]. He accordingly invited Jacob over to his place on the pretext of having business to discuss. Jacob fell into the trap . . .'[7]

We will never have enough information to write a full biography of this extraordinary man, but someone needs to write a good novel.

10

Comfortable asylum?

Encounters with white settlers, 1824–5

He [Francis Farewell] had made Natal the shining objective towards
which courageous men would direct their thoughts, their dreams of
fortune and their slow-moving but resolute trek-oxen pulling their
heavily-laden wagons. He had set the pattern and given the lead to the
rising tide of white infiltration from the south into darkest Africa.
Elizabeth Paris Watt, *Febana* (1962, 309).

Francis Farewell, Henry Francis Fynn and their companions were
astonished at the order that Shaka commanded. Whether the gathered
populace at kwaBulawayo was there to participate in post-campaign cleansing
or in some other ritual event, or had been expressly called to greet the whites,
is arguable. James Stuart gave a fillip to the myth of the gently civilised
Europeans, stranded like Robinson Crusoe in 'darkest Africa', in a footnote
to *The Diary of Henry Francis Fynn*:

Shaka, whose heart had been mysteriously touched by the advent of
British settlers to his shores, converted the occasion into a grand and
dramatically planned festival. We cannot but think these warm-hearted
exhibitions of regard should be attributed in the main to two
influences seemingly trivial in themselves: (*a*) Jacob [Msimbithi]'s
previous lengthy contact with worthy officers of the Royal British
Navy; (*b*) Fynn's discreet, courageous and humane bearing during the
weeks he was striving to open up communication with Shaka. His

307

spontaneous humanity straightway disarmed all suspicion and even caused him to be taken as typical of the race he belonged to.[1]

'Mysteriously touched', indeed. Jacob Msimbithi's longest period of contact with officers of the navy had been through the bars of Robben Island prison. He had been only too glad to escape them. The 'warm-hearted' and 'spontaneous humanity' may as logically have belonged to Shaka. We need look no further than the above passage for a succinct expression of the deliberate omissions, delusions and racial prejudices that have underpinned the conventional portrayal of the Zulu chieftain for 180 years.

The Zulu themselves were certainly under no illusions about the nature of these white visitors. However initially exciting and even potentially threatening their arrival might have been, it would be soon enough recognised that, as DINYA comments: 'The first Europeans who came to Natal were persons in debt or in poor or questionable circumstances at the Cape.'[2] It was they who were looking for what Farewell would later term a 'comfortable asylum' and, briefly and in rather perverse ways, they would find it 'under Shaka's armpit'.

BULLETS AND PURGATIVES

The visitors were made to feel their absolute dependence on Shaka's bounty:

[T]he whole Country as far as we could See round us was covered with Droves of Cattle and people the King came up to us and desired us not to be afraid of his people who was then comming up in small divisions each bringing cattle before them singing & dancing while comming with them and the Cattle being assorted of their different Colours each coloured Cattle being driven separate as also the different shaped horned Cattle which were turned in numbers of different shapes by Art as also many with 4–6 and 8 horns some of which stood upwright on the head and others hanging loosely down others also their whole Bodies covered with pieces of Skin hanging down which had been cut out of the animal Skin leaving the pieces hanging in 3 or 4 Inch lengths after they had continued 2 hours shewing their cattle they Collected together in a Circle and Sang & danced to the War Hoop . . . [The] women now enetered the Krall dressed in long [word illegible] each having a long thin stick in their right hand which they moved to the Tune of the song they had not danced many minutes before they were obliged to make room for the ladies of the Seraglio, being [word not clear] about 150 who were termed Sisters they danced in parties of 8 to 4 each partie having different coloured Beads which were crossed from the Shoulders to the Knees each with a Bunch of Black feathers in the head & four Brass Collars fitting close around the neck the King joining in the dance was accompanied by the Men which lasting half an hour he made a long Speech which was interpreted for us by his Interpreter Clamber Amanze [Hlambamanzi also known as Msimbithi] asking us if ever we had seen such order in any other state . . .[3]

This passage is badly written but the details are vividly recalled. There was one respect, and one respect only, in which the whites did have something of power to offer: '[A]t 7 O Clock', continues Fynn, 'we sent off 4 Rockets and fired 8 guns which from fear he [Shaka] only sent people to look at and would not himself appear out of his Hut.'[4]

However, it would not be long (a day, if we can believe Fynn) before Shaka was cogently arguing that muskets had their limitations: hardened shields could deflect the balls if they were fired from a distance, and the musketeers took so long to reload that warriors would cover the intervening space, whereupon 'we without Shields would drop our guns and attempt to run but from our inability of running as fast as his soldiers can must inevitable fall into their arms'.[5] Nevertheless, the power of the musket was palpable, as Fynn demonstrated later that day on a 'Sea Cow' – a hippo.

This foreshadowed a different kind of war-of-bullets: a war on the animal population. The acquisition of ivory was a primary desire for the whites, and it would prove to be a serious sticking-point in their relations with Shaka. It would also not be long before Shaka was employing these gunmen to help wage his own wars against other people. Though the presence of firearms may not always have been decisive, it certainly contributed to Shaka's self-confidence in his raids of the next four years.

That is how short a time was left to him – and he almost didn't survive even that long.

Fynn and Farewell liked to portray themselves as having a singular power over Shaka in another respect, too: their possession of medicines. Fynn claimed that Shaka had heard that Fynn had all-but-miraculously 'cured several Sick Invalids' amongst Mbikwana's people. He informed Fynn that he had rheumatism, and discussed medicines for a couple of hours.[6] (Stuart converted this into a wholly fraudulent, fictionalised 'conversation' in the *Diary*,[7] calculated mainly to show up Shaka's despotic caprice. Fynn's entire medical experience consisted of a short period as a 'lob-lolly boy' – a general factotum – at a London hospital.)

Rheumatism in such an otherwise superbly fit man potentially indicates that Shaka was older than the whites said.

Far from being overawed by the Europeans' potions, Shaka put them to the test. He got Fynn to 'treat' a minor chieftain in order to observe the result. He demonstrated some traditional medical procedures to Fynn, arguing that they were, in fact, better. With a kind of nasty playfulness, which (as far as it is possible to tell from dubious but numerous anecdotes) seems to have been a prominent aspect of his character, he tested the purgatives in exuberant quantities on some of his *isigodlo* women. He also tried them out, much to the amusement of the other whites, on Peterssen – 'the consequences of which to a person of 63 years of age requires no further relation'.[8]

It comes as little surprise, then, that most of the white men wanted to leave. Fynn was persuaded to stay on while Farewell, Peterssen and the others returned to Port Natal. According to Fynn, Shaka gave the party a rousing send-off. Farewell promised to send more medicines up to kwaBulawayo.

A 'DANGEROUS WOUND'

The temptation for the historian at this point is to begin to rely very heavily on the relatively dense white accounts. They have that familiar narrative feel; they have that air of eyewitness veracity. They are *documents*, attractively specific, dateable. The danger of focusing on these sources is that we fall into the very myth that the adventurers and their successors tried to spread: that they were central to Shaka's life.

In fact, they were not. These men spent very little time in Shaka's presence. He was in command of a large and expanding territory in which a great deal was happening, very little of it to do with the whites. Their arrival was momentous, in the sense that they would prove (as Elizabeth Paris Watt's smug epigraph at the start of this chapter says) to be the vanguard of a much more dangerous influx of settlers, traders, trekkers, missionaries, reprobates, administrators, and armies of soldiers. This influx would do its best throughout the rest of the century to destroy the Zulu nation altogether. However, in and of themselves, these few money-grubbing traders were a rather hapless, squabbling and only intermittently useful presence on the outermost fringe of Shaka's consciousness. Only in the final year of Shaka's life would they make an impact on events out of all proportion to their meagre numbers.

Having said this, it is useful and necessary to spend time on the details of their accounts for a number of reasons. Firstly, they do give us details of character and of everyday happenings in Shaka's reign that are largely missing from the Zulu oral accounts. However, in the same way as we do with the Zulu sources, we have to read these written versions as equally infected with political and cultural biases, memory lapses, storytelling conventions, and outright lies. The personalities and agendas of these men did much to shape their portrayal of Shaka. This is fascinating in its own right because, secondly, their accounts *are* the *fons et origo* – the source and origin – of much of the Shaka mythology. In describing and critiquing both their activities and their writings , we can see the mythology in the process of being made. That, too, is 'Shaka in history'.

So, let's remember that Henry Francis Fynn was only on the outermost edge of the next major event in Shaka's life. Indeed, the Zulu accounts don't even bother to mention Fynn's presence. Literally, he was (he said) shuttered in a smoky hut at kwaBulawayo, reading until the afternoon light gave out. Then he ventured out into a scene of dancing and revelry, lit by bunches of reeds burning dully in the dark. Suddenly Fynn 'heard a shriek and the lights immediately extinguished which was followed by a general bustle & cry'.[9] It turned out that Shaka had been stabbed through the left arm and slightly through the ribs.

Fynn immediately places himself at the centre of the action, fighting his way through to a hut where Shaka lay moaning. The *inkosi* was spitting blood:

'By what chance it had escaped the Lungs,' Fynn wrote, 'I could not account for'[10] – a statement that shows just how meagre was his knowledge of anatomy. Apart from Fynn, we have only one other alleged eyewitness. MAQUZA contradicts Fynn, saying that Shaka was stabbed in the *right* arm. This is possible – but then again MAQUZA was only about four years old at the time, so we can't place too much weight on *that* memory.[11] Anyway, as Fynn himself admitted, he had nothing more effective to apply to the wound than camomile tea. Shaka no doubt recovered on his own, aided by the ministrations of his own doctors' bleedings and herbal poultices.[12]

Fynn said that the assassins were immediately thought to be Ndwandwe (he calls them 'Zwide's people', which they still were even though Zwide was way up in Pedi country by now). The Ndwandwe, of course, had every reason to try to assassinate Shaka. According to Fynn, about 1 000 Zulu warriors set off and destroyed a few Ndwandwe settlements.[13] However, not a single Zulu tradition agrees with Fynn's version.

The assassination attempt was a well-remembered event amongst Zulu informants. They disagree with each other on the details, but the consensus is that Shaka was indeed stabbed at Gibixhegu or kwaBulawayo.[14] Shaka pulled the assegai out of the wound himself; the weapon was found to be rounded at the end of the haft in a style immediately associated with the Qwabe people. The Qwabe were blamed, and something of a purge was said to have ensued. A particular man was even pointed out as the suspect, one Sikwayo, once an *induna* of the dead Qwabe chieftain Phakathwayo.[15]

Would some disaffected Qwabe have tried to assassinate Shaka? There is tentative evidence that Zulu-Qwabe relations were troubled after Phakathwayo's death. Shaka's uncle Nxazonke is said to have fought the Qwabe more than once.[16] Zulu kaNogandaya, Shaka's Qwabe favourite, may have had some rivalry with Sithunga, a Qwabe notable to whose sister Zulu was married.[17] Zulu is said to have had an exchange with Shaka that probably reflects some of the complex tensions involved:

One day in the assembly at Bulawayo Shaka asked, 'Is Magcansa here?' (Magcansa of the Ncwana people was brother of Zulu.) 'Is Mbewu here?' (Mbewu of the Mbedwini people.) The men of the assembly replied, 'Yes, *Ngasita*.' Shaka said, 'Take them and kill them.' Upon

which Komfiya [Zulu] stood up and said, 'Ngasita!' Shaka looked at
him and said, 'What is it, Komfiya?' The latter replied, 'Hau, Nkosi!
Why did I come here to the Zulu country? Why, when the people
with whom I came from the Qwabe country are being killed? Why do
I konza? Do I not konza for them?' Shaka said, 'Sit down, Komfiya;
you have spoken. Let them go.'[18]

There are some other hints. Masuwana, a warrior of Shaka's and induna at
Vungameni umuzi, liked to get certain Qwabe killed by Shaka through telling
tales about them.[19] At one point Shaka is said to have had some Qwabe
men's eyes taken out,[20] although this seems confused with an atrocity
committed by Dingane in 1833, and its veracity is dubious.[21] Several more
sweeping statements are made: for instance that Shaka said that the Qwabe
should be killed off ('You will recognise them by their great love of
quarrelling'), because they were continually stirring up strife.[22]

Several informants do assert that a number of Qwabe fled after the
assassination attempt,[23] and that Shaka rounded up Qwabe people living at
kwaBulawayo and killed them. A punitive impi was sent out, told that the
Qwabe could be recognised by the way they pushed firewood into the fire
with their right arm, or lengthwise. When caught, they must be stabbed in
the left side, as Shaka had been. 'Many members of the tribe were accordingly
killed,' said JANTSHI, and 'the people scattered in all directions to hide
themselves'.[24] There were even informants who heard that Shaka tried to
fill up a whole donga with Qwabe corpses.[25] Some said that the donga was
the Thathiyana Gorge, a place associated with the mythical split between the
Qwabe and the Zulu, which no one has ever located.[26] In other words, it is a
legend. MBOVU concluded hyperbolically: 'So vast was the massacre that the
whole people left Zululand to settle in Natal'.[27]

However, it seems clear that any such exodus did not happen in 1824, but
rather, if at all, on two other occasions. The strongest indication is that the
main displacement of Qwabe people had actually taken place earlier. For
instance, when Zulu kaNogandaya was asked by Shaka if he would fight Qwabe
people, he was said to have done so with the Mgumanqa ibutho, which was
gathered for the purpose; this dates it to before 1820.[28] The Qwabe were said
to have been 'broken up' before the Ndwandwe clashes (that is, before 1820),
and large numbers apparently left for the south after Phakathwayo's death.[29]

On the second exodus, large numbers did flee into Natal under Nqetho himself, but this was to escape Dingane, not Shaka.[30] Even then, 'the greater bulk of the Qwabes had remained behind in Zululand'.[31] Mamfongonyama, Phakathwayo's true heir, was one of those who remained amongst the Zulu right into Mpande's reign.[32]

In short, at the time of the assassination attempt, most Qwabe evidently remained in the area under Nqetho. Shaka may well have taken advantage of the situation to purge a few enemies, including some Qwabe. However, even Fynn, who was horrified at the few killings that he did claim to have seen around him, didn't say that there was wholesale slaughter. Some alleged culprits were swiftly caught and killed, their right ears cut off, and their bodies dumped about a mile from the *umuzi*. (We are not told who they were.) There, in a general paroxysm of grievance and anger, people poured in by the thousand to beat the bodies and gradually bury them under a huge pile of sticks. The ears were ceremonially burned. The wearing of ornaments and the shaving of heads was temporarily banned.[33]

Despite all the subsequent finger-pointing at the Qwabe, informants are virtually unanimous that it was neither the Qwabe nor the Ndwandwe who were responsible. The Qwabe in general, and Sikwayo in particular, were being slandered; the blunt-hafted Qwabe assegai was a ruse. One account names Ntintinti kaNkobe as the assailant – and he was of the isiPhezi *ikhanda*, 'where his [Shaka's] brothers lived'.[34] Ntintinti was presumably a brother of Bhibhi and Ndlela kaNkobe (also known as Sompisi); Ndlela was one of the few great *izinduna* of Shaka's retinue to survive Dingane's purges – regard that as suspicious if you will. The assassination attempt had taken place right at the *isigodlo* gate, in the heart of the complex, a place that no Qwabe outsider could have reached. In reality, informants insist, the attempt had been driven by Shaka's own brothers, Dingane and Mhlangana, possibly aided by the *inceku* Mbopha – the very men who would finally murder Shaka four years later.[35]

'FULL POSSESSION IN PERPETUITY'

The white traders were able to take advantage of the wounding of Shaka almost immediately. If Fynn sidelined Farewell in his account of this visit,

Farewell, in his despatch to the Cape governor, omitted to mention Fynn at
all. Farewell had sent some medicines up to kwaBulawayo and, hearing about
the assassination attempt, returned in person, accompanied by the master of
the *Julia*, W.H. Davis. Hence Farewell could claim that *he* – not Fynn – had
saved Shaka's life from his 'dangerous wound'. In return for this and some
doubtless trivial gift of 'beads, brass, cloth etc', he obtained from Shaka a
'sale and grant' of land, entailing 'full possession in perpetuity' for the 'sole
use' of Farewell and of 'his heirs and executors'. The document (see Box 7 on
page 317 for the full text) was dated both 7 *and* 8 August 1824, and was
signed by a huge scrawl representing, we presume, Shaka's very first contact
with the mystery of writing. Below it were the 'marks' of 'Umbeguarn,
Chaka's uncle' (Mbikwana), 'Umsega' (Msika?), 'Euntclope' (Mhlophe?), and
'Clambermarnze, king's interpreter' (Hlambamanzi-Msimbithi). The single
breathless, rambling sentence underlined the whites' main fears through its
very repetitions: that Shaka really, really *had* done it of his 'own free will',
and that he really, really was in full command of the whole territory from
Port Natal to Delagoa Bay.

A large part of the Shaka mythology would be based on this one sentence
alone.

Farewell was also obviously afraid that someone might interrupt his
schemes, and so tried to insulate himself against any interference, including
from Shaka. At the same time, with astonishing arrogance, he seemed to
expect Shaka to keep them in food and labour, virtually in perpetuity, as
well.

A coda, asserting Shaka's full comprehension through Msimbithi's
translation, was countersigned by Farewell, Fynn, Davis, Henry Ogle, and
August Zinke. The illiterate Goliat Fire, Frederick Daster and Joseph Powell
added their marks. A second rider, signed once more, asserted a third time
that the translation had been accurate and comprehended.

Farewell clearly foresaw that this matter of translation could become a
legal sticking-point. He also understood that some deft *mis*-translation was a
very useful tool. It is practically impossible to believe that either Shaka or
Msimbithi, whatever the latter's command of English, could have realised
the implications of this jargon-laden document. (Fynn had already
encountered the limitations of Msimbithi's mediation in trying to argue with

Shaka about the merits of musketry and the demerits of having a white skin or being locked up in prison.[36]) There are other anomalies. We have no independent verification that Ogle, Zinke, or Powell had returned to kwaBulawayo with Farewell. It may be significant that Farewell, in his covering letter to Somerset, dated the land grant 27 August, not 7 (or 8) August. Was it just a slip of the pen, or does it indicate that the document was drawn up, or perhaps 'completed', at a later date than it pretends, that is, back at Port Natal? Why is it Farewell, who was *not* present to give 'kind attention to me [Shaka] in my il[l]ness from a wound', who gets the land grant, while Fynn apparently gets nothing? In Farewell's letter, he calls it a 'sale and grant'. Was it a 'sale' – 'in consideration of divers[e] goods received' – or a 'grant', a gift of gratitude? If it was a sale, what exactly was paid for it? We are not told.

Farewell's ambitions are plain enough: 'commercial pursuits' along with (a somewhat vacuous afterthought) 'a wish to obtain a knowledge of this country'.

> The portion granted me affords every prospect of being a most desirable one for settlers . . . [M]any of that class at the Cape (particularly agriculturalists) who it appears have been living in great distress would here find a comfortable assylum and the means of benefitting themselves, as well as the English nation, by forming a colony . . .[37]

Moreover, he none too humbly submits that he is the man to be in charge:

> I trust your Lordship will see the propriety of my being vested with some authority over persons residing here as without it it will be impossible to prevent irregularities amongst themselves as well as the natives which could not fail but be attended with fatal consequences.[38]

Despite the muddled sentence, Farewell's arrogance, his perception that 'his' community was more than capable of 'irregularities', and a slyly threatening tone, are clear enough. He then lied that there were no people of consequence already living there:

Box 7

Shaka's 'grant' to Farewell

I, Inquos Chaka, king of the Zulos and of the country of Natal as well as the whole of the land from Natal to Delagoa Bay which I have inherited from my father, Kenyargacarchu, for myself and heirs, do hereby on the seventh day of August in the year of Our Lord eighteen hundred and twenty-four, in the presence of my chiefs of my own free will and in consideration of divers[e] goods received, grant, make over and sell unto F.G. Farewell and Company the entire and full possession in perpetuity to themselves, heirs and executors, of the port or harbour of Natal known by the natives name, Bubulongo, together with the islands therein and surrounding country as herein described, viz., the whole of the neck of land or peninsula in the SW entrance and all the country ten miles to the Southern side of Port Natal, as pointed out, and extending along the sea coast to the Northward and Eastward as far as the river known by the native name, Comgclote, and now called Farewell's river, being about twenty-five miles of sea coast to the North East of Port Natal, together with all the country inland as far as the nation called by the Zulos, Gowungneu, extending about one hundred miles backward from the sea-shore, with all the rights to the rivers, woods, mines and all articles of all denominations contained therein, the said land and appurtainances to be from this date for the sole use of said Farewell and Company, their heirs and executors, and to be by them disposed of in any manner they think best calculated for their interests, free from any molestation or hindrance from myself or subjects, in witness whereof I have placed my hand, being fully aware that the so doing is intended to bind me to all the articles and conditions that I of my own free will and consent do hereby in the presence of the undermentioned witnesses acknowledge to have fully consented and agreed to in behalf of F.G. Farewell as aforesaid and perfectly understand all the purport of this document, the same having been fully explained to me by my interpreter Clambamarnze and in the presence of the two interpreters Goliat and Frederick before the said F.G. Farewell, whom I hereby acknowledge as the chief of the said country with full power and authority over such natives that like to remain there after this public grant, promising to supply him with cattle and corn when required, sufficient for his consumption, as a reward for his kind attention to me in my ilness from a wound.

(Signed) CHAKA, King of the Zulos, X His mark

Native Witnesses: (Signed) UMBEGUARN, Chaka's uncle, X His mark, UMSEGA, X his mark, EUNCLOPE, X His mark, CLAMBERMARNZE, king's interpreter, X His mark

We the undersigned were present when the aforesaid king Chaka made the above grant or sale of land to F.G. Farewell, which was done of his own free will and consent in presence of a number of his chiefs and people when he appeared to fully comprehend the purport of the said document and the reason of his being required to place his mark of signature thereto by means of his own interpreter, Clambermarnze, a native of the country who speaks good Dutch as well as English, and two other interpreters who understand both languages. The conversation was carried on in our presence and the above marks and signature of the king and chiefs affixed, in witness whereof we hereunto affix our hands and seals as well as to our full belief and knowledge that the aforementioned Chaka has full power to make the said grant, being acknowledged by all the country which we have passed from Natal as their true and lawful king and possessed of the land hereby granted, in consideration of which Mr F.G. Farewell has to our knowledge given sundry goods consisting of beads, brass, cloth, etc.

(Signed) Interpreters GOLIAT FIRE, X His mark, FREDERICK DASTER, X His mark

(Signed) W.H. DAVIS, Master sloop Julia, H.F. FYNN, Super Cargo, CARL-AUGUST ZINKE, HENRY OGLE, JOSEPH POWELL, X His mark

We the undersigned interpreters hereby declare that we have fully explained the true intent and meaning of the annexed document to Inquos Chaka, king of the Zulos, and that he clearly understood the reason of his being required to sign it and of his own free will and consent granted and sold the said land to Mr F.G. Farewell as stated in the manner described and mentioned therein.

(Signed) CLAMBERMARNZE, X His mark, GOLIAT FIRE, X His mark, FREDERICK DASTER, X His mark

Witnesses: (Signed) W.H.Davis, H.F. Fynn

The territory he has made over is nearly depopulated, not containing more than three or four hundred inhabitants who appear much pleased at the manner of its disposal, of which they have been informed by Chaka. The climate seems perfectly healthy with a good soil fit for any purposes and well wooded and watered, four rivers of magnitude running through it, besides several smaller streams.[39]

As it would be for the propagandists for the Great Trek, the perception of 'depopulated' areas was a direct prerequisite for their reoccupation by whites. Partly this was a matter of wishful thinking, partly a matter of cultural preconceptions. The whites expected to find landscapes as populous as England's – or even the western Cape's – and were then hard put to reconcile the language of Shaka's great kingship with the general sparseness of the population. They therefore assumed that the warlike Shaka must have killed everybody off. It suited them to think that. In later appeals for land from the governor, Fynn also insisted that the '60 persons' found living on the Bluff were 'in a most distressful and famished condition' due to Shaka's attacks.[40] To some extent, this may have been true; as we've seen, this was part of the area ravaged by the iziYendane. There is a fair bit of evidence from Zulu and Thuli informants that the immediate vicinity of isiBubulungu had been devastated.[41] The contradictions between accounts may be because the damage was patchy, and the travellers' impressions were varied – and then could be used at will to support whatever was motivating them.

In this way, a tangle of contradictory mythology began. The myth proposed that the region had been thoroughly 'depopulated' by the murderous Shaka himself, and that the people remaining were both Shaka's craven vassals whom he could simply order about, *and* refugees from his ongoing tyrannies, whom the whites could then magnanimously 'rescue' – with Shaka's blessing. This makes no sense whatsoever.

The myth of brutal depopulation rested uneasily alongside a portrayal of Shaka as a reasonable and accommodating person who was happy to have white people taking over large expanses of his country as a reward for their intrinsic goodness and (as Fynn wishfully claimed) because he 'could not help but acknowledge our superiority'.[42]

The fundamental fraudulence of the land grant – whether or not Shaka actually signed it – lies in its total opposition to Shaka's understanding of land use. As we have seen, Shaka simply would not have thought of 'land rights' and 'possession' in the way that Farewell did. In the first place, he didn't 'own' that land – 25 miles on either side of the port and 100 miles inland. Part of it was already under the jurisdiction of Magaye and Mathubane. These chieftains and their followers remained in place, and were never in any way seen to be subordinate to the whites. Other parts of the 'grant', stretching all the way back across the Drakensberg, had not been incorporated into the Zulu polity at all: they were still largely under the entirely independent sway of the Chunu, Thembe, Bhaca and Ngwane.

(It's potentially possible that Shaka was happy to commit a legalistic fraud himself – 'giving away' land that wasn't his in the first place. It's unlikely, though. Moreover, how they could have arrived at an agreement of the scale of the 'grant' is a mystery, since Shaka wouldn't have understood miles, and the whites wouldn't have known where to locate the delimiting border with the 'Gowungneu' – just possibly a seriously garbled version of 'amaNgwane'.)

The various conversations with Shaka recorded by the whites, tainted though they are with mockery and distaste, show Shaka to have been quite astute enough to have steered clear of any such arrangement. Most likely, he agreed to let the whites establish themselves at isiBubulungu, as he would have known Port Natal, and assigned some people to help them build a small settlement. In time he would, as with any other local headman, demand some sort of tribute. He would negotiate trade terms with the new community, and employ them in his wars, willingly or not. In most respects, he would have treated them as he would have any other group that strayed into his ambit and wanted to *khonza*. On the one hand, he tried to overawe them with his power and, on the other, he generously supplied them with the means to survive. The whites, for their part, had neither any concept of how, nor at first any wish, to *khonza* in this fashion. Their attitude would soon change.

In another respect, Shaka realised that the whites were different. They had guns; they had different medicines; and they offered a range of trade goods that were superior to those he had been getting from Delagoa Bay. They paid obeisance to a different king. He was, if we can credit Fynn's and Isaacs's accounts, fascinated by the image that he received of King George the Fourth, repeatedly comparing himself to what he was told about the

king. He asked the traders to send up a carpenter to build him a house on
King George's pattern – and then took a wicked delight in showing how the
European gimlet and nails bent and broke on native ironwood.[43] He conceived
of the possibility of meeting King George himself one day and, to that end,
(if we can believe Farewell at this point) 'expressed a wish of sending two of
his chiefs to the Cape for the purpose of being better acquainted with the
English nation'.[44] This was likely the seed of the 'embassy' of 1828. Whether
it was originally Farewell's or Shaka's idea we will never know.

Back at Port Natal, the white party celebrated their new acquisition in
the best way that they knew how: '4–6 Rockets & 20 rounds of Musketry
were fired in taking possession of the Grant of Land given by Chaka to Mr
Farewell in the name of his Majesty King George the fourth'.[45]

'SISTERS OF THE SERAGLIO'

In the course of both the revelry of their reception, and the tumult of the
assassination attempt, Fynn and his companions had the opportunity to note
the presence of certain apparently privileged women. Some of them were
practically choking on heavy brass neck-rings that signalled their status. They
were the inkosi's 'sisters', Fynn was told, members of the isigodlo – which
untranslatable word the whites could only approximate with 'seraglio'. The
parallel of the Middle Eastern sheikh's 'harem' stocked with 'concubines'
(both words used by Fynn) was almost entirely misleading. Mistranslation
(both of words and concepts) and ignorance of what they were seeing was,
not unexpectedly, the common experience. Still, Fynn did get to sense that

> Shaka's innovations were not confined to the expansion, organization,
> discipline and efficiency of his army, vast, complex and mobile as it
> was, nor was his time and attention wholly occupied by the campaigns
> or deeds of his warriors and the numerous direct and indirect
> consequences thereof. He was shrewd enough to see that the success
> of his system, as a whole, and the many far-flung and exacting
> operations he was always engaged in depended, to no small degree,
> on the way in which the relations between the sexes were controlled.

Among his extraordinary developments in this connection were the
royal *izigodlo* or seraglios . . .[46]

This is more likely to be James Stuart's voice than Fynn's, and so rather
better informed. Even so, it perhaps underestimates how deeply integrated
the so-called 'military' and the more 'domestic' controls were in Shaka's
increasingly centralised polity.

I've already remarked on the importance of the institution of the *isigodlo*.
It was not an entirely new concept: chieftains had always had some power to
distribute women, to domestically enslave them, and to dictate marriage
patterns. Shaka refined these accepted practices in ways that meshed intricately
with other methods of centralising his control: the formation of *amabutho*
and *amakhanda*; the elevation of important women, the *amakhosikazi*; his
control of trade items of finery and status; the development of centralised
rituals; the distribution of responsibility for cattle and agriculture amongst
his *izikhulu* (most important family elders) and the *izinduna*. By the time that
the whites arrived in 1824, these aspects of Shaka's rule were clearly well
developed.

(It's obviously a bit artificial to separate them off from each other, though
I have done so, and I spread my discussions throughout the book, in order to
emphasise that the development of the various facets of Shaka's rule was
happening all the time, in between and in tandem with the more famous
'military' campaigns and political manoeuvrings.)

The *isigodlo* was both a physical architectural feature and the group of
people who lived within it. Physically, it denoted the innermost and most
tightly guarded enclosure of a large *umuzi*. It was closed off with a vicious-
looking palisade at the highest end of the *umuzi*, furthest from the main
gates. The gateposts were carefully selected *mtombothi* wood, durable and sweet-
smelling; screens (*izihonqa*) of *uklele* wattles were topped by a layer of *ugagane*
thorns.[47] Inside, neat compartments, screened off and swept meticulously
clean, each with a hut or huts, gave the impression of 'an intricate labyrinth'.[48]
The young Charles Rawden Maclean – also known as John Ross, who claimed
to have had uniquely privileged access to Shaka's *isigodlo* – was able to take a
'peek' beyond the first 'spacious square':

We observed before us another gateway in the side of the square, fronting the one by which we entered, that leads to another oblong enclosure, more spacious than the former, and containing a dozen or more huts, still more elegant of construction and of still larger dimensions. The floor of this enclosure is of glassy smoothness, with a polish that reflects the image like a mirror. A continuation of enclosures of this last description, with more or less huts in them, and of different shapes, some semi-circular and some triangular, which together complete the internal economy . . .[49]

It was divided into the 'black' reserve (*isigodlo esimnyama*), where the *inkosi* slept amongst the highest-ranking women and those women named the *umdlunkulu*; and the 'white' reserve (*esimhlophe*). The white reserve was itself divided into two: the *imvoko* side, which housed 'royal' children and other dependent children lately attached to the chiefly family, and the other side which housed lower-ranking dependants, usually termed *izigqila*, or battle-captured menials – domestic slaves.

The *isigodlo* was tightly guarded. The body of the *inkosi* himself had to be protected against both actual invasion (or assassination attempts) and against magical malpractice. In particular, the *inkosi*'s bodily emissions – faeces, hair shavings, semen, and spittle – had to be carefully contained and disposed of. Urine was caught in a calabash and carried away by a small girl. In this way, even the most basic functions of the *inkosi*'s life were carefully regulated, even ritualised, by the select staff of the *isigodlo*. The women themselves had to be guarded, against both untoward abduction and escape: most of them hadn't asked to be there in the first place, and most were prevented from freely expressing their physical desires. Some of these women had been presented in tribute by their prominent fathers; these were the *umdlunkulu*.

The *umdlunkulu* enjoyed a certain status: for them at least the *isigodlo* was a rather comfortable asylum. The word also meant 'great hut', that closest to the *inkosi*'s own, and highest in status. These women had various privileges, such as using their own entrances and paths, and eating certain choice parts of a beast. Particular ornaments distinguished them: girdles of *umbedle* leaves, large red and green beads around the loins and strung from the ears, and brass *isongo* rings on their arms. The *amakhosikazi*, those closest to the *inkosi*, were marked by the brass neck-rings noted by Fynn, and bangles on the upper arm.[50] They grew fat as pigs, groused one informant; they made the mats wet where they sat. When they went to a river to wash they would be accompanied by armed men, and if you chanced upon them you had to fall flat on your face in respect.[51]

The *umdlunkulu* were essentially high-class payments in tribute to the *inkosi*. It was a system developed out of the long-established *lobolo* arrangement, which involved the obligation by a junior house to transfer the eldest daughter to the senior house in return for cattle or other payment. This was called *ukwethula*. The richer a man, the more such dependent women he could attract. They would be brought up in the household as *umdlunkulu*, his to dispose of in marriage as he pleased. Since the richest men were those patronised by Shaka, and they were generally of the closest collateral clans, they got a lot of young women to dispense. It was a way of expanding the influence of the Zulu élite without the *inkosi* himself having to marry. At the same time, Shaka himself got a lot of *lobolo* payments, as did the core chieftains in their turn. In this way, wealth – mostly expressed in cattle and secondarily in beads – also became more centralised and élitist.

While some *umdlunkulu* probably did have a lot of time to laze about, enhancing the impression of a sensual 'harem', most were in reality *izinqila* – captives – who had to work hard, collecting firewood, hoeing the gardens, fetching water, and emptying chamberpots.[52] This was mostly an extension of the normal division of labour at the homestead level. There, women were conventionally responsible for agricultural production, pottery and mats, thatching of huts, and the rearing of children. Under Shaka, more women were either doing this for the contingents of men gathered at the *amakhanda*, or for the *inkosi* himself. 'The girls used to leave the *isigodhlo*, three and four at a time, to cultivate the fields. When there was *amabele* (sorghum) to be carried from the gardens one might see a large number of girls going out to fetch it. They used to be accompanied by say one *inceku* [*inkosi*'s male attendant].'[53]

How much was produced specially in this way, and how much the *imizi* or *amakhanda* were fed by surplus or requisitions from nearby homesteads, the oral record is too sparse to say. What is clear, as Carolyn Hamilton has shown, is that grain production was at least as important as cattle rearing, and in some ways was even more important. Beef was not the staple diet, but a form of conspicuous consumption. Slaughtering was relatively rare, and highly ritualised. Maclean noted that men liked to head off to the *inkosi's* place, 'their principal object being to feast on the royal bounty, when tired of the milk and vegetable diet at their homes, for it is a rare occurrence that a Zulu can find it in his heart to kill one of his own flock'.[54] Even at the *amakhanda,* 'one had to fight for one's food . . . This would take place when beasts were killed'.[55] Cattle-raiding was not primarily for food: it made possible the redistribution of the means to transferable wealth in women and influence.

Consequently, women's labour was vital to the survival of the polity. The women of the central *isigodlo* were equally vital to the *inkosi's* survival. They worked the nearby '*inkosi's* fields' and brewed his personal beer. Once in a while, some or other of the one or two hundred *isigodlo* women would be called into the *inkosi's* hut for his pleasure.

SHAKA'S SEXUALITY

When A.T. Bryant made an ill-judged jibe about 'the stumpiness of a certain organ' (misreading a very ordinary insult that need have no actual relation to truth or length[56]), he inaugurated a century of prurient speculation about the (mal)functions of Shaka's penis.

> He [Shaka] was unquestionably a latent homosexual, and despite the fact that his genitals had more than made up for their previous dilatoriness, so that he always took great pride in bathing in full public view, he was probably impotent.[57]

This categorical judgement by Donald Morris is only the pinnacle of this kind of speculative rubbish. As we've seen, Shaka may well have had wives when amongst the Mthethwa, but chose for political reasons to pass them on, along with (possibly) a son or two. He also chose thereafter not to take formal wives, or to create acknowledged heirs. (Even this is not wholly unanimous. GXUBU's father Luduzo was a Hlubi of Shaka's iziMpholo *ibutho,* formed c.1816; Luduzo insisted that one Mzepeti was a 'wife' of Shaka's, though she bore no offspring.[58]) Although the informants are unanimous that Shaka's avoidance was done for political reasons, it has been assumed by most later writers to have been the product of some grotesque personal pathology.

The first white observers were greatly exercised in their speculations about Shaka's sex life. Fynn claimed that Shaka had 5 000 'concubines' in his 'seraglios'[59] – as if these women all existed solely to satiate his personal desires. No doubt, sexual services were sometimes required from these women, but we know almost nothing about it. (The general public was not even allowed to watch Shaka eat or bathe, let alone have sexual intercourse.) One anecdote relates an insult thrown many years later at Cetshwayo's mother Ngqumbazi. Ngqumbazi was accused of being 'a woman who had borne an illegitimate child, a woman who smelt of the vagina, a woman already used and rejected who had been married to Shaka (for she was a sweetheart of Shaka's)'.[60] Even if the insult is outrageously untrue and politically motivated, it says something about how Shaka was remembered. Very occasionally pregnancy did result, and Fynn hints at one such case.[61] Most reasonably, Maclean said that there were several offspring who were quietly farmed out to distant families, to live in 'great retirement and obscurity'. He had even met a couple of them.[62]

Another tale tells that Shaka once had an *inceku* hold a torch over him while he *hlobonga*'d with a lover. The informant adds: 'This was not done for fear of making the girl pregnant, for all such girls were killed.'[63] Others later went on to claim that Shaka regularly murdered his own babies and their mothers, being paranoid about the threat of son-successors. Though the death sentence was undoubtedly meted out for apparently minor infringements, it is difficult to believe that it was a habitual practice – despite stories such as this one:

Once on the day of the *umkosi* [first-fruits ceremony] Shaka saw a pretty girl from another part of the country. He sent his *izinceku* to go and summon her. The girl came, and he spoke to her. The girl said, 'I don't like you.' When he forcibly took hold of her, she cried. She hurled an insult at him, saying, 'I don't want you; you have an ugly nose, an *isifonyo* [like] a muzzle put on a calf to prevent it sucking.' He said, 'What did you say?' She said, 'I really do not want you. Rather than sleep with you, I choose to die.' He said, 'Kill her.' She was taken away outside to be put to death, and was duly killed.[64]

Another famous story would also be portrayed as the product of Shaka's warped sexuality. This is the legend of him cutting open a pregnant woman 'to see how the foetus lay'. Here is one of the more detailed versions:

Shaka once met a woman at the Mbozamo when he was living at Dukuza, and asked her for a drink of water. She was a wife of Mdungu kaSobongela's following. She, not knowing Shaka, refused, saying, 'Why don't you go and lap up water in the stream [like a dog]?' Shaka later on saw this woman, and directed men to seize her and cut her open to see what sort of position the foetus took in the womb.[65]

Most informants thought that the ghastly event had happened only once.[66] However, in certain fervid imaginations it spiralled into larger numbers, becoming a habit.[67] Kutshwayo kaNzwakele is said to have reproved Shaka for doing it.[68] One informant even thought that it became a cornerstone of Shaka's 'state policy', leading directly to his assassination.[69] In the wildest version of them all, it was said that Shaka filled up a whole donga with pregnant women because Nandi had died;[70] here the pregnant woman story joins up with the Thathiyana Gorge story and enters the realm of total fantasy. An additional source of exaggeration was James Saunders King's assertion, made in 1826, that *any* women found pregnant were 'instantly killed'.[71] As we will see, King's sundry accusations in this article had very specific purposes. Nevertheless, credulous foreigners such as Donald Morris would later write, with a sneering tone borrowed from Bryant, that Shaka 'developed a mild interest in embryology' and butchered a 'hundred' women in this way.[72]

This is a superb example of what we would now call an 'urban legend' in the making.

There are a number of ways of explaining the legend's origins. It has to be said that there were perfectly acceptable and well-known ways of aborting foetuses with traditional herbs – and Shaka would ordinarily have used these methods.[73] It may be that one such abortion is the core of truth behind the story, but we have no way of knowing.

Even if there *was* some original incident, it was clearly picked up later
and wildly magnified. The most obvious explanation for *that* is that it was
pumped up by Dingane's propaganda campaign of the 1830s. Dingane
claimed that Shaka had killed one of *his* wives, and that was why he had
assassinated him. Alternatively – or additionally – the foetus story may have
emerged in tandem with the one about Shaka's alleged murder of his own
mother – probably another slander spread by Dingane in order to discredit
his predecessor.

As a further example of how the story could migrate, a Swazi informant
related how Shaka had asked Sobhuza of the Dlamini-Swazi for a wife. He
was given Sobhuza's first-born daughter Mpandeze. She fell pregnant, so Shaka
had her killed. The only problem with this is that the informant is hopelessly
muddled: it was Zwide who got the wife, not Shaka.[74]

In short, these bizarre accusations are at best unverifiable, and at worst
complete fabrications. Of one thing we can be sure: there was nothing amiss
with Shaka's organ.

NOT QUITE AMAZONS

Once the various insinuations of sexual depravity were believed, they assumed
a life of their own and came to be seen as governing *all* of Shaka's attempts
to control the ways of his women. A more sensible explanation is, however,
easy to find in the politics of the situation. Shaka was building a centralised
élite whose ascendancy depended to a large degree on who married whom.

Controls over sexuality and marriage prospects were indivisible. Hence
izigodlo women were rigidly guarded against sexual waywardness. This was
doubtless to keep young women pure and intact for their future husbands.
(This attitude persists to some degree, as evidenced by recent calls in certain
quarters for systematic 'virginity-testing', especially in the face of the Aids
pandemic.) Even under Shaka the system wasn't inflexible, though obvious
infringements could meet with dire consequences:

> Shaka would give the order permitting girls to go as they liked to
> their lovers. Even if a girl stayed six days with her lover it was all right.
> It was not an offence to Shaka; it was good. What was an offence was

if a man spoiled a girl. For she belonged to the king in her regiment, as did the youth. He would now be spoiling a member of a regiment. They would die; they would be killed.[75]

Fynn exaggerated the level of such controls to the point of absurdity: 'It has been no uncommon occurrence for a regiment of soldiers and another of girls to be surrounded and slain on the slightest suspicion of intercourse; in which case sometimes not less than 3,000 people would suffer, whereas, in fact, only a very few, and possibly none at all, were guilty.'[76] Only a few of these alleged massacres would have wiped out Shaka's entire army.

Just a page or two later, Fynn was more accurate and sober in his writing. In cases of disgrace, 'the male relatives of the girl are obliged to forfeit cattle'. He added, 'in no palace of Europe is greater decorum, order and etiquette observed than in these seraglios and their various compartments'.[77] Fynn was particularly impressed with the styles of finery, regularity of dance, and compositions of songs that characterised the appearance of the 'regiments' referred to in the above quotations – Shaka's female amabutho.

Shaka also attempted to regulate women's affairs beyond the strict confines of the isigodlo. The female ibutho appears to have been a genuine innovation on his part, though it wasn't as thoroughly applied as Fynn thought. (Dingiswayo was said to have married women off by decree, but not as far we know in 'regiments'.) A small number of female amabutho were allied with some of the male amabutho for a time. On the one or two occasions when Shaka actually went on campaign with his army, he took some of these women with him. The Mcekeceke ibutho – Shaka's first – went on the second Mpondo expedition, under Magaye and Zihlandlo; it was said that some women actually fought, and subsequently wore izuqu, medicated string necklaces, showing that they had killed.[78] We have no further details on such Amazon-like activities. These women were probably more important as support units, cutting shields and bearing spare assegais, water and food.

First and foremost these female units seem to have been intended as another means of regulating reproduction (rather than sexual activity as such) and marriage. The Mvutwamini were of the same age-grade as the Fasimba, and were obliged to marry men from that unit; others were allowed to hlobonga only with men of the older amabutho, such as the Mbelebele, esiKlebhe and

Bulawayo.[79] They became effectively organised maids-in-waiting, or *izingodosi*:
women who had been betrothed but not yet *lotsholwa*'d.[80] As it happened,
Shaka never *jutshwa*'d, or released for marriage, those few female *amabutho*
he had formed: the Mcekeceke, the Ntshuku (same call-up as the Mgumanqa),
the Mvutwamini, and the Cenyane (same call-up as the Mbonambi). All were
jutshwa'd by Dingane, some having to marry the old men of the oldest
amabutho.[81] Though the female *amabutho* continued to play a role in subsequent
Zulu administrations, in Shaka's time their application seems patchy, and
couldn't have affected a great number of women. Like many of Shaka's
institutions, they were fully active only in the relatively limited areas under
his direct command.

MEN AMONGST THE WOMEN

Women were not the only people who were allowed into the confines of the
isigodlo. There were also, for instance, the *izinceku*. An *inceku* was a personal
aide, a bodyservant, who had a particularly important part to play, involving
a high degree of trust. He was not a mere menial. BALENI kaSilwana, for
instance, was made an *inceku* only *after* he was appointed an *induna*,[82] although
this was in Mpande's day, so caution is necessary in reading back. His duty
was to carry the *inkosi*'s personal ornamented milk-pail; to supervise the
cutting of his meat; to pour water, drawn from prohibited springs, into the
inkosi's mouth without spilling it;[83] to carry important messages, to spy.
Nohadu (old-style spelling Noradu) was an *inceku* to Shaka, and related this
revealing anecdote to his son MTSHAPI:

> One day Noradu went to gather green maize for the *inkosi*. He came
> back with it to the *isigodhlo* and gave it to the girls there. The *inkosi*
> had been putting people to death in the cattle enclosure. As Noradu
> turned about, the *inkosi* was just turning from the enclosure on his
> way back to his hut. They bumped into each other at the gate. Noradu
> fell to the ground in fright, exclaiming, '*Bayede!*' He turned to look at
> the *inkosi*, and saw that smoke was coming from Shaka's mouth. As
> he turned Shaka asked, 'Here now, Noradu! This food of mine, do
> you people wash before you touch it?' 'Father, indeed we wash. We
> wash every time we cross a river. If a man needs to urinate, he does so

only after putting down the *inkosi*'s food. When he has quite finished urinating he will wash before taking up the *inkosi*'s food.' Shaka said, 'I ask because no sooner had I eaten the food from your place than I vomited, and vomited and vomited!' He clapped his hands behind his back as he uttered the last 'vomited'. 'Who went to gather this food?' '*Inkosi*, it was Mlindazwe (an *inceku*) who went to gather it.' The *inkosi* said, 'Wo! You are saved!' Noradu slipped away. Behind him smoke was still coming from the *inkosi*'s mouth. He turned his back, belched, and went off into the Black *isigodhlo*, where entry was prohibited.[84]

Another such attendant was the man who shaved the *inkosi*. A man named Manokotsha shaved both Shaka and Dingane. He had to dance about the lordly personage, taking three or four scrapes between sentences, catching the hairs in a small basket, deftly applying water to the headring, hoping against hope to inflict no accidental damage.[85] Mlahla, the father of Stuart's informant MBULO, was at one time appointed to hold a shade-shield over Shaka on a hot day.[86]

Even for favourites, behaviour within the *isigodlo* could be fine-tuned to the point of torture. LUNGUZA, a Thembu who was born just when his chieftain Ngoza took off for the south around 1822 or 1823, remembered crawling into the *isigodlo* at the heels of his father Mpukane. Mpukane seems to have had a most peculiar relationship with his *inkosi*. Shaka had appointed him *induna* with Jobe's Sithole people, who were closely related to him. Mpukane, a recognised hero with a battle-scarred chest, was to teach Jobe how to fight. Shaka looked on Mpukane 'as a dog that would not allow the enemy to get near its master Shaka'. With characteristically barbed humour, Shaka said that he therefore had to eat his meat like a dog, and beer 'was to be given to him to drink as he lay down on his back, in beer baskets'. In this way Mpukane 'got to be very stout'.[87]

This bizarre ritual was apparently continued under Dingane, when LUNGUZA joined his father. LUNGUZA could recall very richly the textures of *isigodlo* life. He would be guided through a particular door, flanked by *izinceku*, and bear left to a screened-off hut, where he would find up to 30 *umdlunkulu* seated with the *inkosi* at the back.

I would find my father lying down on his stomach like a dog, eating meat on eating mats before him, biting it off without in any way using his hands. This meat would often be about to go bad and even have maggots, for that was the kind preferred there. Meat was kept a day or so before being cooked. There would also be baskets of beer alongside him, from which he would be helped to drink . . . baskets made of *lala* palm leaves. I would lie a yard or two behind my father. He was fed by the *izinceku*; the *umdhlunkulu* would feed me. I was given some of the *uvili* dish as it was called, i.e. of clotted blood cooked and ground up and then mixed with fat; it becomes the rich, drinkable dish known as *ububende*. This was the *umdhlunkulu*'s great dish, what they partook of daily. I received it of course in a large earthenware saucer, beautifully smooth and polished (rubbed with a smooth stone). The *uvili* was given to me warm. I drank it as if afraid of it or afraid to show that I was drinking . . . .[88]

There was also the strange cripple or dwarf Mhayi (or Mhaye). Shaka apparently liked cripples and idiots. Mhayi, three-foot-six high with bandy legs, was a Qwabe *imbongi* – praise-singer – in Phakathwayo's time. He went on to *bonga* Shaka, Dingane and Mpande in turn, a kind of court jester. Shaka favoured Mhayi with wives now and then, even though Mhayi was the kind of man who would go to a woman and order, 'Show me your vagina!' He would then exult, 'This is food for the *umnumzana!*' or tease them, 'Oh, there's nothing there.'[89] Not that he would have dared to do this to a woman of the *isigodlo* itself, even though he was allowed in there. One of his jobs was to strip certain fibres (*izinsinga*) from a beast's foreleg for the *inkosi*, presumably for string.[90] Mhayi was eventually killed by Mpande, it was said simply for having *bonga*'d three chiefs.[91]

Favoured *izimbongi* – praise-singers – were also amongst the select few to luxuriate in close physical proximity to the *inkosi*. The institution of the *imbongi* was already in existence, but his role became more prominent as the *inkosi*'s power grew. The favoured *izimbongi* would be present at all major functions and most minor ones, announcing the *inkosi*'s presence, stimulating the army to battle-pitch, eulogising the presence of the ancestors and joining the living with them. According to MELAPI,

Shaka's *izimbongi* were differently dressed. One would put on two bushbuck horns in front at the top of the forehead; another would have an *impiti* hairstyle made at the back of his head and have it painted red (like a woman), the hair twisted in front and falling slightly over the face, with a woman's leather skirt on; another would put on two headrings, one at the back and the other at the front. The man with the horns, as he *bonga*'d, would go about the crowds collected round and pretend to butt or stick them as a beast would. Those standing about would scramble away – the noise would resound – as if afraid of being hurt.[92]

The *izimbongi* were inescapable. 'An *imbongi* might *bonga* at night. Or he might get up with the dawn and *bonga*, leaving off only for meals, and go on all day long until sunset. He would *bonga* right at the upper end of the cattle enclosure and close to the *isigodhlo*. He would *bonga* till his voice failed.'[93] Their commentary, which was by no means always flattering to the subject, was an important indicator of the health of the polity.

[The *imbongi*'s] assessment of the chief is not blindly adulatory. He has the ability to inspire strong emotions and also to sway opinion. If he criticizes excesses in the behaviour of the chief, he also exhorts his audiences to mend their errant ways. He is loyal especially to the chiefdom; he is the bard, the tribal poet . . . he functions therefore as a herald; he is a cheerleader, custodian of lore, mediator, prophet, literary virtuoso. His essential role is, however, political, concerned with the well-being of the polity.[94]

The *izibongo* pronounced the subject's pretensions to immortality. So, as Dingane's *izibongo* put it:

Though people may die, their praises remain.
These will remain and bring grief for them,
Remain and lament for them in the empty homes.[95]

The *izibongo* were an accumulation of spontaneous epithets, references to actual events, and lines stolen from the praises of the conquered. Although most of the commentary would have been invented and conferred by the *izimbongi* themselves, Shaka seems to have had a considerable degree of influence over which words were included, dropped, replaced, or tabooed (*hlonipha'd*). He replaced 'Lufenulwenja' with 'Ndabezitha', which he had stolen from the Mbatha (or the Khumalo), for example. Here's a sample of Shaka's *izibongo*, with its mix of inherited lines, references to events long forgotten, and vividly metaphorical epithets both adulatory and critical:

> Dlungwana son of Ndaba!
>   Ferocious one of the Mbelebele brigade,
> Who raged among the large kraals,
> So that until dawn the huts were being turned upside-down.
>   He who is famous as he sits, son of Menzi,
> He who beats but is not beaten, unlike water,
> Axe that surpasses other axes in sharpness;
> Shaka, I fear to say he is Shaka,
> Shaka, he is the chief of the Mashobas.
> He of the shrill whistle, the lion;
> He who armed in the forest, who is like a madman,
> The madman who is in full view of the men.
> He who trudged wearily the plain going to Mfene;
> The voracious one of Senzangakhona,
> Spear that is red even on the handle.[96]

Of the *izimbongi* who might have invented or sung these praises, we have only two names: Mshongweni, and Mxhamama kaSotshaya of the Sibisini clan.[97] The latter was also a personal attendant of Shaka's – and/or an *induna* of kwaDlangezwa – and was killed by Shaka's assassins.[98] We know little about these men and, in the end, it is the *izibongo* themselves – running to several hundred 'lines' in the Cope collected version – that survive and attest to Shaka's political centrality.

'Praises are like photographs,' said the informant MQAIKANA, 'they correspond to Europeans' photography.'[99]

Though the *isigodlo* was kept quite secretive and separated by rituals and armed guards, its rhythms were felt throughout the community. Proximity

to it signalled importance. So it was that favoured chieftains such as Zihlandlo
or Magaye had their own huts nestled up against the *isigodlo* palisade. The
cattle-enclosure adjoining it was the venue for the most important events.
The *isigodlo*'s activities dictated those of many around it, such as the cadets
who were training up for entry to their *ibutho*. BALENI's summary of the cadet's
life shows how integrated 'military', 'domestic' and 'agricultural' activities
were:

> Anyone who sees the milk-pail come from inside the *isigodhlo* might
> shout, '*Zi jubekile!*' There would be one, two or three boys to drink at
> one cow, for they stood all about in the cattle enclosure. There would
> be no rushing at the cattle, for the cows had all been appropriated.
> The calves would be let out on the above signal being given. All the
> cattle which the boys of the kraal drink from are king's cattle. They
> are all herded by these boys. The oxen were kept separate; they were
> herded separately in the field by men. These men used to be given
> the foreleg of the animal on a beast's being killed. Many boys herded
> the cattle. Those for the *isigodhlo*'s use grazed separately. They were
> herded by two boys.
>
> The cadets used to collect firewood and thornbush for the *isigodhlo*.
> The thorns are very painful. The thornbush would surmount the
> *isigodhlo* fence. Cadets also hoed the fields, carried the *amabele* when
> it was being reaped, and threshed it . . .
>
> They used to perform war dances at the meeting-place in the cattle
> enclosure. They would do this alone. They have no assegais, only sticks
> and small- and large-knobbed kieries. They also practiced [*sic*] stabbing
> at plant bulbs while herding at the river. They used to eat lung. The
> fat on top of a beast's heart – *ubedu* – was eaten only by the leading
> herdboys . . .
>
> Cadets *kleza*'d [drank from the udder] for two or three years, when
> they were *butwa*'d. They would have their kraal built. They would be
> given a name. When first *butwa*'d they would go to the king's kraal to
> attend the men's assembly. This would last only one day. The king
> would present them with cattle which they would take off to their
> military headquarters and there slaughter. It would be after that they

would come together and build their kraal. The giving of these cattle is to make them mature; they are given meat.[100]

It is little wonder, then, that Shaka kept as close an eye on the cattle themselves as possible. This was the case even in distant parts, such as the area under Mathubane's jurisdiction. Infringements of reportage and etiquette could be unforgivingly punished – as in this incident, when the combination of a missing beast and a dialectal slip of the tongue from a Thuli lowlander, one of the amaLala, provoked Shaka's anger:

> Bambalele was sent by Gcamatshe, who was in charge of the herdboys, to report to Shaka that the cattle were dying. One beast was not reported at once; there was a delay of about a year or so. Bambalele was with another. When they came to Shaka, Bambalele said, 'I am reporting on the cattle of our place, the place of Nansi [a dialectal variation of 'Nandi', Shaka's mother]. Shaka asked, 'Who is Nansi?' Bambalele's friend said at once, 'Ndabenkulu.' They reported and returned home and told their friends, and congratulated themselves on their escape. Presently Matubane visited Shaka, who said, 'Did you kill the fellows who spoke of me as Nansi?' Matubane answered, 'I have not done so.' Shaka said, 'I've a good mind to kill the lot of you off.' Matubane thereupon sent a man to the person in charge of the cattle to say, 'Put this matter right' . . . The two were thereupon put to death.[101]

In summary, then, the isigodlo was the nerve-centre of the polity. It was where the main decisions were taken, and where many of the main rituals were conducted. Its secrecy and inaccessibility were an index of the degree of stratification that was opening up between the Zulu leadership and the general populace. Marriage arrangements, class and ethnic differentiations, manipulation of genealogies, distribution of cattle, control of rituals and language-use, all combined with the military structures to enhance political control and centralisation.

THE BEST TERMS OF FRIENDSHIP

Shaka was not the only leader in the area to be portrayed as extremely brutal. Macingwane kaLubhoko of the Chunu was described in terms reminiscent of the worst depictions of Shaka:

> It was a matter of common knowledge . . . [He] was an evil monster, who killed his own children, and put others to death without mercy . . . sufficiently powerful to conquer other clans . . . terribly cruel . . . killing [his sons] because he saw that they would become men and contend with him.[102]

Perhaps this illustrates more stereotyping. As we've seen in Chapters 6 and 7, Macingwane had managed to avoid any serious clash with Shaka, moving first to the Mvoti river area, and then, in about 1822, to the Mkhomazi. There, some 200 kilometres south-west of kwaBulawayo, he felt safe enough to re-establish himself. Perhaps, as Magema Fuze alleges in the quotation above, he had to murder his own sons to do it. He certainly had time to establish his *umuzi* iGqunu, and to raise at least one more *ibutho*.[103]

Shaka was not about to let him rest. Perhaps he felt that Macingwane was becoming a threat, although he was too far off to be a serious one. More likely, Shaka saw the Chunu polity as a promising target for a cattle-raid. The supply of cattle was probably now low amongst the small clans south of the Thukela, and the 'amabece' raid against the Mpondo in mid-1824 had proved a near failure. With the death of Ngoza in late 1824, and *perhaps* in December of Madikane of the Bhaca as well (the relative dating of these events is very difficult to be sure of, given the sparseness of the evidence), the possibility of wider resistance seemed slight. The northern marches were relatively quiet; the army was growing; doubtless a lesson or two had been learned from the first long-distance raid against the Mpondo. In general terms, it makes more sense that Shaka would have launched his shattering raid on Macingwane in 1825, not 1822.

Besides, Shaka could call on a little more help from an unexpected quarter. Magema Fuze recalled it this way: '[I]n that campaign when Shaka was in pursuit of Macingwane, it was he [Fynn] who accompanied him and travelled with the Zulus as far as Pondoland. There Shaka left him with a regiment, to serve as the caretaker of that country, as its governement [sic]'.[104]

It has to be said that this is the only direct evidence that we have that Fynn might have been present on this campaign. It may be that Fuze is confusing things – as he does at other points – but it does help to make sense of some other aspects.

Fynn later portrayed himself as making a couple of terrible, food-deprived journeys south along the coast towards the Mpondo. On his first attempt he had failed to get more than a few miles down the beach, encountering almost no people and scavenging rotting fish off the strand. He got back to find that Peterssen and some of his company had sailed in the *Julia*. Ten others were waiting for her to return for them.

Fynn also found a request from Shaka to make another journey up to kwaBulawayo. There, to his surprise, he found residents of Delagoa Bay in attendance, bringing gifts to Shaka and, we assume, trade goods. One of the visitors even knew Fynn. (Such was the well-developed network; Farewell would shortly send a man to Delagoa Bay himself, protected by an escort supplied by Shaka.[105]) Fynn recalled:

> The King requested me to relate the particulars of my journey to the westward which in my absence he had heard of he laughed heartily at my relation of it asking how I could expect to travell without his assistance as the whole of my trouble had been occasioned by him having Killed the whole of the inhabitants of the surrounding country telling me it was just what I deserved for attempting to travel among nations from whom I could not possible reape any benefit and could terminate in no other result than being murdered by them . . .[106]

So were the 'nations' actually present to murder him – or not, having been wiped out already? At any rate, Fynn found it impossible to explain himself or to argue with Shaka: 'I might have saved my breath on that Occasion as in many others as I found I was talking to a King who had no Idea of the extent of his power and being assured that his commands were stout [?] reason and law he commanded me not to make a second attempt.'[107]

Of course, Shaka had a rather better '[i]dea of the extent of his power' than Fynn had. Fynn claimed that he then made another trip to the Mpondo

– both unauthorised and unsupported – in the company of Davis, the master of the *Julia*. The vessel had now returned and was in the process of being cleaned up at Port Natal.[108] If the almost tedious detail of this part of Fynn's narrative can be believed, he and Davis seemed, in fact, to encounter quite a number of people, some of them engaging in conflict with others further inland.[109]

By contrast, Fynn's treatment of his subsequent obligatory visit to Shaka occupies no more than a couple of lines. Shaka 'as before was angry with me for visiting strange Nations which he assured me would be my ultimate ruin'.[110]

Despite his allegedly awful experiences on the 'depopulated' southern coast, Fynn is so keen to resume 'business' there that he says nothing at all about the *Julia*'s departure on 1 December 1824, with the remaining ten Afrikaners of Peterssen's disgruntled party. The ship also carried six elephant and forty-nine hippo tusks and twelve 'dried wolf skins', apparently the sole fruit of Farewell's hunting activities of several months.[111]

The *Julia* was never seen again.

Farewell's party only learned of the loss when another ship, the naval cutter *York*, under Lieutenant Edward Hawes, dropped anchor off Port Natal in May 1825. Although the Port Natal settlers were 'much in want' of certain supplies, and hadn't made much progress towards cultivating a garden, Hawes found them to be in fine fettle. They were 'living on the best terms of friendship with the natives and under the protection of the king, Inguos [*inkosi*], Chaka', who had assigned a contingent of 100 people to keep an eye on them. Apart from the Port Natal grant which we have already seen, Farewell told Hawes that Shaka had also granted him a tract 'one hundred and fifty miles to the NW of Port Natal' (the St Lucia area, presumably). Copies of these grants had been sent to the governor, Farewell claimed, but they never transpired. This grant was even more fraudulent than the first.[112]

It was, in fact, Shaka who was keeping the tiny colony alive.

For his part, Fynn, by his own account, was facing a mini-trial. Faku and the Mpondo were accusing him of being a spy for Shaka. This was logical enough: Fynn had come from that direction; they had seen him use salt, which they'd only heard of being used around the Thukela river; and they had also heard that Shaka himself was of white extraction, so Fynn must be one of his relatives. Once he had talked his way out of that corner, Fynn retreated eastwards a short distance to a people whom he calls the 'Amatucens',[113] and quickly established a homestead.[114]

The next several months disappear between the lines of Fynn's 'Notebook'. Suddenly he is well established, with a large haul of ivory that Shaka's men are carrying out for him. At the same time, 'spies' are suspected as arriving from inland, possibly belonging to 'Madigarn': Madikane.[115] Forerunners of Shaka's forces are also in the Umzimkhulu area. What are we to make of this?

Firstly, it seems unlikely that Fynn would have been able to set himself up so rapidly and in this way without Shaka's support. In other writings, Fynn was clearly concerned to portray himself both as operating with Shaka's permission, *and* as independent of him. In his later years he invented other 'land grants' from the Zulu chieftain as he desperately tried to make good. We have to see almost all of his writings in this light. He was also desperate to avoid the accusations, current even during Shaka's lifetime, that the whites were acting as mercenaries for Shaka. This might explain the odd gaps in the 'Notebook'. I remind you here of Fuze's understanding that Shaka *established* Fynn at the Umzimvubu river, according him some kind of jurisdiction and support force. Indeed, Fynn was known amongst the Zulu as Shaka's *isicaca sempi*, 'poor destitute of the army'.[116] Shaka had also given him permission to set up a building or little *umuzi* at Ensimbini on the Mlazi river (just south of present-day central Durban). How did Fynn earn Shaka's trust?

Secondly, what were these inland disturbances? They coincide interestingly with a fresh influx of apparently rootless invaders into the northern reaches of Xhosa country. These people were becoming known to settlers along the Cape Colony frontier, 400 kilometres westwards, collectively as 'Fetcani': marauders. The authorities, relying on sporadic reports from the isolated missionaries who had ventured into Xhosa territory, were perpetually puzzled about these people. Some appeared to come from directly north, harried by Griqua and Bergenaar raiders; others came from the north-east or east, and so were lumped together as 'Mantatees'.[117] What is particularly interesting about the reports of May 1825 is that some of these new 'Fetcani', who had been encountered in considerable force raiding the Thembu Xhosas east of the Swart Kei river,[118] is that they, in turn, were being 'driven from their own land by a people of yellow complexion with black beards and long hair and who were armed with swords'. The writer here – the famous poet and philanthropist Thomas Pringle, at that time farming beneath the Winterberg – decided that these 'long-haired people must certainly be the Portuguese, tho it is odd that they are not described as being armed with fire-arms rather than swords'.[119] This is possible, though hardly conclusive, and it would be a very long way, even for Portuguese slavers. It does, nevertheless, coincide with the continued upsurge in slaving from the Mozambique coast. Just how far away and how long ago these long-haired marauders had been encountered, Pringle couldn't say.

There is a third interesting item. As we saw earlier, Madikane of the Bhaca was said to have died in December 1824, at the time of the solar eclipse. Most historians have been seduced by this lovely and useful coincidence. Perhaps the oral traditionalists were, too. Perhaps they were a few months out. However, there is no further mention of Madikane in the record. If the eclipse date is correct, it must be Fynn who was wrong (or covering up): it was not Madikane, but Macingwane still marauding in the region. He (or someone) had already, some months before, sent a few 'Ficani' raiders into the Transkei area. Now they were falling upon the Thembu with greater ferocity. They were not merely an army, since (according to Pringle) they were accompanied by women and children. Instead, they were a people on the move, both raiding and looking for somewhere to live. They were 'Fetcani' marauders transforming into 'Mfengu' or 'Fingoes' – from the phrase *siyam fenguza*, 'we need help, we are hungry'.[120]

Was this, in fact, the moment when Shaka sent out another long-distance raid, with some white and 'Hottentot' gunmen in support, and crushed Macingwane for good, sending a ripple of refugees and of secondary raiding towards the colony?

The evidence is thin, and largely circumstantial, but this is my hypothesis, for what it's worth. White travellers were involved in these inland disturbances earlier than we previously thought. 'Thompson' – possibly Alex Thompson of Farewell's party – was present at the death of Madikane. Long-haired men with swords (or guns) and horses were responsible for harrying men, women and children westwards. Traders were also beginning to make their way through.[121] Shaka was now fully capable of carrying out such a far-reaching raid. Fynn, needing support for his own ivory enterprise, and perhaps attracted by the prospects of booty (cattle, slaves for himself or for export, women), helped out in whatever way he could or was obliged to. This was to establish the pattern for the future. He half admitted what was going on: Shaka's spies were also present in his area at the same time, and Shaka was threatening an attack (though Fynn says that the threat was against the Mpondo, it would be another three years before Shaka seriously contemplated any such thing). It was – I suggest – against the Ngwane that the 1825 raid was aimed.

This is one account of the clash:

> Shaka appeared on the scene with his army, which he personally accompanied, taking up a position on the Pateni hill [south-west of present-day Richmond] as the army went forward to attack Macingwane. Macingwane, finding he was no match for Shaka, immediately moved off with his stock, women and children across the Mzimkhulu and Ingwagwane [rivers] to a district about Insikeni mountain, where there was a forest [40 kilometres north of present-day Kokstad]. The cattle and children, also the *impi*, took refuge in the forest. Before the mountain was a plain on which the Zulu army was drawn up and where it was given its instructions. Macingwane himself went and took up a position on the very top of a mountain, going to a point, and from there he observed Shaka's tactics. Shaka himself was with his forces – for he never failed to accompany them in person until the occasion of his assassination, when the army was away in the north-east. The Zulus then moved forward and *tshaya*'d *ingomane*, i.e. simultaneously struck their shields loudly, and so loudly that the cattle in the forest became terrified and emerged into the open. This was the signal for closing in. The Zulus entered the forest, fought and defeated the Cunus, killing off even women and children without exception. In the meantime, Macingwane, seeing the game was up, came down the mountain and fled to Pondoland. Thus Shaka got the whole of the Cunu cattle.[122]

Macingwane disappeared. A few of his people probably continued south and west to 'become Mfengu', intersecting with the 1825–6 influx of Tswana or

Sotho 'Mantatees'; others went back into Zulu country, saying that they would rather *khonza* Shaka than any amaLala of lesser worth than themselves. Some *khonza*'d Mfusi, the son who was already in favour with Shaka.[123] Macingwane's mantle – either deliberately bestowed before he died, or by default – fell upon his son Pakade, who initially *khonza*'d Zihlandlo. (Later, probably under Dingane, Pakade would set himself up more firmly amongst the Zulu.) Other Chunu milled about, chasing rumours that Macingwane was still alive. Shaka did not interfere with their wishes; they must join their chief if they wanted to, he said. Then, disappointingly, they heard that Macingwane had been eaten by 'cannibals' at Nsikeni. In the end, it was Shaka to whom they submitted.[124]

This was the first raid – almost the only one – that approximates the stereotype of the Zulu onslaught: a major 'nation' actually destroyed and scattered. Were women and children really massacred? Maybe; there is scarcely a major war zone in history in which this hasn't sometimes happened. Quite likely many women were raped, as Zulu warriors fulfilled the vile and virile custom of 'wiping the hoe'.[125] Despite these actions, a substantial number of Chunu were willing to go on living under Shaka, and he welcomed them.

As thanks for their assistance, the whites were rewarded, as they would be again in the future, with cattle, hunting rights, and women. The 'best terms of friendship', as so often, were those of mutual profit. As Fuze summarises it: 'To these white people Shaka gave girls from his [*isigodlo*], who became their wives. They bore them many children, now comprising several clans, and those clans are still known [in 1920] by the names of their fathers. They are distinguishable by being white, but they are black in all other respects.'[126]

'DISTRESS AND PRIVATIONS'

Only Francis Farewell seems (as far as we know) to have held himself aloof from these marital arrangements. He alone amongst the adventurers had a white wife back in Cape Town.

Catherine Farewell had heard from her husband via Lieutenant Hawes of the *York*, and was doubtless relieved to hear that he was healthy. Someone else refused to believe it: James Saunders King. He had been in London in the latter part of 1824, complaining to Earl Bathurst about how he had been excluded from the guano trade on the St Croix islands off Algoa Bay. By mid-1825 he was back in Cape Town, scheming. On 9 August King wrote to Governor Henry Somerset, proclaiming that he was about to set off for Port Natal in the brig *Mary* for 'the express purpose of relieving Mr Farewell' who was 'labouring under very great distress and privations'.[127] This – as King knew from Hawes – was nonsense.[128]

King wanted two eight-pound guns and a dozen stand of arms, with ammunition. More importantly, he hoped that 'if Mr Farewell should feel inclined to introduce to the Cape of Good Hope a chieftain or others from Port Natal', the Cape government would be nice enough to grant permission.[129] Here he's latching onto an idea first mooted by Farewell back in September 1824 – the germ of the ill-fated, eminently suspect 'embassy' of 1828. King's activities were already suspect: he had tried to ship both arms and cases of beads illegally from another vessel, incurring the irritation of the customs men at 'the extreme irregularity of [King] first asking to pass an import without payment of duties and then an export of gunpowder to the borders of the colony without . . . permission'.[130] He eventually got away with fifteen muskets, a case of musket-balls, and five barrels of gunpowder from another ship (ironically named *Olive Branch*) in addition to two twelve-pound cannon and twelve muskets from the government stores.[131] Such was the character of a man who would do much to spread a badly skewed view of Shaka to the rest of the world.

King sailed in the *Mary*, almost crossing paths with Captain Owen in the *Leven*, making his final return from the vicinity of Delagoa Bay.

On 1 October 1825 the *Mary* was lying keeled over and breaking up in stormy surf on the sandbar of Port Natal.

Box 8

The depopulation myth

Historian Shula Marks showed many years ago how white settlers drew heavily on early travellers' perception that vast regions of southern Africa had been 'depopulated' (mostly by Shaka), thereby opening them up for settlement with no moral consequences. What gradually developed into the apartheid ideology of 'native homelands' depended on this perception. Marks quotes, for instance, a 1977 South African Department of Information pamphlet: 'After the frontier wars of the 18th and 19th centuries and large-scale depopulation of the interior as a result of the wars of genocide committed by the Zulu king Chake [sic] the Whites and Blacks by and large retained the respective White and Black homelands into which the country had come to be divided'.[1]

As far as I know, however, to date no one has bothered to map precisely what areas were *said* to have been depopulated by Shaka's armies. This may not be quite the same as what he *did*: both Zulu and white sources exaggerated the scale of destruction and movement. The descendants of victims of Zulu raids or attacks liked to exaggerate the scale of their victimhood; the Zulu themselves the scale of their power; and the white settlers the scale of 'black savagery'. Yet even if, for the argument's sake, we take such reports as we possess more or less as they stand, a remarkably precise – and remarkably limited – impression of the centres of violence can be generated.

One useful source is the collection of potted tribal histories collected by Theophilus Shepstone in the early 1860s and printed in Bird's *Annals of Natal*. These tiny clans are often represented in these histories as having been 'scattered' or largely (though almost never completely) annihilated by 'Chaka'. If we trace them as far as we can on Bryant's map of the pre-Shakan distribution of peoples, the following becomes clear. The whole area allegedly denuded was quite small (maybe 80 kilometres across at most), and within that the destruction was patchy, since many clans continued to live there unmolested, as did some remnants of the peoples attacked. Indeed, of the 94 tribes listed, only a little over half (51) were described as having been 'scattered'; the other half had a very different experience. (The clans listed as 'destroyed' are marked on Map 10 on page 346. Compare this to historian G.M. Theal's 1891 map of 'Territory almost depopulated by the Zulu wars before 1834', which extends north right across the Limpopo, south-west to the Mzimvubu river, and north-west across the Modder.[2])

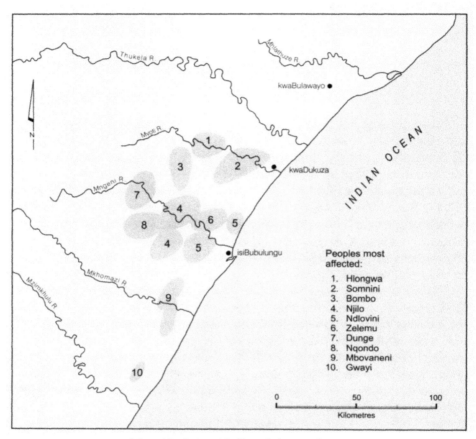

Map 10: Areas of alleged depopulation

Shepstone's information is problematic in many ways,[3] but let's assume for the moment that, as he asserted, considerable devastation did happen south of the Thukela. This area correlates pretty well with that so described, in much more vague terms, by some local informants,[4] by the first white settlers, and independently by subsequent travellers. Francis Farewell, sometime in 1825, travelled inland of Port Natal, probably up the Mngeni river, and wrote that there were signs of 'thousands' of people having been slaughtered.[5] Since there were unlikely to have been many thousands living there in the first place, this is certainly exaggerated. Both Fynn and Isaacs depicted patches of the region inland of Port Natal, and between the port and the Thukela, as having been depopulated. So did Charles Rawden Maclean.[6] That it was very patchy is confirmed, despite the rhetoric, by Isaacs himself, who depicted the countryside in the vicinity of the Mngeni river as littered with 'innumerable fragments of human skulls', but two pages later, described the very same area, as 'thickly inhabited', though the people there 'had greatly suffered from the incursions of Chaka'.[7] This was echoed by several independent later travellers, including Allen Gardiner in early 1835.[8] Gardiner did not explicitly blame Shaka, though American missionaries, travelling to Dingane a year later and noting the same lack of inhabitants, did attribute the situation directly to him.[9]

There seems little doubt, then, that a quite focused region between the Mngeni and Thukela rivers suffered an extreme form of raiding or attack – an *izwekufa* – in Shaka's time. As I have argued (see pages 277 to 280), this was precisely the area represented in Zulu sources as the sphere of the iziYendane *ibutho*'s partly unauthorised raiding. This may have been exacerbated by these small clans' vulnerability to (previously underestimated) raiding by the Mkhize on one side, the Mpondo on the other, and to sundry internecine conflicts that were stimulated to murderous proportions as Zulu raids made living more difficult. (Such stories of cannibalism as we have – see Box 4 on page 223 – arose from precisely this region.) In due course, white-sponsored slaving might have further worsened this situation. Peoples moving west or north-west out of the coastal strip ran into longer-range Ngwane raids for cattle, drought, and the disruptions caused by Chunu, Thembu and Bhaca migrations; many of them never fully reconstituted themselves, were scattered and absorbed into other polities.

In sum, some brief, intense but still patchy depopulation occurred. It comprised part slaughter, part capture, part absorption into migrating units or into the Zulu state itself, part dispersal, and part exaggeration.

We have no records whatsoever of similar depredation happening elsewhere within Shaka's sphere of influence.

The Zulu were not the only human marauders in the 'Natal' area, though for a time they were doubtless the main ones. There is also another, non-human candidate, one that has been almost totally ignored by the historians: smallpox. The evidence is thin, but sufficient for the speculation that at least some people died of this foreign malady as early as 1589.[10] There were outbreaks in the neighbouring Cape Colony in 1713, 1755, and 1767. A further outbreak in 1812 was definitely caused by infection from a slave ship.[11] There were several documented outbreaks throughout the subcontinent, some of them associated with droughts that had coincided with, and helped to stimulate, the incursions of slavers. This was certainly the case in southern Mozambique between 1822 and 1832, when slaving from Delagoa Bay was building to a crescendo; slave ships from there periodically carried smallpox to Brazil.[12] More precisely, Andrew Smith, travelling towards the Thukela in 1832, noted smallpox scars on both Mpondo and Zulu peoples' faces and bodies; he learned that large numbers of Mthethwa had died from a smallpox outbreak perhaps sixteen years previously (around 1816).[13] One Zulu informant, NHLEKELE, remembered that the Msweyi people near the Mfolozi river died off from some such disease at what I take to be about the same time.[14]

Finally, Shaka himself is intriguingly connected with it, through the story of the white metal armbands or neck-rings. One story is simply that one of Shaka's wives developed sores under her brass neck-rings, sickened and died. Shaka subsequently got some of these neck-rings together and buried them near the Khangela *umuzi*.[15] Another version claims, however, that some armbands or neck-rings were fashioned from a strange new 'white' metal. Sickness developed in the land, supposed to have been smallpox; some *izinyanga* divined the white rings as the cause; so these were collected and buried.[16] The original source of this version was Henry Francis Fynn, and it must be treated cautiously. There is no reason, of course, to exclude common and fatal diseases from the everyday lives of the early Zulu, and smallpox may just have been one of the more devastating. It might explain why so many bodies were never buried.

11

Wars with words and guns

In control, 1825–6

When he [Shaka] entered on a war with a power, his whole mind and soul were irrevocably bent on annihilation; he had no redeeming qualities; mercy was never for a moment an inmate of his bosom; he had indulged in the sacrifice of human blood, and nothing could sate his monstrous appetite.

> Nathaniel Isaacs, *Travels and Adventures* (1836, I 266–7).

Shaka . . . dealt with rival tribes and enemies mercilessly, marching entire regiments off a high cliff above the Indian Ocean to plunge to their deaths on the rocks below, and killing an estimated two million people in a decade of conquest.

> Geoff Hill, *The Battle for Zimbabwe* (2003, 44).

In September, after the first rains or *uMandulo* – the 'first-fields moon' – the seeds of the staple cereals, *amabele* (sorghum) and *uphoko* (millet), would be planted. In mid-summer both crops and weeds sprouted, birds and beasts raided, and men and women all worked hard in the fields. The process culminated in the harvests, signified by the 'first-fruits' or *umkhosi* ceremony.

[The *umkhosi*,] the greatest of Zulu festivals, took place once in each year, being preceded by a smaller dance known as the *inyatelo*. It was sometimes called the great *umkosi* of the gourd. The *izinyanga* used to prepare in good time for the great feast, procure medicines and gourds some days before they were actually required by the king. An ordinary

Zulu, a commoner, could always tell when this *umkosi* was about to take place, for in the first place it was at the beginning of the new summer season, then by the size of the moon, and when it got to a certain size they would go for the gourd. Then he might tell by the dancing (*keta*) of *amabuto*, which always took place just before. It seems the exact day was fixed by the king in consultation with his doctors, though it depended chiefly on the moon, which the king did not ignore.

The great concourse of people would begin arriving from the various *amakanda* between say the hours of four and six in the latter part of the afternoon, and encamp. The *umkosi* was invariably characterised by quarrelling and fighting among the different regiments, when *indunas* used to interfere and strike about among them with sticks right and left. About dawn the next morning very early, *amabuto* would go and call the king to strike the gourd. The king, having put on a covering of green rushes, would come with the *isigodhlo*; he would come to the *amabuto*, all assembled. He comes with the gourd in his own hands, and is accompanied by the *izinyanga* who are doctoring him. He passes through the gate, and, having come up to the *amabuto*, at the instant the first rays of the rising sun are shot forth he spits the medicine at the sun. He then, the *amabuto* having already begun to sing or chant as the king approached, as they continue singing, suddenly throws the small gourd he carries up into the air and catches it as it falls, and the great ceremony is over; the gourd for that year has been struck.[1]

This is a description of the *umkhosi* ceremony as it happened in Mpande's time, but there is no reason to doubt that it occurred in much the same way in Shaka's reign, too.[2]

THE LANGUAGE OF RITUAL

One of Shaka's less well-recognised achievements was that he centralised the control of various ceremonies to an unprecedented degree. He waged war not only with the assegai, but also with rituals and words.

The *umkhosi* gathering was only the most important of these rituals. Shaka's appropriation of it would be obvious to all from the moment of its announcement. The informant BALEKA said: 'My father told me of a chant sung by the regiment appointed to fetch Shaka from the *isigodhlo* to bring him to the men's assembly in the cattle kraal; this during an *umkosi*. "Come down! Bird which devours others; come down! You who overcame the chiefs; come down! Come here!"'[3]

Just as it was a mark of exceptional favour to be granted your own *isigodlo*, it was a mark of favour if you could run your own *umkhosi*. Shaka made it essentially the *inkosi*'s prerogative. As Eileen Krige puts it:

The king is thus the leader in all agricultural operations, and at certain times, such as at the sowing of the seed and the eating of the first-fruits, he is strengthened with medicines so as to ensure a good harvest. Indeed, on no occasion is the king's position as a representative of the tribe as a whole, and as a person on whom the strength of the army and success of the crops depends, more clearly seen than at the national First-fruits ceremonies.[4]

The *umkhosi* was also an occasion for a military parade, with much rivalry between units; for discussion of general policy with the elders and *izinduna* in the *umphakathi* (the conclave of great men[5]); and for the *juba*ing of girls (although evidently Shaka himself never got around to doing this). Then, it seems, the men would scatter to their homesteads, to be gathered together only as occasion warranted, or when the campaign season began in February or March.[6]

The *umkhosi* was only the greatest of the many agricultural ceremonies in which the *inkosi*, with the full panoply of ritual medicines and the involvement of the ancestors, was obliged to take part. For obvious reasons, rain-making was also an important one. The *inkosi*'s role in rain-making ceremonies was central. Here, too, Shaka was able to use the ceremonial to enhance political power. 'To make quite sure of getting rain . . . the Zulu kings generally kept rain-doctors who helped them when prayers to their ancestors proved of no avail.'[7] Shaka seems to have inherited rain-makers of the Gasa people, who had been scattered by Macingwane's Chunu before Shaka's accession, and had *khonza*'d Senzangakhona.[8] Shaka did not necessarily always see eye-to-eye with them, as is captured in one story, which is probably apocryphal since the whole people is collapsed into one man named Gasa. 'Gasa' used to make rain in this way:

> He had eight pots, which were carried by as many men. [Gasa] would go to the foot of a cliff and speak to his fathers. . . . Then when Gasa came away from the cliff he would be like a very sick person, one sick for the thing he had asked for. It was said that he sweated, he cried, he was depressed, he was humble, from wanting the thing that he had asked for. Then he would emerge and summon the eight men. The pots would be placed in a reed hut (*uhlaka*). Then to the side a firestick would be twirled, for a fire was needed. When fire appeared, Gasa himself would rise and light up wood already there and arranged under all the pots. Smoke came forth, and incense (*impepo*) too, and rose up. With the rising of the smoke a cloud would appear in the sky. He would see that this plea had been heard, and would now wait for the rain.[9]

When Gasa failed once too often to produce more than empty thunder, Shaka had him killed. According to Stephen MINI, Gasa actually belonged to a people called the amaZolo, who either claimed ancient ancestry with the Zulu, or had been scattered by them, or both. 'The amaZolo were the owners of the sky; they were the rainmakers; they were addressed as "*Zulu! Dhlangamadhla* [a great ancestor]!" . . . The Zulu took from them the power of sovereignty.'[10] MINI is probably exaggerating the past glories of his Zolo people, but the implied connection between rain-making and other forms of the *inkosi*'s power is authentic. (This was later confirmed when Dingane slaughtered the Gasa rain-makers, whom he rightly saw as particularly sympathetic to Shaka; rain-making and kingship were virtually synonymous.[11])

All of these occasions would be accompanied by copious beer-drinking. The brewing of that beer from grain grown in the *inkosi*'s own fields was a particularly important activity, invested with rich ritual import, for the *isigodlo* women.[12]

Although the *umkhosi* was an indication that in many respects cultivation held precedence over cattle in the economy,[13] it was also an occasion to display the fruits of that other main branch of economic wealth. Henry Francis Fynn described the importance of cattle as follows:

> Each kraal is supported by the King's cattle, these being in the same manner formed into regiments, assorted to each regiment according to the colour of the shields worn by them. When the cattle arrive from an enemy, they are assorted and sent to their respective regiments. At such a time each individual drives away one or two, or as many as he can in the general scramble. This entitles him to their milk which is for his support while he remains with the regiment. Sometimes they are allowed to take these cattle to their private kraals. In such case they may be called together at a moment's notice to be given as individuals or to be slaughtered without the knowledge of the possessor, the milk being the only remuneration for their services during their lives. The whole of the cattle taken in war are the sole property of the King, who gives away tens, fifties or hundreds to chiefs, favourites and private servants. The common soldiers have little or no expectations of such favours.[14]

In this manner, cattle distribution contributed to the distinction between the élite and the commoners. Cereal crops could be stored, but not transported very far over that rugged terrain; they had to be grown fairly close to the concentrations of *amakhanda*. Cattle, by contrast, could move. They were mobile wealth: Shaka's reign seems to span a shift from beads to cattle as the main currency of *lobolo*. Cattle were also, in their way, more vulnerable to raiding and to disease. As in other aspects of his politics, Shaka needed to – and was able to – enforce to a large degree new controls over cattle. He also worked the other way round, using cattle as a tool to 'pay for' new controls. The traditional operation of *ukusisa* – the placing of cattle in the care of a dependant, who has certain rights of usufruct as well as certain obligations – was interwoven into the *inkosi*'s spreading network of centralised patronage.

> The king's cattle were scattered (*sisa*'d) all over the country. They were *sisa*'d by the *indunas*. A man would have a certain number *sisa*'d,

generally one or two, and when these increased, even though the birth of a calf was premature, or a calf might be still-born, they must at once be reported, when the *indunas* might direct one of the cattle there to be given to some other man who had no cattle, and the same order would be observed there. A man was held responsible with his life for the king's cattle. If any were stolen or lost or made away and not reported, or, if reported and the explanation was not satisfactory, he would be killed. By this system every beast belonging to the king was known and recorded in the minds of the *indunas*. No man ever attempted, would dare to attempt, to deceive, for he feared his neighbours would inform against him. . . . It was an unheard of thing for any man to refuse to take charge of cattle *sisa*'d to him by the king. Dingane and Mpande *sisa*'d very freely, especially Mpande; Shaka placed them at special kraals (*inhlohla*), and also with men. It is clear that cattle were *sisa*'d to men because in Shaka's day cattle were *jutshwa*'d, i.e. formal permission was given by the king that people to whom they were *sisa*'d could milk them for their own use. Cattle were *jutshwa*'d year by year by Shaka at the time when calves left off sucking and new ones were born.[15]

No doubt, such tight control also contributed to the fantastically rich vocabulary that had developed to describe the nuances of colouring and character, even the horn shapes, of the Zulu's most treasured resource.[16]

As important to emerging senses of identity and loyalty were the names of the *amabutho* (see Box 9 on page 389). These were equally rich and playful, their own meanings amplified by nicknames. The Mgumanqa *ibutho*, for example, was known as 'That which stands threateningly in the patch of burnt grass', and when it was sent down to Port Natal to keep a closer eye on the whites, it acquired the nickname or *ithakazelo* 'uKhangela-amaNkengane' ('keep an eye on the vagabonds'). The Fasimba was 'The rough tongue of a beast'; the Bhekenya, 'A person with angry, noisy tongue'; the uGibabanye, 'Take out the others'; and so on.[17] The verbal language was extended by the language of physical symbols: incisions in the body, bird feathers, hairstyles, and bangles. These symbols, too, were mostly controlled by the *inkosi*:

Iminaka . . . were large, roughly made copper rings allowed by the king to be worn. Anyone allowed to wear them could not remove the rings except with the permission of the king obtained through the *izinduna*, and permission would be sought only in cases of urgent necessity. Hide was put between the neck and the metal to prevent it burning and chafing. A man would be compelled to wear it for three or four months at a time and, when once on, it would have to be kept on night and day. It would have to be polished while still round the neck – polished with hide. It looked very well, and sometimes as many as four of these heavy rings would be put round one man's neck. Some of this was native copper; some of the metal came from Delagoa Bay. A whole regiment might be given permission to wear *iminaka*. The Izimpholo, for instance, wore *iminaka*.[18]

In these and other ways the *amabutho* distinguished themselves from each other, and their warrior role from their own everyday lives. This intensified and became more ornate as, after 1825, Shaka's activities became more aggressive. The growth of such military accoutrements undoubtedly increased internal and international trade.

There's also an interesting case in which the search for new ways of making distinctive ornaments backfired. Fynn told the story of how during Shaka's reign a disease broke out and some *izinyanga* – traditional doctors – were called in. They divined that the cause lay within bangles of a curious white metal. The bangles were retrieved; the disease disappeared. William LEATHERN, our informant here, speculates that it was some alloy of lead and silver.[19] The disease was possibly smallpox (see Box 8 on page 345). Fynn claimed to have found amongst people along the Mzimkhulu river bangles of solid silver, obtained from some northern conquered people.[20] However, he also piled myth upon myth, once giving his friend William Bazely a one-pound neck-ring he claimed had been obtained from the body of the very woman Shaka had cut open to see the foetus; her head had had to be cut off.[21]

Genealogies and praises

If the élitist symbolic languages of warriorhood contributed to one aspect of stratification within the Zulu polity, the languages of clan and belonging comprised another. This involved the manipulation of both genealogies and clan-praises. What kind of ancestry you had – or pretended to have – and whose praises you adopted or were allowed to adopt, registered in the public ear your degree of closeness to the centre. This was intricately connected to the patterns of marriage alliances.

Shaka was born into a system in which new family lines were customarily created by being formally split off from the parent line. Generally speaking, members of a particular family or clan had to marry those of another quite distinct one. This is the principle of exogamy. In essence, exogamy avoided inbreeding, mollified potentially aggressive neighbours, spread wealth, and created stronger links between disparate peoples. All of these measures continued to be useful to a polity bent on centralising, but these splitting-off aspects were also potentially disruptive. In practice, just *how* the distinction between one family genealogy and another was made was rather malleable.

There were two different ways in which the splitting-off could happen: *dabuka* ('to get torn off') and *dabula* ('to tear off'). *Dabuka* was usually meant to achieve an independent political existence for the section concerned. It would be led away to build a new settlement elsewhere, but it would hang on to a residual tie to the parent section by retaining its praises or *izibongo*. *Dabula*, by contrast, involved the new section creating additional *izibongo* of its own; it might move no further away from its parent sections either politically or geographically, but intermarriage would thereafter be permissible. The language of praising was the crucial difference. MANGATI puts it this way:

> In the separating off of a section of a chiefdom (*dabula*ing) there must be shedding of blood, i.e. violence. As regards a girl, she is deflowered with the penis, which is regarded as like an assegai, for it draws blood; the same as regards an *inkosi* or chief, when assassinated or wounded by some portion of his own tribe. In each case, there being effusion of blood, there is *dabula*ing or creation of a new order, separation from the parent tribe, after which intermarriage may lawfully occur.[22]

The blood-letting didn't have to be quite so literal, as in this account of the *dabula*ing of the Biyela collateral clan: 'Mvundhlana was the great head of one branch of the Zulu tribe. As time went on and they became rather distantly related to the Zulu house, the Zulu chief *dabula*'d them seeing they had beautiful girls, upon which Mvundhlana's people became the Biyela.'[23]

It does seem to come down to sex – and to the political implications of who gets it.

As James Stuart pointed out, the Zulu, particularly in Shaka's day, created new clans (*dabula*'d) with unusual frequency, 'which amounts to saying that it resorted to endogamy in a manner somewhat more precipitate than was the custom in other tribes or what was the custom prior to Shaka's day'.[24] In short, Shaka tried to concentrate political power amongst a limited number of family groupings by encouraging greater *in*breeding. Most of the collateral clans were *dabula*'d during Shaka's reign. Some then fabricated genealogies to give the impression that they had originated separately. They included the Biyela, the eGazini, the emGazini, the Ntombela, the Mdlalose, and the Mpangisweni. While 'no longer "Zulu" (the *isibongo* having the meaning of "the heavens"), they lacked the crucial abilities of the Zulu proper to intervene . . . on behalf of the nation . . . in the heavens as the source of rain, and in the control of lightning'.[25]

It's difficult to draw boundaries between these clans, partly because they were already so closely interrelated, partly because they were still in the process of forming. It was still a very shadowy, muddled process – and not only because our information is thin. Nevertheless, the leading men of these clans retained the authority of their birth.

It would be instructive to see *where* Shaka deployed these clans' leaders, but we have few leads in this regard (see Box 10 on page 391).[26] Here are the few who we are certain were elevated to prominence by Shaka. From the emGazini collateral clan, Hlati kaNcidi was a prominent warrior of the iNtontela;[27] Mdlaka kaNcidi was the *induna yezwe*, chief of the nation, who led several of Shaka's major campaigns and was *induna* at esiKlebheni.[28] These two were thus stationed in the Zulu heartland. Of the Biyela, Mvundlana kaMenziwa was the head, and *induna* of Mqumanqa.[29] Mvundlana's brother Solatsha might also have been an *isikhulu* – a respected elder – under Shaka.[30] Of the Mdlalose, Ndengezi kaKhuzwayo was a great warrior, but apparently never an *induna*.[31] Of the Ntombela, Dambuza kaSobadli was second-in-command to the great Mdlaka; Lukwazi kaZwana is listed as amongst Shaka's *izikhulu*, but seems only to have come into real prominence under Mpande.[32]

That's all we know. These men are easily outweighed in numbers by others from neighbouring peoples. Consequently, while there is much to recommend the notion that Shaka was trying to build up a tightly élitist core of Zulu adherents, he was evidently having a hard time doing so. He also had to rely on much more tenuous ties of marriage and bought loyalty. His strategies were, perhaps inevitably, rather ad hoc. Obviously it was in his interest to create entities that were subordinate to him but which, unlike *dabuka*'d sections, shared no part of the Zulu *izibongo*. This meant that they had no ideological lever with which to unseat the *inkosi* or his family. Any family that remained geographically close and/or retained the Zulu *izibongo*, could pose a serious threat to the Zulu leader. One such family branch was that of Mudli who, as we've seen, had to be sharply, even murderously, dealt with right from the start, and deprived thereafter of the possibility of producing any pretenders to power.[33] Accordingly, Shaka manipulated the language of praises and belonging to minimise the threat and close the ranks of the central families.

Another, closely related rhetorical resource that Shaka adapted to fashion his new élite was to manipulate the *ithakazelo*: the address-names of various groups. We've already touched on one example : the notion of being *ntungwa* (see Chapter 1, page 18). A fantastic patchwork of fragmentary clans could be at least partially united through the assertion of a common identity such as *ntungwa*. The various groups' *ithakazelo* could be manipulated, acquired in exchange for goods and services, or simply stolen. Shaka was good at this. He got the *ithakazelo* 'Gumede' and 'Nguni' from the Qwabe, and 'Ndabazitha' from the conquered Mbatha (substituting the latter for the insulting '*Lufenwuljana*'). As for *ntungwa*, it may originally have been a Khumalo term. However, as Shaka popularised and empowered it, a number of groups began to assert that they were also *ntungwa*, and to connect it with the legend of having originated 'upcountry'. The other related terms – *Nguni*, *Lala* – were similarly massaged:

> These expressions came into vogue principally in Shaka's day . . . Shaka called those in Zululand who *tekeza*'d amaLala, whilst those of Natal

he spoke of as iNyakeni, i.e. those who also *tekeza*'d. He used to insult
us [Cele] and frighten us by saying that we did not have the cunning
to invent things out of nothing, like lawyers. . . . He said that we were
Lala because our tongues lay (*lala*) flat in our mouths, and we did not
speak in the Ntungwa fashion.

He spoke of them as iNyakeni because they had dirty habits and
did not distinguish between what was good and what was bad. A person
of the iNyakeni did not pay respects to chiefs, nor did he wash or
keep himself neat. . . .

These names Lala and Nyakeni may have been and probably were
in existence long before Shaka's day, but it was in his day that they
came to be widely known . . .[34]

Similarly insulting was the idea that the term *amaLala* 'arose in Shaka's time
because they went about hiding and eating *imihlakanya* woodborers'.[35]
Geography, accent, social habits, ethnic disdain, military inferiority: all of
these aspects were encompassed by the language of rearranged power. Shaka
was widely credited with bringing new meaning to much of the language of
identity:

Ho! Ofe!' is equivalent to '*Ho! Wenzani!*'[What do you think you're
doing?] and is said by the amaNtungwa whenever they head off
anything. They had a separate dialect of their own, these Kumalo
people. It was altered by Shaka. . . .

The amaNtungwa speak of themselves as being abaNguni. Shaka
however put an end to this as he said he was umNguni. He was
addressed as, '*Mnguni, Mnguni* of our people!' The amaNtungwa
thereupon became afraid of applying this word to themselves. . . .

[T]he name umNguni is a precious one to the people of Zululand,
being used as one of the profoundest and most reverential salutations
to the Zulu kings, who conquered all the tribes of these parts. Shaka
was the first to appropriate the appellation . . .[36]

Manipulation of the *ithakazelo* at the 'clan' level was closely tied to Shaka's
appropriation of another established feature of Zulu self-awareness: the

izibongo. These 'praises' had always been sung for prominent figures, for the group as a whole, for the ancestral 'shades', for local animals, for the cattle, and so on. Shaka used this to his advantage. The number of praises that he accumulated was a measure of his status and power; it would be interpreted as such by anyone who heard them. He acquired other people's praises, such as the salutation '*Bayethe!*', along with the 'royal ceremonial song' (*ingoma*), which he was said to have taken over from Zwide – a verbal equivalent to leaping over a defeated foe.[37] He got '*Ndabezita!*' from the Chunu.[38]

At the same time, Shaka appropriated the authority to bestow praises on others. This applied to individuals and to units. The iNtontela *ibutho*, for instance, was granted the name 'Amehlakamboni' as an '*isitakazelo* or name given after something good or worthy done in war'.[39] He also extended another common linguistic practice, that of *hlonipha*. This complex phenomenon essentially involved tabooing a word that had acquired a disrespectful echo.[40] It was said, for example, that Shaka *hlonipha*'d the word *itshaka* – the intestinal disease snidely alleged by some to have been the cover for Nandi's pregnancy – and replaced it with *iqagane* or *iqangala*.[41] In another instance: 'Shaka first called the Gibabanye the uPoko regiment, but as he used to take *upoko* beer and that was his food, he decided to withdraw this name.'[42] The same kind of thing occurred with regard to the Ndabenkulu *ibutho*, which was first called the Velabakuze (*ukuvela*, to appear, and *ukukhuza*, to express surprise). Shaka said, 'That expression is one which refers to me, for wherever I appear people are startled.'[43] Another example, handed down by a Hlubi informant, brings us back to where we began, at the *umkhosi* ceremony. Nowhere is the close relationship between language and power better expressed:

> The word *igagane* only came into vogue after Shaka began to reign, for it was forbidden to hold the *umkosi* ceremony. It used to be *umkosi* among our tribe [the Hlubi] previously to Shaka. We were prohibited from practising the custom as it was intended our tribe should become extinguished in order that Shaka's nation should be augmented.[44]

Informants cite many more examples of this process. Shaka – like powerful leaders everywhere – was fully aware that forging a unified polity involved much more than simply inflicting violence on your neighbours.

Language of a different order must have been an ongoing vexation in dealing with those new neighbours, the pale intruders at isiBubulungu.

PALE-SKINNED VISITORS

In early October 1825, Shaka was informed that a ship had gone aground on the sandbar at isiBubulungu and broken up. There were a number of new white men now stranded there, salvaging what they could from the wreck. Farewell – perhaps already known amongst the locals as 'Febana' – had been away engaged in what Captain Owen, dropping in on the Port Natal party in September, had called a 'destructive war raging in the country'.[45] Charles Maclean, one of the new castaways, found that 'Mr Farewell and the male portion of the party were absent, with the chief of the country's forces, against a neighbouring tribe in the north-east, called the Izee-can-yon'a.'[46] This was presumably Sikhunyane, newly installed chieftain of the Ndwandwe. Maclean recounts Farewell's view of the battle in some detail, leaving no doubt that Sikhunyane was who he meant.[47] However, it's clear from other sources that the main confrontation with Sikhunyane was still nearly a year away. Maclean, writing 30 years later, was confusing wars. So was this 1825 war the one against Macingwane's Chunu, related in Chapter 10? It's more likely that the 'old king' who was defeated was Macingwane, rather than Sikhunyane, who was still quite young. Alternatively, there was more than one confrontation with Sikhunyane, which is the impression that the traditions give. Besides, Farewell, as we'll see shortly, wasn't present at the final Sikhunyane fight at all.

Whichever raid it was, the important point is this: Farewell and the whites were already engaged in Shaka's campaigns. Moreover, Maclean noted, 'no compulsory measures had been adopted to force the white men to join the Impee [impi]',[48] that is, they had participated voluntarily.

Farewell was back at Gibixhegu/kwaBulawayo when Shaka heard of the wreck of the *Mary*. He was sent down to report, and to bring back representatives of the new arrivals. Farewell arrived at Port Natal on 20 October, on the heels of Fynn, who had also returned after an eight-month absence and with a load of ivory. There they found, amongst others, three more characters who would prove to be of huge importance in the development of the Shaka mythology.

Launching a skewed portrayal

James Saunders King, who had hired – and now lost – the *Mary*, we have already met. The other two – whom we've also had occasion to mention a few times – were mere boys who all but adored King.

Nathaniel Isaacs was barely seventeen, a rather bereft but energetic Jewish lad from Liverpool. He had had a torrid passage out. He was abused by the ship's captain (his own veiled account suggests buggery), and was desperately grateful to be rescued by King in St Helena. The wreck of the *Mary* inaugurated a three-year stay for Isaacs at Port Natal, after which he would write his two-volume work, *Travels and Adventures in Eastern Africa*, published in 1836. Though apparently based on a journal, the original has been lost.[49] Isaacs remained semi-literate all his life, and the book was largely the work of some anonymous ghost-writer. (This was not unusual for the time: Thompson's contemporaneous *Travels and Adventures in Southern Africa* was ghost-written by the poet Thomas Pringle.)

It's difficult to say just where Isaacs's personally venomous agendas end, and the fantasies of an English armchair-traveller begin. The *Travels* is a hugely problematic source, riddled with lies and misunderstandings. Nevertheless, it launched the portrayal of Shaka as an utterly irredeemable monster, the residues of which remain stuck like tar to many present-day perceptions – as the epigraphs to this chapter, for example, testify. Consequently, while Isaacs's account is deeply dubious as a source, it is also unavoidable.[50]

Isaacs later became a full-time slave-trader in West Africa, owning a personal slaving station on an island off Sierra Leone. We have to wonder if he didn't begin to learn his trade, so to speak, on the ridges inland of isiBubulungu. By the same token, we can speculate whether his even younger fellow castaway, Charles Rawden Maclean, didn't discover in the same place exactly the opposite. Maclean developed so profound a distaste of human trafficking that as an adult he became a lifelong, obsessive, even violent *anti*-slaving campaigner in the Caribbean.[51]

Maclean, a mere fourteen when he staggered out of the wreckage of the *Mary*, became even more legendary than his older companions. By some obscure linguistic chemistry, he became known as 'John Ross'.[52] Like Isaacs, he seems to have found in James Saunders King something of a foster-father figure. However, Maclean offers a partial corrective to Isaacs's diatribes and to the posthumous doctoring of Fynn's writings, as well as to the vicious collaboration between Isaacs and Fynn to sully Shaka's name. It's partial because he apparently never finished his account, which was published in the relatively obscure *Nautical Magazine* in the 1850s (and a biography of Shaka that he mentions writing hasn't surfaced); partial because his accounts made little impact until the South African critic and historian Stephen Gray resurrected them in the 1980s;[53] and partial because he is sometimes prone to the same cultural blindnesses and defensiveness.

On 20 October 1825, gathered at the shabby, half-built 'very primitive, rude looking' Fort Farewell, adorned rather than guarded by a couple of 'dismounted and neglected' cannons,[54] were the five white men who would do most to disseminate to the credulous outside world their peculiarly skewed portrait of Shaka.

The *inkosi* was expecting a visit from them. Consequently, on 26 October Fynn, Farewell and King set out for kwaBulawayo. Isaacs and Maclean were left to explore the vicinity and to meet Mathubane.[55] The party was received (Maclean heard later) 'in a friendly manner, but with that air of haughty indifference which might be expected from the Napoleon of Eastern Africa'.[56] James King, who also wrote an account of this visit, concurred: when Shaka was not in 'en-daba [*indaba*]' – in conference – he 'cast off his stern look, became good-humoured, and conversed with us through our interpreters on various subjects'.[57] Fynn wrote only that within an hour of their arrival,[58] Shaka was commanding them to demonstrate the power of their firearms on some unlucky elephants passing by. Protests were brushed aside, and a sailor 'Jack' was fortunate to fell an elephant, as much by chance as design. '[We] could [hardly] believe our eyesight,' said Fynn.[59]

Fynn was then abruptly requested to visit Shaka's ailing grandmother. She was 80 years old and dying of dysentery (or so Fynn diagnosed). Fynn's opinion that she had no hope of recovery caused Shaka to 'cry bitterly'.

Msimbithi, on hand to interpret, told Fynn of Shaka's 'affectionate conduct towards his Grandmother and that he would frequently when visited by her wash her Ears & Eyes which were much affected from age cut her nails to[o] & treat her as a Father would a Child'. Fynn professed that he could hardly believe this – 'untill a longer acquaintance assured us off [sic] it' – since Shaka had what he called such 'an opposite character'. The tidings of her death caused Shaka 'to contemplate some minutes in deep silence till his feeling burst upon him and he cryed loudly which set the nation in a general uproar'. After a day of such mourning – the customary openness of which would no doubt have unnerved the characteristically emotionally reserved Englishmen – they departed to return to isiBubulungu.[60]

If we were to follow only Fynn's published *Diary*, we could be forgiven for thinking that Fynn and Shaka were on the most intimate terms:

> He received us in the most affable manner and gave us two bullocks to slaughter. We managed to pitch our marquee and tents by sunset. Shaka then sent for me. I was taken into his seraglio. This was now his regular practice whenever I visited him, and he rarely allowed me to leave before twelve or one o'clock, owing to the intense interest he took in the different subjects he questioned me about.[61]

This was, however, inserted by Stuart; the intimacy is pure fiction. So is the 'marquee' (they were given huts, King said). Even more misleadingly, Stuart deliberately substituted for 'opposite character' (meaning merely contradictory or stubborn) the phrase 'unfeeling disposition'.

At this point, the whites' opinion of Shaka was almost entirely favourable. King penned perhaps the best-known (because so rare), but frustratingly brief portrait of Shaka:

> Chaka is about thirty-eight years of age, upwards of six feet in height, and well proportioned: he is allowed to be the best pedestrian in the country, and, in fact, during his wonderful exercises this day he exhibited the most astonishing activity: on this occasion he displayed a part of the handsomest beads of our present.[62]

This tells us remarkably little, and underestimates his age. In return for his gift of beads, Shaka sent the white men away with 107 cattle to keep them going for a while.

King would not see Shaka again for another year; Fynn would not see him for another eight months. It would be largely left to Nathaniel Isaacs to fill the gap.

Isaacs doesn't help us much in divining what Shaka was doing over that year. In addition, his portrait of Shaka's character cannot be taken at face value. Accepting his dates, Isaacs made four brief visits to Shaka between December 1825 and November 1826 – spending a total of just 44 days at kwaBulawayo.[63] This was time enough for Isaacs to form *some* sort of impression, but it is an impression seriously hampered by ignorance and cultural prejudice on the one hand, and by retrospective rewriting on the other.

It was only to be expected that the untutored Isaacs should be horrified, disgusted and bemused by what he saw around him. Isaacs admits that 'not understanding [Shaka] I was led about like a child'.[64] Shaka seemed to Isaacs to do nothing but discuss war (though nothing warlike actually happened until mid-1826), and entertain himself with dancing and reviewing his cattle. Isaacs failed, unsurprisingly, to comprehend the ritual and societal significance of any of these activities. He also did not comprehend the reasons behind the executions that he claims to have witnessed:

> The sanguinary chief was silent; but from some sign he gave the executioners, laying one hand on the crown and the other on the chin, and by a sudden wrench appeared to dislocate the head. The victims were then dragged away and beaten as they proceeded to the bush, about a mile from the kraal, where a stick was inhumanly forced up the fundament of each, and they were left as food for the wild beasts of the forest, and those carnivorous birds that hover near the habitations of the natives.[65]

It is doubtful whether the shocked Isaacs really did follow for a mile to see what happened. Three men, he wrote, were executed in this incident. In April Isaacs got embroiled in an outburst of mourning for a deceased chieftain, and claimed that a number of people were killed for not crying adequately; a day or two later he saw seven men executed, again for crimes he couldn't work out.[66] In July, he claimed that 'great arguments' with the king resulted in eight people being instantly killed, though in fact the 'cause for this [he] could not comprehend'.[67] This brings the total so far to maybe twenty deaths – a figure that is perhaps just credible. Summary justice was common enough, and as acceptable amongst the Zulu then as it was amongst the English of the same period (a man could be executed at Newgate for stealing bread in the 1820s; only the manner differed). Some of James Stuart's informants even regretted the ending of such a system; national discipline had eroded as a result, they felt.

In his account of his fourth visit, however, Isaacs – or his ghost-writer – launches into an account of a massacre. It's an unusually long, ornately judgemental, and rather muddled flight of fantasy. Shaka is now suddenly depicted as deliberately designing 'one of his usual inhuman executions, or horrible butcheries'. Only Isaacs seems to see these coming (he now, quite against the evidence in his own account, claims to have 'before been witness to similar proceedings'). Shaka pretends to gather people to build a new 'kraal'; he then informs them that he had a dream about a number of his boys 'having violated the purity of the imperial seraglio'. Shaka is now, Isaacs claims, 'revengeful and unappeasable', a 'diabolical tyrant' embarking on an 'unexampled sanguinary massacre of unoffending beings'. The result of some complicated planning (to every twist of which Isaacs seems rather improbably to be privy): 170 boys and girls, some of them sick, all of them innocent, 'indiscriminately butchered'. Nowhere is the fictionality of this account more evident than here:

> The king at first beat his aged and infirm mother with inconceivable cruelty, and to the astonishment of all, as he had ever manifested towards his parent a strong filial affection. He then became in such a violent and savage rage, that, knowing his want of temper to discriminate objects, and apprehending something for my own personal safety, I withdrew to my hut.[68]

Can this be the same individual who supposedly had cold-bloodedly planned the massacre – or indeed, the same man whose intelligent enquiries, Isaacs himself had written, 'manifested a shrewdness which we little expected to find in an unlettered savage'?[69] I don't think so. Fynn would relate so similar an accusation that we have to conclude that these passages are a product of the later, infamous pact between Fynn and Isaacs to 'make [Shaka] out to be as bloodthirsty as you can'.[70] In fact, as he had had no personal 'ocular demonstration' (in the phrase of the day), Fynn generalised Isaacs's account: 'it has been *no uncommon occurrence* for regiments of soldiers & females to be surrounded & slain on the slightest suspicion of intercourse, in which sometimes not less than 3 000 people suffered where only a few possibly were guilty'. Fynn also claimed that on one occasion 'sixty boys under twelve years of age [were] despatched before breakfast'.[71] James King further related a hearsay story that once Shaka was informed that a certain chief 'had been proved a coward' (though King could assert with all the authority of the ignorant that 'in reality' he had merely been 'overpowered and defeated'). Shaka wiped out the chief and his entire establishment, sparing only women and children. King further pontificated, 'I could also relate many other instances of his barbarity, but they go to such an enormous extent, I feel unwilling to mention them, lest they should be discredited.'[72]

In truth, none of these 'eyewitnesses' could validly claim to have seen anything of the sort. There is no firm evidence here for more than a handful of selective executions. To be fair, these must have been unnerving enough. Isaacs may well have been right that at least some executions were designed specifically to frighten them; Shaka would not have been the first strongman to discover the political value of the occasional random execution.

Isaacs could also have resented being made fun of. On his first visit to Shaka he found him entertaining a Portuguese visitor from Delagoa Bay. Isaacs gathered that the man was employed in some 'military office' but claimed merely to be purchasing cattle. It's an interesting moment: symbolic, almost, of the swing that Shaka would start to make from Delagoa Bay to Port Natal as his main trading centre. Shaka had great fun making arbitrary marks on paper and teasing the two Europeans when they couldn't decipher them. He tried to get them to wrestle. He later enjoyed the joke of scaring his white visitors, while on a hunt, by pretending that they were about to be charged by buffalo.[73] With a sense of humour like that, we might discern greater irony than Isaacs did in Shaka's approval of King George the Fourth's widowed status. Shaka said, 'I see it is the custom of all warriors to abstain from cohabiting with women.' Isaacs adds disdainfully, 'This was said with a smile, and indicated that he did not accord with the precept, nor profit much by the example', since he almost immediately disappeared into his 'palace' with a bevy of compliant girls.[74]

The other persistent theme of Isaacs's account is the rigidity of the hierarchy. He attributed this entirely to Shaka's tyrannical power, missing its history and its subtleties. He did, however, note with some acuteness Shaka's body language, his seating position at the head of the cattle enclosure on a rolled-up mat, his concern not to show too much enthusiasm in public about the whites' paltry gifts. He observed the subservience of the women and the character of their brass ornaments. He also noticed the behaviour of the people who attended Shaka. This passage, although probably refurbished by the ghost-writer, retains a certain credibility:

> Three boys came [to Shaka] with water, carrying it over their heads with their arms extended, which I perceived was the usual way they bore everything to the king. One held a broad black dish before him, while another poured in water for his majesty to wash, and a third stood ready with a further supply in case of need, holding it in the position before described, without daring to put it down.
>
> Chaka, while bathing from head to foot, conversed with his people near him. After this was concluded, another attendant came, bearing a basket, which he presented at arm's length. His Majesty took from it a sort of red coloured paste, with which he ornamented, or rather besmeared his body, but kept rubbing until the whole had disappeared. After this another attendant came with some greasy substance, which the king likewise applied to his body, over which he rubbed it, and this gave him a fine glossy appearance.[75]

Despite the bulk of Isaacs's accounts, there is quite frankly not much more of cultural or historical value to be gleaned from them. He was perceptive but blinkered. He rightly but dimly perceived that dreams, communication with the ancestors, and medicinal curses played some part in Zulu society. He tended to dismiss these things with an ill-concealed sneer; we will have to turn again to the Zulu sources to understand more fully Shaka's involvement in these vitally important areas.

Isaacs also noted Shaka's fascination with methods of warfare, especially firearms. He tended either to exaggerate Shaka's interest, or to reduce it to merely childlike curiosity. In reality, Shaka's experiments with guns on vultures and buffaloes were serious enough. They became almost legendary amongst Zulu people:

> Shaka used to have European guns tested by setting them cattle to aim at at various distances. He was fond of seeing the power of a gun, and his intention was to send a regiment of men to England who there would scatter in all directions in order to ascertain exactly how guns were made, and then return to construct some in Zululand.[76]

It was only logical, in Shaka's view, to extract tribute from the whites in the form of firepower for his campaigns. After all, he was doing enough to support them.

As the whites' own accounts show clearly, Shaka consistently gave them cattle to eat. They weren't always very good at feeding themselves, it seemed. They nevertheless were able, with Shaka's help, to establish quite substantial communities.

Zulu perceptions

Fynn first set up an *umuzi* named Mpendwini, near the Mbokodwe stream, in present-day Isipingo. As DINYA recorded it, 'Shaka presented Fynn with three lots of cattle which were driven to his home (Port Natal), one herd after the other, to enable Fynn to set up a kraal.'[77] At least one batch of cattle was his reward for participating in the Sikhunyane campaign.[78] Fynn became known as 'Mbuyazi' or 'Mbulazi', usually translated as 'Long-tailed finch of the Bay' or something similar. This sounds innocuous enough, except that it refers to the 'butcher-bird', the Fiscal shrike, notorious for impaling its live prey on thorns. In short, Fynn was 'The Killer', as the traveller Andrew Smith recorded.[79] Or, as one of his companions' sons put it, Fynn 'was the one given permission [by Shaka] to kill others'.[80] Fynn and his followers became known as the *iziNkumbi* – The Locusts.[81] Fynn acquired an *induna*, Juqula kaNqawe, and other adherents. One was Pambo (or Ngungwini) kaMngane of the Xolo people: 'This man Pambo used to go about with Mbuyazi when going to join Shaka's *impi* with guns.' Another fighter who likewise went with them was one Mrabula (or Coywana).[82] (So much for Isaacs's and Maclean's strident denial of the missionary Stephen Kay's accusations that *any* of the whites had been acting as mercenaries; Maclean was probably the only one who did not.)

Of course, as far as Shaka and the Zulu were concerned, Fynn's aggressiveness was all to the good; he was useful and therefore admired, hence the tenor of his *izibongo*:

> Prince of the Bay!
> Finch that came from Pondoland.
> Traveller who will never go home.
> Ahungered, he eats the spinach of the river.
> (Finch who does not beg like the Kafirs)
> Throbbing as if it were the heavens thundering.
> Bull calf with the broad body,
> Feathers, now growing, now falling out.
> Tamer of the evil-tempered elephant.
> Who was pregnant with many young ones,
> Who increased river by river . . .[83]

These praises were printed as an epigraph to *The Diary of Henry Francis Fynn*. They allude to Fynn's aggression, to his hunting, to his shaving and growing his whiskers, and to the area that he acquired, more or less in local 'warlord' style.

Fynn also acquired 'four or five' wives, but we have been left with none of their names. His eldest daughter was named Nomanga. A son, Mpahlwa, was born during the Sikhunyane campaign in August 1826. He must have been conceived around December 1825, which shows that Fynn hadn't wasted time in settling in.[84] A son, and perhaps other children, died during his flight from Dingane in 1831.[85] 'Wohlo and Mbuyazi [Henry Ogle and Fynn]', according to DINYA, 'had the largest number of wives.'

Sexual intercourse with these wives took place on the Zulu plan; that is, any woman required would be specially sent for. She would at nightfall come to the man's house. The man would not go about to each woman's hut from time to time, carrying his blanket with him, as less important men are in the habit of doing.[86]

This makes a mockery of Ogle and Fynn's defence against Kay's accusations that they had also 'gone native'. In fact – as Kay alleged – they adopted native dress. Fynn habitually wore an *umutsha* leather loincloth when he visited Shaka; it was the dress-code, and Fynn conformed.[87]

Henry Ogle built up three *imizi*; one of his sons, who eventually took charge, was named 'Tshaka' after the Zulu *inkosi*.[88] That these *imizi* were also at Shaka's pleasure is reflected in MCOTOYI's perception that one *umuzi*, eZembeni, was 'Wohlo's *and* Shaka's'.[89] Shaka thought of Ogle as his *isicaca sasendlini* – the 'poor one of the home'.[90] John Cane (Jana) was also prolific. King (Kamu Kengi) built an *umuzi*, Esihlengeni, on the Bluff,[91] and gathered a small force of his own.

Farewell, who faithfully took no wives, built a more 'European' enclosure of *uhluma* wood, named Isinyama. (It stood where the courthouse was later built.) He soon gathered some adherents. Among them were Jadilili kaPudwa of the local Thuli people, Ndandane kaMantiyane of the Maphumulo, and Mdliwa kaMagoda of the nearby Khanyaweni.[92] It's debatable whether these people had been ravaged into poverty by Zulu or iziYendane raids, or were appointed by Shaka. The reality is perhaps a mix of the two. All of the whites would claim that they had rescued destitute refugees. It became part of their very identity. William BAZELY told James Stuart: 'Fynn, I know for a fact, saved thousands of the homeless wretches who were wandering about the country, a prey to wild animals and, worse, wild animals of their own species – cannibals.'[93] It is virtually impossible that these few whites, who couldn't even get a proper garden going and were riven with factional squabbles, would on their own have had the resources to rescue anyone. Moreover, if there were 'thousands' of these people, the country would hardly have appeared so depopulated. There were probably never more than a few thousand living there even in its prime. Rather, the reverse was true: Shaka sent people to them, and allowed them to gather a few wanderers and to breed children, not out of some quasi-mystical intrinsic respect, but because he could then demand tribute in the form of ivory and firepower.

In mid-1826, he began to call for their presence again.

THE SIKHUNYANE ATTACK

'Shaka has overcome you, for you are an old man. He will not overcome my age-grade.'

These were, you might recall, the boastful words of Sikhunyane, Zwide's son and heir. Once Zwide had died in mid-1825, Sikhunyane apparently lost no time in renewing the Ndwandwe threat to the Zulu. We hardly have a clue about what happened in the old Ndwandwe area, just south of the Phongolo river. The scattered Zulu amakhanda along Shaka's northern boundary, if it can be called that, seemed not to suffer any attacks, but full Zulu control scarcely crossed the Black Mfolozi.

In any event, Sikhunyane started re-establishing a coherent Ndwandwe presence just north of the Phongolo, in the eZindololwane hills. What the balance of aggression and counter-aggression was is difficult to see now. If we can trust James Saunders King on this point, by the end of 1825, or at the latest the first few months of 1826, Sikhunyane had already made several attacks, 'but they had always been repulsed'.[94] And if we can trust Nathaniel Isaacs's chronology, the first intimation that he got that Sikhunyane was pushing south in threatening numbers was in April 1826.[95] At the time, Isaacs was – at Shaka's behest – making bizarre but sterling efforts to manhandle a boat across country from isiBubulungu to kwaBulawayo. The impending Ndwandwe attack, Isaacs insinuates, is why Shaka needed the boat: it would be available for him to escape in. Unhappily for this plan, at one of the stops, the boat broke free of its moorings and was lost down the flooded Thukela river.

Meanwhile, messengers were braving the surging rivers to call all available fighting men, white and black, to defend the capital.[96]

Fynn recorded that on his arrival at kwaBulawayo, he saw 'Umpoonjas', a brother of Sikhunyane's who had defected to khonza Shaka. This was presumably Somaphunga kaZwide.[97] According to JANTSHI, Somaphunga khonza'd only after Sikhunyane's defeat,[98] although the process of khonzaing may have involved longer negotiations than the sources suggest. Somaphunga's defection may well evidence a succession dispute within the Ndwandwe polity, of which Shaka decided to take advantage.[99]

If Isaacs's timing is at all reliable, Shaka was not so pressured that he could not make further inquiries about the properties of certain medicines, marvel at the *Mary's* figurehead (which, scratching for gifts, the whites had carried all the way up from the wreck), have fun with his women, and observe an attempt to shoot some vultures. According to Isaacs, Shaka was only going to make his advance on Sikhunyane at the full moon. Shaka did not participate in whatever skirmishes were going on, receiving reports on how close the enemy had got, and at one point interpreting a wind-blown flurry of small white flowers as 'a sign the enemy had retreated from his position'. While the 'war' was going on, they shot at buffalo and humorously discussed God, reviewed cattle, and welcomed three more 'regiments of boys', all with black shields, some 6 000 of them in Isaacs's estimation:

> The respective corps were distinguished by the shape and ornament of their caps. One regiment had them in the shape of Malay hats, with a peak on the crown about six inches high, and a bunch of feathers at the top. Another wore a turban made of otter-skin, having a crane-feather or two on each side; and the third wore small bunches of feathers over the whole head, made fast by means of small ties. Thus accoutred and distinguished, they entered the gate, ran up to the kraal, halted in front of the palace, and saluted the king . . .[100]

Only when the *impi* had returned, bringing with them booty of cattle, did Shaka let Isaacs go. By 17 April he was back at Port Natal, disappointed to find that the naval vessel the *Helicon* had called in the meantime, and borne away his father-figure, James King.

Back in Cape Town, King was negotiating for another vessel. He had arrived there on the *Helicon* with a seventeen-year-old lad from the Zulu country, who apparently had been taken aboard at Port Natal, but not permitted to disembark before they left.[101] His name was probably Nasaphongo, and he was classified a 'servant'.[102] King applied to purchase a schooner, *Frances*. He was sick, he said; he needed a quick reply.[103] 'The crew of my wrecked vessel are now wandering for sustenance amongst the tribes inhabiting the coast at Natal,' he wheedled; 'as the delegate of British seamen in distress in a savage land I throw myself upon the government of this colony.'[104] It is little wonder, then, that he inserted a passage in his July article for the *South African Commercial Advertiser*, which I have already quoted (on page 327), abruptly maligning Shaka's 'despotism'. It was more fiction than fact, drummed up on the spur of the moment to support his case that his comrades were in deep trouble. Eventually, on 22 July, he signed a contract with his usual business partner, John Thomson, to hire a 93-ton schooner, *Ann*, on condition that she be back within three months. It was only on 6 October that the *Ann* arrived at Port Natal.[105]

In the meanwhile, King's comrades had been off fighting Sikhunyane in earnest.

The summons from Shaka had come on 13 June. It was preceded, according to Isaacs, by another internal fracas in the trader community. One of two 'Hottentots', Michael, who had gone with Fynn to see Shaka, had drunk himself on native beer into a rowdy state and provoked an unseemly scuffle. Shaka, says Isaacs, 'pursued a very impartial course', though when the unruly Hottentots actually assaulted Fynn, he was inclined to have them simply killed. He allowed Farewell to exercise his leader's rights, however, and the miscreants got off with lashes, in good Royal Navy style.[106]

This bit of idiocy was overshadowed by the call to general arms. Shaka had evidently decided to take the fight to Sikhunyane, again (I suspect some doctoring of Isaacs's text here) at the full moon, so it was another month before anyone actually left Port Natal. Isaacs was first requested to take Shaka the Europeans' tent, which (in Isaacs's rather patronising view) Shaka thought 'would strike his enemy with dismay and panic'.[107] There is no evidence that it was ever used for this purpose. The oddities of chronology may also, as Wright speculates, indicate that the whites were portraying more aggression from the Ndwandwe than actually existed, in order to conceal the outright aggression of their own northward raid: 'It was Shaka's response not to an actual Ndwandwe invasion but to the threat of one, and also to the possibility that Sikhunyana was giving support to his internal enemies.'[108]

Shaka was busy drilling troops, seventeen *amabutho* numbering some 30 000 men in Isaacs's untutored estimation (or fevered imagination). As already mentioned, Isaacs then tried to leave, but Shaka had other ideas. Isaacs presents the incident as the whimsy of a tyrant, but there was more to it than that. The account is inadvertently revealing:

> I had no alternative but to return or excite the king's wrath, I chose the former, when his majesty began to abuse us, and told me that we were liars, and were afraid of war. I said we feared nothing but our King, who had sent us to get ivory, and to make friends; we therefore did not like to disobey his orders. 'Well,' said he, 'if you want to make friends you will go with me to engage my enemies, and then you will have me for your friend; but if otherwise, you will make me your enemy.' I saw that he was determined I should accompany him to meet his opponents; I, therefore, told him that I was willing to go with him, but that I must first return home to prepare for the expedition. He agreed, telling me to return with Lieutenant King's party, and that he did not wish Mr Farewell to come, as he was too much like an old woman.[109]

Shaka's logic scythes through the white boy's fraudulent appeal to King George the Fourth's entirely irrelevant laws.

Fynn's arguments, as he recounts them in the 'Notebook', are so similar that I suspect further collusion between the two writers. Fynn's account is both more cryptic and more politically fraught.[110] He also claims that he argued with Shaka about the legal propriety of their fighting for him, but 'our explanations as to our Countrys laws only proved to us by his answers that the more willing we appeared to go with him the better it would be as his replies to our arguments became unpleasant'. In Shaka's view, 'it was a custom of *his* Country when the King went in person to war every able man in his dominions should proceed with him'. And when Farewell refused to give Msimbithi, the ubiquitous interpreter, a musket, it was 'taken from [him] by force'. Shaka did ease the tensions a little by then reassuring the whites that they wouldn't have to fight, just go with him.[111] Little of this rings true. Fynn had already violated the laws of his country on several counts, and it would not be the last time that he, Farewell, Isaacs and other of their followers, both white and black, fought alongside Zulu warriors. They may have been dependent on Shaka, but they were also in it for gain; and fight they surely did.

The Zulu force set off to confront Sikhunyane sometime in September 1826. There is a curious account of the Zulu departure, rich with the symbolism of war-dress and of uprooting, and indicative of the care taken to doctor the army satisfactorily:

> Shaka said to Zihlandhlo, 'Shall we hold a dance together?' Zihlandhlo then collected his people and went to Shaka who was at Bulawayo. Shaka directed Zihlandhlo to sleep there. Next day Shaka sent a messenger to tell Zihlandhlo to go to the meeting-place (isigcau), a place on a hill nearby, where the dancing was to go on. Zihlandhlo went to the spot. People then arrived from Shaka, wearing horns on their heads, like cattle. The people then fought in imitation of bulls fighting. Other people went on all fours, in imitation of dogs fighting. Others came carrying reed pipes; these they played by blowing into them. After this Shaka himself appeared with his men. He came into the semi-circle which had been formed. The Zulus then danced. Shaka exclaimed after a while, 'This is no meeting place, my mnawe.' Shaka then passed on with his troops to search for another spot where the ground resounded. On coming to another spot he tried it but said again, 'This is unsuitable.' And so they went on and on till they had gone some 20 miles or so. He came to a garden of ripe mabele. He then pointed with his stick and gave a loud whistle. The troops took hold of the mabele plants and pulled them out. Still carrying the plants, they performed an inkondlo dance. He then directed them to put them down. The inkondlo was then performed in the garden (no longer a garden!). Shaka then said, 'O! My mnawe, I am going to war. I am making war on Sikhunyana. He has returned, for I drove out his father.' He then prepared the army, and went off with it in the night. That is, he started straight from there on his expedition. He did not rest until dawn, having walked through the night.[112]

They first headed for Nobamba, the ancestral heartland umuzi where the troops, as tradition dictated, would first gather to be doctored for war. The divisions were then sent off by a variety of routes, spies fanning out ahead of them. Boys (carriers known as *udibi*) and women came on behind – a complement of 50 000 in total, Fynn exaggerated.[113] Dust hung about them; thirst raged; some boys were trampled to death in a rush for a slick of marshy water. Farewell (who had come along after all) got stamped on by a cow and retired from the field. They marched in 'immense bustle & confusion' until nine at night, camping at the settlement of 'a once powerful nation, the Isindani, of whom no more than 150 or 200 souls now remained'.[114] They crossed a treeless plain; men died of cold in the night. Finally, they rested for two days amongst forests on the edge of Ndwandwe territory, in a huge cave on a mountain named 'Ingualla qua Hawana' (Inqaba ka Hawana) or Hawana's Cave 'from the Chief of that name who some years back revolted and defended himself from attack by the capabilitys [sic] of the Cave'.[115] For the first time in a while they ate corn, plundered from enemy granaries. Shaka had recently called up the Bhekenya *ibutho*:

> When he got to within two or three miles of Sikhunyana, who had taken refuge in a stronghold with stones about it, on the opposite side of the Mhlongamvula stream, he gave orders to the Bekenya boys to scatter and seize *amabele* from the neighbouring kraals and gardens. He told them to bring it back and cook it where he was. Numbers complied, but many did not. They slept in the gardens etc and only got back early next day just as he was sending out his *impi*. He ordered all those who had not come back to go into a gully where they were all killed, then he proceeded to attack Sikhunyana.[116]

Is this merely another donga legend? At any rate, the following day they began to gather for the impending battle.

Fynn is extremely vague about the geography, but Zulu informants are more or less agreed that the encounter took place at eZindololwane, north of the Phongolo river where it is joined by the Bivana and Mtolo rivers.[117] Shaka was not without local support: he had come to an agreement with Manzini kaTshana of the Zungu, who had defected from Zwide.[118] Otherwise, we know almost nothing about who took part, other than the Nomdayana *ibutho*.[119] The three substantial accounts that we do have of the battle – Fynn's,

Maclean's and MBOKODO's – are considerably at variance, and it's interesting
to lay them beside each other. For military enthusiasts who are keen on
studying exemplary tactics (or on proving Shaka a military genius), the
eZindololwane battle is a disappointment.

Shaka prudently retired to a nearby hilltop to watch proceedings, pulling
back later into the forest itself. He learned of the battle only by report. Possibly
Zihlandlo was with him. Shaka said to him, 'As for you, my *mnawe*, you shall
guard me. I shall send the whole of the Zulus to Sikhunyana.'[120] Possibly
Manzini of the Zungu was with him, too.[121] Fynn's version is singularly
unedifying:

> The hill from which we had first seen the enemy presented to our
> view an extensive valley, to the left of which was a hill separated by
> another valley from an immense mountain. On the upper part of
> this there was a rocky eminence, near the summit of which the enemy
> had collected all his forces, surrounding their cattle; and above them
> the women and children of the nation in a body. They were sitting
> down awaiting the attack. Chaka's forces marched slowly and with
> much caution, in regiments, each regiment divided into companies,
> until within twenty yards of the enemy, when they made a halt.
> Although Chaka's troops had taken up a position so near, the enemy
> seemed disinclined to move, till Jacob had fired at them three times.
> The first and second shots seemed to make no impression on them,
> for they only hissed, and cried in reply, 'That is a dog.' At the third
> shot, both parties, with a tumultuous yell, clashed together, and
> continued stabbing each other for about three minutes, when both
> fell back a few paces. Seeing their losses about equal, both armies
> raised a cry, and this was followed by another rush, and they continued
> closely engaged about twice as long as in the first onset, when both
> parties again drew off. But the enemy's loss had now been the more
> severe. This urged the Zulus to a final charge. The shrieks now became
> terrific. The remnant of the enemy's army sought shelter in an
> adjoining wood, out of which they were soon driven. Then began a
> slaughter of the women and children. They were all put to death.[122]

Charles Rawden Maclean's version, heard second-hand and related apparently from memory much later, needs to be treated cautiously, but it's intriguingly different in its nuances from Fynn's. Maclean – having presumably been informed by Fynn in the first place – ironically seems more likely to be closer to the truth:

> It appears that the battle was fought in the night, so that the services of the fire-armed men on that occasion were not called into requisition. The enemy fought with great obstinacy and bravery, equal in every respect to the Zulus, but the superior discipline and practice of the latter in war prevailed over the more uninitiated forces of the Izeecanyana [Sikhunyane]. The latter were beaten and almost totally annihilated, no quarter being given or received. The brave fellows, even when wholly discomfited, scorned to seek safety in flight, and even the women stepped into the ranks and filled up the gaps occasioned by their falling husbands; the old chief alone, at the earnest persuasion of a handful of devoted followers, saved himself when the field was irretrievably lost.[123]

Maclean was told that too much confusion in the dark was avoided by the Zulu having a countersign (as they did in the 'kisi' battle), giving them a distinct advantage. Only one Zulu was mistakenly shot by a 'Hottentot' in the mêlée. At the end, according to Maclean, some 3 000 Ndwandwe were dead, and about half of the 5 000 Zulu warriors involved.[124] The discrepancy with Fynn's allegation of the numbers involved is striking. It is likely that Fynn deliberately exaggerated them in his writings.

MBOKODO offers something slightly different and, in tactical terms, rather less deft:

> After being prepared, the troops left, forming two horns, and surrounded that mountain. Before they could surround the mountain, Sikhunyana escaped. Shaka saw him flee. The two horns met and began stabbing one another, for the people, being very numerous, did not know one another. But they soon discovered, and desisted. Sikhunyana himself had escaped, but his impi had been hemmed in.

'Kill off every soul,' said Shaka, 'woman and child.' He wanted nothing of Sikhunyana's to survive. The *impi* went and finished them all off. Shaka then directed the troops to follow after Sikhunyana, but they failed to overtake him. [125]

This does not reflect particularly well on Shaka's supposed military genius. A clash of brave but uninteresting attrition; or – in the *one, solitary* case in which Shaka's forces *might* have used the 'classic' horns formation – they end up stabbing each other. Indeed, if we are to believe MAGOJELA, the victory wasn't won by the Zulu at all, but by the Zungu forces of Mfanawendhlela kaManzini, with his amaNketshane *ibutho*. Shaka then saw them as a threat, and would later call Manzini to kwaBulawayo, and kill him. [126]

A fourth brief version, little more than an anecdote, is footnoted by James Stuart in *The Diary of Henry Francis Fynn*, a story concerning the hero Nohadu (or Noradu), an *inceku* to Shaka (and to his successors). It was related by the hero's son: [127]

Among the regiments directed to attack Sikhunyana's army, when concealed in the forest, was one called Izimpholo, of which my father, Nohadu was a member. As it charged Sikhunyana's forces appeared at the edge of the forest drawn up in wall-like formation. As the Izimpholo got close up, the enemy flung a shelf of assegais at them. (The assegais coming simultaneously and horizontally from so many looked like a shelf.) One of these struck Nohadu in the ankle. His assailant turned quickly (like the others) to retreat into the forest, but only as quickly to become entangled in monkey-ropes at the edge of the forest. Seeing this, Nohadu, instead of stopping to withdraw the assegai, rushed, assegai and all, after his foe and forthwith stabbed him to death. Shaka happened to see all this, also the colour of Nohadu's shield, from the hill where he was watching the battle. When all was over, discussing the various incidents, Shaka remarked, 'Whose was that *hemu* (light and dark shield) I saw at the edge of the forest?' Nohadu being present, claimed it as his. This proved to be indeed the case. Shaka, thereupon, directed his war doctor to look for a suitable beast for his hero to kill and so conform to yet another Zulu custom known as *ukuncinda*. [128]

Apart from this perhaps apocryphal boast, we know little more about the participants in the battle. We also do not have enough information to even begin to reconcile the differences between these accounts. It was largely a success for the Zulu forces, evidently, though at the cost of considerable exhaustion. To add insult to casualties, the main target – Sikhunyane himself – got away. Some informants do claim that Sikhunyane was captured and killed,[129] but according to NGIDI, he went off into Mzilikazi's territory, and built an *umuzi* at Nhlabangekanda, a stream near the Nzwabuhlungu, where he would eventually be attacked by Dingane.[130]

Fynn thought that the whole Ndwandwe nation numbered maybe 40 000, and estimated that 60 000 cattle were taken. How he could calculate this in the confusion – in which he says himself 'parties of 3, 4 and 5' were swarming about 'killing cattle and cutting off the tails of others to make their war dress'[131] – is difficult to say. We have to balance this against Maclean's recollection that only 1 500 head were captured.[132] Even if we assume that we're seeing Fynn's usual exaggeration, and we halve the numbers involved, the Sikhunyane attack was a major expedition on Shaka's part, perhaps the most ambitious of his reign. That firearms were involved remains probable, despite the denials. That Fynn was himself involved in the fighting is implied in the tradition that he was rewarded with some of the so-called 'Usuthu' cattle captured in the raid.[133] Shaka was already using Fynn as another client-chief to help control and plunder specific areas in the south. The use of firearms in battle was a new bonus.

The aftermath of the eZindololwane battle has attracted several stories of Shaka's brutality. Even if we accept them at face value, it seems to be the *only* occasion in all the encounters reviewed in this history where a slaughter of women and children is unambiguously said to have been ordered by Shaka. All other references to this kind of behaviour are generalities that simply can't be credited. Maclean, however, makes no mention of any such massacre, only that the crops of this largely agricultural people were razed to 'a barren and desolate wilderness', and in this way the Ndwandwe 'entirely annihilated'. In any case, there *were* survivors who, Shaka proclaimed, 'should be spared and received as his children, and worthy of becoming the companions of Zulu warriors'. Indeed, adding 'these brave men to his band of warriors' was Shaka's 'primary and only motive'.[134]

Shaka is also said to have killed off malingerers: 'When the troops got back, Shaka said to Zihlandlo, "Some people fell on their backs; others shuffled around with bent knees, pretending to be ill".'[135] As for the killing of cowards, we have only Fynn's testimony, which must be treated with extreme caution:

> Early next morning Chaka arrived, and each regiment, previous to its inspection by him, had picked out its 'cowards' and put them to death. Many of those, no doubt, forfeited their lives only because their chiefs were in fear that, if they did not condemn some as being guilty, they would be suspected of seeking a pretext to save them, and would incur the resentment of Chaka. No man who had been actually engaged in the fight was allowed to appear in the king's presence until a purification by the doctor had been undergone. This doctor gave each warrior certain roots to eat, and to every one who had actually killed an enemy an additional number. To make their bravery as public as possible, bits of wood are worn around the neck, each bit being supposed to reckon for an enemy slain. To the ends of this necklace are attached bits of the root received from the doctor, part of which had been eaten; they then proceed to some river to wash their persons; and until this has been done, they may not eat any food except the meat of cattle killed on the day of battle. Having washed, they appear before the king, when thanks or praise are the last thing they have to expect; censure being loudly expressed on account of something that had not been done as it should have been; and they get well off if one or two chiefs and a few dozen soldiers are not struck off the army list by being put to death.[136]

Fynn, concerned mostly to underline his own gentle humanity and Shaka's abominable ferocity, related one more incident:

> During the afternoon [after the battle], a woman and a child of the defeated tribe, the latter aged about ten years, were brought before the king, and he made every enquiry respecting Sikhunyana: what had been his plans when he heard of the intended attack, and what

was the general feeling as to its result. To induce her to set aside all fear, he gave her some beer and a dish of beef, which she ate, while giving all the information she was possessed of. When her recital was finished, both mother and child were sentenced to instant death. Being present, I begged the life of the child, that it might become my servant. An application to save the life of both was little likely to succeed.[137]

Whatever the truth and scale of these incidents, Shaka had clearly delivered a shattering blow to the Ndwandwe polity. Having evicted the father, he had now crushed the son. Probably many Ndwandwe khonza'd and stayed in the area; others fled. It was this event, at any rate, that all but destroyed Ndwandwe memory, and explains why so little in the way of Ndwandwe oral tradition has survived. In addition, it may well be that some of them were reduced to destitution and sold off to the slavers. Although we have no direct evidence for this, it is otherwise difficult to explain how the structure of the polity, which had been the most persistent in the region, so comprehensively vanished.

It seems simplistic – indeed untenable – to attribute its disappearance entirely to a single massacre ordered by Shaka.

TRADE WARS

It is more than possible that Delagoa Bay slavers were then within striking range of the defeated Ndwandwe. We left our discussion of the Delagoa Bay situation at around the end of 1823 (see Chapter 8, page 252). What had happened there since? How deep was Shaka's involvement?

The settlement made by Captain Owen in Delagoa Bay in 1823, having been subsequently destroyed, a connection is stated to have been formed between the Portuguese and the French slave traders, and a marauding system commenced, the object of which was the capture of peaceable tribes inhabiting the interior of that part of Africa, to which cause has been attributed the appearance since 1823, of great numbers of starving people upon the frontier of the Cape Colony.

The slave traders at Delagoa Bay, are said to have gone out in armed parties to drive off their cattle, and destroy their grain, in the expectation that a large proportion of these wretched people would repair to the coast, in quest of subsistence, where they might be seized and embarked in the slaving vessels. A vessel of this colony (the 'Walter Farquhar'), engaged in the slave trade at Bourbon, was wrecked on her return from Delagoa Bay on the southern coast of Madagascar, and 116 negroes taken from her were brought to Mauritius by His Majesty's ship Ariadne, and condemned in the Vice Admiralty Court in 1825.[138]

On 28 August 1825, Captain W.F.W. Owen of the Royal Navy sailed for his last time into Delagoa Bay. If he had been in any doubt about the volume of slaving from this misbegotten port before, he wasn't now: 'In every succeeding visit since our first arrival at Delagoa, we had observed that the natives were becoming still more unhappy; many, it appeared, had voluntarily sold themselves into slavery in order to avoid the miseries of starvation: for so great had been the ravages of the Hollontontes . . .'[139]

'Voluntarily' sounds a bit simplistic. The dynamic is better captured by the case of Makhasane, the long-lived Tsonga leader who 'paid tribute first to Zululand' but when famine struck, 'arrested some of his people and sold them [as slaves] for food'.[140] The fundamental factor was that, whatever the normal ravages of climatic fluctuations, famine was deliberately brought about by human warfare, in order to create slaves. As we saw, figures are sketchy, but those that we do have suggest that between 1820 and 1822 trade boomed, coinciding with the movement of the 'Ndwandwe' slavers towards the Bay. About 13 000 slaves a year were being exported from Mozambique and the minor ports. There was a slight dip between 1823 and 1827, with a resurgence in 1828 (24 000 that year) which extended into the 1830s.[141] The dip may be deceptive: in 1826–7 alone, at least 35 French vessels bore slaves away from Quelimane, maybe 7 000 people in all, and it seems likely that the smaller ports suffered similar expansion.[142] These figures don't isolate Delagoa Bay's contribution, but there is every reason to suppose that the Bay followed the general trend. By 1825 slaves were its main export; substantial volumes of beads and bangles were coming in. Though most of the slaves were probably coming from Soshangane, north of the Bay, we don't know how far *he* was raiding or trading for his slaves.

Many of the slaves were now going to Brazil. Between 1795 and 1811, the east African ports had provided only 3 per cent of Rio de Janeiro's slave imports. Between 1825 and 1830, this had risen to 25 per cent.[143] During this same period, Rio alone received 4 031 recorded slaves from Delagoa Bay. Added to this are other Brazilian ports like Pernambuco and Bahia, as well as the trade on French vessels to the Arab world, India, and the Mascarene islands. (Owen narrowly missed a French slave vessel in the Bay in August 1825, carrying 130 slaves bound for Bourbon [Réunion]; and just before that a particularly infamous Mauritian slaver named Dorval.[144]) In 1828 alone, twelve *known* French vessels left Delagoa Bay, carrying 2 400 slaves between them.[145] Add the Dutch, North American and Caribbean complements, which remain uncalculated but were probably substantial. (The Americans' presence in the Indian Ocean was obvious enough to make them appear to some to be *the* major threat to British maritime control.) In addition, there were the clandestine shipments that no one, anywhere, ever recorded. Patrick Harries's estimate of 1 000 slaves a year being shipped from each of the east coast ports during the 1820s begins to look conservative. Consider, finally, a contemporary observer's view that for every slave shipped five people died, and the impact on inland populations begins to look quite devastating. John Cane, passing though from Port Natal to Delagoa Bay in July 1827, reported that the hinterland of the Bay was decimated.[146]

Moreover, it's highly unlikely that the slaves all came from the immediate vicinity of the Bay, any more than the ivory did. They also came from well inland.[147] As we've seen, trade links practically spanned the subcontinent. Mzilikazi, living by the mid-1820s at the headwaters of the Vaal, had been (Dr John Philip reported) engaged in 'constant wars' with 'slavers on the coast'.[148] Philip didn't think that Mzilikazi himself was engaged in slaving, but in other accounts Mzilikazi is said to have kept in quite close touch with the Jere and Gaza groups and regarded them as 'relatives', so it is not impossible. At the same time, he was beginning to get harassed by slaving raiders, armed and on horseback, from the west: Bergenaars, Griquas, and Taung. The north-western fringes of Shaka's sphere of influence were becoming increasingly subject to a pincer movement of slavers and ivory hunters, with the effects rippling down as far as the headwaters of the Thukela. As we've already mentioned, marauders were even penetrating along the foothills of the Drakensberg and as far as the headwaters of the Kei river, alarmingly close to the colonial border.

In the meantime, however, there was plenty of traffic, both peaceful and not so peaceful, to and from Delagoa Bay along the coastal trade routes. There were people from Delagoa Bay offering tribute to Shaka at Gibixhegu in September 1824.[149] Isaacs found that Portuguese or mestizo trader already mentioned at Gibixhegu in 1825.[150] More white men from the Bay were reported approaching Shaka's *umuzi* at kwaBulawayo in late 1825.[151] (They were given, apparently, a cool reception by Shaka.) A Zulu raiding party 'north-west of Delagoa', probably along the upper reaches of the Phongolo river, ran into 'yellow people on horses' almost unquestionably raiding for slaves, in March 1827; and, later that year, another hunting party from the Bay was encountered by Isaacs on the Mhlathuze river.[152] Zulu contacts up the coast were extensive but peaceful, if it's true that Makhasane's people were in some respects adopting Zulu habits such as the headring – even as they were adapting certain Portuguese quirks to local use.[153]

The Port Natal traders themselves were getting though to the Bay. Farewell sent a man there under Shaka's protection in early 1825.[154] In mid-1826, Shaka handed a letter to Isaacs from Delagoa Bay, written by a Captain Cooledge of the brig *Salisbury* and addressed to Farewell. Cooledge was hoping to drop in on Port Natal. We are not told why.[155] Both Charles Rawden Maclean and John Cane made their way to the Bay in 1827; both found their way aboard French slave ships. Cane, by his own account, had been 'sent on a mission by Chaka', not by the white community.[156] He also (inadvertently, he claimed) offloaded some people onto his slave-ship.[157] Whatever the adventurers might have said, it wasn't that difficult to get to Delagoa Bay. The fourteen-year-old Maclean devoted only three lines to the 'long and somewhat perilous' journey. He found the Bay itself a hellhole.[158]

The question arises, naturally, of whether the Port Natal whites were *actively* engaged in the slave trade – and whether Shaka himself was. In the case of the whites, the probability is high, but the case remains largely circumstantial. Opportunities certainly existed, as did the motive. Though the traders extracted a substantial amount of ivory, it hardly appears to have been enough to sustain them. They tried to acquire uncontrolled access to points of the coast outside Shaka's reach: Fynn in Mpondo territory, King at the mouth of the Mlalazi, which he tried unilaterally to annexe by raising a flag. Most tellingly – though only tantalisingly so – it was reported in June 1826 that slaves had been loaded onto French vessels off the Transkei coast – precisely the area in which Fynn was operating at the time.[159] By 1830, Isaacs at least was unquestionably running guns, and it must be suspected that the process began earlier.[160]

As for Shaka, it can be surmised that he would have been willing to release sworn and captured enemies on his furthest boundaries to slave traders, but given his general policy of trying to gather people up, it seems to me unlikely that he would have slaved on his own account on any great scale. With the exception of the Sikhunyane attack, there is no sign that the Zulu really had the opportunity to offload slaves at Delagoa Bay itself. Other trade items were certainly flowing, and it is possible that slaves were going, too, alongside or even as carriers of ivory or metal. Fynn, writing in the 1830s, claimed that the 'unsettled state' of the country in Shaka's reign meant there were fewer 'blacksmiths' than before. There was nevertheless internal and external trade, working together:

> [T]he iron which is now seldom or ever worked from the Ore is brought to the smith by the person wanting work done which has been taken from the Enemy or picked up at the old habitations and only the work is paid for at an average of an Hefer for 12 Hoes[;] 2 strings of Beads that will encompass round the waist for an Assegai[,] and a string as long as a mans arm for a Neadle or Razor . . . the working of Brass is at an average of 50 or 60 Balls or Beads for a cow[,] and 4 strings of Beads for a Brass collar for the neck[;] the Brass as well as the Iron has been for the most part taken at different times from the Enemy but immense quantities are brought from Delagoa Bay by the natives which they purchase from the Portuguese for Ivory & Slaves . . .[161]

There is, however, no harder evidence. My suspicion is that the isiBubulungu whites' attempts to trade in slaves, along with running guns and trying to subvert his ivory trade controls, was part of what made Shaka increasingly irritated with them. His initial policy, to use the Englishmen as counters in a broader trade and power game – to play them off against the Portuguese, and to gain more direct access to independent English resources – was gradually undermined by their own criminality.

In any case, by late 1826 Shaka, continuing despite his victory over Sikhunyane to feel insecure in the north (the ongoing slave-wars themselves undoubtedly being a perpetual worry), was already contemplating a further move south.

Box 9

Shaka's *amabutho*

It is difficult to compile a complete list of Shaka's *amabutho*: as with his settlements and his *izinduna*, surviving information is scattered and sometimes irreconcilably contradictory. Moreover, units frequently shifted, changed names, or were absorbed one into another, so often our attributions of their relative importance and chronology must remain tentative.[1]

abeSutu	'At our place in the Zulu country we are never satisfied, for we have nothing but bones to crunch'; stayed at Dlangezwa *ikhanda*.
uBhekenya	Formed *c.*1826; went on '*Eyokutshinga*' raid and Mpondo campaign in 1828; shields of black cattle with stomach markings.
Dlangezwa	'The stand of last season's grass'; slightly younger than the Mqumanga; used in the 'Mvuzane fight'.
Dlangubo	Possibly a section; was at the 'Mvuzane fight'.
esiKlebhe	Inherited; elderly men; grey shields, black and white hairs mixed; fought at the 'Mvuzane fight'.
Fasimba	'Distant haze of hills'; Shaka's first own *ibutho*; went on both Mpondo and 'Bhalule' campaigns; all-white shields.
Fojisa	Shields from black cattle with white stomach markings.
Gibabanye	Younger; members still unmarried *c.*1824 when Shaka visited Magaye; formerly the uPoko; shields black with white marks on the sides.
iNtontela	Inherited; combined with Dlangubo by Shaka; 'the eyes of Mbonwa, which saw the Ndwandwe in the river'; was in the 'Mvuzane fight'.
isiPhezi	Older men when first formed under Shaka; had to cut off their headrings.
iziKwembu	Uniform dun-coloured shields (probably section of a larger formation).
iziNyosi	Possibly formed by Shaka, but so named by Dingane in 1828.
iziYendane	Mostly Hlubi; all-red shields; fought at the 'Mvuzane fight'; raided as far as Thuli country; broken up by Shaka.

Jibingqwange	Followed Fasimba in age; had to cut off headrings; speckled grey shields.
Mbelebele	'The headrest of our mothers'; inherited; was at the 'Mvuzane fight' and later campaigns; red-and-brown shields.
Mbonambi	No information; possibly a section.
Mgumanqa	'Which stands threateningly in the stand of burnt grass'; Zulu kaNogandaya's unit; fought at the 'Mvuzane fight'; red shields spotted with white, like the eggs of the *uqelu* bird.
Mkhandlu	Disbanded by Shaka for failing in the first Mpondo expedition.
Mnkhangala	Possibly called up by Senzangakhona; absorbed as a section into other formations.
Ndabezibona	So named because from birth all Shaka saw was *izindaba* (troubles); probably a section of a larger formation; black shields with some white.
Njanduna	Taken over from Magaye of the Cele; killed off by Dingane.
Nqobolondo	Probably a section; *izinsasa* shields, speckled on black.
Tshoyisa	Section of Fojisa; red shields with white markings from upper legs.
uBulawayo	No information.
uGubetuka	No information; probably a section of a larger formation.

Female *amabutho*

Cenyane	Age-grade of Mbonambi; called up at kwaDukuza; took part in the Mpondo campaign in 1828; allowed to marry by Dingane.
Mcekeceke	Age-grade of isiPhezi; Shaka's first; allowed to marry by Dingane.
Mvutwamini	Age-grade of Fasimba; marked with incisions on inside of calf.
Ntshuku	Age-grade of Mgumanqa.

Box 10

Shaka's *izinduna*

In the compilation of this list I differ from Carolyn Hamilton in a number of inclusions and exclusions.[1] Evidence of whether a man was an *induna* under Shaka or Dingane is often ambiguous. Of the thirty known *izinduna* listed here, five came from close collateral clans, eight from genealogically fairly close peoples, and seven from absorbed peoples – a fair representation of Shaka's balances of power (the origins of the other ten are not known).

Dambuza kaSobadli	Alias Nzoba; iWombe *ibutho*; Ntombela collateral clan; second in command to Mdlaka in Shaka's time; became ranking *induna* in Dingane's time; fought at the battle of Ncome in 1838.
Duzi	Makanya people.
Khokhela kaMncumbata	Ndwandwe; became *induna* of White Hlomendlini; lived under Zulu kaNogandaya; died in Dingane's attack on Mzilikazi in 1836.
Klwana kaNgqengelele	Caya/Buthelezi; headed Mbelebele *ibutho* on *amabece* campaign; continued to do so into Dingane's and Mpande's reigns.
Lukhilimba kaMbasa	Commanded Mdadasa *ibutho* against Zwide; banished to Port Shepstone area.
Madabulela kaQumbumbete	Langeni; *induna* of Bekenya *ibutho*; died on 'Eyokutshinga' raid in 1826.
Mangena kaNokupata	*Inceku* to Shaka; possibly *induna* alongside Mdlaka on 1824 raid against Madikane.
Manqondo kaMazwana	Magwaza section of Langeni; Bulawayo *ibutho*; present at Nandi's burial; became more prominent under Dingane.
Manyundele kaMabuya	Accompanied Shaka and Fynn in pursuit of Ngoza.
Mapitha kaSojiyisa	Mandlakazi; iWombe or Mnakangala *ibutho*; fought Ndwandwe; given Ndwandwe territories in trust; accompanied Shaka on *ihlambo* campaign.

Maqoboza kaMbekelo	Nzuza; *induna* of kwaDlangezwa *ibutho*; killed on '*Eyokutshinga*' raid.
Masawuzana kaMteli	Qwabe; *induna* at Vungameni *umuzi*.
Mbikwana kaKhayi	Langeni; *induna* of Mgumanqa *ibutho*; accompanied Shaka at accession; present at Nandi's burial; wounded at Shaka's assassination and moved away; died at home on the Ngoye.
Mbilini kaCungeya	Mkwanaza section of Mthethwa; *induna* at Nodwengu; Mqumanga *ibutho*; went on Mpondo campaign; survived into Mpande's reign.
Mbuya kaNsungane	Xulu; *induna* of Mkhandlu; killed after Mpondo campaign for cowardice.
Mdlaka kaNcidi	Mdlalose collateral clan; *induna* at esiKlebheni; *induna yezwe* ('*induna* of the nation'); led Mpondo campaign and '*Eyokutshinga*' raid; killed by Dingane in 1829.
Mfetshe kaMutiwensanga	Mthethwa; *induna* of Fojisa and/or Gibabanye *ibutho*.
Mjanyelwa	Cele; died shortly after Shaka.
Mpangazitha kaMncumbata	Ndwandwe; brother of Khokhela; Fasimba *ibutho*; became more prominent under Dingane.
Mthobela kaMthimude	*Induna* of ekuWeleni *umuzi*; oversaw Magaye's Thuli raid.
Mvundlana kaMenziwa	Mdlalose/Biyela collateral clan; possibly *induna* of Mgumanqa, under Dingane of iziNyosi; accompanied Shaka on Mpondo campaign.
Mxamama kaSotshaya	*Induna* of kwaDlangezwa; accompanied Shaka on Mpondo campaign; killed alongside Shaka.
Ndlela kaSompisi	Ntuli section of the Bhele; *induna* of whole army; responsible for making the *inkatha*; killed by Dingane, ostensibly for saving Mpande.
Ngomane kaMqomboli	Caya section of Mthethwa; went on Mpondo campaign.

Nomapela	Ndwandwe; *induna* on *amabece* campaign in 1824; killed on Dingane's Swazi foray.
Nombanga kaNgidli	*Induna* of Fasimba; great warrior under Shaka; killed at Ncome river in 1838.
Nquhele kaMqudlana	Mthethwa; headed Mthethwa section that *konza*'d Shaka on Zwide's attack; made *induna* at Empangiweni; Shaka admired him as being as good-looking as a woman.
Sotobe kaMpangalela	Sibiya; accompanied King's 'embassy' in 1828; became second-ranking official under Cetshwayo; died *c*.1856.
Zidunge kaMbikwana	*Induna* of Fasimba, then uBhekenya *ibutho*; went on Mpondo campaign in 1828.
Zulu kaNogandaya	Qwabe; great warrior on Ndwandwe and Mpondo campaigns; fled on Dingane's accession.

12

Moved by grief?

Tending towards aggression, 1826–7

'You kill for your own delight. You are on your way to becoming a
bloodthirsty madman. You are just a savage after all.'
                              Nickie McMenemy, *Assegai!* (1973, 171).

Shaka's southward move from kwaBulawayo to kwaDukuza was surely one
of the most important shifts of his reign – just as important as his first
move southward to Gibixhegu/kwaBulawayo.

> Shaka built his principal Natal kraal where Stanger now stands and
> called it Dukuza. The reason for the name is that when he was at
> Gibixegu kraal in Zululand he was stabbed by Ntintinti kaNkobe.
> The assegai, which he drew out, he recognised as belonging to Sipezi
> where his brothers lived (he had distributed to them this kind of
> assegai). It struck him high up the arm (right, I fancy) above the elbow
> and therefore penetrated the arm and just touched the side. It was
> prevented by his arm from entering his person or side, i.e. it *dukuza*'d.
> *Dukuza* means going astray, going by the way which is not the desired
> one.[1]

MAKEWU's implied explanation for Shaka's move to kwaDukuza is just one of
many theories – most of which can be regarded as unsatisfactory.[2] No one
has really explained why Shaka moved south, rather than, say, north back

into emaKhosini or Mahlabathini, which as far as we can tell were areas by now securely within Zulu control. If the assassination attempt was the reason, why exactly should it have been? If we are correct that the attempt was made in 1824, why would Shaka have waited two or more years to move? It doesn't quite add up.

Yet move he did, in the wake of the 1826 Sikhunyane campaign. He built his new residence on the site of an old *umuzi* of the Cele chieftain Dibhandlela. KwaDukuza was positioned on the summit of a rounded hill overlooking all the other *imizi*, above the Nzololo stream flowing into the Mvoti river, not far from the coast. It was a move to about halfway between kwaBulawayo and isiBubulungu, some 80 kilometres from either place.

> The kraal at Dukuza was a very large one, and was called Fasimba at its nether part and Dukuza in front. The magistracy [of Stanger, now kwaDukuza again] stands on the very spot where the *isigodhlo* was; and on the near side of the house which Mr Wheelwright used to occupy when magistrate here is the spot at which the kraal stood in which Shaka was assassinated. The grave is close to the same place and has a thorn tree growing about or on it.[3]

Nowadays, there is a small museum on the hilltop, several tall acacia trees, and a large grey rock on which Shaka is reputed to have sat while conducting councils.

Shaka established the new 'capital' with the full co-operation of his old friend Magaye. According to Magaye's son, MELAPI, 'When Shaka built Dukuza he said to my father he was to make up songs and that they would hold dances together.' MELAPI, who you will recall was a small child at the time, said that they indeed danced and sang together. Shaka composed this song:

> *Kukuluku*, the cock crowed,
> Who placed it there?
> Vutani and Gubetuka praised him,
> The husband enters,
> You must carry *imincwazi* berries,
> I am not a goat to be made terrified in the kraals,

I am not a gate-keeper such as is selected by kraal-owners;
I am a great warrior there in the Zulu country,
I am foremost in the place of headrings.[4]

Magaye responded with a song of his own, which we have already heard (on page 258). 'With what nations are you going to make war?' he asked. Both songs express sentiments that may well sound more boastful than Shaka actually felt at the time.

THE 'HIDE-AWAY'

We can propose both positive and negative reasons for the move southwards. The positive scenario goes something like this: Shaka, having crushed Sikhunyane, was feeling more secure than he had ever done about his northern territories. He now felt free to start expanding aggressively towards the south. His final raids are a sign of this increased confidence and strength. Moreover, he was shifting towards the Port Natal whites as his primary trading conduit. They were closer than the Portuguese at Delagoa Bay, and everything 'Hlambamanzi' Msimbithi and others must have told him about the British colony far to his south-west would have indicated that the British were a more powerful and viable trading partner. Possibly there were also resources around kwaDukuza that outstripped the value of those around kwaBulawayo – more elephants, perhaps. This positive scenario is founded on attractions *to* the kwaDukuza area, in conjunction with expansionist ambitions.

A more negative scenario is founded on repulsion *away from* the kwaBulawayo area. KwaBulawayo may have been running low on available resources such as grazing or firewood. Far from feeling secure about the north (the negative scenario continues), Shaka continued to feel *insecure*. His victory over Sikhunyane had exhausted his forces; he was aware that the violence emanating from Delagoa Bay was, as we have seen, escalating. Though the whites and their trading links (still more potential than actual) were attractive, they were also proving to be a nuisance; they were increasingly in need of closer control. Their attempts at ivory trading were certainly getting out of hand, even as they became potentially more profitable for the *inkosi* himself.

Of course, there might well have been a combination of positive as well as negative reasons working together. Such evidence as we have – and it's surprisingly thin – tends to support the negative rather than the positive scenario. As we will see, apart from consolidating settlements in already friendly Cele territory in the vicinity of kwaDukuza, Shaka made no major aggressive or colonising forays southwards for another two years. The naming of the place is one possible clue: if indeed 'dukuza' means something like 'Gone astray', or 'One who has gone astray', that would indicate insecurity rather than triumph. However, the name may simply have been borrowed from a predecessor in the Mahlabathini area.[5]

Henry Francis Fynn dates the move only to the end of 1827, after (and because of) the death of Shaka's mother Nandi.[6] By contrast, Nathaniel Isaacs indicates a move of about a year earlier, around October 1826. The two may not be wholly contradictory; there may well have been several phases to the move over the period of a year. Isaacs, whose translation may be untrustworthy, thought that the name meant 'hide-away'. His account doesn't give an impression of any haste: it was a measured response to northern pressures, 'appropriate', Isaacs considered, 'to his design of *occasionally* being absent from his palace at Umbulalio [kwaBulawayo], or from a wish of his people that he should retire, while they attacked his enemies'.[7] In addition, if Isaacs's chronology is correct, Shaka was by no means abandoning the northern marches. There were still some north-bound campaigns to come.

The impression here is nevertheless that the primary purpose of the move was defensive, arising from a sense of unease. MAKEWU's account, on page 395, though unlikely to be strictly true in an historical sense, may still hold a clue. Several informants claim that Shaka left the kwaBulawayo area because he regarded it as the 'country of cats', of the *impaka*.[8] Cats were always regarded with suspicion. The *impaka* (wild cat) was particularly feared, a cat possessed by *umthakathi* 'as a "familiar", and sent by him on villainous errands'.[9] Axel-Ivar Berglund explains:

> The Zulu idiom *ubuthakathi* implies two fields of evil. Firstly, it refers to an incarnate power geared towards harm and destruction which manifests itself through humans and, either directly or indirectly, is addressed to fellow human beings. The manipulators of *ubuthakathi*

are termed *abathakathi* [sing. *umthakathi*]. . . . Secondly, *ubuthakathi* is associated with the embedded neutral powers of materia, *imithi*, the manipulation of which is geared towards evil ends.[10]

We have already come across some stories of people trying to 'bewitch' each other through *imithi* (semen, water, even shadows). Sickness and death were (and are) frequently associated in the first instance with *ubuthakathi*. An agent or 'witch' is immediately sought. Their cunning is endless: '*ubuthakathi* is always on new roads', as one of Berglund's informants put it. Such witches must be killed if discovered; they can sometimes be detected by the presence of a 'familiar', usually an animal companion. The *impaka* is the most powerful and feared familiar of all.[11]

Although Shaka seems to have displayed a certain scepticism about the political motives behind some accusations of witchcraft, there is no reason to suppose that he didn't share the basic belief system. Here is a version of one of the most fascinating stories of his reign: the story of the blood-sprinkling trick:

Shaka made *ububende* [blood from a slaughtered beast] and sprinkled [it] on the doors in the *isigodhlo* at Bulawayo because he had had enough of people being killed because they were alleged to be *takata*ing [concocting evil medicines]. He summonsed doctors to smell out who had done this. At the same time a wild cat (*impaka*) which had given birth at Maqwakazi hill made its way into Bulawayo kraal in search of mice (*izimpuku*). Shaka thereupon summoned doctors from far and wide to see how it was that there was blood about the doors of the *isigodhlo*, and what the meaning could be for so uncanny an animal visiting his kraal. Doctors came and smelt out Dingana, also Mhlangana, and Dingumtoli kaMqubata; they smelt out also Ngqojana, also Mfihlo, also Sopana. Upon this Shaka dismissed them and said they were to go away to sleep. Other doctors were called up: Ntando kaMbaba of the Dube people, who said, 'It was done by the heavens above,' and Nyanda kaMazenyane of the Cele people, who said, 'It was done by the heavens above.' Mutsha of our Langeni people was next called, who said, 'It was done by the heavens above' [meaning

Shaka himself]. Then Ndhlovudawana of the Gcwensa people, of the
Mtetwa people, was called, who replied like the three others just
mentioned.

Shaka then referred to the *impaka* incident. These doctors then
said it had given birth at Maqwakazi and had two young. They said it
had not been driven by any person (i.e. bewitched etc into coming)
but had come merely in search of rats. It was *takata*ing no one. Shaka
said to the Fojisa regiment that it was to go and see where the *impaka*
came from in order to find out if the doctors were wrong. The Fojisa,
true enough, found the wild cat, and about sunset returned with it
and its young. The *impaka* was caught and killed. The former doctors
who had smelt out Dingana, Mhlangana etc were then called back.
Whereupon Shaka instantly put to death every one of the doctors
who had erred . . .[12]

I may be reading too much into this, given that it's only one of many variants.
Nevertheless, the conjunction of the *impaka*, embodying the fear of invasive
evil, and the smelling-out of Shaka's own brothers, especially Dingane and
Mhlangana – precisely those men already accused of trying to assassinate Shaka
– is powerfully suggestive. NGIDI's retelling above may be no more than a
retrospective allegory for, on the one hand, Dingane's machinations against
Shaka and, on the other, Shaka's apparent blindness to those machinations.
It is certainly one of the mysteries of these later years that Shaka appears to
be oblivious to the threat. Perhaps this is one clue that he wasn't so blind,
that moving away from the 'country of the cats' was indeed an attempt to
outmanoeuvre his brothers. There is some support for this in a statement by
the Port Natal trader John Cane:

Chaka's people are represented [by Cane] as dissatisfied and disposed
to revolt in consequence of his cruelty and constant wars. Chaka is
sensible of this disposition of his people to free themselves from his
yoke and has removed his kraal within one day and a half's journey
of Port Natal with the view of taking shelter with Farewell's party in
the event of his people throwing off their allegiance.[13]

This is mostly nonsense: the timing is wrong; Shaka's 'people' were certainly never so single-minded, and, by 1828, as we will see, Shaka was far too angry with the whites to 'take shelter' with them. However, there may just be a smidgen of truth in the impression of internal dissent being one motivation for the move.

There is no reason to doubt that Dingane was plotting Shaka's downfall. It's in the nature of conspiracies, of course, that everything is hidden; we haven't much to go on. We will have to rely on just a few more tiny clues about what was happening.

Beyond these speculations, we know nothing for certain. In any event, my reading of the situation is that it is a feeling of insecurity rather than arrogant imperial confidence that underpins Shaka's eventual move – lock, stock and *isigodlo* – to kwaDukuza.

A SKIRMISH IN THE NORTH

For some months now, the steep slope of isiBubulungu had been echoing to the sounds of mallets and saws. The tiny white community had already lost several of its members: the mate of the wrecked *Mary*, John Norton, had in December 1825 absconded with the *Mary*'s longboat. 'Cowardly,' Isaacs called Norton.[14] James Saunders King, Norton reported after he got back to Port Elizabeth, 'used every means to prevent my sailing, but I persevered.' The community was fine, but needed tools, Norton said, 'tho they have nothing to dread from the natives – they are to all appearances quite harmless'.[15]

Tools were needed to build a new boat. Since King had had his eye on the timber of isiBubulungu from his very first visit, he had probably always intended to build one, out of the reach of the Cape bureaucracy. Though he still had the whaleboat,[16] the wreck of the *Mary* obviously made this even more desirable. King was not building a mere escape boat for a dozen castaways; he had decided to build a 42-tonner, nearly twice the size of the ill-fated *Julia*.

It's uncertain to what extent Shaka approved of this venture. At first King characteristically tried to conceal it – a futile enterprise. However, he probably couldn't have done it at all without forced labour – slaves – assigned by Shaka from the local Thuli population.[17] Shaka was as interested as the whites were in opening up communications with the Cape. That this was the case is indirectly suggested by the fact that the vessel was to be named the *Chaka*. (That King resented this is suggested by his renaming it *Elizabeth and Susan* the moment it crossed the sandbar.)

At any rate, throughout 1826 and into 1827 work slowly progressed under the supervision of the *Mary*'s carpenter, Hutton. Tools doubtless arrived with the *Helicon* in April 1826, and more with the schooner *Ann* in October. Nathaniel Isaacs was at Port Natal when the *Ann* arrived, bearing James King – and none other than Mrs Elizabeth Farewell, in search of her miscreant husband. Farewell himself got back to Port Natal on 21 October, falling immediately into an altercation with King. Isaacs doesn't say what it was about but, ever loyal to King, he blamed it on Farewell's 'selfishness'.[18] One result of the spat was that both men refused to return to see Shaka. Hence, Isaacs was appointed to take King's presents of ostrich feathers, beads, a brass crown and other trifles to Shaka: his fourth visit.

He took with him young 'Nasophongo', who had returned with King from the Cape, and arrived at 'Umboolalio, formerly Gibbeclack' on 8 November. Shaka admired the crown, sniffed at the feathers, and expressed regret that he could see neither King nor Mrs Farewell. Isaacs found Shaka filled with triumph at his recent military victory: he had 'now destroyed the most powerful tribe with which he had ever contended, and, in fact, the only one that could have held out so long. They had often come in collision, and each party had been successively defeated.'[19]

Shaka wasn't finished with the north. Even as he was (according to Isaacs's chronology, anyway) making the move to kwaDukuza, he was planning a couple of smaller campaigns for which he wanted white firepower.

It is quite possible that Shaka was also becoming increasingly worried about the whites' activities. He was concerned that Fynn had apparently tried to smuggle ivory away from the Mzimkhulu area aboard the *Julia*; far from helping Fynn, as both Fynn and Isaacs alleged, Shaka confiscated the ivory.[20] Isaacs also hinted that Shaka was concerned about illegal elephant hunting in the Mkhize region when Isaacs made a trip in late 1826 to Zihlandlo's territory.[21] To add to Shaka's concern, as soon as Isaacs returned to Port Natal, he joined James King on a foray up the coast to the Mlalazi river mouth. Fynn had just returned from that area with 700 pounds of hippo ivory. They passed the iNtonteleni *ikhanda* and Mbikwane's *umuzi*. King judged the river mouth an excellent point from which to trade with 'Madagascar, the Isle of

France, and the Cape of Good Hope'.[22] (The main merchandise that was going *out* to either of the first two places from the Thukela-Phongolo catchment was slaves.) Consequently, King and Isaacs mounted the Union Jack on a conspicuous sand-dune and proclaimed the area theirs – or as Isaacs disingenuously put it, 'taking possession of it as a grant to us from Chaka to inherit'. I find it difficult to believe Isaacs's account of Shaka's reaction when they got to kwaDukuza:

> The king was glad to see us; we made him acquainted with our design of surveying the river, and of making a settlement there if we should find it navigable. He quite approved of our object, seemed much pleased with it, and promised Lieutenant King a large grant of that part of the country, with an exclusive right of trading in his dominions.[23]

(This is probably the supposed 'grant' from Shaka that King would flaunt the following year at Port Elizabeth. It was a fraud.)

Shaka was doubtless mystified, too, by the whites' internecine squabbles. The fall-out between Farewell and King was 'of a pecuniary nature', as Isaacs delicately put it. He declined to elaborate in his *Travels*, but added:

> One thing, however, became evident: this contention, which brought on a division of sentiment, interest, and operations, was in the sequel detrimental to the general good; as petty jealousies and envious feelings increased so much, as to render it somewhat difficult for either to carry on a communication with [Shaka], without perplexing or exciting a man so sensibly alive to conflicting representations.[24]

More obviously exasperating for Shaka was that Michael and John, Farewell's two 'Hottentots', were in trouble again. This time it was more serious than a drunken brawl: they had raped at gunpoint the wife of a local chieftain of some consequence. King and Isaacs went immediately to kwaDukuza, where Shaka received them 'very coolly'. He threatened to kill the whole lot of them, but relented, especially after John Cane arrived with Farewell's apologies. Nevertheless, something had to be done to appease the offended parties; Shaka's solution was to call them all up to attack the Bheje Khumalo.[25]

At least, this is Isaacs's explanation for the whites' involvement. Fynn's account and chronology of this little raid are entirely different. He claimed that the Bheje and Mlotsha groups, 'In an unsuccessful attack on Chaka' at some unspecified date, had been 'cut off from the main body, and were induced to join Chaka.' Shaka had dealt with them 'kindly at first, but the moment their former king [Mzilikazi? Sikhunyane?] had been subdued, and they could have no opportunity of revenge, they were attacked'.[26] This doesn't make much political sense. Probably the Khumalo, or parts of the Khumalo, had khonza'd Shaka, integrating even to the extent that they began to adopt their accent.[27] In other ways, they had resisted Zulu rule. As far as the whites were concerned, this was a cattle- and captives-raid.

The Bheje attack is at least remembered by Zulu informants, although so briefly that it must have been a relatively minor fracas. The Mlotsha attack, by contrast, probably never happened at all. According to Fynn, on the way back from fighting Sikhunyane, a detachment of the Zulu army attacked Mlotsha in his stronghold on Mpondwana mountain. Set like a carbuncle in the centre of a plain, it boasted only two accessible passes, 'guarded by men who hurled down masses of rock on their assailants', the women supplying them from behind. Caught by surprise and unprovisioned, Mlotsha meekly succumbed.[28]

However, there is no other account of this attack, and Bheje's case is so geographically and tactically similar to Mlotsha's that I suspect the two have become confused in Fynn's faulty or deceitful memory. According to him, the Bheje Khumalo had 'succeeded in cutting to pieces one of Chaka's regiments', a recently butwa'd unit whose name Fynn translates as 'Dust'.[29] Isaacs also stated that the Bheje had 'successfully repelled every attack of the Zoola chiefs, and had recently destroyed a whole regiment of Chaka's bravest warriors'.[30] If so, Shaka had every reason to hire gunmen to dislodge them. 'Ten would be quite sufficient,' Shaka said. For his part, Isaacs unconvincingly wrote: 'We did not hesitate, being glad of this alternative to appease the monarch, and soften the wrath of his people; and more especially as it was to save our own lives, which otherwise might be forfeited.'[31]

Isaacs, Cane and Brown, two unnamed seamen, three of 'Mr Farewell's people', two interpreters and two natives, all musket-armed, travelled to kwaDukuza and then to the umuzi of Shiyabantu, through Zihlandlo's territory to his brother Manzini's on the Thukela, and across it into what Isaacs vaguely describes as 'an irregular, rugged and sterile tract'. This was presumably the Ngome.[32] The enemy was located. No one really wanted to fight; the Zulu troops, claims Isaacs, were more afraid of Shaka than anything. When an attack was finally pressed, on 7 February 1827, the Zulu detachment abandoned the musketeers on the slopes of Bheje's hill, where, in Isaacs's account, a muddled series of skirmishes ensued. In contrast to Fynn's account, here it doesn't appear to be an assault on anything like a concentrated redoubt. They came across 'some huts, which [they] burnt, and killed their dogs'; they were held off with stones and assegais. The upshot of the day's action was that Isaacs got a barb in his bottom. (This wound at least was remembered in one Zulu tradition.[33])

The following day the Zulu *impis* ranged themselves up to press the attack, but the Bheje surrendered before they got shot at again. They would give up their cattle, their tribute, and even 'ten maidens' for the use of the sailors.[34] Such Zulu traditions as we have are sketchy, but make a little more of Zulu valour. BALENI claims that his uncle Nomnanzi managed, after an unsuccessful initial assault, to enter by the sole entrance to Bheje's stronghold and heroically killed two men.[35] Another account asserts that the Zulu warriors got into the redoubt using *zungulu* monkey-rope creepers. This is cunning, but rather too close to a certain legend of Khumalo origins to be quite credible.

One way or another, it was not a grand operation, and perhaps only one of the better-remembered cattle- and captive-seeking raids of Shaka's final years. Although Shaka teased Isaacs about the wound he'd received in his behind – he must have been running away, so he really ought to be killed for cowardice – he rewarded him with the usual handful of heifers. The whites kept the women;[36] this was the true source of at least some of the settlers' 'refugees'.

That Isaacs suffered a high level of guilty defensiveness about this operation is evident in his extended and self-contradictory attack on Stephen Kay: 'the terror of our arms', Isaacs claims, '*saved* the spilling of human blood, and the horrible massacre that always accompanied Chaka's wars'.[37]

By early to mid-1827, the northern regions perhaps more or less subdued for the moment, and his presence at kwaDukuza firmly established, Shaka was turning his attention to the south again.

'THE *IMPI* OF WRONG-DOING'

Between the raid on Macingwane in mid-1825 (assuming that I am right on this obscure campaign) and mid-1828, nothing much was happening in the southern marches at all. The white traders were, as we have seen, causing a certain amount of consternation along the coast. No doubt Zulu *impis* continued to raid and extract sporadic tribute from the small polities south of the Mngeni river. This river, just north of isiBubulungu/Port Natal, was now effectively the southern Zulu boundary. Shaka concentrated on establishing *amakhanda* in the Cele area. His reach extended as far as isiBubulungu itself, and he would start building cattle-posts between there and the Mzimkhulu, where Fynn was now established in some strength. However, there is no evidence that Shaka ever tried to colonise the area south and west of the lower Mngeni, as he had done in the Mhlathuze valley or Mahlabathini, or even in formerly Ndwandwe territory north of the Mfolozis. Mostly it appears that he amused himself by travelling around the immediate area:

> Shaka used to be very fond of going about visiting places. He sat very little indoors. He frequently used to sit by, and look at, the sea, and when it was sunset he used to start off home at a run, and his *incekus* were obliged to keep up the running, which was not stopped until Dukuza was reached.[38]

There was one exception to this relative quiescence. The evidence for this expedition is particularly thin, perhaps because the participants tried subsequently to cover it up. It's important, however, for the faint light that it casts on Zulu internal politics. An *impi* set out, it seems, to 'fetch' Matiwane of the Ngwane.

You will recall that we last saw Matiwane disappearing over the escarpment of the Drakensberg, in about 1823 (see page 258). His force had remained relatively cohesive; he was powerful enough to extract tribute from Moshoeshoe of the Sotho, amongst others. He had gathered a heterogeneous band of people – original Ngwane, Hlubi, Sotho and others – who jostled for grazing and peace in the Caledon river valley with Sekhonyela, Moshoeshoe and Makhetha. They suffered raids from Mzilikazi, on the one hand, and Griquas on the other, and in turn raided into northern Xhosa territory in order to replace cattle.[39] These were the raiders known generically as the 'Fetcani', often conflated with the Zulu, or even with Shaka, since they spoke a Zulu-related dialect, built huts on the Zulu beehive pattern, and similarly pierced their ears. This would cause huge confusion, and meant that Shaka was landed with the blame for a great deal that had been no concern of his at all. (It's worth slipping in here John Cane's observation, made in 1828, that 'Fetcani' being driven into towards the Colony had been pursued not by Shaka, but by 'Omsilicosan' – Mzilikazi.[40]) The identity of the 'Fetcani' is clear from the account heard from a young 'Fetcani' in July 1827:

> I belong to a tribe on the other side of the Great (Orange) river. Our principal kraal (pointing North East) is distant five days journey from this. Where we cross the Orange river is about half way. Our people consist of two tribes formerly distinct, 'Masutu' [Zulu plural: amaSutho] and 'Manguana' [amaNgwane]. Our great chiefs are Maheta [Makhetha] and Mattuana [Matiwane]. We are very numerous, fought battles with many tribes and beat them all but Chaka's (the Zulus). Chaka beat us some time ago and took our cattle. We heard that the Tambookies [Thembu] had cattle. We sent out Fetcanie (army or, as translated, commando), beat the Tambookies often and took their cattle . . . Our Fetcanie consist of young men, no men having wives and no women accompany it. We purchase our wives and the young men can only get them by fighting and taking cattle to pay for them. We never saw white people, we never heard of them. We are not cannibals. Our property consists in cattle. Chaka took it from us and we will fight and take cattle wherever we can find them.[41]

We could hardly ask for a more lucid explanation. There is only one ambiguous sentence: 'Chaka beat us *some time ago*'. It seems unlikely that the 'Fetcani' would still, four years later, be trying to replace cattle taken in the last raid we noted, back in 1823 on the headwaters of the Thukela. There must have been another raid by the Zulu since, and there is really only one candidate:

The *eyobutshinga* [sic] *impi* fetched Matiwane kaMasumpa. It was not
caused to offer praises to the spirits (*tetwa'd*) by Shaka. Mdhlaka kaNcidi
was *induna* of the *impi*. Maqoboza kaMbeleko of the Nzuza people
and Madabulela kaQumbumbete died with this *impi*; they were killed
by the amaNgwane. Maqoboza was *induna* of the kwaDhlangezwa.
Madabulela was *induna* of the uBekenya regiment. The regiments
Ndabenkulu, Bekenya and Dhlangezwa simply decided to go after
Matiwane without orders from Shaka, without being *teta'd*. They
formed themselves into a raiding or marauding party.[42]

Eyokutshinga impi: 'the *impi* of wrong-doing, of villainy'.[43] Rather like the
iziYendane *izwekufa* earlier, the kind of raiding that most conforms to the
violent stereotype is precisely that of which Shaka *disapproved*. It's possible
that this was a party said to have been sent by Shaka 'to the iNyoka pass in
the Amaxosa country beyond the Pondos to build him a kraal there'. This
seems an unlikely project in itself, but it was possibly linked to Shaka's growing
interest in what was happening along the Cape Colony boundary. The party
came back with some looted cattle (said to be Mpondo cattle), but without
having set up the outpost – much to Shaka's anger.[44] Did they, in fact, divert
to the north?

Or was it the raiding party that Isaacs says he observed returning in April
1827? Once again, though, the details differ:

They had been absent about three months on an expedition to the
westward, not fighting any particular tribe, but maintaining a kind of
predatory warfare, contending with all, and plundering as they
advanced. In this expedition the Zoolas penetrated N.W. of Delagoa
Bay. They arrived at an immense river or lake, and travelled on its
banks for a fortnight in an easterly direction, with a river to cross, but
could not find anything like a fording place. They met with some
yellow people on horses, who compelled them to return.[45]

Some 'Armasootoos' (abeSotho) ambushed part of this force and killed them,
so they 'suffered losses of chiefs and men, but on the whole returned with a
considerable booty in cattle, the main object for which the Zoolas go to war'.[46]
There is no sign in Isaacs that Shaka disapproved of this apparently very

long-range venture – but also no independent evidence that it happened at all. We are left with the *eyokutshinga impi*.

There is some support for a Zulu raid on the Ngwane from other, non-Zulu sources. This includes the French missionary D.F. Ellenberger's book *History of the Basuto*. Like many of these compilations, this work has been disparaged in recent scholarship. Nevertheless, Ellenberger includes his version of an account bearing some resemblance to that of the *eyokutshinga impi*. It is also backed up by a few other Ngwane and Sotho sources. According to this account, Moshoeshoe, ensconced amongst the mountains of present-day Lesotho, was in the habit of sending tribute to Shaka in the form of feathers and skins. When this tribute dried up suddenly, Moshoeshoe excused his omission by blaming Matiwane for blocking the way. Shaka himself then sent out an *impi*, commanded by his brothers Dingane and Mhlangana. They moved out, according to Ellenberger, around the end of 1826; in February 1827 they attacked Matiwane's *inyanga*, Zulunga, and killed him. Ellenberger goes on:

> Satisfied with their victory, the Zulus crossed the Caledon at Maseru Drift, in search of the cattle of the Amangwane, which were then scattered about in various herds from Masite and Makhoarane and on to Kolo, Mafeteng, Thabana Morena, Siloe, and even farther south, Matuane himself being at Ngope Khubelu (Blasball Spruit).
>
> The Zulus halted at Qeme, passed on to Masite and Thabane Morena, and attacked the Amangwane at Likhoele. They were not very numerous, but their discipline and valour were of a high order, and they easily defeated the Amangwane, who fled towards the Caledon.[47]

A member of Matiwane's 'Ushee' *ibutho* named Moloja later related his experience:

> When we arrived at Kononyama [Vier Voet], our regiment proposed to attack the Zulus, but the regiment of the White Shields [the married men] refused to join, and went elsewhere to capture cattle. But they did not escape defeat; for the first regiment of the Zulus fell upon them and put them to flight, while we, soldiers of the Ushee, were

fighting near Ladybrand against the rest of the Zulus. We were very weary, having fought all day; but on our return, we encountered the first regiment of the Zulus, who had defeated our White Shields, near the reed bed between Modderpoort and Ladybrand. We joined battle with them, and Dingaan received a spear-thrust in the chest. Well was it for us that they were as weary as we, and we sank upon the ground for very weariness, being able to slay no more, and cursed each other as we sat there. At last the Zulus struggled to their feet and staggered off like drunken men, driving the cattle before them, and we had not the strength left to stop them.[48]

Matiwane retreated across the Caledon, and in a few months' time would descend upon the Thembu once again.

Is it possible to reconcile this account with NGIDI's version of the *eyokutshinga impi*? Did Shaka order this raid, or not? Was Dingane in charge, or Mdlaka? There may be some significance to the information that Mdlaka, the alleged *induna* on this wayward *eyokutshinga impi*, had some previous connection with the iziYendane.[49] Was this raid an extension of the Hlubi-inspired revenge which, I argued earlier, impelled the 1823 Zulu attack? And was this new raid the misdeed that caused the remains of the iziYendane, then patronised by Nandi, to flee after her death (see below)? Why was it that such remnants of the iziYendane were precisely those that Dingane used as an emergency military force to consolidate his power after 1828?[50]

I'm not sure that we possess enough information to answer all these questions. The Ngwane and Sotho, naturally enough, would have assumed that Shaka had authorised the raid, and so they give this impression. It seems highly unlikely that Mdlaka, one of Shaka's most trusted men, would have gone off on such an unauthorised mission. There is, furthermore, no sign of a later compact between Dingane and Mdlaka; indeed, Mdlaka was murdered by Dingane. Perhaps NGIDI was simply wrong on this detail. It may be significant that there is no sign of this raid in either Shaka's or Dingane's *izibongo*, as might be expected. However, there seems little reason to doubt that *some* sort of raid happened.

There is perhaps room here to speculate that in fact Dingane and Mhlangana, the brothers who were already in conspiratorial opposition to

Shaka, decided to conduct a raid of their own, to gain their own kudos, their own cattle, and their own sense of independence. It was, however, a dangerously long way to go for these things; could it have been worth it? The case must remain extremely speculative, but it is almost the only information that we have as to what Dingane was doing in these years.

Unhappily for Matiwane, it was not the last time that these two leaders would meet.

'THE EVIL-DOER CRIED LIKE A LITTLE GIRL'

Up to this point in his history, Shaka certainly appears as arrogant, aggressive, and unnervingly tough. He had killed a lot of people, albeit in a conventional and (for the times) acceptable manner. There is, however, no obvious indication that he might have been pathologically insane; indeed, most of the time he comes across as eminently pragmatic. However, in the last year or so of his life – it is often said – he became unhinged. This was Fynn's view, and it became almost standard in the histories:

> [Shaka's] inclinations until the defeat of the Endwandas [Ndwandwe] had been suppressed from the fear of his subjects quitting him, but now having defeated the only remaining formidable enemy & having nothing to fear from any other quarter imagined his extensive power placed him in perfect security his real character began to develop itself. Hitherto he had in a great measure acted on the system of his protector Tingiswio [Dingiswayo] but blending a more rigid despotism keeping his subjects in perpetual awe & continual astonishment from the variety and of his exploits & brilliancy of his achievements, but after this event a reign of terror commenced, his excessive cruelties over leaped all bounds.[51]

'This event' – the alleged breaking-point – was the death of his mother. Grief supposedly undid him.

Nandi died in early August 1827,[52] at her own *umuzi* Nyakumubi, situated close to kwaBulawayo. Fynn, characteristically, places himself at the centre of the drama. He may have been around, though no Zulu informant ever testified to his presence there. According to Fynn's earliest version (he wrote several), he and Shaka had been out hunting elephants. They had returned to supervise the building of a new residence when news of Nandi's illness reached them. Shaka sent doctors. The news got worse. They then marched for some six hours through the night to reach her.

> Chaka requested me to pay her a visit. Cattle were at the same time ordered to be killed as an offering to her spirits. On my arrival at her hut which was crowded to excess with native doctors several of whom had to move out before I could enter it [sic]. Being an exceedingly hot day, sufficient to sicken one of the strongest constitutions I recommended at least half of her medical attendants and nurses to make room for a little air which being done gave me an opportunity of seeing my patient. I soon perceived she had little or no hope of living, being then in the last stages of dysentery. I returned to give Chaka my opinion. He requested me to go back again and observe if there was any change. On my returning I had not been there ten minutes before she expired . . .[53]

There is no comparably detailed deathbed account from the Zulu sources. Fynn may well have been right about the cause of her demise, but the convulsion of mourning that followed rapidly bred other rumours.

The convulsion began with Shaka himself. As people began to strip off their ornaments as a sign of grief, Shaka appeared in his war dress and daubed with coloured clays. He stood, Fynn wrote, 'several minutes in a most mournful attitude, his face laying carelessly over his shield on which dropped his tears as they fell using his right hand to wipe them away. His form altogether having the appearance of Innocence in distress, would have claimed compassion from the hardest heart.'[54] At last, a shriek wrung itself from him, a signal for a general paroxysm of sympathetic grief. The physical extravagance – the wailing, the throwing of the body on the ground – was and is conventional enough in African circles. Likely, it would have profoundly alarmed the European observer. Shaka is said to have howled, 'All such as behold me, I suppose have mothers to go to': he felt bereft, singled out, at a disadvantage now.[55]

People began to compete in demonstrating their grief. Cattle were slaughtered but not eaten – left for the vultures and dogs.[56] Some people started to kill others, allegedly for not grieving. No doubt long-standing vendettas were opportunistically satisfied. At first, Shaka seems to have been oblivious to the carnage, if carnage it was. The day after Nandi's death, according to Fynn, Shaka ordered the killing of an aunt who had long been opposed to Nandi. A dozen attendants also perished. A chieftain who went down to the river to drink was killed.[57]

These few cases apart, Shaka is not recorded as having given the order for any killing at all. When, in the evening, he heard about the bodies left lying along the river, he put a stop to it.[58] Meanwhile, groups had fanned out across the countryside, killing those alleged to have failed to mourn; people rubbed snuff in their eyes to stimulate the tears. Nathaniel Isaacs, at that moment returning along the coastal route from the Mlalazi river, ran into one such marauding group, who attacked a village and burned some women and children to death in their huts, because their headman 'had not gone to the king's residence to mourn for the queen mother'. The headman himself, that morning at dawn, had resisted the attack but had finally been speared to death in a grain pit. A 'most inhuman and savage exhibition,' swore Isaacs. 'But to whom is such an act of unexampled barbarity to be attributed, but to the insatiable monster who ordered the attack?'[59]

It is far from clear, however, that Shaka *did* order these wider attacks. In Fynn's shock, and Isaacs's (or his ghost-writer's) purple prose, lie the roots of subsequent exaggeration. Fynn mentions no figures in his original manuscripts, except '12 or 14' people killed on the third day.[60] Only in a much later manuscript does Fynn claim that 7 000 were killed, a figure that can safely be dismissed as ludicrous.[61] Within a year or two, though, rumours had spread to missionaries in the Cape Colony that Shaka '*all most every day* let kill ten till twenty, who from the Doctor are marked to be bad people; and on the day where his mother died, nearly 2 000 men was killed'.[62] It is also far from clear how far the killing spread. Isaacs decided that after all it might be polite to go and commiserate with Shaka, and he remarked on seeing a number of freshly killed corpses on his way to kwaBulawayo. He attributed them to Shaka himself, and assumed, without any further evidence, that this was happening all over the country.[63] Some Zulu made the same assumption.[64]

There was probably *some* killing, enough to cause a ripple of distress, and perhaps to intensify nascent political dissent. If the informants can be believed, Shaka later, for political reasons, did away with several individuals under the pretext of their having failed to mourn, or for violating the food and sex taboos that were instituted. For a short period, people could eat milk and curds, but not *amabele* grain, and had to refrain from intercourse. Food belonging to one Masawuzana was spotted being brought into kwaBulawayo; Masawuzana lied that it was destined for his brother Mnongose, who then innocently suffered Shaka's death-knell.[65] Another man, one Nquhele, was killed for being slow to arrive at the mourning – but *not* on Shaka's orders.[66] Some people took the opportunity to ingratiate themselves: Mxamama of the Sibisi people informed on non-mourners, who were then killed off for being 'defiant'.[67] Spies went about inspecting faeces exposed by bush-fires to see if anyone was eating grain.[68] More whimsically, according to one story, an *inceku* of Nandi's, Mqumbela, cried for two days. On the third day Shaka said, 'Give him rest; he is tired. His mother is dead, he has been crying for a long time. Happy is the man who has a mother.' So they 'gave him his quietus'.[69]

Perhaps more importantly, some of the rump of the iziYendane *ibutho* – Nandi's personal charge – fled, expecting some retribution now that their patroness was dead.[70] This doesn't really make much sense unless they had already been up to no good – which, as I proposed in the previous section, might just be right. The iziYendane flight was evidence of some strains, connected with Dingane, within the Zulu polity. Dingane himself may well have been responsible for a rumour that sprang up almost immediately – that Shaka had murdered Nandi himself.

With *this* anecdote the slur of madness really begins. It became widespread in Zulu circles, and it eventually bred any number of improbable stories connected with Shaka's sexuality. It's worth underlining that there is *no* direct evidence – not even from the white traders who might have been expected to pounce on such a juicy morsel – that the story was current in Shaka's own lifetime. They were happy to spread it abroad later: Fynn, against his very own evidence, loved to tell the tale anyway:

The story goes: He, Shaka, questioned [Nandi] about a son that one of the women had had. He supposed that Nandi was hiding this son

away. Some say she denied it and turned round to get some straws or
wood to feed the fire with, the hut being dark, and he in his rage,
stabbed her up the fundament with a sharp stick, through her leather
skirt. This penetrated some inches up the anus. He told her if she
divulged it he would have her torn limb from limb and eaten by the
dogs of the kraal. So it was always supposed she died of enteric fever
or typhoid, which natives call *intsheko*. . . . After stabbing her he went
off next day to hunt. This hunt had been organized before he stabbed
her. A messenger was sent to say Nandi was dead. As a matter of fact
she was dying. As soon as he received the news Shaka cried, and natives
said, 'The evil-doer cried like a little girl'.[71]

William Bazely claimed that he had heard this from both Fynn and Zulu
men. He also alleged that Fynn suppressed this version 'for fear of what
people would say in England'. This makes no sense whatsoever. Fynn simply
liked the story, untrue though it was. (NGIDI does exactly the same, denying
that Shaka killed Nandi – and then relating the tale anyway with a deceptive
wealth of circumstantial detail.[72])

Versions of the story are wildly variable, but almost all centre on the
notion that Shaka discovered Nandi trying to shelter a son of his, conceived
by one of the *isigodlo* or *umdlunkulu* women. Infuriated, he killed the baby,
and the mother, and Nandi. He is variously described as stabbing his mother
up the anus, in the stomach, in the armpit; with an awl, or a stick, or a small
assegai.[73] Or he sent an *inceku* to do the dirty work for him, tying her leather
apron around the wound so that he could pretend she was dying of typhoid.[74]
Or he set an *inyanga* on her, magically making her bleed through the nose
and ears.[75] Or she was strangled.[76]

The whole thing was a fabrication. MADHLEBE, one of the few informants
who could claim to have been present, albeit as a child, insisted that Nandi's
death was natural.[77] MKEHLANGANA almost certainly has it right: 'Nandi did
try to conceal a child, but Shaka neither killed her nor caused so much
mourning in order to conceal the fact.'[78]

The aftermath likewise was hugely exaggerated. Fynn's account that the
mourning prohibitions went on for a whole year and reduced the country to
waste is not borne out, though it was picked up by one or two colourful Zulu

accounts.[79] Likewise, Fynn's claim that no one could approach Shaka for 'six months' is nonsense.[80] Isaacs, for one, was present at kwaBulawayo when, on 7 September, Shaka went into the forests 'to perform the national ceremony of discarding the mourning dress', and thence to a river for 'customary ablutions'. Mourning thus ceased exactly a judicious month – one 'moon' – after the death. In one anecdote, Shaka's extravagances during the mourning period were quickly brought up short by his own people. Gala kaNodade went to complain, 'What are you killing your country for?' Shaka said, 'Here is one who inspires me with courage,' and gave him two cows.[81] Whatever impulsive and opportunistic killing happened, it was hardly genocidal.

Nandi was buried at Matheko, near Eshowe. Fynn heard, though he wasn't allowed to witness it, that 'ten maidens' were buried alive with her; other of his informants denied it.[82] One Zulu source states that three old women, Nandi's own *izinceku*, and some girls were buried with her to cook for her in the afterworld, as 'persons of her rank cannot die alone', but this is not reliable.[83] At any rate, dirges were chanted. The great men – Nxazonke, Tshangane, Bantwana, Mbikwana, and Ngomane – were present at the burial. Fynn was later able to hear Ngomane making a hyperbolic speech to the nation, telling them

> that the result of Nande's death was not yet known; that the word Nande which implied anything nice should never more be used and instead of the word nande should be used umtote; that she was the mother of an elephant, the mother of a lion, a tiger or the mother of wild beasts (alluding to the praises of Chaka) and seeing that now had died the she-elephant with small breasts that they must not be surprised if the heavens and earth came together and the nation be crushed; there could not be expected to be any more gathering of corn nor breeding of children; that nothing now surrounded them but death and destruction and locusts would cover the earth and no man should live.[84]

Fynn took all this quite literally, and recorded that 'orders were given that not a grain of corn should be planted that year and that every woman found in the family way should be put to death. The order for murdering all pregnant women was strictly attended to the whole year following . . .'[85] There is nothing elsewhere in the records to bear this out. Nothing in the tales of genocidal madness stands up to scrutiny. Shaka suffered an understandable spasm of grief; he went through the conventional taboos of the mourning period; and he set about planning an *ihlambo* – cleansing – campaign in Nandi's honour, which would take nearly a year to mature.

'DREAMS AND NECROMANCY'

The 1975 *Guinness Book of World Records* provides an extreme incarnation of the famous 'blood-sprinkling trick', which we have already encountered:

> The greatest 'smelling-out' recorded in African history occurred before Shaka (1787–1828) and 30,000 subjects near the River Umhlatuzana, Zululand (now Natal, South Africa) in March 1824. After 9 hours, over 300 were 'smelt out' as guilty of smearing the Royal kraal with blood, by 150 witchfinders led by the hideous isangoma ['witchdoctor'] Nobela. The victims were declared innocent when Shaka admitted to having done the smearing himself to expose the falsity of the power of the diviners. Nobela poisoned herself with atropine ($C17H23NO3$) [*sic*], but the other 149 witchfinders were thereupon skewered or clubbed to death.[86]

This version is a text fascinating for its multiple distortions and inventions. Most of its entirely fictional detail is drawn from Ritter's novel, *Shaka Zulu*. This is not to say that something like it didn't happen at all. It was perhaps first recorded by the missionary James Callaway in his 1870 book *The Religious System of the Zulus*. As we've noted, there are many variants of it in *The James Stuart Archive*. What the truth of it might have been, and what the story might tell us about Shaka's relationship to spiritual and magical practices, is a difficult issue.

Of this much we can be sure: Shaka believed in the spiritual realm as much as anybody in his polity. These beliefs would have coloured almost all his waking, and some of his sleeping moments.

This realm of spirituality, 'magic' and 'witchcraft' (it is dangerous trying to apply European terms) is the most opaque to the outsider (including myself), and I will attempt no more here than to point out how vital it must have been to Shaka's entire world-view. We cannot simply ignore it, or pretend that it was something just tagged onto pragmatic politics. In a world-view that regards the 'material' and the 'spiritual' as seamlessly interfused, spirituality *is* politics.

We have touched on numerous aspects already: Shaka washing himself over his father's hut, the medicinal preparation (*tetaing*) of the army before leaving on campaign, the divinatory throwing of the sticks into the sea, the careful preservation of bodily materials against the threat of bewitchment, and calling on the rain-doctors at the annual *umkhosi*. When Shaka bathed, doctors

> strengthened him with magical arts and decoctions of various vegetables prepared for that purpose, during which all persons who had lost their relatives by death were obliged to purify him in order that they might be admitted into his presence by taking the gall of a live calf from its side and sprinkling it at the entrance, poor people throwing a brass ball or a few beads which became the perquisites of the menial servants.[87]

Almost every single daily act in Zulu ordinary life had then, and in many places has still, its spiritual dimension, its religious significances. There is in this society no clear boundary between 'spiritual' and 'material'. The presence of the ancestors – the shades – was constant, their appeasement an unremitting task, both a pleasure and a necessity. On the negative side, 'witchcraft' and other damaging 'magical' practices were perpetual, ineradicable fears.

'Smellings-out' of potential or suspected 'witches', evil-doers bringing down sickness or death, certainly happened. Here is a general account by LUNGUZA, one of Stuart's informants:

> The most frequent cause of people being killed was through the holding of a smelling-out. This took place by people standing all around the

doctors. The wizards would run and prance about within the circle. They are carrying shields and assegais. Those forming the circle carry shields (small) and possibly also assegais. These things they place on the ground, and when appealed to by the wizards, strike the ground with rough, knobbed sticks – straight sticks (fighting sticks) are not used – shouting, '*Izwa! Izwa!*' Only those appealed to shout, '*Izwa!*'; those from whom the wizard has just come or turned do not then beat and shout. The doctor says to those he immediately addresses, 'There is an *umtakati* [an evil-doer, a 'witch'] here among you,' and calls on them to beat with their sticks. The heartiness of the response of those addressed would depend on their opinions as to whether there was or was not an *umtakati* among them. If the nature of the response was feeble, the doctor would hesitate and not declare that there was an *umtakati* among them. He then turns to others who possibly become very excited and beat in the loudest manner. The wizard would then go on smelling, smelling, smelling, and then leave them. No-one would be killed.

A report would then be sent to the king. This report would be that the doctors smelt out so-and-so and so-and-so, for those in the circle are not a mixed gathering but are grouped according to their *imizi*, and are not intermingled. The doctors declare in the circle, 'So-and-so, you *takata*!', giving the name of the person or persons smelt out. Those smelt out are in the circle. There is no chance given them of running away, nor would they attempt to run for there was nowhere to run to. They would not be put under arrest. The king would then give the order as to who of those smelt out are to be killed, and they would then be killed, say two or three days after the smelling out. They are not killed on the first day. . . . After the chief had given the order that anyone was to be killed he would be tied up behind his back with thongs. He would be kept until those sent to kill him had arrived. The executioners would take him out of the kraal, 100 yards or so, and then kill him and leave him there. These people had their heads twisted to the back so that the neck breaks. In the case of others, stones might be got and he be battered to death with them. Others might have thongs tied around their necks and then be dragged off to the place of execution, and this string would be struck with a stick till it got tighter, and so the victim would be throttled.

The more important persons smelt out would be surrounded during the night (just before dawn). In other cases the surrounding took place as it was getting dark. One would see a kraal burning shortly after sunset whereupon, not knowing at the time what had happened, you would say, 'So-and-so's kraal is burning,' and this would turn out to be the kraal at which an *umnumzana* had been killed. This man would be stabbed; his children too would be killed, including women and of course males, for the whole place would be killed off.[88]

This describes a brutal system: a system with deep spiritual significance, but also prone to abuse, both by what we today would call 'state-sponsored terrorism', and by the practitioners, the *izinyanga*. LUNGUZA, who witnessed a smelling-out during Dingane's reign, also related a version of Shaka's 'blood-sprinkling trick'. He hints that it was done because the *izinyanga* were killing off too many of Shaka's own warriors.[89] Socwatsha also thought that Shaka had done it for political reasons, and thereby 'checked a growing abuse'.[90] If we can credit another anecdote, Shaka was canny enough to pit *izinyanga* against one another in other ways, too:

Mqalana was Shaka's *inyanga* from the Swazi country. Shaka one day called Mqalana and Ngazi to produce their medicines to see who had the most. Mqalana, on inspecting Ngazi's drugs, was able to give the name of each one. Ngazi, however, could not give the names of Mqalana's in any satisfactory manner. Mqalana then said to Ngazi, 'Do you give the king this medicine, Ngazi?' referring to *iloyi* (a particular drug). Ngazi assented, 'Yes, I do.' Mqalana replied, 'The king will kill all the people if you give him this medicine.' Shaka then directed both doctors to do up their medicines and go home. But Ngazi, instead of going home, entered another hut, whereas Mqalana went home. After Mqalana had gone off, Shaka again called Ngazi. He said, 'Why does Mqalana speak in this way? Can you kill him? Yes, kill him!' Ngazi replied, 'Let the king find me a sheep if I am to kill him.' Shaka sent for one, a large ram. Ngazi took a drug and bit it as he held the sheep. He then blew the medicines into the sheep's nostrils. He then told Shaka it should be forwarded to Mqalana at his home as a present. The sheep was sent accordingly, and duly arrived. He [Mqalana] was told, 'Here is a sheep, a present for you from the king.' Mqalana directed it should be killed at once and the spleen cooked. . . . Mqalana called for the cooked spleen. He took down a spoon and put it into the food and raised it to his mouth. No sooner did he take the first mouthful than he fell dead on the spot.[91]

There are hints here of power struggles behind the scene, but so detached from any specific time period or political context that there is no telling what the account might conceal. The passage does at least show the Zulu perception that Shaka, far from being either a thorough-going sceptic *or* an unquestioning superstitious puppet, as various writers have proposed, was a 'believer' at least to the extent of being able to manipulate traditional beliefs and medicines to his own advantage. As one informant noted: 'For when a man had repeatedly been given presents of cattle and these had multiplied, people would come and say he had enormous herds of cattle and accuse him of overshadowing the king. Upon this he would be accused of being an *umThakathi* [one who uses supernatural forces for evil] and killed.'[92]

Possibly something similar lies behind the story of Mbiya.

We know nothing about Mbiya except that he was an old Mthethwa man, prominent in Dingiswayo's time. He gained some position of favour under Shaka, so that when he died in 1826 or 1827, Shaka was deeply saddened.[93] Thereafter, according to Fynn and Isaacs, Mbiya literally haunted him. Whether Fynn and Isaacs independently related the same incident, or borrowed the story one from the other, together they made a comprehensive mess of understanding it. They both used it to demonstrate Shaka's (in their view) absurd attachment to 'dreams and necromancy'[94] – and (equally interesting from our point of view) demonstrated a relationship to each other that shows how myth and prejudice work together to create 'history'.

Despite (or, rather, because of) the whites' distortions, the incident is worth lingering on. The presence of the ancestors or 'shades' was, and still is, a constant and undeniable psychological and ritual presence in Zulu society. Dreams in particular are an ever-present conduit to the ancestral realm, a guide to the desires of the shades. As Axel-Ivar Berglund explains: 'The important role played by dreams in Zulu thought-patterns cannot be over-stressed. Without dreams true and uninterrupted living is not possible. There is cause for anxiety when people do not dream. . . . In dreams the shades become very real, concrete and intimate.'[95] Moreover, dreams were closely associated with the 'calling' of a diviner to his or her profession.[96] This is also implicit in the story of Mbiya.

Fynn's version of the story is as follows. A few months after Mbiya died, it was reported that Mbiya's spirit (*idlozi*), in the form of 'a homeless snake', had appeared, and intended to visit Shaka. The *inkosi* sent chiefs to investigate; on several occasions, the *idlozi* conversed with the chiefs. It even sent them to find snuff, accurately directing them to hidden boxes. They satisfied themselves that it really was Mbiya's spirit. Shaka prepared himself – and a special hide kaross – for a personal visit. What appeared, however, was an old woman, 'pretending to be the spirit in question'. Shaka 'soon put a stop to this by declaring her to be an impostor and ordering her to go away'. Nevertheless, he argued that Mbiya himself must have sent her, 'owing to his not wishing, for some reason or other, to appear himself'.[97]

Fynn then tells an entirely separate anecdote about how (during this same period) a certain Cele man first fell ill, then disappeared. He reappeared some months later, long-haired, dishevelled, and claiming to have been taken away by a lion. The lion had breathed on him, relieved his pains, and then taken him gently underground to the world of the spirits. There he was surrounded by a multitude of dead chiefs and even some of his own deceased wives, all living in happy luxury. This man became an eccentric but trustworthy favourite of Magaye and of Shaka. He was 'accidentally killed by some Zulus when chasing stolen cattle in 1828'.[98]

Fynn refrains from passing any particular judgement on these events. Isaacs, however, conflates the two separate incidents, claiming that the man in the second anecdote also saw, in particular, the shade of Mbiya in the underworld, and brought back a message from him. Isaacs connects this up with Shaka's original dream of Mbiya, in which Mbiya instructed Shaka as follows:

[Shaka's] father Esenzengercona [Senzangakhona] was very angry with the Zoolas for losing their fame, and not being 'schlanger-nee-pee-lie' [*uhlakaniphile*], that is 'more shrewd and cunning,' and superior to their neighbours; – that the nation was getting too large and required constant employment; – that there were plenty of enemies yet to conquer before they could 'booser' [*ukubusa*] (make merry) and enjoy themselves: that Umbeah had also told him he was living very comfortably under ground . . .[99]

The second messenger (the old woman vanishes from Isaacs's account), dressed in 'a piece of bullock's hide, covering his hind part from hip to hip, and fastened in front with pieces of cord reaching to the joints of his knees, and thickly studded with brass balls', thereafter hung around Shaka's residence constantly, being given the appellation of 'prophet'. He was not, in this version, accidentally killed by Zulu people, but was carried off by a leopard, and heard from no more.

There's no point in trying to reconcile these accounts. Isaacs's version is driven by his main aim: to vilify Shaka. The whole ceremony, Isaacs claims, 'was nothing but an imposition to elate the people with a spirit for war. It was designed by Chaka, and the individual who did the executive part was instructed in the character'[100] – a charade, adding deceitfulness to monstrosity. It prepares the reader for Isaacs's tour de force of Gothic fantasy:

> Thus the eve of going to war was always the period of brutal and inhuman murders, in which he seemed to indulge with as much savage delight as the tiger with his prey. When he had once determined on a sanguinary display of his power, nothing could restrain his ferocity: his eyes evinced his pleasure, his iron heart exulted, his whole frame seemed as if it felt a joyous impulse at seeing the blood of innocent creatures flowing at his feet; his hands grasped, his herculean and muscular limbs exhibiting by their motion a desire to aid in the execution of the victims of his vengeance: in short, he seemed a being in a human form, with more than the physical capabilities of a man; a gaint [*sic*] without reason, a monster created with more than ordinary power and disposition for doing mischief, and from whom we recoil as we would at the serpent's hiss or the lion's growl.[101]

Coming from someone who practically owed his life to Shaka, this is a supremely ungrateful and near-hysterical piece of invective.

'ACTS OF MADNESS'

Various observations by Fynn work to some degree to counteract Isaacs's vindictive monomania:

> In their haste a group of men passed within five yards of Shaka, not having noticed him till they got to within that distance. He looked upon them so fiercely as to make them run back, whereupon he vociferated his usual oath, 'Mnkabayi!' in so violent a manner as to bring them to a momentary stand. He then ordered an attendant to single out a man and stab him. . . . The moment the assegai pierced the body Shaka averted his head, his countenance betraying something like a feeling of horror, but we had not proceeded more than a mile when two other unfortunates experienced the same fate.[102]

Whatever his faults may be, Fynn at least has the merit of recognising that Shaka's personality was a complex one. Indeed, Fynn found it baffling: 'Such opposed kinds of conduct in one person appeared to me to be strange, but I afterwards became convinced that both the contradictory dispositions, delicate feeling and extreme brutality, were intimately blended in him.'[103]

My own aim is not to whitewash Shaka. No one ever said that he was a gentle pacifist. For many, if not most people, Shaka had an undeniably ferocious reputation – even his supporters thought so. There's likely to be at least *some* truth in all of the accusations of unbridled violence.

Shaka's *izibongo* – the praises that were chanted in his presence – are one indication of what people felt: he was called, for instance, 'the wrong-doer who knows no law',[104] and 'The violently unrestrained one who is like the ear of the elephant'.[105] 'That man used to play around with people,' said BALEKA.[106] Shaka was widely attributed with introducing a previously unknown savagery into warfare, killing women, children, and cowards with little restraint: 'Chiefs are responsible for acts of madness', complained LUGUBU.[107] Shaka 'did not hold trials, he simply killed a man off'.[108]

At the same time, Shaka's tough kind of rule was bound to breed enemies prepared to say just about anything about him. Many anecdotes about his viciousness were almost unquestionably misattributed. Usually these were transferred from Dingane. We have already seen one or two cases; here is another to prove the point. Shaka is accused by at least two informants of killing Mathubane, Shaka's own Thuli client-chief, over a cattle dispute, and installing a younger appointee, Mnini.[109] Both these informants, interestingly, are Thuli, and they are wrong. *Dingane* killed Mathubane, as MAZIYANA's detailed account makes quite clear.[110] It's improbable that this is simply a case of misplaced memory. Either Dingane himself, or Dingane's supporters, had spread the story that it was Shaka who had killed his own favourite. The story would have found willing ears amongst disaffected Thuli.

Seeds of slander planted by Dingane or others easily found resonances in the minds of other prejudiced commentators. Here is another, milder example. Shaka once – with that mixture of political pragmatism and malicious humour which I venture to isolate as part of his personality – decided to 'play a trick' on the iziMpohlo *ibutho*:

> As the sun was going down, Shaka called out inside the *isigodhlo* (this was either at Bulawayo or Dukuza), 'Summon the men of the *umpakati*; let them put on their finery. Let them dress up, and go and *soma* [dally sexually with their girlfriends].' (A prohibition had been placed on them; they had been made the king's wards or *imvokwe*. The order had been given that they should not have connection with the girls.) They put on their finery, and scattered; not one of them remained. They disappeared completely. Shaka said, 'Hau! How empty the place is! Where has everyone gone?' 'Au, Nkosi, there is not a single man left.' 'So they went off when they heard my order? So, in spite of my prohibition they still want the girls?' 'Au, Father, there is not a single one of them left.' 'Weu! Let a force go out to eat them up.' He then summoned the Mbelebele regiment and ordered them to eat up the Izimpohlo. They were to carry away their cattle. 'Put the spade (*ifotsholo*) in! I saw one at Dukuza. When you arrive, and you see a herd of cattle at a home, drive them all away. Put the spade in!' The force ate up their cattle. After this had happened a man of the Izimpohlo came forward and said, 'Our cattle have been eaten up. We were given the order deliberately; it was he who gave us permission to go and *soma*. Seeing there were so many, will they all return?' . . . The king exclaimed, 'Hau! We! Son of Mqomboyi! They have poured even their

ungazi medicines on themselves; they have brought even their witches' cats! No! And their words, "Will they all return?"'(holding his hands behind his back, and bending right down to emphasize the words). Smoke came from his mouth. He went on repeating, 'No! And their words "Will they all return?".' He went on at this for an hour.[111]

The temerity of the iziMpohlo in querying the decision apparently 'frightened Shaka'; his response was to slaughter their cattle; none were returned. The man who had first uttered the fateful question fled, turning at the brow of the hills and shouting back, 'The destructiveness of the Zulu people has risen up against them!' Quite what was behind this prank-turned-nasty, if it's true, is arguable. In later retellings, however, what was perhaps a whim, perhaps a way of reducing a unit's overweening arrogance, would become an example of wayward and murderous destructiveness on Shaka's part, when it was nothing of the sort.[112]

The validity of many such individual cases melts away under scrutiny. Other anecdotes are hopelessly general or decontextualised, and at best can never be verified.

Only a small cluster of 'cruelty' anecdotes can unequivocally be said to have arisen within Shaka's lifetime, and those were made up by James Saunders King in the throes of one of his commercial conspiracies. They were all but repudiated by him later. A few of them appeared, as we have seen, in mid-1826, in the Cape Town paper *The South African Commercial Advertiser*, and were reprinted the following year in George Thompson's book, *Travels and Adventures*. Apart from the pregnant women story that we've already noted, King had only one other substantive accusation:

Several months before my departure from Nathal [sic], he [Shaka] was informed that a chief, who had under him about 450 men, had proved himself a coward (which was in reality nothing more than having been overpowered and defeated). The king sent for him and all his people to his own kraal, where every man was put to death: the lives of the women and children only were spared, and many of them were added to his seraglio.[113]

This event, if it happened – and even King could not claim to have witnessed it – would become equally blown out of proportion. Shaka would be represented as killing cowards all over the place. It may be that what King had heard about was Shaka's uncompromising disciplining of the iziYendane, or alternatively of the *amabutho* involved in the aberrant *eyokutshinga* foray. Either way, *at the time*, King could not validly represent the killing of cowards as habitual. The more common method of dealing with cowards was probably that outlined by Fynn: '[the] cowards were ordered aside from the warriors to whom the beef was given hot[, t]he refuse & fragments being given to the cowards, having been previously soaked in cold water'.[114]

Isaacs's and Fynn's accusations, as far as we can tell, were all written up well after the event. We have seen most of Isaacs's accounts already. Fynn also alleged a further three cases. First, that a servant of Shaka's, named by Fynn as 'Gosa and Gosa' (Ngozangoza?), or 'wound and wound, which name he had acquired from the numerous wounds inflicted on him by Chaka was in one instance compelled to continue acclamations of praise and make oath that he was never hurt by Chaka, who was all the while burning him with a firebrand on his neck'.[115] Second, that Shaka and Dingiswayo both pretended to have female 'periods', during which cattle and people would be killed;[116] and third, that Shaka put to death one of his sisters for having taken a pinch of snuff out of his snuff box.[117]

These events, even if true, do not affect many people. Nevertheless, enough wild and vicious stories were circulating through the Cape Colony in 1827 and 1828 to provoke some disbelief. Shaka, noted one correspondent, 'is declared a determined, a systematic, and a practiced plunderer, raising no corn, breeding no cattle, and procreating no children'. Such a portrait was only to be expected, the writer wryly noted, from the 'prejudiced channels' of his enemies, and should be treated with 'considerable caution'.[118] A few months later, another writer said sensibly:

> The frightful stories told of King Chaka, and which have for several years appeared in the English newspapers uncontradicted, are, we have reason to believe, mere fabrications. His enormous army, his shocking barbarities, and his projected conquests, partook too much

of the marvellous . . . If Chaka cut down his subjects like hay, we
suspect his army would dwindle to something less than thirty thousand
men.[119]

It's also worth noting another demurral, from our most level-headed
eyewitness. Charles Rawden Maclean didn't minimise Shaka's executions,
but felt that many of them were not solely Shaka's doing. They were
'prompted by degrading superstitions' or 'at the instance of a cringing and
cowardly scoundrel named Mbopha, a confidential servant'.[120] (Now that's
an interesting piece of information, given Mbopha's role in Shaka's
assassination.) Maclean, though 'far from vindicating cruelties, with many of
which Shaka can be justly charged,' vehemently denied the genocidal
allegations that appeared, for instance, in Stephen Kay's 1833 Travels and
Researches in Kaffraria. Kay, despite being keen to rubbish the Port Natal
traders' reputations, was happy to regurgitate the stories of mass-murder of
regiments and children spun by James Saunders King. These 'monstrous
absurdities,' Maclean fulminated, 'supplied either by the fertility of the writer's
brain or from exaggerated and evil report,' were themselves a 'monstrous
injustice'. Shaka's alleged 'slaughter of the children is a portion of that history
which was never heard of at Natal up to the death of him who is represented
to have perpetrated that atrocity!'[121] He is surely correct.

What do the Zulu sources reveal? It's possible, of course, that the whites
drew on a strand of local, 'Zulu' antipathy to Shaka. (Some Zulu sources, for
instance, also claimed that Shaka habitually slaughtered cowards.[122]) Well,
there is the infamous Thathiyana Gorge story, a place that, as we've already
seen, can't be located – and neither can its victims. It might have been the
Qwabe;[123] it might have been another group of ill-fated warriors, a 'portion
of a regiment' being punished (the iziYendane, perhaps).[124] At least one
informant thought that it was in fact Dingane who tried to fill the gorge
with corpses.[125] If there was ever a core of truth in the story, it's lost to us.

Shaka was also said to have deliberately killed people in order to feed the
vultures. 'The vultures are hungry,' he would say, 'they must be given food'.[126]
There's a story that Shaka was reproved for the practice by Ngqengelele.[127]
(There is always someone around to reprove him.) However, several

informants, including BALENI who is no lover of Shaka, claim that it was Dingane who did this, at kwaMatiwane.[128] Doubtless the bodies of the executed were left out in the bush or on a hillside to be cleaned up by natural undertakers; it's easy to see how the perception might have arisen. As it stands, the attribution of this practice to Shaka as policy is dubious.

There is the story that Shaka blinded two or three Qwabe men and left them to fend for themselves. These men were named by one informant as Matshongwe, Nhlanganiso and Mpezulu.[129] Fynn wrote that two chiefs – 'Machongwa and Umsoka' – had been charged with witchcraft and blinded, dying shortly afterwards.[130] Mashongwe was cited by another informant as being a Qwabe, the only survivor of an incident, after Phakathwayo's defeat, in which Shaka, apparently in some sort of competitive spirit, set some Qwabe warriors on to kill each other. Shaka blinded him, and he died much later. The same informant, NGIDI, relates in some detail that Nhlanganiso, named as Shaka's victim above, was in fact blinded by Dingane – and that it was not the only time that Shaka's successor did this.[131] Once again, we have a single crime attributed to both men. I suspect that this is another of Dingane's acts being read back into Shaka's time, perhaps by Dingane himself. As for Mashongwe, another long, almost certainly apocryphal story was told about him:

Matshongwe and Nhlanganiso were once sent by Shaka to spy upcountry, in the Transvaal above Swaziland. They went, and on getting to that country they found many bucks. On seeing the buck they supposed them to be cattle. They returned, and told the king, 'We have seen the cattle; there are great numbers up-country.' An *impi* went out, and travelled a great distance searching for the cattle. Seeing a number of buck in the distance they said, 'There they are.' The *impi* went forward, and discovered that they were buck. This was reported to Shaka . . . The king became angry, and cried, '*Weu*! I did not send you out to find buck and mistake them for cattle. This is the fault of you people, Matshongwe. You failed because you did not go close enough to see properly. This is the end for you. Seize them and take out their eyes . . .[132]

Shaka is said to have made up a nasty song about the blinding:

> You do not ask the askers for us to agree with them,
> We went and took out their eyes,
> They went floundering about, falling into dongas.[133]

Even more viciously, it was alleged that the toxic sap of the euphorbia was rubbed into the gaping sockets.[134] It is possible that Mashongwe's case contains a kernel of truth – but one sanctioned by the norms of combating witchcraft.

Other anecdotes of Shaka's alleged murders – the more detailed ones, interestingly – are obviously conducted for reasons of honour. You will recall the case of Bambalele and his friend, who failed to report a dying cow and inadvertently (and fatally) insulted Shaka's mother. Questions of honour shade indistinguishably into questions of discipline, security, and even popular expectation. Maclean, who was sympathetic but admitted that Shaka made 'many bloody sacrifices of his people', attributed the brutality to a clear, even unwilling pragmatism, not to madness:

> As proof of Shaka's sentiments and concern for us, I recollect his saying very seriously to me one day, 'Jackabo (the name he always called me), if it was not for me I fear there is scarcely an umfogasann [umfokozana] (a common man, or an expression of the lower order of the natives) but would rejoice of having the opportunity to kill my white people. Oh!' he continued, 'they are a bad people; I am obliged to kill a few to gratify the rest; and if I were not to do it, they would think me an old woman, a coward, and kill me themselves. I have been often told by my Indaba (Council) to kill you wild beasts of Mlungus . . .[135]

Many executions were certainly punishment for simple criminality. Theft was punishable by death. For instance, Gcugcwa, a chief of the Wosiyana people, was caught stealing cattle near the Thukela. He was tied across a gate and Shaka ordered that the cattle that Gcugcwa was so fond of be driven across him and trample him to death.[136] This is without doubt nasty, but also, in the circumstances, poetically just.

These anecdotes reflect a leader utilising customary practices – including death sentences – to achieve a consolidation of his power and control, rather than a tyrant pathologically addicted to cruelty for its own sake. There are, however, a cluster of other one-off anecdotes that might be said to expose a truly sadistic streak. In the examples that follow, few of them are attributable to any particular time, person, or place, and the majority are therefore completely unverifiable.

Shaka killed a pretty girl who had the nerve to tell him that he was ugly, with a nose like an *isifonyo*, a calf's leather muzzle.[137]

'Shaka used to kill a man just because he was ugly.'[138] A second version attaches this to one man, a half-brother named Sankoye, whom Shaka banished because he was ugly, but who later rather stupidly wandered back; he was put to death.[139]

A man who put a feather in his ear and turned it round and round would be killed.[140] (Or, at least, Shaka lewdly joked: 'To what is he trying to compare the sensation of tickling his ear with a feather?'[141])

A girl called Nomlethi was killed for putting on airs and walking through Shaka's cattle at the *umkhosi* ceremony.[142]

A man named Lubhedu was killed just for laughing.[143]

Shaka would kill people dancing out of time at dances.[144]

Once Shaka asked some boys of an *ibutho* whether anyone brought them food; when they replied in the negative, he ordered them to go and kill their negligent mothers.[145] (Whether the order was carried out is not recorded.)

Shaka killed the informant MKANDO's uncle Samvu because Samvu had shaved his head before Shaka did.[146]

Madla kaNombanda was accused of saying, 'Why shouldn't we Mbonambi *ibutho* who *hlabana* so much (ie are so plucky in battle) be given cattle?' Shaka had him tied to a tree, a fire was made under him and he was burnt alive (although this may have been connected with a general disciplining of this unit for grumbling).[147] A similar death-by-fire was said by Fynn to have been meted out to a man named 'Impesan', accused of witchcraft.[148]

Shaka ordered his *izinduna* to 'sharpen' their assegais on a man's forehead. The man did not die.

Even on a thorough combing of the testimonies, these accounts are pretty much all we have. Are they the tip of an iceberg of cruelties that have gone unrecorded? Or are they exaggerations of crimes of a lesser order? They are not to be dismissed out of hand, but I lean towards the second possibility. Like many of the much later white fantasies, some of these Zulu traditions are probably inventions, too. Nevertheless, it's hard to avoid the imputation of a cruel edge to Shaka's conduct. Perhaps the best that we can do is to lay these anecdotes of nastiness and malice alongside the almost equally numerous anecdotes of his generosity and judiciousness, stories which have been all but buried up to now.

'LIBERAL WITH CATTLE'

Shaka is just as often displayed as generous, amused, intelligently perceptive, accommodating, and flexible, as he is depicted as cruel and capricious. He was liberal with the whites: regularly giving them meals, cattle, porters, men to help cut timber, hunters, and ivory. Fynn comments:

> [Shaka] was inflexible in his resolves, severe in his discipline and the terror of his enemies. Of the soldiery, notwithstanding his atrocities he was the idol and to a conquered enemy where he had no suspicion of witchcraft he was liberal and lenient. The sacred characters of ambassadors from his most inveterate enemies, even in the ardour of conflict, he always respected and ensured their safety. To the brave he was liberal to excess, to the cowardly merciless and cruel. Vain, haughty, imperious and cruel to his subjects to the Europeans he was affable and kind, anxious to know their wants only to alleviate them, possessing a perpetual thirst for knowledge which he received with caution and conversed with a shrewdness and policy which would not have disgraced many civilized beings. On the loss of the Mary and on the deaths of Capt. King and Mr Hutton his manly features evinced that sincere sorrow which showed he was not altogether divested of the finer feelings of humanity.[149]

Shaka was equally generous with many of his own people. He would give cattle to families setting up new homesteads, and reward his warriors fulsomely for their bravery, 'ten, twenty, and thirty cattle' at a time.[150] Doubtless, much of this liberality was politically motivated, but it often seems to extend beyond that. One informant, MBULO, relates that his father was rewarded by Shaka for killing off a predatory 'giant' holed up amongst some precipices. The victorious stalwart was allowed to choose ten heifers as his reward. When another five beasts moved to follow the selected ones, which the herdboys tried to drive back, Shaka said, 'No! Leave them; they are simply following my hero.'[151] Shaka liked to reward strength and athleticism: he offered a large calf to anyone who could lift it onto his shoulders (it was won by Manqondo kaMazwana);[152] and he rewarded a white sailor, Ned Cameron, for daringly performing a nautical jig or two.[153]

On occasion his generosity even extended to the enemy. After the defeat of Sikhunyane, according to Maclean, 'on hearing of the gallant defence made by the enemy, [Shaka] departed from the general rules in Caffrarian warfare by proclaiming that all of the enemy who had survived and made their escape should be spared and received as his children, worthy of becoming the companions of Zulu warriors'.[154] As we've seen repeatedly, this was, in fact, his policy. The strategy was, in Maclean's view, purely pragmatic:

> The policy of adding these brave men to his band of warriors, to strengthen and promote his success in future schemes of conquest, might be considered as the primary and only motive in the savage chief for exercising the act of mercy, were it not known that courage always had been a sure passport to Shaka's favour and esteem.[155]

Shaka was also not oblivious to criticism: 'Zidunge, son of Mbikwana, *induna* of the Bekenya *ibutho*, used to reprove Shaka when in his opinion he was wrong, and Shaka would desist.'[156] Young Maclean also depicts himself grandly as having prevented Shaka from committing many executions.[157] Apart from such (slightly suspicious) self-congratulations, Shaka is regularly depicted as letting people go who might otherwise have been killed off:

> On one occasion, when Shaka, in the presence of his counsellors, had ordered a man to be put to death on some pretext or other, he

said to him, 'Tell me, So-and-so, now you are on the point of being put to death, which among the things you are leaving behind, do you consider the most delightful?' 'A little child, your majesty, that has just learned to smile,' replied the poor wretch, 'a brave young maize plant just about to burst into bloom; and best of all, the king.' 'So well, Zulu,' exclaimed the despot, 'has the man spoken, he deserves not to die. Release him!'[158]

Whether this appealed to Shaka's sentiment or his vanity is impossible to say. A more detailed version of the same story is more revealing of Zulu mores:

Once, at the royal *umuzi* Bulawayo, a man was caught *takataing* [concocting evil medicines] against someone of the *umpakati* [men of the *inkosi*'s inner circle] during the night. He was arrested. The matter was reported to Shaka, who expressed great surprise that anything of this sort should go on in his *umuzi*, and directed the culprit to be brought before him. . . . 'How is this?' 'Sir, it is in consequence of having been inoculated as a child by my father to the end that I should follow this practice. He inoculated me on the anus.' 'Well, then,' said Shaka, 'now that you are about to die, say what things of surpassing beauty you leave behind on earth.' 'In the first place, oh son of Senzangakhona,' replied the poor wretch, 'I leave the king whom, merely to converse with face to face, is an inexpressive [sic] delight; next, the smile of a little child that has just learnt to sit up by itself; and lastly, the young shoot of a mealie plant, to look on which is enchanting, especially when seen with one's head brought so as to view the tops of a whole field.' Shaka, pleased with the compliment to himself, then directed that he was to be taken away and have the place where he had been inoculated excised, whilst his medicines, particularly those which he had, on Shaka asking him, pointed out as what he poisoned others with, were to be taken and burnt, and their ashes strewn on the Umhlatuze river to be carried off towards the sea. . . . The man was thereupon allowed to live. Never again did he resort to his former practice; the king's treatment had cured him completely.[159]

This is perhaps apocryphal, but is supported by several other instances in which Shaka draws back from the death penalty. For example, there was Mpitikazi (whom we have encountered on page 167), the Langeni man who on Shaka's succession advised the Langeni to flee or be killed by Shaka: Shaka let him go on Nandi's request.[160]

Maclean also recalled a case in which a man who had been executed in one of the traditional ways – by having a wooden skewer driven up his anus – somehow extracted the stake and crawled back to Shaka who, impressed, spared him and had him treated.[161] Here's another account that demonstrates Shaka's generosity:

A woman, dirty and without a good skirt to wear, came to Shaka. Shaka expressed astonishment and said, 'Mame! Does your husband *konza* me?' The woman said, 'He does, my father.' 'Why then, mother, do you go about naked?' 'My husband is poor, *inkosi*.' Shaka said, 'Mdhlaka, pick out two heifers which are dripping milk, with full udders. Pick out also for me a fat ox with "udders" (ie through being so fat)'. The two heifers and the ox were fetched. . . . The king said, 'These heifers, take them off, and mix up some fat. I give them to you; I do not impose on you any kind of responsibility in regard to them. When they calve, pour the fat in one calabash and smear it on yourself. The other cow must furnish curds so that you can get fat and not go on being as dried-up as you are. I give you this ox and call your husband to whatever *ikhanda* he may be attached. Tell him that I have given you these cattle. Say that the king says he must kill this ox, skin it, and make you two coverings, two skirts. The meat to be cooked for the fat is plentiful and must be used for softening these things. You will have a calabash of fat.' Shaka then directed a man to be sent along to drive the cattle to the woman's home. The man in due course came to give praises to the king. Shaka reprimanded him for allowing his wife to come to the great one's place not properly dressed. 'You do me a dishonour,' he said, 'I want the women to bear the looks becoming the wives of those who *konza* me.' . . . Shaka said, 'Seize hold of so-and-so!' 'Only wait and let me praise the king,' said the man, thinking he was about to be killed. The man said, 'It is good that I am being killed by our king, "the ferocious one from whom people do not court trouble".' Shaka said, 'Leave him, he is praising his king . . .' Shaka then gave him cattle.[162]

Here's a more whimsical tale:

Shaka once sent out a heifer with two men to different parts of the country. Their instructions were to ask people in the usual way for snuff, and the first person who gave the snuff without having denied having any was to be given the beast. Many persons were approached. At last a woman, on being asked, took out a snuff box and, in knocking out the snuff, said, 'But there isn't very much, I'm afraid.' She was given the heifer.[163]

On a related note, it was said that once at kwaBulawayo, Shaka rose and allowed his shadow to fall across Mepo kaNgwane of the Ngcolosi people. Mepo was too afraid to move, though he knew that the shadow would be fatal to him. Shaka was laughing and joking obliviously. Mepo did indeed sicken and die; Shaka expressed great concern and regret, ordering his men to carry Mepo home to be tended there.[164]

Even Fynn, recounting a journey across Zulu country with Shaka's army, described how Shaka waded into a flooded river and stood in the middle helping little boys across.[165]

If these stories can be cautiously summarised, we arrive at the picture of a leader who is severe, even aggressive, but not inflexible. The picture is, however, unstable. No one, least of all the Zulu people themselves, can agree. Perhaps MAYINGA is closest to the tenor of the time: '[Shaka] was always talking of war. He snuffed a good deal. The old regime was good, even though the king killed off frequently. We used to think the king was having sport and we thought but little of it. He never seemed in earnest'[166] – which couldn't have been much comfort to the people whose necks were broken.

Box 11

The 'mfecane' debate

Variations on the words *Fetkanie, Ficanie,* and *imfecane* appeared in the 1820s and 30s, applied to the roving bands of marauders – sometimes Ngwane, sometimes Bhaca, Sotho, Ndebele/Khumalo, Mpondo, once or twice Zulu – who harassed the peoples of the Transkei region from about 1822 onwards. There seems no doubt that it was a Xhosa word (*-feca,* to crack or bruise), and never one that the Zulu applied to anything they themselves were doing.

Only in the 1880s did the first instance of the word being used to denote a whole process or event appear. It was in this sense that historian Eric Walker used it in his 1928 book, *A History of South Africa* – exactly a century after Shaka's death. John Omer-Cooper, then at Ibadan in Nigeria, entrenched it in his influential 1960 survey, *The Zulu Aftermath.*

The concept of 'the mfecane' as some kind of cohesive movement or period was rooted in the nineteenth-century view of the 'wars of Shaka', the edges of which the first white settlers (and their historians) encountered. Shaka was almost wholly blamed for sending other 'tribes' scattering across the subcontinent, taking destructive 'Zulu' methods of warfare with them. The repercussions continued after Shaka's death, but its roots were cut off when he died. Such was the stereotype.

Omer-Cooper dressed the process up in a new politically correct garb of 'Afrocentric' state-building initiative. It was, in his view, a fundamentally locally organised 'revolution' and he did not radically question this Zulu-centred picture. His account, indeed, included little new empirical research, and continued to use slightly watered-down variants of the apocalyptic rhetoric previous writers had used to describe Shaka's alleged devastations.

It was essentially Omer-Cooper's view of the 'mfecane' as a more or less isolated, Zulucentric, albeit more positive phenomenon that was critiqued in the 1980s by Julian Cobbing, an historian based at Rhodes University in Grahamstown. (Graham's Town, as it was then known, was ironically a hub for much of the initial myth-making about the Zulu in the 1820s and 30s.)

From 1983 onwards, Cobbing produced a number of unpublished papers questioning the very foundations of the concept of the 'mfecane'. This culminated in his only formally published paper on the subject, 'The Mfecane as Alibi', in the prestigious *Journal of African History* in 1988. Cobbing argued that blaming

Shaka for the violence was empirically wrong; the main cause of the violence was the slave-trade emanating from Delagoa Bay, in time exacerbated by slaving raids from the east and north. Cobbing focused on two 'battles' – Dithakong in 1823 and Mbholompo in 1828 – as test cases. In both instances, he asserted, the essential dynamic was the desire for slave labour on the part of Europeans, missionaries and Cape Colony officials alike. This motive was covered up, then and subsequently; a massive verbal and textual campaign was launched to blame regional violence entirely on someone else: Shaka was picked out as the main culprit. In short, according to Cobbing, the 'mfecane' was a kind of alibi for European depredations.

The acerbity of Cobbing's tone, the insinuation that even present-day academics were implicated in this ongoing conspiracy of silence, and the far-reaching ramifications of his views for southern African history generally, provoked howls of protests from established historians. In particular, he was accused repeatedly of misusing evidence, suppressing disagreeable material, and drawing outrageously untenable conclusions. For a while, the 'mfecane' debate was the most exciting furore to have affected South African historiography for decades. Cobbing continued to defend and refine his position, here and there admitting to errors of fact or judgement, but sticking to his main points: that the slave-trade was deeply implicated in general regional violence, that this had begun long before Shaka, that Shaka's polity was at least initially primarily defensive, and that mainstream white historians had collaborated to conceal these unpalatable facts.

The debate culminated in a colloquium held at the University of the Witwatersrand in 1991. A selection of papers from the colloquium was eventually published as *The Mfecane Aftermath* – a deliberate echo of Omer-Cooper's title. Insurmountable disagreement with the editor Carolyn Hamilton, a long-time student and collaborator of John Wright's, unhappily meant that no contribution was included from Cobbing himself – the very man who had started the debate. This was amongst a number of possible reasons why the wind suddenly seemed to go out of the controversy.

The lull was not at all because the question was settled. Reactions to Cobbing's thesis were deeply divided. A number of his students (including myself) continued largely to support him. Archaeologists such as Thomas Dowson and Simon Hall were excited and mainly supportive. By contrast, mainstream historians, including Omer-Cooper, demurred in varying degrees. Omer-Cooper tried to preserve the idea of the 'mfecane' as a suitable umbrella term, though he could do it only by changing its definition. Jeff Peires, an erstwhile colleague of Cobbing's at Rhodes, attacked him particularly acidly over the Mbholompo issue, accusing him of deliberately ignoring African source material. Illogically, Peires blamed Cobbing for having 'paralysed' the debate, and asserted a need for resurrecting the 'old paradigm', supported by more research.

The historians, including Cobbing himself, thereafter drifted off into other areas of research, leaving the whole thing unresolved. Even now, great areas of detailed empirical research still need to be done. Only Carolyn Hamilton, working in a more interdisciplinary mode, produced her book *Terrific Majesty*, and I, working from a literary angle, produced a complementary (if not always congruent) Ph.D., published as *Savage Delight: White Myths of Shaka*. There have been two short interventions by Elizabeth Eldredge, an American historian, and some muted revisionist noises from generalists such as Robert Ross (British) and Norman Etherington (Australian). (Even this excites resistance: Peires has attacked Etherington's new overview, *The Great Treks*, with unnecessary vituperation.) South African mainstream historians have remained virtually silent – with the exception of John Wright, a professor of history at the University of KwaZulu-Natal, Pietermaritzburg.

Wright has done more than anyone to lay the foundations of future studies of early Zulu history. If Cobbing has provided unprecedented spark and controversy, Wright has been patiently building up a series of journal articles, a Ph.D., encyclopaedia chapters, and – not the least of his achievements – editing *The James Stuart Archive*. Wright has tackled both the empirical details of Shaka's times, and the conceptual sweep of 'mfecane' studies. His voice is unrelentingly level-headed – a scholar difficult to disagree with. It is hard to differ, in the end, with his judgement that, though the Cobbing thesis can be faulted at numerous points, it has proved magnificently valuable in one way: 'Zulu' history can no longer be simplistically divorced from a wider regional history, even a 'world' history, and Shaka can no longer be simplistically blamed for a savage outburst of self-consuming, purely black-on-black mayhem. What began as an upsurge of violence well before Shaka's time continued afterwards, merging all but seamlessly into the patterns of violence that accompanied increasingly militarised European colonisation. The misleading and politically overcharged labels of 'Afrocentric' and 'Eurocentric' processes or approaches must be abandoned, along with any notion of some clearly defined, geographically and chronologically bounded 'time of troubles' coincident with Shaka's reign.

As a concept, the 'mfecane' can be consigned to its proper place: an ancillary 'box' dealing with the ephemera of historiographical debate and its museum pieces.

13

White mischief

Frontier rumours, 1827–8

If death had not put a stop to his ambitious career [Shaka] would assuredly, ere this, have exterminated every tribe of Kaffirs up to the Colonial border. The numbers whose death he occasioned have been left to conjecture, but exceed a million.

Stuart and Malcolm, *The Diary of Henry Francis Fynn* (1951, 20).

In August 1827, the Eastern Cape settler Thomas Philipps wrote from Graham's Town (now Grahamstown) - nearly 1 000 kilometres west of kwaDukuza:

There seems now no doubt that the aggressions of the Mantatees and all the other Tribes on each other is solely occasioned by the operation of that monster Chaca. He rules with despotic sway as far as Delagoa Bay down to Port Natal, and whenever he thinks proper to set off on one of his plundering and murderous excursions either North or South, he sets the whole of the Tribes in motion, he robs those nearest to him, murders, and burns their habitations. . . . [T]here appears no present remedy for it.[1]

This is perhaps the earliest potted version of the regional history that would become known as the 'Mfecane', pictured as a massive disturbance solely attributable to Shaka. Cape Governor Bourke wrote in a similar vein to the Colonial Office a month or two later: 'A powerful chief named Chaca, whose

territory stretches from Port Natal to the Indian Ocean to the 25th degree
of East longitude, has already threatened them [the Xhosa] with attack and
from the large force he has organized and the discipline he is said to maintain
he appears likely to become a great conqueror'.[2] (Twenty-five degrees 'East'
is about 50 kilometres *west* of Port Elizabeth; Bourke's geography is an
absurdity.) At the same time, the colonial commander Colonel Henry
Somerset claimed that he had heard from a Thembu chief named Powana
that Shaka was 'coming on'; Powana had been told so by the 'Fetcanie'.[3]

The eastern colonial border descended into a frenzy of alarm and
speculation.

'CONTINUED STATE OF ALARM'

As we've already seen (on page 407), the one thing that is now quite clear
about the 'Fetcanie' incursions is that they were *not* Shaka's Zulu. This is
evident even in the following fuzzy account, written on the same day as
Somerset's letter, 31 August 1827. It was penned into his journal by a
missionary at Wesleyville, William Shaw:

> The country has been kept in a continued state of alarm for some
> time past in consequence of the near approach of a large marauding
> tribe from the Interior; – for several years past there has been
> continual wars among the interior tribes both of Bootshoannas &
> Caffres originating in the restless Spirit of some powerful chiefs not
> far from Delagoa Bay . . . [T]he near approach to Caffreland & to
> part of the Colony, of a large and powerful tribe whose object appears
> to be War and plunder, they have come a considerable distance from
> the interior and are the same people who for several years have caused
> so much confusion among the various tribes of southern Africa. They
> are called by the Caffres *Fikaanie* . . .[4]

The implication here is that Shaka was by no means solely responsible for
the disturbances. (Shaw also mentioned drought as a factor in the latest round
of aggressions – a further indication that drought tends to stimulate scattering
and mobile raids, rather than centralisation.[5]) In 1827, Matiwane and the

Ngwane were the primary raiders. As we have seen, they had been pushed west and then south by a combination of, first, Zwide, later Shaka, possibly Dingane's raid, and Bergenaar and Griqua raiders from the north-west. Another source, drawing on the evidence of John Cane, stated explicitly that it was 'not Chaka that drove the Fetcanie upon the Caffres', but 'Omsilicosan' – Mzilikazi.[6]

Nevertheless, as the Port Natal traders fed misinformation to the Cape press and officials, the threat became increasingly identified with Shaka himself.

How damaging these raids really were, and how much was unnecessary panic, is hard to say. William Shaw noted in the same journal entry that the local Xhosa didn't seem to be taking the invaders terribly seriously, never having been worsted in battle yet. There was also much exaggeration. As the border agent Mackay wrote from the Kei river in July 1827, 'It is . . . true that on many recent occasions they [the Thembu] have suffered from the attacks and inroads of that tribe [the Fetcanie], but, on the other hand, I am bound to state my firm conviction that their natural irresolution and timidity magnify the slightest appearance of danger into a real cause of terror.'[7] A few days later, having encountered a 'Fetcanie' force he estimated at 5 000, with more lurking in the vicinity, Mackay was able to interview a 'Fetcanie' (in fact, Ngwane) captive. This is the man whom we quoted earlier (see page 407), who said that 'Chaka' had taken their livestock 'some time ago', obliging them to raid further afield for cattle.[8]

In the meanwhile – these panicky missives notwithstanding – the colonial border area had lapsed into quiet.

As for Shaka, what *was* he up to?

WHITE MISCHIEF

Shaka was at home, mourning. His troops were at ease. Ironically, he *was* planning a foray to the west, but this would take several months more to mature. No one in the Cape knew about it until after it had happened. He was also probably working on the idea of sending some of his men on an 'embassy' to the Cape.

Zulu informants also liked to think that the 'embassy' idea was Shaka's, and that it was he who instructed King to build the boat that would take his representatives.[9] It did emerge that sometime in 1826 Shaka had sent a four-horned bullock down to Port Natal as a present to be conveyed to the governor whenever it proved possible. The bullock was entrusted to King, but it never reached its intended recipient: King killed it because he wanted the fat to grease the launch of the boat.[10]

Shaka may even have momentarily considered going to the Cape himself. In one possibly apocryphal story, he and his chief *izinduna* threw sticks in the sea, and let the sea's caprice decide the matter. As on the other occasion when he did this with Zihlandlo (see page 195), Shaka's stick was never found. Partly on the strength of this, he chose his number one ambassador – Sotobe kaMpangalala – to make the journey.[11]

In fact, the idea was older. Farewell had mooted it in one of his first communications with the Cape in 1824. King had mentioned it again the following year. Ironically, Farewell got excluded from the embassy in the end. This was because of the petty but vicious conflict within the Port Natal community, particularly between King and Farewell.

Right from the start, these two hard-headed men had jockeyed both for access to market resources and for Shaka's favour. Isaacs coyly covered up the details of these disputes in his book, but more came out in a plaintive deposition made by Isaacs and the carpenter Hutton in Port Elizabeth in May 1828.[12] According to them, Shaka gave King two bullocks and an elephant tusk after the *Mary* was wrecked. Farewell, who had been allowed to do all the talking, appropriated them for himself. They also claimed that King had refused all presents from Shaka, saying that he hadn't come to trade, only to rescue his friend Farewell – an astoundingly transparent lie. Farewell later stated that this rescue was only 'nominally' King's purpose: 'in reality almost ever since his arrival every endeavour has been made by himself and party to undermine my interest here'.[13] Farewell himself, having delivered a present from King to Shaka, was in turn accused of having smuggled away the return gift of 70 head of cattle.[14] If King had indeed given over to Farewell the primary right to negotiate with Shaka as a safety measure, as Isaacs claimed, he was right to feel grievously betrayed.[15] Quite clearly, however, King's desire for personal gain overrode any other loyalties, including any obligation to Shaka.

Another dispute arose over the building of the new boat. In their 1828 deposition, Hutton and Isaacs claimed that when the *Helicon* took King back to the Cape, King and Farewell squabbled further over the debt that Farewell now owed. Farewell promised to supply King's people with cattle while he was away. The moment King was gone, however, Farewell 'endeavoured to seduce the natives away from us that the king [Shaka] had given to assist in drawing timber out of the forest'. Moreover, he tried to starve them.[16]

When King got back in the *Ann* in October 1826, Farewell apparently refused to pay half the charter, as he had promised, adding the mystifying comment that 'Mr King had better send the present of feathers, the crown etc., to the king (Chaka) himself otherwise himself and party would be killed,' and observed that 'it matters not who sends them as the king is aware everything comes from me'.[17] After this provocative arrogance, Isaacs and Hutton tried to persuade King to trade independently, which wouldn't have been difficult since he was doing it anyway. This explains King and Isaacs's manic scrounging for ivory on their own, and also, more importantly, their subsequent land claims.

In their 1828 deposition Hutton and Isaacs seemed to be in accord, but in his later book Isaacs accused Hutton himself of being part of the problem. Quite what Hutton's 'extraordinary conduct' was, Isaacs characteristically doesn't say.[18] Probably he threatened to down tools for some reason. King's reaction was to threaten to burn the boat in its stocks and 'force' a way overland to Delagoa Bay, where he would somehow get his hands on a vessel. The bluster evidently didn't impress: the problem was patched up, it seems, and work on the boat resumed.[19]

Perhaps because the boat was the key, it was James Saunders King who ended up taking the embassy from Shaka to the Cape. Farewell claimed that he 'did all in [his] power to prevent their going until the pleasure of government was known,' but found himself subverted by the misinformation of Jacob Msimbithi.[20] (The fact that the 'embassy' didn't go on any of the other vessels that called in at Port Natal is intriguing; King had somehow managed to control the process, and so was able to conceal his own motives from Shaka.) At noon on 24 July 1828, Isaacs wrote in his book, Shaka summoned himself, Fynn and King into the innermost enclosure of his *isigodlo* – an extraordinary (and, I must add, unlikely) privilege. Shaka seemed 'peculiarly grave', looked at them 'sternly, but with a wily air, as though he wished to communicate something, yet feared to do so'. When he broke his silence, it was to say 'that he should like to cross the water to see King George, but feared that he would not receive a welcome reception'. He would therefore send a chief, 'under the charge of Lieutenant King', once the vessel was finished, and 'he would send two elephant's teeth as a present to King George, to show that he desired to be on terms of amity with him'.[21]

In this way, Isaacs makes the embassy idea out to be Shaka's. This is an oversimplification. Almost certainly the whole thing was pressed by King as a way of outflanking Farewell. Given that Shaka was getting irritated by the dispute between the two white men, and perhaps by Farewell's own selfish behaviour, the Zulu leader may have been quickly swayed into colluding in the scheme. As for the two elephant tusks, Isaacs attempts to counter the dispute over the ivory that subsequently arose. According to him, King protested that two tusks were not enough; Shaka responded that he would supply more, Farewell having kept a whole lot in his store.[22] In other words, Isaacs was claiming that the extra ivory was for King, not the King. This was a lie.

While waiting for the boat to be completed, the whites meanwhile spent most of their time hunting or trading independently for ivory. On 13 September, after the first phase of mourning for Nandi was over, King sent Isaacs back to Shaka for the present of ivory, anxious to get it before Farewell objected. Isaacs found that Shaka was already planning a cleansing, or ihlambo, campaign against the Mpondos – part of the ongoing ceremony of mourning for Nandi that would, as convention demanded, run for about a year. Shaka was concerned to know whether the Mpondos might have firearms. (This is a measure of how trade had developed in that area, primarily through Fynn. There were probably more weapons around than anyone has acknowledged.) On his way back to Port Natal, Isaacs ran into trouble extracting sustenance from some of the local people. He only got his way after shooting at them with a barrelful of Indian corn and threatening to tell Shaka. There are other hints that the whites' presence, and the arrogant way in which they conducted themselves, was beginning to generate resentment. Their sometime interpreter Jacob Msimbithi had also, according to Isaacs, tried to persuade the Zulu youths accompanying Isaacs to desert; the ubiquitous Msimbithi seems to have popped up again at Port Natal, where Shaka wanted him killed in case he 'would incense the Governor of the Cape'. Isaacs also accused Jacob of unspecified 'bad conduct'. However, the whites spared him, apparently out of the goodness of their hearts, and he would join them on the impending 'embassy' to the Cape.[23] The truth of this is highly questionable; all the evidence points to the *whites* wanting to kill Msimbithi, whom they portrayed as being consistently against them.

Back at Port Natal, disputes continued. Isaacs as usual doesn't reveal what they were, and tries to dismiss them as 'trivial', no more than what you would expect from crusty sailors – but he expends two whole pages of his book saying this in tellingly evasive prose. The King-Farewell difference was obviously the running sore. In his book Isaacs says merely that Shaka showed favour to King, Fynn and himself, while displaying 'a cool indifference' to Farewell.[24] In the 1828 deposition, he is more open (or exaggerated). Farewell had tried to fill Shaka's ears with lies directed against King, which 'would have led to the *murder* of the whole party' had Shaka not shrewdly divined the truth. One day, King fell ill at Farewell's premises (what he was doing there is a mystery). Hutton visited the sick man, upon which Farewell 'said to Mr Fynn (placing a pistol in his bosom), "Don't you think I had better go to that damn'd rascal?".' Whether the rascal was King or Hutton isn't clear. In addition, John Cane had quietly informed them that Farewell was threatening, once King's boat had sailed, to kill off the whole of his (King's) establishment.[25]

In this poisonous atmosphere, King and Hutton's new boat was launched. As Isaacs, or his ghost-writer, romantically wrote, she 'glided gently into the sea, floated on the bosom of the ocean, and brought up her bows to the billows, as if evincing the desire to take a longing farewell of the spot that had given her birth'.[26] It was 10 March 1828. She was initially named *Chaka*, but this was changed to the *Elizabeth and Susan* the moment she reached the open sea. At any rate, the means of escape, and of getting Shaka's delegation to the Cape, was afloat.

There is no clear idea about what Shaka hoped to gain from the enterprise, apart from certain supplies. As we'll see shortly, the Cape officials who received the 'embassy' couldn't discover a clear purpose either. Perhaps it was no more than the exploratory foray outlined by the informants: 'to go and find out what the English people's home was like'.[27] This may – as Cape officials also suspected – have been a euphemism for military spying. At any rate, a combination of circumstances and the machinations of James Saunders King would derail whatever diplomatic purpose the 'embassy' may have been intended to serve.

Sotobe, appointed by Shaka to represent him on this exploration, was an aggressive but respected elder. He was old, about the age of Jama, Shaka's grandfather, and had begun his career herding cattle at Nobamba. He had grown into a big, very dark man, with a prominent forehead and his headring mounted far on the back of his head. He became the *induna* at iNtontela, where he was largely excused from campaigning because he could count cattle. He was red-eyed and humourless; people who laughed in his presence were likely to get a grindstone pitched at their heads. He wouldn't eat meat unless it was fat, and liked it pounded first to a juicy tenderness. He would upbraid people loudly, so the *inkosi* could hear, and was permitted to kill miscreants without Shaka's permission.[28]

Shaka told Sotobe to take a favourite wife with him – he took Ntombintombi – and his trusted attendant, Mbozamboza. Several other Zulu people accompanied him, named by John Cane as Managarda, Pangia, Nomama, Macomba, and Mushleiva.[29] There was also Hutton, King and Isaacs, Jacob Msimbithi, and another interpreter (King's own), Klaju kaNomdayi of the emaThulini.[30] Sotobe took his dancing dress, assegai, headband resplendent with the regal crane feather, and oxtails for adorning his arms, and boarded a white man's boat for the first time in his life.

Was Shaka aware of what his emissaries would encounter? Did he ever think that the white men would become a serious threat? It's difficult to believe that he did not have a fair idea, even if Xhosa boasts and Jacob Msimbithi's misinformation led him to think that the whites wouldn't make a particularly formidable foe. According to Farewell, Shaka had examined several Xhosa people from the frontier region: 'One man said that his country had been at war ever since he could recollect but they still had their cattle, and the white people always ran away before he could get near them.'[31] Descriptions such as this would hardly have frightened him off. In addition, Mbozamboza, Sotobe's attendant, and others were said to have spied as far as the Cape Colony's eastern frontier.[32] Shaka probably knew quite a lot. Everything suggests that from his point of view, he would be wise to take tentative and cautious steps, and preserve amity with the whites at all stages.

The embassy's purpose was to establish that amity. In retrospect, of course, such hopes were futile. One anecdote grants Shaka greater foresight than he perhaps had:

> At Dukuza, while Shaka was sitting in company, he pointed to the cattle in the kraal and said, 'No ordinary man will inherit those cattle; none but a great man will get them. The day I die the country will be overrun by locusts; it will be ruled by white men. The stars will be bright in the sky. While I am still taking care of you, you alone will smell one another out. Afterwards, men will be smelt out as *umtakati* by their own wives; wives will smell out their husbands.' Just as he finished speaking thus, he suddenly exclaimed, 'There is Sotobe,' seeing a ship holding its course at sea. Sotobe had just left and was on his way towards the Cape. My [that is, JANTSHI's] father was present when Shaka spoke as stated, and he added that, as he spoke, Shaka was seated in the cattle kraal and pushed the manure dust about slightly with the fingers of each hand when moving backwards and forwards as if to emphasize his words.[33]

THE *IHLAMBO* CAMPAIGN

A conventional part of the extended mourning process for Nandi was to launch a serious raid for cattle – their capture was a kind of a tribute to the dead woman. The raid also had all the advantages of replenishing stocks during an apparently tough climatic time, of extending patronage into some new areas of the Zulu polity's southern marches, and of keeping the warriors' enthusiasm fired up; they hadn't done much all year. MQAIKANA explains, with reference to a later chieftain's death and burial:

> Had Europeans not been in the country there would have been ritual burial victims (*umgando*), for a chief is not buried alone. A chief must not remain there [in the grave] by himself. Those killed were men, not women. After this burial a ritual hunting party would go out. First, there would be a 'black' hunting party, ie. one still in mourning and not doctored. After doctoring, there would be a 'white' hunting

party. This would then go forth and raid some tribe's cattle. This was a very general custom.[34]

When exactly Shaka launched the campaign isn't clear. Isaacs makes no mention of it before his departure in the *Chaka/Elizabeth and Susan* in late April. The month of May would have been about the time that the rivers started to drop after the summer rains, and the crops had been planted and were maturing.[35] It was the right time to attack. This more or less correlates with what Fynn says,[36] and with the rumours that would filter back to the Cape frontier.

Shaka accompanied his army part of the way. He took several *amabutho*, including the Mgumanqa and a unit of girls, the uNkisimana, who had been recently *buthwa*'d at kwaDukuza.[37] He crossed the Mzimkhulu and halted, taking up a position at or near Fynn's *umuzi*, protected by the Fasimba. The main body went on ahead under the command of Mdlaka and Ngomane. Other *izinduna* were Mxamama, Mbikwana, Sekethwayo of the Mdlalose, Maphitha, Mbilini of the Mthethwa, and the irrepressible Zulu kaNogandaya.[38] Faku and the Mpondo apparently chose not to fight, but retreated towards the Drakensberg and into the country of the amaBomvana people, leaving the Zulu forces to rustle their cattle at will. Only one account implies that there was a clash:

> The army . . . fell upon the Mpondo country, and went about eating up the cattle everywhere. It then came back with the light brown (*mdubu*) cattle; all of them were of this one colour. The *inkosi* said, 'Now do you see what I told you? I told you to go to the Mpondo country, where you would find many cattle.' For all those from Fabase's country [Ndwandwe territory] had been slaughtered, those which warded off famine. When they returned with the *mdubu* beasts he made them presentations of cattle. After this the land was peaceful. 'Go, take them to your mothers and to your wives.' By now the crops were ripe. Some people [prematurely?] ate the new crops, swelled up, and died. They took the cattle to their homes.
>
> The Mpondo then followed up their cattle. The army was summoned again and told, 'The Mpondo have come. They have camped in the forests near their place.' Shaka's army then went off

and encountered them in the forests. It flung a volley of small assegais at them, assegais which were black on one side and white on the other. The assegais were poisoned, so that even if they did not penetrate, even if they simply cut a person, he would die. They scattered the Mpondo and drove them into the forests. The army returned. The *inkosi* said, 'Because of this I am now going to give the order permitting you to marry.'[39]

Some of the cattle came from as far as the Mthatha river, at Maphozi near the sea.[40] The missionary William Shrewsbury, at Butterworth, heard that the Zulu troops had swung inland first and actually picked up the cattle as they turned east again along the coast. Shrewsbury added that Shaka, 'intoxicated with success (for immense herds of cattle were taken)' sent a peremptory message to Hintsa, 'demanding a present of Oxen from him' which would have served as 'an acknowledgement of him [Shaka] as a liege lord'. Hintsa haughtily told him that he had better sharpen his assegais.[41] While this much may be true, one thing is clear: this raid by Shaka's forces caused minimal physical damage to the people in Mpondo territory, never went anywhere near the colonial frontier, and never had any intention of doing so. Fynn probably gives a fairly accurate impression of the negotiating process (although we can take his alleged influence in it with more than a pinch of salt):

Owing to the knowledge I had of Faku, Shaka asked me one morning if I thought, were he to withdraw his army, Faku would consent to becoming his tributary. I replied in the affirmative and recommended, as an inducement, the return of the girls who had been captured and sent to him by the army, and refraining from destroying more corn. To this he assented. He accordingly sent messengers to Faku with proposals for peace, at the same time returned the females as proof of his bona fides; he, moreover, directed his army to withdraw and to stop destroying the corn. Several chiefs of petty tribes in Faku's neighbourhood, with messengers from Faku, returned with the army to thank him for his liberality in thus sparing their lives. They were rewarded with presents of cattle . . .[42]

Why then – as we'll see in a moment – was the Cape border region in a paroxysm of panic? Something else was going on.

As far as Shaka was concerned, the most dramatic and dangerous event of the raid occurred (according to two accounts) on his way home. At a lower drift of the Mkhomazi, Shaka went and sat on a flat rock on the river bank. His brothers Dingane and Mhlangana and others were with him. The main *impi* was busy crossing further upstream. Dingane and Mhlangana, and possibly Mbopha, Shaka's *inceku*, closed in on him, pretending to kneel in supplication, but intent, in fact, on assassinating him then and there. Fortunately for Shaka, they were interrupted. A man named Lucunge, an *induna* of the Cele chief Magaye's, chanced by. Seeing Shaka there, he tried hastily to withdraw, but Shaka spotted him and summoned him over. Lucunge knelt. Shaka then ordered those present to 'sharpen' their assegais on Lucunge's forehead as if it were a grindstone. Blood flowed. Lucunge continued to praise Shaka. He was then released, having unwittingly saved the Zulu chief's life – at least for the time being.[43]

Complex plotting was afoot. Dingane was almost certainly using the raid as a cover to mobilise Mpondo support for a murderous coup. There is another version of this assassination attempt, which might be confused in the informant's mind with the 1824 incident, but which nevertheless contains some intriguing details:

> Dingane sent to the Pondo chiefs and advised them to follow and come and ask Shaka for cattle to give milk to the children, and also to give them dung, 'so that they should not be troubled by fleas'. 'Follow him and he will give you cattle. Follow him and there will be peace.' A chief, Myeki, chief of the Jali, went to Shaka whilst stationed at Nyenyezini, a low-lying place near the Mzimkhulu, where he found Shaka's forces performing the hunting-dance (*gubaing*). At this night-dancing Shaka was stabbed in the back slightly, near the shoulder-blade. Inquiry was made and it was stated Gcugcwa had done it. Gcugcwa was not there at all; Shaka's brothers, Dingane and Mhlangane must have done this.[44]

Myeki and some others were the ones who went on to *khonza* Shaka at kwaDukuza later.[45] They would be present when the assassination finally took place; Myeki was rewarded by Dingane with some of those very same light-brown cattle. These details are suspicious, to say the least. Moreover, both Fynn and MAHAYA agree that Shaka was staying at or near Fynn's *umuzi* at the time. Indeed, Fynn much later made a rather curious admission. There was 'little doubt,' he wrote, 'that the intention of killing Shaka had been long in contemplation. As I have since understood, it was intended to have taken place at my residence during the attack on the amaMpondoes, at which time both brothers [Dingane and Mhlangana] remained behind with Shaka feigning sickness, when an opportunity was wanting to effect their purpose.'[46] Is that phrase 'As I have since understood' a cover-up for his full knowledge that an attempt was to be made at this point, in June 1828 – or even for his connivance (as Julian Cobbing has suggested)?[47]

The passage in itself is insufficient evidence for a firm conclusion, though it certainly provides indirect support for the Zulu accounts of a thwarted attempt in the vicinity of Fynn's *umuzi* on the Mzimkhulu. However, there are hints of other connections that tie Fynn, Dingane, and various minor disaffected elements to the assassination plot. Fynn also mentions that 'Bechuanas' were present at the eventual assassination, this being his term for Hlubi people or iziYendane,[48] whom we have already seen colluding with Dingane. Another minor chieftain implicated in this tangle of relationships is Fodo kaNombewu of the Nhlangwini (or Hlangwini). Fodo would also be present at the successful assassination, 'presenting tribute' of crane feathers. The Hlangwini were already known for their combative nature; they fought often with their neighbours, the Bhaca, and Fodo's predecessor and father Nombewu was, according to one informant, 'the first to be an *imfacane*, i.e. an *impi* that goes along with its women and children in a fighting manner'.[49] They were not, in short, mere victims of Shaka's depredations, as Allen Gardiner understood it in 1835, although they had also been attacked by Madikane.[50] Fodo himself – short, bewhiskered, left-handed, thin-armed – was well known as a compulsive fighter.[51] The Hlangwini were so peripatetic that they were sometimes referred to as '*abathwa*', like the Drakensberg Bushmen. They came to supply Fynn with poison and began to work for him as elephant hunters.[52] Thus the Hlangwini became the primary component of Fynn's iziNkumbi (Locusts) followers, the 'people of Vundhlazi'; Vundlase was Fynn's 'great wife'.[53] They continued to act as troopers for the Fynn clan into the 1830s,[54] at the same time as acting as a client-chiefdom to Dingane.[55] This ambivalent relationship was already being forged through 1827 and 1828.

Taken together, these details add up to a case that is circumstantial but compelling: in early to mid-1828, Dingane, together with dissident fragments of the Zulu forces including iziYendane elements, was colluding with Fynn, Fodo of the Hlangwini and Myeki of the Jali to have Shaka killed.[56]

As for Gcugcwa, he was then accused of stealing some of the Mpondo booty; he and two others had diverted some cattle from posts near the Thukela. (Shaka had begun distributing them to posts ranging from Lukhilimba's on the Mzimkhulu to the Cele *umuzi* kwaShiyabantu on the Mvoti.[57]) The thieves made off towards the sea, then turned up the Thukela until they got past Maphumulo and headed for Ntunjambili (Kranskop). Shaka sent an *impi* in pursuit; they caught Gcugcwa at the very top of Ntunjambili mountain, and dragged him back to Shaka. 'I see you, Gcugcwa,' Shaka greeted him. 'We see each other,' Gcugcwa replied. 'You see me; tomorrow they will see you, too.' He knew what was coming. Shaka ordered him to be tied down across the entrance to the cattle enclosure. 'He is so fond of cattle,' said Shaka, 'let him be trampled to death by them.' So he was, until there were only mangled remains.[58]

If it's true, this incident forms an ironic postscript to the *ihlambo* campaign.

ENTERTAINING AMBASSADORS

On 4 May 1828, the *Elizabeth and Susan* sailed into Algoa Bay and convulsed the embryonic settlement of Port Elizabeth with excitement. The port's Customs Officer, D.P. Francis, was greatly impressed by Hutton's shipbuilding effort, and thought that James Saunders King should be accorded the 'greatest praise for his industry, workmanship and perseverance'.[59] King was, however, already in trouble.

Within a couple of days of his arrival he had let slip that he intended to head back east to the frontier fort-hamlet of Graham's Town, with the 'ambassadors' in tow. There was no serious officialdom to see there. He might have wanted to make a courtesy call on Fynn's family, who had recently moved there – but the company of the Zulu chiefs was scarcely necessary for that. A clutch of ambitious travellers based in Graham's Town, led by one Benjamin Green, had within days heard that the 'ambassadors' intended to head back to Zulu country overland, and thought that it would be fun to join them.[60] King, it appeared, had no intention of seeing the Cape government.

There has to be a strong suspicion that his real intention was to strengthen overland links between Port Natal and the Cape; it was, after all, only a two- to three-week journey. It would be the obvious way of sidestepping Shaka's trade control, and perhaps of feeding war captives into the eastern Cape's desperate shortage of forced labour.

The local Civil Commissioner, J.W. van der Riet, was based in Uitenhage, just outside Port Elizabeth. He was not about to let a group of unknown Zulu warriors, already carrying a reputation for ferocity, wander through the British military lines, assessing their strength. He told King that he would have to stay where he was; the government would gladly pay the embassy's board and lodging.[61] King's reply immediately plunged the enterprise into confusion. The principal, Sotobe, he asserted, was to proceed to *England*

> for the purpose of explaining to our government the friendly disposition of Chaka towards our nation, also to ascertain whether the Zulos are likely to meet with the least opposition should he make his attack upon the tribes contiguous to this colony which, from his power and the determined bravery of his warriors, I am persuaded that success awaits him should he not meet with opposition from our forces.[62]

This was the first that anybody had heard of Shaka contemplating any such thing, and the allegation was to have dramatic consequences. King continued:

> The minor chief Umbosomboser has instructions from his king to return immediately to report the safe arrival of the former, their reception, etc., with any satisfactory information that our government may be pleased to offer for Chaka's guidance.
>
> Chaka at the time of my leaving Natal was collecting his armies to attack the Hammapondoes, a nation near St Johns (or Umsomfooto

[Umzimvubu]) river, about one day's journey from Hinser [Xhosa chieftain Hintsa], Eastward, and he expresses no wish to proceed further after the defeat of the former nation until the pleasure of His Britannic Majesty's Government is known, which induces me to ask the favour of the chief paying a visit to our forces at the frontier to enable one of them to return agreeable to Chaka's wish, which, in all probability, might prevent his nearer approach, save thousands of souls and otherwise form a saving to our government.[63]

So which of the two chiefs – Sotobe or Mbozamboza – was to go to the frontier, which overland, which to England, which back with King by sea – since he said that he was holding his vessel in readiness to take Mbozamboza back as soon as possible? The settler Thomas Philipps had gained the impression that one 'ambassador' was slated to go to England – but King had also lied that Shaka had organised 10 000 men to hunt elephant for him, a scheme that had been interrupted only by Nandi's death.[64] Why was there such a sense of urgency? To add a little more pressure, King made another extraordinary claim: he had 'been compelled . . . to leave hostages' for the embassy's safe return.[65] Since Farewell had had little or nothing to do with this ambassadorial venture, the only real candidate for hostage status was Henry Francis Fynn.

Fynn later said that he was a 'hostage'. As we've seen, he certainly did not act like one. He behaved as if he were a free agent, going down unescorted to his Mzimkhulu residence and pretending to be totally surprised when Shaka turned up, the army looming behind him. According to Fynn, Shaka stayed with him until the army returned from the *ihlambo* raid. Then they went back to kwaDukuza together. This is demonstrably false. The extended narrative of this journey, packed with arbitrary murders, is an invention, riddled with inconsistencies.[66]

Back at Port Elizabeth, the government didn't know quite what to make of King's delegation, and requested that the whole party proceed to Cape Town to see the governor. They were not to be allowed anywhere near the frontier.[67] King now prevaricated: he thought that a visit to the frontier would impress the chiefs with a show of military might; he wanted to get Mbozamboza home smartly, or the 'consequences may prove serious'; his boat was too small to go safely to Cape Town and he wanted to wait for another ship.[68] There were, in the meantime, no signs of trouble from Shaka at all; the frontiers seemed stable enough for the authorities to give permission to Benjamin Green and company to proceed into the interior, though reports were filtering through of renewed 'Fetcanie' activity further to the north-east.[69] (These turned out to be drought- and locust-stricken people from a branch of the Orange river, who by the end of the month had retired 'unmolesting and unmolested'.[70])

Days passed during which the chiefs were more or less trapped at Mrs Robinson's boarding-house. The governor's secretary, Lt. Col. Bell, chastised Van der Riet for not going to Port Elizabeth himself, and told King that if he wanted to take Mbozamboza back by sea that was up to him. He authorised giving Mbozamboza some 'trifling presents', to the value of ten pounds. *He obviously wasn't taking this diplomatic foray too seriously.*[71]

If King really did want to leave, he was prevented from doing so by the intrusion of a ridiculous knot of red tape. The *Elizabeth and Susan*, the government decided, was a foreign vessel that had been built in a foreign port, and was therefore not entitled to a sailing register, and without the register she was entitled to none of the privileges of a British coaster.[72] King was incensed; if he left for Natal without it, he would be subject to piracy on the high seas from all and sundry, he wailed to the governor himself.[73] To Van der Riet he protested that he was *not* wanting to go back to Natal for any 'sinister motives'; evidently he had raised suspicions somehow. He emphasised as usual his 'heavy losses and long sufferings'. He even suggested that the 'liberality' of His Majesty's government might like to make 'any reward they may conceive the sacrifice of my time and prospects to the public service may entitle me to, and in proportion as the mission of these chiefs may ultimately prove to the interests of this colony'.[74] He went up to Uitenhage himself, chiefs in tow, to impress upon Van der Riet the horror posed by Shaka who, having maybe defeated the Mpondos already, might be descending upon the frontier even as they spoke. Moreover, a ten-pound present for Shaka was derisory; he, King, had already laid aside eight *hundred* pounds' worth of gifts. For someone who had portrayed himself as being all but bankrupt, this was a remarkable achievement.[75]

A week later, King's threats of an invasion by Shaka suddenly seemed to take on some substance. A report came through from William Shrewsbury, the Wesleyan missionary at Butterworth, written on 12 June: various sources, including Hintsa had heard that 'Chaka' had crossed the Mzimvubu river, and was approaching 'with a very numerous body of men divided into 8 companies, each of which is supposed to be 2 or 3,000 strong, and the whole population before him is described as being in motion, the chief Maxabisa, who lives beyond Fako and near the river Zimvuba, having been routed . . .'[76]

That same day – although he could not have heard this particular report yet – Mbozamboza apparently tried to escape. No one recorded just what had happened, but the idea must have been to set him on the road back to Shaka. It seems highly unlikely that King didn't know about the attempt. Mbozamboza may have been stimulated by King now refusing to sail to Port Natal without the precious register. The Cape government moved quickly to distance themselves from diplomatic entanglement: they underlined their view that 'the persons with whom King Chaka has held communication on this matter are not authorised agents of the British government', and that King in particular was entirely unreliable. Did these men 'have any credentials whatever'? That said, the Cape government repeated that it desired friendly relations with Shaka; if the chiefs were the genuine article, and wanted to come to Cape Town, an arrangement could be made to take them overland.[77] At the same time, the government made moves to cut King out of the loop altogether. A Major A.J. Cloete was dispatched to negotiate.[78]

On the frontier, Somerset discovered, there was for the moment no sign of Shaka: all was 'in a state of tranquillity'.[79] He interviewed the Xhosa chieftain Ngqika ('Gaika') on 21 June. Ngqika appeared to know something of Shaka's movements, but 'seemed a good deal surprised that Chaca should not have communicated with the colony thro the medium of the Kaffer tribes'. He, too, was rightfully suspicious of this 'embassy'.[80] The implication is that Shaka had had no intention of moving in this direction in the first place. The Civil Commissioner (and sometime commando leader) W.B. Dundas, cancelled a proposed trip eastwards to bolster the resolve of Hintsa, the Xhosa chief who was allegedly Shaka's next target. There was no need. Another missionary, W.R. Thomson on the Tyume river, said that he had

heard a vague rumour about Shaka, and that there had been some
'consternation' among the Mpondos, but he saw no 'particular anxiety
manifested in [his] neighbourhood'.[81]

Nevertheless, Shaka's reputation worried Major Dundas: 'I fear from
the impetuosity of his character and the difficulty of keeping together a great
number of warlike savages that his intentions are immediately to assail the
less warlike Kaffres . . . and he will hardly await the return of his messenger
to begin his attacks . . .' Dundas then repeated Shrewsbury's information
about eight disciplined divisions, and imagined that they would attack 'many
points at the same time'. This was pure speculation, and showed a contradiction
very frequent in white views of the Zulu: on the one hand, they were thought
of as completely uncontrollable savages and, on the other hand, as a highly
disciplined force controlled by the iron will of a tyrant.[82]

On the strength of such speculation, the Cape government authorised
an expedition, led by Dundas, 'to procure an interview with Chaka', with a
view to telling him that the British would tolerate no such attack on the
western Xhosa.[83] In fact, Shaka's forces, as we have seen, had turned around
at the Umzimvubu before mid-June. This was confirmed by the missionary
at Theopolis, William Brownlee.[84] Before retiring, Shaka had, according to
Kay, apparently conveyed the threat to some nearby Xhosa leaders to return
in 'three moons', and not go home until he had 'seen and conversed with
his white friends, viz. the English in the Colony'.[85]

Whether this threat actually came from Shaka himself, or was in any way
serious, is debatable; the important thing is that the colonists *believed* it to be
so.

The news that the colonial forces would oppose any attack on the Xhosa
seemed to take James Saunders King by surprise. He had been outflanked by
Cloete, who had secured an independent interview with the chiefs. Clearly
King had primed them on what the stories were: they too thought that Shaka
'had determined to overrun all the Kaffer territories between his own
dominions and our frontiers in order to become our ally'. They insisted that
Shaka wanted only to be friends, not to annihilate the Xhosa (they would be
allowed to retire with their cattle). King 'thought the Governor would rather
assist their king in getting rid of Hintza and the other border chiefs than
lend them any aid against Chaka'. However, their plans were 'completely

deranged' by news of this invasion; it was a total surprise to them. They also 'knew' that 'Shaka' was advancing with eight divisions; Shrewsbury's news had filtered through, almost certainly via King. As they acknowledged, they were 'much, if not entirely, influenced by Capt King's opinions'; he was, after all, their only friend, their 'protector' in this very strange place. They didn't want to go anywhere without him. Isaacs, who claimed to have witnessed at least one of these conversations, thought Cloete peremptory; he made the chiefs 'uneasy'.[86]

As for King, Cloete's feelings were mixed. He didn't wish to suspect King of evil motives, but at the same time thought that his 'notions of Chaka's power and strength and [his] *good opinion of and confidence in the king's personal character* are such that were they to be implicitly received as the guide in treating with Chaka [they] would mislead the government into serious errors'. This was a complete reversal of King's earlier assertions of rampant tyranny. And when Cloete tried to cut a deal with King, and basically pay him to sail the chiefs home, King inexplicably resisted.[87] Everything suggests that he was working according to his own agenda, and attempting to wriggle through the net of authority and away.

He also seemed determined for some reason to get Mbozamboza across the frontier. Cloete made a quick trip up to Graham's Town. He returned to find that on the night of 3 July Mbozamboza and one of the younger Zulu men had taken advantage of his absence; they had packed their war dress and left. Evidently they were caught, and brought back by King and Isaacs – but it seemed to Cloete that King himself had taken the Zulu 'some little distance from the town' in the first place, and that Sotobe, his denial notwithstanding, had known about it. Cloete threatened to lock them up if they tried again. As Cloete had discovered in Graham's Town, rumours were strengthening about a Zulu incursion across the Umzimvubu. Dundas was going to go ahead with his expedition to try to 'interview' Shaka, though the frontier commander, Colonel Henry Somerset, didn't yet feel that there was sufficient need to mobilise a military force.[88] However, Mbozamboza's second attempt at escape was almost certainly precipitated by the thought that Zulu forces might be relatively close to the frontier.

Colonial impressions of Shaka's intentions had now reached hysterical levels. Shrewsbury wrote on 30 June:

The chief Tshaka, or Chaka . . . is coming down the coast upon the Caffres with immense Hordes of people under his command. No engagement has yet taken place, but Hintsa has resolved to fight . . . in a plain near the Bashe . . . Chaka appears to be a Prince of unbounded ambition & a Monster of Cruelty. One of his principal commanders bears the name Umbulawe, that is *The Murderer* or the Killer of Men. The troops under him are compared to locusts for number. They are drawn out in several divisions, distinguished by the colour of their shields; or the White, Red, Black shields &c: one division goes forth to the fight; & the others come to their aid, or reserve themselves for securing plunder, as circumstances may dictate. Within the last month, Chaca's army has routed, or dispersed, two Chiefs lying beyond us, and forced Dapa to retire; so that nothing seems now to remain . . . . 'The Wild B[east?] Chaka is tearing the prey, the River is dyed with Blood, and he is hunting Fako from the Mountains to the Sea.' Last year Fako defeated a part of Chaka's forces, and slew his son; hence against him he is stimulated by Revenge as well as ambition. He continually cries out, 'Where is Faku's *gall?* And where is his mother? Bring her to me, that I may cut off her hands & feet, for bearing so worthless a Son.' And as he advances in his victories he says, 'I seek the head of Hintsa, & the Horses of the white peoples.' [By a few days ago] the Enemy had advanced to within 70 Miles of Butterworth & a little more than 20 of the place Hintsa designed to give him battle . . .'[89]

As it turned out, there *had* been an incursion. William Shaw, Shrewsbury and another missionary named Davies had ventured from Hintsa's place on 24 June, and ridden as far as the Mthatha river. There, on 2 July, they found the aftermath of considerable violence: 'Houses burnt, crawls [kraals] destroyed, Bones scattered around and the skeletons of such has [sic] fallen by the enemy, and birds of prey picking the flesh that remained.'[90] The amaBomvana people had been hard hit.[91] This attack, according to Shrewsbury, had happened on 29 June. However, Shrewsbury did not say that the attackers were Shaka's Zulu; they were 'Fetcanie'.[92] As Dundas ascertained when he got to Hintsa's a few days later, another group of invaders had 'established themselves in winter quarters beyond the Umtata about 20 miles, where they will remain until they shall have consumed the cattle they have stolen'.[93] In other words, they were *not* the hit-and-run bulk of Shaka's army, who had already retreated east again. These people were settled in for the duration. So who were they?

Part of the answer lies in a postscript that Shrewsbury scribbled at the bottom of his letter of 2 July to Somerset: 'PS. It is currently reported that there is a white man amongst the Fetcanie who assists them with fire-arms.'[94] Shrewsbury had already, quite unknowingly, identified this man, in the long letter quoted above: 'Umbulawe, that is *The Murderer*', Mbulazi, or Mbulazwe. It was Henry Francis Fynn.

This was confirmed when Dundas's party finally reached Faku's *umuzi* on 18 July. Thirteen emissaries of Shaka's, who had been negotiating the Mpondos' new tribute obligations, had left some ten days before.[95] Meanwhile, the force that attacked the Mpondos

> had been accompanied by a party of armed Englishmen . . . That Fynn was present with the invading army was verified to me beyond a doubt as a man who had been wounded by a shot from a gun in both thighs was brought to me, who said that the person who shot him afterwards saved his life and dressed his wounds and then told him that his name was Fynn . . .[96]

Another independent observer, a traveller named Shaw (who is not to be confused with the missionary), later asserted that 'Chaka's people would never have attacked Fakoo's people and the frontier Kaffers had they not had the advantage of the fire-arms and the countenance of English people from Natal.'[97]

The whole thing was very murky. As we have seen, Stuart's collected traditions record no such major depredation against the Mpondos or other Xhosa peoples, as we might expect them to. There is no record of Shaka's forces trashing Faku's main *umuzi*, or of killing dozens, or destroying corn, huts and women, or carrying off children, as Dundas and the missionaries described. This sounds rather like a classic slave-raid.

There are two ways of interpreting this 'Zulu' incursion. The first option is that Zulu forces, ordered by Shaka, *did* attack across the Mzimvubu and as far as the Mthatha, and were merely accompanied by Fynn and his group of European and 'Hottentot' gunmen. Somehow – inexplicably – this attack has been left out of the traditions. The second possibility is that Shaka's own forces retired, leaving Fynn, with his own private army and/or renegade Zulu soldiery, to advance further, plundering cattle and people, with Fynn spreading the rumour, or simply allowing the impression to develop, that this was still Shaka's enterprise. (This would have been easy to do, given the established fear of Shaka and Fynn's former service with him.) This implies that Fynn's own *impis* were more extensive than we've been led to believe. (However, it's doubtful that Fynn could command eight divisions; possibly this referred to Shaka's original raid, from which Fynn extended a smaller, but more destructive, attack across the Mzimvubu.)

Almost everything points to the second possibility. William Shaw's comment that 'Mbulazwe' was the *commander* of the forces indicates that Fynn was leading the expedition, not just helping out. Intriguingly, Bertram Bowker, who accompanied Dundas to Faku's place, recalled that the Mpondos had burned 10 000 pounds of ivory 'to prevent the enemy getting it'.[98] The only 'enemy' who would have wanted it in the first place would have been Fynn and company. Francis Farewell wrote later that Shaka's positive orders to his forces were to go nowhere near the whites, and that they had not gone beyond the Mpondos, having 'no wish whatever to molest the English'.[99] Farewell also admitted that he had 'sent a man' (Henry Ogle) to accompany the expedition, he claimed, 'in case they should see white men and not be able to make them understood'. The self-contradiction here is plain – and is exposed by another lie, that Ogle had 'never fired a musket in his life'. This is precisely what Farewell is concealing: that Ogle was a hired gunman.[100] In short, there is much to support the humanitarian John Philip's perception (only somewhat exaggerated) that 'Farewell and others have stirred up war wherever they have gone' and that '[t]o Farewell's establishment at Port Natal we are to trace the devastations of Shaka'.[101]

The inference is that Fynn and King had planned from the beginning to take advantage of Shaka's Mpondo raid and of his desire to send men to assess the situation in the Cape; it all provided (they hoped) a perfect cover, and it explains a great deal of their future projection of violence generally onto Shaka. It is difficult to know what they thought they were achieving, if it was not slaving. This was just the sort of strategy long since practised by the Portuguese. (When John Cane came through some months later, he was particularly concerned 'to prevent the supposition of jealous natives' that he had sold his Zulu companion 'for slaves'; the Zulu knew all about the threat of slaving from these white men.[102]) The flaw in the plan, if such it was, was that they believed that the colonial government, having been at war with the Xhosas for so long, would not oppose an attack on them from the east.

Fynn's own obvious lying afterwards is negative evidence for this reading of the matter. Whichever way we look at it, the events made nonsense of King's claim that Fynn had been left behind as a 'hostage'. John Cane, who was at or near Port Natal throughout this flurry, confirmed later that there was no talk of hostages, and there was no threat of death to the whites there at all. Moreover, he said that the 'embassy' had been King's idea from the start.[103] Fynn tried to cover his tracks in a letter to Somerset, written after the 'embassy' had returned. After King's departure in May, Fynn said, he had gone back to his umuzi 160 kilometres away on the Mzimkhulu. That didn't sound like someone who was a hostage. In due course Shaka arrived with his army to raid the Mpondo and (Fynn claimed) 'the nations to the Westward as far as the European settlements'. Fynn says that he advised Shaka against raiding the Xhosas, who were (and this is where the retrospective lie is obvious) 'allies of the colony'. It is difficult to believe that, as Fynn asserted, Shaka then meekly withdrew and sent the army off north instead. If we follow Fynn's chronology carefully, as he outlines it in this letter, Shaka's withdrawal would have happened around late May or early June. The emissaries to Faku must have been in Mpondo territory around the middle of June. This may be right for Shaka's main body, but, as we've seen, Fynn was with raiders still operating in early July.[104] This also does not agree with Fynn's later, longer, and even more confused rendition. He claims there that the Zulu army crossed the Mthatha, while he stayed behind at his own place engaged in 'warm argument' with Shaka and teaching him how to cook pancakes on a frying-pan. Well, we know he certainly wasn't doing *that*. He implies here again, however, that there was no outright attack on Faku, only a demand for tribute, and that, in fact, Shaka's men did *not* attack the border peoples[105] – but someone did. Fynn then tries to find a way out of this contradiction by blaming somebody else altogether:

It may perhaps be here necessary to mention that Matewan's tribe were lying up the Umtarte [Mthatha], before the Zuloes appeared about there and the great consternation which the whole Frontier was thrown into in consequence of Chaka's approach gave Matewan an opportunity of attacking the Frontier tribes and taking their cattle as they fled supposed to be a division of Chaka's army. The Colonial forces, in consequences of the report of Chaka's intending to invade the Colony with Fynn at their head induces them to come and meet this formidable enemy but they had returned and the Colonial forces misled by their interpreters they asking where the Umfetcarnies marauders were instead of Chaka's force were by the Caffers led to Matewan . . .[106]

Fynn is partly accurate here, though his main aim is to defend himself against the charge of leading this invasion; he uses what could only have been his *subsequent* knowledge of the Matiwane incident to shield himself. It doesn't quite work: Matiwane was indeed raiding once more into Thembu territory, but that encounter took place much later than Fynn implies here. It was also further north-west, and there is no suggestion in Ngwane sources that they ever attacked Faku.[107]

(Isaacs also attempts to cover for his friends, saying that Fynn, Ogle and the others were 'sent out' with Shaka's forces under compulsion. However, in the next breath he avers that Farewell and Fynn remained at the Mzimkhulu with Shaka. This we know to be untrue. He added an unlikely aside about some cover story of Shaka's about his half-brother Ngwadi having stolen some cattle and needing firearms to retrieve them. Fynn of course dissuaded Shaka from attacking the frontier Xhosa, and all the reports of violence were inventions of frontier peoples trying 'to excite the commiseration of the European settlers'. There is a little too much boasting, born of relief at having got away with it, in Isaacs's depiction of Dundas's subsequent attack on 'the inexperienced, harmless and inoffensive tribe' of Matiwane and his return 'to their colony, inflated with the triumph they had achieved' – though he was closer to the truth than even he realised.[108])

The most likely scenario, in short, is that there were *three* major forces involved in all this: Shaka's, which had withdrawn by early June, apart from

negotiators who returned to exact tribute; Fynn's, which raided westwards as
far as the lower Mthatha until well into July; and Matiwane's Ngwane who
were trying to encamp as a whole nation, practically, on the *upper* Mthatha.
The colonial communication system was as yet incapable of distinguishing
such complexities.

Another unlikely land claim

In the meantime – for the whole of July – the 'embassy' languished in Port
Elizabeth. Sotobe got drunk and quarrelled with Jacob Msimbithi.[109] King
was getting increasingly entangled in his own deceptions. He now claimed
that he had been '*compulsorily involved*' in the whole enterprise by Shaka. He
alleged that his only thought was really for the 'thousands of unfortunate
creatures between [Shaka] and the colony . . . who are likely to experience a
fate that Humanity cannot contemplate'.[110] He threatened to leave
immediately. Go then, retorted Cloete.[111] Cloete and King had words in the
street, with a bemused Collector of Customs, D.P. Francis, looking on. Cloete
implied that the government was too poor to pay for all this, and King would
have done better to have left the embassy behind. King felt 'wounded'. He
was going to take a 'decisive step'. He would now 'furnish a suitable present
with the return of my vessel at my own risk'. He would take Sotobe home 'if
compelled'. At the same time, however, he said that he was trying to organise
his own departure to England aboard the *Duke of Bedford* – 'as a duty I owe to
the humanity and kindness of king Chaka, a friend of nearly three years
since the wreck of my unfortunate vessel in his territory'.[112]

The government, for its part, was still trying to find out exactly what the
embassy was there for. They tried to keep the options open; Sotobe could
still come to Cape Town. A ship – the *Helicon* – was finally to be dispatched,
with some presents 'of no great bulk' for Shaka from the governor, obviously
in the hope that the chiefs could simply be taken away and forgotten about.[113]
When Cloete pressed Sotobe for clarity, the Zulu chief said, 'What is the use?
My saying only makes me appear a liar, saying one thing to you and then
when Captn King comes and talks and talks, saying another thing to him.
You white people must talk together.' In the end, Cloete could only regard
the mission 'chiefly as one of compliment, bearing *assurances* of Chaka's
friendly feeling'.[114]

Since King was again threatening to return to Natal immediately, Cloete mulled over possible gifts: medicines, definitely; fireworks, maybe. Meanwhile, Cloete added, King was now trying to take greater control, portraying himself as 'the *chief* of Chaka's messengers'. Cloete was now convinced that King 'was aware of Chaka's determination under any circumstances to subjugate our Caffer tribes, to which he would have had the colonial govt submit'.[115] This is to say, King had known there would be some kind of raid all along. He was trying to bolster his flagging reputation by getting affidavits from his white friends and threatening to leave the following week; Cloete said that he might not be able to sanction that. Oh, do stop quarrelling, sighed the governor's secretary.[116]

In the confusion, the mood of the Zulu ambassadors swung between fear and apparent contentment. The movement of a burgher force up to the frontier galvanised Sotobe and Mbozamboza to gather their belongings with a view to making another escape attempt; Cloete was obliged to call on the magistrate 'for the assistance of his constables'.[117] A few days later, Sotobe appeared in a conciliatory mood:

> hitherto his mind had been much oppressed, that he had looked on me [Cloete] with suspicion and distrust, that he was now convinced that I was the proper person to place entire confidence in and was, in reality, the only one that could do anything; that, therefore, he had come for the express purpose humbly to solicit that I would allow him and all his party to go back as soon as possible, that he was most desirous to return home immediately and that he would rather promise to come back if I wished it, that he did not know, or rather could not understand, what the people he had come with were at, that he had been like a wounded deer, crippled in all he had said before, if it were not natural that when a blow was aimed at one side of your head he would guard it, if at the other side he would ward it off, but now that he had come through the rain on purpose to place every confidence in me . . .[118]

King (who might have put Sotobe up to this move in the first place) chose to conclude that it was Cloete's intention to separate him from the chiefs altogether 'against their free choice'. In desperation he suddenly produced

what he hoped would be his trump card. This was a most extraordinary
document, purporting to have been dictated by Shaka himself. It is datelined
'At Chaka's principal residence, Umlololilo February 1828' (the name possibly
a miscopying by the notary of 'Ubullalio' – kwaBulawayo). It is worth
reproducing in full here:

> I, Chaka, king of the Zulas, do in presence of my principal chiefs now
> assembled, hereby appoint and direct my friend, James Saunders King,
> whom I now create chief of Sugooso [kwaDukuza?] kraal, to take under
> his charge and protection Sotoby, one of my principal chiefs, Karchey
> my body servant, Jacob my interpreter and suite. I desire him to convey
> them to His Majesty King George's dominions to represent that I
> send them on a friendly mission to King George and, after offering
> him assurances of my esteem and friendship, to negotiate with His
> Britannic Majesty on my behalf with my chief Sotoby a treaty of friendly
> alliance between the two nations. Having given them, the said J S
> King and Sotoby, full instructions and invested them with ample
> powers to act for me in every way as circumstances may seem to them
> most beneficial and expedient, I request my friend King to pay every
> attention to the comforts of my people entrusted to his care, and I
> solemnly enjoin him to return with them to me in safety and to report
> to me faithfully such accounts as they may receive from King George.
>
> I hereby grant him, my said friend J S King, in consideration of the
> confidence I repose in him, of various services he has already rendered
> me, presents he has made me and, above all, the obligations I am
> under to him for his attentions to my mother in her last illness, as
> well as having saved the lives of many of my principal people, the free
> and full possession of my country near the sea coast and Port Natal
> from Natal Head to the Stinkein river, including the extensive grazing
> flats and forests, with the islands in Natal harbor and the Materban
> nation, together with the free and exclusive trade of all my dominions,
> and I hereby confirm all my former grants to him.[119]

The document was adorned with a massive fishbone scrawl purporting to be
Shaka's mark, and countersigned by 'John Jacob, Interpreter' (your guess is
as good as mine as to where that 'John' came from), and Nathaniel Isaacs.

Cloete quite rightly was flabbergasted that King hadn't produced this document in the beginning. King's explanation only amplified the illogicality and increased the suspicions:

> I had intended to reserve the production of the . . . document and the disclosure of other important matter connected with it until, in a personal interview with the Lieutenant Governor, by impressing upon the mind of His Honor the formidable and increasing power and resources of the Zulo nation, I could pave the way for the reception of this mission in a manner suitable to the occasion or, in case it should continue to be considered only in the light of a begging visit to the colonial government by a tribe of common Caffres, and which it appears to me as still to be treated, to avoid the ridicule of appearing the principal in such a mission by withholding this document until some corroborative proof should arise to display its real importance, and your treatment of me from the very first stage of your interference with the chiefs as well [as] the unfavourable aspect which my correspondence with the colonial government at the same time assumed, determined me on no account to produce it to you, whose authority to interfere on the part of the colonial government I have to this moment strictly no right to recognize. I feel now compelled to do so in the last extremity . . .[120]

It makes absolutely no sense that King should have feared 'ridicule' to be seen as the principal. The signatories are hardly above suspicion; all three were in Port Elizabeth together. And why didn't Sotobe sign it? Why is this astounding, previously unheard-of land grant appended to the instructions for the embassy? Why is there no sign of the compulsion that King was supposed to be under? King had never helped Nandi. It was the first mention of a formal 'treaty'.

When this pompous piece of chicanery was read out to John Cane on 13 November 1828, he practically snorted with derision. He intimated that King had drawn it up himself. Shaka *had* made a land grant to King, but that was in the St Lucia area, 'eastward of Port Natal about 86 miles'.[121] A grant had already been made of the Port Natal harbour region and the islands to

Farewell; there was no way that Shaka would have granted its use twice. Another grant had also been made to Fynn in the region of the Mzimkhulu river.

None of these grants, it has to be stressed, would in Shaka's view have constituted giving the land away wholesale. The novelist Alan Scholefield, albeit in fictional mode, expressed the reality neatly in *Great Elephant*:

> No one *owned* or *gave* or even *bartered* land after the European fashion. All the land belonged to Chaka, who kept it for his people; it was their inheritance and their heritage; it *was* the people. What he had done, in fact, was to allow us to live on a piece of *his* land for as long as *he* cared.[122]

As for King being made chief of kwaDukuza,[123] Cane thought that this was impossible, since King's presence would then be continuously required to lead the army's most active units.[124] The whole thing is patently a forgery.

As Cloete dismissed the ploy out of hand, King raged:

> The chiefs have this moment emphatically expressed themselves on the subject. 'We came here,' they say, 'the friends of the white people and we are now sent back like rascals. We now see what the white people are.' Good God! Is this the feeling with which they are to be returned? Is this the way a British government treats so interesting and important a mission? No!'[125]

The 'hostages' King had left were 'now placed in jeopardy'. He had often ventured his life; he would do it again; he would accompany the *Helicon* in his schooner; he would provide presents at his own expense. The colonial government's presents, he claimed, were paltry alongside what Shaka could get from Delagoa Bay (an interesting snippet) - especially as they were 'in hourly expectation' of Shaka's turning up on their doorsteps.[126] (This was nonsense; the frontier seemed quiet; Benjamin Green had once again been given permission to proceed into the interior.[127]) Cloete was unimpressed. He did 'not feel disposed to oppose [King's] personal wishes,' he said.[128] King was free to go.

The governor was also not taken in. He wrote, probably quite accurately: 'It appears probable that they [the Zulu ambassadors] hoped to be allowed to return overland and thus to reconnoitre the Caffre country, or otherwise that they were mere instruments in the hands of the Englishmen who brought them.'[129] Bourke eventually offered the opinion: 'I have little doubt that those designs were fomented and encouraged by King and the English of his party at Port Natal for their own interested purposes . . . Englishmen who by their fire-arms contributed to the success of the plunderers and shared in the plunder as their reward.'[130] Cloete was ordered to break off all communication with King: 'his conduct in this matter has been such as to render it impossible for this Govt to place any confidence in him'.[131]

As it happened, this was easily done: much delayed, the *Helicon* had finally arrived. King had managed to cadge 90 pounds of gunpowder to take with him.[132] The *Helicon* also carried some presents for Shaka – a trivial circumstance that would generate a disproportionate amount of controversy. The presents consisted, apparently, of three packages, 'two of which are intended for king Chaka, the one containing a small assortment of medicines, etc., and the other various articles of ornament, dress, etc., which have been selected, in the absence of all information on the subject, as being probably acceptable to the king.' The third package contained a few small presents for the Zulu envoys.[133] Against this very modest offering, King claimed that he would contribute 2 000 Rix Dollars' worth of goods.[134]

At three o'clock on the afternoon of 7 August, the chiefs boarded the *Helicon* 'in high good humour'.[135] They were on their way home, having achieved precisely nothing.

'IGNIS FATUUS' – THE ELUSIVE INKOSI

Cowper Rose, then temporarily settled in the Eastern Cape, wrote sardonically of the border situation in the 1820s: 'there are rumours constantly afloat of some mighty force of countless thousands, that is approaching the settlement: the ball, not of snow, gathering as it rolls, a combination of many tribes, and all cannibals – an immense advantage this, in warfare, as it prevents the necessity of a commissariat'.[136]

'Chaka' was apparently one of these mighty forces. Rose's tongue-in-cheek characterisation of Shaka as 'the restless Alexander of Southern Africa' would become another irresistible trope. Rose then outlined an alternative scenario, one completely opposed to the ever-increasing 'ball, not of snow' of the previous paragraph, the kind of 'domino' effect that would become a staple of 'mfecane' proponents in later historiography:

> The country of a distant tribe suffers drought, their harvest withers, mortality prevails among their cattle, and to save the remainder, it becomes necessary to seek a more favoured tract: rendered desperate by hunger and hardship, they attack a neighbouring horde, overcome it, deprive the unhappy wretches of all means of existence, who, in turn, are forced to play the same game with their most tempting neighbour, until at length these petty movements among the remote savages reach some tribe in communication with those upon our frontier, the tale . . . loaded with interesting exaggerations . . .[137]

These were the two quite incompatible stereotypes of 'native depredation' that bedevilled the colonial imagination: the 'mighty force' versus the 'domino effect'. Rose rightly noted: 'These stories have frequently no foundation, sometimes a slight one.'[138]

Still, he should perhaps not have taken all of them as 'laughingly' as he did. What Major Cloete did not tell the Zulu ambassadors, as they boarded the *Helicon* in Port Elizabeth, was that there *had* just been another clash in the interior with – as people still insisted on thinking – Shaka's forces. The story is not strictly relevant to Shaka's life, but it's an illuminating sideshow. We left Major Dundas in the previous section consulting with the ravaged Faku. Dundas had then retired towards the Mbashe river to link up with the Xhosa chief Vusani (proper name Ngubengcuka). En route, somewhere near the present town of Umtata, he encountered what he thought to be a major concentration of 'Fetcanie'. On 26 July, some sort of running encounter happened; Dundas claimed 60 or 70 of 'the enemy' killed for only one 'Tambookie' – more of a massacre than a battle, evidently. As missionary Stephen Kay noted, Dundas never made contact with a main body; it seems doubtful that there ever was one.[139] As Thomas Philipps put it later, Dundas encountered people who are now said to have been only herding their Cattle. They engage them without enquiring whether they are Chaka's Troops, take a great number of Cattle and drive the People flying before them. Major Dundas, full of his Victory, and forgetting his Character of Ambassador, comes back to our advancing Army and informs Col Somerset that he may return, for the Enemy are gone.[140]

They captured some 25 000 cattle. Dundas himself began to doubt his antagonists' identity:

> I was uncertain . . . whether the intruders were Chaka's people or not, and it was not until after the affair of the day that I learned from some Tambookie girls, who had been carried off by the Fichanies and who in the confusion escaped, that they were undoubtedly Chaka's people who had themselves given out that they were Manguanas [Ngwane?] . . . [T]he dress and arms of the enemy, together with the systematic mode in which the business of plundering was conducted, proved beyond a doubt that the intruders were Zoolos and that Chaka had artfully contrived for some politic purpose to make it believed that they were not so.[141]

This was rapidly proven to be wrong. Commandant J.S. van Wyk at the Klipplaats river soon noted that the intruders (perhaps, given their huge stock of cattle, best described as hopeful settlers) 'were not Chaka's people but another tribe, the names of whose chiefs are as follows: 1st – Matekwana [Matiwane]; 2nd – Makesana; 3rd – Mageta. They act, however, in the same manner as Chaka.'[142] The Ngwane had indeed raided the Thembu with considerable destructiveness, and had possibly (according to one informant) gone as far as the Mzimvubu.[143] And it may have been Matiwane who was doing the deceiving, telling his people to describe themselves as 'Magagadhlana' (though this disguise never seems to have been picked up by the whites).[144]

The Ngwane seemed to have expended all but their last strength in these raids. After the skirmish with Dundas, they launched a counter-raid and recovered some of the cattle. They then were reported as having 'hutted themselves' on the upper Mthatha and 'brought up their wives and children'. Ngubengcuka and Hintsa were massing people and calling on the whites and on Faku for support. Henry Somerset, turning around and arriving with a new force, reconnoitred the position. He was *still* thinking of the intruders as Shaka's 'Zoolahs'.[145] In fact, Somerset was accumulating a huge force: over 500 armed white soldiers and burghers, joined by Xhosa and Mpondo warriors – some 26 000 in all, he calculated.[146] Somerset claimed that there were some 20 000 'Fetcanie' in the vicinity, some of whom were 'warmly engaged' with gunfire, but the main event, on 27 August, was an indiscriminate attack on various 'huts' as well as the slaughter and carrying away of women and children. In his official report, Somerset congratulated himself on 'rescuing' a handful of these victims. The missionary J. Davis, however, interviewed an NCO involved in the engagement, who testified there had been no sign of a main body of 'enemy' at all, only a 'general slaughter' by the accompanying Xhosa and the plunder of some 28 000 cattle.[147] Even this evaded the truth: Somerset himself had fallen on the villages with cannon, small-arms and sabres:

> numbers, gaunt and emaciated by hunger and age, crawled out of their miserable sheds, but with pitiable apathy sat or lay down again, as if heedless of their fate . . . the field presented a scene indescribably shocking: old decrepit men, with their bodies pierced, and heads almost cut off; pregnant women ripped open, legs broken, and hands severed from the arms for . . . the armlets, or some trifling ornament, little children mutilated and horribly mangled . . .[148]

This inglorious affair was subsequently termed the 'Battle of Mbholompo'. It is little wonder that the colonists were keen to project gratuitous violence onto others who lived out beyond the borders, people who couldn't argue back.

Most interesting in Somerset's report, for our purposes, was the vague but suggestive testimony of one captured woman, the 'wife of Oolana, a heemraade [*induna*] of Matuana':

> The nation with whom we had been engaged is called Maceesa, their great chief or captain is called Matuana, they come from the Sootou

country to the Northward of Chaka. Chaka had formerly fought with them and they were driven in a North West direction, and attacked numerous tribes whom they conquered and destroyed untill they arrived in the Tambookie country. They consider themselves a powerful and independent nation, Chaka never having been able to subject them. . . . The first tribes they attacked were under the Captain Bunyami [Bungane?] whom they called Ozueeda's or Osmeeda's [Zwide's]. Chaca had formerly attacked these people. . . . The reason the Maceesa nation murder women and children is stated by this woman to be that the custom has been adopted by them from seeing Chaca's people do so.[149]

If confirmation were needed, Shrewsbury, who had tagged along on the attack, reaffirmed that these people were not Shaka's, but Matiwane's, previously established near the headwaters of the Thukela; they were the same people who had passed near Butterworth a year previously. Shaka never had anything to do with this frontier flurry; as one acerbic correspondent to the *South African Commercial Advertiser* later said: there the authorities were, floundering about after '*ignis fatuus*', while all the while Shaka was 'quietly seated on his own hearth'.[150]

Shaka would never again venture westwards, not even disguised as somebody else. Even as Dundas and Somerset were rampaging around the Mthatha area, Shaka was conducting his last military venture.

A PROBLEM OF PRESENTS

Meanwhile, the ramifications of the ill-fated 'embassy' were still sputtering on. The chiefs had wanted King on board the *Helicon* with them as they left Port Elizabeth, so Isaacs followed in the *Elizabeth and Susan*. On 17 August they hove to off Port Natal, a heavy surf running. King was looking ill, Isaacs said; they had to carry him to his residence at 'Mount Pleasant'. On 19 August Isaacs offloaded the presents that the Cape government had sent to Shaka. They broke open the boxes, and found a rather paltry offering: some useless sheets of copper, a piece of scarlet broadcloth, some medicines, a few knives and other gaudy toys. To this, according to Isaacs, King added a 'valuable looking-glass which cost 120 rix-dollars, a quantity of beads, and variety of little amusing trifles'.[151] It took them a while to get going, but after a few days Isaacs eventually reached kwaDukuza with the presents, to face an incensed Shaka.

First, the gifts were regarded as pathetic; Shaka looked on them with an 'ineffable contempt'. Second, he was deeply suspicious that the box had been broken open without his consent; even Sotobe had not been present (Isaacs contradicts himself on this point). A list that should have been in the box wasn't. That man King was, Shaka fumed, 'like a monkey, he wants to peep into everything'. Still, the mirror was better than anything the government had sent. Shaka speculated that King had been poisoned by them. Third, there was no macassar oil, on which, according to Isaacs, 'all his hopes and interest seem to have centred'. There's no telling whether the following account by Isaacs contains any truth, but it has a certain vivacity of detail:

At Chaka's desire I opened the chest; when he told me, with a sagacious look, and apprehensive of being seen or overheard, to observe if anyone was coming. Finding all still, and that we were not perceived, he dextrously took out a case of lancets from the chest, and began to examine the black case, which was neatly ornamented with a gilt etching. This, I presume, he took to contain the miraculous, or sacred medicine, for which he so anxiously sought; for he ingeniously conveyed it under his mat on which he reposed, and in his opinion quite unobserved by me. He afterward desired me to hand him everything separately, and to explain to him the use of each article; he looking on with intense eagerness and anxiety. The first package was bark, which I told him was a specific in cases of fever, and of a strong and efficacious property in cases of debility; he replied, in a sulky tone – 'I am strong enough: do you think we are such weak things as you are?' I then handed to him some ointment, the properties of which were healing, and were applied to sores or wounds; when on looking at it, he, with a sort of savage grin, observed – 'do you think we are such scabby fellows as you are?' The next was spirits of lavender, which, when I explained to him, was to revive the spirits in case of depression, he took it significantly; and asked 'if I thought they ever wanted anything to exhilirate [sic] them, or that they were ever dull?' After having handed to him every article, and given to him a description of the appliances of each, and received his petulant replies, he, in a kind and gentle mood asked me for the 'medicine he wanted', namely the ointment for changing the colour of the hair; for, said he, 'these are of no use to my subjects: they are not troubled with the disorders you mention; the best medicine for them is beef – and when my people are not able to eat, they are of no use to me.' After again repeating, 'the medicine I want is the stuff for the hair;' and perceiving that I had not got it, he turned round on his mat on which he was reclining, and fell into a sound sleep.[152]

In the morning Isaacs was freshly upbraided for not bringing the oil, and for putting King up to 'roguery'. Shaka said he had heard that King had spent all his time in Port Elizabeth carousing with the women, instead of doing his business.[153] Isaacs, in turn, upbraided Sotobe and Jacob Msimbithi for misleading the *inkosi*. What actually passed between Sotobe and Shaka has been lost to sight, apart from two amusing snippets.

One thing Sotobe had apparently been impressed by was 'the place where water comes out of a hole (*intunja*)' – a pump.[154] He was also said to have brought back another box of gifts:

[Sotobe] returned, bringing a whitish box with him containing two cats, one male, one female. These were intended for Shaka, as the Europeans had observed that mice were eating the regiments' shields. The box was closed down when it reached Shaka. He had it broken open with an axe; the two cats came out alive. He was much surprised. Shaka was grateful that he was given the cats. But at first, until explanation was given as to the purpose they were to satisfy, he was alarmed at the mewing of the cats in the evening. The cats were not killed. When Shaka left Zululand to go to Dukuza, he left the cats behind, calling Zululand the 'country of cats'.[155]

However, it was another present – one which Isaacs did not mention at all – that exercised Shaka's patience much more than the hair oil. This was the discovery that all the ivory that he had given King for the governor had somehow disappeared. The chiefs had seen it landed at Port Elizabeth, but not afterwards. It was a substantial load, both hippo and elephant: according to John Cane, 69 tusks, or about two tons' worth; and according to the Zulu envoy Makhombe, 'a heap 3 feet high and 6 feet broad'.[156] Obviously King had sold it all for himself. (This was confirmed later, when Cane was instructed to inform Shaka that King had 'delivered 2 elephant's teeth as Chaca's present to the Governor and disposed of the rest of the teeth as his own private property'.[157]) Shaka also seemed to believe that King was solely responsible for his chiefs never having seen the governor; he would 'now take no notice whatever of anything Mr King or party might assert'.[158] He regretted not sending an independent letter earlier, and fumed: 'all of you [white people] would tell me anything for the sake of elephant's teeth'.[159]

Shaka's solution to the obvious failure of King's 'embassy' was to send another ambassador, John Cane, and this time overland. Cane left kwaDukuza on about 6 September, accompanied by Mbozamboza and another unnamed chief, two boys, two soldiers (Monakali and Makhombe), and an Mpondo guide.[160] The two chiefs turned back at Faku's. The rest of the party had to disguise themselves to avoid attack, met up with the itinerant trader Shaw, and gradually made their way via the mission stations towards Graham's Town. Cane walked into Butterworth on 29 September, after twenty-odd days on the trail, and finally got to Graham's Town on 8 October. He bore a letter from Farewell, and several requests from Shaka: medicines (castor oil, tartar emetic and salts), blankets, warm clothing, dogs, oxtails, and macassar oil. Some of these requests were contained in another letter, signed by Shaka himself and secreted in a bullock-horn. Shaka, his illiteracy notwithstanding, had quickly learned to employ the white man's modes of communication: he also requested a seal engraved with his name, and sealing wax, to secure his mail.[161] He also wanted an officer from the British sent to him, 'as the several statements made by Mr Farewell and Captain King are of a very contradictory nature'. He desired nothing but friendship, and would even consider setting aside some land for a settlement between Natal and the Mzimvubu river.[162]

Through the soldier Monakali (each one of his ambassadors had been independently instructed to press the point), Shaka conveyed that he wanted the government to know he was angry with King, whom he suspected of pilfering his gifts. He was particularly concerned to know what had become of the 'very large present of ivory which he [had] sent by Captain King as a present to King George'. He had also assembled another gift of ivory at Faku's place, intended for the Cape government who, he hoped, would not support Hintsa in the latter's offensive comments to him. He reiterated that he wanted various medicines, hatchets and knives, a brass plate with clasps to attach to his forearm, and a few bottles of macassar oil, 'a private request to the government which Chaca is desirous should not be revealed to his people'.[163]

The Cape government took this second embassy more seriously. It would not be long before Cane, Monakali and Makhombe would stand before the governor himself in Cape Town. By then, however, events had already overtaken their leader.

14

Death and the aftermath

1828

Whereupon the monster of a myriad crimes rolled over in the dust
and gave up his ghost to Satan.
    A.T. Bryant, *Olden Times in Zululand and Natal* (1929, 662).

We have encountered many gaps and mysteries in this study of Shaka. There is a great deal that we do not know, and never will know. We do not know quite when he was born. We cannot be sure about the trajectory of his childhood. We know almost nothing about his career under Dingiswayo. We do not know much about the daily routines of his life. Maybe two times out of three, we cannot be sure that the anecdotes told about him are true. We can gain little solid insight into his 'character' – something that every biographer likes to be able to summarise: 'Yes, he was like *this*', or, 'No, his personality would not allow *that*'. The material for a trustworthy 'biography' of Shaka simply does not exist.

WHAT DO WE KNOW?

Against all of these gaps, I've tried to make some educated guesses. A great deal of the micro-politics of Shaka's reign is, paradoxically, clearer than the character of the man who implemented them. The following, I think, is close to unquestionable. Shaka was not responsible for much of the violence in the Thukela-Phongolo catchment between 1780 and 1830. He was

482   MYTH OF IRON

remarkably successful as a leader, but he was neither the genius nor the tyrant that he has been made out to be. He made mistakes; he lost battles. He killed what today we would regard as a large number of people, but almost always for political or disciplinary reasons. He may have exhibited occasional cruelty, but he was far from genocidal. He inevitably made some enemies within the polity. He laid many of the foundations for what would be regarded as the 'Zulu nation', but he was far from unifying all the diverse peoples of the region seamlessly. He had made his mark on a considerable stretch of territory, but more through client-chiefs than through direct colonisation. Negotiation, patronage, marriages, ritual, language and propaganda were as important to his vision as coercive violence. The degree of his control was liable to be exaggerated. The informant NDUKWANA pictured the Zulu polity this way:

> The boundaries of Zululand were the Income river on the north-west to where it enters the Mzinyati, from there along the Mzinyati to the Tugela, then along the Tugela to the sea; on the north-east the Pongola was the boundary (it was the first boundary in Shaka's and Dingane's reigns . . .) Thence to uBombo along the Pongolo, and then, on the east of the uBombo, the Mkuze river to the sea . . .[1]

This is close, but not close enough. It's also not nuanced enough. The Thukela would later be seen as the boundary because that's where the invading whites drew it. During Shaka's last years, the Thukela, up to the confluence with the Mzinyathi, would be better pictured as the central thread of the polity. North of the Thukela the Zulu exercised strong control up to the Mfolozi rivers, and light control beyond them towards the Phongolo. To the south of the Thukela, they exercised strong control in the lower Mvoti valley and in the coastal belt as far south as isiBubulungu/Port Natal, but south of the Mngeni river asserted only sporadic raiding dominance. Inland, they exercised indirect control through client-chiefs, especially Jobe of the Sithole and Zihlandlo of the Mkhize. The strength of Zulu power in any one area, the central core excepted, fluctuated over time, depending on Shaka's own movements (which were consistently southwards), and the availability of larger military expeditions (see Map 11 on page 483).

We can also be sure that the rise of the Zulu polity can at no stage be accurately read independently of the global influences of trade, slaving, and

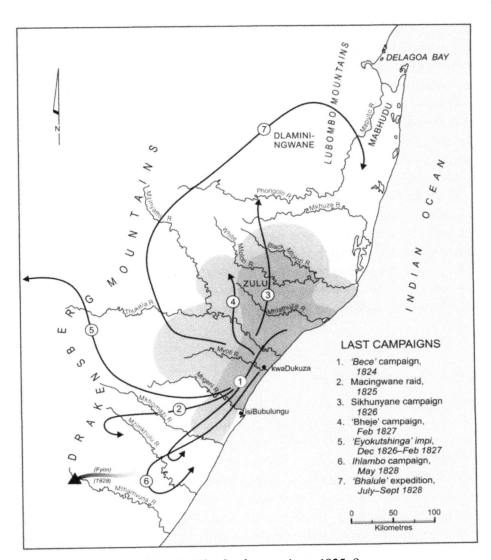

Map 11: The final campaigns, 1825–8

white settler ambitions. While the minutiae of such influences – at least until
1824 – remain extremely elusive, they can no longer be discounted. 'Zulu
identity' was being transformed and shaped by those influences even as Shaka
was forging it; it was as fluid as the fortunes of his *impis*.

Finally, we can be sure that the sources on Shaka's career are patchy,
often prejudiced, and always politically 'embedded'. We need to know – and
can have just as much fun getting to know – *how* the portrayals of Shaka
came to be recorded or written, by whom, when, and why. In some ways, this
creates even more gaps and mysteries, but that is the nature of history.

Now, in the last few weeks of Shaka's life, we encounter two of the
strangest and most intractable of all the questions haunting his reign. The
first mystery is: why, just a few days after his forces had returned from the
ihlambo campaign against the Mpondo, did Shaka send them on an apparently
madcap new expedition way off to the north-east? The second mystery is:
how was it that he apparently didn't notice that his brothers were trying to
kill him, and do something about it? Why was he unable to prevent his own
death?

SWEEP UP THE RUBBISH

Amidst Shaka's more successful military campaigns there had been failures
and retreats and rebellious units overreaching their mandate. However, there
was never a campaign that appears so obviously misconceived as the so-called
'Bhalule' expedition, otherwise known as the *ukhukhulela ngoqo* – the Sweep-
up-the-Rubbish Campaign. It was called this because Shaka is said to have
ordered every last man to go on it, even the old and the crippled, the rubbish.
'Call up all the riff-raff,' Shaka is supposed to have ordered, 'let no one
remain behind, not even old men with bad knees'.[2] They were sent off, the
usual story goes, to raid Soshangane, then living well north of Delagoa Bay,
and came to grief on the Bhalule (or Olifants) river, which crosses the present-
day Mpumalanga province into the Kruger National Park.

This is far beyond the Zulu forces' normal range – as aberrant, in its way,
as Dingane's *eyokutshinga* raid north of Lesotho. If it's true, either Shaka had
completely lost his mind – as the informant MELAPI heard: Shaka had
bunguleka'd, gone crazy, giving such an order[3] – or something else very
desperate had pushed him. What little is told about this venture is so strange

and contradictory, however, that I suspect it's not Shaka's head that needs examining, but the accounts themselves.

The most interesting feature of the evidence is this: the white accounts (mainly Fynn's and Isaacs's) assert that the Zulu attacked Soshangane and were beaten. They travelled 1 000 kilometres or more 'to attack a tribe he [Shaka] thought to be rich in cattle and other things', according to Isaacs.[4] (These 'other things' are never specified. Trade goods? Or slaves, which were Soshangane's main export?) By contrast, the traditions recorded by Stuart say nothing of the sort.

How do we explain this discrepancy? What could have happened out there?

White accounts

Fynn gave two quite different, very garbled accounts of the return of the Zulu forces of the Mpondo *ihlambo* expedition and the dispatch of the 'Bhalule' expedition. In one, he claims that Shaka was angry that the army had not gone as far as the Colony – when (by Fynn's own account) he had ordered them not to. Fynn as usual puts this down to Shaka's own inexplicable caprice. The army was obliged to camp for three days, and forbidden to eat even the 30 000 cattle that milled about them. Fynn then relates an all-but-unintelligible story about himself and Ngomane trying to cover up an insult to Shaka allegedly committed by 'certain chiefs east of the Zuloes'. Ngomane didn't want the exhausted army to be sent out again. At a meeting about this alleged insult, someone unnamed stood up and said, 'every time a war was proposed', Shaka's army 'expected a defeat, but they had now become so used to conquer under his command . . . that they were now willing to face whatever enemy might offer [sic]'.[5] This is mixed in with the death of 50 cattle, which they were also trying to explain away. Why was Fynn involved in this at all? Something very murky is going on.

In Fynn's account, the army does finally assemble before Shaka, and the captured cattle are paraded, sorted, and distributed – 'excluding those taken by the Umquindein [amaQadini?] to which were added some of the cattle taken by the natives in our service, being three small droves in the taking of which one Armumpondo had been shot'.[6] (This is as close as Fynn gets to admitting that he and his people *had* been involved in the Mpondo raid –

but it is a crucial admission.) The army then is appropriately doctored, washes in the sea, and spends several days on the road home to kwaDukuza. Shaka kills off numerous people for arbitrary reasons on the way. Two days after Fynn leaves kwaDukuza to return to Port Natal, the 'Bhalule' expedition is sent off.[7]

Fynn doesn't state when the expedition left. The chronology in the 'Notebook', such as it is, differs from that of his second account, a letter he wrote on 9 September 1828, in which he claimed that the army had been given only *four* days' rest.[8] If the chronology that I followed in Chapter 13 is correct, the tail end of the Zulu force had pulled back from the Mpondo in early June, and hence would have left for the 'Bhalule' in late June at the outside. However, we know that Fynn was still in Mpondo territory in July; so either (as I argued in Chapter 13) he was *not* with Shaka at all when the latter was going back to kwaDukuza; or there was a much greater gap between the two campaigns than he says. Bryant, by contrast, dates the 'Bhalule' expedition's departure to late July.[9]

The expedition – Fynn goes on – had some 'skirmishes' on the way, attacking 'Nkantolo and Sindane, two tributary chiefs', for alleged infringements of the mourning ceremonies, heading thence 'to Shoshangane's, 80 miles to the north-east, beyond Delagoa Bay and near 500 miles from Dukuza'.[10] When it reached the Phongolo river, the force was cut off by Sobhuza of the Swazi, leader of 'a tribe which had several times joined the Zulus and as often revolted, intercepting all messengers and killing them, protecting himself from the Zulus by the capabilities the caverns of that country afforded him'.[11] Fynn exaggerates the relationship: 'joined' and 'revolted' are too strong. Just possibly Sobhuza (also known as Somhlolo) had played it safe in the past and offered Shaka some form of conciliatory gesture, as Makhasane of the Tembe had. This is far from implying that Shaka ever *controlled* Sobhuza. Indeed, the most that can be said is that there was desultory contact. Some Swazi marriages were secured by Zulu *izinduna* such as Masiphula, Mnyamana and Sekethwayo.[12] There's a tradition that Sobhuza was once invited by Shaka to visit him, either at Mbelebele *umuzi* or at kwaBulawayo. 'After discussing their business, whatever it was, Sobuza returned to his country. This shows,' the informant MSIMANGA adds, 'that Shaka did not put chiefs to death as a matter of course, especially where they

acknowledge his supremacy'.[13] There is another similar visit story, related by
a Swazi informant. I want to linger on this story because it ends on an event
that possibly gives us a clue to what happened on the 'Bhalule' expedition.

Even Shaka the Zulu heard of his [Sobhuza's] virtues, and consequently
there came messengers from Shaka to Somhlolo's [Sobhuza's] royal
residence. They came to invite Somhlolo to visit Shaka, so that Shaka
could satisfy himself of the virtues, as he had heard of Somhlolo's
admiration by other people. Some people did not favour the invitation,
because they suspected that Shaka would murder their king. But
Hlophe of Mabhongane favoured the invitation, confident that no
harm would befall him. The Swazi then agreed to Hlophe's suggestion.
Preparations were made and the king started for Zululand. When he
neared Shaka's palace there was an abrupt change in the weather – a
thunderstorm was brewing. The Zulu call that 'the elephant rumbles'.
During the period of the thunderstorm Somhlolo arrived at Shaka's
palace. Unfortunately Shaka had caught 'flu. After Maphokela and
another man had returned from Shaka after reporting the arrival of
the king, Shaka sent his *indvuna* [sic] and mother to greet the son of
Ndvungunye and assure him of safety, also saying that he would perhaps
see him tomorrow. Shaka's warriors were full of malice, and they
danced and cried out that Shaka should give the command to kill
Somhlolo. But the guests were given ten head of cattle and were
assigned to a nearby homestead for lodging. Before they could undo
the mats to prepare for sleep, Somhlolo told his escort that they should
wait for a moment. There was then a torrent in Zululand. Somhlolo
asked his people to go out and look at the sky. On their return they
told him that the king was fully clad. Then Somhlolo asked his escort
if they had seen the warriors dancing in their anxiety to kill him, and
if they thought that they would see the next daylight. He himself
suggested that they had rather depart then and there. They went out.
The cattle were resting. They touched one of them, and then they
went off into the night. All night long they went on their way. Just
before dawn they were about to cross the Pongolo river. It was still
raining, but not on the Ngwane [Swazi] party who were walking on

dry land. Across the Pongolo they spotted a hillock with caves. They got there, slaughtered one beast and undid their sleeping mats. Some flayed the beast while others prepared for sleep. Just then they looked across the river, in the direction which they had come, and they saw a great army there. The Zulu could see the cattle but could not readily see the Swazi. Suddenly, in the overflowing river there floated a big tree, which was being washed down by the flood. The anxious Zulu army began to throw assegais over the flooded river. All the assegais they threw did not cross the river, but were washed away. Then there came another regiment of Zulu. The latter urged the first regiment to cross the flooded river. They decided to attempt it. This was the first heavy rain experienced on Zulu soil after six years of drought. Unfortunately their courage led them to their death – all were washed away downstream and drowned. None managed to reach the Swazi. Those who remained on the bank of the river remorsefully remarked that their fellow warriors were just chasing the *mhlengas* (a term of abuse).[14]

I want to extract four details from this rather fascinating account. First, there's the drought, to which I'll return in a moment. Second, there's the mention of Shaka's mother, which might date this visit to 1827 or before (although the 'mother' may not be Nandi; the reference could be to Mnkabayi or one of the other *izinkosikazi* 'mothers').[15] Third, there's a correlation between the mention of protecting caves here and in Fynn's account. Fourth, and most crucial, is the flooded river incident. In Isaacs's version, the Zulu encounter Soshangane's army, to whom their presence has been betrayed by a renegade chieftain. Soshangane roughs up the Zulu in a surprise night attack. The Zulu counter-attack, whereupon 'many of them having escaped the spear jumped into the river, with an intention to cross, but were drowned from the force of the current'.[16] It's a curious cross-over, and I speculate that in Isaacs's account a fleeting skirmish with the Swazi has been elevated and distorted into an all-out battle with Soshangane.

To brush the carpet in the other direction, so to speak, a detail from Isaacs's account ironically all but proves that the very battle he relates could *not* have been with Soshangane, who was indeed then ensconced somewhere north of Inhambane, just south of the Limpopo. However, Isaacs places the scuffle on the 'Marfumo', or Maphutha river, which flows from the *south* into Delagoa Bay itself.[17]

Finally, amongst the white accounts, Francis Farewell had a slightly different version, related to Captain Aitchison in December 1828:

> King Chaca about five months ago, previous to Cane's leaving Natal, sent a force of 30,000 fighting men to the Eastward and Northward of Mozambique for the express purpose of weakening *his tribe* with a view to his punishing them with greater brutality. This force marched with provision only for the advance and orders to fight for their future sustenance. The tribe against whom they proposed to war, hearing by some unexpected chance of their intention, drove off the whole of *their cattle* and quietly awaited the invaders, whom (a party of 8,000) they took by surprize [sic] and cut to pieces. The remaining 20,000 were subsequently reduced from famine and other casualties to a mere nominal force.[18]

Farewell's geography is too vague to be of much use, though it roughly correlates with Soshangane's location. His proposal that the whole thing was designed to satisfy some whim of Shaka's brutality – to deliberately weaken the tribe – is too ridiculous even to consider. In any event, in another letter he had written to Major Dundas just a week before, Farewell tellingly contradicts himself. The Zulu force was sent 'a considerable distance the other side of the Portuguese at Delagoa Bay', he alleges – but at another point says that Shaka had sent the army only 'some hundred miles to the Eastward', which is to say perhaps as far as the vicinity of the Bay.[19]

In sum, the white accounts are so contradictory that I am tempted to discard them, although certain details do tantalisingly echo the Zulu sources.

Zulu versions

The Zulu oral testimonies are thinner and also somewhat contradictory, but they do suggest a very different story. They agree that a contingent was sent off to the north-east more or less immediately after the *ihlambo* campaign. A

couple of accounts claim, interestingly, that Shaka dispatched at least part of
the force even before he had left the Mzimkhulu river – Fynn's place.[20] Only
then did Shaka go home to kwaDukuza and gather together all the old men
and send them in the tracks of the first body. Many people hid away in the
bushes to avoid the call-up.[21] After they had gone Shaka belatedly realised
that he was left with no one to protect him: the old – all the 'white' – warriors
were recalled to guard him. (In Fynn's account, so were some youngsters,
who were then formed into an ad hoc unit nicknamed the iziNyosi – the
Bees.[22] Not one Zulu source supports this: the iziNyosi was not formed in this
manner.[23])

   That Shaka should make himself vulnerable in this way is improbable. In
addition, it's unlikely that even he would have been able to order virtually
his entire people to hike off 800 kilometres or more to the north. The 'entire
people' did *not* go, anyway. Units attached to Zihlandlo and to Ngwadi certainly
remained behind as did some contingents loyal to Dingane. Within months,
even weeks, of the assassination, Dingane was able to deploy substantial forces
– forces which, if we were to take the 'Bhalule' story seriously, would no
longer have existed. Nevertheless, Shaka seems to have been left more
vulnerable than usual.

   Zulu sources are also fragmentary on what path the 'Bhalule' army took.
Most likely they travelled below the Drakensberg escarpment,[24] and then
headed east into southern Swazi territory. They may have attacked someone
named Nhlanganiso on their way.[25] In the informant NGIDI's opinion, they
reached the Mbuluze river in present-day Swaziland, the bailiwick of Swazi
chiefs Mampontsha and Matshekana. Here the army was *thethwa*'d, doctored
for battle. It was at this point, on the Mbuluze river, that Shaka's brothers
Dingane and Mhlangana, bent on murder, turned back.[26]

   The Zulu expedition didn't go anywhere near Soshangane. After they
had clashed with the Swazi, they almost certainly swung east and south through
Machakane's territory on the Mafumo or Maphutha river and past Delagoa
Bay (country *through which* Soshangane had passed and which was still
associated with Soshangane in the minds of distant southerners). The Zulu
army then moved further south along the coast to head for home. This is
reinforced by the most telling indication of all: no Zulu account relates any
clash with Soshangane himself. The Zulu force did not get anywhere near

any place identifiable with the word 'Bhalule'. It was only much later that A.T. Bryant identified it with the Olifants river.[27] There *is* a place still named Bhalule at the junction of the Olifants and the Limpopo, now in the Kruger National Park. The Bhalule, according to Doke and Vilakazi, is the Crocodile or Limpopo river, even further north – and no one suggests that the Zulu force went *there*.

In my opinion, however, both possibilities seem too far north.

I suggest, instead, that the word *bhalula* or *bhalule* simply means 'to go to a far country', or to 'tramp across uninhabited country': this generality has been wrongly pinned down, by both white and Zulu commentators, to a particular place.[28]

Did Fynn, Isaacs and company invent the Soshangane scenario, then? If so, why? Were there actually more rational, communally agreed on reasons for the expedition? There are, I think, three or four possible scenarios. None is entirely satisfactory, but they are also not necessarily mutually exclusive.

'Bhalule' scenarios

The first scenario is connected with the reason that I proposed for the *ihlambo* campaign: drought and hardship. The cattle raided from the Mpondo were useful, but inadequate. Some of them may even have been left behind.[29] More were required, and someone to the north had them. If so many people were in fact dispatched on the campaign, it speaks of serious deprivation at home. At least one account notes that the area between the Zulu and Mpondo polities had been denuded of crops – by the iziYendane initially, possibly by white-led raids subsequently. Later on, Dingane, contemplating a similar foray, ordered the planting of crops in that region precisely to prevent a repetition of Shaka's mistake.[30] There was ongoing severe drought and famine along the southern Mozambique coastal areas through 1827 to 1829 or 1830.[31] Writers in the eastern Cape Colony also noted that groups from the interior were being pushed by drought.[32] It seems to have been particularly widespread. Shaka was simply after more supplies of food.

The problem may have been exacerbated by another factor: theft. We've already seen Gcugcwa stealing a portion of the Mpondo cattle. Some accounts relate that Hlangabeza of the Ntshalini people also absconded. Hlangabeza

had resisted and even attacked Shaka before.[33] He did not present himself to
accompany the *ihlambo* force, and he was clearly bent on eloping now, with
both people and cattle. This was the immediate object of the 'Bhalule' force,
led by Mdlaka. They did indeed hunt Hlangabeza down: they found his
temporary shelters erected alongside a forest, attacked in two prongs before
dawn, and wiped them out. Hlangabeza escaped, hid in a pond, but was spotted
by young *udibi* bearers and was speared to death in the water. Only then did
the Zulu force proceed to its further object.[34] This is reinforced by Mtshapi,
who claims that the initial purpose was to 'fetch the red cattle of the
umkandhli' – the Mpondo cattle were famous for their russet colour.[35] Mtshapi
adds one little phrase that has significant implications: 'an ox bellowed'. This
indicates that, far from being a capricious idiot, Shaka was obeying deeply
cherished beliefs, the call of the ancestors. Mtshapi explains:

> There were two ways of getting permission to start hostile proceedings:
> (a) by the king dreaming that his ancestors agree to their being entered
> on; (b) by an ox bellowing at night, it may be long after all have gone
> to sleep.... [The ox] would be identified, and such ox would be called
> *Izwandaba* [that which 'hears a matter', and prognosticates], not a
> given ox, but any one. On this occurring the king would give the
> order for the *umpakati* [circle of elders] to come into the kraal there
> and then, where a semi-circle would be formed and the great chant
> sung, viz. the *uhawu*. And there and then the king might issue his
> orders that the impi is to go and attack such and such a tribe, eg. the
> Swazis, whereupon preparations for leaving would at once ensue.[36]

This is exactly what happened on this occasion. Mtshapi's account is the only
really nuanced one that we have. It's chronologically muddled, and the army's
ignorance of local trees seems unlikely, but the overall picture is of a landscape
ravaged by drought, locusts and need.

> The army duly went off to the Balule. After travelling a great distance
> it came to a broad valley, where it camped. It had been marching
> through open country where there was no wood to be found. It had
> had to drive its cattle on without being able to slaughter them, for it

was a problem to find wood for roasting the meat. Then they came to the valley, where there was abundant wood. But it was wood of the *umdhlebe* tree. They roasted much meat with the *umdhlebe* wood. Because of this the whole army was seized with stomach pains. When it arrived, the *umdhlebe* tree [a species of poisonous euphorbia, *synadenium capela*, one replete with folkloristic associations, but one also common throughout the catchment, unlikely to be unknown to these troops; therefore, this aspect of story is more likely legendary than factual] was crying out, 'Meh!' like a goat. As it cried out it exuded blood, like that of a person bleeding. The men of the army roasted meat; they were hungry. They had been surviving on *umncwazibe* berries. . . . When this happened the advanced section of the army went forward. The rest remained behind where they had made their fires. While matters were in this state the vanguard went off; it captured the red cattle and came back with them. In capturing the cattle it had reached a place infested with locusts. All those men who had remained in the camp died. They were red locusts. The remaining section of the army brought the cattle back to the king. As it arrived the locusts poured into Zulu country. They finished off the grass and the people's crops. The king then said, 'Wo! What is to be done on account of this? I hear there is food to be found in the country of Fabase, in the direction of Soshangane's. Let the army prepare for war, and go and fetch seed from Fabase's country, so that the country can revive at planting time.' The *izinduna* replied, 'The king is right to give orders for seed to be fetched, for the people have been made weak by hunger; they are very thin. They are even roasting their shields.' The king ordered, 'No! Let the army prepare, and go and fetch seed. The men must shift for themselves. People will not save themselves by simply remaining in their homes without planting.' So the army went off, and fetched seed. The king then ordered, 'Go and search for the cowdung . . .'[37]

This depicts a complex and desperate *series* of expeditions for sustenance, not the vague, simplistic, one-off foray of the white account. There is no mention here at all of the army going all the way to Soshangane himself.

The aim of replenishing stocks of cattle and grain might overlap with a second goal: to serve some purpose in the trade with Delagoa Bay. There seems little other reason for the Zulu venturing so close to the port, and slaving by 1828 was booming.[38] This is one possible explanation for the strong presence of the whites' units on the force. It may also be the explanation for why the whites portrayed the expedition as an attack on Soshangane, rather than a venture virtually to Delagoa Bay itself. Trade in other goods with Delagoa Bay had declined in early 1828, and now that the outlet at Port Natal appeared to be unravelling, Shaka may have wished to reassert his options in that direction. This possibility places Isaacs's complaint that Shaka 'had an extreme aversion to anything like commercial traffic' and was 'decidedly opposed to any intercourse, having for its object the establishment of a mercantile connection with his subjects', in a different light. In Isaacs's jaundiced view, Shaka's 'whole soul was engrossed by war, and he conceived that anything like commerce would enervate his people and unfit them for their military duties'.[39]

We have accumulated enough evidence, I think, to show that, in fact, Shaka was intensely interested in commerce, but on his own terms. His concern was to control trade, not to suppress it. His problem was that Isaacs and company were becoming uncontrollable; hence his renewed interest in Delagoa Bay. (Dingane would take advantage of this realignment immediately after his accession, finding the Port Natal traders just as troublesome and unpredictable as Shaka had. He quickly moved the Zulu 'capital' back north again.) Given this growing antipathy, it was in the whites' interests more generally to represent Shaka as doing something especially crazy.

John Cane (who had left Zulu country for the Cape before the 'Bhalule' expedition returned) provided what is to my mind the clinching piece of evidence. Cane (incidentally echoing NGIDI, cited earlier) indicated that the Zulu had actually gone after one 'Omchuaguan'. The Portuguese were, however, supporting this chieftain's people, having supplied them with muskets; this had brought the Zulu force up short.[40] 'Omchuaguan' is almost certainly not Soshangane, but Machakane (or Matshekana), the Matoll chieftain who had long had dealings with the Portuguese, and who in 1828 was forcibly taking over the region just west of Delagoa Bay.[41] He was both rich and threatening to the trade routes. Shaka wished to attack him, and knew that gunmen would be necessary. No engagement seems to have transpired. Perhaps already demoralised by the unexpected Swazi clash, and outbreaks of malaria, the allegedly invincible Zulu army backed off. Direct evidence is lacking, but this scenario makes to my mind the greatest circumstantial sense.

A third possible scenario involves Shaka's personality more directly. The expedition was punitive. Shaka was angry as he had been disobeyed again. You will recall that according to one account, he had sent forces to establish an *umuzi* on the border of Xhosa territory. The force went, having been ordered not to touch the Mpondo. They nevertheless raided Mpondo cattle, which they then brought back – without having established the settlement. In fury Shaka sent the whole lot of them off to the Bhalule.[42] This still hinges on an aberrant, if not insane decision on Shaka's part, and it doesn't explain why all the old men should have had to go, too. Still, there are other hints of a punitive element. One is supplied by Fynn, who notes that two peoples, the 'Contelo and the Isendarns' were attacked by the expedition. The 'Contelo' had disobeyed the post-Nandi funeral prohibitions, and the 'Isendarns' had once been 'Spies & Guides' to Shaka. Were they the lingering, rebellious rump of the iziYendane, who were being attacked for their connection with Dingane?[43] Maybe Shaka was punishing his forces for *not* getting to grips with the Mpondo: since there had been no fighting with them, the Zulu were still obliged to satisfy the funerary glory of Nandi.[44] Or was Shaka angry because (as JANTSHI's father told him cryptically) 'Faku had taken the assegai that was red from stabbing people, had slaughtered a beast with it, and had tossed it into a storage pot'? This was apparently an insult; some sort of honour had to be retrieved.[45]

Although these hints of a punitive aspect are intriguing, they amount to little in the way of a coherent explanation, and may have been an element in only one of a number of concurrent events.

A fourth scenario is a more conspiratorial one. It makes better sense, but is also less provable. It's curious that units, *amavuyo*, from the Port Natal traders' groups were amongst those sent off: Dlemula, Jadilili, Mhabula, Ndandane of the Maphumulo, Ngungwini, Funwayo, Mhuyi, Sipongo (who was in charge of James Saunders King's isiHlanga *vuyo*) all went, from both

King's and Farewell's establishments.[46] These were precisely the people most likely to have accompanied Fynn on his southern raids. Was Shaka trying to get them out of the way for a while, along with his brothers Dingane and Mhlangana?[47] Was he perhaps aware, after all, that his brothers and maybe the whites were conspiring against him?

We've already seen Dingane apparently trying to make a deal with the Mpondo, in the wake of the second failed assassination attempt. Fynn, as we saw, was also in the vicinity. At the very least, Fynn had exceeded Shaka's mandate (again). It's possible that elements of the various *amabutho*, along with the various peoples whose loyalty Fynn had already purchased,[48] had joined him in the foray across the Mzimkhulu, further exciting Shaka's suspicions. Were Fynn, Farewell and Dingane, and perhaps Ngomane, colluding together? The white contingent was under some suspicion already when the embassy left for Port Elizabeth, and then in deep trouble after its return. They had every motivation now for getting rid of Shaka. Getting *them* out of the way until he knew the outcome of the 'embassy' to the Cape would be one way of dealing with the problem. It doesn't seem to me a particularly effective way, and I'm not wholly convinced by this scenario. There are hints here, though, that the main expedition was not so much a cause of the internal dissension, as a complex product of it.

None of these four scenarios makes complete sense of the scattered evidence that we have. We know that an expedition – or, probably, more than one – went out. However, we don't know exactly what it consisted of, how many went, what route it took, what it was meant to achieve, or why it ran into trouble. That it did get into difficulties is certain, and the clash with the Swazi was only the first of them. DINYA said that his father, of the Dukuza *ibutho*, went, and died on it.[49] MKEHLENGANA's father was more lucky. He injured his foot on the way and Shaka allowed him to return.[50] JANTSHI's father Nongila almost died, but made it back.[51] Shaka's one half-brother who stayed with the expedition – Nzibe – died of fever, *imbo*.[52]

Quite where or why the army ran into trouble we don't know. Was it breathing the fumes of *umdhlebe* trees that did them in, as in the account above;[53] or did they camp somewhere in the sweating lowlands for long enough to get malarial fevers, as others have assumed?[54] The first option seems very odd; the incubation period of malaria makes the second seem unlikely, too. Isaacs wrote that local chieftains deprived them of food; they died – of 'hunger, sickness and fatigue'.[55] Isaacs claimed, exaggeratedly, that 'upwards of 15,000' of them perished this way. They were said to have been reduced to eating their shields, soaked in water. They fought no one and straggled back, shattered, in twos, threes, and fives.[56]

Whatever the reasons for the expedition, one result was that Shaka was left relatively unprotected. Somewhere along their journey, possibly near the Swazi borders, Dingane and Mhlangana had turned back, murder on their minds. The rest of the army – like John Cane and the second embassy – returned to find that events at home had outstripped them.

'THE LAND WILL SEE LOCUSTS . . .'

When John Cane arrived in Graham's Town on 8 October 1828, he had a long discussion with the civil commissioner of Albany, Captain Campbell. According to Campbell's report, Cane represented Shaka's people 'as dissatisfied and disposed to revolt in consequence of his cruelty and constant wars'.[57] This was certainly true of *some* of the people – including the whites. However, all the evidence suggests that resistance to Shaka's rule was much slighter than we might suppose. Wars had *not* been constant. Cane's statement – made in supposed ignorance of what was happening back at Port Natal and kwaDukuza – is just one more indication that he had already anticipated what was brewing.

The first thing that had happened – on 7 September – was that James Saunders King had died. Any number of reasons were given at the time, ranging from a liver complaint,[58] to 'grief and dysentery',[59] to being 'broken hearted'.[60] In his book, Nathaniel Isaacs mourned the passing of his father-surrogate in a long passage soggy with conventional sentiment.[61] King believed, said Isaacs, that Cane had gone off to harm him. Farewell refused to come to the dying man's side, sending only a note: 'a poor, frivolous, unnatural, and ungrateful excuse', wrote Isaacs. Farewell, as we saw, had already threatened to kill King and his party. If he did not actually murder King at this point,[62] Farewell's studied neglect certainly helped him along. King died, according to Isaacs, while requesting Isaacs to deliver him a lethal dose of laudanum. Fynn's account, by contrast, is remarkably dry.[63]

Then, strangely, John Hutton, the big, truculent carpenter, also died. Here there's a substantial discrepancy between Fynn's and Isaacs's versions. Fynn says that Hutton died just 'a few days' after King, and before Shaka. Isaacs claimed in a letter to the governor that he died *after* Shaka, on 23 October – and then in the *Travels* changed this to only sometime in November.[64] The discrepancy may be trivial. Or not. It certainly becomes of major importance that we know exactly where the whites were in the days leading up to Shaka's assassination. According to Isaacs, both he and Fynn went up to kwaDukuza to inform Shaka of King's death, undergoing various purification rituals.[65] Shaka regretted having 'abused' King; it was Farewell's fault. Isaacs reports Shaka as saying that he thought some 'black man' had poisoned King; Fynn wrote: 'Shaka was, however, glad to be able to say that an *umnumzane*, ie. a gentleman, had died a natural death and not by the hands of his people or himself . . .'[66] This radical change of opinion is not explained.

Shaka proposed recalling Cane's overland mission, and sending Fynn and Isaacs on yet another, by sea. They objected, given the bad blood over the last one. After a couple of days, Shaka sent them back to Port Natal. Things were distinctly uncomfortable for the whites: Shaka had become radically suspicious of all of them, and rumours that he wanted to kill them off circulated alarmingly. (Or so the whites said; it gave them at least a certain satisfaction in seeing him assassinated.[67]) As Fynn put it dryly, 'Mr Isacs [*sic*] was not treated as well as usual'.[68] Despite this, much later (and only in his book), Isaacs incongruously claimed that

> As a remuneration for the presents he had received from me, as well as for my attention to his people on the last mission, and for the wound I had received in the war against Ingoma, he created me chief of Natal, and granted to me the tract of country lying from the river Umslutee to the river Umlass [Mdloti to Mlazi], a space of twenty-five miles of seacoast and one hundred miles inland, including the bay, islands, and forests near the point, and the exclusive right of trading with his people.[69]

This was at least the third time that Shaka had allegedly ceded this same stretch of country to one or other of the white adventurers. Nothing about this emerged at the time; it was another fraud. Anyway, Fynn, Farewell and Isaacs were back in Port Natal when they heard the news of the assassination – that is, if we believe their later accounts.

The assassination had been heralded by the unexpected return from the *bhalule* expedition of Shaka's brothers Dingane and Mhlangana. 'Are you returning on your own?' inquired the surprised Shaka. The brothers, ominously, made no reply.[70]

There are almost as many theories about who instigated the final assassination plot as there are informants.

One version holds that it was *all* the brothers: Dingane, Mhlangana, Mpande, Ngqojana, Mfihlo, Mqubana, and others.[71]

Another opinion is that it was primarily Dingane, who said, 'This person Shaka is causing us distress. He is continually making us go out to war, and we cannot eat the new crops in the home of our mothers. We should kill him . . .'[72]

Then there is the theory that it was started by Mbopha kaSithayi, Shaka's personal attendant, who greeted Dingane's return: 'Hau! So you are here, children of the king? You are troubled by the madman. As soon as you returned from Pondoland the order was given to move on. Are you not going to stab him?'[73]

Another version maintains that it was really the great king-maker, aunt Mnkabayi who persuaded Mbopha to do the dirty deed, and then arbitrated the result.[74]

Or, it was the whites who put Dingane and company up to it, in the hope of benefiting from the result.[75]

In addition, there are versions that are various combinations of the above.

Why would anyone want to assassinate Shaka at all? The most important factor to look for is obviously motive. Naturally, a slew of reasons has been given. A common one was that Shaka had sent the army off again just at a time when they needed to reap and store the latest harvest.[76] We can credit this up to a point, although Shaka was surely not solely responsible: it's hard not to believe that this would have been only a pretext – perhaps a premeditated one.

Was Shaka's cruelty the prod? There seems little reason to doubt this as a contributing factor – although there is every reason to doubt Farewell's assertion that 'During the absence of this [*bhalule*] force Chaca fancied he could with impunity go to greater lengths in acts of cruelty than he had ever yet ventured upon and ordered 2 000 females to be destroyed at the rate of about 300 p[e]r diem'.[77] This would later be embellished to include some women belonging to Dingane himself – hence his involvement in the assassination.[78]

Who was supposed to be carrying out these multiple executions, if Shaka had no warriors left even to defend him? If anything can be said to implicate Farewell in the plot, it is precisely this ridiculous allegation (combined with those that he made about the *bhalule* expedition itself, as we saw on page 489 in the previous section). At the very least, we must put it down to one of the many stories of Shaka's atrocity spread by both the whites and Dingane's spindoctors in the succeeding months and years, stories that they invented in order to cover their own tracks.

So was it merely one of those 'palace coups', so common to royal rule the world over? Was it a case of a thwarted, surly brother, biding his time, now finding or creating the opportunity, needing no other reason than his own ambition? The brothers' resentment may have gone back to their own boyhoods: one account claims that Shaka was hidden during his later youth not from his father, but from his brothers.[79] Dingane and the other brothers seem to have been relatively sidelined by Shaka. They were given their patrimonies but played no obviously prideful place in the hierarchy. Fynn claimed, dubiously, that the brothers were not permitted even to be 'known as his relatives'.[80] This is probably exaggerated: Dingane was occasionally to be seen at the head of the Fasimba *ibutho* with their all-white shields.[81] Fascinatingly, Charles Rawden Maclean asserted that Shaka had entered into an 'arrangement' with Dingane, that Dingane would succeed him. This explained why Shaka denied himself any heirs. Dingane, Maclean thought, had simply 'become weary of waiting for the removal of his brother, Shaka, in the ordinary course of nature'.[82] Add the stress of drought, the absence of a crucial segment of Shaka's warriors, a stock of real or imagined cruelties, and the tacit or active collusion of firearm-wielding whites – the moment was certainly ripe.

Whether or not Dingane had widespread support is another matter.

The manner in which the assassination itself unfolded will always be open to dispute. We can't be certain exactly when it happened. According to Isaacs

– whose chronology is the most nuanced that we have, but must still be treated
with caution – it happened on the night of 22 September 1828. The usual
date given is 24 September, based only on Fynn's memory;[83] Farewell said 23
September.[84] We'll never be quite sure. As with his date of birth, this equally
crucial date of Shaka's biography will remain shadowy.

We also don't know exactly where it happened, whether it was within
kwaDukuza or another cattle enclosure. No eyewitness accounts emerged.
Fynn's version is the most detailed, suspiciously so:

> [I]n the middle of the day on which he was killed being the 24th
> Septr 1828 he dreamed that he was ded [sic] and Umbopo was serving
> another king on waking he told his dream to one of his Sisters who
> . . . afterwards told Umbopo the circumstance who knowing that in
> consequence he would not have many hours to live urged the two
> confederates [Dingane and Mhlangana] to take the first opportunity
> which shortly occurred when some Caffers ariving from the outskirts
> of the nation with Cranes feathers which the king had sent them for
> in which they had delayed much time Chaka came out of his Hut and
> went to a small krall about 50 yards from Dugusar called Inyarka
> moobie where these people that brought the feathers sat before
> him . . .[85]

Fynn's notebook fades to illegibility for a few lines, but if we follow James
Stuart's extrapolation of it, Shaka demanded in 'a severe voice' what had
delayed them. Mbopha then uncharacteristically did the same, brandishing
a stick. The visitors fled.

> Chaka seing [sic here and elsewhere] them run asked Umbopo what
> they had done to be driven away Umhlengana & Dingarn having
> hid themselves at the back of the small fence . . . standing having an
> hidden assegai under the kaross seing . . . the people run and the king
> by himself stabbed him throu the back by the left shoulder Dingarn
> . . . also and stabbed him Chaka having only time to ask what is the
> matter, children of my father but the three together stabbed him . . .[86]

If this is anything like correct it suggests a set-up. Who were these visitors? The word 'Caffers' could be Xhosa or Mpondo (the opinion of some Zulu informants, too).[87] As I noted in Chapter 13, they were almost certainly the 'opposition Mpondo' under Myeki of the Jali and Fodo of the Nhlangwini, who were in the habit of presenting tribute in the form of crane feathers. Myeki at least would be richly rewarded with cattle later. They were there as a deliberate distraction.

The extant Zulu traditional accounts are quite short by comparison and vary in detail. This is a typical one from DINYA:

> The Pondos had come from Faku with a small drove of oxen in order to tender their allegiance; . . . some of these cattle were killed in order to be eaten; . . . Dingane, Mhlangana and Mbopa arrived at night-time; . . . seeing the messengers from Faku the following morning talking to the king (seated on his 'throne'), he [Mbopha] ran up to them and struck them with the stick end of his assegai; he did this to rouse Shaka's anger, Shaka of course being helpless without his forces; the Pondos ran off at once for their homes, leaving their assegais and the meat which was cooking for them unconsumed . . . Shaka said when stabbed, 'Is it the sons of my father who are killing me? How is this, seeing I never put to death any of my brothers ever since I became king? You are killing me, but the land will see locusts and white people come.' He then fell.[88]

There are multiple other variations on – and disagreements about – this basic scene. No, it wasn't cattle, it was crane feathers. No, Mbopha didn't beat the messengers, he beat the cattle.[89] Mbopha gave Shaka's spears to Dingane beforehand, a gesture both practical and symbolic.[90] No, he just hid them away.[91] Mbopha stabbed Shaka in the back; no, he threw an assegai from a distance.[92] No, Mhlangana stabbed first.[93] Shaka pulled the spear out and ran for the gate where he was cut down by another man.[94] Dingane stabbed him, too; no, Dingane just held him down.[95] Actually, Shaka said, 'Are you stabbing me, the king of the earth? You will come to an end through killing one another.'[96] No, he said, 'The land will be overrun by the swallows, the white people, you kill me but the land will be destroyed, the sky will be white with stars.'[97] Actually, he knelt in the dust and 'in the most supplicating manner besought them to let him live that he might be their servant'.[98]

And so on.

The fact that no one, either then or now, could verify any of this, contributed directly to the success of the coup. They had made an end of Shaka – the most self-assured and successful local leader of his time – and they could now say pretty much what they liked about him.

THE RED ASSEGAI

At some point during Mpande's reign in the 1840s, the royal *umuzi* of kwaNodwengu was convulsed by the unusual spectacle of two snakes – one marked like a python, the other green and white – writhing in battle along the fences. It was immediately interpreted as the returned spirits, the *amadlozi*, of Dingane and Shaka, fighting each other after death, just as they had in life.

> These kings, Dingane and Shaka, fought each other; they chased each other up and down the fence at the door of Masipula's hut, and finally dropped onto the ground in the yard. They began as the sun was getting warm, and continued until midday. They twined round each other, with first one on top and then the other. They were red with blood from biting each other.
>
> Then Masipula said, 'Let the king be told.' The king then ordered all the *izinduna* to go down to look. [The snakes] fought and fought. Men returned to the king to say, 'Hau! They are still fighting, *Nkosi*, even now.' Then he ordered, 'Chase the evil-doer of Mgungundhlovu [that is, 'Dingane']. Catch it, and burn it, and throw the ashes into the Mfolozi.' The *izinduna* were trying to intervene in the fight, calling out, 'Our pardon, kings! What is happening?' Then Mpande's order arrived, 'Drive off that evil-doer of Mgungundhlovu. So he is fighting with Shaka when it was he who finished off the sons of Senzangakhona? He used to say that he had killed Shaka for troubling the people; in fact it was he who finished off the Zulu house.'[99]

The snake representing Dingane was driven off, and a fire prepared. An *inyanga* named Giba went off to fetch appropriate medicines. Suddenly, the fire flared, caught the doorposts and the thatch of the huts; it threatened to spread to the *isigodlo*, and was brought under control only with difficulty.

> The king then ordered that the *izinyanga* should be consulted as to what had caused the fire. The *izinyanga* said that it was because of the kings, Shaka and Dingane, who had been fighting there in the home. Dingane had asked, 'Am I now going to be put to death by the *izinyanga*?' and Shaka had asked, 'Why were my wounds not soothed with gall?' [Mpande] ordered that cattle should also be fetched from Dukuza. In addition, cattle from Nodwengu were taken to Dukuza, and others to Bulawayo, to Mbelebeleni, and Siklebeni. The king ordered that all the *amakanda* cattle should be taken and the ancestors praised, in order to placate them.
>
> The king said, 'Hau! Do you see how this crafty fellow has destroyed the *umuzi*? He is one whose locusts are roasted last (*intete zosiwa muva*)'. . . . From this we saw that Dingane had spoken with two tongues; for he had said that he had killed Shaka for troubling the people when in fact it was he who had finished off the country. He had ordered the house of Senzangakhona to be killed off for the vultures, for they were hungry. It was the bewhiskered one from Mgungundhlovu who had killed people off for them.[100]

In the end, the 'Dingane' snake was merely caught, defanged, and released. It's a fascinating episode, revealing at once the depth and intensity of Zulu beliefs in the presence of their ancestors, the centrality of the leaders to their well-being, and the prevalent opinion about the relative merits of Shaka and his fratricidal successor. It could as easily have been Dingane and his supporters, rather than the white invaders, who were the 'locusts' that Shaka supposedly foresaw in his dying prophecy.

Of course, Shaka's prophetic last words we can safely consign to the realm of encrusted legend. However, they are 'correct' in terms of any reading of the terrible aftermath.

The details of the assassination itself were nevertheless important: they would dictate the thinking around the succession. A period of confusion ensued. The two brothers had to be ritually purified with a bullock's gall. They immediately almost came to blows over who was to drink and sprinkle the gall first. Shaka's body was left overnight before being placed in a grain pit within the enclosure. He was buried with all his favourite belongings, and was guarded over by a dozen stalwarts, who would eventually become virtually a family group of their own.[101] Mbopha temporarily took over the day-to-day running of things.

The main question was whether Dingane himself had actually struck a fatal blow. If he had, the reasoning went, he would not be eligible for the leadership. However, if he had indeed put a spear in, the fact could and would be covered up; the aftermath suggests that this is exactly what happened. All eyewitnesses, it seemed, had been killed off: 'the chiefs who were with [Shaka], and who had attempted to escape, . . . were arrested in their flight, and put to death'.[102] Fynn names these men as 'Ingnasconca, uncle to Nandi, and Nomxamama' – Nxazonke and Mxamama kaSotshaya, who had been with Shaka right from his accession. Another Shakan right-hand man, his Mthethwa 'father' Ngomane, was wounded and put out of action for a while.[103] Ngidi also names Ntendeka, *induna* at Dlangezwa, as being killed at this point.[104] Even those who helped to bury Shaka, there in the centre of the enclosure, were killed – they were *umgando*, 'stones of the king', to be buried with him. The exception was one Ngunuza kaNsiyana of the Langeni, who leaped on top of Shaka's hut, *bonga*'d him loudly, then stabbed his way through the circle of would-be executioners and fled to Faku's Mpondo.[105]

The debate about the succession took time. It was held before Ngqengelele, the premier elder; Nomcoba, Shaka's by now powerful half-sister; and Mnkabayi. It was confused, since Mhlangana had in some eyes been Sigujana's heir; he would have succeeded to the chiefship had Shaka not intervened on Senzangakhona's death. Mhlangana was said to have jumped over Shaka's dead body as a sign that he considered himself the successor.[106] However, Shaka had given Dingane considerable power over an area north of the Thukela, apparently favouring *him*.[107] Rightly or wrongly, it was decided that Mhlangana had lost his claim as he had done the killing. He could 'not rule with a red assegai'. Dingane, ostensibly, was clean.

To add to the complexity, neither Dingane nor Mhlangana was Shaka's own heir-designate in any case: the heir seems to have been Ngwadi, Shaka's other half-brother and full brother to Nomcoba. Ngwadi had been given considerable authority by Shaka, and was spoken of as Senzangakhona's child rather than Gendeyana's. Ngwadi 'seemed disposed to dispute the right to the throne', and Dingane moved swiftly against him. According to Isaacs, it was Mbopha himself who led the force in; Ngwadi put up a fierce fight, but he and his people, perhaps 2 000 of them, were wiped out.[108]

Even before Mnkabayi and the council ratified him as the new incumbent, then, Dingane was taking steps to secure his position. Not even his fellow conspirators were safe.

There were numerous minor quarrels between Dingane and Mhlangana. Much depended on the opinion of the army. They waited for the *bhalule* contingents to return. Mhlangana (Fynn's version goes) couldn't bear the suspense, seeing there 'appeared more hope for his Brother than himself'. Dingane spotted him sharpening an assegai. That's for me, he thought. He got Mbopha to make discreet inquiries; Mbopha assured Mhlangana he was really on his side, but they would have to wait for the army to return and give its approval; murdering Dingane wouldn't help him if the army didn't like it. Mhlangana settled down – but was promptly dragged from his hut and dispatched by some of Dingane's heavies.[109] Or he was killed 'by order of Nomcoba and Mkabayi together'.[110]

In the initial stages, there was no sudden exaltation of Dingane, nor ecstasy that Shaka was gone. When the tattered remnants of the *bhalule* force returned, they were understandably aghast. They 'caused Dingane etc to be surrounded and questioned as to who had killed Shaka'. Dingane and Mhlangana accused Mbopha; Mbopha was then stabbed to death. Had Shaka's army returned whole, says NDUKWANA, 'all the above-mentioned [brothers] and others unnamed would have been killed as well'.[111] In the end, the warriors had little room to manoeuvre. One particular individual, Masawuzana, is recorded as having survived the expedition; he offered beasts to the spirits in lament at Shaka's death – and was promptly killed off by Nowela kaMtheli on Dingane's orders.[112]

Almost everyone else, for the time being, accepted the inevitable: Shaka was dead, and Dingane looked set to take over.

For their part, the white adventurers at Port Natal – whatever role they had played in the assassination – greeted it with unrestrained delight. Fynn wrote, with telling contradictoriness, that it was just as well Shaka hadn't seen the return of the army, since 'His independence of self-control would have hurried him to such acts as would have compelled the nation to revolt and destroy him, or suffer in some terrible way.' In other words, Shaka had had it coming. Alternatively, he went on, if the campaign *had* succeeded, there would have been even more mayhem, and the army would not have 'borne the murder of Shaka as quietly as they did'. So was the army on Shaka's side or not? At any rate, Fynn celebrated, 'there were few who did not bless the spirits of their forefathers for allowing them to enter their huts and rest themselves'.[113]

Nathaniel Isaacs likewise claimed that Shaka's death 'had given so general a satisfaction throughout his dominions, that it was likely to give to the natives a period of repose from the vexations and casualties of war, and from the terror which the savage decrees of the late king constantly created'.[114] He summed up his views of the differences between the two rulers:

> The Europeans . . . are bound to admit that Dingan is a man differently constituted from his predecessor Chaka, the warring elements in the latter made him a ferocious savage; whilst the calm and reflecting Dingan, his successor, is deliberative and calculating, though bold and energetic. He never sought to gratify the feelings of revenge from the mere love of cruelty, though at times he was implacable, and perhaps unrelenting; on the other hand, he had those perceptive powers, that were likely to promote the ultimate good of his people, of which Chaka was destitute. Thus the one was hated by his subjects, whilst the other is likely to be esteemed . . .[115]

Farewell – for the moment the main conduit of information to the Cape Colony – agreed: 'I have no doubt but Chaka's death will add greatly to the happiness of the nation', he wrote. The impression was given, in contrast to all the evidence, that Dingane was 'mild and peaceable'.[116]

John Cane, who had at least the virtue of some independent opinion, asserted more accurately that Dingane was 'weak, cruel and capricious'.[117] It would not be long before the white adventurers all realised that their collusion in the assassination had backfired horribly.

A NOVEL ENDING

The trouble with history, of course, is that it never ends. History is always unfolding into its own future. The present is always lengthening the retrospective view. By the time I finish typing this sentence (let alone by the time this book goes to print), another distortion of the iron myth of Shaka will doubtless have been read or aired somewhere around the world. The picture of him will have been further entrenched, or altered, if only ever so slightly. The story – or, more accurately, the story*telling* – of Shaka does not end with his death. His reputation – however conceived – soldiers on. His name is repeatedly evoked, not only in the continuous reconstruction of the Zulu sense of identity, but in spheres quite removed from it: attached to the prow of a new South African navy frigate, for example; or at the erstwhile film-set, tourist attraction 'Shakaland'; or in Professor Mzilikazi Khumalo's musical, *Ushaka*, the 'first symphonic/choral repertoire work in Zulu', an opus 'meant to be an appeal to the great king to forgive the nation that he cursed' with his dying words.[118]

Of course, all the characters who survived Shaka continued to flourish or suffer in his shadow. I shall 'end', therefore, as a Victorian novel might, with an overview of these subsidiary characters, for through their careers we can build one perspective on how Shaka's life and death affected the future.

Most important for the future of the Zulu people were Shaka's two successor brothers: Dingane and Mpande.

Dingane went on to rule the Zulu people for another twelve years. He became most famous for slaughtering Piet Retief and his party at Mgungundlovu, and for failing to resist the Boer invasions at the 1838 Battle of Blood (Ncome) River (which certain die-hard Afrikaners continue to celebrate even today). These events have obscured the complexities of his internal politics. Though he set about relaxing some of Shaka's marriage restrictions, he retained the essentials of the structures that Shaka had founded: the *izigodlo*, the *amabutho*, and the *izinduna*. He continued the pattern of raiding widely for cattle – indeed, even more aggressively – against the Bhaca, against Mzilikazi, and against the Swazi. He even attacked and wrecked Delagoa Bay itself in 1833, in aggressive but unsuccessful pursuit of trade and slaving opportunities.

He had a hard time holding the components of Shaka's Zulu polity together. In the first place, supporters of Shaka had to be eliminated. Indeed,

Dingane's rule initiated a period of virtual 'civil war' (the phrase is Nathaniel Isaacs's).[119] Once he had killed off all the eyewitnesses to Shaka's assassination, Dingane murdered anyone who might lay claim to ascendancy. Not only Ngwadi, but all of Shaka's other brothers – except a very young brother, Gcugcwa, and Mpande – were murdered: Mfihlo, Ngqojana, Mqubana, and more.

Over the coming months, even years, Dingane set about eliminating most of Shaka's major pillars of state. Several of Shaka's client-chiefs were shortly attacked, killed, and replaced by Dingane's appointees: Magaye of the Cele, Zihlandlo of the Mkhize and his brother Sambela, Mathubane of the Thuli, and Nzwakhele of the Dube. Mvundlana kaMpumuza, another high-ranking man of Shaka's who 'could have struck even Ndlela or Dambuza in Dingane's presence', was killed on a pretext.[120] The whole Njanduna *ibutho*, one of Shaka's favourites, was killed off or scattered.[121] The Qadi people under Dube were attacked and subdued.[122] The informant NDUKWANA's father, Mbengwana, was murdered on Dingane's orders for mourning Shaka, and his Impanganiso people were thrown over a cliff at kwaNganga.[123] Mdlaka, the most high-ranking Shakan warrior, was assassinated within the year.[124] The informant NDONGENI's father, Xoki kaCamela, was killed for siding with Mhlangana.[125] Sihayo of the Nyuswa, another Shakan tributee – killed.[126] Macingwane's heir, Mfusi – killed.[127] Dingane eliminated most of the Gasa people living among the headwaters of the Black Mfolozi, because they were Shaka's doctors.[128] Matiwane, destitute after the disaster at Mbholompo, came looking to *khonza*. Dingane installed him on some land, with cattle to keep him quiet, but eventually put him to the spear, too, in June 1830, at kwaMatiwane – the very spot where Piet Retief and his ill-fated commando would be butchered a few years later.[129] These are just the victims we know about.

By contrast, supporters of the assassination were promoted. For instance, Sotobe was given semi-autonomous jurisdiction over territory north of the Thukela, but his loyalties wavered onto Mpande's side eventually.[130] Jobe of the Sithole continued to hold position; so did Maphitha, the client-chief Shaka had installed north of the Mfolozis. He, too, would turn against Dingane eventually. These few men aside, Dingane's purge was unforgiving and thorough.

Sundry components of Shaka's polity uprooted and fled, mostly southwards into Mpondo country, or to Natal as it came increasingly under white power: 'many broke away south'.[131] One was Shaka's 'son', Zibizendlela, who would eventually die amongst the Mpondo people. Nzwakhele of the Dube concealed him in his flight, with fatal consequences.[132] That favourite of Shaka's and irrepressible fighter Zulu kaNogandaya fled south too, in 1839, afraid amongst other dissatisfactions of also being accused of concealing Zibizendlela. He initially sought refuge with Henry Ogle ('Wohlo') at Port Natal, and survived until just before the Anglo-Zulu War of 1879.[133] Gaqa and Mbikwana, Shaka's loyal *induna*, were wounded and fled.[134]

Dingane's reign unravelled entirely when Mpande himself absconded in 1839. He took 17 000 followers over the Thukela to make compact with the Boers against the *inkosi*, his own brother. Mpande had been raised amongst the Cele in Dibhandlela's day, and continued to cultivate his friends in that southern corner. He had always had leg trouble, a protruding bone (*umcoboka*); this and an appearance of stupidity, perhaps, saved him.[135] Ndlela kaSompisi was said to have protected him: 'The king is surely not going to kill this scrofulous thing, this thing that runs to its mother when the king is preparing for war?'[136] Or, it was said, Mpande was born of an *emsizini* connection, that is, of a one-night stand performed by the *inkosi* after tasting the new crops; this condemned him to inferior status.[137] He was seen – decidedly incorrectly – to be politically innocuous.

Mpande finally gave Dingane and his declining popularity the death blow in a pitched battle on the Thukela in 1839. This was the melancholy climax of the civil war that followed Shaka's assassination. Dingane fled north across the Phongolo with a few faithful supporters. There he was fatally wounded by the local Nyawo people in a swift raid. Mpande went on to rule the Zulu for another 32 years.

Amongst the characters who had carried Shaka's power for him, and had to flee from Dingane, was Nqetho of the Qwabe. His subsequent career is perhaps best documented (and deserves a whole study on its own). It underlines just how tenuous Shaka's control had been.

Nqetho had built up considerable power and a number of *amabutho* under Shaka's wing. Some said that he was an *itshinga*, an evil-doer, of the same ilk as Shaka. In early 1829 he gathered a body of followers (Isaacs thought 5 000) and a massive herd of cattle, including some of the Mpondo cattle brought back on the *ihlambo* campaign, and headed south. As an act of gratuitous vandalism, he cut off the tails of a whole lot of Zulu cattle to decorate his warriors with. Dingane hastily drew together a number of people, called them the Hlomendlini, and the uFasimba *ibutho* under Mpangazitha, and sent them in pursuit. Nqetho tried to persuade, or even force, Magaye of the Cele to go with him, but Magaye's people wouldn't let him. At the very least, Magaye allowed Nqetho to pass through, and the Hlomendlini killed Magaye for this. A number of people died on Dingane's orders for trying to follow Nqetho: the informant Mbovu's mother Mamadu-njini was one, Nowela kaMteli was another. In a series of skirmishes, the heaviest on the Mlazi river south of Port Natal, Nqetho beat off the pursuing Zulu. Mpangazitha himself was wounded on the side of the head. Nqetho tried to set himself up amongst the Mpondo, who initially welcomed him. However, he was unwilling to settle; he became a marauder, never planting crops. He was joined by other refugees, some of Matiwane's Ngwane amongst them.[138] He also attacked Myeki, the Jali chieftain with whom Dingane had colluded over Shaka's assassination. Eventually the Mpondo, followed up by the Bhaca, decimated his plundering bands, and he wandered north to die in solitude and destitution – not unlike his main adversary, Dingane himself.[139]

One victim of Nqetho's marauding was another ally of Dingane's: Francis Farewell. His brief story is worth detailing for what it tells us of the burgeoning colonial interest in Natal.

Isaacs and Farewell fled immediately after Shaka's assassination, arriving in Port Elizabeth in the *Elizabeth and Susan* on 16 December 1828. The vessel was instantly impounded by customs. Although the adventurers tried to portray this trip as a calm and collected trade venture, Cape officials recognised it as a 'flight in consequence' of Shaka's death.[140] Isaacs and Farewell were petrified that the whole thing would backfire on them, not because of hostility from Dingane – there wasn't any – but because, contrary to their claims that the whole Zulu nation was exulting at Shaka's demise, a serious 'civil war' threatened.[141]

Despite this, Isaacs was confident that 'the nation is now in a state of profound peace' – another bit of wishful thinking. He and Farewell proceeded to concentrate on nothing but successful trade and annexation. Farewell did not impress Captain Aitchison, the government's man on the spot in Port Elizabeth. Aitchison had been interviewing the trader Shaw, who had gone overland to Port Natal and also returned, panicked by the turmoil, on the *Elizabeth and Susan*. The Port Natal group was a bunch of liars, Shaw said. 'In fact,' wrote Aitchison,

> truth seems to be utterly unknown to the whole party. I do not like Mr Farewell's appearance – he certainly does not speak out like an upright honest man and, moreover, he looks very much like a drunkard. I endeavoured to ascertain from him what were the advantages contemplated by an intercourse with this colony but failed in eliciting anything like a satisfactory reply. All he seems to wish is that *he* should be vested by gov[ernmen]t with some authority to give him more influence than any other of the settlers and that 10 or 12 families be sent to form a young settlement there.[142]

Farewell proceeded to Cape Town to speak to the governor. Lowry Cole was equally unimpressed:

> I find it impossible to attach any credit to the contradictory statements of Lieut[enan]t Farewell or King . . . as these persons seem in their intercourse with Chaka to have had no other object in view but their own personal advantage and as far as I can judge from their proceedings they do not appear to be very respectable characters. Lt Farewell . . . is very desirous to induce the government to form a settlement, but even in his own interested statement he shows no ground whatever to make it appear desirable in any point of view. The harbour is insecure and fit only for small craft and scarcely any article of trade is to be procured there except a scanty supply of elephant's teeth.[143]

'Elephant's teeth' were provoking more mayhem back in Port Elizabeth, where John Cane was putting in claims for some of the ivory brought back on the *Elizabeth and Susan*; and another drunken crew member, one Whitehead, got into fisticuffs over what he asserted was *his* share, which the customs' man wanted to confiscate. Meanwhile Farewell was claiming that the Zulu people who had come with Cane, and who were still languishing in Fort Beaufort, 100 kilometres east of Graham's Town, were *his* servants.[144] They should not leave without him. Or they could go with Aitchison, if he ever went. Or they might go with Henry Fynn senior – Henry Francis Fynn's father – who, with two other sons, Frank and William, was also poised to head overland to Port Natal. Fynn senior was suddenly revealed to be bankrupt, so there was a bit of a problem. Meanwhile, the government was washing its hands of the whole mess:

> [The governor] will oppose no obstacle to either of the parties returning to Natal or to the elder Mr Fynn joining his son there, providing there be no claims against him to prevent his quitting the colony, but as *that* son has assisted one native tribe with his fire-arms against another for his own purposes only and as there is too much reason to believe that the late movement of the Zoolahs against the Caffre nations was mainly brought about by the instigation of European subjects of H[is] M[ajesty] who thereby caused an infinity of trouble and expence [*sic*] to the colony H[is] E[xcellency] desires it may be made fully known to every person who may obtain permission to proceed into these countries that he will consider all those who foment or take part in the quarrels of the native tribes as having forfeited all claim to any protection . . .[145]

Farewell's response was to formulate a private annexation plan with a Cape Town advocate and businessman, Saxe Bannister.[146] They presented an abridged version of their agreement to the governor that was blatant in its aims. They wanted 'pecuniary advantage'; lands annexed for 'forts, roads and other public purposes'; half a million acres for 'an association to aid in civilizing the natives'; unspecified acreages for Farewell and Bannister themselves, plus more for anyone else who joined up; and 'town lots at Natal [for] Mr Farewell's faithful followers'. Its projected advantages were derisory: 'A means of civilizing the natives near the Cape of Good Hope'; 'Support to missions at Lattakoo' (1 500 kilometres away); 'Cheap additional security to British interests'. Most ironic of all was: 'Furnishing some means of checking the occasional misconduct of these traders'. As for 'civilizing the natives', the document was tellingly self-contradictory: 'The aborigines shall be undisturbed in their liberties', *but* would somehow at the same time be subjected to 'good rules', and 'care shall be taken to withdraw them from heathenish customs and from indolence'.[147]

It is worth contemplating these motives, since they are the impulses that would govern the white invasion and settlement of Natal.

Importantly, for our story, this was all based on the alleged land grant from Shaka of 1824, a copy of which Farewell and Bannister judiciously attached.[148]

The governor told Farewell to get lost.[149]

Farewell decided within days to return to Port Natal. He asked for 100 pounds of gunpowder – a request that was, amazingly, approved.[150] Meanwhile, John Cane also left for Port Natal, leaving behind him a debt of some £22 for clothing furnished to the Zulu envoys.[151] It took Farewell some months to organise himself; it was 17 September before he could report back to the Cape Colony on his activities. He had reached the Bashee river, where he had unexpectedly bumped into John Cane, heading back to the Cape yet again, with an elephant tusk from Dingane to the governor. Dingane had still not been formally installed, but had been named as Shaka's successor. Farewell correctly wrote, 'He seems to have murdered a great number of his people and to have shed more blood than Chaka was accustomed to do . . .'[152]

Farewell found the country nearer to hand also in upheaval. Nqetho was raiding, being joined by Makhanya people and by fugitive Ngwane – those who had not chosen to chance their luck with Matiwane's overtures to Dingane. Faku was gearing up for a scrap or flight. The traveller Green's wagons were being held hostage. Back at Port Natal, things were acrimonious as usual: Fynn was trying to take over Farewell's land, it seemed, on the strength of a forged document by which he could have it if Farewell wasn't back in six months. Anyway, Farewell, displaying that absurdly British mix of humanitarian hubris, declared: 'I shall endeavour to hold communication with them [Nqetho's Qwabe] and prevent them molesting their neighbours.'[153]

On 25 September he wrote again from Shepstone's mission at Morley. Several white men had gone ahead of him, all evidently dreaming that Shaka's death was going to introduce a halcyon age of free trade. Shaw was back there; two men named Southey and Stub (Stubbs?) had supplied gunpowder

to another group of white and 'Hottentot' elephant hunters. This group had
had some violent encounter with Nqetho's raiders, and one of them, Klaas
Lochenberg, had been killed. It seemed that Nqetho himself had been
wounded in the exchange.[154] This obviously put following whites like Farewell
in a very precarious position. Nevertheless, he pressed on to Faku's and
beyond.[155]

He didn't get very far.

On 12 October, John Cane reported the outcome – 'the most melancholy
occurance that ever happened in Caffraria':

> We had opened a communication with [the Qwabe] from Faku's and
> received for answer the most flattering offers of friendship with two
> head of cattle for our present use and Cato [Nqetho] expressing a
> wish to see Mr F[arewell] he complied with his request, depending on
> their honour which I always supposed, as well as Mr F[arewell], to be
> strictly just but, alas, we were deceived.
>
> On their arrival at the kraal they observed every mark of friendship
> and gave them a cow to kill. At midnight they surrounded their tent
> and committed the fatal act. Three natives escaped and gave us
> intelligence. I had intended to have stood and protected what property
> we should have taken in our waggon but was basely deserted by all the
> Hottentot people and was obliged to fly into the bush. I returned to the
> waggon in the evening. Such a destruction I suppose was never seen
> in Caffre land. They had taken about 5,000 lbs of beads, every article
> of cloathing [sic] and whatever could be of service to them. Faint hopes
> are entertained that Mr F[arewell] was made a prisoner. The interpreter
> saw Mr F[arewell] and Mr W[alker] lying before the tent and some
> Caffres standing over Mr F[arewell], but whether they were binding
> him or in the act of assassination he is not positive.[156]

Assassination it was, of course. It may have been displaced revenge for
Lochenberg's attack. According to Isaacs, writing from hearsay, it was the
result of an ivory dispute. Farewell was insisting on progressing to Dingane.
Jealous and enraged, Nqetho ordered 'his best regiment' to surround the
tent; they cut all the ropes, and speared Farewell, Walker and Thackwray to
death through the canvas.[157]

However it happened, it was a significantly bloody tailpiece to Shaka's story.

Most of the other Port Natal whites who remained in Natal met similarly dramatic ends. Thomas Halstead was murdered by Dingane alongside Piet Retief at kwaMatiwane. Henry Ogle initially fled Port Natal, but soon returned. Despite being illiterate, he became a prominent figure at Port Natal. He was responsible, amongst other deeds, for killing the ambiguous figure of Jacob Msimbithi, Hlambamanzi, after a dispute with Dingane.[158] As he had done under Shaka, Ogle joined armed Zulu raids, including that against Ncaphayi of the Bhaca.[159]

John Cane's relations with Dingane were rocky. Zulu kaNogandaya scattered Cane's people in 1831 for failing to hand over some cattle, but in 1837 Cane was still around to send 30 armed men to help Dingane's abortive raid on the Swazi. After Dingane razed the nascent settlement of Port Natal to the ground, Cane threw in his lot entirely with the invading Boers. He led a commando into Zulu country and burned several important imizi to ashes, including that of his erstwhile ally, Sotobe. In April 1839 he was part of the so-called 'Grand Army of Natal' that attacked Zulu kaNogandaya's umuzi of Ndondakusuka. They were trapped there by the Zulu army and slaughtered, Cane amongst them.[160]

There were those who got away. Nathaniel Isaacs fled with the others in 1828. He went on to cement connections with American and Madagascan slavers, travelling with them to the Comores in 1831. The following year he made a totally bizarre proposal to the Cape government that they permit the military occupation of Natal by a Madagascan warlord named Ramanataka.[161] When that failed, he made contact with G.C. Redman, a one-time chairman of the South African Land and Emigration Association, and issued a 'Prospectus' encouraging people to settle in Natal.[162] Despite this, he seems never to have returned to the region. In 1836 his rewritten *Travels and Adventures in Eastern Africa* cemented Shaka's reputation as a megalomanic monster almost beyond redemption. By the 1840s, Isaacs was established in Freetown, Sierra Leone, trading groundnuts, smuggled rum – and slaves. He bought a small island, Matakong, off the West African coast, from which he could forge illicit treaties with mainland chieftains and avoid customs' interference. He married twice, the second time to a formidable, slave-trading

Afro-American. He barely escaped arraignment on slaving charges, and in his will left Matakong to a son, before dying peacefully at Egremont, Cumbria, on 26 January 1872.[163]

By contrast, Charles Rawden Maclean became a toughly Protestant professional mariner. Within a decade of leaving Natal in 1829, he had achieved his master's ticket; he bought a vessel, the *Susan King*, plying the London to Caribbean routes. He made the Caribbean island of St Lucia his home. Between 1853 and 1857 he contributed extensively to the *Nautical Magazine*, including the 37 000 words of his memories of his time with Shaka, which we have found so useful a corrective to the venom of Isaacs and Fynn. Maclean developed a keen sense of human rights and campaigned against slavery in the Caribbean – one of the slave-trade's most notorious beneficiaries. After a series of setbacks, he died in St Lucia on 13 August 1880.[164]

Of all the white opinions of Shaka, Maclean left one of the more measured: 'Shaka was a man of great natural ability, but he was cruel and capricious; nevertheless it is possible he has left behind something more than the terror of his name . . .'[165]

Finally, let's see what happened to the man of whom we have heard so much: Henry Francis Fynn. Despite himself, Fynn also penned one of the more nuanced summaries of Shaka's character:

> [Shaka] was inflexible in his resolves severe in his discipline and the terror of his enemies[. O]f the soldiery notwithstanding his atrocities he was the Idol and to a conquered enemy where he had no suspicion of witchcraft he was liberal and lenient. The sacred character of Embassadrie from his most inveterate enemie even in the [heat?] of the conflict he always respected and ensured their safety[. T]o the brave he was liberal to an excess to the cowardly merciless and cruel. Vain, haughty, imperious, and cruel to his subjects, to the Europeans he was affable, and kind, anxious to know all their wants only to alleviate them, possessing a perpetual thirst for knowledge which he received with caution, and conversed, with a shrewdness and policy which would not have disgraced many civilized beings . . .[166]

Who else has recognised Shaka's policies as following the 'sacred character of Embassadrie'? On most other occasions, however, the self-serving Fynn wrote the most horrendous lies about his one-time patron. Much of the time he was trying to get the Cape and then the Natal authorities to give him some land. He repeatedly referred to a grant of territory from Shaka. The government wasn't fooled. Although they continued to employ Fynn, who by the 1830s was an acknowledged Zulu expert, they always regarded him with some suspicion. Between 1834 and 1856 he was variously hired as agent or 'magistrate' to the Mpondo, the Zulu, and the Thembu Xhosa. He was violent – he executed Lukhilimba in cold blood, and was later accused of doing the same thing to chiefs in the Kat river region of the Eastern Cape. He was accused of running guns and stealing cattle under the cover of his frontier official's status. He was hauled up before two commissions of inquiry, narrowly escaping censure on both occasions. He was, Governor Harry Smith once raged, 'a greater ass and Don Quixote than one could possibly conceive'.[167] Like Isaacs, he abandoned a whole clan of coffee-coloured children bearing his name. He died, virtually destitute, in Durban on 20 September 1861.

All this, and more, was swept under a romanticised veneer by white settler historians. They took Fynn's voluminous though clumsy and ungrammatical writings at face value, even (or especially) after 1950, when Stuart and Malcolm published The Diary of Henry Francis Fynn. As I have been concerned to show throughout this book, the production of the Diary has proved, as Julian Cobbing rightly put it, 'one of the major disasters of South African historical literature'.[168] It represents the extraordinary capacity of a century of South African historians to swallow massive discrepancies, fictions and cultural bias without ever questioning the quality of the source, or enquiring into how it got into print, or why the language is used in the way it is. Part of a long process of systematic misrepresentation, the Diary has done both Shaka and native peoples in this country a profound disservice. The unbelievable yet unquestioned mythic status of Shaka – as either superhuman hero or satanic monster – is South Africa's most prominent monument to blindness, prejudice, and failure of scholarship. I hope that this book helps a little to dislodge this astonishing 'myth of iron'.

'I AM A SEED'

No doubt we will always look back on Shaka's rule with mixed emotions, as did James Stuart's Qwabe informant MBOVU kaMtshumayeli. Some 70 years old when he talked to Stuart in 1903, MBOVU was a *kholwa*, a Christian convert. His father had been a Shakan loyalist, although he refused to entertain Nqetho when he came looking for support on his way south. Mtshumayeli did, however, join Mpande in his defection in 1839, when MBOVU was just old enough to milk cows. MBOVU's subsequent career and testimony contains all the tragic and poignant ironies of South African history. He knew he had entered a profoundly different world from the one he'd been born into when Shaka's body was scarcely cold. 'I no longer belong to the old generation,' he said. 'I am a seed that has dropped to a new state of civilization. I take but little interest in former affairs.'[169]

Nevertheless, he evidently took an intense interest in the affairs of 1903. He was clear-eyed enough to see the parallels between what Shaka did and what the British government was doing: Shaka 'established colonies like Europeans'.[170] Politics being what it was (and is), he could not see why he should not participate in the violent ways either of Shaka or of the present government. MBOVU, Stuart wrote,

> said he was anxious to obtain permission to hold a gun; that, aided by the influence of Mr Titren, late Resident Magistrate, Umlazi Division, at the recommendations of his missionary, he had sent in an application to the Government – last year I think – which had been refused on the ground that the Government had already authorized the keeping of 100 guns by natives and did not propose to increase that number . . . Mbovu cannot understand how his application came to be refused as he is loyal, and seeing he was born in the colony and passed all his life here, never having been convicted of any crime. . . . [He] went on to observe that the natives would have liked to help repel the Boers who invaded Natal in the late war but their assistance was not asked. A time will come when the British people, finding themselves in trouble, will be glad of the assistance proffered, but it will not be given as it will be too late.[171]

That is a stroke of prescience to measure against Shaka's alleged dying prophecy about the coming of the swallows – the whites. There is, finally, no blunter statement of the ironies embedded in the demise of Shaka's world, than this one: 'Government is expanding, every few years. The Government resembles Shaka, for he never got tired. Its army is money.'[172]

Notes

Chapter 1: **Stones from a distant grave**

1. I have been drawing here on archaeologists' accounts of the fourteenth-century site of Moor Park, just west of the Thukela river; see, for example, Whitelaw, 'Southern African Iron Age', 452.
2. See, for example, Diamond, 'How Africa became Black', in *Guns, Germs and Steel*, 376–401; Newman, *The Peopling of Africa*, 186; Vogel and Vogel, *Precolonial Africa*, 435–8.
3. See Vansina, 'The Bantu Expansion'. It is interesting to note that scholars now feel the same scepticism about a wholesale migration of immigrants through the Americas (see Luis Alberto Borrero and Colin McEwan, 'The Peopling of Patagonia', in McEwan, Borrero and Prieto, eds., *Patagonia*, 32–6).
4. Some of these herders may have been what are usually called 'Khoikhoin', who might well have 'developed' through the same admixture of movement and interbreeding. After all, South Africa is the site of some of the oldest human beings yet discovered (see Hall, *The Changing Past*, 32–45; Phillipson, *African Archaeology*, 188).
5. No one has properly been able to date the San or Bushman rock paintings of the Drakensberg. Most are probably quite recent, but similar examples further south in the Cape have been dated to 12 000 years ago. The oldest known rock art is from Namibia: a staggering 27 500 years old (Deacon and Deacon, *Human Beginnings in South Africa*, 165).
6. It is possible to see a similar effect, over the last couple of hundred years, in the way African and Indian words have infiltrated the terminologies of their English conquerors (see Prins and Lewis, 'Bushmen as mediators'; Jolly, 'Interaction between South-eastern San').
7. According to recent studies, modern Zulu people share 45 per cent of crucial genetic markers with Kgadikgadi San. The Xhosa, further south, share 60 per cent (see Nurse, Weiner and Jenkins, *The Peoples of Southern Africa*, 144). It has to be said that the genetic situation is much more complex than these blunt figures suggest. Nurse et al. tend problematically to retain models of 'Bantu migration' and the 'Mfecane'.
8. Bryant, *Olden Times*, 286; Prins and Lewis, 'Bushmen as mediators'; Wright, 'Sonqua, Bosjesmans, Bushmen, abaThwa'. Intriguingly, certain pygmy people in the present Democratic Republic of Congo are called 'Batwa', too.
9. This presupposes that groups of people were quite firmly separated off from one another, for considerable lengths of time, to allow the differences to mature. But what we think of as the differences varies, depending on what criteria we choose.

10. The term 'Bantu' remains controversial. In the anthropological literature, it has somehow crept northwards from its southern African origin, now referring to a great language group covering most of Africa south of the Sahara. Linguists theorise about a 'proto-Bantu' from which all the present dialects are derived. Like Indo-European, 'proto-Bantu' – or 'siNtu' – no longer exists. It is a deduced, imaginary construct (see Hombert and Hyman, *Bantu Historical Linguistics*).

11. 'Nguni', which is now used to include the Zulu, Xhosa, Ndebele, Ngoni, and Swazi languages, has also never been more than a linguist's term of convenience. It has almost nothing to do with bloodlines, and little correlation with the way the local people actually used it.

12. Fuze, *Black People*, 42.

13. MBOVU 42. Names in small capitals refer to informants contained in *The James Stuart Archive*.

14. MAHAYA 115.

15. MAGIDIGIDI 84; Socwatsha, James Stuart papers, File 9, item 51, 13–17.

16. DINYA 98.

17. BALENI 29.

18. JANTSHI 176.

19. NDABAMBI 176.

20. MANGATI 203; MAZIYANA 281.

21. One informant lists the following as Ntungwa: Bhele, Khumalo, Mabaso, Ntuli, Sithole, Thembu (MBOVU 42). According to another, only the Khumalo were really Ntungwa. When the Khumalo gave food, the recipient originally responded, 'E Mntungwa!' (MABONSA 12). The Hlubi, Ngwane, Mangweni and Bomvu were also called Ntungwa by some (MAZIYANA 277; LUNGUZA 297). Some considered it a difference in dialect: 'I say *inhlatu* [python] because I am Ntungwa; the Zulus who are abeNguni say *inhlwati*' (LUNGUZA 335).

22. MAHAYA 115.

23. MAZIYANA 281.

24. MAGIDIGIDI 84.

25. MRUYI 38.

26. See Note 13 above.

27. MAZIYANA 281 (emphasis added).

28. BALENI 29.

29. MAYINGA 254; MAGEZA 70; MAZIYANA 280.

30. MRUYI 38.

31. Hamilton and Wright, 'The Making of the *AmaLala*', 16.

32. I'm reminded here of those Shona-speaking Zimbabweans who, despite the dramatic recent reduction of whites' presence in their country, emerge from private-school education and enter my South African university without a trace of Shona accent.

33. *Lala* means to lie down; MADIKANE 55.

34. MELAPI 75.

35. MAGIDIGIDI 97.

36. MELAPI 87.

37. MADIKANE 55.

38. Hamilton and Wright, 'The Making of the *AmaLala*', 18–19.

39. MADIKANE 54-5; MKANDO 158; DINYA 118; MAHAYA 130. So the amaLala included the Nyuswa, Ngcobo, Qadi, Cele, Thuli, Dunge, Phumulo, Hlongwa, Bombo, Langeni, Ngcolosi, Mphumuza, Zondi (MBOVU 42), the Kabeleni, Nxamalala, 'and others further south' (MADIKANE 55).

40. MQAIKANA 3.

41. There were, for instance, various peoples who were regarded as standing outside them altogether: the Ndwandwe were thought of as having originated with the Swazi (LUZIPO 354). Other notions of origin connected peoples, including the Zulu, with the Suthu across the Drakensberg (MKEHLANGANA 215), sometimes in conjunction with the other terms, sometimes in opposition to them.

42. For a discussion of ethnicity in the Zulu context, see Maré, *Brothers Born*, 6-25.

43. JANTSHI 176.

44. Shipwreck survivors of 1686 recorded the names 'Magoses [Xhosa], Makriggas [Griqua], Matimbas [Thembu], Mapontes [Mpondo], and Emboas [Mbo]' (Bird, *Annals*, 47). No Zulu yet, but this account is hardly comprehensive or conclusive. See also Etherington, *Great Treks*, 23-4.

45. JANTSHI 174. For some reason, this insult stuck. One example can be found in this piece of handed-down doggerel: 'He looked at the dog's *isigonogono* [anus], which had a stick of the amaNtungwa thrust into it; look up [*pezulu*]' (NDHLOVU 200), which was supposed to indicate that the Zulu had come from the north. Shaka had to deal with the ugly slight which had become part of the Zulu 'praises', their *izibongo*. He abolished the idiom, replacing it with 'Ndabezitha' and 'Zulu' – implying, rightly or wrongly, that 'Zulu' was actually Shaka's invention. The word Zulu itself would, at some point still unclear, come to be associated with height, even 'the heavens'. 'The People of Heaven' was probably first recorded in 1833 by the missionary Stephen Kay (*Travels and Researches*, 402; see also Isaacs, *Travels and Adventures in Eastern Africa*, I 263). Doubtless this is little more than etymological vanity. Either way, it reflects the perception that the Zulu arose from a small, even despised clanlet into a great, self-congratulating nation.

46. Bryant, *Olden Times*, 32-5.

47. David Beach, using Shona genealogies, found himself having to build in margins of error of at least twenty years either way, making it exceptionally vague (Beach, 'Generational Dating'; see also Vansina, *Oral Tradition as History*, 182-5).

48. MBOVU 25; MMEMI 239, 259 denies it.

49. MAZIYANA 277; MAGIDIGIDI 84; NGIDI 31.

50. MBOVU 45.

51. MAGIDIGIDI 97; compare MAZIYANA 277 who connects it with the Hlubi; and JANTSHI 175-6 who attributes it to the 'ancient Zulu people'.

52. Sometimes Zulu is called Zulu ka[son of]Ntombela, but most think 'Ntombela' was a praise-name, an *ithakazelo*, for Malandela, not another person. The name gave rise to a place near Nobamba, kaNtombela.

53. MAZIYANA 281; MGIDHLANA 105.

54. MAYINGA 255.

55. MBOVU 25.

56. MMEMI 239.

57. See Hamilton, 'Ideology', 164.
58. We will meet the bolshy Makhanya people later; suffice it to say they never stooped to linking their genealogies to those of the Zulu, and their versions survived the collapse of the Qwabe polity in the 1830s. For a detailed argument along these lines, see Hamilton, 'Ideology', 152–64.
59. MAYINGA 255.
60. JANTSHI 176.
61. MAYINGA 255.
62. Lugg, *Historic Natal*, 123.
63. Lugg, *Historic Natal*, 117–18, 123.
64. JANTSHI 174.
65. NDUKWANA 279.
66. Webb and Wright, *A Zulu King Speaks*, 3.
67. MTSHAPI 76.
68. MTSHAYANKOMO 115–16 (slightly edited).
69. MTSHAYANKOMO 116–17 (slightly edited).
70. MTSHAPI 75–6; compare MGIDHLANA 108.
71. NDHLOVU 200.
72. MAYINGA 252. The earlier leaders are also sometimes credited with this achievement, mind you, so we can't be certain (MGIDHLANA 110).
73. MMEMI 259; MANGATI 203.
74. LUZIPO 355–6.
75. NDHLOVU 214.
76. MADIKANE 49.
77. MKANDO 109. Mntaniya was apparently a daughter of Zingelwayo of the Sibiya people; though MKANDO contradicts himself (159), saying she was a wife of Senzangakhona, as does JANTSHI 200; also 178, 190.

Chapter 2: Under pressure
1. LUGUBU 290.
2. Bird, *Annals*, 42.
3. See Morris and Preston-Whyte, *Speaking with Beads*; Stevenson and Graham-Stewart, *South-east African Beadwork*; Smith, 'Struggle for Control', 185–9.
4. Jill Kinahan's *Cattle for Beads* is a study of such trade in Namibia; as far as I know, no such study has been done for the south-east coast.
5. Bird, *Annals*, 40.
6. See the essays by Simon Hall, Neil Parsons and Andrew Manson in Carolyn Hamilton, *The Mfecane Aftermath*.
7. These are better-evidenced, mostly from Portuguese sources, and are well documented in two unpublished theses: Alan Smith, 'Struggle for Control', and David Hedges, 'Trade and Politics'.
8. What do I mean by 'states'? In Western eyes, a state is basically stable, centralised. It has recognisable hierarchies, organs of government, a system of justice and taxation, organised

military support, capital cities, firm boundaries. It has some sort of ethnic, linguistic, cultural and ritual cohesion. It has *size*. How such states come about in the first place is an area of intense debate. Shaka's Zulu are often cited as an example on which theorists indiscriminately, sometimes ignorantly, draw. Jared Diamond's discussion in his readable book, *Guns, Germs and Steel*, is an example. Diamond's generalisations need constantly to be qualified, but this comment is of relevance: 'Contrary to Rousseau, such amalgamations never occur by a process of unthreatened little societies freely deciding to merge . . . Leaders of little societies, as of big ones, are jealous of their independence' (Diamond, *Guns, Germs and Steel*, 289). I agree; but not with Diamond's crude division of 'merger under threat of external force' as against 'merger by conquest', in which he takes the Cherokee confederacy of the United States south-east as an example of the former, and Shaka's Zulu as an example of the latter. Archaeologist Martin Hall rightly regards the very term 'state' as too loose to be of analytic value in our context (Hall, *The Changing Past*, 74). Hence, throughout this book I prefer to use the rather prissy but useful word 'polity'.

9. Bird, *Annals*, 59.
10. *The Oxford History of South Africa* edited by Monica Wilson and Leonard Thompson (Oxford: Clarendon Press, 1969), to cite just one example.
11. My thanks to John Wright for encouraging me in this effort.
12. Boxer, *Tragic History of the Sea*, 70-1.
13. These were given as 'the Temboes, the Mapontemoussee, the Maponte, and Matimbas, the Malihryghas' (Bird, *Annals*, 41, 47).
14. Vigne, *Guillaume Chenu de Chalezac*, 36.
15. Norman Etherington, partly following Bryant, has suggested that there was once a large, all-inclusive 'state' known as the 'Mbo'. The evidence is extremely tenuous, though (Etherington, *Great Treks*, 23-4, 34-5).
16. JSA III 361.
17. Giba 152.
18. Smith, 'Struggle for Control', 78-9.
19. Hedges, 'Trade and Politics', 141, 135.
20. Mahungane 144, 146.
21. Hedges, 'Trade and Politics', 138-9, 144.
22. Hedges, 'Trade and Politics', 153.
23. Arbousset and Daumas, *Narrative*, 165.
24. Bonner, *Kings, Commoners*, 9; Etherington, *Great Treks*, 80.
25. Wright, 'Pre-Shakan Age-group Formation', 26; Wright and Manson, *The Hlubi Chiefdom*, 1-10.
26. Arbousset and Daumas, *Narrative*, 33. Two different groups named 'Ngwane' should not be confused: one mutated into the Dlamini-Swazi; the other remained Ngwane, migrating westwards under Matiwane.
27. Luzipo 354.
28. Nhlekele 127.
29. Hamilton, 'Ideology', 110-11.
30. Hedges, 'Trade and Politics', 129.
31. Hamilton, 'Ideology', 116-17.

32. Hamilton, 'Ideology', 118.
33. Hamilton, 'Ideology', 118.
34. This is according to Henry Francis Fynn, the first literate man to record the tale (Bird, *Annals*, 62). For an intriguing, but I think untenable, theory about Dingiswayo's succession, see Argyle, 'Who were Dingiswayo and Shaka?'; also Koopman, 'Dingiswayo Rides Again'.
35. Bryant, *Olden Times*, 78. John Wright correctly notes that subsequent historians tended to ignore Bryant here ('Pre-Shakan Age-group Formation', 25).
36. Wright, for one, repeatedly refers to this wave (without quite explaining what it was or how it started) as 'a major social upheaval', 'a time of social crisis' ('Pre-Shakan Age-group Formation', 26).
37. Omer-Cooper, *Zulu Aftermath*, 24.
38. An analogy is the eighteenth-century French slavers' myth that there was a region of fantastic overpopulation in the middle of West Africa, named Nigritie, in relation to which the slave trade was as much a solution as a product (Harms, *The Diligent*, 16–17).
39. See Simon Hall and Neil Parsons in Carolyn Hamilton, *Mfecane Aftermath*.
40. Etherington estimates less than a million, unevenly spread through the whole region in the eighteenth century – 'only the roughest of guesses', he admits, but the best thumb-suck we're likely to get (*Great Treks*, 25). The overpopulation thesis was propounded by Max Gluckman in three early papers (1940, 1960, 1974), and more or less swallowed whole by subsequent historians. See also discussion in Gump, *Formation of the Zulu Kingdom*, 42–6.
41. Bird, *Annals*, 35, 46.
42. Patrick Manning notes that in Africa, the introduction of maize 'corresponded to areas of heavy slave trade', but 'was neither more productive nor more nutritious than the crops it replaced' (Manning, *Slavery and African Life*, 56). There is no convincing evidence to support James Gump's assertion that 'Conceivably, maize diminished crop versatility for Zululand farmers and likely contributed to the ecological disequilibrium'; the weakness of Gump's point lies in that sly shift from 'Conceivably' to 'likely' (*Formation of the Zulu Kingdom*, 60).
43. Gama 142; Hedges, 'Trade and Politics', 39, 41.
44. Diamond, *Guns, Germs and Steel*, 284.
45. Ballard, 'Drought and Economic Distress'.
46. Bryant, *Olden Times*, 63, 88.
47. Etherington, *Great Treks*, 36.
48. As was, for example, the storage of grain for years in underground bins, which was noted in the 1680s, and continued to be used into modern times (see Bird, *Annals*, 46). In central Sudan at almost the same time, drought caused 'widespread displacement' and many deaths, not gathering together (Manning, *Slavery and African Life*, 57); the situation was similar in Angola (Miller, *Way of Death*, 155–6). 'Droughts were the major cause of fission' in Tswana societies, Thomas Tlou and Alec Campbell demonstrate (cited by Parsons, 'Prelude to *Difaqane*' in Hamilton, *Mfecane Aftermath*, 323). In northern Mozambique, too, in times of drought large groups became 'very vulnerable' (Isaacman, 'The Sena', in Miers and Kopytoff, *Slavery in Africa*, 116). It remained the case in Zululand itself even in the 1880s, when civil war aggravated drought to the point of starvation (Guy, *Destruction of the Zulu Kingdom*, 232).

49. Hall, 'Dendroclimatology'. Hall himself has moved far beyond this early paper's perspectives.
50. Newitt, *History of Mozambique*, 252-4; Smith, 'Struggle for Control', 212. The evidence is not 'ample', as Gump (*Zulu Kingdom*, 65) claims; he bases his case entirely on Bryant.
51. Guy, 'Ecological Factors', 110.
52. Guy, 'Ecological Factors', 114.
53. Jantshi 102.
54. Guy, 'Ecological Factors', 104-5.
55. 'Their land is in common, each grazing his cattle or cultivating the ground where he likes; they may also remove from place to place, provided that they remain within the boundaries of the kingdom' (Bird, *Annals*, 46).
56. As Guy argues in 'Ecological Factors', 114. Centralised states are rarely more efficient in anything except enhancing the belly-lines of those who command the centre; it was no different in the new Zulu polity.
57. Hall, *The Changing Past*, 126.
58. Bird, *Annals*, 43.
59. See Hedges, 'Trade and Politics'; Smith, 'Struggle for Control'; also Alan Smith's articles, 'Delagoa Bay and the Trade of South-east Africa' (1970), and 'The Trade of Delagoa Bay as a Factor in Nguni Politics' (1969).
60. Boxer, *Tragic History*, 66.
61. Boxer, *Tragic History*, 173-4, 181.
62. Bannister, *Humane Policy*, xii.
63. Boxer, *Tragic History*, 201, 245ff.
64. Bird, *Annals*, 27ff.
65. Bannister, *Humane Policy*, xiv.
66. Bannister, *Humane Policy*, xv.
67. 'Dampier's Voyages', in Botha, *Collecteana*, 129-30; compare Gill, *The Devil's Mariner*.
68. Hedges, 'Trade and Politics', 120.
69. Bannister, *Humane Policy*, xviii.
70. Smith, 'Struggle for Control', 62; Bannister, *Humane Policy*, xxiii.
71. Smith, 'Struggle for Control', 71.
72. Bannister, *Humane Policy*, xxxvii.
73. Hedges, 'Trade and Politics', 141.
74. Smith, 'Trade of Delagoa Bay', 179.
75. Bowditch, *Discoveries of the Portuguese*, 19-20; Prior, *Voyage*, 41.
76. Smith, 'Struggle for Control', 182-4.
77. Smith, 'Struggle for Control', 150-60.
78. Smith, 'Trade of Delagoa Bay', 173.
79. Bird, *Annals*, 42. The metal wasn't always imported: European traders were sometimes surprised to find that locally mined copper was better than the imported stuff. Metals went both in and out of south-east Africa.
80. Baleni 24.
81. Mahungane 148.
82. Smith, 'Struggle for Control', 151, 179, 191.
83. White, *Journal*, 37, 48-9. The impact of American 'whalers' will not be known until a

more thorough sifting of maritime archives in Savannah, Boston, Mystic Port, etc. is undertaken.

84. White, *Journal*, 41.
85. White, *Journal*, 28.
86. Smith, 'Struggle for Control', 79.
87. The cannibalism issue is a fascinating one. Some oral traditions of cannibalism date to the pre-Shakan years, a few to the years of his rule, some later. We have no hope of verifying these stories, most of which (as James Stuart thought) sound like 'fairy tales' at best. Almost certainly, however, the word was used metaphorically, to mean raiders or slavers. This was the way Henry Callaway understood it in the 1860s: 'It is probable that the native accounts of cannibals are for the most part the traditional record of the incursions of foreign slave hunters' (Callaway, *Nursery Tales*, I 159; cited in Cobbing, 'Grasping the Nettle', 15). The connections between slaving and stories of cannibalism – from both sides – have been amply demonstrated elsewhere (see, for example, Harms, *The Diligent*, 299–300). If such destructive raiding was as widespread as the many tales of 'cannibalism' seem to indicate, we need to ask why such raiding was happening with such intensity, and in so organised a fashion. Drought may well be an associated cause, but it's hardly sufficient on its own.
88. Gray and Birmingham, *Pre-colonial African Trade*, 17.
89. Compare elephant hunting organisation further north; the Makua hunted communally, the hunt being highly ritualised. This provides some basis for trade-orientated hunting, and greater societal cohesion, but there is no evidence of anything similar amongst the Thukela-Phongolo peoples (Alpers, *Ivory and Slaves*, 11–17).
90. Bannister, *Humane Policy*, xxviii.
91. Alpers, *Ivory and Slaves*, 106.
92. See, for example, Hamilton, 'Ideology', 127.
93. These links also represent a gap in the research; most east coast studies, including Alpers, Clarence-Smith and Beachey, tend to stop at Mozambique Island or Sofala, and simply assume that Delagoa Bay is excluded from the system. Portuguese historian Alexandre Lobato, for example, claimed that Delagoa Bay 'was one of the rare parts of Mozambique that did not export slaves [because] the region had never been influenced by the ideas, habits and customs of the Moors' (cited in Harries, 'Slavery, Social Incorporation and Surplus Extraction', 311). Most studies also begin in 1800. More archival work is needed here.
94. Etherington, *Great Treks*, 31.
95. Smith, 'Struggle for Control', 154.
96. Smith, 'Struggle for Control', 174.
97. In what follows, I am indebted to Cobbing's work, though I differ frequently in my emphases and conclusions.
98. Miers and Kopytoff, *Slavery in Africa*, 11, 66, 72.
99. Cooper, *Plantation Slavery*, 32.
100. Manning, *Slavery and African Life*, 79.
101. Ross, 'The Last Years of the Slave Trade to the Cape Colony' in Clarence-Smith, *The Economics of the Indian Ocean Slave Trade*, 211; Mackeurtan, *Cradle Days*, 78.

102. Stein, *The French Slave Trade*, 121, 124. In 1735, there were 648 slaves in Mauritius; in 1777, more than 25 000, and nearly twice that by 1797 (Allen, *Slaves, Freedmen*, 13).
103. Teelock and Alpers, *History, Memory and Identity*, 115.
104. See *Report of the Commissioners of Inquiry upon the Slave Trade at Mauritius*, 20, 23. On the Madagascar trade, see especially Campbell, 'Madagascar and Mozambique in the Slave Trade', in Clarence-Smith, *The Economics of the Indian Ocean Slave Trade*, 166-93; also Bloch, 'Modes of Production and Slavery in Madagascar', in Watson, *Asian and African Systems of Slavery*, 100-34; and Pearson and Godden, *In Search of the Red Slave*, the astounding story of Robert Drury, who was himself made a slave in Madagascar for fourteen years, between 1703 and 1717, and returned there later as a slaver himself. What the Madagascar case makes abundantly clear is the close articulation between militarised 'states' and slavery.
105. Smith, 'Struggle for Control', 41.
106. Boxer, *Tragic History*, 115, 152-7.
107. Mackeurtan, *Cradle Days*, 74.
108. Smith, 'Struggle for Control', 71-2, 91, 97, 110-16.
109. Pearson and Godden, *In Search of the Red Slave*, 193. This was still a small proportion of the world's total: of the 192 000 Africans arriving in British Caribbean colonies in the period 1658-1713, only some 4 600 came from 'SE Africa' (Eltis, *The Rise of African Slavery in the Americas*, 245). This was set to change radically within a century, that is, by Shaka's time.
110. Bannister, *Humane Policy*, xxxii; Mackeurtan, *Cradle Days*, 74-5.
111. Bannister, *Humane Policy*, xxxv.
112. Thanks to Ann Smailes for this comparison.
113. Thompson, *African Diaspora*, 87-8.
114. Cited in Thompson, *African Diaspora*, 85 (emphasis added).
115. The notion of 'diffusionism' – the idea that people learn to do new things from one another – is sometimes disparaged by historians. As an educator, I have less of a problem with this; arms races and fashion rages elsewhere are ample demonstration of the phenomenon.

Box 2: Dr Cowan disappears
1. Campbell, *Travels*, II 247; entry for June 1813. I am especially indebted to Jürg Richner for directing me to sources for this Box.
2. Burchell, *Travels*, I 50.
3. Campbell, *Travels*, II 247, 264.
4. Stockenström, *Autobiography*, I 182.
5. Burchell, *Travels*, I 50.
6. Bird, *Annals*, 62-3.
7. Stuart and Malcolm, *Diary*, 5.
8. Bryant, *Olden Times*, 93.
9. Stockenström, *Autobiography*, I 40.
10. See Legassick, 'The Griqua', 206.

11. Bryant, *Olden Times*, 91–2.

12. Ritter, *Shaka Zulu*, 16.

13. Greisbach, 'Limpopo', 211.

14. Kirby, *Diary of Dr Andrew Smith*, I 406; entry for 5 May 1835.

15. Morris, *Washing of the Spears*, 41.

16. *Beaver* logbook, National Maritime Museum, Greenwich, RUSI/NM/180/10, vol.10.

Chapter 3:   Behind the matting screen

1. BALEKA 5.

2. NGIDI 29.

3. MBOVU 31; MMEMI 243.

4. BALEKA 11; NGIDI 29.

5. JANTSHI 188; NDHLOVU 201.

6. Bird, *Annals*, 64.

7. NDHLOVU 218.

8. MKANDO 150.

9. Cope, *Izibongo*, 76.

10. Cope, *Izibongo*, 76–80.

11. Isaacs, *Travels*, I 262.

12. Cope, *Izibongo*, 74.

13. NDUKWANA 289; JANTSHI 189.

14. BALENI 22.

15. If Thimuni was about eighteen at the time of his call-up, and was 'on his back', a newborn babe, when Shaka took power and killed Thumini's father Mudli, this would date Shaka's succession to about 1808 (see NDHLOVU 199).

16. NDHLOVU openly disapproved of other aspects of colonial methods. He advocated a return to traditional ways of political life, while enthusing about book-education for all. At least some of his statements evidently draw on white-created myths about Shaka that he must have imbibed in Natal: a classic case of a 'feedback loop'.

17. See NDHLOVU 198, 200–1, 207–8, 212–13. For background, see Colenbrander, 'The Zulu Kingdom 1828–1879', in Duminy and Guest, *Natal and Zululand*, 105–8.

18. NDHLOVU 219–21 (slightly edited).

19. NDHLOVU 231.

20. NDHLOVU 206, 217.

21. NDHLOVU 221.

22. Stuart and Malcolm, *Diary*, 12.

23. Bird, *Annals*, 64; Fynn KCM Ms1230, 278; Isaacs, *Travels*, I 263.

24. See JANTSHI 179; BALEKA 5; NDHLOVU 215.

25. MAPUTWANA 230.

26. NGIDI 42.

27. MBOKODO 19. See also MTSHAPI 87 on naming: 'In the Zulu country a child . . . is named by its father. The name does not come from the mother, for she might *qopa* [talk at cross-purposes with] the child's father.'

28. NGIDI 78; MAYINGA 246. I'd love to emphasise this point by calling the boy 'Sikiti' from here on, but will retain the name Shaka to avoid confusion. It's also possible that the boy acquired several different names at once; this would be quite normal practice.
29. JANTSHI 177.
30. See Shooter, *Kafirs of Natal*, 249; Grout, *Zulu-land*, 71; Fynn, KCM Ms1230, 278.
31. Bird, *Annals*, 164.
32. MRUYI 38; MADIKANE 47.
33. NDHLOVU 221-4 (slightly edited).
34. JANTSHI 178; MKEBENI 199; BALENI 32; BALEKA 5; MMEMI 248; FUZE 45; Yenza JSP File 57, item 10, 1.
35. NDHLOVU 232-3.
36. JANTSHI 178.
37. For example, MAYINGA 246.
38. MRUYI 38.
39. MADIKANE 47.
40. JANTSHI 188.
41. BALEKA 5; BALENI 32; MAYINGA 246; MRUYI 38.
42. BALENI 32; though there may have been similar mutterings about Dinuzulu's succession; see NDUKWANA 293.
43. MKEHLANGANA 220.
44. NDHLOVU 215.
45. NGIDI 29; MAYINGA 247.
46. MMEMI 248.
47. MADIKANE's education creates its own problems. He recycles Shepstone's story of Godongwana/Dingiswayo going off to Cape Town and meeting white men, getting his idea of enrolling regiments from there – another classic feedback loop (see Note 16 of this chapter).
48. MADIKANE 47, 50, 53, 61.
49. Probably Hlathi kaNcidi, who was heroically wounded in the 'Mvuzane fight' against the Ndwandwe (MANGATI 209).
50. MADIKANE 59, 61.
51. MADIKANE 51; compare 47.
52. The implication is that if the child had been female, there would have been less of a problem.
53. MADIKANE 47.
54. Compare JANTSHI 189; MKEHLANGANA 218. M.M. Fuze thought that the group of boys, the *intanga*, which Senzangakhona was with in the bush when he met Nandi, was in fact preparing for circumcision (Fuze, *Black People*, 43).
55. Isaacs, *Travels*, I 263.
56. Fynn, 'Notebook', 72-3.
57. Fynn, KCM Ms1230, 277-8. Since Senzangakhona went on to have numerous children in short order, this doesn't make sense entirely, but there may be something in it. Amongst those sons, according to Fynn, was shortly born 'Umfogas' [Mfokazi or Mfokozana], Dingane's elder brother and designated heir (KCM Ms1230, 278). Compare MKEHLANGANA

217–18; possibly an alias of Sigujana (Mangati 205), since Mfokazi seems to disappear from the record.

58. Wright, 'Pre-Shakan Age-group Formation', 26.
59. Mkando 160–1.
60. Lunguza 301; Mkando 161.
61. Jantshi 195; Magidigidi 94; Melapi 76; Ndukwana 265.
62. Mini 128.
63. Mkehlangana 215.
64. Lunguza 301.
65. Mtshebwe 160.
66. Mangati 204.
67. Mabonsa 20.
68. Mabonsa 19–20.
69. Krige, Social System, 116.
70. Here I am partly following John Wright's argument in 'Pre-Shakan Age-group Formation', 27–8.
71. Stuart and Malcolm, Diary, 268–9.
72. Mnkonkoni 284; Gama 140.
73. Mmemi 248.
74. Madikane 54; Magidigidi 94; Ngidi 68.
75. See Wright, 'Control of Women's Labour in the Zulu Kingdom', in Peires, Before and After Shaka, 82–99.
76. As Carolyn Hamilton points out: 'The oral record consists primarily of formally recounted traditions, delivered by men, about men, and concerning the male dominated spheres of politics and warfare'. Much of my argument in these paragraphs is drawn from the relevant chapter of Hamilton, 'Ideology', 422ff.
77. I recognise that there's no direct evidence to support this contention. Elsewhere, however, the sexual imbalance resulting from slaving is well attested, including in Mozambique in the 1790s: see Manning, Slavery and African Life, 79.
78. Jantshi 190; Mayinga 254.
79. Hamilton, 'Ideology', 444.
80. Jantshi 196.
81. Mkando 152. Such an umdlunkulu could look forward to considerable independence in her later life, as well as a certain power, symbolised in her four brass neck-rings.
82. I don't really support Carolyn Hamilton's suggestion that a primary purpose of the isigodlo was to fill the 'vacuum' left by the inkosi's lack of his own children. Most izigodlo were owned by married chiefs; Shaka and Dingane were unusual.
83. Mgidhlana 107. Similarly, Nomantshali kaZigulana of the Ntuli, a member of Shaka's umdlunkulu, was given to his brother Mpande; she bore him a child, Mthonga, and became an important inkosikazi herself (Hamilton, 'Ideology', 431–3; Baleni 27–8, 39). But we need a much more thorough survey of marriages than Hamilton gives, or than I can supply here. I am also not convinced that even a thorough combing of the sources would yield a statistically adequate number of examples.

Chapter 4: Escaping the father

1. Freud, 'Dostoevsky and Parricide', 183.
2. Bryant, *Olden Times*, 67.
3. Bryant, *Olden Times*, 66-7 (emphasis added).
4. Gray, *The Natal Papers of 'John Ross'*, 110.
5. Yenza, JSP file 57, item 10, 1.
6. BALEKA 5; JANTSHI 179, 188-9; MADIKANE 48; MRUYI 38.
7. NDUKWANA 330; compare Bryant, *Olden Times*, 63; but MKANDO (151) denies this.
8. NDHLOVU 203, 215-16; others again deny it.
9. Holden, *Past and Future*, 11; and others deny it.
10. NGIDI 59.
11. MTSHAPI 87.
12. MRUYI 38.
13. MADIKANE 48; MKANDO 151; NGIDI 30.
14. MKANDO 151.
15. NGIDI 83.
16. Though MAYINGA contradicts himself here (compare 247, 248).
17. MAYINGA 247.
18. Bryant, *Olden Times*, 49, 63.
19. MKEBENI 200.
20. BALEKA 4-5 (slightly edited).
21. NGIDI 30; MKANDO 151.
22. MBULO 51.
23. JANTSHI 188.
24. Hedges, 'Trade and Politics', 147.
25. Smith, 'Struggle for Control', 210.
26. Hedges, 'Trade and Politics', 145.
27. Hamilton lays great emphasis on this alleged expansion in the cattle trade as a reason for the rise of the Mthethwa, but the evidence seems to me to be non-existent; see 'Ideology', 126-8.
28. Hedges, 'Trade and Politics', 156-61. *What* they were defending themselves against, Hedges does not try to explain.
29. The Jere, under Zwangendaba, and the Gaza, under Soshangane, would go on to become fully fledged slaver-states; most likely the seeds of their involvement were being planted in this period (Hedges, 'Trade and Politics', 165). The evidence for all of this is extremely scanty, though.
30. Hedges, 'Trade and Politics', 185, 191.
31. Wright and Manson, *The Hlubi Chiefdom*, 4-9.
32. MABONSA 12.
33. Compare Bird, *Annals*, 62; Stuart and Malcolm, *Diary*, 8.
34. Hedges, 'Trade and Politics', 185-6. Some - notably A.T. Bryant - even pushed it as late as 1808, but this was solely in order to make the mythical meeting with Dr Cowan possible (see Box 2 on page 74).
35. Hamilton, 'Ideology', 107-9.

36. Generally speaking, I am favouring the long, slow accretion view of this history, rather than the abrupt, explosive one.
37. Hamilton, 'Ideology', 111.
38. Stuart and Malcolm, *Diary*, 7.
39. Amongst them Hedges, 'Trade and Politics', 153; Smith, 'Trade of Delagoa Bay', 184; Cobbing, 'Mfecane as Alibi', 506.
40. Hamilton, 'Ideology', 108. Some of Matshwili's testimony did find its way into a Zulu reader that Stuart compiled, *uBaxoxele*, but with what accuracy it is impossible now to say.
41. White, *Journal*, 36, 47.
42. Smith, 'Trade of Delagoa Bay', 183-5.
43. This was in the hills east of present-day Melmoth, and not very far north of where Shaka would eventually establish kwaBulawayo.
44. Hedges, 'Trade and Politics', 187.
45. Hamilton, 'Ideology', 123-9. It is not possible to sequence all these activities securely to either before or after 1800; see also Chapter 5.
46. JANTSHI 176.
47. BALENI 19; MQAIKANA 23.
48. BALENI 18, 22. James Stuart's own opinion of his informant was that BALENI was less reliable than his brother Nonqeta kaSilwana, who did not 'require to think of things', as BALENI did (34).
49. MGIDHLANA 105; MAGOJELA 104; Bryant, *Olden Times*, 29.
50. BALENI 16-22; NDUKWANA 341, 378.
51. MKANDO 151; though at least one older member, Nduvane, might have been; MANGATI 204.
52. MADIKANE 50.
53. MKANDO 166.
54. The iWombe would include Nzobo kaSobadhli of the Ntombela people, eventually one of Dingane's chiefs; Mapitha kaSojiyisa of the Mandlakazi; and Ndengezi kaKuzwayo of the Mdlalose, later a great warrior under Shaka (MANGATI 201, 204, 210; NDUKWANA 282, 316; MADIKANE 52).
55. MAYINGA 253.
56. MANGATI 208.
57. MELAPI 81.
58. NGIDI 42, 49, 59. Otherwise James Stuart's informants give us no information about her at all. Bryant, *Olden Times* (46-7, 56) claims she was of the Nzuze people, and that she eventually committed suicide during the 1879 Anglo-Zulu War. She is the subject of Cecil Cowley's fictionalised *Kwa Zulu: Queen Mkabi's Story* (1966), which is almost entirely reliant on Bryant's snippets and cannot be said to have any independent validity as a source.
59. Bryant, *Olden Times*, 52.
60. Bryant, *History of the Zulu*, 72. The area is still called Hlabisa today, between the Mfolozi and Hluhluwe game reserves. Bryant names Songiya's father Ngotja (Ngotsha) as an *inceku*, personal attendant, to Senzangakhona (73).
61. Bryant, *Olden Times*, 52. Bryant claims that Bakuza was the first choice of heir, but was killed early on. I have not found independent evidence for Sondaba or for this son.

62. BALENI 23; compare Bryant, *Olden Times*, 46–52; *Dictionary*, 35.
63. Bryant, *History of the Zulu*, 35.
64. Some say Sigujana was Mpikase's son, resulting in a rather different scenario in the succession dispute (for example, NGIDI 49). Bhibhi is more commonly attested.
65. MANGATI 204–6.
66. MANGATI 202 (slightly edited).
67. Bhibhi would survive both Shaka's and Dingane's reigns, but in the 1840s would run foul of politics under Mpande. Although Mpande wanted her alive, she was killed by dissident units, stabbed to death amongst the bushes of the amaQongqo hills, north of the upper Mkhuze river (MANGATI 204).
68. BALENI 22.
69. Krige, *Social System*, 69.
70. Krige, *Social System*, 73.
71. SEME 271–2.
72. MAYINGA 251 (slightly edited).
73. NDUKWANA 330.
74. See Bryant, *Zulu People*. MAYINGA's account goes on relate that Shaka then sent out a force of men to kill the chief, Nzombane kaMathomela, who lived near oSungulweni, near present-day Eshowe, and lift his cattle. Only when they came back did Shaka *thomba*, or come out of seclusion. Is this some sign that Shaka had been unable to perform this vital, integrating ceremony at its proper time, that it had to hammed up later? My guess is that MAYINGA is squashing together two different events: the original emission, and a much later attack. The only other record we have of Nzombane of the Bomvu, is when he was attacked by the great warrior Zihlandlo, at Shaka's behest, well into Shaka's reign (MBOKODO 12; compare Bryant, *Olden Times*, 411).
75. Krige, *Social System*, 88–95.
76. Krige, *Social System*, 81–5.
77. MKANDO 160.
78. Only Bryant, out on a limb as usual, says he did (*Olden Times*, 49).
79. NGIDI 29.
80. MAYINGA 246. But that may be MAYINGA's opinion as much as Senzangakhona's.
81. JANTSHI 179 (slightly edited).
82. NDUKWANA 330.
83. Isaacs, *Travels*, I 264 (emphasis added).
84. MKANDO 160.
85. NGIDI contradicts himself slightly on this point (58, 94).
86. NGIDI 30. Nsindwane ran away when Shaka came to power, and eventually joined the white settler William Fynn (NGIDI 58).
87. NGIDI 29; MMEMI 270; NDHLOVU 206. Bryant (in another uncorroborated but perhaps here significant account) asserts that Shaka refused to return from the Langeni to get his *umutsha* (*Olden Times*, 63).
88. NDUKWANA 352.
89. MMEMI 271.
90. NGIDI 49.

91. NGIDI 42.
92. MMEMI 270.
93. NGIDI 53; compare Tununu, JSA File 70, 94-9. Fynn relocates Dingane's impropriety and flight to Shaka's reign (Stuart and Malcolm, *Diary*, 16).
94. NGIDI 58. Although, that Shaka could drink milk there at all, is also symbolic of a certain belonging.
95. NGIDI 44, 55, 66, 94.
96. NGIDI 66. Almost certainly many others were using it, too.
97. NGIDI 31.
98. Holden, *Past and Future*, 12.
99. NGIDI 31, 43. Some such story might have spawned Fynn's mistaken assertion that Makhedama was Nandi's 'father' (Stuart and Malcolm, *Diary*, 13).
100. MADIKANE 48.
101. NGIDI 58.

Chapter 5: Waiting in the wings

1. MADIKANE 48.
2. JANTSHI 190.
3. MAGIDI 79; Ngomane is MAGIDI's father.
4. JANTSHI, 180 and 190, contradicts himself on this point.
5. MKEBENI 197.
6. NDHLOVU 227.
7. Hedges, 'Trade and Politics', 199-200.
8. Wright, 'Dynamics of Power', 158, 178.
9. The debate is encapsulated in the graph that Cobbing provides, comparing his surmise with that of Elizabeth Eldredge (Cobbing, 'Overturning the "Mfecane"', draft, 15). Eldredge argues that there was practically no slaving up to 1820 or so, when there was a sudden expansion. On the whole, I am inclined to support, with qualifications, Cobbing's circumstantial argument that there was most likely *some* slaving and other trade before 1810, for which we lack concrete evidence.
10. Eldredge, 'Sources of Conflict', in Hamilton, *Mfecane Aftermath*, 130-1.
11. Smith, 'Struggle for Control', 327.
12. Smith, 'Struggle for Control', 324.
13. Eldredge, 'Sources of Conflict', in Hamilton, *Mfecane Aftermath*, 132; compare *RSEA* IX, 14, 16.
14. Manning, *Slavery and African Life*, 79-80.
15. *RSEA* IX, 1. Both Cobbing and Eldredge try to suck more precision out of this report than it can sustain.
16. Bonner, *Kings, Commoners*, 20-6. Bonner's chronology is extremely fuzzy for these years.
17. This argument has been suggested by Hedges for this region ('Trade and Politics', 145-52), and by Peter Delius for the Pedi polity further north (*The Land Belongs to Us*, 19). As Delius warns: 'On the basis of existing research and evidence, however, this explanation cannot claim to be more than a derivative and tentative hypothesis' (42). Such a scenario would

also incidentally make nonsense of the claim that a major 'Madlathule' drought/famine around 1802–3 had any great effect on events.

18. Historians regularly use such phrases without being able to say what the contentions were about.
19. Bird, *Annals*, 63.
20. See, for example, Hedges, 'Trade and Politics', 153.
21. The exact timing of this, as my mention of it also in Chapter 4 indicates, is impossible to pin down.
22. Hamilton, 'Ideology', 123–4.
23. Wright, 'Dynamics of Power', 174. Nqoboka also later became a prominent *induna* under Shaka (MMEMI 258).
24. These paragraphs essentially follow Carolyn Hamilton's reading; she draws mainly on Bryant and James Stuart's unpublished 'Life of Tshaka' (KCM, JSP file 53). The original sources remain obscure.
25. Hamilton, 'Ideology', 128–9.
26. Bryant, *Olden Times*, 100.
27. NGIDI 67.
28. NDUKWANA 326.
29. Bird, *Annals*, 64.
30. NDUKWANA 333.
31. MAGIDI 79.
32. NGIDI 67.
33. See discussion in Hedges, 'Trade and Politics', 173–6.
34. MMEMI 243, 264.
35. MBOVU 29–30.
36. MMEMI 243–5; Hamilton, 'Ideology', 125.
37. MAYINGA 247; NGIDI 55, 67.
38. MBOVU 36. MMEMI (246) says that Nomo died at Dingiswayo's.
39. NGIDI 67; MMEMI 257.
40. Bird, *Annals*, 149.
41. NGIDI 94.
42. BALEKA 5.
43. MKEBENI 197. It was later embellished by James Stuart for his Zulu reader *uVesekithi* (1938; translation at KCM 53311/2), and thereupon became ineradicable legend.
44. MKEBENI 198.
45. NDHLOVU 205.
46. NGIDI 53, 90.
47. MAGIDI 80.
48. NGIDI 41.
49. See MELAPI 85–6; MANGATHI 216; JANTSHI 198; NDHLOVU 218; Socwatsha JSP File 70, 101.
50. DINYA 103.
51. MAYINGA 247.
52. MAYINGA 247.
53. MADIKANE 61.

54. MBOKODO 19.
55. NGIDI 42.
56. MTSHAYANKOMO 123–4; compare MAGIDI 80, who claims Nkomo was killed because he did not hold a dance or give Dingiswayo a gift of cattle when *he* visited.
57. LUGUBU 292.
58. Compare Bryant, *Olden Times*, 224. Shaka is, however, said to have attacked Nkomo much later (MANDHLAKAZI 180).
59. JANTSHI 181.
60. MRUYI 36. NDHLOVU (204) supports the shadow incident.
61. JANTSHI 181.
62. MRUYI 37; compare NDHLOVU 204.
63. MRUYI 37.
64. NGIDI 53.
65. MADIKANE 48; MKEBENI 198.
66. MTSHAYANKOMO 123; JANTSHI 182.
67. MAGIDI 80.
68. Leslie, *Among the Zulus*, 94.
69. MKEBENI 199.
70. MADIKANE 48 (emphasis added).
71. MKEBENI 199.
72. SIVIVI 375.
73. BALENI 16.
74. JANTSHI 195.
75. NGIDI 42.
76. NGIDI 36.
77. MKEBENI 199. Fynn claimed that one of the *amahubo* songs was of Shaka's own composition, 'in which he set forth his warlike views' (Bird, *Annals*, 65). Stuart later edited in the following song, though there is no evidence whatsoever that this is what happened:

> Ohah! O-o-hah!
>   Who is it that opposes us?
> When we stab we proceed forward,
>   While there are some who retreat,
> The aged must be separated and put in the rear.
>   Do you not see they impede the King's army?
> They were men formerly,
>   But now our mother's mothers.
> We must find petticoats to wear.
>   See, they go out of three roads:
> As it comes they are seen
>   Painful is it to be said I am a commoner.
> I am at a loss for a pit to run away
>   In front and rear there are all enemies.

This, it might be argued, gives us certain insights into several aspects of Shaka's rule, but nothing at all into the accession of power, where Stuart places it. Stuart also added in the inaccurate notion that Shaka was supported by Macingwane of the Chunu (Stuart and Malcolm, *Diary*, 14).

78. NDHLOVU 205, 230.
79. Bird, *Annals*, 65. Stuart, in the published *Diary*, added the imaginative detail of Ngwadi spearing Sigujana to death in a river while he was bathing; Stuart and Malcolm, *Diary*, 14; compare NGIDI 66.
80. MAGIDI 80.
81. NGIDI 42. NGIDI also names Mudli kaNkwelo, Sojisa kaJama, and Renqwa as being supportive of Shaka's candidature (59).
82. JANTSHI 199; evidence of NDUKWANA.
83. MADIKANE 48.
84. NDUKWANA 307, 330.
85. BALENI 19.

Chapter 6:   Laying the foundations
1. Stuart and Malcolm, *Diary*, 13.
2. MAGIDIGIDI 94. Leslie (*Among the Zulus*, 94), thought that Senzangakhona died in 1820; such is the range.
3. Wright, 'Dynamics of Power', 174.
4. Hamilton, 'Ideology', 335.
5. NDUKWANA 282.
6. LUZIPO 356; NGIDI 58; NDUKWANA 263, 282, 346, 348, 357.
7. MKANDO (159) lists Ngqengelele's *imizi* as: KwaGociza, Ematungweni, Ensukaze, and eMahlabaneni.
8. BALEKA 12.
9. His sons also became *izinduna*: Klwana was old enough to fight against the Ndwandwe under Shaka, and still young enough to fight the Boers at Blood River in 1838, commanding Dingane's Mbelebele regiment. Mnyamana became one of Cetshwayo's principal *izinduna* (LUZIPO 357; NDUKWANA 345; NDUNA 2; NGIDI 76).
10. MKEHLANGANA 211; MKOTANA 225.
11. MKOTANA 226.
12. MKEHLANGANA 214.
13. MMEMI 246, 258, 270.
14. MKEHLANGANA 217.
15. JANTSHI 196; MAGIDI 79. Unfortunately, MAGIDI, a son of Ngomane, has very little to tell us of his father. Another son of Ngomane's, Magwababa, was a prominent warrior under Dingane (NGIDI 80).
16. JANTSHI 190.
17. Leslie, *Among the Zulus*, 94.
18. NGIDI 54; compare MELAPI 81; Wright, 'Dynamics of Power', 180ff.
19. MAYINGA 255.

20. Hamilton, 'Ideology', 248.
21. MMEMI 259.
22. LUGUBU 283. In fact, LUGUBU says that the Buthelezi were living on the Thukela river near Ladysmith. This is so wildly wrong that we have to be a little suspicious of his account.
23. MADIKANE 60-1.
24. NDUKWANA 289.
25. JANTSHI 186.
26. NDUKWANA 279, 330.
27. 'Buffer zone' may also be a misleadingly military term: these intervening peoples were as much a conduit for communications as they were a barrier.
28. Hamilton, 'Ideology', 248-50. Hamilton argues that the core Zulu area in the Mkhumbane valley was becoming overcrowded by Shaka's 'army'; this may have been a factor later, but it is unlikely in this initial stage.
29. Leslie, *Among the Zulus*, 94-5. Of all the many stories with which Leslie found himself 'overdosed' in the 1850s and 60s, the 'Zoongoo' dispute emerged for him as the most memorable.
30. NGIDI 40.
31. NGIDI 40, 90.
32. MKEHLANGANA 210-11.
33. MMEMI 258.
34. MTSHAPI 61; MPAMBUKELWA 293; Bryant, *Olden Times*, 25; and compare Bryant's somewhat fanciful rendition of the conflict, 175-7.
35. BALENI 22.
36. Bryant, *Olden Times*, 147.
37. There was also Somaphunga, Nqabeni, Myomo, Nomahlanjana, Dayingubo, Mphepha, and Nombengula (LUZIPO 354).
38. LUZIPO 354-5.
39. Bonner, *Kings, Commoners*, 27. Compare MABOLA 7; MADIKANE 51.
40. Bonner, *Kings, Commoners*, 27-8.
41. Wright, 'Dynamics of Power', 178; compare Bryant, *Olden Times*, 172-3.
42. Bryant, *Olden Times*, 138.
43. Van Warmelo, *History of Matiwane*, 62.
44. See especially *Report of the Commissioners of Inquiry upon the Slave Trade at Mauritius*, 14-17. At least 30 000 slaves had been smuggled into Mauritius by the early 1820s (Allen, *Slaves, Freedmen*, 14).
45. *Report of the Commissioners*, 16
46. *Report of the Commissioners*, 16, 38. But see Campbell, 'Madagascar and Mozambique in the Slave Trade of the Western Indian Ocean 1800-1861', in Clarence-Smith, *The Economics of the Indian Ocean Slave Trade*, who doesn't even list Delagoa Bay as a source port for the Madagascar entrepôt.
47. See Wright, 'Dynamics of Power', 200-1. Also Alpers, *Ivory and Slaves*, 209-11; Beachey, *Slave Trade*, 13-14; Manning, *Slavery and African Life*, 82, 137-8. Though I disagree with Manning's timing, his assertion that the inland wars associated with Shaka helped to *cause* the upsurge in slaving is worth attending to.

48. *RSEA* II 471, 475, 478.
49. Smith, 'Struggle for Control', 225.
50. Owen to unknown, 15 April 1823; National Maritime Museum, Greenwich; COO/3A, MS 52/061.
51. Smith, 'Struggle for Control', 222, 226, 227, 232. Smith, despite his own evidence, nevertheless claims that 'Before the fourth decade of the nineteenth century, the increasingly specialised commerce of the interior of south-eastern Africa was not affected by a trade in slaves' (344).
52. *RSEA* II 472.
53. Smith, 'Struggle for Control', 342.
54. BIKWAYO 68.
55. Smith, 'Struggle for Control', 344.
56. Van Warmelo, *History of Matiwane*, 64.
57. Wright, 'Dynamics of Power', 213–14.
58. See MABONSA 19.
59. Stuart and Malcolm, *Diary*, 318.
60. For example, Theal, *History of South Africa*, 376–82.
61. MABONSA 25.
62. MABONSA 13.
63. MABONSA 29.
64. MABONSA 19.
65. LUZIPO 354.
66. MAGEZA 71.
67. MAZIYANA 273; NGIDI 76. He also survived into Dingane's and Mpande's reigns (MMEMI 258; MELAPI 82), though he was 'already quite advanced in years' when he arrived (MKEHLENGANA 216). He was killed in ugly circumstances in 1839 (DINYA 102; MAQUZA 237; MKOTANA 222; Bird, *Annals*, 541–2).
68. MKANDO 162.
69. Stuart and Malcolm, *Diary*, 17. This is not, however, in Fynn's original (Bird, *Annals*, 65–6).
70. BALEKA 7 (slightly edited). Mpitikazi went on to fight in Shaka's later campaigns, and died around 1888.
71. NGIDI 61.
72. NGIDI 61.
73. MAHASHAHASHA 108 (slightly edited).
74. MTSHAPI 69.
75. NGIDI 39.
76. NGIDI 72.
77. MKANDO 159.
78. MKOTANA 228. Unfortunately, the story about her is a sad though unlikely one; she wet the bed, made the *isigodlo* smelly, and Shaka tested her father by getting him to kill her.
79. NGIDI 49.
80. They did not disappear even under Dingane, who killed Nxazonke alongside Shaka, and wounded Mbikwana. Succession disputes over a self-consciously Langeni entity went on into Mpande's reign (NGIDI 64–5).

81. See, for example, BALEKA 11.
82. See MBOVU 39, 41; MCOTOYI 57; MADIKANE 52; MSIME 50.
83. NGIDI 67; MELAPI 81.
84. Bird, *Annals*, 150. Another account has it, though, that Sihayo was killed not by Shaka, but by Dingane for exhibiting too much independence (MSIME 49).
85. MELAPI 81.
86. However, MBOVU (33) alludes to this dispute without bringing in Shaka at all; JANTSHI (186) claims Shaka attacked Mapholoba, which must have been earlier, but places it after 1826 and Sikhunyane, which is not possible.
87. This is according to Dube's own son, MADIKANE (47); JANTSHI (183) claims that Shaka attacked the Qadi without provocation after he had dealt with Mzilikazi, but that they continued to live there and pay tribute. They were still there under Dube until Dingane attacked them (MANDHLAKAZI 191).
88. MQAIKANA 23.
89. BALENI 17.
90. Fuze, *Black People*, 52.
91. Cope, *Izibongo*, 130.
92. MAGIDIGIDI 89; Fuze, *Black People*, 52.
93. MQAIKANA 24.
94. MAYINGA 251.
95. Cope, *Izibongo*, 130.
96. MADIKANE 61; Wright, 'Dynamics of Power', 242.
97. BALENI 18.
98. MAGIDIGIDI 85.
99. NDHLOVU 205.
100. MMEMI 270.
101. See my discussion in Chapter 8 of Wylie, *Savage Delight*.
102. BALENI 17; MAZIYANA 269.
103. Hamilton conflates what I take to be different events, and implies that both the scorched earth retreat and the 'kisi' battle took place before the Phakathwayo event (Hamilton, 'Ideology', 172).
104. MAZIYANA 269.
105. DINYA 115; MAZIYANA 296. This was probably only the first of such assertions; as one informant puts it, the Maphumulo were 'incorporated by degrees' (Bird, *Annals*, 150).
106. NGIDI 55.
107. Bird, *Annals*, 149.
108. KAMBI 210.
109. MBOVU 29; MMEMI 260.
110. KAMBI 208; MBOVU 29.
111. Cope, *Izibongo*, 146.
112. Hamilton, 'Ideology', 155ff.
113. Hamilton, 'Ideology', 157.
114. MBOVU 35.
115. MBOVU 35–6.

116. MESENI 100; MMEMI 241.
117. JANTSHI 182. It's highly unlikely that this would have happened immediately after Shaka's accession, as JANTSHI implies, JANTSHI's sense of timing never being too reliable.
118. MANDHLAKAZI 177–8. An ongoing quarrel is encapsulated in another version of the fighting-over-clay-bulls story, this time involving Shaka and Phakathwayo as boys; a legend (NDHLOVU 226).
119. MAKUZA 168.
120. JANTSHI 182–3.
121. MAKUZA 168–9.
122. MMEMI 240–2.
123. JANTSHI 183.
124. MMEMI 264.
125. MANDHLAKAZI 178. Cobbing, drawing on a dubious reference in *The Diary of Henry Francis Fynn*, uses the confusion over how Phakathwayo died to speculate that he was sold off as a slave, but I find no evidence to support this. Compare James Stuart's summary, interpolated into *The Diary of Henry Francis Fynn*, 16–17.
126. MBOVU 43; MMEMI 249.
127. MAKUZA 169.
128. MESENI 100. Bryant is uncertain whether Nqetho was in fact a son of Khondlo (*Olden Times*, 391).
129. MMEMI 249.
130. MESENI 100. Another version says that Vukubulwayo was initially left in charge, before he absconded to the Ndwandwe (Bird, *Annals*, 150).
131. MMEMI 261.
132. MMEMI 242–3.
133. MESENI 100.
134. KAMBI 210; MMEMI 243, 257.
135. 'James Langa', *Shaka*, 70. 'James Langa' is the pseudonym of Geoffrey Bond, whose novella was originally published in 1961 as *Chaka the Terrible*, then reworked slightly in 1982 for greater political correctness.
136. LUNGUZA 303; DINYA 104; KUMALO 213; MELAPI 84.
137. Their estimate (*JSA* I 94n) is probably based on the assumption that Shaka came to power in 1816; two years after his accession sounds right, hence in my chronology *c.*1814. That it was *butwa'd* before the early Langeni incidents is implied by the story of BALEKA's father Mpitikazi (see page 167), a Langeni of the Fasimba.
138. LUNGUZA 303; NDUKWANA 269. They would only regain their headrings under Dingane (NDUKWANA 276).
139. NDUKWANA 333.
140. NDUKWANA 350.
141. JANTSHI 180; MAGIDIGIDI 95.
142. MAGIDIGIDI 94.
143. MAYINGA 249.

Chapter 7: 'The bulls of the herd have met'

1. NDUNA 1.
2. NDUNA 1.
3. MKEHLANGANA 211.
4. NDUNA 2.
5. NDUNA 1–2 (edited for brevity); compare DINYA (101–2) for a slightly different version.
6. NDUNA 3. NDUNA then conflates this with the final confrontation on the Mhlathuze river; compare JANTSHI 183.
7. MKEHLANGANA 211, 217.
8. Perhaps the following derivation of the word *kisi* is also an indication that this wasn't necessarily too serious a fight: 'The saying "kisi fighting" originated among the Chunu . . . . They threw assegais at one another as if they were boys. Such a manner of fighting was said to be that of "kisi", for as one was about to fling his assegai he would shout, "Kisi!" at his foe . . .' (BALENI 17). Another version has it that Shaka cut reed whistles (*amavenge*) for the men to use as signals (NGIDI 68).
9. Cope, *Izibongo*, 178.
10. MANDHLAKAZI 175; MKOTANA 223.
11. Compare MKEHLANGANA 210; MKOTANA 222. Zulu married three of the informant DINYA's sisters.
12. MKOTANA 222–3.
13. MANDHLAKAZI 181.
14. MANDHLAKAZI 183.
15. MMEMI 270.
16. KAMBI 211.
17. MMEMI 241–2. MMEMI, Mbokazi's nephew, is the only informant to attest to Mbokazi's existence, and he may be exaggerating his role.
18. MBOVU 36.
19. Hamilton, 'Ideology', 180–3.
20. MELAPI 78.
21. NGIDI 55.
22. Hamilton, 'Ideology', 135–6.
23. MMEMI 270. According to Wright, the Mgumanqa was formed around 1819 of youths born *c.*1790 (JSA III 229). I would date it a year or two earlier.
24. BALENI 33–4.
25. For some details dating to Cetshwayo's time but probably not much different from Shaka's, see MPATSHANA 315ff.
26. Compare NDUKWANA 363: 'No man was allowed to wash inside the cattle enclosure.'
27. Isaacs, *Travels*, I 139.
28. MBOKODO 6.
29. JANTSHI 186; this would make sense only if it happened while Shaka was with Dingiswayo.
30. Cope, *Izibongo*, 158.
31. MANDHLAKAZI 192–3.
32. MBOKODO 6.
33. NDUNA 7.

34. Cope, *Izibongo*, 156–60.
35. Mbokodo 11.
36. Mandhlakazi 193.
37. Mbokodo 11.
38. Mbokodo 15.
39. Madikane 53.
40. Mbokodo 15.
41. Mbokodo 8–11.
42. Mbokodo 15.
43. Mbokodo 6.
44. Cope, *Izibongo*, 158.
45. Mbokodo 6.
46. Mbokodo 13.
47. Mqaikana 22–3.
48. Lugubu 281, 285.
49. Lugubu 282.
50. Lunguza 298–9. Compare Lugubu 282. Ngidi (37, 59, 70) claims that the uBhekenya were only *butwa*'d just before the Sikhunyane attack, that is, in 1826; either he or Lunguza is wrong on this detail, then. The time lapse evident between these campaigns indicates long-term struggles, rather than short, sharp evictions and movements.
51. Compare Mqaikana 27; Lunguza 299. To confuse matters further, there seem to have been *two* Nomagagas.
52. Bird, *Annals*, 144; informant not named. This Jobe is presumably Jobe kaGece of the Sithole, then living just north of, and so possibly tributary to Ngoza.
53. Hamilton, 'Ideology', 255–7.
54. Magidigidi 84, 85, 87.
55. Mbokodo 12, 18.
56. Bird, *Annals*, 130–3.
57. Mgidhlana 107.
58. Mandhlakazi 175; Bird, *Annals*, 132.
59. Bird, *Annals*, 133.
60. Mandhlakazi 193.
61. Madikane 55.
62. Mageza 69.
63. I take this view despite what Maziyana says (295–6), that the attacks on Mande of the Cele and others happened *before* the Zwide confrontation.
64. Ndukwana 279.
65. Mandhlakazi 185–6.
66. Jantshi 177.
67. Nhlekele 128.
68. Makuza 170.
69. Ndukwana 331.
70. Bird, *Annals*, 65.
71. Makuza 170–1.

72. MAKUZA 171.
73. NGIDI 54.
74. NDHLOVU 230.
75. MANDHLAKAZI 176.
76. See, for example, Hamilton, 'Ideology', 137–8; Wright, 'Dynamics of Power', 179; Bryant, *Olden Times*, 164–5; Stuart and Malcolm, *Diary*, 11.
77. NGIDI 62; he is compressing events.
78. NHLEKELE 130.
79. Bryant, *Olden Times*, 202–3; Wright, 'Dynamics of Power', 188.
80. MGIDHLANA 105, 107; MMEMI 259.
81. NDUKWANA 363, 378.
82. Somveli's flight may have been as late as 1821 (see Hedges, 'Trade and Politics', 205). See pages 240 to 242. There's an interesting epilogue to this. In about 1880 Sitimela, a son of Somveli, returned from the north. Some Mthethwa wanted to recognise him as the rightful heir of Dingiswayo's line; others not. Mlandela punished those who had offered cattle to Sitimela, but the latter gathered considerable support and Mlandela had to flee across the Mhlathuze river to shelter with that maverick 'white Zulu', John Dunn (NDUKWANA 355–6; compare NHLEKELE 127–8).
83. JANTSHI 182.
84. NEMBULA 12–13.
85. Hamilton, 'Ideology', 262–3; NDUKWANA 278.
86. This is a diversionary but interesting story in relation to Shaka's childhood 'bullying':

    > When Makoba and Zungu were children they had curds poured into their hands. Makoba ate up all that was put in his hand, whereas Zungu would take one mouthful and throw the rest away, or let it fall through his hands on the ground. This was then interpreted to mean that Makoba was a glutton and would be mean, whereas Zungu would be content with little and leave some for others; hence it was right he should become the chief notwithstanding Makoba's seniority. And so it happened (MAGOJELA 105).

    In short, this anecdote illustrates curd-pouring as a metaphor, not 'history'.
87. MAGOJELA 104.
88. Hamilton, 'Ideology', 250.
89. MELAPI 81.
90. Hamilton, 'Ideology', 247–8.
91. Wright, 'Dynamics of Power', 186.
92. Cobbing, 'Jettisoning the Mfecane', 11.
93. MAPUTWANA 230.
94. NDHLOVU 230; compare MADIKANE 52.
95. BALEKA 5; BALENI 17.
96. DINYA 103; MMEMI 271. Interestingly, MMEMI says that Shaka was 'advised' to do this; even this was not his idea.
97. MMEMI 271.
98. JANTSHI 184.

99. BALENI 17; MANDHLAKAZI 180-1.
100. MMEMI 271; MANGATI 208; compare Bryant, *Olden Times*, 205-6.
101. LUGUBU 284.
102. BALEKA 5.
103. For other versions of this famous event, see NDHLOVU 229; NDUNA 2-3; Fuze, *Black People*, 55. For more discussion see Wylie, 'The Feather Stood Quivering'.
104. BALENI 17, 18.
105. DINYA 103.
106. MMEMI 271.
107. Bryant, *Olden Times*, 206.
108. JANTSHI 186.
109. MMEMI 271.
110. MAGIDIGIDI 95.
111. LUNGUZA 303.
112. NGIDI 36.
113. MANDHLAKAZI 177; compare NDUKWANA 330.
114. MANDHLAKAZI 180.
115. NGIDI 36-7.
116. MAYINGA 249.
117. MANGATI 199, 209.
118. MADIKANE 47, 60.
119. NGIDI 37; SIJEWANA 334.
120. MAGIDIGIDI 94-5.
121. MAYINGA 249.
122. LUNGUZA 312.
123. MAYINGA 249.
124. LUNGUZA 303.
125. MKANDO 148.
126. MAGIDIGIDI 85, 95.
127. MAYINGA 249. It may later have absorbed whatever was left of the iNtontela (JANTSHI 180).
128. LUNGUZA 303; MAYINGA 249.
129. MAGIDIGIDI 95: as a Chunu himself, he might be exaggerating their participation.
130. NDUNA 3.
131. DINYA 103.
132. MADIKANE 52.
133. BALENI 18; compare MANDHLAKAZI 181.
134. MANGATI 209; compare Bryant, *Olden Times*, 207.
135. BALEKA 12.
136. JANTSHI 174-5.
137. JANTSHI 195.
138. JANTSHI 193.
139. JANTSHI 184-200.
140. JANTSHI 186, 193, 201.
141. MKEBENI 196. Compare MMEMI 263; NDHLOVU 227; NDUKWANA 263; MAYINGA 24; for reiterations of the same idea.

142. NGIDI 68.
143. MELAPI 87.
144. MANDHLAKAZI 187.
145. BALENI 35.
146. MAYINGA 247.
147. JANTSHI 187.
148. JANTSHI 187.
149. NGIDI 60.
150. NDUKWANA 294.
151. Isaacs, *Travels*, I 205.
152. *RN* II 9.
153. NDUKWANA 263.
154. MMEMI 271.
155. BALEKA 13; MPATSHANA 327.
156. NDUNA 4.
157. NDUNA 4.
158. Leslie, *Among the Zulus*, 118.
159. Leslie, *Among the Zulus*, 119–23.
160. MADIKANE 61. There are also some very strange legends, apparently emanating from Lemba people in Zimbabwe, about Shaka and Zwide. According to these stories, some Lemba people travelled south, via the Shangaans, who are said to be Shaka's 'fathers-in-law', carrying their particular expertise with medicines. These medicinal skills they taught to Shaka, who subsequently used them against Zwide. However, these accounts are totally unsupported by anything else in the records (see Von Sicard, 'Shaka and the North').
161. Wright, 'Dynamics of Power', 183.

Box 4:   Cannibal tales
   1. Warner, *No Go*, 10.
   2. Fuze, *Black People*, 7.
   3. MQAIKANA 14.
   4. Stuart and Malcolm, *Diary*, 22.
   5. BALENI 34.
   6. DUNGWA 126.
   7. MAZIYANA 277.
   8. BAZELY 53–5; LUNGUZA 301, 306; MBOVU 27; MKANDO 161; SHEPSTONE 394.
   9. MAGIDIGIDI 85, 87.
  10. MAHAYA 113.
  11. MELAPI 81; JANTSHI 201; MBOVU 26.
  12. JANTSHI 201; MABONSA 31.
  13. BAZELY 60; DABULA 90; LUNGUZA 299; MABONSA 24; MANGATI 202; MBOVU 27. Compare Bryant, *Olden Times*, 58, 347, 377, 552; Bird, *Annals*, 132.
  14. Stuart and Malcolm, *Diary*, 320.
  15. MKANDO 162.
  16. MQAIKANA 5.

Chapter 8:   Holding the centre

1. Isaacs, *Travels*, I 87.
2. BALENI 24.
3. Bird, *Annals*, 76; Isaacs, *Travels*, I 61.
4. Whitelaw, 'Preliminary Results', 107–8. Compare Van Schalkwyk, 'oNdini'.
5. Fynn, KCM Ms1230, 315; compare Stuart and Malcolm, *Diary*, 30.
6. This is Carolyn Hamilton's argument ('Ideology', 350), though the evidence she cites doesn't bear it out. She refers to Bryant, but Bryant in fact says (again wrongly) that the 'nickname' Gibixhegu was only applied to the Bulawayo *umuzi* in 1826 (*Olden Times*, 587). It was never 'rebuilt on the coastal plain', as Hamilton, citing Isaacs, states ('Ideology', 351); in fact, Isaacs makes it clear that, after crossing the 'Great Water' of the Thukela, he approached Shaka's homestead through 'mountainous country' (*Travels*, I 57–8, also 87. The Thukela is wrongly footnoted as the 'amaTigulu' in Hermann's edition of *Travels*).
7. MAYINGA 253; compare MADIKANE 59.
8. NGIDI 79.
9. NGIDI 58.
10. MAYINGA 253.
11. NGIDI 59; Bryant, *Olden Times*, 586–7, says that the Gibixhegu-Bulawayo move was from the western to the eastern side of the valley, but if NGIDI is right, it was more likely the other way round.
12. MELAPI 85.
13. SIJEWANA 335; Tununu, JSP, File 60, Nbk 23, 1–9.
14. Socwatsha, JSP, File 58, Nbk 22, 21.
15. Hamilton, 'Ideology', 352. Or, rather, what would later be Dingane's Khangela, originally Phakathwayo's *ikhanda* Emtandeni (NGIDI 39; MMEMI 259).
16. NGIDI 33–4; SIJEWANA 334–5; Socwatsha, JSP, File 70, 6–8.
17. JANTSHI 184. Hamilton's suggestion that there was ecological exhaustion in the Makhosini area is unsupported by precise evidence; and her assumption that the move happened after Zwide's defeat is, I think, incorrect (but compare NGIDI 79). There may, as she proposes, have been a 'pull factor' in the environmental attractions of the coastal region – forests and sweetveld grazing - but then the Zulu would hardly have moved to a less favourable region ('Ideology', 354).
18. MELAPI 85.
19. NGIDI 59; compare SIJEWANA 333.
20. Isaacs, *Travels*, I 60, 268; he calls it 'Gibbeclack', or 'drive the old men out'.
21. Gray, *Natal Papers*, 61; Maclean writes 'Umbollalili' for kwaBulawayo. Maclean later visited kwaDukuza, way to the south, but still thought of the mountains as the Bulawayo range.
22. There is some evidence for iron-working at kwaBulawayo (Whitelaw, 'Preliminary Results', 108).
23. MMEMI 257.
24. MANDHLAKAZI 179.
25. The missionary Allen Gardiner claimed that all principal *izinduna* under Shaka had the power of life and death, which Dingane curtailed to only three (Gardiner, *Narrative*, 94), but the available evidence does not support this claim.

26. LUNGUZA 314.
27. Gardiner, *Narrative*, 94.
28. NDUKWANA 311.
29. NDUKWANA 316.
30. MAYINGA 257–8 (slightly re-ordered).
31. MAYINGA 257.
32. MAYINGA 257 (emphasis added).
33. Bonner, *Kings, Commoners*, 27–8.
34. Stuart and Malcolm, *Diary*, 248.
35. Owen, 'The Bay of Delagoa', *RSEA* II 468.
36. Bonner, *Kings, Commoners*, 28; Delius, *The Land Belongs to Us*, 22–3.
37. Delius, *The Land Belongs to Us*, 17–19.
38. NGIDI 70. Zwide was thought to be over 50 in 1819.
39. NDUKWANA 363, 377.
40. NDUKWANA 277–8.
41. Hamilton, 'Ideology', 366.
42. Hamilton, 'Ideology', 444.
43. MANGATI 216, MAYINGA 252.
44. MAYINGA 256.
45. SIVIVI 372.
46. BALENI 20; NGIDI 34.
47. Gardiner, *Narrative*, 123.
48. Laband, *Rope of Sand*, 63.
49. Hamilton, 'Ideology', 446 (no source given).
50. MABONSA 20.
51. NGIDI 84.
52. NDHLOVU 232. The fact that several *amakhosikazi* are credited with ruling esiKlebheni may mean that they sometimes ruled in conjunction with each other, or that they were periodically moved around – Shaka's attempt, perhaps, to destabilise any faction-building.
53. NDUKWANA 360.
54. NGIDI 34; Hamilton, 'Ideology', 443–6.
55. Cope, *Izibongo*, 172–3.
56. Hamilton, 'Ideology', 365, following Jeff Guy, writes 'Ntlaka'; there was no such person.
57. MAPUTWANA 230.
58. Guy, *Destruction*, 36. See also SIVIVI 374.
59. NGIDI 33.
60. Hamilton, 'Ideology', 366.
61. MANGATI 213; MANGATI himself saw Maphitha at his eNkungwini *umuzi* during Mpande's reign; he was by then already too old to go and *khonza* in person.
62. Hamilton, 'Ideology', 219–21.
63. NDUKWANA 282.
64. Hamilton, 'Ideology', 221–2. Hamilton lists four of Maphitha's *imizi*, though drawing on what source, and over what time period, is unclear.
65. LUNGUZA 343.

66. Ndukwana 358.
67. Cope, *Izibongo*, 202.
68. Ndukwana 321.
69. Ndukwana 357.
70. Liesegang, 'Migrations', 321-2.
71. Mtshwebe 158; Madikane (53) derives it from a hill on which the Mthethwa first built.
72. Mahaya 116.
73. Ngidi 70.
74. Nhlekele 130.
75. This is also Hedges's surmise; he draws on a letter by Governor Matoso of 11 July 1821; 'Trade and Politics', 205.
76. *RSEA* II 468-9.
77. Owen, *Narrative*, I 126. Smith argues that 'Nyambose' must be 'the same person' as Zwangandaba, but only by way of misunderstanding the name 'Nyambose' ('Struggle for Control', 250n).
78. Liesegang, 'Migrations', 322.
79. Owen, *Narrative*, I 79.
80. Liesegang, 'Migrations', 322.
81. See Liesegang, 'Migrations', 324-9.
82. Only one account makes this identification: that of a hapless missionary named William Threlfall, who tried to set himself up in the pestiferous lowlands inland of Delagoa Bay in 1823. Threlfall identified the 'Bratwahs' specifically with Shaka's Zulu – but I suspect doctoring of his journal by Samuel Broadbent, in whose hagiographic account this item appears (Broadbent, *Missionary Martyr*, 69-100). An original journal for this part of Threlfall's career has not come to light; the journal held at SOAS ends abruptly in 1821.
83. Broadbent, *Missionary Martyr*, 84.
84. Smith, 'Struggle for Control', 269.
85. Owen, *Narrative*, I 214-18.
86. Owen, *Narrative*, II 20; Smith, 'Trade of Delagoa Bay', 187.
87. Stuart and Malcolm, *Diary*, 47. This remained the case well into the nineteenth century.
88. Smith, 'Trade of Delagoa Bay', 186.
89. Ndukwana 357; the exact timing of the Maphitha-Mbopha quarrel is, however, unknown. On ivory: Philip to Brink, 13 April 1824, *RSEA* IX 42. Alan Smith's impression is that 'Most of the ivory which reached the export market at Delagoa Bay originally came from Zululand' ('Struggle for Control', 268).
90. Fynn, 'Delagoa Bay', *RSEA* II 482 (emphasis added). Compare this to the *Diary*, which states much more categorically: 'I had already noted that the natives of Delagoa appeared to be in great dread of the Orentonts. I found out that these people, the Orentonts or Hottentots, belonged to the Zulu tribe, under Shaka, and were a very powerful nation' (Stuart and Malcolm, *Diary*, 42). The orthography alone is enough to raise suspicion of doctoring.
91. *RSEA* II 468-9; Smith, 'Struggle for Control', 249.
92. Owen, *Narrative*, I 71.
93. Madikane 59.

94. Mᴘᴜᴛᴡᴀɴᴀ 230.

95. Mʙᴏᴠᴜ 45.

96. Mᴋᴇʜʟᴀɴɢᴀɴᴀ 216.

97. Even excellent historians such as Philip Bonner still succumb to the 'mfecane' stereotype in saying that '*splinters* of the Ndwandwe state *flew off* in all directions' and '*sped* north' (Bonner, *Kings, Commoners*, 29 [emphasis added]). Carolyn Hamilton likewise preserves shards of the stereotype in calling these absconding groups 'recalcitrant' or 'dissident'; but Shaka had no intrinsic *right* to rule them in the first place.

98. Etherington, *Great Treks*, 120.

99. Owen, *Narrative*, I 80.

100. Owen, 'The Bay of Delagoa', *RSEA* II 470.

101. Smith, 'Struggle for Control', 250-6.

102. Etherington, *Great Treks*, 120.

103. The treaties were dated 4 August and 23 August 1823; Owen claimed that they were 'forced on' him, even though the country had lapsed into a brief peace at that point (Smith, 'Struggle for Control', 267).

104. Owen, *Narrative*, I 255.

105. Owen, *Narrative*, I 270.

106. Broadbent, *Missionary Martyr*, 72-3.

107. Owen to unknown, 15 April 1823. National Maritime Museum, Greenwich, COO/3A, ms 52/061.

108. Stuart and Malcolm, *Diary*, 43.

109. *RN* I 30-3.

110. Owen, *Narrative*, I 292-3.

111. Owen, *Narrative*, I 301.

112. Owen to Philip, nd. *RN* I 34.

113. Owen to Philip, nd. *RN* I 34; also *RSEA* II 478.

114. Owen, *Narrative*, I 302.

115. Nourse to Croker, 26 September 1823; *RSEA* IX 32. This has created difficulties for researchers looking for the precise origins of Mascarene island slaves, for instance, but it's a reasonable surmise that 'the ports of [both] Inhambane and Delagoa Bay . . . provided slaves from its hinterland for the Mauritius plantations' (Teelock and Alpers, *History*, 115). The case of the notorious slaver, the *Walter Farquhar*, which was wrecked on the Madagascar coast in 1823, en route from Delagoa Bay to Mauritius, is one indication (*Report of the Commissioners of Inquiry upon the Slave Trade at Mauritius 1829*, 38).

116. Owen to Croker, 9 October 1823; *RSEA* IX 32-3 (emphasis added). Compare Liesegang, 'A First Look', 463, who estimates only 5 000, but this is official customs receipts only.

117. Liesegang, 'A First Look', 463.

118. Etherington, *Great Treks*, 121. See also the discussion in Cobbing, 'Grasping the Nettle', 17-18.

119. Etherington, *Great Treks*, 122.

120. Newitt, *History of Mozambique*, 244; Etherington, *Great Treks*, 116-17.

121. *RSEA* II 474.

122. *RSEA* II 26.

123. *RN* II 18.
124. Stuart and Malcolm, *Diary*, 48.
125. Etherington, *Great Treks*, 120.
126. Philip to Brink; *RSEA* II 42; Arbousset and Daumas, *Narrative*, 107.
127. JANTSHI 182.
128. Rasmussen, *Migrant Kingdom*, 12; Moffat, *Matabele Journals*, I 29.
129. Thomas, *Eleven Years*, 156-7. This is the version so readily repeated in the popular literature.
130. NDUKWANA 264; MADIKANE (60) even thought that Mzilikazi was an *inceku* of Shaka's at esiKlebheni, responsible for milking.
131. MADHLEBE 46. MADHLEBE says that Jinjana was associated with Mashongwe of the Qwabe whose eyes Shaka took out, possibly dating this to late 1824.
132. LUNGUZA 307.
133. Cope, *Izibongo*, 132.
134. Thomas, *Eleven Years*, 156-8.
135. JANTSHI 183.
136. NEMBULA 13.
137. Smith, *Diary*, II 260-1.
138. Smith, *Andrew Smith's Journal*, 277. Etherington's citation of this (*Great Treks*, 162) confuses the chronology, however.
139. Bryant, *Olden Times*, 422; Campbell, *Mlimo*, 33. Campbell's version is derived from an Ndebele informant, who claimed that Mzilikazi 'applied for leave to attack Somnisi, a Basutho chief'. Shaka approved, sending one 'Qozo' to oversee. When Qozo demanded the cattle, Mzilikazi told him that Shaka would have to come and get them himself, and defiantly cut off the tops of Shaka's messengers' feather head-dresses. Neither Qozo nor Somnisi are attested to elsewhere.
140. Campbell, *Mlimo*, 41-2.
141. See Bird, *Annals*, 68; Rasmussen, *Migrant Kingdom*, 25.
142. MAGEZA 73.
143. NDUNA 5. By contrast, DINYA (101) claims that Khokhela joined Shaka's Njanduna *ibutho*.
144. NEMBULA 13.
145. Campbell, *Mlimo*, 44.
146. Etherington, *Great Treks*, 161-2.
147. See also Wright, 'Dynamics of Power', 190-1; Cobbing, 'The Ndebele', 15-16.
148. MADIKANE 60.
149. JANTSHI is as unreliable as usual in stating that Shaka attacked Mzilikazi shortly after Phakathwayo (183); and Campbell is equally aberrant in suggesting that it was after the defeat of Sikhunyane, that is, in 1826 (Campbell, *Mlimo*, 32).
150. Cope, *Izibongo*, 132.
151. MABONSA 13-14.
152. It was here, in 1823, that the Ngwane would catch up with them again. See Etherington, *Great Treks*, 127-8; Wright and Manson, *The Hlubi Chiefdom*, 17-18. Mpangazitha died in the Caledon valley in battle in *c.*1825.
153. Bryant (*History of the Zulu*, 33) may be half-right that in 1819 the Ngwane were 'ejected by the routed Ndwandwe', which is to say Zwide (or possibly Nxaba), on the move north.

154. Bryant, *History of the Zulu*, 33–5; compare *Olden Times*, 357; Wright, 'Dynamics of Power', 219–20.

155. Bryant, *History of the Zulu*, 35; Bird, *Annals*, 142.

156. NGIDI 82.

157. MANGATI 213.

158. Hamilton, 'Ideology', 261. Hamilton's chronology of Bhele history is muddled and the assertion that Shaka 'was forced' to launch a campaign to stop Bhele cannibalism is dubious – though even some Bhele people remembered themselves as 'cannibals' (MABONSA 24; MANGATI 202). See Box 4 on page 223.

159. Wright, 'Dynamics of Power', 284–5. He dates this to probably 1823. See Stuart and Malcolm, *Diary*, 319; Peires, 'Matiwane's Road to Mbholompo', in Hamilton, *Mfecane Aftermath*, 213–40.

160. Etherington, *Great Treks*, 130.

161. MABONSA 26.

162. MELAPI 73.

163. MABONSA 17, 26.

164. Nourse to Croker, 5 January 1823; *RSEA* IX 19. This doesn't quite gel with Owen's claim that he left Delagoa Bay for St Lucia, Madagascar and Mozambique on 5 November 1822 (Owen, *Narrative*, I 160).

165. Their movements are worth including here in some detail as they were the first channel by which misinformation about Shaka would filter into European literatures.

166. Owen, *Narrative*, I 252.

167. CA, GH 1/8, no.605.

168. Fynn, NA A1382/17/8. This document was incorporated into Fynn's published *Diary*, with interesting editorial changes: Farewell became 'venturesome' rather than 'speculative', the *Princess Charlotte* was 'wrecked' rather than sold, and Fynn/Stuart – here as elsewhere – covers up the rivalry, amounting eventually to detestation, which 'sprang up' between the two adventurers (Stuart and Malcolm, *Diary*, 51–2).

169. *RN* I 7–8, 12–13.

170. *RN* I 9–10.

171. Nourse to Somerset; *RN* I 1, 19–20.

172. On earlier history of these two, see Owen, *Narrative*, I 59, 81–3; Stuart and Malcolm, *Diary*, 180–3; Isaacs, *Travels*, II 209–11.

173. Owen, *Narrative*, I 253–4.

174. Stretch to Read, 8 May 1843; Read to Philip, 8 May 1843; Macmillan Papers, Rhodes House, Oxford, 1330, 1334. I am indebted to Julian Cobbing for this reference.

175. Fynn lists the *Cockburn* as amongst Owen's vessels, though if his dating is correct, the *Cockburn* had already been irretrievably wrecked in Table Bay (Owen, *Narrative*, I 243), and Owen's third vessel was then in fact the *Albatross*.

176. Stuart and Malcolm, *Diary*, 37–9. Compare Fynn's earlier account contained in *RSEA* II 479ff.

177. *RN* I 19–20.

178. SACA 11 July 1826; Thompson, *Travels*, II 406; Stuart and Malcolm, *Diary*, 53.

179. Farewell to Somerset, 1 May 1824, Bird, *Annals*, 71–2.

180. Owen, *Narrative*, I 222.

Chapter 9:   Southward bound

1. Bryant, *Olden Times*, 500; DINYA 98.
2. NGIDI 57. Beware the alleged purity of 'oral traditions'. MQAIKANA tells another funny story set in this spot:

   > Shaka, on one occasion, when his troops were at the Sibubulungu (Port Natal), asked his *induna* how it would be if his troops, when attacking or when dancing at the royal kraal, were to imitate the waves which came breaking in onto the shore, one after the other. The *indunas* said it would be an excellent arrangement. The warriors were accordingly ranged to front the oncoming breakers and told to imitate and stab them . . . And when they got back to the royal kraal, they adopted evolutions which resembled those of the sea . . . (MQAIKANA 27).

3. Stuart and Malcolm, *Diary*, 58-9.
4. Stuart and Malcolm, *Diary*, 64-5.
5. MBOKODO 12-13. He states that the litany of murders happened 'when Zihlandhlo returned' from the Sikhunyane expedition in 1826, but in several cases they must have happened earlier. If Bryant's distribution is roughly right, they all take place within a fairly restricted area – from the middle of the Thukela's south bank to the headwaters of the Mngeni, excluding the coastal area.
6. MBOKODO 13-14.
7. MADIKANE 53; MAQUZA 237. Isaacs is certainly exaggerating in saying that Shaka took away 'all the young warriors to complete his own regiments' (*Travels*, I 149; emphasis added).
8. MBOKODO 8-10 (slightly edited for brevity and clarity).
9. Wright, 'Dynamics of Power', 237-8.
10. Isaacs, *Travels*, I 149.
11. This latter expedition incidentally chased a son of Mathomela's, one Magwaza, into the arms of the Mkhize, where Zihlandlo adopted him. Part of the Ngcobo moved south under a minor chief, Mahawule; the old Mathomela elected to stay in the country of his birth, where he was eventually devoured by wild animals (Fuze, *Black People*, 73).
12. MTSHAYANKOMO 114; compare Bryant, *Olden Times*, 491, 511-12, 548.
13. Bryant, *Olden Times*, 550.
14. MBOVU 45.
15. MABONSA 21; also Bryant, *Dictionary*, 712, cited in JSA II 305n.
16. Bird, *Annals*, 133; MQAIKANA 10.
17. Wright, 'Dynamics of Power', 230.
18. Bird, *Annals*, 133; compare Isaacs, *Travels*, I 148; Wright, 'Dynamics of Power', 234.
19. SINGCOFELA 342.
20. SINGCOFELA 342.
21. SINGCOFELA 339. SINGCOFELA dates this to 'before the mourning for Nandi' (1827), but it's more likely to have happened some years before that.
22. Bird, *Annals*, 127.
23. Wright, 'Dynamics of Power', 231; Bird, *Annals*, 133-4. It was possibly such a remnant that was found still in a state of frightened mountain-top resistance by Isaacs in 1825 (*Travels*, I 146-7).

24. Wright, 'Dynamics of Power', 232; Bird, *Annals*, 134.
25. BALEKA 11. The reference to kwaDukuza, if credible, would date this to after 1826.
26. MAZIYANA 296.
27. MAZIYANA 296. MAZIYANA was born in around 1827 in the isiBubulungu (Port Natal) area, which was hard hit by the iziYendane.
28. Apart from the violence, there were some reports of a more caring attitude:

> Shaka's *impi* did actually attack Xesibe in his original tribal lands. Xesibe and his people got into a natural fastness and successfully defended themselves for a whole day, morning till night. When the Zulus had withdrawn for the night, Xesibe said to his people, 'It is impossible for me to fight two and three more days with the Zulus; they are much too powerful.' Upon this he quitted his stronghold. It so happened that just before attacking him, the Zulus had seized a large number of cattle from the Nadi tribe . . . . Xesibe came across these and, seizing them, put them with his own. His people remonstrated, saying that he ought to give them back to the Nadi people, but he said, 'No, I have only captured what had already been captured by the Zulus; therefore they are rightly my property.' However he was afterwards . . . prevailed on to give them back to the Nadi people, then hiding in the adjoining forests . . . . When, on the following morning, the Zulus came to renew the attack against Xesibe at the stronghold, they found it completely deserted (MQAIKANA 23).

29. Bryant, surprisingly, has nothing at all to say about this unit, until in 1829 when, according to him (*Olden Times*, 667–8), Dingane gathered a crowd of 'menials and cattle-herders' from the Natal area known as iziYendane (mop-heads) into an emergency military force. I suspect that these were the remnants of the original wayward marauders, who in the early 1820s may well have been helping Dingane to pursue his own agendas in the south, as he was to continue to do through Shaka's reign.
30. MQAIKANA 13, 16, 28–9.
31. Wright, 'Dynamics of Power', 242–4.
32. Bryant, *Olden Times*, 267; compare Cope, *Izibongo*, 92.
33. For some detail, see Bryant, *Olden Times*, 267–70.
34. MAHAYA 113.
35. MQAIKANA 23.
36. Bryant, *Olden Times*, 270; compare Wright, 'Dynamics of Power', 284–5.
37. Wright, 'Dynamics of Power', 240.
38. MQAIKANA 17.
39. LUGUBU 286–7; see also LUNGUZA 298–9.
40. MADIKANE 51.
41. DINYA 98.
42. MAHAYA 113.
43. See Gamede, 'Oral History', 67–8; evidence of P. Mjoli.
44. Bird, *Annals*, 132.
45. MAHAYA 113.

46. MQAIKANA 8-9.
47. MAHAYA 117-19. Compare Peires, 'Matiwane's road to Mbholompo', in Hamilton, *Mfecane Aftermath*, 222n; Wright, 'Dynamics of Power', 305. There is an intriguing hint in Fynn's writings that Matiwane of the Ngwane might also have been involved in killing off Madikane – and an even more intriguing hint that a white man, a 'Mr Thompson', was present at the event (Stuart and Malcolm, *Diary*, 319). The best candidate for this man is Alex Thompson, Farewell's companion and the man who exchanged blows with Jacob Msimbithi on the beach at St Lucia; I can, however, find no independent verification of his presence in the Mkhomazi area in 1824-5, though Fynn was not far off.
48. MELAPI 79.
49. DINYA 95; MAGEZA 69.
50. MAGEZA 68; MAQUZA 236.
51. MAGEZA 68.
52. MELAPI 74; MTSHWEBE 159.
53. MELAPI 77.
54. MELAPI 77.
55. MAGEZA 71.
56. DINYA 115.
57. MAZIYANA 295-6.
58. DINYA 115.
59. DINYA 115.
60. MAGEZA 71.
61. MELAPI 78-9.
62. MAGEZA 71, 73. Another of Dibandlela's sons, Mkwebi, was said to have gone to the Ndwandwe, too; but on Zwide's defeat preferred to *khonza* Mzilikazi. This didn't put him entirely beyond Shaka's reach after all. However, the timing of this account doesn't make much sense; it may refer to an earlier stage of the ongoing dispute.
63. MELAPI 79; DINYA 116.
64. MELAPI 93; MTSHWEBE 159.
65. DINYA 117.
66. DINYA 117.
67. MELAPI 72.
68. MTSHWEBE 158.
69. MAQUZA 236-7; MAZIYANA 296; NGIDI 34, 70.
70. MAZIYANA 282, 286, 296. Further Thuli source material is included in Grout, *Zulu-land*, and Shooter, *Kafirs of Natal*.
71. NGIDI 63.
72. MELAPI 84.
73. MAZIYANA 297.
74. Mnini would take over during Dingane's reign, after Dingane had Mathubane murdered, forming a number of *amabutho* of his own (MAZIYANA 273, 292, 293).
75. MAGEZA 71.
76. MABONSA 22.
77. MAZIYANA 296-7.

78. MAZIYANA 272-3.

79. LUGUBU 282. The timing is wrong if we credit the solar eclipse dating (discussed on page 286). This expedition must have left the Thukela in about April 1824.

80. MAZIYANA 272-3. MQAIKANA (27) testified that the Mkhandlu *ibutho* was mauled by the Mpondo, possibly on this campaign. LUGUBU (282), by contrast, claims that the Zulu contingent met with no actual resistance.

81. MAZIYANA 273.

82. MAZIYANA 275.

83. MAZIYANA 270.

84. Stuart and Malcolm, *Diary*, 198-205; compare BAZELY 57-8.

85. Isaacs, *Travels*, I 44-5.

86. Isaacs, *Travels*, I 257.

87. MAHAYA 115. See also Taylor, *Caliban Shore*; Stuart and Malcolm, *Diary*, 111-14.

88. MAZIYANA 268-9.

89. MCOTOYI 54.

90. DINYA 97.

91. Fynn, 'Notebook', 8.

92. Fynn, 'Notebook', 45; Stuart and Malcolm, *Diary*, 111.

93. MAZIYANA 268.

94. MAQUZA 235.

95. Isaacs, *Travels*, I 55; also 65, 112, 120.

96. DINYA 96-7. DINYA was born at Magaye's *umuzi* Mhlali in about 1826, which is to say about two years after the events that he describes here.

97. *RN*, I 2.

98. *RN*, I 35-6.

99. KCM 24997, 46. The published *Diary* is more circumspect: 'a few days in connection with Farewell, Petersen [sic] and Hoffman were enough to convince me that the necessary confidence which should exist in such an undertaking did not prevail' (Cf. NA A 1382/ 17/8; Stuart and Malcolm, *Diary* 56-7).

100. King to Bathurst, 10 July 1824; *RN* I 40-2.

101. KCM 24997, 46-7. Fynn wrote several versions of this visit at different times; the purposes and dates of their composition are not clear. One version is in James Stuart's typescript (KCM 24997) closely related to Ms1230. Another is in what I call Fynn's 'Notebook', which starts only midway through this visit to Shaka. This often ungrammatical account was slightly 'fixed up' and printed in Bird's *Annals* (75ff); and more extensively rewritten by Stuart for the *Diary* (65-77).

102. Stuart and Malcolm, *Diary*, 61.

103. Quoted in Stuart and Malcolm, *Diary*, 54.

104. Fynn, 'Notebook', 2.

105. Farewell to Somerset, 6 September 1824; *RN* I 37 (emphasis added).

106. Stuart and Malcolm, *Diary*, 73.

107. Fynn, 'Notebook', 2.

108. Fynn, 'Notebook', 5.

109. DINYA, 97.

110. Owen, *Narrative*, II 222-3; compare Fynn, 'Notebook', 2-3; Gray, *Natal Papers*, 71-2; Stuart and Malcolm, *Diary*, 180-2 for a somewhat different version.
111. Fynn, 'Notebook', 6.

Box 6: The astonishing career of 'Swim-the-Seas'

1. See Hazel Crampton, *The Sunburnt Queen*. (Jacana, 2004).
2. Stuart and Malcolm, *Diary*, 180-3.
3. Isaacs, *Travels*, II 225.
4. Owen, *Narrative*, I 59, 82; Stuart and Malcolm, *Diary*, 182n.
5. Mbovu 25; Mcotoyi 58; Mkotana 222.
6. Stuart and Malcolm, *Diary*, 184.
7. Stuart and Malcolm, *Diary*, 189-208; see also W.M. Fynn to Thompson, 21 July 1831; *RN* I 197-200; and H.F. Fynn to Thompson, 21 July 1831; *RN* I 202-7.

Chapter 10: Comfortable asylum?

1. Stuart and Malcolm, *Diary*, 76n.
2. Dinya 99.
3. Fynn, 'Notebook', 3-4; compare Bird, *Annals*, 77; Stuart and Malcolm, *Diary*, 73.
4. Fynn, 'Notebook', 4.
5. Fynn, 'Notebook', 10.
6. Fynn, 'Notebook', 6.
7. Stuart and Malcolm, *Diary*, 76-7.
8. Fynn, 'Notebook', 7.
9. Fynn, 'Notebook', 12.
10. Fynn, 'Notebook', 13.
11. Maquza 232.
12. Fynn, 'Notebook', 12-15. Compare Stuart and Malcolm, *Diary*, 83-4.
13. Fynn, 'Notebook', 15, 20.
14. Ngidi (39, 62) says that Shaka was stabbed at esiKlebheni, but later agrees that it was at kwaBulawayo. Compare Thununu, JSP file 60, nbk 25, 5.
15. Makuza 169.
16. Ngidi 65.
17. Mandhlakazi 183.
18. Mandhlakazi 188-9.
19. Dinya 100.
20. Baleka 7; Madhlebe 46; Stuart and Malcolm, *Diary*, 29.
21. See also Ngidi 89-90; *JSA* I 13-14n; Stuart and Malcolm, *Diary*, 226.
22. Baleka 8; Baleni 16. Carolyn Hamilton ('Ideology', 185ff) argues that the assassination attempt was perpetrated by Qwabe 'dissidents', that Shaka pursued a policy of 'appeasement' with the Qwabe under Nqetho, who, along with Zulu kaNogandaya, became increasingly tyrannical. The information that she draws on — the same that I'm using here — to my mind doesn't adequately support her case. Interestingly, Mmemi, our most reliable Qwabe

informant, is very detailed on pre-Shakan Qwabe internal politics, and on post-Nqetho developments, but has very little to say about the Qwabe during Shaka's reign – probably because nothing much was happening.

23. KAMBI 209.
24. JANTSHI 194.
25. MBOVU 43; MELAPI 80; MMEMI 249.
26. For example, BALENI 19.
27. MBOVU 43.
28. MANDHLAKAZI 180.
29. BALENI 16; MBOVU 42; KAMBI 209; NDUKWANA 284.
30. MELAPI 82.
31. DINYA 105.
32. KAMBI 209.
33. Fynn, 'Notebook', 16. It's difficult fully to credit Fynn's account of people beginning to kill one another for not showing sufficient grief or for putting spittle in their eyes; it sounds too close to his account of Nandi's later death to be quite credible. Indeed, I wouldn't be surprised if Fynn made the whole story up; the version of his visit he offered elsewhere – written for 'your Excellency', probably the Cape governor – makes no mention of the assassination attempt at all (KCM 24997, 47). This needs pointing out in the light of Julian Cobbing's speculation that the whites were, in fact, involved in the assassination plot or plots; he suggests that some of this account may be Fynn 'writing back' from a later bid made at his own umuzi (Cobbing, 'Mfecane as Alibi', 502n; see also page 453). There seems little reason, however, to doubt the traditions' collective impression that an assassination was attempted at kwaBulawayo around this time. The dating doesn't rely wholly on Fynn, but on Farewell, too – who was not seeing eye-to-eye with Fynn at that point. We need to take seriously, however, accounts that Shaka moved to kwaDukuza because of the assassination attempt; two years seems a long time to wait to do so. MAKEWU (161) states that kwaDukuza was so named because Shaka's arm had deflected the spear from his ribs, made it go astray (dukuza'd).
34. MAKEWU 161.
35. MAKUZA 169–70; MESENI 100; NGIDI 39.
36. Fynn, 'Notebook', 10.
37. Farewell to Somerset, 6 September 1824; RN I 37–8.
38. Farewell to Somerset, 6 September 1824; RN I 37–8.
39. Farewell to Somerset, 6 September 1824; RN I 37–8. He later claimed that there were 'not more than 250 people', including 100 sent by Shaka (Cape Town Gazette, 4 June 1825; RN I 51).
40. Stuart and Malcolm, Diary, 60n. The self-interested nature of many of Fynn's writings is obscured in Stuart's compilation.
41. For example, MAZIYANA 273; see Box 8 on page 345.
42. Fynn, 'Notebook', 11.
43. Fynn, 'Notebook', 19.
44. Farewell to Somerset, 6 September 1824; RN I 37.
45. Fynn, 'Notebook', 20.

46. Stuart and Malcolm, *Diary*, 24.
47. NDUKWANA 316, 370.
48. Stuart and Malcolm, *Diary*, 25.
49. Gray, *Natal Papers*, 119.
50. BALENI 38–9. This might be the origin of *inkhosikazi* Mawa's praise-name: 'she whose neck is made of brass' (NGIDI 42).
51. LUNGUZA 310.
52. BALENI 45; MKANDO 162.
53. BALENI 45–6.
54. Gray, *Natal Papers*, 81.
55. MKANDO 162. See discussion in Hamilton, 'Ideology', 433–6.
56. See, for example, MABONSA 72.
57. Morris, *Washing of the Spears*, 46.
58. GXUBU 158.
59. Stuart and Malcolm, *Diary*, 299.
60. BIKWAYO 66.
61. Stuart and Malcolm, *Diary*, 300.
62. Gray, *Natal Papers*, 111.
63. MMEMI 245. The incident sounds like common male voyeurism to me.
64. BALEKA 11.
65. NGIDI 40. See MELAPI 85, who names a different woman altogether. There is also another very similar story, in which Shaka cuts open the nasty woman to see 'what kind of *heart* so unhospitable a person had'. It was found – not surprisingly – to lie up against the lung. (BALEKA 10).
66. BALEKA 7; BALENI 30; MMEMI 245; NDABAMBI 175.
67. JANTSHI 195.
68. NDHLOVU 219.
69. MELAPI 85.
70. LUNGUZA 337.
71. SACA, June 1826; reprinted in Thompson, *Travels*, I 247–8.
72. Morris, *Washing of the Spears*, 106.
73. MAQUZA 232.
74. GIBA 149–50.
75. BALEKA 12.
76. Stuart and Malcolm, *Diary*, 25.
77. Stuart and Malcolm, *Diary*, 27.
78. NGIDI 41, 56.
79. NGIDI 69.
80. Doke and Vilakazi, *Dictionary*, 464: *lotsholwa*, a man on whose behalf others have passed over *lobolo*. Compare MKANDO 146.
81. LUNGUZA 315, MKANDO 146. The implicit resentment underlying these accounts indicates the extent to which age-grouping was still a strong element in the organisation.
82. BALENI 35.
83. BALENI 37.

84. MTSHAPI 64–5.
85. LUNGUZA 318.
86. MBULO 51. This same Mlahla, his son boasted, was rewarded by Shaka for killing off a 'rascal', a 'giant of great strength' who preyed on his neighbours from a mountaintop (MBULO 51).
87. LUNGUZA 301, 324.
88. LUNGUZA 320.
89. MANDHLAKAZI 179.
90. NGIDI 32.
91. MELAPI 87.
92. MELAPI 87.
93. BALENI 30.
94. Jeff Opland; cited in Brown, *Voicing the Text*, 92. For an extended analysis of Shaka's *izibongo* see Brown, 75–115.
95. Rycroft and Ngcobo, *Praises of Dingana*, 25.
96. Cope, *Izibongo*, 88.
97. Socwatsha JSP File 20, 6–8; Brown, *Voicing the Text*, 89.
98. NGIDI 64.
99. MQAIKANA 28.
100. BALENI 34.
101. MAZIYANA 294.
102. Fuze, *Black People*, 52–3.
103. MQAIKANA 24.
104. Fuze, *Black People*, 52.
105. *RN* I 51; *Cape Town Gazette*, 4 June 1825.
106. Fynn, 'Notebook', 22–3.
107. Fynn, 'Notebook', 23.
108. The *Julia* had left Algoa Bay on 23 September 1824; she left Port Natal again on 1 December (*RN* I 48, 50).
109. Fynn, 'Notebook', 25–44.
110. Fynn, 'Notebook', 44–5.
111. Notarial Deed, 27 June 1825; *RN* I 52–4.
112. Hawes to Moorsom, 16 May 1825; *RN* I 49–50.
113. Stuart glosses 'amaNtusi' (Stuart and Malcolm, *Diary*, 114).
114. Fynn, 'Notebook', 46–50.
115. Fynn, 'Notebook', 51.
116. MAZIYANA 269; MCOTOYI 57.
117. For discussion of this complex term, see Etherington, *Great Treks*, 133–5.
118. Or 'Tambookies', as the white settlers insisted on calling them; not to be confused with Ngoza's Thembu.
119. Pringle to Forbes; *RN* I 61. There is an outside possibility that these people were the iziYendane, with their long proto-dreadlocks hairstyle, though the beards and swords make it unlikely and they had probably already been disbanded.
120. Mostert, *Frontiers*, 606. The question of the origins of the 'Mfengu' remains under-researched. Even Alan Webster, in his 1991 groundbreaking thesis on the Mfengu, does

not adequately penetrate the mist of generalisation spun by settler raiding and slaving. Some of the earliest arrivals, wandering into Thembu territory in 1824, may have been Zizi from the foothills of the Drakensberg, displaced by Ngwane and Chunu raids (Thompson, *Travels*, I 180–2). Zizi or Chunu offspins are, however, unlikely to have been the battle-club and hook-wielding marauders ravaging the Queenstown area at the same time (Thompson, *Travels*, I 184–5). A Xhosa informant in 1910 said that 'Fingoes' with 'big holes in their ears' – certainly a feature of Zulu-related people – arrived from the east, 'chased by Shaka', to settle with Hintsa's Xhosa (Berning, *Historical 'Conversations'*, 112, evidence of Mdandala). Others were thought of as amaMbo; the big influx was associated with Matiwane in 1828 (Berning, *Historical 'Conversations'*, 115, evidence of Mruhe). Still others, who wandered around in three or four fragmented sections, called themselves Hlubi; a substantial group under Langalibalele remained amongst the Zulu, and would lead later 'rebellions' against white rule; and at least one segment, including Pamla, grandfather of George Cory's informant Theodore Ndwandwa, arrived in the Butterworth area in around 1825. Some others were Bhele, likewise displaced by the Ngwane rather than directly by Shaka (Berning, *Historical 'Conversations'*, 118, evidence of Ndwandwa). It nevertheless became a kind of shorthand to blame everything on Shaka. Overall, the numbers of 'Mfengu', at least before 1828, were probably small. Most eventually 'came' from amongst the Xhosa people themselves.

121. One was John Thackwray. If the chronology of Fynn's 'Notebook' (50) is even roughly accurate, Thackwray was at the uMzimkhulu river in April or May 1825 – several months *before* he asked official permission to go there (Thackwray to Somerset, 4 October 1825; *RN* I 76). Communications in all directions were open, albeit slow.

122. Mqaikana 24.

123. Mqaikana 26.

124. Magidigidi 85. Magidigidi, a Chunu, was born at Shaka's *umuzi* Nobamba in about 1825, when they had been 'given refuge' amongst the Zulu (90).

125. This custom was explained by Singcofela 344:

> The wiping of the hoe (*ukwesul' isikuba*): done by those who have killed, i.e. they will rape a woman; 2 or 3 may rape the same one. They may do this to a woman of *any* tribe a long way from their own, even though not of that against which they are fighting. This woman may give birth to a child, and such child, it is said, has an *umkangu*, i.e. a mark of a different colour from the rest of the body . . . this custom is observed in regard to either married women or girls, just what comes, and if they cannot find a woman or girl, they will get a young *umsenge* tree and 'wipe off' (*sulela*) in that. It is wrong to have connection with one's own people until the 'hoe' (*isikuba*) has been 'wiped' . . .

126. Fuze, *Black People*, 52. On the subsequent history of the Fynn clan, see Bramdeow, 'Henry Francis Fynn'.

127. King to Somerset, 9 August 1825; *RN* I 67.

128. Unless there were communications happening between King and Farewell that have not been documented – as is certainly the case at other points in the history – King could not

have known anything other than Hawes's report. That Hawes *was* King's source is implied by Fynn in his 'Notebook' (52).

129. King to Somerset, 9 August 1825; *RN* I 67.
130. Wilberforce to Plasket, 20 August 1825; *RN* I 72–3.
131. *RN* I 68–71.

Box 8: The depopulation myth

1. Marks, 'Empty Land', 8.
2. Theal, *History of South Africa*; reproduced in Etherington, *Great Treks*, 336.
3. See Wright's detailed discussion of this documentation, 'A.T. Bryant and the "Wars of Shaka" '.
4. For example, MQAIKANA 8.
5. Kirby, *Andrew Smith and Natal*, 64.
6. Gray, *Natal Papers*, 99.
7. Isaacs, *Travels*, I 108, 111.
8. Gardiner, *Narrative*, 24.
9. Kotze, *American Missionaries*, 110.
10. Alden and Miller, 'Out of Africa', 198.
11. Burrows, *History of Medicine*, 64, 102; Smith, 'Khoikhoi Susceptibility', argues that these were less damaging than other factors such as land loss and famine.
12. Alden and Miller, 'Out of Africa', 209.
13. Kirby, *Andrew Smith and Natal*, 49, 107.
14. NHLEKELE 130.
15. BALENI 23. See also the longer version in Stuart's *uVusekithi*, Ch. 21, trans. E.R. Dahle, KCM 53314.
16. LEATHERN 278.

Chapter 11: Wars with words and guns

1. NDUKWANA 271.
2. See Fynn's description in Stuart and Malcolm, *Diary*, 304–5.
3. BALEKA 10.
4. Krige, *Social System*, 248–9.
5. There is some disagreement over the exact meaning of *umphakathi*; see *JSA* III 20.
6. Hamilton, 'Ideology', 440.
7. Krige, *Social System*, 247.
8. MAYINGA 251.
9. MINI 136.
10. MINI 134.
11. MAYINGA 250. MAYINGA's father was one of the few to survive these killings. Incidentally, the legend that Shaka once approached the Swazi 'queen' Mujaji to make rain for him is not supported by traditional accounts. See also Berglund, *Zulu Thought-patterns*, 54ff, for more on rain-making ceremonies.

12. Hamilton, 'Ideology', 441.
13. A certain 'silence on agriculture in the oral record is reflected in the neglect of agricultural production by scholars of the Zulu kingdom' (Hamilton, 'Ideology', 435).
14. Stuart and Malcolm, *Diary*, 284. Fynn also accused Shaka of using the *umkhosi* as an occasion for mass murder, but we can safely ignore him here.
15. NDUKWANA 270.
16. See Poland, *The Abundant Herds*. Amongst these were the so-called 'royal whites' – *inyonikayiphumuli*, or 'the bird that never rests' (the all-white cattle egret). This refers to Cetshwayo's time; Poland's wonderful book does not confirm the popular perception that Shaka started this all-white herd.
17. Koopman, *Zulu Names*, 97ff.
18. DINYA 109.
19. LEATHERN 278.
20. Fynn, 'Notebook', 108-9.
21. BAZELY 53.
22. MANGATI 214.
23. MANGATI 208.
24. Cited in Hamilton, 'Ideology', 214.
25. Hamilton, 'Ideology', 225.
26. Many of those listed by Hamilton ('Ideology', 226-7) are either wrong, or were elevated by later leaders, not by Shaka (compare Box 10 on page 391).
27. MANGATI 209.
28. MVAYISA (165) says that Mdlaka kaNcidi was *induna* of the Mdlalose.
29. Interestingly, Mvundlana is also recorded as being Mdlalose; these clans were so closely interrelated that the boundary between them is blurred (MMEMI 268).
30. NDUKWANA 377.
31. MADIKANE 52.
32. NDUKWANA 318; SHEPSTONE 298.
33. Hamilton, 'Ideology', 225.
34. MADIKANE 54-5.
35. MKANDO 150; compare DINYA 118.
36. MAGIDIGIDI 97.
37. MADIKANE 53; compare DINYA 104.
38. DINYA 104.
39. MADIKANE 47.
40. For detail see Krige, *Social System*, 30-1; MKANDO 154.
41. MAPUTWANA 230. This isn't evidence that Shaka's name originated in this way, only that he objected to the closeness of sound.
42. MAYINGA 248.
43. MAYINGA 248-9.
44. MABONSA 25.
45. *Cape Town Gazette*, 16 June 1826; *RN* I 91.
46. Gray, *Natal Papers*, 49.
47. Gray, *Natal Papers*, 67-8.

48. Gray, *Natal Papers*, 49.

49. For the one extant scrap of paper that might have been part of it, see Wylie, *Savage Delight*, 101–3. Also Wylie, *Savage Delight*, 83–100, for a fuller discussion of Isaacs and his writing.

50. It is not wholly without valuable information. I have found no reason to doubt that the dates of *Travels and Adventures* are roughly accurate (Isaacs had less need to lie about those). However, I treat with extreme caution all the content and opinion, especially the retrospective chapter 'History of Chaka', which is outrageously unbelievable. It suited many later whites, including the indefatigable A.T. Bryant, to believe it nevertheless.

51. I am following an idea of Stephen Gray's here; Gray has done a wonderful job of unpacking the Maclean mythology in several articles, his novel *John Ross: The True Story*, and his edition of Maclean's writings, *The Natal Papers of 'John Ross'*.

52. In Durban you will still find the John Ross Highway, the *John Ross* tugboat, and the John Ross Building on the dockfront, not far from where the first whites made their settlement.

53. Elizabeth Paris Watt, in her racist, racy, but well-researched novel *Febana* (1962) mentioned Maclean's accounts; so did Brian Roberts in his often acute and underrated history, *The Zulu Kings* (1974); but otherwise Maclean has been largely lost to sight.

54. The description of Fort Farewell is Maclean's (Gray, *Natal Papers*, 62).

55. Fynn's 'Notebook' (51) gives the impression that he had already just paid a visit to kwaBulawayo, after which Shaka had 'lent' him 60 men to carry his ivory to isiBubulungu. At this point he reports learning of Zwide's death and the succession of Sikhunyane. There is no sign of either tension or friendship between Fynn and Shaka at this point. The exact movements of both Fynn and Farewell remain somewhat conjectural.

56. Gray, *Natal Papers*, 71. An early example of this common but misleading comparison.

57. Extract in Isaacs, *Travels*, I 47–52; since no original journal of King's has survived, the extracts that Isaacs and Maclean both used must be treated with some caution.

58. This occurred the following morning, according to King (Isaacs, *Travels*, I 49).

59. Fynn, 'Notebook', 53. (What he'd been using all this time to kill elephants south of isiBubulungu he never says.)

60. Fynn, 'Notebook', 53–4.

61. Stuart and Malcolm, *Diary*, 119–20.

62. Isaacs, *Travels*, I 50.

63. 3–12 December 1825, 3–17 April, 19–27 July, and 5–14 November 1826. See Isaacs, *Travels*, I 58–63, 87–100, 114–16, and 127–38 respectively.

64. Isaacs, *Travels*, I 58.

65. Isaacs, *Travels*, I 62.

66. Isaacs, *Travels*, I 89, 92.

67. Isaacs, *Travels*, I 116.

68. Isaacs, *Travels*, I 131.

69. Isaacs, *Travels*, I 93.

70. Isaacs to Fynn, December 1832; in Kirby, 'Unpublished Documents', 67.

71. Fynn, KCM Ms1230, 311, 314 (emphasis added).

72. King, in Thompson, *Travels*, II 249.

73. Isaacs, *Travels*, I 59, 95.

74. Isaacs, *Travels*, I 99.

75. Isaacs, *Travels*, I 61–2.
76. JANTSHI 200; compare MAKEWU 162; MAKUZA 166; MAYINGA 259.
77. DINYA 98; compare JANTSHI 189. As we have seen, Shaka also helped Fynn to set up a post near the Mzimkhulu river.
78. MAZIYANA 269.
79. Kirby, *Andrew Smith and Natal*, 33, 38.
80. John OGLE (Wohlo's son) 218.
81. MBOVU 41; MELAPI 74. Although Isaacs, Farewell and Ogle certainly fought under Shaka, they were so frequently at loggerheads with Fynn they did not become *iziNkumbi* as such: this appellation referred mostly to Fynn's own Cape 'Hottentot' gunmen, his various local adherents, and after 1829 the coteries of his brothers.
82. MCOTOYI 58, 67.
83. Stuart and Malcolm, *Diary*, epigraph.
84. OGLE 217.
85. BAZELY 59, 61. Fynn later abandoned this burgeoning 'coloured' family, marrying two white women in succession.
86. DINYA 110–11.
87. MBOVU 44.
88. Possibly Tshaka was Fynn's son (MKANDO 187).
89. MCOTOYI 56 (emphasis added).
90. MCOTOYI 57.
91. MAZIYANA 267.
92. MAZIYANA 268. These men, plus a full company (*viyo*) of fighting men from King's *umuzi* were called up on Shaka's 1828 'Bhalule' campaign.
93. BAZELY 56.
94. SACA, 18 July 1826; also Thompson, *Travels*, II 243. King visited Shaka in December 1825; he left Port Natal in April 1826; the article was published in July. It is unclear at which point King heard about Sikhunyane, or when he means by 'now' in his statement, 'now [the Zulu] are preparing an advance against them'.
95. Isaacs, *Travels*, I 79. The name reads 'Inconyarner', in Isaacs's text – a mistranscription of 'Iseconyarner'; compare Fynn's identical spelling in 'Notebook', 54. Isaacs's editor wrongly speculates 'uNkonyane' in a footnote.
96. Isaacs, *Travels*, I 79–80. Fascinatingly, Isaacs mentions in the briefest of asides that their messenger had seen 'four vessels standing to the westward'. Were they sailing by, or waiting for something? We'll never know.
97. Fynn, 'Notebook', 54. Incidentally, Fynn says nothing, as Isaacs relates, about running into the mourning ceremonies for a revered chief, in which people were being slaughtered for failing to cry (again). I suspect that this is another later insertion, filled with references to Gold Coast 'Obeah' and other customs of which the young Isaacs was certainly ignorant at the time. They are calculated to further the book's largely fictional portrait of Shaka as an 'inhuman monster' of 'savage rage'. The underlying impulse – in 1836 when the book was published, anyway – was made pretty clear: 'it is much to be wished that . . . a dissemination of more civilised notions should be attempted . . . as may eventually root out these savage and brutal propensities' (Isaacs, *Travels*, I 89–90). In other words, colonise the brutes.

98. JANTSHI 186.

99. Wright, 'Dynamics of Power', 341.

100. Isaacs, *Travels*, I 91, 97, 99.

101. Acland to Collector of Customs, 6 May 1826; *RN* I 86.

102. See Isaacs, *Travels*, I 127. According to MELAPI, 'Siphongo' was an *induna* of King's, a Zulu, not a local Thuli. He may thus have been an appointee of Shaka (MELAPI 85).

103. King to Plasket, 26 May 1826; *RN* I 86.

104. King to Plasket, 2 June 1826; *RN* I 87.

105. For further discussion of the whites' accounts in this period, see Hamilton, *Terrific Majesty*, 36–71. Another energetic, but often inaccurate general critique of the whites' behaviour is Louis du Buisson's *The White Man Cometh*.

106. Isaacs, *Travels*, I 104–5.

107. Isaacs, *Travels*, I 114.

108. Wright, 'Dynamics of Power', 341–2.

109. Isaacs, *Travels*, I 117.

110. He also conflates the arrival of the *Helicon* with this later adventure. The 'Notebook', having 'lost' some months, abruptly restarts in May 1826. See also Stuart and Malcolm, *Diary*, 122, where Stuart inserted this date.

111. Fynn, 'Notebook', 55. Compare the somewhat smoothened version in Bird, *Annals*, 86ff.

112. MBOKODO 12.

113. Bird, *Annals*, 87.

114. Bird, *Annals*, 87; 'a hundred or two' in the 'Notebook' (57). The name there appears to be 'Isendarns'; Stuart in the *Diary* (124) glosses 'Iziyendane', a 'Bechuana tribe'; this may mean the remains of the Hlubi people still living there.

115. Fynn, 'Notebook', 58; this bit is missing from the Bird version. In the *Diary* (125), Stuart places this twenty miles to the east of Utrecht. The cave-riddled mountain, also known as Khambula, was also the site of much fighting in the Anglo-Zulu war of 1879; see Laband, *Rope of Sand*, 270–7.

116. NGIDI 70.

117. JANTSHI 186; MAGOJELA 104; NDUKWANA 276. MBOKODO (12) says 'Mhlongamvula mountain'; NGIDI (65–6) says that this was where they camped.

118. MAGOJELA 104.

119. NDUKWANA 276.

120. MBOKODO 12.

121. MAGOJELA 104.

122. Bird, *Annals*, 88–9. Compare 'Notebook', 56–61.

123. Gray, *Natal Papers*, 67–8.

124. Gray, *Natal Papers*, 68.

125. MBOKODO 12.

126. MAGOJELA 104.

127. This is almost certainly MTSHAPI kaNohadu, though the incident doesn't appear in MTSHAPI's testimony in *The James Stuart Archive*; see *JSA* IV 106ff.

128. Stuart and Malcolm, *Diary*, 127n. The fact that the Izimpholo *ibutho* was constructed by Dingane from fragments of Shaka's units after 1828 casts some doubt on the account.

129. Jantshi 186; Nduna 4.
130. Ngidi 79; compare Isaacs, *Travels*, I 128.
131. Fynn, 'Notebook', 61.
132. Gray, *Natal Papers*, 68.
133. See Bryant, *Zulu People*, 329.
134. Gray, *Natal Papers*, 68-9.
135. Mbokodo 12
136. Bird, *Annals*, 89. Isaacs also alleges the killing off of cowards, but can offer no eyewitness credibility.
137. Bird, *Annals*, 89-90; compare Fynn, 'Notebook', 62. What actually happened to the child, Fynn doesn't say.
138. 'Inquiry', 38; compare Moorsom to Christian, 24 May 1825; *RN* I 65-7, where the wreck of the *Walter Farquhar* is also mentioned, amongst other links between the coast and Madagascar slavers; also Gwyn Campbell, 'Madagascar', on the Madagascar trade. That the Port Natal traders were at the very least becoming aware of these connections is evidenced by Nathaniel Isaacs's 1832 attempt to forge a bizarre plot whereby a well-known Malagasy slaver, Ramanataka, would actually annex Natal (*RN* II 226-31).
139. Owen, *Narrative*, II 218.
140. Mahungane 143.
141. Liesegang, 'A First Look', 463.
142. Madeiros and Capela, 'La traite', 258.
143. Harries, 'Slavery', 313n.
144. Owen, *Narrative*, II 218.
145. Madeiros and Capela, 'La traite', 258.
146. Campbell to Bell, 10 October 1828; *RN* II 18; compare *RSEA* I 474, 488.
147. Madeiros and Capela disagree, but adduce no evidence to support their view ('La traite', 280).
148. Macmillan, *Bantu, Boer and Briton*, 33n.
149. Fynn, 'Notebook', 22-3.
150. Isaacs, *Travels*, I 58-62.
151. 'Private letter', *Cape Town Gazette*, 6 January 1826; *RN* I 80.
152. Isaacs, *Travels*, I 205.
153. Kirby, *Andrew Smith and Natal*, 76.
154. *RN* I 51. This was presumably John Cane, not the sailor Joseph Powell, who was later reported as having disappeared en route to the Bay (Isaacs, *Travels*, I 183; Mackeurtan, *Cradle Days*, 108), since Powell was apparently still at Port Natal in May 1825 (*RN* I 50).
155. Isaacs, *Travels*, I 95.
156. *RN* II 18.
157. Isaacs, *Travels*, I 182-5; Gray, *Natal Papers*, 65; Statement of John Cane; *RN* II 169.
158. The journey would become another legend: the brave 'John Ross' gets vital medicines through to Port Natal in the nick of time, etc. Isaacs started it:

> When I look at his youth and reflect on the country through which he had to pass, and that he had to penetrate through wild, inhospitable, and savage

tracks, in which the natives had never been blessed with the sweets of civilization nor the light of reason . . . I cannot but conceive the journey of this lad as one that must be held as exceedingly bold (Isaacs, *Travels*, I 186).

It couldn't have been an easy trip, but, in fact, Maclean had a substantial escort of Zulu men with him, supplied by an avuncular Shaka, and he took a lot less than the six months that he claimed (eighteen days one way, according to Isaacs). Moreover, there were travellers and vessels going through constantly. The *Helicon* had visited Port Natal in April 1825. The other settler Henry Ogle testified that a man named Griffiths had been coasting up and down in a boat called the *Frances*; this had mysteriously disappeared around 1826; Griffiths later turned up plying some unspecified trade between Sofala and Mombasa. The possibility that he was slaving between Port Natal and Delagoa Bay can't be dismissed (Statement of Henry Ogle; *RN* II 168-9). It was the same boat that King had tried to buy in 1826, specifically for the Natal trade (*RN* I 86-8).

159. *South African Chronicle*, 6 June 1826. We must entertain the probability that the early Delagoa Bay visits played a part in setting this up.

160. See Campbell to Bell, 26 November 1830; *RN* II 172:

[A]n American schooner named *St Michael* . . . entered Port Natal where she remained five or six weeks and landed a quantity of muskets, cutlasses, gunpowder and salt, which have been left under charge of one of the crew named Nathanial Isaaks [sic], . . . who . . . is stated to be instructing the natives in the use of fire-arms . . .

161. Fynn, 'Notebook', 105-6. It is not entirely clear, however, whether this 'immense' trade refers to Shaka's time or to the time of Fynn's writing, when this was certainly true. Fynn's *Diary* contains a couple of further cryptic references to the Zulu people slaving, but I haven't located an original document, and I regard the whole chapter in which they appear with some suspicion (Stuart and Malcolm, *Diary* 48, 55-6).

Box 9:   Shaka's *amabutho*
1. Compare list in Knight, *Anatomy of the Zulu Army*, 262-4, for slightly differing construction.

Box 10:   Shaka's *izinduna*
1. Compare list in Hamilton, 'Ideology', 390-2.

Chapter 12:   Moved by grief?
1. MAKEWU 161. Compare JANTSHI 194, evidence of NDUKWANA.
2. See, for example, Wright, 'Dynamics of Power', 345.
3. MAKEWU 161.
4. MELAPI 72-3.
5. BALENI 31. Similarly, Dingane later moved the name to a new location in emaKhosini as a home for Shaka's *idlozi* spirit (Webb and Wright, *JSA* IV 389, Note 128). It also acquired another nickname, Kwa Masangomabili, 'The place of the two gates' (MMEMI 270).

6. Fynn, 'Notebook', 71; Stuart and Malcolm, *Diary*, 137. Compare NGIDI 35.

7. Isaacs, *Travels*, I 137-8 (emphasis added).

8. NGIDI 35; MAQUZA 235. MAQUZA wrongly attaches this to the story that Sotobe brought cats back from the Cape in 1828, and that Shaka only moved to kwaDukuza then. The connection between cats and the Europeans is nevertheless intriguing.

9. Bryant, *Dictionary*, 480; cited in *JSA* V 114.

10. Berglund, *Zulu Thought-patterns*, 266.

11. Berglund, *Zulu Thought-patterns*, 269, 279-80. As I write this, South African newspapers report an increase in attacks on elderly women accused of being witches (see, for example, *ThisDay*, 23 December 2003, 1).

12. NGIDI 40-1. This story exists in multiple variations, and has been adapted by popular writers in all sorts of ways. See also BALEKA 9; JANTSHI 192, 195; LUNGUZA 330, 334-5; NDUKWANA 267; Socwatsha JSP File 70, 17 (and further discussion in the text).

13. Campbell to Bell, 10 October 1828; *RN* II 18.

14. Isaacs, *Travels*, I 103.

15. Norton to Plasket, 19 January 1826; *RN* I 80-1.

16. *RN* I 85; whether this was the one lost down the Thukela is unclear.

17. MAZIYANA (267) probably wrongly gives the initiative to Shaka: 'Shaka asked Kamu Kengi [King] to build a boat . . .' Compare MCOTOYI 66.

18. See Isaacs, *Travels*, I 135-6.

19. Isaacs, *Travels*, I 128. Even Isaacs, unlike later popular myth-makers, realised that Shaka's *impis* were not invincible.

20. 'Extracts from a Private Letter', *Cape Town Gazette*, 6 January 1826; *RN* I 79-80.

21. Isaacs, *Travels*, I 149.

22. Isaacs, *Travels*, I 154.

23. Isaacs, *Travels*, I 152-5.

24. Isaacs, *Travels*, I 135.

25. Isaacs, *Travels*, I 157-8.

26. Bird, *Annals*, 90; Fynn, 'Notebook', 63.

27. MAGIDIGIDI 97.

28. Bird, *Annals*, 90. This account is unsupported elsewhere. It would have involved an unlikely eastward deviation along the north bank of the Phongolo, to the vicinity of present-day Jozini. The only Mlotsha attested to in *The James Stuart Archive* is a Bomvu chieftain, Mlotsha kaMatomela, who migrated to the Basuto around 1828 (SINGCOFELA 345). Bryant's account is wholly based on Fynn, and it's possible that Fynn is thinking of later attacks on one Mlotsha in the 1830s (Bryant, *Olden Times*, 602-3).

29. This is presumably the uBhekenya. Stuart changed this to ' "Warmth", or in the Zulu "Motha"' in the *Diary* (129); compare Bird, *Annals*, 90; Fynn, 'Notebook', 63, is illegible at this point. No other *ibutho* fits. In editing Fynn's *Diary*, Stuart, in one of his more vigorous pieces of doctoring, inserts a whole account, rather obviously derived from Isaacs, to bring it all into line. Fynn makes no mention of white involvement here.

30. Isaacs, *Travels*, I 159 (emphasis added).

31. Isaacs, *Travels*, I 159.

32. BALENI 18; Isaacs, *Travels*, I 174.

33. MAZIYANA 267.
34. Isaacs, *Travels*, I 166–71.
35. BALENI 18.
36. Isaacs, *Travels*, I 179.
37. Isaacs, *Travels*, I 174–9 (emphasis added). See also discussion in Wright, 'Dynamics of Power', 347–8; Hedges, 'Trade and Politics', 236–7.
38. MAKEWU 163.
39. Etherington, *Great Treks*, 130–2.
40. Campbell to Bell, 10 October 1828; *RN* II 18.
41. Mackay to Plasket, 8 August 1828; *RN* I 133; cited in Etherington, *Great Treks*, 156.
42. NGIDI 54; see also Webb and Wright, *JSA* V 104, Note 186.
43. NGIDI 54.
44. MAKEWU 163.
45. Isaacs, *Travels*, I 180. The 'immense river' is a bit of a mystery; the 'easterly direction' may be incorrect. If it was the Orange river, the 'yellow' mounted men might have been Griquas.
46. Isaacs, *Travels*, I 180.
47. Ellenberger, *History of the Basuto*, 176.
48. Ellenberger, *History of the Basuto*, 176–8. Compare Moloja, *Cape Quarterly Review*, 1881–2; see differently worded version in Peires, 'Matiwane's Road', in Hamilton, *Mfecane Aftermath*, 219. Also Arbousset and Daumas, *Narrative*, 307; Van Warmelo, *History of Matiwane*, 26–8.
49. DINYA 103.
50. MQAIKANA 26.
51. Fynn, KCM Ms1230, 310.
52. This dating is based on Isaacs; Fynn claimed that it happened in June (KCM Ms1230, 273); Stuart adjusts this loosely in the *Diary*, 131.
53. Fynn, KCM Ms1230, 273; compare Fynn, 'Notebook', 66; Stuart and Malcolm, *Diary*, 132–3.
54. Fynn, KCM Ms1230, 274.
55. MCOTOYI 67.
56. Fynn, KCM Ms1230, 274.
57. Fynn, KCM Ms1230, 275.
58. Stuart and Malcolm, *Diary*, 135; compare Fynn, 'Notebook, 69.
59. Isaacs, *Travels*, I 197–8.
60. Fynn, KCM Ms1230, 275.
61. KCM 24997, 34; Stuart and Malcolm, *Diary* 134.
62. Kayser to London Missionary Society, 18 October 1828; SOAS LMS Records Box 11, Folder 2b.
63. Isaacs, *Travels*, I 199–200.
64. For example, JANTSHI 194–5; MBOVU 31.
65. DINYA 100; compare MELAPI 85.
66. NDUKWANA 327.
67. BALENI 19.
68. LUNGUZA 307.

69. Lunguza 311.
70. Mabonsa 21. A Langeni relative of Nandi's, Ngunuza, was also said to have fled to the Mpondo at this time, though no reason is given (Mbovu 31).
71. Bazely 57.
72. Ngidi 35, 72.
73. Baleka 8; Magidi 8; Maquza 232; Ndukwana 330.
74. Lunguza 311.
75. Mgidhlana 109.
76. Mabonsa 22.
77. Madhlebe 45.
78. Mkehlangana 218.
79. Ngidi 35.
80. Fynn, KCM Ms1230, 276.
81. Socwatsha, JSP File 70, 102. Gala was later murdered by Dingane for expressing regret at Shaka's death.
82. Fynn, KCM Ms1230, 276.
83. Ndukwana 292. According to the same informant, a comet – an *ubaqa* (literally, a torch) – appeared in the sky, and people threw pieces of burning wood at it; but he appears to be confusing this with the later burial of Mawa; see Ndukwana 305.
84. Fynn, KCM Ms1230, 276
85. Fynn, KCM Ms1230, 276. This became intertwined with the various cutting-open-the-pregnant-woman stories; that it was untrue is all but confirmed here.
86. McWhirter, *Guinness Book of World Records* (Guinness Publishing: Enfield, 1975), 195.
87. Fynn, KCM Ms1230, 313.
88. Lunguza 333-4 (slightly edited for brevity). The words 'doctor' and 'wizard', so different in their connotations in English, are Stuart's translations of *isangoma* or *inyanga*.
89. Lunguza 330-1. He also names three *izinyanga* who 'smelt' correctly and were spared, all of them Dladla people; compare those named in Ngidi's version, cited earlier in this chapter. Informants like to claim that diviners of their own folk were the honest and clever ones.
90. Socwatsha, JSP File 70, 17.
91. Jantshi 192 (slightly edited for brevity).
92. Baleni 19.
93. Compare Stuart and Malcolm, *Diary*, 32 and 308.
94. Stuart and Malcolm, *Diary*, 31.
95. Berglund, *Zulu Thought-patterns*, 97-8.
96. Berglund, *Zulu Thought-patterns*, 136.
97. Stuart and Malcolm, *Diary*, 31-2; another version on 308.
98. Stuart and Malcolm, *Diary*, 33-4. Suffice it to say that these – the appearance of an *idlozi* snake; the calling of a diviner to the underworld of the shades – are fairly common phenomena in Zulu belief.
99. Isaacs, *Travels*, I 277-9.
100. Isaacs, *Travels*, I 279-80. Bryant (*Olden Times*, 634-9), spins this out even further, and connects it to Shaka's alleged rampant sexuality. See the discussion in Wylie, *Savage Delight*, 176-8.

101. Isaacs, *Travels*, I 281.
102. Stuart and Malcolm, *Diary*, 152; compare Fynn's rather less eloquent but substantially similar original, 'Notebook', 86. Stuart, characteristically, omits Fynn's crucial phrase 'as an example', which makes Shaka's political and disciplinary logic clearer.
103. Stuart and Malcolm, *Diary*, 151-2. This is probably just, though it's largely Stuart's formulation, not Fynn's; compare Fynn, 'Notebook', 85.
104. MAGIDIGIDI 96.
105. BALEKA 8.
106. BALEKA 12.
107. LUGUBU 290; but note well: 'chiefs', not just Shaka. Compare LUNGUZA 314.
108. MELAPI 87.
109. MBOVU 41; MCOTOYI 65-6.
110. MAZIYANA 293-4.
111. MTSHAPI 92-3; he is relating the eyewitness account of his father Noradu. The word *ifotsholo* is derived from the English 'shovel', reminding us that this account is not a pure pre-colonial product.
112. A.T. Bryant, relating the tale in jocular fashion in *Olden Times* (641), highlights it as an unusually *humane* act on Shaka's part. E.A. Ritter, claiming to draw on alternative sources for *Shaka Zulu* (178), found the whole story improbable – and for once he might be right.
113. Thompson, *Travels*, II 247-8.
114. Fynn, KCM Ms1230, 308.
115. Fynn, KCM Ms1230, 315.
116. Fynn, KCM Ms1230, 315.
117. Stuart and Malcolm, *Diary*, 151; Fynn, 'Notebook', 85.
118. *The Colonist*, 19 August 1828; Hamilton, *Terrific Majesty*, 46.
119. *SACA*, 15 December 1828.
120. Gray, *Natal Papers*, 110.
121. Gray, *Natal Papers*, 109-11.
122. MELAPI 87. See Carolyn Hamilton's argument in *Terrific Majesty*. However, *all* the Zulu sources whom Hamilton cites are James Stuart's informants; although some of them were all but eyewitnesses themselves, their testimonies were only being *recorded* in the 1890s and 1910s, by which time their memories may have been seriously compromised by stories arising well after Shaka's death. Nevertheless, the essential point is taken.
123. MBOVU 43.
124. BALENI 19; compare BALEKA 7; MANGATI 217.
125. MKHEBENI 205.
126. MANGATI 217; he was said to have been copying someone else, one Mxamama.
127. NDUKWANA 263.
128. BALENI 19, 29; compare BALEKA 7; JANTSHI 195.
129. BALEKA 7.
130. Fynn, KCM Ms1230, 315. Bryant (*Olden Times*, 614-15) offers a lurid necromantic version, dating it, on no obvious evidence, to late 1828.
131. NGIDI 89-90. Confirmed by Bryant (*Olden Times*, 615n), who also names Mgoduka and Mpezulu as Dingane's victims.

132. MASUKU 239. There is no corroboration for such a mission by these particular men.
133. MELAPI 86.
134. MELAPI 86.
135. Gray, *Natal Papers*, 72. The very existence of such an *indaba* or council has been virtually erased from the historical record. Many of Shaka's decisions were almost certainly not his alone.
136. MELAPI 81; MMEMI 246; Stuart, *uTulasizwe*, Ch. 36, trans. E.R. Dahle, KCM 53299.
137. BALEKA 11.
138. BALEKA 12.
139. JANTSHI 179.
140. BALENI 17.
141. MCOTOYI 67.
142. MADIKANE 58.
143. MADIKANE 59.
144. MADIKANE 62.
145. MCOTOYI 66.
146. MKANDO 184.
147. NGIDI 40.
148. Fynn, KCM Ms1230, 314.
149. Fynn, KCM Ms1230, 316.
150. MELAPI 87.
151. MBULO 51.
152. MADIKANE 50.
153. Gray, *Natal Papers*, 132.
154. Gray, *Natal Papers*, 68.
155. Gray, *Natal Papers*, 68.
156. NGIDI 65.
157. Gray, *Natal Papers*, 113.
158. MANDHLAKAZI 189. The language here already bears the imprint of James Stuart's prejudices.
159. MANGATI 214.
160. BALEKA 7.
161. Gray, *Natal Papers*, 130.
162. DINYA 114.
163. MADIKANE 50; also NGIDI 67.
164. MCOTOYI 55-6.
165. Fynn, KCM Ms1230, 278.
166. MAYINGA 248.

Chapter 13:   White mischief
1. Philipps, *1820 Settler*, 325.
2. Bourke to Goderich, 15 October 1827; *RN* I 151-3.
3. Somerset to Bourke, 31 August 1827; *RN* I 142. 'Powana' is probably Bawana; see Peires, *The House of Phalo*, 89.

4. SOAS, World Mission Society archive, Box 301, microfiche 57, 59; Hammond-Tooke, *William Shaw*, 83-4.
5. Compare Philipps, 27 February 1828, *1820 Settler*, 328.
6. Campbell to Bell, 10 October 1828; *RN* II 16-17.
7. Mackay to Plasket, 26 July 1827; *RN* I 119-20.
8. Mackay to Plasket, 8 August 1827; *RN* I 132-5; compare Philipps, *1820 Settler*, 324.
9. MAZIYANA 266.
10. 'Statement of John Cane', 10 November 1828; *RN* II 28-31.
11. MAKUZA 166-7.
12. 'Notarial Deed', 24 May 1828; *RN* II 36-8.
13. Farewell to Dundas, 10 September 1828; *RN* II 10.
14. *RN* II 37.
15. Isaacs, *Travels*, I 135.
16. *RN* II 37.
17. *RN* II 38.
18. Isaacs, *Travels*, I 181; entry for 15 April 1827. I speculate that it may have had something to do with the arrival of another boat 'from the Kowie [river in the eastern Cape]', which had come up on 'Speculation, taking Stores etc to purchase the Ivory collected' (Philipps, 19 March 1828, *1820 Settler*, 334).
19. It was at this point that Maclean made his own trip to Delagoa Bay, with Shaka's help (see page 386).
20. Farewell to Dundas, 10 September 1828; *RN* II 10.
21. Isaacs, *Travels*, I 191. Fynn makes no mention of this meeting.
22. Isaacs, *Travels*, I 192. Fynn claims that Shaka also promised to send King George six young girls (Stuart and Malcolm, *Diary*, 141; compare Fynn, NA A 1382/17/7). We hear nothing more of them, however.
23. Isaacs, *Travels*, I 201-11. See Fynn's extended portrait of Msimbithi in Stuart and Malcolm, *Diary*, 196-8.
24. Isaacs, *Travels*, I 209-10.
25. *RN* II 38.
26. Isaacs, *Travels*, I 211.
27. MAKEWU 162; MELAPI 73.
28. MAYINGA 247, 252-4, 257; MELAPI 81.
29. Statement of John Cane, 10 November 1828; *RN* II 28-31.
30. MAZIYANA 266-7.
31. Farewell to Somerset, 10 September 1828; *RN* II 8-9.
32. Cloete to Bell, 27 June 1828; *RN* I 185-6. Compare Philipps, *1820 Settler*, 337; JANTSHI 186.
33. JANTSHI 198.
34. MQAIKANA 21.
35. MTSHAPI 82.
36. Fynn, KCM Ms1230, 277.
37. MAZIYANA 274. A unit not mentioned elsewhere; Stuart thought it was another name for the Icenyane (see MKANDO 146).

38. Mmemi 245-6. Mmemi also names Sotobe as being present, but obviously if my timing is right he couldn't have been. Compare Stuart and Malcolm, *Diary*, 144, where Fynn also mentions Maphitha's presence. Fynn claims that Shaka told the army to 'exterminate the whole of the tribes between him and the Colony' – and then gave secret orders to Maphitha not to. The general confusion in Fynn's account reflects his need to cover up his own role.
39. Mtshapi 82.
40. Mahaya 110.
41. Shrewsbury to WMS, Box 301, microfiche 62.
42. Stuart and Malcolm, *Diary*, 146-7. In fact, as we will see, the role of Fynn and of some of those 'minor chiefs' was much darker than this.
43. Dinya 95; Mcotoyi 55.
44. Mahaya 110.
45. This may be the 'Umyaykie' mentioned by William Shaw as having supported Faku in rebuffing a 'Fetcani' attack in early 1828 (Hammond-Tooke, *William Shaw*, 132).
46. Stuart and Malcolm, *Diary*, 156.
47. Cobbing, 'Mfecane as Alibi', 511.
48. Stuart and Malcolm, *Diary*, 124, 156; compare Fynn, 'Notebook', 57.
49. Mahaya 113-14.
50. Gardiner, *Narrative*, 312.
51. Mqaikana 19.
52. Qalizwe 249.
53. Mkando 185, 194.
54. Ogle 218.
55. Mqaikana 7-8.
56. I am particularly indebted here to discussion in Cobbing, 'Grasping the Nettle', 29; and 'Tainted Well', 49-51.
57. Melapi 83.
58. Mmemi 246.
59. Francis to Bell, 9 May 1828; *RN* I 154.
60. Green to Bell, 9 May 1828; *RN* I 154-5.
61. Van der Riet to King, 8 May 1828; *RN* I 156.
62. King to Van der Riet, 10 May 1828; *RN* I 156-7.
63. King to Van der Riet, 10 May 1828; *RN* I 156-7.
64. Philipps, 13 June 1828, *1820 Settler*, 337-8.
65. King to Van der Riet, 10 May 1828; *RN* I 156-7.
66. Stuart and Malcolm, *Diary*, 141, 143-52.
67. Bell to Van der Riet, 15 May 1828; *RN* I 158-9.
68. King to Van der Riet, 24 May 1828; *RN* I 163-4.
69. Bell to Commandant of the Frontier, 16 May 1828; *RN* I 160; Somerset to Bell, 22 May 1828; *RN* I 160-1.
70. C. Mill to Bell, 30 May 1828; *RN* I 166.
71. Bell to Van der Riet, 29 May 1828; *RN* I 164.
72. Bird to Bell, 30 May 1828; Bell to Francis, 30 May 1828; *RN* I 165-6.
73. King to Bourke, 6 June 1828; *RN* I 167-8.

74. King to Van der Riet, 6 June 1828; *RN* I 168-9.
75. Van der Riet to Bell, 7 June 1828; *RN* I 169-70.
76. Shrewsbury to Somerset, 12 June 1828; *RN* I 173-4. It is this information that is reflected in Somerset's note to Dundas, 15 June 1828; *RN* I 173; and in Stephen Kay's journal entry, written at Mount Coke on 18 June; WMS Box 301, microfiche 60. In other words, there was a single source, which was only partly right, for the rumour. Further rumour, or James Saunders King, would pump this up to *30 000* Zulu poised on the Mzimvubu (Philipps, 13 June 1828, *1820 Settler*, 338).
77. Bell to Somerset, 13 June 1828; CA, CO 4893, 254.
78. Bell to Cloete, 14 June 1828; *RN* I 172-3.
79. Somerset to Bell, 20 June 1828; *RN* I 175.
80. Somerset to Bell, 27 June 1828; *RN* I 184.
81. Thomson to Somerset, 25 July 1828; *RN* I 184-5.
82. Dundas to Bourke, 20 June 1828; *RN* I 175-6.
83. Bell to Dundas, 21 June 1828; *RN* I 180-1. This order was issued before the council had received Dundas's opinion that such an expedition seemed no longer necessary.
84. Brownlee to Campbell, 2 July 1828; *RN* I 197.
85. Kay, Journal, 23 June 1828; WMS Box 301, microfiche 60. Compare William Shaw's journal entry for 25 June 1828 (Hammond-Tooke, *William Shaw*, 129). Philipps also heard that the chief Vusani had received a message from Shaka: 'I hear you are a strong man, I am coming to see if it is true' (Philipps, 13 June 1828, *1820 Settler*, 338).
86. Isaacs, *Travels*, I 216ff. The detailed conversations that Isaacs claims to recall verbatim don't add much to our understanding; they are probably fictitious.
87. Cloete to Bell, 27 June 1828; *RN* I 185-6 (emphasis added).
88. Cloete to Bell, 4 July 1828; *RN* I 191-3.
89. WMS Box 301, microfiche 61.
90. Kay, Journal; WMS Box 301, microfiche 60.
91. Shaw to Somerset, 8 July 1828; *RN* I 204-5.
92. Shrewsbury to Somerset, 2 July 1828; *RN* I 203-4.
93. Dundas to Somerset, 7 July 1828; *RN* I 227.
94. *RN* I 204.
95. See also Shaw's journal entry for 23 July 1828 (Hammond-Tooke, *William Shaw*, 136).
96. Dundas to Somerset, 15 August 1828; *RN* I 271-8.
97. Somerset to Bell, 16 January 1829; *RN* II 77-8.
98. Mitford-Barberton, *Holden Bowker*, 57. Bowker also 'remembered' that the raiders were 'a regiment of Zulus under Natawana [Matiwane?] that had deserted from Dingaan'. This is tantalising but unreliable.
99. Farewell to Somerset, 10 September 1828; *RN* II 8-9.
100. Farewell to Barrow, 15 March 1829; *RN* II 133. OGLE's own son indicated that his father habitually accompanied Shaka's *impis* on their raids (OGLE 218).
101. Quoted in Macmillan, *Bantu, Boer and Briton*, 19.
102. 'Statement of John Cane', 4 February 1829; *RN* II 96.
103. 'Re-examination of John Cane', 11 November 1828; *RN* II 32.
104. Fynn to Somerset, 9 September 1828; *RN* II 74-5.

105. Fynn, KCM 24997, 27–8.
106. Fynn, KCM 24997, 40. James Stuart, who typed up this script, noted in the margin that Fynn sometimes wrote of himself in the third person.
107. See Peires, *House of Phalo*; Van Warmelo, *History of Matiwane*, 50–4. However, see Hammond-Tooke, *William Shaw*, 132.
108. Isaacs, *Travels*, I 227–8.
109. Isaacs, *Travels*, I 216.
110. King to Cloete, 5 July 1828; *RN* I 211–12; also King to Van der Riet, 13 July 1828; *RN* I 219–20.
111. Cloete to King, 5 July 1828; CA GH 19/3, 167.
112. King to Cloete, 11 July 1828; *RN* I 213–14.
113. Bell to Cloete, 11 July 1828; *RN* I 207; Bourke to Skipsey, 13 July 1828; *RN* I 218–19.
114. Cloete to Bell, 18 July 1828; *RN* I 227–9.
115. Cloete to Bell, 11 July 1828; *RN* I 209–10.
116. King to Cloete, 18 July 1828; *RN* I 229–30; Cloete's reply; *RN* I 230; Bell to Cloete, 18 July 1828; *RN* I 234–5.
117. *RN* I 229.
118. Cloete to Bell, 25 July 1828; *RN* I 237–8.
119. Copy made by notary John Anthony Chabaud, 29 July 1828; *RN* I 247–8. The man 'Karchey' is a bit of a mystery. Isaacs never mentions the document at all.
120. King to Cloete, 29 July 1828; *RN* I 246–7.
121. 'Statement of John Cane', 13 November 1828; *RN* II 33.
122. Scholefield, *Great Elephant*, 36.
123. Fynn also claimed, retrospectively, that this was so – in which case why had *he* not countersigned this document? (Fynn, KCM 24997, 36).
124. 'Statement of John Cane', 13 November 1828; *RN* II 33.
125. King to Cloete, 29 July 1828; *RN* I 246–7.
126. King to Cloete, 29 July 1828; *RN* I 246–7.
127. Bell to Somerset, 30 July 1828; *RN* I 250.
128. Cloete to King, 30 July 1828; *RN* I 248.
129. Bourke to Huskisson, 1 August 1828; *RN* I 251.
130. Bourke to Huskisson, 26 August 1828; *RN* I 268–9.
131. Bell to Cloete, 8 August 1828; CO 4893, 291–2.
132. Van der Riet to Evatt, 2 August 1828; *RN* I 253.
133. Bell to Cloete, 15 July 1828; *RN* I 223.
134. *RN* I 247.
135. Cloete to Bell, 7 August 1828; *RN* I 255.
136. Rose, *Four Years*, 62.
137. Rose, *Four Years*, 62–3.
138. Rose, *Four Years*, 63.
139. Kay to WMS, ? August 1828; WMS Box 301, microfiche 62.
140. Philipps, *1820 Settler*, 345.
141. Dundas to Somerset, 15 August 1828; *RN* I 271–8.
142. Van Wyk to Somerset, 21 August 1828; *RN* I 261–2.

143. Moloja, cited in Peires, 'Matiwane's Road', in Hamilton, *Mfecane Aftermath*, 233.
144. Mhlanga, cited in Peires, 'Matiwane's Road', in Hamilton, *Mfecane Aftermath*, 234.
145. Somerset to Bourke, 23 August 1828; RN I 265-6.
146. Cobbing, 'Mfecane as Alibi', 502n.
147. Davis to WMS, Box 301, microfiche 62.
148. Stockenström, *Autobiography*, 279-80; Kay, *Travels*, 330-1.
149. Somerset to Bourke, 29 August 1828; RN I 88-91.
150. SACA, 13 December 1828.
151. Isaacs, *Travels*, I 230-1.
152. Isaacs, *Travels*, I 237-8.
153. Isaacs, *Travels*, I 240.
154. NDUNA 5.
155. MAQUZA 235. This doesn't really correlate with the move to kwaDukuza. It's probably apocryphal, though not impossible; the Europeans, after all, brought more horses back with them, and had always had dogs.
156. 'Statement of John Cane', 10 November 1828; RN II 28-31; 'Statement of Macomba', 11 November 1828; RN II 31-2. Fynn said 86 tusks (Stuart and Malcolm, *Diary*, 143).
157. 'Memorandum for John Cane'; RN II 43.
158. Farewell to Dundas, 10 September 1828; RN II 11.
159. 'Statement of John Cane', 10 November 1828; RN II 30.
160. The 30-year-old 'Managarda' was also named as being in the party; 'Statement of Managarda', 10 November 1828; RN II 27-8; Cane listed his five companions as 'Managarda, Pangia, Nomama, Macomba, and Mushleiva'; RN II 30.
161. Shrewsbury to WMS, 30 September 1828; Box 301, microfiche 62; Campbell to Bell, 10 October 1828; RN II 16-17; Farewell to Dundas, 10 September 1828; RN II 10-13; 'Message from Chaka'; RN II 20.
162. 'Statement of John Cane', 7 October 1828; RN II 19. If this was not just another white ploy for land, it would nullify any other 'grants' Shaka is supposed to have made.
163. 'Statement of Monagali', 8 October 1828; RN II 19-20.

Chapter 14:   Death and the aftermath

1. NDUKWANA 315.
2. MTSHAPI 80.
3. MELAPI 83.
4. Isaacs, *Travels*, II 19.
5. Fynn, KCM 24997, 39.
6. Fynn, KCM 24997, 40-1.
7. Fynn, KCM 24997, 41; compare 'Notebook', 87; Stuart and Malcolm, *Diary*, 145-53.
8. RN II 75.
9. Bryant, however, also proposes *two* 'Bhalule' campaigns, the first in 1827. There is no oral traditional support for this earlier one, and they sound so similar that he is certainly wrong (*Olden Times*, 604, 626).

10. Stuart and Malcolm, *Diary*, 153. I can find no independent confirmation of the existence of these chiefs; in fact, James Stuart inserted them. These distances also do not make great sense.

11. Stuart and Malcolm, *Diary*, 153.

12. GIBA 149-50. GIBA (Sobhuza's son) does call Zwide's Ndwandwe 'Zulus', though, occasioning some confusion. Sobhuza was said to have given his daughter Mphandzeze to Shaka as a wife (but she was killed when found to be pregnant); but she was probably given in fact to Zwide.

13. MSIMANGA 41.

14. Bonner, *Kings, Commoners*, 38-9.

15. In another tradition, Shaka's mother is said to have restrained Shaka from harming Sobhuza (Bonner, *Kings, Commoners*, 241). At any rate, Shaka seems to have been inclined to be hospitable in this case.

16. Isaacs, *Travels*, II 19-20.

17. This echoes one (wrong, but significant) tradition that Soshangane was at this time located on the Mkhuze river, between Delagoa Bay and St Lucia (JANTSHI 187).

18. Aitchison to Bell, 19 December 1828; *RN* II 60 (emphases in original).

19. Farewell to Dundas, 10 September 1828; *RN* II 11.

20. MAYINGA 249.

21. MAYINGA 250.

22. Fynn, KCM 29447, 42; 'Notebook', 87; Stuart and Malcolm, *Diary*, 153.

23. Unit names change confusingly, but the consensus seems to be that the Ingcobinga *ibutho* or section was formed earlier by Shaka, and only after Shaka's death was this thrown together with other units by Dingane, who then called the collection iziNyosi (LUNGUZA 304; MAGIDIGIDI 95-6; MAQUZA 235; MCOTOYI 55).

24. MAYINGA 250.

25. MAYINGA 250. There is no other information on 'Nhlanganiso' – just *possibly* these were the dissident Nhlangwini people under Fodo.

26. NGIDI 75.

27. Bryant, *Olden Times*, 604-6.

28. Doke and Vilakazi, *Dictionary*, 22.

29. BALEKA 6.

30. MQAIKANA 8.

31. Liesegang, 'Migrations', 336; Newitt, *History of Mozambique*, 258-60.

32. For example, Hammond-Tooke, *William Shaw*, 87.

33. NDUKWANA 279.

34. DINYA 95; compare MCOTOYI 56.

35. MTSHAPI 80; the *umkandhli* were women of the *isigodlo* who had washed – or menstruated.

36. MTSHAPI 77.

37. MTSHAPI 80.

38. Liesegang, 'A First Look', 463.

39. Isaacs, *Travels*, I 284.

40. Campbell to Bell, 10 October 1828; *RN* II 17-18. Compare NGIDI (75), who with a broad brush classifies 'Matshakane' as Swazi.

41. Smith, 'Struggle for Control', 285. Smith claims that Shaka and Soshangane clashed well north of the Bay at Bilene, but presents no coherent evidence or detail to support this (305–6).

42. MAKEWU 163. The timing of this Xhosa venture is very elusive.

43. Fynn, 'Notebook', 87; KCM 29447, 42.

44. MKEHLANGANA 217.

45. JANTSHI 187; but why not avenge himself directly on Faku? This doesn't make much sense to me.

46. MAZIYANA 297.

47. Wright, 'Dynamics of Power', 368. Alternatively, the whites' contingents were going along for their own purposes, such as offloading slaves at the Bay, but there is no real evidence for this.

48. See MAZIYANA 275.

49. DINYA 95.

50. MKEHLENGANA 217.

51. JANTSHI 187.

52. JANTSHI 191; MAYINGA 250.

53. MTSHAPI 80; BALEKA 6.

54. JANTSHI 187.

55. Isaacs, Travels, II 21. 'Doctor' Bryant quite arbitrarily diagnoses 'malignant dysentery'.

56. JANTSHI 187.

57. Campbell to Bell, 10 October 1828; RN II 16–17.

58. Aitchison to Bell, 19 December 1828, RN II 59–60.

59. Stephen Kay, cited in Isaacs, Travels, I 248.

60. Isaacs to Cole, 19 December 1828; RN II 56–9.

61. Isaacs, Travels, I 243–6.

62. Julian Cobbing has suggested this option ('Grasping the Nettle', 28). It seems to me unlikely that Isaacs would have covered up a murder, whatever his professed scruples about protecting the dead – though even then he alludes darkly to 'knowledge' about Farewell that he will not divulge (Travels, I 249).

63. Stuart and Malcolm, Diary, 155.

64. Stuart and Malcolm, Diary, 155; Isaacs to Cole, 19 December 1828; RN II 58; Isaacs, Travels, I 291.

65. Stuart and Malcolm, Diary, 155; Isaacs, Travels, I 255.

66. Stuart and Malcolm, Diary, 155; then echoed by Isaacs (Travels, I 256); a curious discrepancy in Isaacs's version. As usual there must be more here than meets the eye.

67. For example, Stuart and Malcolm, Diary, 157.

68. Fynn, 'Notebook', 88.

69. Isaacs, Travels, I 256.

70. JANTSHI 187.

71. JANTSHI 187.

72. MKEBENI 199. In MKEBENI's version, it is Sigujana being addressed, but we can be fairly sure that Sigujana died on Shaka's accession; it is probably Mhlangana who is meant; see the argument in JSA III 200.

73. BALEKA 6; Gray, *Natal Papers*, 111.
74. Fuze, *Black People*, 71–2.
75. Cobbing, 'Grasping the Nettle', 28–9.
76. MBOVU 31.
77. Aitchison to Cole, 19 December 1828; *RN* II 60; compare Stuart and Malcolm, *Diary*, 156, where Fynn says 400 to 500 were killed.
78. Campbell to Bell, 19 December 1828; *RN* II 52.
79. MRUYI 38.
80. Stuart and Malcolm, *Diary*, 156.
81. Gray, *Natal Papers*, 124.
82. Gray, *Natal Papers*, 111.
83. Fynn, 'Notebook', 90; Stuart and Malcolm, *Diary*, 156.
84. *RN* II 60.
85. Fynn, 'Notebook', 90. Stuart, for what it's worth, translated the name as 'Nyakomubi or Ugly Year' (Stuart and Malcolm, *Diary*, 156).
86. Fynn, 'Notebook', 90–1; compare Fynn's letter to Somerset, 28 November 1828; *RN* II 73–4.
87. Interestingly, in the *Diary* Stuart gratuitously changed it to 'Bechuanas' – the name he previously applied to Hlubi or iziYendane – but his reasons for doing this are unclear.
88. DINYA 95–6.
89. MAKEWU 163.
90. MADIKANE 59.
91. JANTSHI 194.
92. MAKEWU 163.
93. JANTSHI 194.
94. MAKEWU 163.
95. JANTSHI 194.
96. MKEBENI 206.
97. NGIDI 43.
98. Isaacs, *Travels*, I 258.
99. MTSHAPI 93–4.
100. MTSHAPI 94.
101. Fynn, 'Notebook', 92.
102. Isaacs, *Travels*, I 258.
103. Fynn, 'Notebook', 91; Stuart and Malcolm, *Diary*, 157.
104. NGIDI 64.
105. NGIDI 43.
106. LUNGUZA 312.
107. JANTSHI 191, 195–6.
108. Isaacs, *Travels*, I 289–90. This figure is exaggerated as usual, but a massacre notwithstanding. Fynn ('Notebook', 93–5) says that 30 out of 400 survived. Compare NDUKWANA 307; MAYINGA 254.
109. Fynn, 'Notebook', 95–6. Compare BALEKA 6. A slightly different version is given by Bryant, involving an actual assassination attempt on Dingane; its source is unknown (*Olden Times*, 669).

110. NDUKWANA 291. Compare JANTSHI 196, who also implicates Ngqengelele.
111. JANTSHI 194.
112. DINYA 100.
113. Stuart and Malcolm, *Diary*, 161–2.
114. Isaacs, *Travels*, I 261.
115. Isaacs, *Travels*, II 30. This was ostensibly written on 29 April 1829, but its mix of past and present tenses shows how it was rewritten in retrospect – an unsettling blend of wishful thinking and deception; it would not be long before Isaacs had to revise this opinion completely.
116. Aitchison to Bell, 19 December 1828; *RN* II 60.
117. Campbell to Bell, 19 December 1828; *RN* II 52.
118. See 'Shaka's Spirit Lives', *ThisDay*, 26 April 2004.
119. Isaacs to Cole, 20 December 1828; *RN* II 58.
120. MAGIDIGIDI 93.
121. MAZIYANA 268.
122. MANDHLAKAZI 191.
123. NDUKWANA 346.
124. NGIDI 89.
125. NDONGENI 239.
126. MSIME 49.
127. MQAIKANA 26.
128. MAYINGA 250.
129. MABONSA 17; MQAIKANA 7; Farewell to Campbell, 17 September 1829; *RN* II 139; Fynn to Bell, 16 June 1830, *RN* II 159–60.
130. Farewell wrongly reported that Sotobe was murdered 'for being one of Chaka's advisers and favourites, as well as several others', though he perceived the general trend well enough (Farewell to Bell, 19 December 1828; *RN* II 61).
131. MAQUZA 236.
132. NDHLOVU 218.
133. MAGIDI 80; MKOTANA 222–3.
134. NGIDI 64.
135. MANGATI 200.
136. DUNJWA 127; compare BALEKA 6. After Mpande defected to Natal, Dingane killed Ndlela for his bad advice – or, more likely, for losing the battle against Mpande's forces in 1839 (Laband, *Rope of Sand*, 117–18).
137. JANTSHI 198, 205.
138. MBOVU 36–8; MELAPI 81–2.
139. MBOVU 38.
140. Campbell to Bell, 19 December 1828; *RN* II 52; this was also based on independent information, contained in an overland letter sent to Cane to inform him of the assassination.
141. Isaacs to Cole, 20 December 1828; *RN* II 58.
142. Aitchison to Bell, 20 September 1828; *RN* II 64. Aitchison had been slated to go overland to see Shaka himself, but now the mission was cancelled.
143. Cole to Murray, 31 January 1829; *RN* II 85–8.

144. A flurry of acrimonious letters later exposed this for the lie it was; see *RN* II 103–7. It did not occur to anyone to wonder whether Cane was intending to feed these people into the Cape labour market – it's difficult to see what other reason the white adventurers could have had for indulging in such violent raiding as they did.

145. Bell to Somerset, 5 February 1829; *RN* II 97–8.

146. Bannister (1790–1877) was a British-born ex-soldier. He became an advocate in Australia where his 'impetuous nature and his stern condemnation of the treatment of the natives' landed him in a duel; he was impossible to work with, and suffered some mental instability. He brought his 'almost fanatical humanitarianism' to bear on the South African situation, writing his best-known polemic, *Humane Policy*, in 1838. This did not prevent him from being a vociferous member of the South African Land and Emigration Association (in which capacity he would doubtless have crossed paths with Nathaniel Isaacs), and writing *A Memoir Respecting the Colonization of Natal* in 1839 (*Dictionary of South African Biography*. Nasionale Boekhandel Beperk: Pretoria, 1968, I 50–1).

147. *RN* II 100–2

148. *RN* II 102. Bannister expanded on this document in a later submission to Sir George Murray, Secretary for Colonies, 12 May 1829; *RN* II 124–30.

149. Bell to Farewell, 2 March 1829; *RN* II 109.

150. Farewell to Bell, 11 March 1829; Bell to Colonial Office, 13 March 1829; *RN* II 117–18.

151. *RN* II 119.

152. Farewell to Campbell, 17 September 1829; *RN* II 139.

153. Farewell to Campbell, 17 September 1829; *RN* II 139.

154. Cane to Campbell, 24 October 1829; *RN* II 143.

155. Farewell to Campbell, 25 September 1829; *RN* II 140–1.

156. Cane to Shepstone, 12 October 1829; *RN* II 142–3.

157. Isaacs, *Travels*, II 13–16; he also includes an excerpt of Stephen Kay's imaginative reconstruction; compare Kay, *Travels*, 386.

158. Maziyana 269.

159. Ndongeni 240–1.

160. Laband, *Rope of Sand*, 77, 85, 93–4; Mkotana 222–3.

161. *RN* II 226–31.

162. Kirby, 'Further Facts', 237–41.

163. Isaacs, *Travels*, I vii–xiii; Fyfe, *Sierra Leone*; Kirby, 'Unpublished Documents', 'Further Facts'.

164. Gray, *Natal Papers*, 6–20.

165. Gray, *Natal Papers*, 135.

166. NA Fynn Papers, file 88.

167. Smith to D'Urban, 15 December 1835; *RN* III 23.

168. Cobbing, 'Mfecane as Alibi', 510n.

169. Mbovu 33–4.

170. Mbovu 44.

171. Mbovu 23.

172. Mbovu 29.

Select bibliography

Archival sources
(CA) Cape Archives, Cape Town.
Cory Library, Grahamstown
(KCM) Killie Campbell Museum Collection, Durban (James Stuart Papers [JSP]; Fynn Papers)
(NA) Natal Archives, Pietermaritzburg (Fynn Papers)
National Maritime Museum Library, London (Owen Papers)
(LMS) London Missionary Society Records, School of Oriental and African Studies (SOAS),
    London
(WMS) Wesleyan Missionary Society Records, School of Oriental and African Studies

Newspapers
Cape Quarterly Review
Cape Town Gazette
South African Commercial Advertiser

Collections of documents
Bird, J., ed. *Annals of Natal, 1495–1945*. Vol.1. P. Davis: Pietermaritzburg, 1988.
(RN) Leverton, B.J.T., ed. *Records of Natal*. 2 vols. Government Printer: Pretoria, 1984, 1989.
Report of the Commissioners of Inquiry upon the Slave Trade at Mauritius 1829. British University
    Press Series of British Parliamentary Papers (Slave Trade 76).
(RCC) Theal, W.McC., ed. *Records of the Cape Colony*. William Clowes: London, 1897–1905.
(RSEA) ——., ed. *Records of South East Africa*. 9 vols. William Clowes: London, 1903.
(JSA) Wright, J.B. and C. deB. Webb, eds. *The James Stuart Archive*. 5 vols. University of Natal
    Press: Pietermaritzburg, 1976–2001.
    Volume 1: ANTEL–LYLE
    Volume 2: MABELE–MAZIYANA
    Volume 3: MBOKODO–MPATSHANA
    Volume 4: MQAIKANA–NDUKWANA
    Volume 5: NDUNA–SIVIVI

Articles, books and theses

Alden, D. and J.C. Miller. 'Out of Africa: The Slave Trade and the Transmission of Smallpox to Brazil 1560–1831'. *Journal of Interdisciplinary History* 18(2), 1987: 195–224.

Allen, R.B. *Slaves, Freedmen, and Indentured Laborers in Colonial Mauritius*. Cambridge University Press: Cambridge, 1999.

Alpers, E.A. *Ivory and Slaves in East Central Africa*. Heinemann: London, 1975.

Arbousset, T. and F. Daumas. *Narrative of an Exploratory Tour of the North-east of the Colony of the Cape of Good Hope*. Struik: Cape Town, [1846] 1952.

Argyle, J. 'Who were Dingiswayo and Shaka? Individual Origins and Political Transformations'. *The Societies of Southern Africa in the 19th and 20th Centuries*. Institute of Commonwealth Studies, University of London, Collected Seminar Papers, Vol.7, 1976.

Ballard, C. 'Drought and Economic Distress: South Africa in the 1800s'. *Journal of Interdisciplinary History* 17(2), 1986: 359–78.

Bannister, S. *Humane Policy: Or Justice to the Aborigines of New Settlements*. Dawsons of Pall Mall: London, 1968.

Beach, D. 'Generational Dating'. In D. Beach. *The Shona and Zimbabwe*. Mambo Press: Bulawayo, 1980: 330–1.

Beachey, R.W. *The Slave Trade of Eastern Africa*. Rex Collings: London, 1976.

Berglund, A-I. *Zulu Thought-patterns and Symbolism*. David Philip: Cape Town, 1976.

Berning, M., ed. *The Historical 'Conversations' of George Cory*. Balkema: Cape Town, 1989.

Bonner, P. *Kings, Commoners and Concessionaires: The Evolution and Dissolution of the Nineteenth-century Swazi State*. Ravan: Johannesburg, 1983.

Botha, C.G., ed. *Collecteana*. Van Riebeeck Society: Cape Town, 1924.

Bowditch, T.E. *An Account of the Discoveries of the Portuguese in the Interior of Angola and Mozambique*. Private printing: London, 1824.

Boxer, C.R., ed. *The Tragic History of the Sea, 1589–1622*. Cambridge University Press: Cambridge, 1959.

Bramdeow, S. 'Henry Francis Fynn and the Fynn Community in Natal, 1824–1988'. MA thesis, University of Natal, Durban, 1988.

Broadbent, S. *The Missionary Martyr of Namaqualand: Memorials of the Rev William Threlfall*. London: Wesleyan Conference Office, nd.

Brown, D. *Voicing the Text: South African Oral Poetry and Performance*. Oxford University Press: Cape Town, 1998.

Bryant, A.T. *A Zulu-English Dictionary: A Synopsis of Zulu Grammar and a Concise History of the Zulu People from the Most Ancient Times*. Mariannhill Mission Press: Pinetown, 1905.

——. *Olden Times in Zululand and Natal*. Longmans: London, 1929.

——. *The Zulu People as They were Before the White People Came*. Shuter and Shooter: Pietermaritzburg, 1949.

——. *A History of the Zulu and Neighbouring Tribes*. Struik: Cape Town, [1911–13] 1964.

Burchell, W.J. *Travels in the Interior of South Africa*. 2 vols. Longman: London, 1822–4.

Burrows, E.H. *A History of Medicine in South Africa up to the End of the Nineteenth Century*. Balkema: Cape Town, 1958.

Callaway, H. *Nursery Tales, Traditions and Histories of the Zulu*. Shuter and Shooter: Pietermaritzburg, 1867.

Campbell, A.A. ["Mziki']. '*Mlimo: The Rise and Fall of the Matabele*. Books of Rhodesia: Bulawayo, [1926] 1972.

Campbell, G. 'Madagascar and the Slave Trade 1810-1895'. *Journal of African History* 22(2), 1981: 203-27.

Campbell, J. *Travels in South Africa*. 2 vols. Westley: London, 1822.

Clarence-Smith, W.G., ed. *The Economics of the Indian Ocean Slave Trade*. Frank Cass: London, 1989.

Cobbing, J. 'The Ndebele under the Khumalos, 1820-1896'. Ph.D. dissertation, University of Lancaster, Lancaster, 1976.

——. 'Jettisoning the Mfecane (with Perestroika)'. Unpublished paper, 1988.

——. 'The Mfecane as Alibi: Thoughts on Dithakong and Mbolompo'. *Journal of African History* 29, 1988: 487-519.

——. 'A Tainted Well: The Objectives, Historical Fantasies, and Working Methods of James Stuart, with Counter-argument'. *Journal of Natal and Zulu History* 11, 1988: 115-54.

——. 'Grasping the Nettle: The Slave Trade and the Early Zulu'. Unpublished paper, 1990.

——. 'Overturning the "Mfecane": A Reply to Elizabeth Eldredge'. Unpublished paper presented to 'The Mfecane Aftermath' colloquium, University of the Witwatersrand, Johannesburg, 1991.

——. 'Rethinking the Roots of Violence in Southern Africa, c. 1790-1840'. Unpublished paper, 1991.

Cooper, F. *Plantation Slavery on the East Coast of Africa*. Yale University Press: New Haven, 1977.

Cope, T. *Izibongo: Zulu Praise Poems*. Oxford University Press: Oxford, 1968.

Cowley, C. *Kwa Zulu: Queen Mkabi's Story*. Struik: Cape Town, 1966.

Deacon, H.J. and J. Deacon. *Human Beginnings in South Africa: Uncovering the Secrets of the Stone Age*. David Philip: Cape Town, 1999.

Delius, P. *The Land Belongs to Us: The Pedi Polity, the Boers and the British in the Nineteenth-century Transvaal*. Ravan Press: Johannesburg, 1983.

Diamond, J. *Guns, Germs and Steel: The Fates of Human Societies*. Jonathan Cape: London, 1997.

Doke, C.M. and B.W. Vilakazi. *Zulu-English Dictionary*. Witwatersrand University Press: Johannesburg, 1958.

Du Buisson, L. *The White Man Cometh*. Jonathan Cape: London, 1987.

Duminy, A. and B. Guest, eds. *Natal and Zululand from Earliest Times to 1910: A New History*. University of Natal Press: Pietermaritzburg, 1989.

Ellenberger, D.F. *History of the Basuto: Ancient and Modern*. Caxton Publishing Co: London, 1912.

Eltis, D. *The Rise of African Slavery in the Americas*. Cambridge University Press: Cambridge, 2000.

Etherington, N. *The Great Treks: The Transformation of Southern Africa, 1815-1854*. Pearson Education: Harlow, 2001.

Freud, S. 'Dostoevsky and Parricide'. In J. Strachey, ed., *The Standard Edition of the Complete Psychological Works* 21, 1955: 175-98.

Fuze, M.M. *The Black People and Whence They Came*. A.T. Cope, ed. University of Natal Press: Pietermaritzburg, 1979.

Fyfe, C. *A History of Sierra Leone*. Oxford University Press: Oxford, 1962.

Gamede, V.W. *The Oral History of the Bhaca of Umzimkhulu.* MA thesis, UNITRA, Umtata, 1992.

Gardiner, A. *Narrative of a Journey to the Zoolu Country in South Africa.* Struik: Cape Town, [1836] 1966.

Gill, A. *The Devil's Mariner: A Life of William Dampier, Pirate and Explorer, 1651–1715.* Michael Joseph: London, 1997.

Gluckman, M. 'The Kingdom of the Zulu in South Africa'. In M. Fortes and E. Evans-Pritchard, eds. *African Political Systems.* Oxford University Press: London, 1940: 25–55.

——. 'The Rise of a Zulu Empire'. *Scientific American* 202(4), 1960: 157–68.

——. 'The Individual in a Social Framework: The Rise of King Shaka of Zululand'. *Journal of African Studies* 1(2), 1974: 113–44.

Gray, R and D. Birmingham, eds. *Pre-colonial African Trade: Essays on Trade in Central and Eastern Africa before 1900.* Oxford University Press: London, 1970.

Gray, S., ed. *The Natal Papers of 'John Ross'* [Charles Rawden Maclean]. University of Natal Press, Pietermaritzburg, 1992.

Greisbach, R.C. 'Limpopo'. *Africana Notes and News* 15(5), 1963: 210–12.

Grout, L. *Zulu-land; or, Life among the Zulu-Kafirs of Natal and Zulu-land.* Trubner: London, 1862.

Gump, J.O. *The Formation of the Zulu Kingdom in South Africa, 1750–1840.* Mellen Research University Press: San Francisco, 1990.

Guy, J. 'Ecological Factors in the Rise of Shaka and the Zulu Kingdom'. In S. Marks and A. Atmore, eds. *Economy and Society in Pre-industrial South Africa.* Longman: London, 1980: 102–19.

——. *The Destruction of the Zulu Kingdom.* Ravan: Johannesburg, 1979.

Hall, M. 'Dendroclimatology, Rainfall and Human Adaptation in the Later Iron Age of Natal and Zululand'. *Annals of the Natal Museum* 22(3), 1976: 693–703.

——. *The Changing Past: Farmers, Kings and Traders in Southern Africa, 200–1860.* James Currey: London, 1987.

Hamilton, C. 'Ideology, Oral Traditions and the Struggle for Power in the Early Zulu Kingdom'. MA thesis, University of the Witwatersrand, Johannesburg, 1985.

——., ed. *The Mfecane Aftermath: Reconstructive Debates in Southern African History.* Witwatersrand University Press: Johannesburg, 1995.

——. *Terrific Majesty: The Powers of Shaka Zulu and the Limits of Historical Invention.* David Philip: Cape Town, 1998.

Hamilton, C. and J. Wright. 'The Making of the *AmaLala*: Ethnicity, Ideology and Relations of Subordination in a Precolonial Context'. *South African Historical Journal* 22, 1990: 3–23.

Hammond-Tooke, D., ed. *The Journal of William Shaw.* Balkema: Cape Town, 1972.

Harms, R. *The Diligent: A Voyage Through the Worlds of the Slave Trade.* Perseus Press: Oxford, 2002.

Harries, P. 'Slavery, Social Incorporation and Surplus Extraction: The Nature of Free and Unfree Labour in South-east Africa'. *Journal of African History* 22, 1981: 309–30.

Hedges, D.W. 'Trade and Politics in Southern Mozambique and Zululand in the Eighteenth and Early Nineteenth Centuries'. Ph.D. dissertation, SOAS, London, 1978.

Holden, W.C. *The Past and Future of the Kafir Races.* William Nichols: London, 1866.

Hombert, J-M. and L.M. Hyman, eds. *Bantu Historical Linguistics: Theoretical and Empirical Perspectives*. CSLI: Stanford, 1999.

Isaacs, N. *Travels and Adventures in Eastern Africa*. 2 vols. L. Hermann, ed. Van Riebeeck Society: Cape Town, [1836] 1936.

Jolly, P. 'Interaction between South-eastern San and Southern Nguni and Sotho Communities *c*.1400–1880'. *South African Historical Journal* 35, 1996: 30–61.

Kay, S. *Travels and Researches in Southern Africa*. John Mason: London, 1833.

Kinahan, J. *Cattle for Beads: The Archaeology of Historical Contact and Trade on the Namib Coast*. University of Uppsala: Uppsala, 2000.

Kirby, P.R., ed. *The Diary of Dr Andrew Smith*. 2 vols. Van Riebeeck Society: Cape Town, 1939.

——., ed. *Andrew Smith and Natal*. Van Riebeeck Society: Cape Town, 1955.

——. 'Unpublished Documents Relating to the Career of Nathaniel Isaacs, the Natal Pioneer'. *Africana Notes and News* 18(2), 1968: 63–79.

——. 'Further Facts Relating to the Career of Nathaniel Isaacs, the Natal Pioneer'. *Africana Notes and News* 18(6), 1969: 237–42.

Knight, I. *The Anatomy of the Zulu Army from Shaka to Cetshwayo 1818–1879*. Greenhill Books: London, 1995.

Koopman, A. 'Dingiswayo Rides Again'. *Journal of Natal and Zulu History* 2, 1979: 1–12.

——. *Zulu Names*. University of Natal Press: Pietermaritzburg, 2002.

Kotze, D.J., ed. *Letters of the American Missionaries, 1835–1838*. Van Riebeeck Society: Cape Town, 1950.

Krige, E.J. *The Social System of the Zulus*. Shuter and Shooter: Pietermaritzburg, 1936.

Laband, J. *Rope of Sand: The Rise and Fall of the Zulu Kingdom in the Nineteenth Century*. Jonathan Ball: Johannesburg, 1995.

'Langa, J.' (aka Geoffrey Bond). *Shaka*. Longmans: Harare, 1982.

Legassick, M.C. 'The Griqua, the Sotho-Tswana and the Missionaries, 1780–1840'. Ph.D. dissertation, University of California, Los Angeles, 1969.

Leslie, D. *Among the Zulus and Amatongas*. Private printing: Glasgow, 1875.

Liesegang, G. 'Nguni Migrations between Delagoa Bay and the Zambezi, 1821–1839'. *African Historical Studies* 3(2), 1970: 317–37.

——. 'A First Look at the Import and Export Trade of Mozambique, 1800–1914'. In G. Liesegang, H. Pasch and A. Jones, eds. *Figuring African Trade*. Dietrich Reiner: Berlin, 1986: 451–65.

Lugg, H.C. *Historic Natal and Zululand*. Shuter and Shooter: Pietermaritzburg, 1948.

Mackeurtan, G. *The Cradle Days of Natal, 1497–1845*. Longmans: London, 1930.

Macmillan, W.M. *Bantu, Boer and Briton: The Making of the South African Native Problem*. Faber and Gwyer: London, 1929.

Madeiros, E. and J. Capela. 'La traite au départ du Mocambique vers les îles françaises de l'ocean Indien'. In U. Bissoondoyai and S.B.C. Servansang, eds. *Slavery in South West India Ocean* [sic]. Mahatma Gandhi Institute: Moka, Mauritius, 1989: 255–77.

Maggs, T. 'The Iron Age Farming Communities'. In A. Duminy and B. Guest, eds. *Natal and Zululand from Earliest Times to 1910: A New History*. University of Natal Press: Pietermaritzburg, 1989: 28–48.

Manning, P. *Slavery and African Life: Occidental, Oriental and African Slave Trades.* Cambridge University Press: Cambridge, 1990.

Maré, G. *Brothers Born of Warrior Blood: Politics and Ethnicity in South Africa.* Ravan Press: Johannesburg, 1992.

Marks, S. 'South Africa: The Myth of the Empty Land'. *History Today* 30(1), January 1980: 7–12.

Mazel, A. 'The Stone Age Peoples of Natal'. In A. Duminy and B. Guest, eds. *Natal and Zululand from Earliest Times to 1910: A New History.* University of Natal Press: Pietermaritzburg, 1989: 1–27.

McEwan, C., L.A. Borrero and A. Prieto, eds. *Patagonia.* British Museum Press: London, 1997.

McMenemy, N. *Assegai!* Macmillan: London, 1973.

Miers, S. and I. Kopytoff, eds. *Slavery in Africa: Anthropological and Historical Perspectives.* University of Wisconsin Press: Madison, 1977.

Miller, J.C. *Way of Death: Merchant Capitalism and the Angolan Slave Trade, 1730–1830.* James Currey: London, 1988.

Mitford-Barberton, I. *Comdt. Holden Bowker.* Human and Roussouw: Cape Town, 1970.

Moffat, R. *The Matabele Journals of Robert Moffat 1829–1860.* 2 vols. J.P.R. Wallis, ed. Rpt. National Archives: Salisbury, 1976.

Morris, D. *The Washing of the Spears.* Sphere: London, [1966] 1973.

Morris, J. and E. Preston-Whyte. *Speaking with Beads: Zulu Arts from Southern Africa.* Thames and Hudson: London, 1994.

Mostert, N. *Frontiers.* Pimlico: London, 1992.

Newitt, M. *A History of Mozambique.* Hurst and Company: London, 1995.

Newman, J.L. *The Peopling of Africa: A Geographic Interpretation.* Yale University Press: New Haven, 1995.

Nurse G.T., J.S. Weiner and T. Jenkins. *The Peoples of Southern Africa and their Affinities.* Clarendon Press: Oxford, 1985.

Omer-Cooper, J.D. *The Zulu Aftermath: A Nineteenth-century Revolution in Bantu Africa.* Longmans: London, 1966.

Owen, W.F.W. *Narrative of Voyages to Explore the Shores of Africa, Arabia and Madagascar.* 2 vols. Richard Bentley: London, 1833.

Pearson, M.P. and K. Godden. *In Search of the Red Slave: Shipwreck and Captivity in Madagascar.* Sutton: Phoenix Mill, 2002.

Peires, J.B., ed. *Before and After Shaka: Papers in Nguni History.* Institute of Social and Economic Research, Rhodes University: Grahamstown, 1981.

——. *The House of Phalo: A History of the Xhosa People in the Days of their Independence.* Ravan Press: Johannesburg, 1981.

Philipps, T. *Philipps: 1820 Settler.* Shuter and Shooter: Pietermaritzburg, 1960.

Phillipson, D.W. *African Archaeology.* Cambridge University Press: Cambridge, 1993.

Poland, M. *The Abundant Herds: A Celebration of the Sanga-Nguni Cattle.* Fernwood Press: Vlaeberg, 2003.

Prins, F.E. and H. Lewis. 'Bushmen as Mediators in Nguni Cosmology'. *Ethnology* 31(2), 1992: 133–48.

Prior, J. *Voyage along the Eastern Coast of Africa . . . in the Nisus Frigate.* Sir Richard Phillips and Co.: London, 1819.

Rasmussen, R.K. *Migrant Kingdom: Mzilikazi's Ndebele in South Africa.* Rex Collings: London, 1978.

Ritter, E.A. *Shaka Zulu.* Longmans: London, 1955.

Roberts, B. *The Zulu Kings.* Sphere Books: London, 1974.

Rose, C. *Four Years in Southern Africa.* Henry Colburn: London, 1829.

Rycroft, D.K. and A.B. Ngcobo, eds. *The Praises of Dingana.* University of Natal Press: Pietermaritzburg, 1988.

Scarr, D. *Slaving and Slavery in the Indian Ocean.* Macmillan: London, 1998.

Scholefield, A. *Great Elephant.* Sphere: London, [1967] 1983.

Shaw, T., P. Sinclair, B. Andah and A. Okpoko, eds. *The Archaeology of Africa: Food, Metals and Towns.* Routledge: London, 1993.

Shooter, J. *The Kafirs of Natal and the Zulu Country.* Standford: London, 1857.

Smith, A. *The Diary of Andrew Smith.* P.R. Kirby, ed. Van Riebeeck Society: Cape Town, 1940.

——. *Andrew Smith and Natal.* P.R. Kirby, ed. Van Riebeeck Society: Cape Town, 1955.

——. *Andrew Smith's Journal of his Expedition into the Interior of Southern Africa.* W.F. Lye, ed. AA Balkema: Cape Town, 1975.

Smith, A.B. 'Khoikhoi Susceptibility to Virgin Soil Epidemics in the 18th Century'. *South African Medical Journal* 75(1), January 1989: 25–6.

Smith, A.K. 'The Trade of Delagoa Bay as a Factor in Nguni Politics 1750–1835'. In L.M. Thompson, ed. *African Societies in Southern Africa: Historical Studies.* Heinemann: London, 1969.

——. 'Delagoa Bay and the Trade of South-east Africa'. In R. Gray and D. Birmingham, eds. *Pre-colonial African Trade: Essays on Trade in Central and Eastern Africa before 1900.* Oxford University Press: London, 1970.

——. 'The Struggle for Control of Southern Mozambique, 1720–1835'. Ph.D. dissertation, University of California, Los Angeles, 1971.

Stein, R.L. *The French Slave Trade in the Eighteenth Century: An Old Regime Business.* University of Wisconsin Press: Madison, 1979.

Stevenson, M. and M. Graham-Stewart, eds. *South-east African Beadwork 1850–1910.* Fernwood Press: Vlaeberg, 2000.

Stockenström, A. *The Autobiography of the Late Sir Andries Stockenström.* C.W. Hutton, ed. 2 vols. Juta: Cape Town, 1887.

Stuart, J. 'Tshaka, the Great Zulu Despot'. *United Empire* 15, 1924: 98–107.

Stuart, J. and D. McK Malcolm, eds. *The Diary of Henry Francis Fynn.* Shuter and Shooter: Pietermaritzburg, [1951] 1986.

Taylor, S. *The Caliban Shore: The Fate of the Grosvenor Castaways.* Faber: London, 2004.

Teelock, V. and E. Alpers. *History, Memory and Identity.* Nelson Mandela Centre for African Culture: Mauritius, 2001.

Theal, G. McCall. *History of South Africa.* Swan Sonnenschein: London, 1891.

——., ed. *Records of South-eastern Africa.* 9 vols. Government of the Cape Colony: Cape Town, 1898.

Thomas, T.M. *Eleven Years in Central Africa*. Rpt. Books of Rhodesia: Bulawayo, [1872] 1970.

Thompson, G. *Travels and Adventures in Southern Africa*. Van Riebeeck Society: Cape Town, [1827] 1967.

Thompson, V.B. *The Making of the African Diaspora in the Americas, 1441–1900*. Longmans: London, 1987.

Van Schalkwyk, L.O. 'oNdini: The Zulu Royal Capital of King Cetshwayo kaMpande (1873–1879)'. In P.G. Stone and P.G. Planel, eds. *The Constructed Past: Experimental Archaeology, Education and the Public*. Routledge: London, 1998.

Vansina, J. *Oral Tradition as History*. James Currey: London, 1985.

——. 'New Linguistic Evidence and "The Bantu Expansion"'. *Journal of African History* 30, 1995: 173–93.

Van Warmelo, N.J. *The History of Matiwane and the Amangwane Tribe, as Told by Msebenzi*. Government Printer: Pretoria, 1938.

Vigne, R., ed. *Guillaume Chenu de Chalezac, The 'French Boy': The Narrative of His Experiences as a Huguenot Refugee, as a Castaway among the Xhosa, His Rescue with the Stavenisse Survivors by the Centaurus, his Service at the Cape and Return to Europe, 1686–9*. Van Riebeeck Society: Cape Town, 1993.

Vogel, J.O. and J. Vogel, eds. *Encyclopaedia of Precolonial Africa*. Altamira Press: Walnut Creek, 1997.

Von Sicard, H. 'Shaka and the North'. *African Studies* 14(4), 1955: 145–53.

Walker, E.A. *A History of South Africa*. Longmans: London, 1928.

Warner, M. *No Go the Bogeyman: Scaring, Lulling and Making Mock*. Chatto and Windus: London, 1998.

Watson, J.L., ed. *Asian and African Systems of Slavery*. Basil Blackwell: Oxford, 1980.

Webb, C. de B. and J.B. Wright, eds. *A Zulu King Speaks: Statements Made by Cetshwayo kaMpande on the History and Customs of His People*. University of Natal Press: Pietermaritzburg, 1987.

Webster, A.C. 'Land Expropriation and Labour Extraction under Cape Colonial Rule: The War of 1835 and the "Emancipation of the Fingo"'. MA thesis, Rhodes University, Grahamstown, 1991.

White, W. *Journal of a Voyage Performed in the Lion Extra Indiaman*. John Stockdale: Piccadilly, 1800.

Whitelaw, G. 'Preliminary Results of a Survey of Bulawayo, Shaka kaSenzangakhona's Capital from about 1820 to 1827'. *Southern African Field Archaeology* 3, 1994: 107–9.

——. 'Southern African Iron Age'. In J.O. Vogel and J. Vogel, eds. *Encyclopaedia of Precolonial Africa*. Altamira Press: Walnut Creek, 1997: 444–55.

Wilson, M. 'Nguni Markers'. In J. Peires, ed. *Before and After Shaka: Papers in Nguni History*. ISER: Grahamstown, 1981.

Wright, J. 'Pre-Shakan Age-group Formation among the Northern Nguni'. *Natalia* 8, 1978: 22–30.

——. 'Politics, Ideology, and the Invention of the "Nguni"'. In T. Lodge, ed. *Resistance and Ideology in Settler Societies: Southern African Studies*. Vol.4. Ravan Press: Johannesburg, 1986: 96–118.

——. 'Political Mythology and the Making of Natal's Mfecane'. CJAS 23(2), 1989: 272–91.

——. 'The Dynamics of Power and Conflict in the Late 18th and Early 19th Centuries: A Critical Reconstruction'. Ph.D. dissertation, University of the Witwatersrand, Johannesburg, 1989.

——. 'A.T. Bryant and the "Wars of Shaka"'. History in Africa 18, 1991: 409–25.

——. 'Sonqua, Bosjesmans, Bushmen, abaThwa: Comments and Queries on Pre-modern Identification'. South African Historical Journal 35, 1996: 16–29.

——. ' "The Wars of Shaka", the "Mfecane", and Beyond'. Unpublished paper, North-eastern Workshop on Southern Africa, Burlington, Vermont, 2002.

Wright, J. and A. Manson. The Hlubi Chiefdom in Zululand-Natal: A History. Ladysmith Historical Society: Ladysmith, 1983.

Wylie, D. Savage Delight: White Myths of Shaka. University of Natal Press: Pietermaritzburg, 2000.

——. 'The Feather Stood Quivering: Oral Tradition, Metaphor and Historiographical Method: A Case Study in the History of Shaka'. Unpublished paper, ISOLA Conference, Chambéry, July 2002.

Index

Simamane (eighteenth-century ruler)   136
Simon's Bay (Simonstown)   260
SINGCOFELA kaMtshungu (Stuart informant)
        278
Sinqila kaMphiphi (Cele man)   168, 269,
        297-8
Sithole (people; see also Jobe)   166, 197,
        270, 278-9, 294, 482
    Ngoza (Thembu) and   284
    Shaka and   199-200
Siyingile (umuzi)   300
slave markets
    American   67, 69, 385
    Brazilian   162, 246, 248-9, 385
    Caribbean   66, 385
    Mascarenes   62, 161, 248-9, 385
slave trade   4, 44, 46, 68-9, 109, 131,
        132, 161-4, 249, 269, 286, 348,
        383-8, 403
    Delagoa Bay and   66-70, 162, 259,
        269, 383-8, 508
    estimated levels of
        pre-1713   529
        1760-90   68, 384-5
        1800-10   132
        1810-20   161-2
        1820-25   248-9
        1825-30   384-5
    female slaves   163
    Madagascar and   68-9, 161, 529
    militarisation and   65-6, 164
    Mozambique and   43-4, 68-9, 162
    Port Natal whites and   69
    trade wars and   383-8
    wars, cause of   66, 70-2, 161-4, 240-
        52, 438
    white-sponsored   347
    Zulu and   383
slavers
    African   67
    Arabic   66-7
    Dutch   67-9, 248
    English   67-9, 248
    French   67, 383, 385
    Port Natal whites   69

Portuguese   67-8, 162-3, 245-50, 383
Spanish   132
Tsonga-Tembe   68-9
VOC Company   68
smallpox   250, 348, 355
Smith, Alan (historian)   59, 131, 242
Smith, Andrew (traveller)   254, 348
Sobhuza (Dlamini-Swazi chief)   160, 235,
        250, 328, 486
Socwatsha   420
Sofala   76
Sojisa kaSenzangakhona (Shaka's half-
        brother)   121, 211, 238, 239
Sokhulu (people)   50, 134
Sokwetshata (Mthethwa man)   111
Somajuba kaSenzangakhona   125
Somaphunga kaZwide (Ndwandwe man)
        235, 238, 372-3
Somerset, Col. Henry   299, 344, 442, 458,
        460-4, 473-5
Somhashi (Bomvu chief)   278
Somhlolo   see Sobhuza
Sompisi (Bhele chief)   118
Somveli (Dingiswayo's heir)   205, 240-1,
        243
Sondaba (Nxamalala chief)   284
Sopana kaSenzangakhona   125, 137
Sophane kaMncinci (Qwabe man)   175
Soshangane (Gaza chief)   171, 241-2,
        244-5, 259, 269, 484-94
Sotho (people)   250, 258, 259, 406, 437
Sotobe kaMpangalala (Zulu induna)   170,
        444, 448, 455, 460, 466-9, 509,
        516
South African Commercial Advertiser   374,
        426, 474
South African Land and Emigration
        Association   516
spears   see assegais
'state'-building   45-50
St Lucia Bay   109, 261, 262
Stretch, C.L.   261
Stuart, James   5-9, 19, 74, 80, 84, 85, 90,
        91, 101, 111, 113, 123, 147, 153,

www.ingramcontent.com/pod-product-compliance
Ingram Content Group UK Ltd.
Pitfield, Milton Keynes, MK11 3LW, UK
UKHW012055110225
454967UK00008B/450